OPERATING SYSTEMS

(A Practical Approach)

OPERATING SYSTEMS

A Practical Approach

◆ Concepts ◆ Principles ◆ System Programming

FOURTH EDITION

For the Students of B.E./B.Tech., M.E./M.Tech. & BCA/MCA

Dr. RAJIV CHOPRA

Ph. D. (Computer Science)

Associate Professor (CSE/IT)

Guru Tegh Bahadur Institute of Technology (GTBIT), Delhi

(Affiliated to Guru Gobind Singh Indraprastha University, Delhi)

S. CHAND PUBLISHING

S. Chand And Company Limited

(ISO 9001 Certified Company)

S. CHAND PUBLISHING

S. Chand And Company Limited

(ISO 9001 Certified Company)

Head Office: D-92, Sector–2, Noida – 201301, U.P. (India), Ph. 91-120-4682700

Registered Office: A-27, 2nd Floor, Mohan Co-operative Industrial Estate, New Delhi – 110 044, Phone: 011-49731800

www.**schandpublishing.com**; e-mail: **info@schandpublishing.com**

Marketing Offices:

Chennai	:	Ph: 23632120; chennai@schandpublishing.com
Guwahati	:	Ph: 2738811, 2735640; guwahati@schandpublishing.com
Hyderabad	:	Ph: 40186018; hyderabad@schandpublishing.com
Jalandhar	:	Ph: 4645630; jalandhar@schandpublishing.com
Kolkata	:	Ph: 23357458, 23353914; kolkata@schandpublishing.com
Lucknow	:	Ph: 4003633; lucknow@schandpublishing.com
Mumbai	:	Ph: 25000297; mumbai@schandpublishing.com
Patna	:	Ph: 2260011; patna@schandpublishing.com

First Edition 2009
Reprints and Revised Editions 2010, 2013, 2014, 2015
Fourth Revised Edition 2016
Reprints 2017, 2018
Reprint with corrections 2019
Reprints 2020, 2021, 2023

Reprint 2024

ISBN : 978-93-856-7635-2 **Product Code:** H3OSY50OSYS10ENAD16R

PRINTED IN INDIA

By Vikas Publishing House Private Limited, Plot 20/4, Site-IV, Industrial Area Sahibabad, Ghaziabad – 201 010 and Published by S. Chand And Company Limited, A-27, 2nd Floor, Mohan Co-operative Industrial Estate, New Delhi – 110 044.

PREFACE

The study of Operating System (O.S.) is very important due to its wide scope in designing application and tools of the operating system that are used in many software applications.

The programmer must be aware of the methods and techniques used by different operating systems. It is desirable to put emphasis on the practical part of the subject rather than only on theory.

The book makes the study of operating systems more interesting and provides concrete knowledge by giving practical examples, experiments in O.S. and several case studies. The book would also be of great use to practitioners to understand the state-of-the-art practices in the industry.

This book is written in such a simple and lucid style that it serves as a self-learning book as it assimilates comprehensive matter on the subject by integrating numerous examples.

This book covers the syllabi of Guru Gobind Singh Indraprastha University (GGSIPU) Delhi, DU, UPTU, PTU, KUD, IGNOU, WBTU, RGTU and many other technological universities. It can be used as a textbook for B.E./B.Tech. (CSE/IT), M.E./M.Tech. (CSE/IT) and MCA & BCA courses of these universities. Sufficient academic rigour and an anendeavour to align the book with the contents of the syllabi of all the universities has been provided.

Salient Features of the book:

- Semaphores have been explored
- More conceptual short questions with answers have been added
- Symbian O.S. is added
- Recent questions and question papers of different universities have been added

I hope the book will cater to the needs of students. It will also be useful to the teachers of the subject.

Any suggestions for further improvement of the book will be highly acknowledged.

Dr. Rajiv Chopra
e-mail: raj_74chopra2004@yahoo.com

ABOUT THE AUTHOR

Dr. Rajiv Chopra, Ph.D. is Assistant Professor in the Department of Computer Science/ IT at Guru Tegh Bahadur Institute of Technology (GTBIT), GGSIPU, Delhi.

He received his Ph.D. in Computer Science from Banasthali Vidyapith University; M.Tech. (IT) from GGSIPU, Delhi; MIT from MAHE, Manipal University and B.E. (Computer Science and Engineering) from SDM College of Engineering and Technology, Dharwad. He has a teaching experience of more than 17 years including one year in software industry. He is teaching information technology at undergraduate level. He has written more than 23 books and reviewed several books and papers. He has to his credit several research papers published in open, peer-reviewed, indexed, refereed international journals and conferences. Dr. Chopra is a life member of ISTE, New Delhi and is a Crezone Certified Ethical Hacker (CCEH), New Delhi.

ACKNOWLEDGEMENTS

A well-informed mind is the best security against the contagion of folly and vice. The vacant mind is ever on the watch for relief, and ready to plunge into error, to escape from the languor of idleness.

First of all, I would like to thank Almighty God for showering uncountable blessings on me. As no task is a single man's effort, various factors, situations and persons integrate to provide the background in the accomplishment of a task. I take this opportunity to express my deep sense of gratitude to all people who have been very cooperative during the preparation of this manuscript. I wish to acknowledge my Director, my colleagues and my students for motivating me to write this book.

I am thankful to the editorial team of S. Chand & Company Pvt. Ltd., New Delhi for their sincere cooperation and generous support in bringing out this book.

Finally, I am indebted to my parents Dr. J R Chopra and Ms Sushma Chopra for their motivation, encouragement and support in the preparation of this manuscript. I would also like to acknowledge my wife Ms Shakti Chopra and kids Arjeesh and Arshitha for their sincere cooperation.

Dr. Rajiv Chopra

CONTENTS

Unit – I

UNIT – II

UNIT – III

UNIT – IV

UNIT – I

CHAPTER 1

Introduction to Operating System

1.0 WHAT IS AN OPERATING SYSTEM?

An operating system (OS) is a layer of software on a bare hardware machine that performs two basic functions :

(*a*) Resource Management.

(*b*) Virtual machine management (User friendliness).

Resource management

A user process accesses several hardware and software resources during its execution:

Examples of resources are CPU, Main Memory, input-output devices and various types of software resources such as compiler, linker, loader, files etc. It is the OS that manages the resources and allocates them to users in an efficient and fair manner.

Resource management encompasses the following:-

(*a*) Time management (CPU, DISK Scheduling)

(*b*) Space management (Main Memory & Secondary Memory).

(*c*) Process synchronization and deadlock handling.

(*d*) Accounting and Status Information.

Virtual Machine Management

An operating system (OS) hides the unpleasant, low-level details and idiosyncrasies of a bare hardware machine and provides users with a much friendlier interface to the machine. To load, manipulate, print and execute programs, high level commands can be used without the inconvenience of worrying about low-level details.

The layer of an operating system transforms a bare hardware machine into a virtual machine with added functionality such as automatic resource management.

Moreover, the user of the virtual machine have the illusion that each one of them is the sole user of the machine, even though the machine may be operating in a multiuser environment.

The virtual machine management encompasses the following tasks:

(*a*) Execution Environment: It includes process creation and management, control, and termination, file manipulation, interrupt handling, support for I/O operations, language support.

(*b*) Error detection and handling.

(*c*) Protection and security.

So, we can say that an OS is a Resource Manager as well as a virtual Machine Manager.

Do we need an OS?

It is not essential to have an OS to use a computer. Some special purpose computer do not have an OS.

For example: Almost all microwave ovens have a small computer chip inside to control the oven. But only a few of the computer chips in microwave ovens have OS.

The OS implements many necessary features that are used by almost every program. It is a good investment to implement them once in OS rather than in each application program. An OS is useful because it contains a library of reusable services. As we know that a general purpose computer must be able to run a wide range of programs. For such a system, an OS is the most natural way to go. Otherwise, each application would have to program its own operating system services. Thus, we conclude that for a general purpose computer system, it is essential to have an OS.

There are two common perspectives of what an operating system is.

One view is that:

- **An OS is a user interface i.e., a program that acts as an interface between the user and the computer hardware.**

or

- **A program that controls the execution of application programs.**

or

- **An interface between applications and hardware.**

Another view is that :

An OS is a **resource manager** *i.e.,* a program designed to manage the computer resources like CPU, memory and peripherals efficiently.

Now, we give a formal definition of an OS.

"An operating system (OS) is an integrated set of systems programs whose major function is to - Manage Resources (like CPU, Memory, Disks etc.), control input and output, schedule jobs, handle errors, provide security, act as an interface between the user and machine"

or

"An OS directs the processor in how to use the system resources and when to execute other programs."

or

"A portion of the OS, called the 'kernel' is resident in the main memory. The kernel contains the most frequently used functions of the OS."

Where does it fit in?

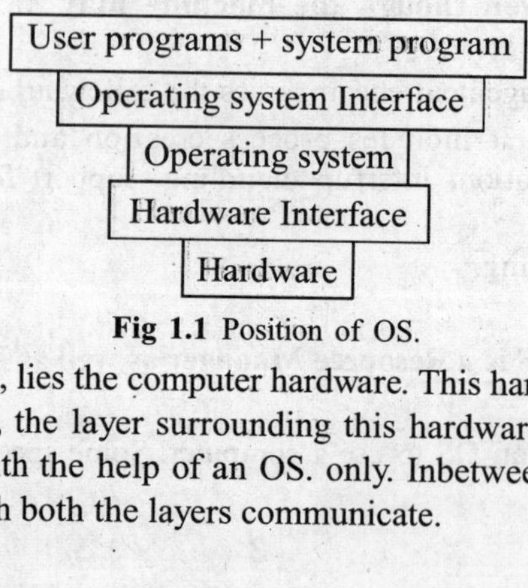

Fig 1.1 Position of OS.

At the core of Figure 1.1, lies the computer hardware. This hardware cannot function without an operating system (OS), So, the layer surrounding this hardware layer is an operating system layer. A hardware interacts with the help of an OS. only. Inbetween these two layers, we have a hardware interface using which both the layers communicate.

An operating system is a program that acts as an intermediatory between the computer user and computer hardware. It provides an environment in which a user can execute programs. The main goal of an OS is to provide convenience and efficiency.

At the top layer, we have the user programs and the system programs like compilers, data base systems, games and business programs.

An OS communicates with this programs via OS interface. **The basic work of the operating system is to control and coordinate the use of hardware among the various application programs for various users.**

The operating systems acts like a government, the government collects money from various sources (like public, companies, taxes etc.) and distributes the money to different development activities. In the same fashion an OS collects the resources from the network environment or within a system and grant the resources to the requesting jobs.

So, the OS acts as a liasion between the computer hardware and application software. **The Application program** requires the OS to carry out hardware related tasks such as printing reports and data storages on the disks. **Please note that the primary goal of the OS is to provide convenience to the user and the secondary goal is to bring efficiency in the operation of the computer system. Also note that, an OS does what the software does**. It implements some desired functionalities by building on the functionalities available in the lower level. **Another point to note is that OS is like hardware in the sense that only one copy of the OS runs at any particular time.**

There are two ways in which one can interact with an OS—

(*a*) By means of operating system call in a program.

(*b*) Directly by means of operating system Commands.

OS calls are like our system calls or predefined functions or subroutine calls. On the other hand, OS commands are the command that are directly run from the prompt. For example, to list files or sub-directories in MS–DOS, we use *dir command.*

Examples of operating systems are as follows—

(*a*) DOS

(*b*) Windows (95/98/2000, NT, XP).

(*c*) UNIX (Sco, Sun Solaris, HP, IBM).

(*d*) Mach

(*e*) Amoeba

1.1 HISTORY OF OPERATING SYSTEMS

Let us summarize the history of an OS in a tabular form below:

Year	Operating system	Features
1. 1940s (First Generation)	No OS	**Utilization :** 7% **Throughput :** 4 jobs/hr. **Productivity :** Good
2. 1950s (Second Generation)	Batch OS	**Utilization :** 90% **Throughput :** 55 jobs/hr **Turnaround time :** A job with l min. time now required 2-3 hrs.
3. Early 1960s	Spooling	**Utilization :** Slower I/O devices

(Third Generation)	(discussed later in section 1.4.1)	**Throughput :** 800 jobs/day **Turnaround time :** 5 mins
4. 1960s and 1970s (Fourth Generation)	Time sharing and batch. Also first microprocessor based OS like MS-DOS	Hard to characterize but turnaround time was few seconds.
5. 1980s	Batch OS disappeared, micros; embedded systems and networks	Hard to characterize
6. 1990s	Distributed systems, time sharing, embedded	Hard to characterize

1.2 MAJOR GOALS OF OPERATING SYSTEMS

Any operating system should meet the following major goals—

(*a*) optimize the use of computer resources so as to maximize its throughput.

(*b*) create a user-friendly computing environment for accessing the computer resources.

When the power of a computer is turned on, the first program that runs is usually a set of instructions stored in Read-only Memory (ROM) that examines the system hardware to check whether all our hardware device function properly or not. This will check our CPU, Memory, basic I/O for errors and stores the result in a special memory location. **This is known as power-on-self test (POST).** Once the POST has successfully completed, the software loaded in ROM (*i.e.*, firmware) will begin to activate the disk drives in our computer. When the computer activates the hard disk drive then the first piece of a system program it finds is the **bootstrap loader.**

What is a bootstrap loader?

The bootstrap loader is a small program whose single function is to load the OS into the memory and allows it to begin operation. The bootstrap loader sets up the small drive programs that interface with control various hardware sub-system of the computer. It sets up the divisions of memory that holds the OS user information and applications. It establishes the data structures that will hold the signals, flags and semaphores that are used to communicate within and between the subsystems and applications of the computer. Finally, it turns control of computer over to the OS.

Therefore, the main OS services are as follows—

- To control basic Input and Output.
- To allocate system Resources.
- To detect equipment failure.
- To manage storage space.
- To maintain security.
- Utilities.

Functionality view of an OS

- To handle hardware details like CPU architecture, keyboards, disks etc.
- To coordinate the working of different parts of a computer.
- To allocate and manage resources for different tasks.
- To store information
- To communicate with other computers.
- To protect integrity and security of stored information.

Application Programming Interface (API) View of an OS-

An OS provides an interface that is used by the developers to get their programs run across different hardware platforms and environments.

1.3 THE EVOLUTION OF OPERATING SYSTEMS

An operating system may process its task serially (sequentially) or concurrently (several tasks simultaneously). This means that the resources of the computer system may be dedicated to a single program until its completion or they may be allocated among several programs in different stages of execution. **This feature of an OS to execute multiple programs in interleaved fashion or different time cycles is know as multiprogramming.**

1.3.1 Serial Processing

In earlier machines like PDP-11, a program coded in machine language (I's and O's) could be entered into the RAM through front-panel switches and executed. The results of execution could be displayed on a set of LEDs, mounted on the front-cover itself. It was very tedious and cumbersome to enter this program of O's and I's through the toggle switches. In case of a power failure, such a program used to disappear and had to be entered all over again.

With the advent of I/O devices like punch cards, paper tapes, magnetic tapes, line printers etc. and with the advent of assemblers and compilers; the concept of serial processing emerged. **Please note that in serial processing, the programs were executed strictly in a serial manner one after another.** The source code (program) written in assembly or high level language on a pack of punched cards could be entered into the computer using punch card reader. Then, the assembler or compiler used to be loaded to translate the source code into an object file. Then the object file used to be linked with library routines to create an executable file, which was then executed and the results were displayed. It is only after this that the next program was taken up for execution in a strictly serial manner.

Advantage of serial processing

(1) Serial processing resulted in a big improvement over the 'bare machine' approach *i.e.*, a machine with no OS.

(2) In serial processing, the OS was limited to only a loader and some I/O device.

Disadvantages of serial processing

(1) The process of development and preparation of a program in such an environment is slow and cumbersome due to serial processing and numerous manual processing.

(2) At a time, only a small subject of resources could be used. So, there was poor utilization of system resources.

Please note, however that it was the concept of serial processing only that led to the new concept of batching jobs of similar types together.

So, we discuss about batch processing now.

1.3.2 Batch Processing

To speed up the processing, the jobs with similar needs were batched together and were run through the computer as a group.

For example: Imagine that the operator received one FORTRAN, one PASCAL program and another FORTRAN program. If he runs them in that order, he would have to set up for FORTRAN program environment (*i.e.*, FORTRAN compiler) then set up PASCAL program and finally, FORTRAN program again. However, if he runs the two FORTRAN programs as a batch, he need to set up only once for FORTRAN thus saving operator's time.

Batching similar jobs increased the system resources utilization a bit but there were still some problems. For example, when a job is stopped, the operator would have to notice that fact by observing the console, determine why the program stopped and then load the card reader or paper tape reader with the next job and restart the computer. During this transition from one job to the next, the CPU sat idle.

To overcome this idle time, **a small program called a resident monitor was created which is always resident in the memory.**

It would automatically sequence the execution of jobs one after the other. It acts as per the programmer's directives given through control cards which certains information like marking of job's beginnings and endings, commands for loading and executing programs etc. These commands belong to job control language. These job control language commands are included with user program and data.

Due to sequencing of program execution and it's automation by batch operating system, the speed discrepancy between the fast CPU and comparatively slow I/O devices such as card readers, printers emerged as a major performance bottlement. Even a slow CPU works in the microsecond range, with millions of instructions per second. On the other hands, a fast card reader might read 1200 cards per minute. **Thus, the difference in the speed between the CPU and its input/output devices may be three orders of magnitude or more.**

The relative slowness of input/output devices can mean that CPU is often waiting for input/output.

For example: An assembler or compiler may be able to process 300 or more cards per second. On the other hand, a fast card reader may be able to read only 1200 cards per minute. This means that assembling or compiling a 1200 card program would require only 4 seconds of CPU time but 60 seconds to read. *Thus, the CPU is idle for* 56 *out of* 60 *seconds* or 93.3 % of the time. **The resulting CPU utilization is only 6.7%. The process is similar for output operations. Please note here that the problem is that while an input/output is occurring, the CPU is idle, waiting for the input/output to complete and while the CPU is executing, input/output devices are idle.**

The improvements in technology resulted in faster I/O devices. But CPU speed increased even faster. Therefore, the need was to increase the throughput and resource utilisation by overlapping input/output and processing operations. Channels, peripheral controllers and dedicated input/output processors brought a major improvement in this direction. Direct memory access (DMA) chip which directly transfers the entire block of data from its own buffer to main memory without intervention by CPU was a major development. While CPU is executing, DMA can transfer data between high speed input/output devices and the main memory. CPU requires to be interrupted per block only by DMA.

There are two other approaches of improving the system performance by overlapping – input, output and processing. They are as follows -

(*a*) Buffering

(*b*) Spooling.

We discuss these one by one now.

(*a*) **Buffering**

It is a method of overlapping input, output and processing of a single job. The idea is quite simple. After data has been read and the CPU is about to start operating on it, the input device is instructed to begin the next input immediately. The CPU and the input device are then both busy. By the time that the CPU is ready for the next data item, the input device will have finished reading it. The CPU can then begin processing the newly read data, while the input device starts to read the following data. Similarly, this can be done for output. In this case, the CPU creates data that is put into a buffer until an output device can accept it.

If the CPU is (on average) much faster than an input device then buffering will be of little use. If the CPU is always faster, then it always finds an empty buffer and has to wait for the input device. For output, the CPU can proceed at full speed until, eventually all system buffers are full. Then the CPU must wait for the output device.

This situation occurs with **input/output bound jobs** where the amount of input/output relation to computation is very high. Since the CPU is faster than the input/output device, the speed of execution is controlled by the input/output device, not by the speed of the CPU.

We shall now explain another form of input/output buffering called as **SPOOLING** (Simultaneous Peripheral Operation Online).

(*b*) SPOOLING

It stands for **S**imultaneous **P**eripheral **O**peration **Onl**ine. 'Simultaneous' means, say if two or more users issue the print command and the printer can accept the requests even if it is printing some other job.

In disk technology, rather than the cards being read from the card reader directly into memory and then the job being processed, cards are read directly from the card reader onto the disk. The location of the card images is recorded in a table kept by the OS. When a job is executed, the OS satisfied its request for card reader input by reading from the disk. Similarly, when the job requests the printer to output a line, that line is copied into a system buffer and is written to the disk. When the jobs is completed, the output is actually printed. **This form of processing is called as spooling.** This is shown below in Fig. 1.2.

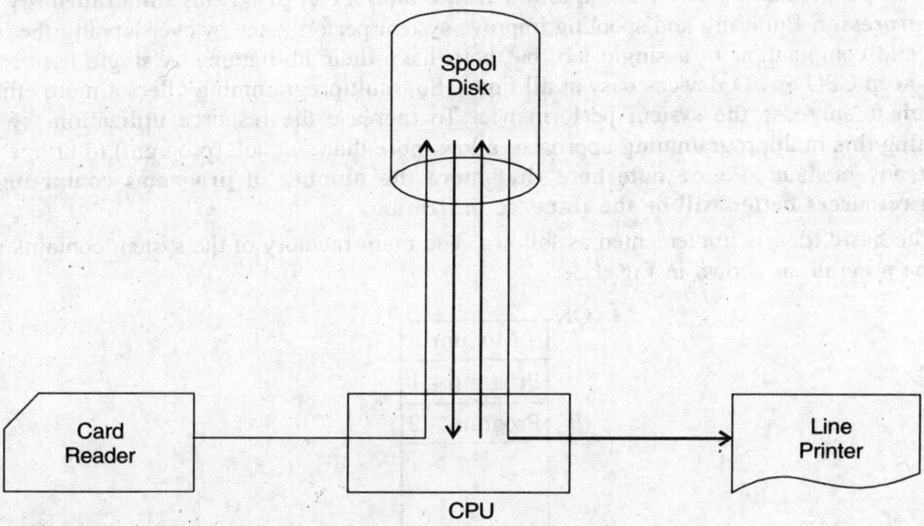

Fig. 1.2. Spooling

Features of spooling

Spooling is used for data processing at remote sites. The CPU sends the data via communication paths to a remote printer. The remote processing is done at its own speed, with no CPU intervention.

Spooling overlaps the I/O of one job with the computation of other jobs. It has a direct beneficial effect on the performance of the system. Spooling can keep both the CPU and the I/O devices working at much higher rates.

Please note here that buffering overlaps input, output and processing of a single job whereas spooling allows CPU to overlap the input of one job with the computation and output of other jobs. Therefore, this approach is better than buffering. Even in a simple system, the spooler may be reading the input of one job while printing the output of a different job.

Advantages of Batch processing

1. Batch processing is particularly useful for operations that require the computer or a peripheral device for an extended period of time and very little user interaction.
2. For batched jobs, the common housekeeping operations, like loading of compiler, were performed only once. Thus, overhead per program got reduced which improved the system utilization.
3. It was with this concept only that job scheduling also started.

Disadvantages of Batch processing

1. No interaction is possible with the user while the program is being executed.
2. Job setup time for it's processing also took lot of time as the tapes/cards need to be mounted.
3. CPU sat idle during the transition from one job to another.
4. Debugging was feasible only offline and it used to be very time-consuming.
5. At any time, it used to dedicate all the system resources to a single program being executed. An executing program may oscillate between computation phase and I/O phase. So, at a time, either CPU will be busy or I/O will be busy. Thus, degree of resource utilization was very low thereby lowering system throughput.

1.3.3 Multiprogramming

Multiprogramming is a technique to execute number of programs simultaneously by a single processor. Buffering and spooling improve system performance by over lapping the input, output and computation of a single job, but both have their limitations. A single user cannot always keep CPU or I/O devices busy at all times. So, multiprogramming offers a more efficient approach to increase the system performance. To increase the resource utilization, systems supporting this multiprogramming approach, allow more than one job (program) to utilize CPU time at any moment. **Please note here that more the number of programs competing for system resources better will be the resource utilization.**

The **basic idea** is implemented as follows. The main memory of the system contains more then one program as shown in Fig. 1.3.

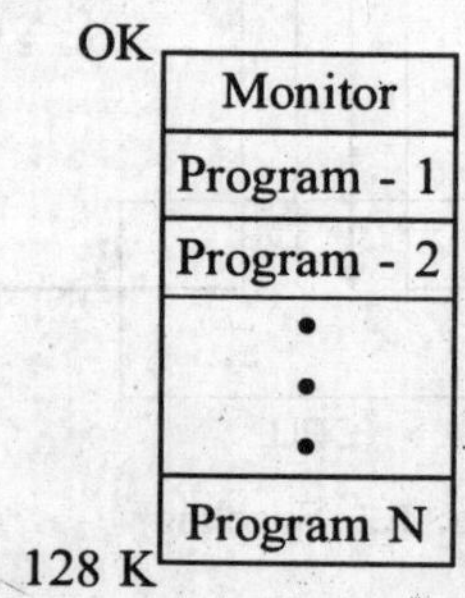

Fig. 1.3. Memory layout in multiprogramming system.

The OS could support for keeping several jobs in the memory at one time. The OS could pick and start the execution of one of the jobs in the memory. Whenever the jobs does not need CPU (*i.e.* the job has to do I/O only) and so the CPU is idle at that time then the OS switches to another job in the memory and CPU executes a portion of it till this job issues a request for I/O or the first one has finished its I/O and so on.

Let us consider an example, say, there are two programs, P_1 and P_2 that are residing in the main memory. The OS picks one of the programs and start executing it. During execution, say, P_1 needs some 100 operations to complete. Then, what happens in a **sequential environment** is that the CPU would sit idle *i.e.*, see Figure 1.4 (*a*) below.

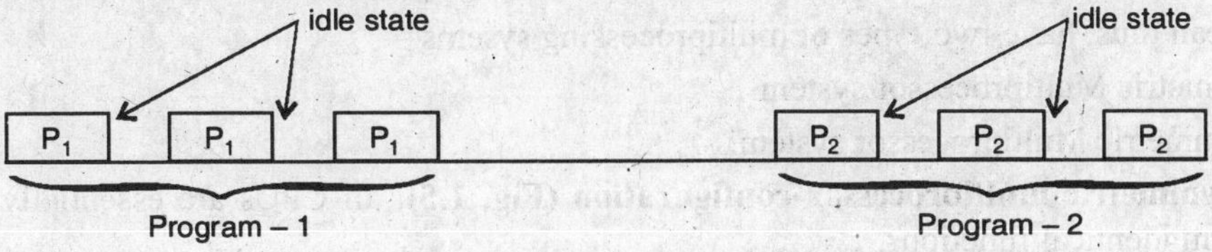

Fig. 1.4 (*a*) Sequential execution of P_1 and P_2

On the other hand, in a **multiprogramming system**, the OS will simply switch over to the next program (p_2). This is shown in Figure 1.4 (*b*) below—

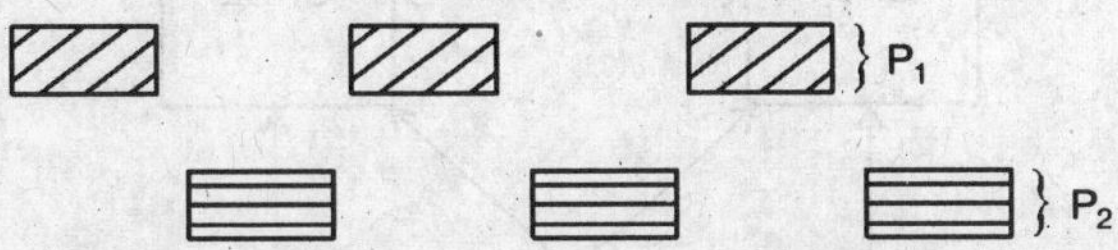

Fig. 4 (*b*) Execution of P_1 and P_2 in a multiprogramming environment

If P_1 is busy with some I/O then it switches to P_2. Similarly, if P_2 wants to do some I/O then it switches to P_3. This goes on. **Please note here that if there is no other program after P_3 (say) then the CPU will pass its control back to the previous programs.**

Another point to note here is that the OS in this case had to be very complex in the sense that now more serious memory management is required. Switching from one job to another is also not very easy.

Multiprogramming has its own advantages and disadvantages too. Let us discuss them one by one.

Advantages of Multiprogramming.

1. High CPU utilization as it is never idle.
2. Supports multiple simultaneous interactive user (terminals).
3. Efficient memory utilization.
4. More CPU throughout.

Disadvantages of Multiprogramming

1. Jobs may have different sizes, so some powerful memory management policy is desired to accommodate them in memory
2. CPU scheduling is must because now many jobs are ready to be run on the CPU.
3. The user cannot interact with the job when it is being executed.
4. The programmer cannot modify a program to study its behavior while the program is being executed.

1.3.4 Multiprocessing

We know that there is a limit on the speed with which a single CPU can operate because the speed of the light (*i.e.* $c = 3 \times 10^8$ m/s) is also limited. If one CPU cannot handle a system's work load then one possible solution is to apply multiple processors to the problem. This is called is a **Multiprocessing environment.**

But the success of this solution depends on many factors. Some of the factors include—

(*a*) Skill of system designer.

(*b*) Can the system workload be best solved using multiprocessors?

We can opt for multiprocessing if we find that the workload is CPU limited and has already saturated a uniprocessor system or we find that our problem involves those calculations which can be solved more easily with multiprocessors. These things are to be kept in mind other wise the performance of a multiprocessor can even be worse than uniprocessors.

We can thus, have two types of multiprocessing sysems—

(*a*) Symmetric Multiprocessor system.

(*b*) Asymmetric Multiprocessor system.

In symmetric multiprocessor configuration (Fig. 1.5), all CPUs are essentially identical and perform identical functions.

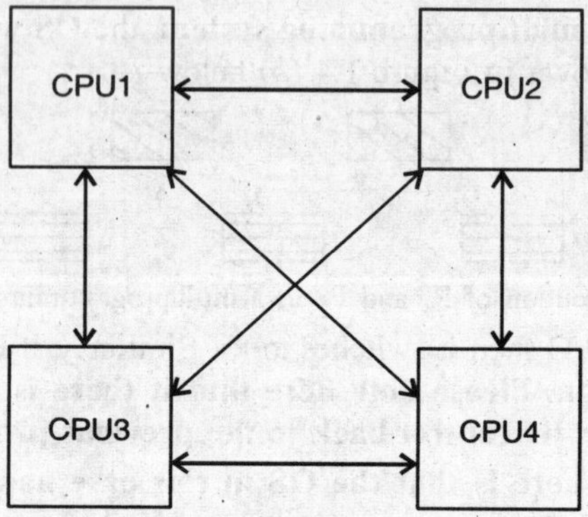

Fig. 1.5. Symmetric Multiprocessing

Herein, any CPU can initiate an I/O operation or can handle any external interrupt and can run any process in the system. So, all the processors are potentially available.

In asymmetric multiprocessor configuration, different processors do different things. We may design in such a fashion that one processor is made a supervisor or Master and it controls other CPUs. This is shown in Fig. 1.6, below—

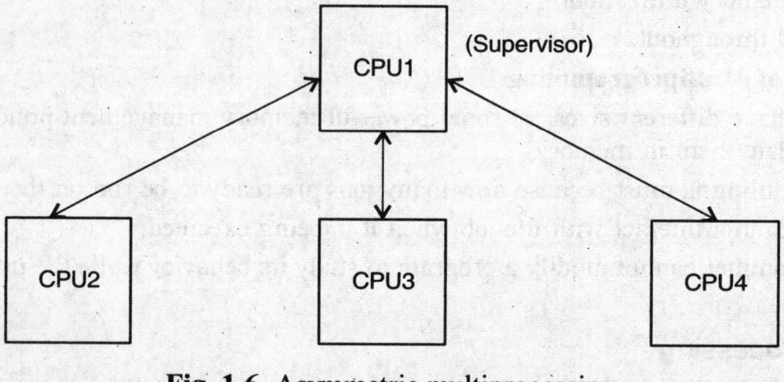

Fig. 1.6. Asymmetric multiprocessing

On one hand, processing may be very fast as then many processors may be available for a single job. On the other hand, processing may be slow because all of the processors (CPU) may not be available to handle peak loads. Also, if the supervisor CPU fails then the entire system will go down.

1.3.5 Time Sharing Systems

These systems are quite interactive that allow user's interaction with the system through OS commands. The user programs can be entered and executed in an interactive mode. Each interactive user is assigned a time slice in a round - robin fashion during which it controls the CPU. During the time-slice, the process gets control of CPU and tries to complete its computation. If the computation is not completed during the assigned time slot then the running process is preempted; then it has to wait for time slot in the next cycle to resume computation from where it was preempted. The time-slot cycle is so adjusted that each user has a feel as if the CPU is assigned to it all the time.

Unlike batch systems, these systems provide quick terminal response and allow online debugging. Each user virtually gets the entire machine. This implies that CPU's time is shared between many user processes. **Please note here that these processes can be of one user or of different users.** This drastically reduced the software development time

Time sharing or multitasking is a logical extension of multiprogramming only. Multiple jobs are executed by the CPU switching between them but switching is so frequent that the users may interact with each program while running. This time sharing or multitasking handles many tasks simultaneously. It is also possible on a system for a single user. *For example,* in window OS, one can open more than one tasks in the running mode.

For a **multiuser system,** the multiple users can submit a request, each through his/her own I/O terminal, to do specific tasks on a system. This is shown in Fig. 1.7 below-

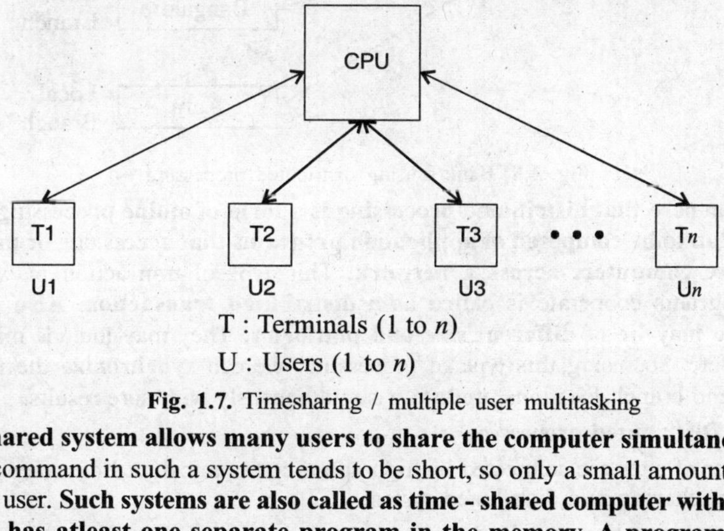

T : Terminals (1 to n)

U : Users (1 to n)

Fig. 1.7. Timesharing / multiple user multitasking

A time-shared system allows many users to share the computer simultaneously. Because each action or command in such a system tends to be short, so only a small amount of CPU time is needed for each user. **Such systems are also called as time - shared computer with the convention that each user has atleast one separate program in the memory. A program that is loaded into memory and is being executed is known as a process.**

1.3.6 Parallel systems

A system consisting of more than one processor that is tightly coupled (*i.e.*, heavy sharing of resources like bus, clock, memory, I/O devices) **is a parallel system.**

A single CPU may be slow. So, a possible solution is to have many CPUs put parallely to execute a single given problem. **This is parallel processing** and such systems are also called as **Supercomputers.**

These systems will increase the CPU throughput (number of jobs per unit time), reduce time required for job execution.

1.3.7 Distributed systems

It comprises of a large central computer to which a large number of remote terminals are attached. We consider two examples to show what is a distributed system and hence distributed processing.

Example 1: Consider that there are two sites- site-1 and site-2. These two sites are connected by some communication links and that the site-1 is having a printer. But site-2 doesn't have a printer. Then site-2 can use the printer at site-1 without moving from site-2 to site-1, by resource sharing that is possible in a distributed system.

Example 2: Consider a bank having its branches throughout India and its head office is in Delhi. Also, we assume that this bank maintains the local data at the local branch and the copy of data of all branches at Delhi. Thus, we say that the data is distributed throughout India. This eases query processing for local customers of a branch and also for global customer.

A global customer is one who moves from one state to another. This is shown below in Fig. 1.8.

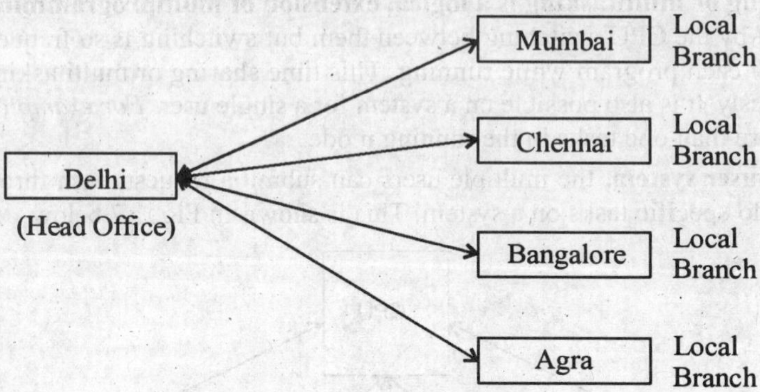

Fig. 1.8. Bank's using distributed processing

Please note here that distributed processing is a form of online processing that allows a single transaction to be composed of application programs that access one or more databases on one or more computers across a network. This type of transaction in which multiple application programs cooperate is called as a **distributed transaction. Also note that the computers here may be of different size and platforms.** They may include microprocessors, minicomputers etc. So, using this type of processing, we can **synchronize** the related data at these regional and branch locations, **update** it simultaneously with sure results.

Advantages of Distributed processing

1. If a number of sites are connected by high speed communication lines, then it allows us to do resource sharing in a distributed system.
2. There is a computation speed-up.
3. Reliability of a distributed system is good.
4. Communications are easy in these systems. E-mails can be sent.

1.3.8 Real Time systems

A real-time system is defined as a system in which the correctness of computations depends not only on the logical correctness of the computation but also on the time at which the result is produced. So, we can say that it has strict time constraints. The inputs, data or outputs should be available within this time period otherwise disasters can happen. Sensors bring data to the computer. The computer must analyse the data and adjust controls to modify the sensor inputs.

For example, some real time systems are like Air-traffic control, medical imaging systems, industrial control systems etc. Also included in this category are automobile-engine fuel injection systems, home appliances controllers and weapon systems.

Please note that in these real-time systems, processing must be done within the defined constraints or the system will fail. For instance, it makes no sense in stopping a Robot's arm once it has already smashed the window of the car that it was building. **Also note that a real time system is considered to function correctly only if it returns the correct result within early time constraint.** We can contrast this to a time sharing system, where it is desirable to respond quickly or to a batch system, where there may be no time constraints at all.

Real Time Systems are put under two main categories—

(*a*) Hard real time systems.
(*b*) Soft real time systems.

We shall tabulate the differences between them

Real time System	Soft Real time system
1. Autonomous error detection for hard real time system.	1. User assisted error detection for soft real time system.
2. These systems have limited utility for rollback/recovery mechanism due to short-term integrity of data.	2. These systems have long-term integrity of data.
3. The data file sizes are small/medium.	3. The data file sizes are large.
4. Their safety is often critical.	4. Their safety is non-critical.
5. Predictable (well defined) peak load performance for these systems.	5. Degraded peak load performance.
Examples:	**Examples:**
(*a*) Air Traffic Control	(*a*) Telecom (Voice)
(*b*) An Embedded system controlling the operation of a refinery.	(*b*) Delayed information about flight path will lose its utility. It is a soft system as it will not be catastrophic but the output loses its utility.

Also note that hard real time systems guarantee that critical tasks will be completed in a given amount of time *i.e.*, **all delays in the system must be bounded.** Please remember that:—

A late response of a process is incorrect and it implies a system failure.

On the other hand, in soft Real time systems, the critical tasks are given **priority** over non-critical tasks. Delays need to be bounded (*i.e.*, predictable) so the critical tasks do not wait forever but these bounds are not as serve as in hard systems.

As in hard real time systems, the **scheduler** plays an important role in soft real time systems also. A careful design of scheduler is required. It must handle priority scheduling and the dispatch latency must be small. **Please note that the smaller the latency, the faster a real time process can start, executing once it is runnable.**

Timeliness requirements are defined by using an average response time. Hence, soft real time systems are characterized by timing constraints that can be—

(*a*) missed occasionally.
(*b*) missed by small time deviations or
(*c*) occasionally skipped altogether.

Please remember that :-

- In soft real systems, late data may still be good data.
- In hard real time systems, late data is bad data.
- A **Firm real time system** is a combination of both hard and soft timeliness requirements. The computation has a shorter soft requirement and a longer hard requirement.

For example: a patient ventilator must mechanically ventilate the patient a certain amount in a given time period. A few seconds delay in the initiation of the breath is allowed but not more than that.

1.3.9 Personal computer system

For a personal computer, we need an OS that performs all basic tasks like reading from keyboard, mouse etc, sending display to monitor and so on. Many OS have been developed for our personal computers.

For example: Windows NT, Window 95, Window 98, Windows XP, OS/2, WIN- 2000, Linux, Mac OS are some OS used commonly on our PCs.

1.4 TYPES OF OPERATING SYSTEMS

Now, we will discuss the general properties, types, applications and merits and demerits of OS. OS can be classified on the basis of type of processing, processor scheduling, memory management, I/O management and file management. The following are the main types of OS.

1.4.1 Batch Operating System

A batch processing environment requires the grouping up of similar jobs which consist of programs, data and system commands. It is the most primitive type of an OS. The programs with large computation time and no user interaction were well served by Batch processing. **For example,** payrolls, forecasting, statistical analysis art, large scientific number crunching programs. User are not required to wait while the job is being processed. They can submit their programs to operators and return later to collect them. But it has two major disadvantages:

1. **Non-interactive environment:** There are some difficulties with the batch system from the users or programmers point of view. These systems allow little or no user interactions. The turnaround time taken between job submission and job completion in these systems is very high. Users have no control over intermediate results of a program. **Please note that this type of arrangement does not create flexibility in software development.**
2. **Off-line debugging:** Another drawback of this approach is that the programs must be debugged which means a programmer cannot correct bugs the moment it occurs.

The typical features of a batch OS were as follows—

(*a*) **Process Scheduling: The allocation strategy for a job/process to a processor is called process scheduling.** These systems used **First Come First Served (FCFS)** Criteria, which provides a fair deal to the jobs but suffers from long average turn-around time and average waiting time. So, to overcome this problem another criteria known as **"Shortest Job Next"** was evolved. So, now jobs with lesser execution time were processed first.

(*b*) **Memory Management:** As shown below in Figure 1.9, the memory is usually divided into two areas. One of them is permanently occupied by the resident portion of the OS and the other is dynamically used to load the transient programs for execution. When one program is over, the new program is loaded into the same area.

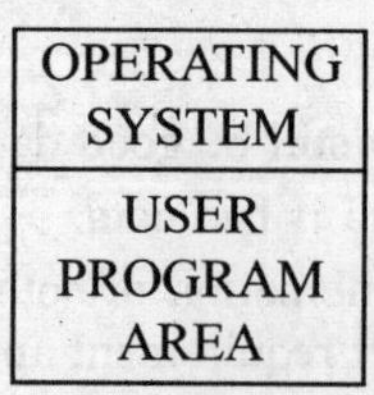

Fig. 1.9. Memory Layout for a simple batch system

(*c*) **I/O Management:** Since only one program used to be under execution at a time, there was no contention for the allocation of I/O devices. *Please note that a simple program controlled I/O approach was good enough to access the I/O devices.*

(*d*) **File Management:** The access to the files is also serial and there is hardly any need of the protection and file access control mechanism. Also since there used to be only on program accessing the files at a time so there was no need of providing concurrency control.

Thus, we conclude that these Batch OS were limited to a loader and some simple device drivers only.

1.4.2 Multiprogramming Operating system

Multiprogramming operating systems are more complex than our batch operating systems. Multiprogramming has a significant potential for improving system throughput and resource utilization with very minor differences. There are three different forms of multiprogramming operating system

(*a*) Multitasking OS.

(*b*) Multiuser OS.

(*c*) Multiprocessing OS.

We shall now explain each in detail.

(*a*) **Multitasking Operating system: A running state of a program is called a process or a task. A multitasking operating system** supports two or more active processes simultaneously. **The concept of managing a multitude of simultaneously active programs, compcting with each other for accessing the system resources is known as multitasking. Multiprogramming OS is an OS which in addition to supporting multiple concurrent process** (several processes in execution states simultaneously) **allows the instructions and data from two or more separate processes to reside in primary memory simultaneously. Please note here that multiprogramming implies multiprocessing or multitasking operation but multiprocessing or multitasking does not imply multiprogramming.** Therefore, multitasking operation is one of the mechanism that multiprogramming OS employs in managing the totality of computer related resources like CPU, memory and I/O devices.

The simplest form of multitasking is called as **serial multitasking** or **context switching.** It means that working on another task will lead to temporary stoppage of first task. **For example,** while a program is running, you decide that you want to use the calculator, so you pop it and use it. When you stop using the calculator, the program continues running even then. This is serial multitasking example.

(*b*) **Multi-user Operating system: It is defined as a multiprogramming OS that supports simultaneous interaction with multiple users.** The multiuser support is necessary for the large company where the data remains same among various user.

The data is stored centrally in one computer called as **server** and all the users can access this data through the terminals called as **client** machines.

For example: A dedicated transaction processing system such as a Railway Reservation system is an example of a multiuser OS. This system supports the hundreds of terminals under the control of a single program.

Some **points to remember** are that—

1. 'Dedicated' means specific for one work.
2. Server is a must for multiuser environment.
3. The clients communicate only via server.

4. User authentication by user-id and password is must.
5. Protection of user's environment is must.
6. Multitasking, without multi-user support, is usually found in real-time systems.

On the other hand, **general-purpose time sharing systems** incorporate the features of both *multiuser* and *multiprogramming OS.* **Also note that multiuser OS does not imply multiprogramming or multitasking.**

(*c*) **Multiprocessing system:** When an OS controls multiple processes at a time, different tasks may be performed on different processors. But all processors are controlled by one CPU only. The OS allows the multiple concurrent processes in execution states simultaneously.

Let us summarize these terminologies now.

The term **'multiprogramming'** means a situation in which a single CPU divides its time between more than one job. Time sharing is a special case of multiprogramming where a single CPU serves a number of users at the interactive terminals.

The term **'multiprocessing'** means multiple CPUs perform more than one job at one time. **Please note here that multiprogramming and multiprocessing are not mutually exclusive.** Some main frames and super computers have multiple CPUs each of which can execute several tasks.

The term **'multitasking'** means a system that runs or appears to run more than one application programs one time. An effective multitasking environment must provide many services both to user and to the application program it runs. Some services are like resource management, which divides computer's time, memory and I/O devices among competing tasks. Other service can be interprocess communication that allows tasking to coordinate their activities by exchanging information.

1.4.3 Time sharing Interactive Operating system

It is a form of multiprogrammed OS which operates in an interactive mode with a quick response time. A time-sharing system allows many users to simultaneously share the computer resources. Since each program takes a very small fraction of time so only small amount of CPU time is needed for each user. **Please note here that as the CPU switches rapidly from one user to another user, each user is given as impression that he has his own computer while it is actually one computer shared among many users.** So, the CPU rapidly switches from one program to another (for one user or many users) automatically and each program is given the attention for a **time quantum** called as **time slice.** The time slice scheduling of CPU for all programs is known as **Round-Robin Scheduling.** Most of the time-sharing system use time-slice (round robin) scheduling of CPU. In this approach, the programs are executed with a **rotating priority** than increases during waiting and drops after the service is granted. **Please note that one program should not be allowed to monopolise the processor. A program executing longer than the system-defined time-slice is interrupted by OS and placed at the end of the queue of the waiting program.**

Examples of time sharing OS—

- CTSS
- Cal
- Multics
- Unix

The main features of time-sharing interactive OS are as follows—

(*a*) **Memory Management:** The memory management in these time-sharing systems provides for isolation and protection of co-resident user programs. Since, the programs are being executed on behalf of different users, they do not involve much of interprocess communication.

(*b*) **I/O Device Management:** I/O management feature of time sharing system must be able to handle multiple users (terminals). However, the processing of terminal-interrupts are not time critical due to the relative slow speed of terminals and users. As required by most multi-user environment allocation and deallocation of devices must be handled in a manner so as to preserve system integrity and provides good, optimized system performance.

(*c*) **File Management:** Since multiple users will be sharing access to multiple files, the file management must provide protection and access control.

1.4.4 Real Time Operating Systems

There are many definitions of Real time OS. Some of them are given below—

"It is characterized by processing activity triggered by randomly accepted external events"

OR

"A real time OS has a well-defined, fixed time constraints. Processing must be done within the defined constraints or the system will fail. A real time system is considered to function correctly only if it returns the correct result within any time constraint."

OR

"A real time system is one in which the correctness of the computations not only depends upon the logical correctness of the computation but also upon the time at which the result is produced. If the timing constraints of the system are not met, system failure is said to have occurred."

Real time OS are used in environment where a large number of events, mostly external to the computer system, must be accepted and processed in a short time or within certain deadlines. Such applications include industrial control, telephone switching equipment, flight control, and real-time simulations. Real time systems are also frequently used in military applications.

Examples of RTOS are—

- Harmony (By National Research Council of Canada).
- MARUTI (By University of Maryland)
- VRTX (Versatile Real-Time Executive by Hunter & Ready Inc.)
- HART (Hexagonal Architecture for RTS by University of Michigan)
- Others like OS9, RTEM (Real Stone Military Arsenal) are examples of RTOS only

A **primary objective** of real-time systems is to provide quick event-response times and thus meet the scheduling deadlines User convenience and resource utilization are of **secondary concern** to real time system designers. It is not uncommon for a real-time system to be expected to process bursts of thousands of interrupts per second without missing a single event. The processor is normally allocated to the **highest priority process** among those, which are ready to execute. **Higher priority process usually pre-empt execution of lower priority processes. This form of scheduling is called as priority based preemptive scheduling** and is used by a majority of real-time systems. Other features of RTOS are as follows—

(*a*) **Memory Management:** In RTOS, there is a little swapping of program between primary and secondary memory. As compared to other types of multiprogramming systems, the memory management m real-time system is less demanding. The reason is that most of the time the process remain in primary memory (programs are ROM resident) in order to provide quick response. The processes, however, have closer interaction in real-time systems. Thus, this provides feature for protection and sharing of memory.

(*b*) **I/O Management:** Time critical device management is one of the major requirements of RTOS. The external events and data have to be accepted and processed, in a highly time-bound manner.

This is implemented using system calls that allow the users to connect the devices and access Interrupt Service Routines (ISRs) directly, so as to achieve a good response time.

(*c*) **File Management: Please note that file management in real-time OS is not very critical. This is because most of the real time databases will be memory-resident.** Some embedded systems may have program and static data on ROM and may not need any online secondary devices at run-time. The dynamic data bases are maintained in ROM. In case of large real-time systems, if at all any files are to be accessed, the the primary objective is fast access rather than efficient utilization of secondary storage.

1.4.5 Network Operating system

A network operating system is defined as a collection of software and associated protocols that allows a set of autonomous computers, which are interconnected by a computer network to be used together in a convenient and cost-effective manner.

Examples of Network OS are

- BSD (Berkeley System Distribution)
- MS LAN Manager.
- WINDOWS-NT
- UNIX
- Lantastic

In a network operating system, the users are aware of the existence of multiple computers. They can login to remote machines and copy files from one machine to another machine.

Some of the main characteristics of network operating systems are as follows—

(1) Each system has it's own private OS (No global OS).

(2) Each user normally works on his or her own system. If he/she has to use a different system then some kind of remote login is required. The OS will not dynamically allocate processes to CPUs.

(3) Users know where the files have been stored. They must use some explicit file transfer commands to more files from one system to another. The OS will not do file management in this case.

Please note that the system has little or no fault tolerance. It means if 5% of the personal computers crash then 5% of the users are out of business.

Network OS offers many other capabilities. It allows the users to access various resources of the network hosts. It controls access to resources so that only users with proper authorization are allowed. It makes a user feel that remote resources are like local resources only. It also provides the online network documentation facility.

Also note that the key issue that distinguishes a network OS from a distributed OS is how much aware the users are of the fact that multiple machines are being used. This visibility occurs in three primary areas—

(*a*) File system.

(*b*) Protection.

(*c*) Program Execution.

The important issue in **file system** is how a file is accessed on one system from another in a network. There are 2 methods to solve this problem-

1. Running a special File Transfer Program (FTP), e.g., UNIX's uucp,
2. Specifying complete pathname.

Protection is another issue. UNIX and many other OSs assign a unique identifier to each user.

Program execution is the third area in which machine boundaries are visible in network operating systems. It deals with the creation of a new process when a user wants to create one.

The question is where this process is created? The answer is that one of the solution is to run a special command from your terminal to cause a program to be executed on a specific machine.

In nutshell, an OS, which includes software to communicate with other computers via a network is known as network OS. This allows resources such as files, application programs and printers to be shared between computers. These OS are specialized to provide the Networking Services. Today's OS come with the networking components built into them. Network OS can be specialized to serve as client/server OS or as Peer-to-peer OS-

Examples of client /server OS

MS-NT Server and UNIX Servers.

Examples of peer-to-peer OS

WIN-NT Workstation and WIN-95 are peer-to-peer network OS.

1.4.6 Combination Operating System

A combination OS will be the one which caters for the needs of a wide spectrum of target environments. **Please note that such OS will not be optimized for a specific environment. This is because sometimes an environment may be a hybrid of such environments,** like the same machine may be used as a software development platform and as a target machine in the real-time environment. So, commercial OS like UNIX are designed in such a way that they serve properly the needs of these various environments. Similarly, say, if batch and real-time jobs are being run simultaneously then we cannot give higher priority to batch jobs. The processes handling real world events and inputs will be given higher priority. Such systems are handled using combination OS only. Thus, now time-slicing and priority-based preemptive scheduling is required which is provided by this combined OS.

1.4.7 Distributed Operating System

A **distributed environment** refers to a collection of autonomous systems, capable of communicating and cooperating with each other through the network, are connected to each other through LAN/WAN. A distributed OS governs such a distributed system and provides a **virtual machine abstraction** to its users. A distributed OS is one that looks to its users like an ordinary centralized OS but runs on multiple independent CPUs. **Please note that the key concept here is transparency.**

It means that the use of multiple CPUs should be invisible to the user, the resource distribution must be hidden from the users and the application programs unless required by the user. **Please note here that the user views the system as virtual uniprocessor and not as a collection of distinct machines. Also note that a true distributed system is one in which users are not aware of where their programs are being run or where their files are residing. It should all be handled automatically and efficiently by the OS.**

Distributed OS often allow porgrams to run on several processors at the same time, thus requiring more complex CPU scheduling algorithms in order to achieve maximum CPU utilization. Also, these distributed systems are more reliable than uniprocessor based system. They perform even if certain part of the hardware is malfunctioning.

Examples of Distributed OS

- Amoeba
- Angle
- Alpha kernel
- Chorus

Advantages of Distributed OS

1. It allows users to access remote resources in the same manner as they do with local resources.
2. Since microprocessors have recently become very cheaper. So it is quite cheap to design these distributed systems. There has been an incremental growth *i.e.*, if there is a need of

5% more computing power then one should just add 5% more processors. **But please note that the system architecture is crucial to the type of system growth.** It is because it is difficult to give each user of a PC another 5%.

3. Distributed systems are reliable. A few parts of the system can be down without distributing users using other devices.

Disadvantage of Distributed OS

It is easy for the communication protocol overhead to become a major source of insufficiency.

Other features of Distributed OS are as follows—

(*a*) **File Management:** Distributed OS supports a single global file system visible from all machines.

(*b*) **Protection:** In a true distributed OS, there is a unique (UID) for every user which should be valid on all machines without any mapping.

(*c*) **Program Execution:** The system chooses a CPU by looking at the processing load of the system or the system always run the process on one specific machine.

1.4.8 Comparison of Network OS and Distributed OS – tabular form

Network OS	Distributed OS
1. In these systems, the control over file placement must be done manually by the users.	1. In these systems, it can be done automatically by the system itself.
2. In network OS, there are various machines each with its oven user-id (UID) mapping.	2. In distributed OS, there is a single system wide mapping that is valid everywhere.
3. We can realize a network OS if we put a layer of software on top of the native OS of individual machines. **Examples:** BSD, MS-LAN MANAGER, WIN-NT etc.	3. A distributed OS governs the operation of a distributed system. **Examples:** Amoeba, Angle, Chorus, Alpha kernel etc.

1.5 FUNCTIONS OF AN OPERATING SYSTEM

The main functions of an OS are explained under different headings for easy understanding.

1.5.1 Process Management

The term '**process**' was firstly used by Daley's and Dennis R. in 1960. A process/task is an instance of a program in execution. ***A program is just a passive entity whereas a process is an active entity.*** A process performs the required functions of its related program. **Please note that a process/ task is the smallest unit of work that is independently schedulable.** To accomplish its task, a process needs certain resources like CPU, memory, files and I/O devices. These resources are allocated to the processes by our OS only. Processes solved the problems introduced by-

(*a*) Multiprogramming batch operations.

(*b*) Time sharing.

(*c*) Real-time transaction systems.

OS has following functions related to the process management:

(*a*) **Process creation:** It involves loading of the program from secondary storage to the memory and to start its execution.

(*b*) **Process scheduling:** It means a process is transferred from the ready-state to a run-state.

(*c*) **Process suspending:** It involves transferring a process from run-state to wait-state.

(*d*) **Process Resuming:** It means transferring a process form wait-state to a ready-state when the I/O request has been completed or an event occurs.

(*e*) To provide process synchronizations for resource sharing among concurrent processes.

(*f*) To provide inter-process communication among concurrent processes.

(*g*) To provide mechanisms for deadlock handling.

(*h*) Process termination is also done by OS only. When a process has finished successfully or when it has committed a fatal error then a process needs termination or deletion. So, now the resources held by the processes are released and process control Block (PCB) is deleted.

Note: Whenever a process is created, its PCB is also created automatically. We will study this in detail later on.

1.5.2 Memory Management

Here, memory means the main memory (RAM). For a program to get executed, it must be mapped to absolute addresses and loaded into memory. So, efficient memory utilization is very necessary here. This is done by our OS. The principle storage management, responsibilities are as follows:

1. **Process isolation:** It means the controlling of one process that interacts with dates and memory of other process.
2. **Automatic allocation and Management:** Memory should be allocated dynamically based on the priorities of the process. otherwise the process waiting will increase which will decrease CPU and memory utilization.
3. **Support of modular programming:** Instead of loading, one big monolithic program, we can load only some modules (if our program is modular). This will increase CPU and memory utilization.
4. **Protection and access control:** Don't apply protection techniques and access control to all the processes. It is better to apply it to important applications only. This will save the execution time.
5. **Long-term storage:** Long-term storage of a process will reduce the memory utilization. So, swapping-in and swapping-out of the processes is to be done.

1.5.3 I/O Device Management

As we know that an OS has a set of **device drivers** i.e., software routines that control respective I/O devices through their controllers. Device drivers are written for Keyboard, Mouse, Monitor, Disk etc. and accordingly these are named as keyboard device driver, mouse device driver and so on. A device driver hides the peculiarities of its I/O device. Also, we know that a device (I/O) communicates with a host CPU through a connection point called as a **port**. A **controller** is an electronic device that controls a port or a bus or a device. A controller will have three things:

Processor + Micro-code + Local Memory

Please note that some devices have their own in-built controllers also, like disk drives. The **main task** of an OS is to collect all the resources (memory, I/O devices) and schedule the resources to the requesting process. This is why an OS is also known as a **resource manager**. Any resource allocation and scheduling policy must consider three factors:

(*a*) **Fairness:** Give equal priority to the demanding processes at the time of resource scheduling

(*b*) **Differential responsiveness:** The OS takes the decisions dynamically based on the classes of jobs and the requirement of jobs.

(*c*) **Efficiency:** The main task of an OS is to minimize the waiting time, minimize the response time and to maximize the throughout.

1.5.4 File Management

Information may be stored on Floppies, CDs, Hard disk, Tapes etc. But for convenience, OS provides a uniform logical view of the information storage. This logical storage unit is known as a **File**. The OS abstracts the logical unit 'File' from the characteristics of the underlying media.

So, OS is responsible for:

(*a*) Creation/deletion of files.

(*b*) Creation deletion of directories.

(*c*) File and directory manipulation.

(*d*) Backing or storing files onto media like tapes.

1.5.5 Secondary Storage Management

The principle online storage medium for storing programs and data is a **disk. Please note that system programs like compilers, debuggers, editors, linkers etc are stored on the disk only and are loaded into the RAM as and when required.** Most of the time we are using this hard disk only. It is the job of an OS to swap-out or swap-in such programs. It is our OS that takes care of—

(*a*) Storage Allocations

(*b*) Free space Management

(*c*) Disk Scheduling

1.5.6 Network Management

A **distributed OS** is an OS that runs on a network of computers. The memory files are **shared** by the number of users in the network from the server.

For example: If 20 nodes are connected by a server through LAN then the OS, files, RAM, processor-slots are all shared by 20 users, from the server. **Please note here that each user thinks that he is running on a single large system with one OS.** The users of a distributed system need not know where their files are on the network.

1.5.7 System Information Protection—Security

System protection refers to the mechanism for controlling the access to computer resources by various users and processes. Since there will be many (multiple) users and hence, multiple process being executed, so there is a need of protection from each other and also protection of OS from the user processes. This is the job of on OS. Generally, three types of protection mechanisms are there-

(*a*) Access control

(*b*) Information flow control

(*c*) Certification

Access Control

It is our OS only that provides read, write or execution access permissions for the files to the users, Without these permissions one cannot access the files.

Information flow control

The OS regulates the flow of data within the system. So, some information should be restricted to the users also.

Certification

The OS provides the priorities and hierarchies to the resources. So, now we can control unauthorized processes.

1.5.8 System structure

The size of OS software (code) was quite small in olden days. But now there sizes have gradually increased.

For example: The size of **WIN-NT OS** is 1,60,000 lines of code (LOC) while that of WIN-2K is 3,25,00,000 LOC.

Now, it is difficult to manage OS with such a huge code. It is difficult to do addressing, OS may be slow in working and performance is also low.

These problems can be overcome, if our OS code is modular and not monolithic. Thus, organizing, debugging and communications become easy now.

1.5.9 Command Interpretation

It is defined as an interface between the user and the OS. When a new job is started in a batch environment or when a user logs in a time-shared system then the **command interpreter** is automatically executed. A command interpreter reads and interprets the control statements. It is also known as a **shell.**

There are two ways in which one can interact with OS—

1. By means of System Commands
2. By means of System Calls.

Method 1: Users may interact with the OS directly by using OS commands. A command provides an interface between an interactive user and the OS. **For example,** if you wish to list files or sub-directories in MS-DOS then you invoke **dir** command.

Method 2: System calls provide an interface between the processes and the OS. User programs receives OS services through a set of system calls only. System calls are usually embedded in the user programs. **For example,** the use of system calls in C or PASCAL programs resemble very much to our pre-defined function or subroutine calls.

Please note that for each system command, there will be an equivalent system call. Also note that the system calls for an OS are listed in the application programs Interface (API) manual.

Based on all these nine (9) functions, the OS is divided into sub-systems each of which corresponds to a software component of an OS.

For example: Process Management Component, Memory Management Component, I/O Management Component, File Management Component and so on.

1.6 CHARACTERISTICS OF MODERN OPERATING SYSTEMS

A modern OS must have five main characteristics:

1. Object-oriented design
2. Multithreading
3. Distributed OS
4. Symmetric Multiprocessing
5. Micro kernel Architecture

We shall now discuss them one by one.

1.6.1 Object-oriented Design

A modern OS must have an object-oriented design (OOD). In this method, an OS creates the objects for each facility. Each object has a set of operations.

1.6.2 Multithreading

A good and modern OS must support multi (many) threading (threads) concept also. A thread is a smaller task of a program that is executed by a processor at a time. The number of independent threads in an application that are executed by the processor at a time is called as multithreading.

For example: When we are typing a MS-WORD document, we can also do spell checking at the same time. These individual tasks are called as threads.

1.6.3 Distributed Operating System

A modern OS must support distributed systems also. A distributed OS should be able to run on a network of computers. It is a collection of processors which do not share memory, clock or I/O devices. Instead, each processor has its local clock and RAM. The users of a distributed system do not know where their files are on the network. User views the system as a **virtual uniprocessor.** A good and modern OS should handle automatically and efficiently all such issues.

1.6.4 Symmetric Multiprocessing

A modern OS should support symmetric multiprocessing also. The OS designed for symmetric processing is called as a **symmetric multiprocessing operating system.** It has its own advantages. Some of these are:

1. **Better throughput:** Throughout means the number of jobs executed by the CPU per unit time.
2. **Better reliability:** Reliability can improve. It means that if one processor fails due to hardware problem even then other processors can continue to work.
3. **Better speeds:** From user's point of view, jobs now will be executed at a faster rate.

1.6.5 Micro-kernel Architecture

A microkernel is a minimal OS that performs only the essential functions of an operating system. System processes will perform all other OS functions. **Please note that here the system processes means servers. And a system which contains the servers are called as the client-server systems/model/architecture.**

1.7 OPERATING SYSTEM STRUCTURE

A system as large and complex, as a modern OS must be engineered carefully if it has to function properly. OS system structure may be of 4 types:

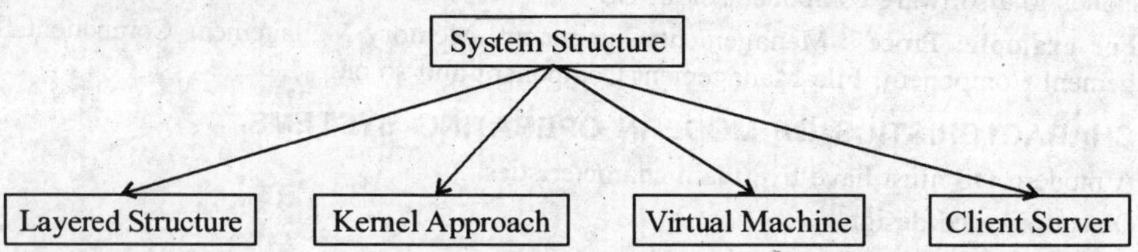

Fig. 1.10. OS Structures

1.7.1 Layered Structure Approach

The OS architecture based on a layered approach consists of a number of layers/levels, each built on top of lower layers.

The bottom layer is the hardware and the highest layer is the user interface.

As the name implies, this type of approach was made in order to use advanced hardware. This was applicable by giving proper hardware support so that the OS could be broken into smaller, more appropriate pieces than those allowed by the original MS-DOS or UNIX. Hence, modular OS were created. The modularization of the system can be done in many ways. The most normal is a layered approach which consists of breaking up of the OS in a number of **Layers** or **Levels.**

The Figure 1.11 shows a typical OS layer, say, layer–N.

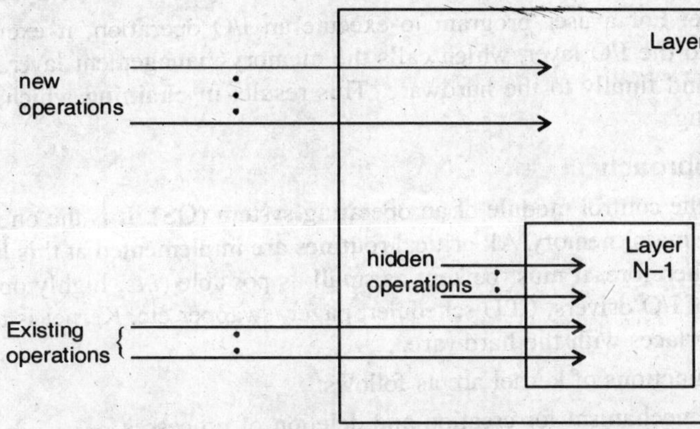

Fig. 1.11. An OS layer

The concept of modularity can be implemented by the layer system. **Please note here that a chain is formed in case of layers such that each uses functions and services of only lower level layers.** The main advantage of this type of approach is debugging and system verification. A systematic approach is followed. The first layer can be debugged without any concern for the rest of the system because by definition, it uses only the basic hardware to implement its functions. As soon as the first layer is debugged, a chain is formed and so on. This process can be very helpful in error detection because we know that error must be in a particular layer, because the layers under it are already debugged. Each layer is implemented using only those operations that are provided by the lower level layers. If a layer does not want to know how these operations are implemented then it just needs to know, what these operations do.

For example: The first system constructed using this approach was the *THE system* built by E.W. Dijkestra in 1968 and his students. The **THE system** was a simple batch OS which had 32 k of 27-bit words. This system was defined in six layers as shown below in Figure 1.12.

Layer–5:	User Programs
Layer–4:	Buffering for I/O devices
Layer–3:	Device Driver
Layer–2:	Memory Management
Layer–1:	CPU Scheduling
Layer–0:	Hardware

Fig. 1.12. Layered structure of THE OS

As is clear from figure 12, the bottom layer (layer-O) dealt with hardware. The higher layer (layer-1) handled allocation of jobs to CPU. The next layer (layer - 2) implemented virtual memory management scheme. Level-3 contained the device driver for the operator's console. By placing it at level-3 and I/O buffering at level-4, above memory management, the device drivers could be placed in virtual memory. Finally, layer-5 was of user programs.

Problems/disadvantages of layered approach

1. **The major problem with this approach is how to differentiate one level from another.** Since a layer can use services of a layer below it, it needs careful planning. **For example:** The device driver for secondary memory must be at a lower level than the memory management routines since memory management requires the ability to use the backing store.

2. **The final problem with this approach is that they are less efficient than other types. Please note that this is because of the formation of chain of layers which delays the whole process.**

For example: For a user program to execute an I/O operation, it excutes a system call which is trapped to the I/O layer, which calls the memory-management layer, through the CPU scheduling layer and finally to the hardware. This results in **chaining** which is a long process and time consuming.

1.7.2 Kernel approach

A *Kernel* is the control module of an operating system (OS). It is the one which loads first and remains in the main memory. All critical routines are implemented at this layer. Since kernel stays in memory, therefore, it must be kept as small as possible (*i.e.*, highly optimized). The OS kernel comprises of I/O drivers, CPU scheduler, pager, swapper etc. Kernel is that part of an OS which directly interfaces with the hardware.

Some main functions of kernel are as follows:

1. It provides a mechanism for creation and deletion of processes.
2. It provides processor scheduling, memory management I/O management.
3. It provides mechanism for synchronization of processes.
4. It provides mechanisms for interprocess communications.

For example: The UNIX OS is based on the Kernel approach. It is shown below in Figure 1.13.

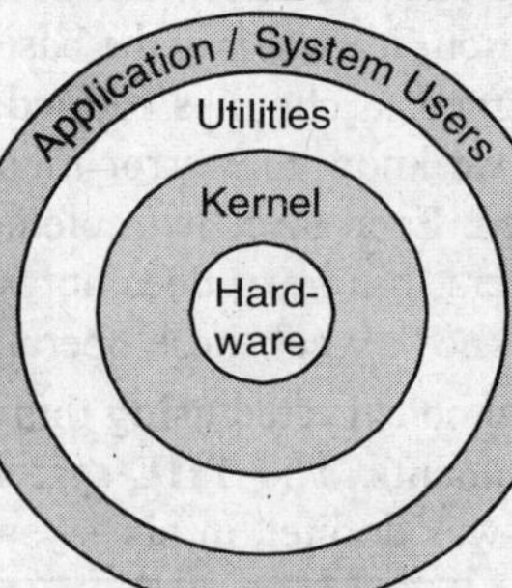

Fig. 1.13. UNIX OS structure

As shown in Figure 1.13, there are two separable parts:

(*a*) Kernel.

(*b*) System programs.

Kernel lies between system programs (or utilities) and hardware. This Kernel uses system calls to perform all its functions-like CPU scheduling, memory management etc. UNIX also supports many system calls. **Please remember that through these system calls, the program utilizes the services of OS (Kernel).**

Shell is an exclusive feature of UNIX. It has a **command Interpreter** which receives and executes OS commands. For OS with GUI (Graphical User Interface) facility, the command processor will interpret mouse operations and executes the appropriate command. **It is also known as a command line interpreter.**

1.7.3 Virtual Machine Approach

It is an approach that creates an illusion of a real machine. The virtual machine creates this illusion by time-multiplexing the system resources among all the users of the machine. A user can also run a single-user OS on this virtual machine. Different OS can run on different virtual machines. **For example,** VM/370 on IBM 370.

An illusion is created by a virtual machine OS that makes a single real machine to appear as several real machines.

Advantages of virtual machine

1. It allows **concurrent running** of dissimilar OS by **different users**.
2. It eliminates certain conversion problem. (This is discussed below).
3. Programs can be developed and debugged for machine configurations that is different from those of host.

   For example: a virtual OS-VM/370 can produce virtual 370 that are different form the real 370 such as larger main memory.
4. The high degree of separation between independent virtual machine provides more security and privacy. The most widely used OS in this category is VM/370. It manages IBM/370 computer and creates an illusion that each of the several users has a complete system 370 (including wide range of I/O devices) which can run different OS at once, each of them on its own virtual machine.

In a virtual multiprogramming system, a single real machine gives an illusion of several virtual machines, each having its own virtual processor, storage and I/O devices possibly with much larger capacities. This technique creates an illusion of a very large memory for program execution.

It is also possible through software, to share files existing on physical disk and several information through virtual communication software.

The virtual machines are created by sharing the resources of physical computer. CPU scheduling can be used to share the CPU and make it appear that users have their own processor. Thus, user are given their own virtual machine. Users can run on their virtual machine. Users can run on their virtual machines, any desired software. **Please note that the virtual machine software is concerned with multiprogramming multiple virtual machines onto a physical machine but need not consider any other software support from user.**

The heart of the system is known as the virtual machine monitor. It runs on the bare hardware and does multiprogramming. However, note that these virtual machines are not extended machines (with more features) but are the exact copies of the bare hardware including kernel, interrupts and everything else the real machine has. That is why each of these virtual machines can run different OSs also.

Applications of virtual Machine system

If we have a network of virtual machines, each of which can send information over **virtual communication network** then such a virtual machine is a perfect vehicle for OS research and development. **Making changes to OS pointers is very dangerous.** Therefore, the current system must be stopped and taken out of use and only then changes should be made and tested. This is called as **system development time.** A virtual machine can eliminate much of this problem. System programmers are given their own virtual machine and system development is done on the virtual machine, instead of, on a physical machine. So, normal system operation is not disrupted for the system development.

1.7.4 Client-Server Model

A *modern trend* today is to move the code up, into higher layers and even further to higher layers so that we can remove the code as much as possible from the OS, leaving below a minimal kernel. Here, the usual approach is to implement most of the OS functions in the user processes. The client process/user process sends a request to the server process by communications between clients and servers. This is what a kernel does. It splits the OS into parts, each of which handles only one facet of the system like file service, process service, terminal service or memory service. This is shown in Figure 1.14.

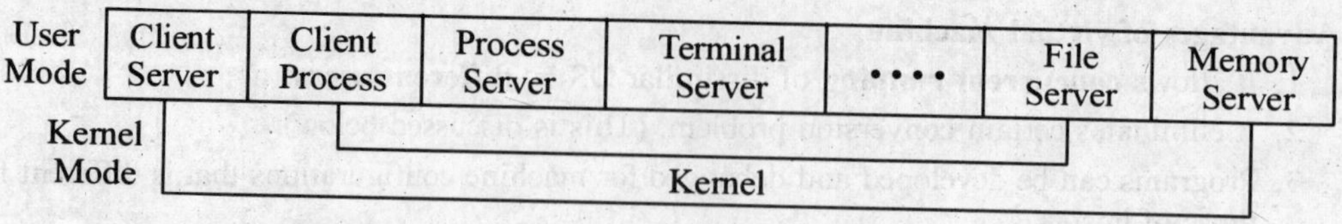

Fig. 1.14. Client-Server Model

This is how each part becomes small and manageable. **Also note that since all servers run as user-mode processes and not in kernel mode so they do not have direct access to the hardware.**

Hence, if a bug in the file server is triggered then the file service may crash, but this will not bring the entire system down.

This model is well adopted in distributed systems also. The client sends a request and reply comes back. He/she is not aware of whether the request message was handled locally in its own machine only or whether it was sent across a network to a server on a remote machine.

1.8 FUTURE TRENDS IN OPERATING SYSTEMS

Due to the development of VLSI chips and due to the reduction in the cost of hardware, multiprocessing will become common and cheaper. Instead of large softwares performing OS functions, micro-codes will be written and implemented. This will make execution faster. The use of distributed OS will increase. Hardware and OS will be designed in such a way that they will be able to execute concurrent programs more efficiently. Developments in the field of software Engineering will make OS softwares more reliable as well as more maintainable. The use of networking OS will also increase as everyday data transmission rates are doubling. All new OS must be supporting multimedia, animations etc in near future.

1.9 CASE STUDY ON TRADITIONAL AND MODERN UNIX SYSTEM

First of all let us see the history of a traditional Unix OS. The first version of unix was developed in 1996 by Ken Thompson of the research group at the Bell laboratories. During the past 25 years, UNIX OS has evolved into a powerful, flexible and versatile OS. It can be used as an OS on all types of computers like single-user personal computers, micro computers, minicomputers and super computers. Today, the growth in use of UNIX OS is termendous. About 20 million computers today use UNIX and more than 100 million people use these systems. This rapid growth is expected to continue. This is so because UNIX is portable, adaptable and simple and supports multi-user and multi-tasking nature. The main features of UNIX are as follows:

1. Ability to support multi users and multi-tasking.
2. UNIX is easily portable from one system to another.
3. It provides excellent network environment.
4. It is adaptable and simple. UNIX utilities are simple and are directed more towards a single function. Unix has an important utility known as a **filler** which is a complex tool.
5. File system in Unix is more of a transparent nature. The file system is hierarchical in mature and works in the time sharing mode.

UNIX Achitecture

Unix architecture has four layers, namely:

(*a*) Hardware

(*b*) Kernel

(c) System call interface (shell)

(d) Application (users) programs/libraries. These layers are shown in Fig. 1.15 below:

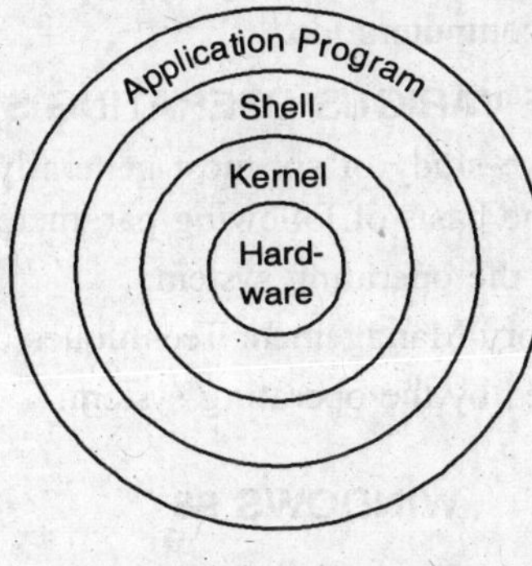

Fig. 1.15. Unix Structure

Kernel: It is the part of OS that interacts directly with the hardware. The OS kernel comprises of I/O drivers, CPU scheduler, pager, swapper etc. Our programs can interact with the kernel through system calls.

Shell: Shell is a program that reads the commands that are entered through the command line and interprets them and sends requests to execute a program. That is why a shell is also called as a command interpreter.

Hardware: It includes various computer parts like clocks, timers etc.

Application program: This layer includes user applications using shell as a programming language. (For more details, students can refer to Section 1.11). On the other hand, **a modern. UNIX System** is shown in Fig. 1.16. In this figure, the outer circles represents functions and an interface that may be implemented in a variety of ways.

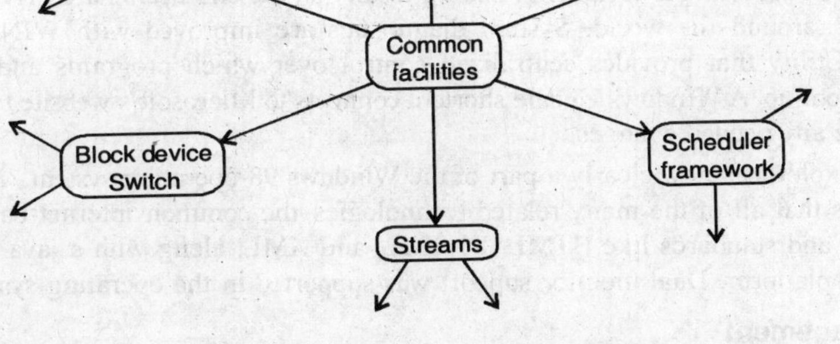

Fig. 1.16. Kernel of a modern UNIX

All unix commands are executed at the shell level. The more advanced versions of unix supports networking via communication links through TCP/IP and also supports the concept of socket formation.

For example: UNIX OS by BSD (Berkeley Software Distribution) is a modern OS. It plays a key role in the development of the OS design theory. System V Release 4, UNIX OS is another modern OS that can work on supercomputers too.

1.10 COMPARATIVE STUDY OF VARIOUS OPERATING SYSTEMS—A CASE STUDY

Given below is the comparative study of six most generally used operating systems these days. The comparison is given on the basis of following parameters:

- **Features:** General Features of the operating system.
- **Memory Management:** Memory Management Techniques used by the operating system.
- **File Systems:** File System Used by the operating system.

WINDOWS 98

History

Windows 98 (WIN/98) was Microsoft's "third version" of the popular operating system Windows; prior versions were Window 3.1 and Windows 95. One should know that Windows 1.0 shipped in November 20, 1985. The term "Windows" refers specifically to the rectangular portion of the screen representing a program, with application-independent format. Windows 98 is a desktop operating system that runs on any of the following **processors:** INTEL, CYRIX, AMD, and PENTIUM. It shipped on June 25, 1998.

Features

The intended purpose of WIN/98 is for desktop use; however it can run on some low-end servers. WIN/98 is a proprietary system owned by a company opposed to an open system. WIN/98 operating system's three primary capabilities (graphics-oriented user interface, multitasking, and hardware independence) are not new, but combining the three into one operating system is. There are two types of system resources: user and GDI (Graphic Device Interface). Both of these resources are limited to a fixed 64KB. This is an example of backward compatibility for 16-bit programs originally written for DOS and WIN/3.X. WIN/98 supports plug-and-play, desktop user profiles, LAN connectivity and peer-to-peer networking architecture, AGP video cards, and DVD drives.

WIN/98's most visible feature is the Active Desktop, which integrates the web browser (Internet Explorer 4.0) with the operating system. Form the end-users point of view there is no difference between accessing a document residing locally on the end-users hard drive or on a web server halfway around the world. System diagnostics are improved with WIN/98's System Configuration Utility that provides centralized control over which programs and settings are loaded during boot-up. A Windows Update shortcut connects to Microsoft's website to scan system files and update any needed changes.

Internet Explorer is now clearly a part of the Windows 98 operating system. What may not be so obvious is that all of the many related technologies–the common internet-based protocols *HTTP* and *FTP* and standards like HTML, DHTML, and XML, along with a java VM–are also now part of the platform. Dual monitor support was supported in the operating system.

Memory Management

Memory management in WIN/98 is improved over the previous version of WIN/98. The major improvement is the change in Virtual Cache a.k.a VCache. VCache is used to store previous used code and data that Windows thinks it might use again. If the code or data is just flushed from memory, but is needed again, it has to be read anew from the hard dive. This is much slower than finding the code or data already in RAM.

One of the improvements in (VCache) management in WIN/98 is the fix of a bug in the pervious version WIN/95. This bug would keep VCache from releasing RAM when needed. The second improvement is that Windows can now execute code or data directly from VCache (Martell User Tips). WIN/98 had a problem of the size of VCache growing and diminishing the amount of available RAM. An improvement was needed leading to the development of a patch, WIN/98 Second Edition. The problem with large amounts of RAM is that VCache size can become large enough that it consumes all of the addresses in the system area. This leaves no virtual memory addresses available for other functions such as opening an MS-DOS prompt.

File System

File system of an operating system is a comparison to a library on the hard drive. WIN/98 uses the FAT (File Allocation Table) 32 and the older FAT 16 format. FAT 32 is an enhancement of the FAT file system that supports larger drives with improved disk space recovery. This file system is incompatible with Microsoft NT's distributed file system. It has new extensions to support the Win32 platform, because it was built to have backwards compatibility for Windows 95. Microsoft supplied the virtual machine manager for developers to take advantage of the last offering of the 32bit DOS based OS from the computer giant. Windows 98 was designed with the 32-bit kernel but runs the WIN 95 16 bit kernel by using thunking. That allows both kernels to coexist seamlessly (Pleas).

WINDOWS 98

Windows 98 is a low quality destop operating system made by Microsoft that urns on Intel/ Cyrix/AMD Pentium and Intel 486DX.

kind	server/mainframe	desktop/workstation	handheld	real time
proprietary custom	low end servers	desktop	not appropriate	not appropriate
current version	**hardware supported**	**number of bits**		
		maximum processors		
98	486 DX, Pentium	24 bits		
		1 Processor		

WINDOWS CE

History

Microsoft released Windows CE 1.0 in November 1996 and released WIN/CE 2.0 one year later (MWH). A version of the Windows operating system designed for small devices such as personal digital assistants (PDA). The Windows CE graphical user interface (GUI) is very similar to Windows 95. Windows CE 3.0 was released in June of 2000. It is now an embedded operating system with comprehensive development tools. It combines the power of Windows and the Internet (PC Museum).

Features

Windows CE was originally developed as an OS system for two different types of apparatuses, interactive TV set-top boxes, and hand held computing devices. It is this OS system that gives the hand-held computing business the "look & feel" of Windows 95/98. It allows the users to use their device in the same way that they would use their Window system at home. This ability was very important due to programs the user would be able to use: Word, Excel, Internet Explorer, File Explorer, and most all of the Microsoft based programs. It virtually gave the user the power of their desktop to the palm of their hand.

Features of version 3.0 now include Inking: it recognizes writing or drawings on the touch screen. Handwriting recognition is supported. It supports all major communication formats, including Infrared, Serial, Telephony, TCP/IP, ICMOP, and ARP. It has SSL built in. It can share its Internet connection and run its desktop on WIN NT or 2000 (Embedded). It has many more features. This allows the device to provide the speed required by the public, while allowing it to be robust enough to give the user the feel of being on his desktop at home.

Memory Management

Windows CE implements almost the full Win32® memory management application program interface (API) available under Windows NT and Windows 98. Windows CE had the feel of Windows 95/98. However, it was much more common to the Windows NT functionality in that it would run the CE programs in 32MB protected memory spaces. This would help prevent the whole system form crashing when one application failed. In addition, by streamlining the Windows CE operating system it allowed the programmer to code the application in a much more cleaner and flexible format. This allowed the programmmers not to worry about the multiple legacy systems that the other versions of Windows had to support.

Chris De Herrera is a long-time CE porponent, website owner, and MSN forum manager. His information reveals the inner workings of the soft white underbelly of Windows CE. **De Herrera writes "Windows CE is able to address as much RAM as the user wants to install in a system. Each application is only allowed 32 MB of RAM and uses preemptive multitasking. Windows CE can multitask up to 32 applications at once."** Further he elaborates on the memory by stating "Program memory is efficiently handled via dynamically allocated 1k or 4k pages depending on the processor used. In addition, Windows CE supports the allocation of shared files stored above the first 1 GB of program space.

Finally, Window CE supports execute is place for ROM based applications to reduce the RAM required to operate the system. **Douglas Boiling shares more on the virtual memory of WIN/CE: "Windows CE devices have as little as 2MB off RAM, with half of that dedicated to file storage. Windows CE applications must pare memory usage to the bone just to survive in such a low-memory environment."** Windows CE does not maintain a page file on a disk; it does have a memory protection scheme that supports page-based virtual memory. The virtual memory functions are the most basic level of memory allocation available to a program.

The CE OS memory system uses the heap method. The heap is the best place to allocate small units of memory, say a hundred to a few thousand bytes. Unlike Windows 3.x with its 64K limits, Windows CE does not limit the heap to any fixed size. The operating system enlarges the heap as allocations are made. As the contents of the heap are freed, the system shrinks the total size of the heap, if possible (Boiling).

File System

On the Microsoft Embedded site, the file system is listed as "Store data in files that exist in directories." Even though that does not list the file structure, other research that was gleaned revealed that it ran the NT file research (NTFS) and an Object Store. The object store is both the data and the procedures to manipulate the data. Available object stress include the file systems, registry, and the database.

The database provides storage and retrieval of database records, with up to four keys and support for transaction logging and rollback. The object store is accessed through the Win32 API. It supports

FATFS, including multiple FAT volumes (up to 99 volumes), Installable block Device Drivers (ATA flash and SRAM drivers included), and Databases on mounted file systems (Windows CE).

WINDOWS CE

Windows CE is a low quality handheld operating system made by Microsoft that runs on Intel/Cyrix/AMD Pentium.

kind	server/mainframe	Desktop/workstation	handheld	real time
Proprietary custom	not appropriate	not appropriate	appropriate	not appropriate
current version	**hardware supported**	**number of bits**		
		maximum processors		
CE98	Pentium	24 bits		
		1 Processor		

WINDOWS 2000

History

Windows 2000 (W2K) is available in four versions. Windows 2000 Professional is the desktop version, for stand-alone use or acting as a client. The other three versions act as servers: Windows 2000 Server will support 2-way SMP (symmetric multiprocessing with 2 CPUs), Windows 2000 Advanced Server will support 4-way SMP and Windows 2000 Data Center Server will support 16-way SMP and 64 GB of physical memory. The history of this operating system began in 1997 and became available to the public in February 2000 (Windows 2000 History). This product has a flavor for everyone from homeowners to a Fortune 500 Enterprise. This is a massive operating system with around 30-48 million lines of code (Thompson).

Features

This operating system was built upon NT technology that combined the familiar Windows 98 user interface. Windows 2000 Server sets a new standard for how well an operating system can be integrated with Web, application, networking, communication, and infrastructure services. Windows 2000 Professional, which will be what this paper concentrates on, is literally crash proof according to Ed Bott at ZDNet. Active Win reports improvements or changes to over 51 key features. Describing these entire features is not in the scope of this paper.

The major premise is entwining the stability and professional features of Windows NT with the usability of WIN 98 into a new operating system that is robust, fast, scalable and secure. ZD Labs was commissioned by Microsoft to compare the reliability of WIN2K, WIN98 and WIN NT. The reliability test conclued that the operating system was much more reliable. Additionally until other operating system developers can provide the standardization the Microsoft has, they will lag the development for working device drivers.

Microsoft engineered the program to be able to install most programs without the need for rebooting. The full 32 bit minimizes the chance for application failures and rebooting. Microsoft implemented the windows Logo program, which is a comprehensive set of standards that ensure system compatibility from third party vendors. The processor and memory is scalable: it supports up to 4 gigabytes of RAM and two symmetric multiprocessors. The Encrypting File System (EFS) encrypts each file with a randomly generated key, which is transparent to the user. Kerberos support is provided. Kerberos is an Internet-standard, which makes it especially effective for networks consisting of different operating systems such as UNIX (W2Keval). Along with those features, all Internet and mobile features have been vastly improved.

Memory Management

Windows 2000 allows the administrator to investigate and resolve memory problems. The Performance Console (System Info Console in WIN98) offers improved control when compared to the other versions of Windows. The Memory performance object consists of counters that describe the behavior of physical and virtual memory on the computer. A performance object is any resource, application, or service that can be measured. Using System Monitor and Performance Logs and Alerts, you can select performance objects, counters, and instances to collect and present data about the performance of system components or installed software (W2KPRKW).

Physical memory is the amount of random-access memory (RAM) on the computer. Virtual memory consists of space in physical memory and on disk. Many of the memory counters monitor paging, which is the movement of pages of code and data between disk and physical memory. Excessive paging, a symptom of a memory shortage, can cause delays that interfere with all system processes (W2KPRKW).

Microsoft improved upon the prior versions of Memory and Cache management. They changed the default size of the paging file to 1.5 times that of the installed RAM (W2KPRK 1289). Cache object counters are similar to the Disk Cachee in the Windows 98 System Monitor, but are named differently. These new Cache object counters display the memory in kilobytes and megabytes.

The Cache performance object consists of counters that monitor the file system cache, an area of physical memory that stores recently used data as long as possible to permit access to the data without having to read from the disk. Because applications typically use the cache, the cache is monitored as an indicator of application input/output (I/O) operations. When memory is plentiful, the cache can grow, but when memory is scarce, the cache can become too small to be effective (W2KPRKW). All of the attributes are adjustable (W2KPRK 1293). One can investigate the source of memory leaks, Kernel-Mode memories leaks, and optimize the memory as needed. This is substantial improvement over the memory problems that plagued WIN98 and NT.

File System

WIN2K supports DOS*, FAT 16*, FAT32 and NTFS. DOS is supported by following the dual-boot procedures supplied from Microsoft, as is FAT16. The NT file system supports large disks up to 2 Terabytes (W2KPRK 114). WIN2K improved NTFS with the following features: Volumes can be increased, Disk Quotas, Encryption, Distributed Link Tracking and Mount Points.

The distributed file system (DFS) is a networking component called IntelliMirror that seamlessly integrates server files onto the desktop. It provides transparency to shared drives on other servers with ease for the end user. Dfs provides a uniform naming convention and mapping for collections of servers, shares, and files. This allows uses to simplify navigation of networked drives or servers. Since DFS maps the physical storage into a logical representation, the net benefit is that the physical location of data becomes transparent to users and applications.

WINDOWS 2000

Windows 2000 professional, Windows 2000 Server, and Windows 2000 Advanced Server are server and workstation operating systems made by Microsoft that run on the Intel/Cyrix/AMD Pentium.

kind	server/mainframe	Desktop/workstation	handheld	real time
Proprietary custom	low quality servers	low quality workstations	not appropriate	not appropriate
current version	**hardware supported**	**number of bits**		
		maximum processors		
2000	Pentium	32 bits (Professional and Server), partially 64 bits (Advanced Server) bits		
		2 (Professional), 4 (Server), 8 (Server Advanced) processors		

WINDOWS NT

History

In 1988, Microsoft decided to develop a "new technology" (NT) portable operating system that supported both the OS/2 and POSIX APIs.

Originally, NT was supposed to use the OS/2 API as its native environment but during development NT was changed to use the Win32 API, reflecting the popularity of Windows 3.0

The first versions of NT were Windows NT 3.1 and Windows NT 3.1 Advanced Server. At that time, 16-bit Windows was at version 3.1. In version 4.0, NT adopted the Windows 95 user interface and incorporated Internet web-server and browser software. In addition some user interface routines and graphics code were moved into the kernel to improve performance with the side effect of decreased system reliability.

Features

Key features of Windows NT are:

- extensibility
- portability
- reliability
- compatibility
- performance
- international support

- **Extensibility** — layered architecture.
  - NT executive, which runs in protected mode, provides the basic system services.
  - On top of the executive, several server subsystems operate in user mode.
  - Modular structure allows additional environmental subsystems to be added without affecting the executive.
- **Portability**— NT can be moved from one hardware architecture to another with relatively few changes.
  - Written in C and C++.
  - Processor-dependent code is isolated in a dynamic link library (DLL) called the "hardware abstraction layer" (HAL).

- **Reliability** — NT uses hardware protection for virtual memory, and software protection mechanisms for operating system resources.
- **Compatibility** — applications that follow the IEEE 1003.1 (POSIX) standard can be complied to run on NT without changing the source code.
- **Performance** — NT subsystems can communicate with one another via high-performance massage passing.
  - Preemption of low priority threads enables the system to respond quickly to external events.
  - Designed for symmetrical multiprocessing.
- **International support** — supports different locales via the national language support (NLS) API.

Windows NT Block Diagram

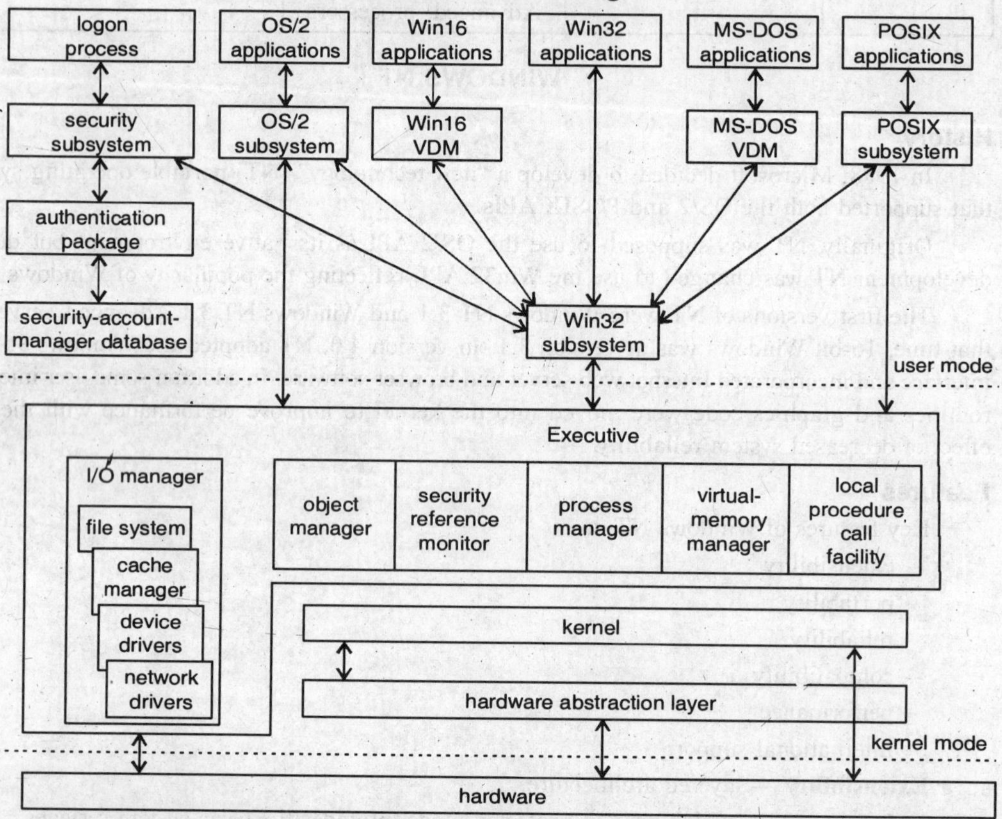

Memory Management

An application can use memory by memory mapping a file into its address space.

- Multistage process.
- Two processes share memory mapping a file into their virtual memory.

A heap in the Win32 environment is a region of reserved address space.

- A Win32 process is created with a 1 MB **default heap**.
- Access is synchronized to protect the heap's space allocation data structures from damage by concurrent updates by multiple threads.

Because functions that rely on global or static data typically fail to work properly in a multithreaded environment, the thread-local storage mechanism allocates global storage on a per-thread basis.

- The mechanism provides both dynamic and static methods of creating thread-local storage.

File System

The fundamental structure of the NT file system (NTFS) is a **volume**.

- Created by the NT disk administrator utility.
- Based on a logical disk partition.
- May occupy a portion of a disk, an entire disk, or span across several disks.

All **metadata,** such as information about the volume, is stored in a regular file. NTFS uses **clusters** as the underlying unit of disk allocation.

- A cluster is a number of disk sectors that is a power of two.
- Because the cluster size is smaller than for the 16-bit FAT file system, the amount of internal fragmentation is reduced.

Important Points about NT File System (NTFS).

- NTFS uses **logical cluster numbers** (LCNs) as disk addresses.
- A file in NTFS is not a simple byte stream, as in MS-DOS or UNIX rather, it is a structured object consisting of **attributes.**
- Every file in NTFS is described by one or more records in an array stored in a special file called the Master File Table (MFT).
- Each file on an NTFS volume has a unique ID called a **file reference.**
  - 64-bit quantity that consists of a 16-bit file number and a 48-bit sequence number.
  - Can be used to perform internal consistency checks.
- The NTFS name space is organized by a hierarchy of directories; the *index root* contains the top level of the B+ tree.
- Security of an NTFS volume is derived from the NT object model.
- To compress a file, NTFS divides the file's data into **compression units,** which are blocks of 16 contiguous clusters.
- For sparse files, NTFS uses another technique to save space.
  - Clusters that contain all zeros are not actually allocated or stored on disk.
  - Instead, gaps are left in the sequence of virtual cluster numbers stored in the MFT entry for the file.
  - When reading a file, if a gap in the virtual cluster numbers is found, NTFS just zero-fills that portion of the caller's buffer.

Comparison of Windows NT File Systems

File System	Advantages	Disadvantages
FAT	Can be accessed when the computer is running a variety of operating systems.	Not protected by Windows NT security or fault-tolerance features.
NTFS	• Provides full file security access control. • Provides fault tolerance via transaction logging. • Automatically generates short file names for compatibility with MS-DOS.	Is recognized by Windows NT only.

WINDOWS NT

Windows NT, Windows NT Server, and Windows NT Server Enterprise Edition are server and workstation operating systems made by Microsoft that run on Intel/Cyrix/AMD Pentium, Intel 80 × 86, and DEC Alpha.

Kind	server/mainframe	desktop/workstation	handheld	real time
Proprietary custom	low quality servers	low quality workstations	not appropriate	not appropriate
current version	**hardware supported**	**number of bits**		
		maximum processors		
5 (2000)	Pentium	32 bits		
		4 processors		

UNIX

History

After three decades of use, the UNIX computer operating system from Bell Labs is still regarded as one of the most powerful, versatile, and flexible operating systems (OS) in the computer world. Its popularity is due to many factors, including its ability to run a wide variety of machines, from micros to supercomputers, and its portability – all of which led to its adoption by many manufacturers.

Like another legendary creature whose name also ends in 'x,' UNIX rose from the ashes of a multi-organizational effort in the early 1960s to develop a dependable timesharing operating system.

The joint effort was not successful, but a few survivors from Bell Labs tried again, and what followed was a system that offers its users a work environment that has been described as "of unusual simplicity, power, and elegance...."

The system also fostered a distinctive approach to software design–solving a problem by interconnecting simpler tools, rather than creating large monolithic application programs.

Its development and evolution led to a new philosophy of computing, and it has been a never-ending source of both challenges and joy to programmers around the world.

Features

The features that made UNIX a hit from the start are:

- Multitasking capability
- Multi-user capability
- Portability
- UNIX programs
- Library of application software

Multitasking

Many computers do just one thing at a time, as anyone who uses a PC or laptop can attest. Try logging onto you company's network while opening your browser while opening a word processing program. Chances are the processor will freeze for a few seconds while it sorts out the multiple instructions.

UNIX, on the other hand, lets a computer do several things at once, such as printing out one file while the user edits another file. This is a major feature for users, since users don't have to wait for one application to end before starting another one.

Multi-user

The same design that permits multitasking permits multiple users to use the computer. The computer can take the commands of a number of users–determined by the design of the computer–to run programs, access files, and print documents at the same time.

The computer can't tell the printer to print all the requests at once, but it does prioritize the requests to keep everything orderly. It also lets several users access the same document by compartmentalizing the document so that the changes of one user don't override the changes of another user.

System portability

A major contribution of the UNIX system was its portability, permitting it to move from one brand of computer to another with a minimum of code changes. At a time when different computer lines of the same vendor didn't talk to each other—yet alone machines of multiple vendors–that meant a great savings in both hardware and software upgrades.

It also meant that the operating system could be upgraded without having all the customer's data inputted again. And new versions of UNIX were backward compatible with older versions, making it easier for companies to upgrade in an orderly manner.

UNIX tools

UNIX comes with hundreds of programs that can divided into two classes:

- Integral utilities that are absolutely necessary for the operation of the computer, such as the command interpreter, and
- Tools those aren't necessary for the operation of UNIX but provide the user with additional capabilities, such as typesetting and e-mail.

UNIX Communications

E-mail is commonplace today, but it has only come into its own in the business community within the last 10 years. Not so with users, who have been enjoying e-mail for several decades.

UNIX e-mail at first permitted users on the same computer to communicate with each other via their terminals. Then users on different machines, even made by different vendors, were connected to support e-mail. And finally, UNIX systems around the world were linked in to a world wide web decades before the development of today's World Wide Web.

Applications libraries

UNIX as it is known today didn't just develop overnight. Nor were just a few people responsible for its growth. As soon as it moved from Bell Labs into the universities, every computer programmer worth his or her own salt started developing programs for UNIX.

Today there are hundreds of UNIX applications that can be purchased from third-party vendors, in addition to the applications that come with UNIX.

How UNIX is organized ?

The UNIX system is functionally organized at three levels:

- The kernel, which schedules tasks and manages storage;

- The shell, which connects and interprets users' commands, calls programs from memory, and executes them; and
- The tools and applications that offer additional functionality to the operating system.

The kernel

The heart of the operating system, the kernel controls the hardware and turns part of the system on and off at the programmer's command. If you ask the computer to list (ls) all the files in a directory, the kernel tells the computer to read all the files in that directory from the disk and display them on your screen.

The shell

There are several types of shell, most notably the command driven Bourne Shell and the C Shell (no pun intended), and menu-driven shells that make it easier for beginners to use. Whatever shell is used, its purpose remains the same–to act as an interpreter between the user and the computer.

The shell also provides the functionality of "pipes" whereby a number of commands can be linked together by a user, permitting the output of one program to become the input to another program.

Tools and applications

There are hundreds of tools available to UNIX users, although some have been written by third party vendors for specific applications. Typically, tools are ground into categories for certain functions, such as word processing, business applications, or programming.

Memory Management

The initial memory management schemes of UNIX were constrained in size by the relatively small memory resources of the PDP machines on which UNIX was developed.

Pre 3BSD system used swapping exclusively to handle memory contention among processes; if there is too much contention, processes are swapped out until enough memory is available.

Allocation of both main memory and swap space in UNIX is done by first-fit method. Sharable text segments do not need to be swapped which results in less swap traffic and reduces the amount of main memory required for multiple processes using the same text-segment.

In UNIX the **scheduler process (or swapper)** decides which processes to swap in or out, considering such factors as time idle, time in or out of main memory, size, etc.

In 4.3BSD, swap space is allocated in pieces that are multiples of power of 2 and minimum size, up to a maximum size determined by the size or the swap-space partition on the disk.

Berkeley UNIX systems depend primarily on paging for memory-contention management, and depend only secondarily on swapping.

Demand paging is a technique which is used when a process needs a page and the page is not there, a page fault to the kernel occurs, a frame of main memory is allocated, and the proper disk page is read into the frame.

File System

The UNIX file system supports two main objects: files and directories. Directories are just files with a special format, so that representation of a file is the basic UNIX concept.

Blocks and Fragments

Most of the file system is taken up by **data blocks,** which contains whatever the users have put in their files.

The **block** and **fragment** sizes are set during file-system creation according to the intended use of the file system:

- If many small files are expected, the fragment size should be small.
- If repeated transfers of large files are expected, the basic block size should be large.

The maximum block-to-fragment ratio is 8 : 1; the minimum block size is 4K (typical choices are 4096 : 512 and 8192 : 1024).

4.2BSD a type of UNIX file system, uses **two** block sized for files which have no indirect blocks:

- All the blocks of a file are of a large **block size** (such as 8K), except the last.
- The last block is an appropriate multiple of a smaller **fragment size** (*i.e.*, 1024) to fill out the file.
- Thus, a file of size 18,000 bytes would have two 8K blocks and one 2K fragment (which would not be filled completely).

Inodes

- A file is represented by an *inode*—a record that stores information about a specific file on the disk.
- The inode also contains 15 pointers to the disk blocks containing the files's data contents.
  - First 12 point to **direct blocks.**
  - Next three point to **indirect blocks.**
    - First indirect block pointer is the address of a **single indirect block** — an index block containing the addresses of blocks that do contain data.
    - Second is a **double-indirect-block pointer,** the address of a block that contains the addresses of blocks that contain pointer to the actual data blocks.
    - A **triple indirect** pointer is not needed; files with as many as 232 bytes will use only double indirection.

Directories

- The inode type field distinguishes between plain files and directories.
- Directory entries are of variable length; each entry contains first the length of the entry, then the file name and the inode number.
- The user refers to a file by a path name, whereas the file system uses the inode as its definition of a file.
  - The kernel has to map the supplied user path name to an inode
  - Directories are used for this mapping.
- First determine the starting directory;
  - If the first character is "/", the starting directory is the root directory.
  - For any other starting character, the starting directory is the current directory.
- The search process continues untill the end of the path name is reached and the desired inode is returned.
- Once the inode is found, a file structure is allocated to point to the inode.
- 4.3BSD improved file system performance by adding a directory name cache to hold recent directory-to-inode translations.

UNIX

UNIX runs on Intel/Cyrix/AMD Pentium, Intel 80486, Intel 80386, Motorola/IBM Power PC, Motorola 680x0, Sun SPARC, HP PARISC, DEC VAX, and ARM.

Kind	**server/mainframe**	**desktop/workstation**	**handheld**	**real-time**
open source BSD UNIX†	small to large scale servers	workstations (for those with UNIX familiarity)	not appropriate	not appropriate
current version	**hardware supported**	**number of bits**		
		maximum processors		
	Pentium, 80486, 80386, 68040, Sun SPARC, SGI MIPS, DEC Alpha, HP PA-RISC	32 bits 4 processors		

LINUX

History

Linux is customarily considered a clone of the operating system Unix, written from scratch by Linus Benedict Torvalds with assistance from a loosely knit team of hackers across the Internet (Newitz). It was started in 1991 while Torvalds was at Helsinki University. In agreement with Stallings et al., the Linux kernel forms the core of the operating system along with other open source developments for UNIX: BSD, and X Window. One must describe Linux in a different manner than one would describe Windows because Linux has grown and developed at a faster rate than Windows did, and it did so as an open development project.

Distribution

It is important to note that Linux is just a kernel; the hoi polloi uses the term Linux as a misnomer for a Linux distribution such as Caldera, Debian or Red Hat. A distribution is the collection of applications, utilities, kerel, and installation software put together and distributed by a group, either a commercial entity like Red Hat Software, or volunteers like the Debian group. Each of these distributions differs in a plethora of ways. **Please note that D. Wheeler has measured Red Hats GNU size in lines of code.** It is comparable with Windows 2000 at 30 million physical lines of code.

The Linux operating system is composed of the Linux Kernel and the GNU (GNU is a recursive acronym for "GNU's Not Unix"; it is pronounced "guh-NEW") subsystems to go with it. So when you say Linux, it's actually more than just the Linux kernel, it is more accurately called the <GNU/Linux systems>.

The GNU C compiler project was started in 1983 by Richards Stallman at Massachusetts Institute of Technology (Hansen). As the development of Linux matured, Torvalds needed volunteers to assist in development and operating system programming.

Features

Linux has all the features that one would expect in a modern fully-fledged operating system, including true multitasking, virtual memory, shared libraries, demand loading, shared copy-on-write executables, proper memory management, and TCP/IP networking. The vast amounts of distributions provide Windows look-alikes and, Windows competitive office suites

Linux started out as a command-line OS much like DOS, without the Windows' GUI that we have come to expect today. X Windows, which urns on Unix, gives Linux a straightforward, Window-like graphic interface that is far more versatile than others you may be using now. And there are two competing Windows-like desktop environments called Gnome and DE that address the needs of the end user, immersing them in a highly configurable, intuitive and robust environment. KDE (K Desktop Environment) is more corporate, while Gnome is fun and highly customizable.

Despite the many improvements in Linux GUI's, one may still have to configure hardware and system devices such as printers, dial-up connections hardware and networking using a bunch of command-line utilities and configuration files. The payoff is that you generally have more power and more options when your program accepts command line commands. However many vendors are designing that process to be user friendly. Linux is far more popular on networks, Web servers, and with other types of Internet appliances than it currently is on desktop systems. The requested data is found in the buffer, it does not have to be read in from disk, thereby making the access time much faster.

The virtual memory in Linux gives each process up to 4GB of memory. Another benefit of this scheme is memory protection. The virtual address spaces are separated from each other. Each process control block stores the upper and lower limits of memory space. A process may not access any space outside of these limits. This prevents one process from affecting another. This is an advantage. It also stops malicious code from being able to corrupt anything else on the system. There is a bit for access associated with each virtual address. If this bit is set so that it only allows reading from that address, on other process can overwrite that protected data! Virtual memory also allows a sharing scheme to be used. Shared virtual memory is also used for things such as dynamic libraries. This means that if a library is used by several processes only one copy of it has to be in memory at any given time. This is another advantage.

All modern computers designed for virtual memory incorporate a special hardware cache called a PTE cache or TLB (Translaion Look aside Buffer), which caches page table entries in the CPU, so that the CPU usually doesn't have to probe the page table to find a PTE that lets it translate an address. PTE cache does not cache normal data, it only caches address translation information from the page table.

The hardware cache in the processor functions like this: the page table is not read directly, but instead caches translations for pages, on an as needed basis. These are the Translation Look-Aside buffers. When the reference to the virtual address is made it will attempt to find a matching TLB entry. If one is found it can directly translate the virtual address into the physical one. If it cannot find one the operating system will use the page table to find the correct physical address and it will then put this translation in the TLB. This type of memory access can actually be slower.

File System

Linux retains Unix's standard file system model, and has had new development for the following file systems:

- ext2fs (From Minix)
- ext3fs (a new journaling file system)

- jfs, (journaling file system)
- reiserfs (based on fast balanced trees)
- vfat (windows based file system)
- xfs (extended file system)

These are currently used and under development. Because Linux is always under development, it can benefit from constant research and testing. There is a plethora of files for mounting other operating systems to the Linux kernels.

The VFAT file system is a Linux file system that is compatible with Windows 95 and Windows NT long filenames on the FAT file system. It does not read the NTFS files system. The EXT2fs is the most feature-full and widely used of the Linux file systems. Other file systems supported are FAT, VFAT, FAT32, UFS, ext2fs, NFSv2, NFSv3, and coda file systems.

The virtual file system is based upon is based upon object-oriented principles. The VFS is comprised of a definitions that define what file objects may look like, and a software layer to manipulate those objects. All types of files are hidden behind this layer of software called the virtual file system.

LINUX

LINUX is a free version of UNIX that runs on Intel/Cyrix/AMD Pentium, Intel 80x86, Motorola/IBM Power PC, Motorola 680x0, Sun SPARC, SGI MIPS, DEC Alpha, HP PA-RISC, DEC VAX, ARM, API 1000+, and CL-PS7110.

kind	server/mainframe	desktop/workstation	handheld	real-time
open source UNIX	small to large scale servers	workstations (for those with UNIX familiarity)	not appropriate	not appropriate
current version	**hardware supported**	**number of bits**		
		maximum processors		
2.4.2	Intel/Cyrix/AMD Pentium, 80486, 80386, 80286 (partial port), 8086 (partial port), IBM/ Motorola Power PC, Motorola 68060, 68040, 68030, 68020, 68000, Sun SPARC, Sun SPARC64 (Ultra), SGI MIPS, DEC Alpha, HP-PA RISC, ARM, API 1000+, CL-PS7110	32 or 64 bits (depending on processor)		
		4 processors		

Chart Showing Comparison of Above Stated Operating Systems

OS / Property	Win 98	Win CE	Win 2000	Win NT	Unix	Linux
Kind	Proprietary custom	Proprietary custom	Proprietary custom	Proprietary custom	Open source	Open source UNIX
Server/ Mainframe	Low end servers	Not appropriate	Low end servers	Low quality servers	Small to large scale servers	Small to large scale servers
Desktop/ Work-station	Desktop	Not appropriate	Low quality workstations	Low quality workstations	Workstations (for those with UNIX familiarity)	Workstations (for those with UNIX familiarity)
Handheld	Not appropriate	Appropriate	Not appropriate	Not appropriate	Not appropriate	Not appropriate
Real-time	Not appropriate	Not appropriate	Not appropriate	Not appropriate	Not appropriate	Not appropriate
Current Version	98	98	2000	5 (2000)	3.4	2.4.2
Hardware supported	486DX, Pentium	Pentium	Pentium	Pentium	Pentium, Sun SPARC, SGI MIPS	Intel/Cyrix/AMD Pentium
Number of Bits	24 bits	24 bits	32 bits (Profession-al) and Server), par-tially 64 bits (Advanced Server) bits	32 bits	32 bits	32 or 64 bits (depending on processor)
Maximum Processors	1 processor	1 processor	2 (Professional), 4 (Server), 8 (Server) Adv-anced) proce-ssors	4 Processors	4 Processors	4 Processors

SUMMARIZED DESCRIPTION OF OTHER OPERATING SYSTEMS

Windows XP

Windows XP is a server, workstation, and desktop operating system made by Microsoft that run on the Intel/Cyrix/AMD Pentium.

Kind	**server/mainframe**	**desktop/workstation**	**handheld**	**real-time**
Proprietary custom	low quality servers	low quality workstations desktop	not appropriate	not appropriate
current version	**hardware supported**	**number of bits**		
		maximum processors		
XP	Pentium	32 bits		
		2 (Professional), 4 (Server), 8 (Server Advanced) processors		

Windows ME

Windows ME (Millennium Edition) is a low quality desktop operating system made by Microsoft that runs on Intel/Cyrix/AMD Pentium.

Kind	**server/mainframe**	**desktop/workstation**	**handheld**	**real-time**
Proprietary custom	not appropriate	desktop	not appropriate	not appropriate
current version	**hardware supported**	**number of bits**		
		maximum processors		
ME	Pentium	24 bits		
		1 processor		

Windows 95

Windows 95 is an obsolete desktop operating system made by Microsoft that runs on Intel/Cyrix/AMD Pentium and Intel 80486.

Kind	**server/mainframe**	**desktop/workstation**	**handheld**	**real-time**
Proprietary custom	low end servers	desktop	not appropriate	not appropriate
current version	**hardware supported**	**number of bits**		
		maximum processors		
95	80486, Pentium	16 bits		
		1 processor		

Windows 3.11

Windows 3.1 is an obsolete desktop operating system made by Microsoft that runs on Intel 80486, 80386 and 80286.

Kind	server/mainframe	desktop/workstation	handheld	real-time
Proprietary custom	low end servers	desktop	not appropriate	not appropriate
current version	**hardware supported**	**number of bits**		
		maximum processors		
3.11	80486, 80386, 80286	16 bits		
		1 processor		

MS-DOS

MS-DOS is a text-based desktop operating system made by Microsoft that runs on Intel 80x86.

Kind	server/mainframe	desktop/workstation	handheld	real-time
Proprietary custom	not appropriate	desktop system for older hardware	not appropriate	not appropriate
current version	**hardware supported**	**number of bits**		
		maximum processors		
8	80486, 80386, 80286 8086, 8088	16 bits		
		1 processor		

PC-DOS

PC-DOS-2000 is a text-based desktop operating system made by **IBM** as an update of the older **MS-DOS.** It runs on Intel 80x86. Only low end servers can run on this operating system.

Kind	server/mainframe	desktop/workstation	handheld	real-time
Proprietary custom	not appropriate	desktop system for older hardware	not appropriate	not appropriate
current version	**hardware supported**	**number of bits**		
		maximum processors		
2000	80x86, Pentium	16 bits		
		1 processor		

MXS

Macintosh OS Server (MXS) is a server operating system based on Rhapsody. MXS is made by Apple Computers and runs on Motorola/IBM Power PC.

kind	server/mainframe	desktop/workstation	handheld	real-time
proprietary UNIX†	small to medium scale servers	workstations (for those with UNIX familiarity)	not appropriate	not appropriate
current version	**hardware supported**	**number of bits** / **maximum processors**		
1.2	PowerPC	64 bits / 2 processors		

Mac OS X

Macintosh OS X (ten) is a desktop operating system based on Rhapsody. Macintosh OS X is made by Apple Computers and will run on Motorola/IBM PowerPC.

kind	server/mainframe	desktop/workstation	handheld	real-time
proprietary BSD UNIX†	small to medium scale servers	general desktop and content creation workstations	not appropriate	not appropriate
current version	**hardware supported**	**number of bits** / **maximum processors**		
10.1.2	PowerPC G3 and G4	64 bits / 2 processors		

Classic Macintosh

Macintosh OS 9, OS 8, OS 7, and OS 6 are desktop operating systems made by Apple Computers that run on Motorola/IBM PowerPC and Motorola 680x0.

kind	server/mainframe	desktop/workstation	handheld	real-time
proprietary custom	small scale servers	general desktop and content creation workstations	not appropriate	not appropriate
current version	**hardware supported**	**number of bits** / **maximum processors**		
9	680x0, PowerPC	32 bits / 4 processors		

OS/2

OS/2 is a high performance desktop and high end operating system made by IBM that runs on Intel/Cyrix/AMD Pentium and Intel 80x86.

kind	**server/mainframe**	**desktop/workstation**	**handheld**	**real-time**
proprietary custom	Warp for small to medium scale servers	client for desktops and workstations	not appropriate	not appropriate
current version	**hardware supported**	**number of bits**		
4.51	80486, Pentium	32 bits		
		maximum processors		
		1 processor		

FreeBSD

FreeBSD is a free version of UNIX$^{\pm}$ that runs on Intel/Cyrix/**AMD** Pentium and Intel 80486.

kind	**server/mainframe**	**desktop/workstation**	**handheld**	**real-time**
open source BSD UNIX$^{\pm}$	small to large scale servers	workstations (for those with UNIX familiarity)	embedded systems	not appropriate
current version	**hardware supported**	**number of bits**		
3.1	Pentium, 80486, 80386, PowerPC, DEC Alpha	32 bits		
		maximum processors		
		4 processors		

NetBSD

NetBSD is a free version of UNIX$^{\pm}$ that runs on Intel/Cyrix/**AMD** Pentium, Intel 80486, Intel 80386, Motorola/IBM Power PC, Motorola 680x0, Sun SPARC, HP PARISC, DEC VAX, and ARM.

kind	**server/mainframe**	**desktop/workstation**	**handheld**	**real-time**
open source BSD UNIX$^{\pm}$	small to large scale servers	workstations (for those with UNIX familiarity)	embedded systems	not appropriate
current version	**hardware supported**	**number of bits**		
1.4.2	Intel/Cyrix/AMD Pentium, 80486, 80386, IBM/Motorola Power PC, Motorola 68040, 68030, Sun SPARC, Sun UltraSPARC, SGI, MIPS, DEC Alpha, VAX, HP PA-RISC, ARM (ARM 26, ARM32, Strong ARM), Cobalt Qube and Raq machines, PC532, SH3 embedded systems	32 or 64 bits (depending on processor)		
		maximum processors		
		1 processor		

OpenBSD

OpenBSD is a free version of UNIX$^{\pm}$ that runs on Intel/Cyrix AMD Pentium, Intel 80486, Intel 80386, Motorola/IBM PowerPC, Motorola 680x0, Sun SPARC, HP PA-RISC, DEC VAX, and ARM.

kind	server/mainframe	desktop/workstation	handheld	real-time
open source BSD UNIX$^{\pm}$	small to large scale servers	workstations (for those with UNIX familiarity)	not appropriate	not appropriate
current version	**hardware supported**	**number of bits**		
		maximum processors		
	Pentium, 80486, 80386, 68040, Sun SPARC, SGI MIPS, DEC Alpha, HP PA-RISC			

GNU Hurd

GNU Hurd is a free open source operating system.

kind	server/mainframe	desktop/workstation	handheld	real-time
open source	small to medium scale servers	workstations (for those with command line familiarity)	not appropriate	not appropriate
current version	**hardware supported**	**number of bits**		
		maximum processors		
	Pentium	32 bits		
		4 processors		

Solaris

Solaris is a UNIX$^{\pm}$-based operating system made by Sun Computers that runs on Sun SPARC and Intel/Cyrix/AMD Pentium.

kind	server/mainframe	desktop/workstation	handheld	real-time
proprietary UNIX$^{\pm}$	medium to large scale servers; corporate databases; supercomputers	workstations (for those with UNIX familiarity)	not appropriate	not appropriate
current version	**hardware supported**	**number of bits**		
		maximum processors		
8	Sun Ultra SPARC, Sun SPARC, Intel/Cyrix/AMD Pentium Pentium, Intel 486DX	64 bits		
		64 processors		

SunOS

SunOS is an older text-based UNIX$^{\pm}$ that runs on Sun SPARC. Solaris is an enhancement of SunOS that includes a graphic user interface.

kind	server/mainframe	desktop/workstation	handheld	real-time
proprietary UNIX$^{\pm}$	medium to large scale servers	workstations (for those with UNIX familiarity)	not appropriate	not appropriate
current version	**hardware supported**	**number of bits** **maximum processors**		
5.8	Sun SPARC	64 bits 64 processors		

HP-UX

HP-UX is a UNIX$^{\pm}$-based operating system made by Hewlett-Packard that runs on HP PA-RISC.

kind	server/mainframe	desktop/workstation	handheld	real-time
proprietary UNIX$^{\pm}$	small to large scale servers; database servers; mainframes	workstations (for those with UNIX familiarity)	not appropriate	not appropriate
current version	**hardware supported**	**number of bits** **maximum processors**		
11.11 (aka 11i v1.0) (for HP PA-RISC) 11.20 (aka 11iv1.5) (for Intel Itanium)	HP PA-RISC (HP9000 workstations and servers), HP Focus (HP9000/500 family), Motorola 680x0 (HP9000/300 family) Intel Itanium	64 bits 128 processors		

OpenVMS

VMS is a high performance operating system made by Compaq/DEC that runs on DEC VAX. Open VMS is an updated version of VMS.

kind	server/mainframe	desktop/workstation	handheld	real-time
proprietary custom	medium to large scale servers; minicomputers; mainframes	workstations (for those with command line familiarity)	not appropriate	not appropriate
current version	**hardware supported**	**number of bits** **maximum processors**		
7.2-1	DEC Alpha, VAX	64 bits Alpha; 32 bits VAX 16 processors		

Tru64 Unix

Tru64 Unix (formerly Digital UNIX) is a UNIX-based± operating system made by Compaq/DEC for the DEC Alpha.

kind	**server/mainframe**	**desktop/workstation**	**handheld**	**real-time**
proprietary UNIX±	medium to large scale servers; minicomputers; mainframes	workstations (for those with UNIX familiarity)	not appropriate	not appropriate
current version	**hardware supported**	**number of bits** **maximum processors**		
5.1	DEC Alpha	64 bits		

ULTRIX

ULTRIX is a UNIX± -based operating system made by Compaq/DEC. ULTRIX has been replaced by Digital UNIX.

kind	**server/mainframe**	**desktop/workstation**	**handheld**	**real-time**
proprietary UNIX±	medium to large scale servers; minicomputers; mainframes	workstations (for those with UNIX familiarity)	not appropriate	not appropriate
current version	**hardware supported**	**number of bits** **maximum processors**		
V4.5	VAX, MIPS	32 bits 6 processors		

IRIX

IRIX is a UNIX±-based operating system made by SGI that runs on SGI MIPS.

kind	**server/mainframe**	**desktop/workstation**	**handheld**	**real-time**
proprietary UNIX±	medium to large scale servers; supercomputers;	workstations (for those with UNIX familiarity)	not appropriate	not appropriate
current version	**hardware supported**	**number of bits** **maximum processors**		
6.5.11	SGI MIPS	64 bits 128 processors		

NeXT

NeXT is a UNIX$^{\pm}$-based operating sysem made by NeXT that runs on Intel/Cyrix/AMD Pentium, Intel 80486, and Motorola 68040. Open STEP runs on Intel/Cyrix/AMD Pentium, Intel 80486, Motorola 68040, Sun SPARC and HP PA-RISC.

kind	**server/mainframe**	**desktop/workstation**	**handheld**	**real-time**
proprietary UNIX$^{\pm}$	small and medium scale server systems; some enterprise systems	primarily for scientific, mathematic, or engineering workstations	not appropriate	not appropriate
current version	**hardware supported**	**number of bits**		
		maximum processors		
	Pentium, 80486, 68040, Sun SPARC, HP PA-RISC	32 bits		
		8 processors		

Rhapsody

Rhapsody is a UNIX$^{\pm}$-based operating system that includes capabilities from the NcXT and Macintosh operating systems. Rhapsody is madc by Apple Computers and will run on Intel/ Cyrix/AMD Pentium and Motorola/IBM Power PC and will have a Run Time Library for Windows.

kind	**server/mainframe**	**desktop/workstation**	**handheld**	**real-time**
proprietary UNIX$^{\pm}$	small to medium scale servers	workstations (for those with UNIX familiarity)	not appropriate	not appropriate
current version	**hardware supported**	**number of bits**		
		maximum processors		
DR 2	Pentium, PowerPC	32 bits		
		4 processors		

AIX

AIX is **IBM**'s version of UNIX$^{\pm}$.

kind	**server/mainframe**	**desktop/workstation**	**handheld**	**real-time**
proprietary UNIX$^{\pm}$	medium to large scale servers; mainframes	workstations (for those with UNIX familiarity)	not appropriate	not appropriate
current version	**hardware supported**	**number of bits**		
		maximum processors		
4.3.3	PowerPC	64 bits		
		24 processors		

MVS

MVS is a mainframe operating system made by IBM.

kind	server/mainframe	desktop/workstation	handheld	real-time
proprietary custom	medium to large scale servers; mainframes	workstations (for those with command line familiarity)	not appropriate	not appropriate
current version	**hardware supported**	**number of bits** **maximum processors**		
5.2	System/360, System/370, System/390	16 bits 2 processors		

NetWare

NetWare "is a dedicated network operating system" that runs on Intel/Cyrix/AMD Pentium, Intel 80486, and Intel 80386.[e16]

kind	server/mainframe	desktop/workstation	handheld	real-time
proprietary custom	small to large scale servers; internal networks	not appropriate	not appropriate	not appropriate
current version	**hardware supported**	**number of bits** **maximum processors**		
5.1	Pentium, 80486, 80386, 80286, 68000	32 bits 4 processors		

BeOS

BeOS is a high performance desktop operating system made by Be that runs on Motorola/IBM PowerPC and Intel/Crix/AMD Pentium.

kind	server/mainframe	desktop/workstation	handheld	real-time
proprietary custom	not appropriate	general desktop and content creation workstations	not appropriate	not appropriate
current version	**hardware supported**	**number of bits** **maximum processors**		
4	Pentium, PowerPC	64 bits 8 processors		

AmigaOS

AmigaOS is an old but popular operating system that is being resurrected. Only low end servers can run on this operating system.

kind	server/mainframe	desktop/workstation	handheld	real-time
proprietary custom	small scale servers	general desktop and video editing workstations	not appropriate	not appropriate
current version	**hardware supported**	**number of bits**		
		maximum processors		
3.5	PowerPC, 68060, 68040, 68030, 68020, 68000, Pentium	32 bits		
		2 processors		

SCO OpenServer

SCO Open Server is a UNIX±-based± operating system that runs on Intel/Cyrix/AMD Pentium.

kind	server/mainframe	desktop/workstation	handheld	real-time
proprietary Sys V UNIX±	small to large scale servers; mainframes	workstations (for those with UNIX familiarity)	not appropriate	not appropriate
current version	**hardware supported**	**number of bits**		
		maximum processors		
5.0.6	Pentium, 80486, 80386	16 bits		
		4 processors		

SCO UnixWare

SCO UnixWare is a UNIX±-based± operating system that runs on Intel/Cyrix/AMD Pentium.

kind	server/mainframe	desktop/workstation	handheld	real-time
proprietary Sys V UNIX±	small to large scale servers; mainframes	workstations (for those with UNIX familiarity)	not appropriate	not appropriate
current version	**hardware supported**	**number of bits**		
		maximum processors		
7.1.1	Pentium, 80486, 80386	64 bits		
		2 processors		

Pyramid

Pyramid uses the MIPS chipset, and did the reference port of SysVr4 to those chips under contract to Unix System Laboratories (USL). Pyramid runs Sys V, release 4.2 (with their own enhancements).

kind	server/mainframe	desktop/workstation	handheld	real-time
proprietary UNIX±	medium to large scale servers; mainframes	workstations (for those with UNIX familiarity)	not appropriate	not appropriate
current version	**hardware supported**	**number of bits**		
		maximum processors		
1.1-[cd] 087.4 for nile and mis series reliant unix 5.43C20 for rm1000	MIPS	32 bits		
		24 processors		

BSDi

BSDi Internet Server (also known as BSD/OS) is a commercial BSD UNIX± for Pentiums and other processors.

kind	server/mainframe	desktop/workstation	handheld	real-time
proprietary BSD UNIX±	small to large scale servers	workstations (for those with UNIX familiarity)	not appropriate	not appropriate
current version	**hardware supported**	**number of bits**		
		maximum processors		
4.0	Pentium, 80486, 80386, Sun SPARC and Ultra-SPARC, PowerPC	32 bits 6 processors		

SUMMARY

In this chapter, we have studied what an operating system is, what are its characteristics, types and the design approaches. We have also seen the basic OS structure. We have also focussed on the trends of future OS designs. Finally, we studied two CASE STUDIES, one on traditional and modern UNIX and the other which compares all OSs.

MULTIPLE-CHOICE QUESTIONS [MCQs]

1. Operating system means:
(*a*) A set of programs which controls computer working
(*b*) A way a computer operator works
(*c*) A way a floppy disk drive operates
(*d*) All of the above.

2. The primary job of an OS is to:
(*a*) Command Resources (*b*) Manage Resources
(*c*) Provide utilities (*d*) Be user friendly

3. When a computer is ON, then its OS software has to reside in-
(*a*) Primary storage (*b*) Main storage
(*c*) AUX storage (*d*) None of the above

4. An OS used by Macintosh computer is-
(*a*) System 7.0 (*b*) AU/X
(*c*) Xenis (*d*) Either *a* or *b*

5. The process of transferring data intended for a peripheral device onto a disk for some period of time is known as-
(*a*) Multiprogramming (*b*) Spooling
(*c*) Caching (*d*) None of the above

6. Two basic types of OS are-
(*a*) Batch and time sharing (*b*) Sequential and real time
(*c*) Direct and interactive (*d*) Batch and interactive

7. A virtual computer is a combination of-
(*a*) Computer hardware + Softwares (*b*) Hardware + Softwares + Processes
(*c*) Computer hardware + OS (*d*) None of the above

8. An OS is an-
(*a*) Application program (*b*) System program
(*c*) AI program (*d*) None of the above

9. A shell is a-
(*a*) Hardware component (*b*) Command Interpreter
(*c*) Part of a compiler (*d*) None of the above

10. A front-end processor is usually used in-
(*a*) Time Sharing (*b*) Multiprogramming
(*c*) Virtual storage (*d*) None of the above

11. Which of the following does not form an OS layer-
(*a*) Kernel (*b*) shell
(*c*) Application Programs (*d*) Critical section

12. A small program which loads OS into the memory is called as-
(*a*) ROM (*b*) Bootstrap loader
(*c*) BIOS (*d*) None of the above

13. A method of overlapping input, output and processing of a single job is-
(*a*) Buffering (*b*) Spooling
(*c*) DMA (*d*) None of the above

14. SPOOLING stands for-
(*a*) Spontaneous primary operation online (*b*) Simultaneous peripheral operation online
(*c*) Small peripheral operation online (*d*) None of the above

15. In soft RTS, data file sizes are-
(*a*) Small (*b*) Medium
(*c*) Large (*d*) None of the above

16. An example of a firm RTS (real time system) is-
(*a*) Patient ventilator (*b*) Moving car
(*c*) Conveyer belt (*d*) None of the above

17. Rotating priority is used in-
(*a*) Round Robin algorithm (*b*) FCFS
(*c*) SJF (*d*) None of the above

18. Which of the following is an example of Real-time OS-
(*a*) UNIX (*b*) MARUTI
(*c*) WIN-NT (*d*) None of the above

19. An example of Network OS is-
(*a*) BSD (*b*) Harmony
(*c*) MS-DOS (*d*) None of the above

20. The term 'process' was coined by-
(*a*) Barry Boehm (*b*) Daley
(*c*) Albrecht (*d*) None of the above

21. PCB stands for-
(*a*) Process common box (*b*) Process control Block
(*c*) Process care Block (*d*) None of the above

22. A controller will have three things
(*a*) Processor + Micro code + Local memory (*b*) Micro code only
(*c*) Micro code + memory (*d*) None of the above

23. The size of WIN-NT OS is about 1,60,000 LOC while WIN-2000 has a size of-
(*a*) 1,25,00,000 LOC (*b*) 2,20,00,000 LOC
(*c*) 3,25,00,000 LOC (*d*) None of the above

24. One can interact with an OS by means of-
(*a*) System commands (*b*) System calls
(*c*) Both *a* or *b* (*d*) None of the above

25. A modern OS that can be used in supercomputers also is—
(*a*) System V Release 4 (*b*) MS-DOS
(*c*) Linux (*d*) None of the above

ANSWERS

1. *a*	2. *b*	3. *a*	4. *d*	5. *b*	6. *d*
7. *c*	8. *b*	9. *b*	10. *a*	11. *d*	12. *b*
13. *a*	14. *b*	15. *c*	16. *a*	17. *a*	18. *b*
19. *a*	20. *b*	21. *b*	22. *a*	23. *c*	24. *c*
25. *a*					

CONCEPTUAL SHORT QUESTIONS WITH ANSWERS

Q.1. What is a partition table?

Ans. A physical disk can be divided into several partitions called **logical volumes.** The data structure that contains the information of different partitions is called a *partition table.* When we need to install more than one OS (say, WINDOWS and Linux then we need partitions. We have different partitioning tools available like PQMAGIC, system commander, Disk Druid etc. A program which manages several bootable partitions and allows user to select one of these OS to boot is called as a **Boot Manager.** For example, PQMAGIC has a boot manager.

Q.2. Explain the Bootstrapping process in IBM PC.

Ans. Bootstrapping: (in IBM PC)

- When a PC is switched on, control goes to the location FFFF0H.
- There lies a jump instruction to the BIOS area.
- After initializing the BIOS, BIOS bootstrap loader is executed. It transfers the 1st physical sector of the disk into location 0000:7C00H and transfers control to it.
- The startup code of the MBR checks which partition is active and based on that transfers the content of the boot sector (1st sector) of the active partition into memory and transfer control to it.
- This program initializes the data structures and loads the OS to the predefined Area and gives control to it.

Q.3. What is an exokernel OS? Give one example.

Ans. Exokernel OS is an OS in which no function is implemented in the kernel space. It passes requests for the resources to the "user space" libraries *i.e.*, a kernel would pass any request to the library only.

For example: MIT exokernel OS.

Q.4. Why do you think that an idleness in CPU occurs?

Ans. The CPU idleness occurs because the speeds of the mechanical I/O devices are internally slower than those of the electronic devices.

Q.5. As OS has typically five layers. Can you mention the objects that are being used at each of these levels. Also specify their typical operations.

Ans. The table below gives the details.

Level/layer	Objects used	Typical operations
Command-language Interpreter (level-5)	Environment data	Statement in the command language
File system (level-4)	Files, Devices	Create, Destroy, Open, Close, Read and Write
Memory Management (level-3)	Segments, Pages	Read, Write and Fetch
Basic I/O (level-2)	Data Block	Read, Write, Allocate and Free
Kernel (level-1)	Process, Semaphores	Create, Destroy, Signal, Suspend, Resume and Wait.

Q.6. List the four steps that are necessary to run a program on a completely dedicated machine.

Ans. The four steps are as follows–

Step–1 : Reserve machine time

Step–2 : Manually load program into memory

Step–3 : Load starting address and begin execution.

Step–4 : Monitor and control execution of program from console.

Q.7. In a multiprogramming and time sharing environment, several users share the system simultaneously. This situation can result in various security problems.

(*a*) What are two such problems?

(*b*) Can we ensure the same degree of security in a time-shared machine as we have in a dedicated machine? Explain your answer.

Ans. (*a*) Stealing or copying one's program using system resources like CPU, memory etc. without proper accounting are such two problems.

(*b*) Probably not, if a machine is shared among various users then the privacy of information is lost. Any protection scheme devised by humans can inevitably be broken by a human. More complex is the scheme, the more difficult it is to feel confident of its correct implementation.

Q.8. What is prefetching? Compare it with spooling.

Ans. Prefetching is a method of overlapping the I/O of a job with that job's own computation. The idea is simple. After a read operation completes and the job is about to start operating on the data, the input device is instructed to begin the next read immediately. The CPU and the input device are then both busy. With luck, by the time the job is ready for the next data item, the input device will have finished reading that data item. The CPU can then begin processing the newly read data while the input device starts to read the following data. A similar idea can be used for output. In this case, the job creates data that are put into a buffer until an output device can accept them.

Prefetching is a user-based activity while spooling is a system-based activity. Spooling is a much more effective way of overlapping I/O and CPU operations.

Q.9. How does the distinction between monitor mode and user mode function as a rudimentary form of protection (security) system?

Ans. Our PC works in 2 modes. One is a monitor mode and the other is user-mode. There are certain privileged instructions that can be executed only in the monitor mode. So, the OS is assured of controlling the entire system at all times.

Q.10. What are the differences between a trap and an interrupt? What is the use of each function?

Ans. An **interrupt** is a hardware generated change-of-flow within the system. An interrupt handler is summoned to deal with the cause of interrupt; control is then returned to the interrupted context and instruction. A *trap* is a software generated interrupt. An interrupt can be used to signal the completion of an I/O to obviate the need for device poling. A trap can be used to call OS routines or to catch arithematic errors.

Let us tabulate the differences

Interrupt	Trap
1. It is due to some sort of external event and is independent of currently running process.	1. It relates to an error/exception condition generated within currently running process.
2. Control is transferred to an interrupt handler	2. If error is fatal, then the currently running process is moved to exit state.
3. *Eg.* I/O interrupt, clock interrupt, memory fault.	3. *Eg.*, Illegal file access.

Q.11. Why is the separation of mechanism and policy a desirable property?

Ans. Policy refers to what should be done.

Mechanism refers to how it should be done.

For example: CPU scheduling

Policy: decides which scheduling algorithm such as FCFS, SJF etc. will be used.

Mechanism: How to implement it? So, mechanism and policy must be separate to ensure that systems are easy to modify. No two system installations are the same, so that installation may want to tune the OS to suit its needs. With mechanism and policy separate, the policy may be changed at will while the mechanism stays unchanged. This arrangement provides a more flexible system.

Q.12. What are the main advantages of the microkernel approach to system design?

Ans. Some advantages of microkernel approach are given below:—

(*a*) Adding a new service does not require modifying the kernel.

(*b*) It is more secure as more operations are done in user mode than in kernel mode.

(*c*) A simpler kernel design and functionality typically results in a more reliable OS.

Q.13. List some categories of privileged instructions?

Ans. Some categories of privileged instructions are as follows—

1. I/O
2. Modifying timer
3. HALT
4. Turning interrupt enable OFF.

Q.14. Define the following terms:—

(*a*) Path (*b*) Pipeline (*c*) Unix's Filter

Ans. Path: Path is a command given to the shell of the OS which changes the working directory.

Pipeline: It is a sequence of processes connected by several pipes in linear fashion.

Filter: It is a program that produces a single input stream to produce a single output stream.

Q.15. Write a short note on system calls?

Ans.

1. A system call is a method used by a process to request action by the OS.
2. It is the interface between the user program and the OS.
3. A system call usually takes the form of a trap.
4. When a system call is executed, it is treated by the hardware as a software interrupt. The control passes through the interrupt vector to a service routine in the OS.

Q.16. The payroll program reads the monthly attendance details of 2000 employees and prints their payroll. Reading a card and printing of a line consumes 200 ms each, while a read or write operation on magnetic page consumes 12 m sec. Salary processing consumes 6 ms of CPU time. What are the program elapsed time and CPU idle time with and without spooling.

Ans. No of input cards = 2000 employees

Total elapsed time (for job) = (*I/O* time + runtime + output *I/O* time)

= 200 ms + 12 ms + 6 ms

= 218 ms

& CPU idle time = (Input *I/O* time + output *I/O* time) – run time

= (200 + 12) – 6 = **206 msec**

EXERCISE QUESTIONS

Q.1. (*a*) Explain the multiprogramming, time sharing and distributed OS.

(*b*) Distinguish between Kernel and micro-kernel of an OS. Describe the essential modules of Kernel and explain the purpose of system calls.

Q.2. Distinguish between single stream batch processing and batch multiprogramming.

Q.3. What is spooling?

Q.4. (*a*) Explain the advantages of multiprocessor system.

(*b*) What are the three major activities of an OS in regard to memory management?

(*c*) What is the purpose of system calls?

(*d*) The client server model is popular in a distributed system. Can it also be used in a single computer system?

Q.5. Define the essential properties of the following types of OS–

(*a*) Batch (*b*) Real time.

Q.6. Give an example of a SPOOLED device. How does it work?

Q.7. An extreme method of spooling, known as staging a tape, is to read the entire contents of a magnetic tape onto disk before using it. Discuss the main advantage of such as scheme.

Q.8. (*a*) What is the main advantage of a distributed system?

(*b*) Describe the differences between symmetric and asymmetric multiprocessing. What are the advantages and disadvantages of multiprocessor systems?

(*c*) What is a device driver? Why is it so important to have a device driver for each device?

Q.9. Define the following terms:—

(*a*) Distributed Systems. (*b*) Real-time Systems.

(*c*) Multiprogramming.

Q.10. What is the main advantage for an OS designer of using a virtual machine architecture? What is the advantage for a user?

Q.11. (*a*) What is an Operating System? Discuss its any four main functions.

(*b*) Discuss the following:—

(*a*) Multiprogramming (*b*) Multitasking (*c*) Time Sharing

Q.12. (*a*) What is a real time OS?

(*b*) Which of the four basic OS modules might be required on a computer system? Explain them briefly.

(*c*) Discuss the properties of the following types of OS:

(*a*) Interactive (*b*) Network (*c*) Distributed

Q.13. (*a*) What is an OS? Discuss its various services.

(*b*) Write differences between:

(*a*) Multiprogramming (*b*) Multiprocessing

Q.14. What are the various types of multiprogramming OSs? Explain with the help of examples. Give one difference between–

(*a*) time sharing systems (*b*) real time systems

Q.15. Define the essential properties of the following types of OS:

(*a*) Batch (*b*) Interactive

(*c*) Time Sharing (*d*) Real Time

(*e*) Network (*f*) Distributed

Q.16. (*a*) What are the three main purposes of an OS?

(*b*) What are the main differences between OS for main frames and PCs?

(*c*) Describe the differences between symmetric and asymmetric multiprocessing.

Q.17. Differentiate between:

(*a*) Interactive and Batch OS (*b*) Multiprogramming and Multitasking.

(*c*) General purpose OS & Real–Time OS.

Q.18. Compare multitasking and multiuser OS?

Q.19. (*a*) What are the essential and desirable properties of an OS ?

(*b*) Explain in brief Real time OS.

Illustrate some areas where they are used.

Q.20. (*a*) What are the advantages of multiprocessor system? Describe the difference between symmetric and asymmetric multiprocessing

(*b*) Differentiate between –

(1) Buffering and spooling (2) System Programs and System calls.

(3) CS systems and Peer to Peer systems.

Q.21. What is the main advantage of layered approach to system design ?

Q.22. Explain two situations in which multithreading provides better performance than a single threaded solution.

CHAPTER 2

Memory Management

2.0 INTRODUCTION

We know that several processes (tasks or jobs) are allocated to a single processor. CPU utilization and performance can be improved further by sharing it among several processes. This is achieved by keeping all the processes in primary memory. Therefore, the sharing of memory is very essential if we want to improve CPU performance. The organization and management of main memory has been one of the most important factors influencing the OS design. Memory management is primarily concerned with the allocation of main memory to requesting processes. Main memory is limited. But no process can ever run before a certain amount of memory is allocated to it. The overall resource utilization and other performance criteria of a computer are largely affected by the performance of memory management module.

Protection and sharing of memory are two important memory management functions. To protect one process from another their address spaces must be spared by the memory management scheme. An active process should never attempt to access erroneously or maliciously the contents of each other's address space. Also, memory management scheme must support sharing of common data or data structure such as a symbol table in compilers or assemblers.

2.1 SINGLE PROCESS MONITOR—A BACKGROUND

It is also called as a **mono programming or uniprogramming system.** It is the simplest memory management approach. The memory is divided into two contiguous areas, first is the lower memory address area for an operating system program (or monitor) and the second is for the user program.

These programs or processes are also known as transient processes which are loaded according to the user's Input. This is shown below in Fig. 2.1.

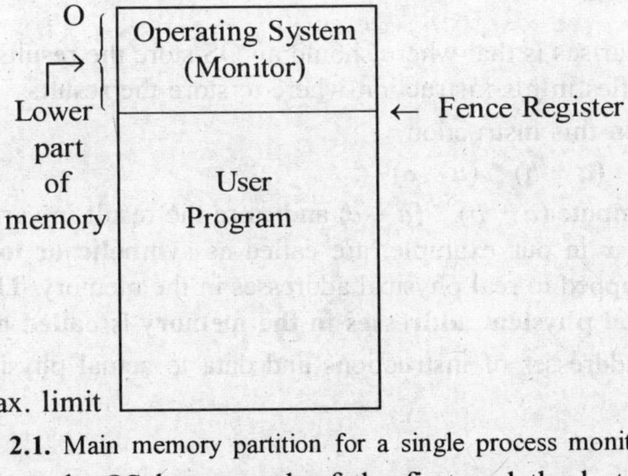

Fig. 2.1. Main memory partition for a single process monitor

In this type of approach, OS keeps track of the first and the last location available for allocation of user programs. **Please note that an OS is loaded either at the bottom or at the top, in order to provide a contiguous area of free storage for a user program.**

Actually, this decision depends upon the location of interrupt vector. Since the interrupt vector is often in low memory so the OS program (or monitor) is kept in low memory as shown above in Fig. 1.

A *transient program* (user process) is only when the OS passes a control to it. After receiving a control, it starts running the program until its completion or termination due to I/O or some error. When this program is completed or terminated, the OS may load another program for execution. This type of memory management scheme was commonly used in single process OS such as PC-DOS, CP/M.

As we already know that protection and sharing of code must be addressed while designing any memory management scheme. But in this approach, sharing of code and data, in a single process environment does not make much sense because only one process or program, resides in memory at a time. Protection is also not an issue in a single process monitor because only one process is in the memory at a time. **However, please note that the protection of OS program from the user code is must otherwise the system will crash down.** And this protection is done by a special hardware mechanism such as a **dedicated register** called as a **Fence Register.**

How Fence Register provides protection?

This is done as follows. The operating system codes usually reside in low memory area as shown in Fig. 1. A special purpose register also called as a **Fence Register** is set to the highest address occupied by the OS code. A memory address generated by the user program to access certain memory location is first compared with the fence register's content. If the address generated is below the fence, it will be trapped and denied permission. Since modification of the fence register is considered as a privileged operation, therefore, only OS is allowed to make any changes to it.

Although this is the simplest approach but due to lack of support of multi-programming, it results in lower CPU utilization. **Please note that since only one program is residing at a time in memory, it may not occupy whole memory, therefore memory is under-utilized. Also note that CPU will be sitting idle during the period when a running program requires some I/O.**

2.2 ADDRESS BINDING

We know that our program is stored in RAM only. Each instruction has to go through different phases. Similarly, a program also has to go through three phases—

(*a*) Compilation phase

(*b*) Loading phase

(*c*) Run phase

The problem that arises is that where should an OS store the results of programs after their execution. A user specifies in his instruction where to store the result.

For example — In this instruction

$$x = (a + b) * (a - c)$$

the user just says to compute $(a + b) * (a - c)$ and store the result in variable, x. Such addresses given by the user, like x in our example, are called as **symbolic or logical addresses.** These addresses need to be mapped to real physical addresses in the memory. **This process of mapping logical addresses to real physical addresses in the memory is called as address binding.**

This binding of addresses of instructions and data to actual physical addresses may take place during—

(*a*) Compile time

(*b*) Load time or

(*c*) Run time

Compile time binding generates absolute addresses. It requires that it must be known at the compile time itself that where will a process reside in the memory. It is quite appropriate choice. Small, simple systems or dedicated hardware. The problem in this approach is that if the starting address of a process in memory changes then the entire process must be recompiled to generate the absolute addresses again.

In load time binding, the compiler generates *relocatable addresses* which are converted to **absolute addresses** at the load time. Process cannot be moved around during execution. Here, in this method of binding, if the starting address of the process changes then it can be accomplished by statically relocating the code. We will study more about relocation in section 2.4.

In run time binding, we can move a process during run time from one memory segment to another. We need a good hardware support here. The total run time of a process also increases. Dynamic relocation is used to achieve it. It has been discussed in section 2.4.

Please note, however, that the address binding for global variables occurs at the load-time whereas the address binding for local variables takes place at run-time.

2.3 LOGICAL VERSUS PHYSICAL ADDRESS SPACE

A **logical address** is the address of an instruction or data as used by a program. It is generated by the CPU. A **physical address** is the effective memory address of an instruction or data that is obtained after the address binding has been done *i.e.*, after logical addresses are mapped to their physical addresses. Such a set of logical addresses used by a program constitutes the **logical address space of the program.** And the set of physical addresses in the main memory which a process actually occupies, constitutes the **physical address space of the process.**

This can be shown in a diagram form also.

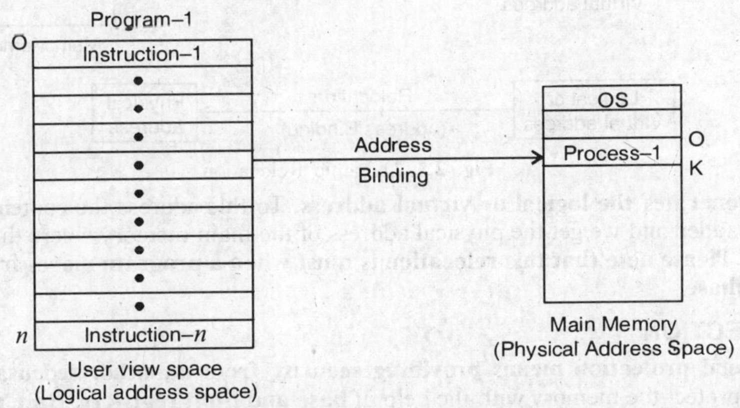

Fig. 2.2. Logical v/s Physical Address Space

2.4 PROGRAM RELOCATION

It refers to the ability to load and execute a given program into an arbitrary place in memory. Relocation is a mechanism to convert the logical (or virtual) address into a physical address. An address generated by the CPU is known as a **logical or virtual address** and that generated by the memory manager is known as a **physical address.** To do this relocation, there is a special register in CPU called as a **relocation register.** Every address used in the program is relocated as follows:–

Effective physical address = Logical address + Contents of Relocation register

MMU or Memory Management Unit is a special hardware which performs address binding, uses relocation scheme.

Relocation is necessary at the time of swapping in of a process from a backing store to the main memory.

There are two basic types of relocation:—

1. Static Relocation 2. Dynamic Relocation

Static Relocation

It is a relocation formed during the loading of the program into memory by a loader. Language translator prepares the object module by assuming virtual address O to be the strarting address of the program, making virtual addresses relative to the program loading address. Once the program is in the memory, values that need relocation are distinguishable from those that do not need relocation. The systems with static relocation in a swapped-out process must either be swapped back into the same partition from which it was evicted or software relocation must be repeated whenever the process is to be loaded into different partitions.

Dynamic Relocation

It implies that mapping from the virtual address space to physical address is performed at run-time. Consider Fig. 2.3 below which shows dynamic relocation.

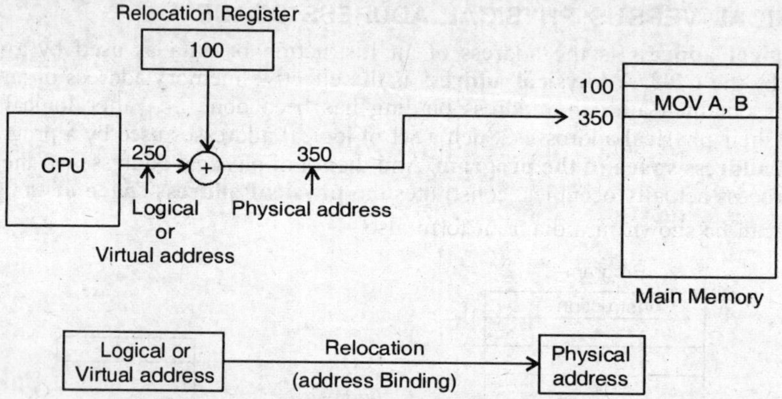

Fig. 2.3. Dynamic Relocation

CPU generates the logical or virtual address. To this address the contents of Relocation Register are added and we get the physical address of the main memory where this program must be relocated. **Please note that this relocation is must when a program moves from compilation to the run-phase.**

2.5 PROTECTION

The word protection means providing security from unauthorized usage of memory. The OS can protect the memory with the help of **base and limit registers. Base registers** consist of the starting address of the next process. **The limit register** specifies the boundary of that job. That is why the limit register is also called as a **fencing register.** Consider Fig. 2.4 below.

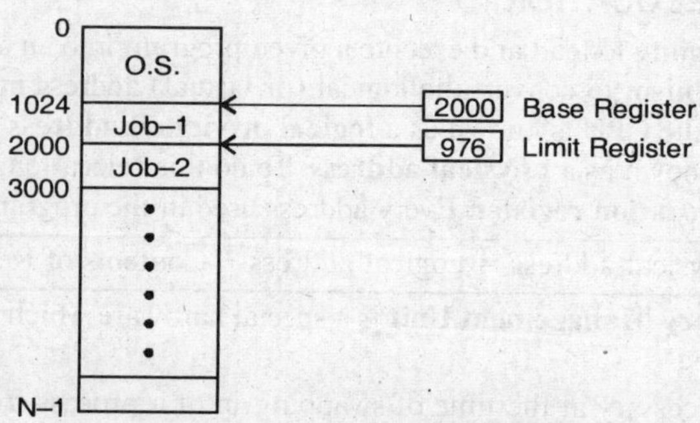

Fig. 2.4. Main Memory Protection

Please note here that the base register holds the smallest legal physical memory address while the limit register contains the size of the process.

Figure 2.5 below shows the hardware protection mechanism with base and limit registers.

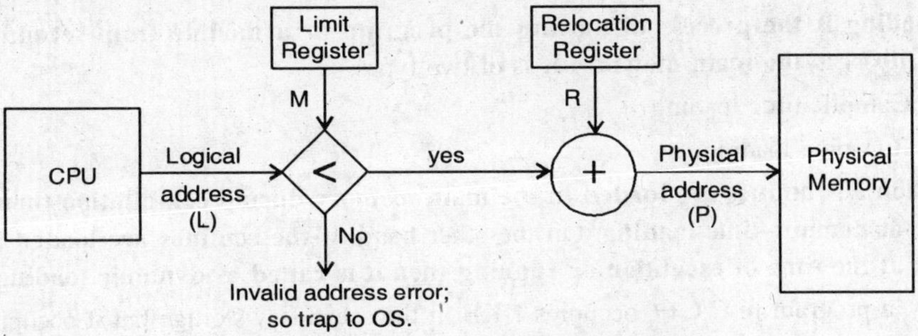

Fig. 2.5. Hardware Protection Mechanism

Explanation:

The Limit Register is initialized to the size M of the currently executing program and the Relocation Register is initialized to the base address of the executing program. When CPU (or program) generates a logical address, this address is compared with the contents of the Limit Register (M). If the logical address (L) < = M, then it is a **valid address** else it is an **'invalid address error'**. So,

if (logical address (L)) < (Limit Register value M)

then physical address (P) = Logical address (L) + Relocation value (R);

else

raise "Invalid address exception & trap of OS."

2.6 SHARING

In general, protection mechanisms are required at the time of access of the same portion of main memory by several processes. **This process of accessing the same portion of the main memory by a number of processes is known as sharing.** *For example,* if, say, 3 users wish to access MS-EXCEL then each user cannot be made to have EXCEL software as then lot of memory will be wasted. Instead one copy of MS-EXCEL can be placed in the server and all 3 users can use it.

2.7 LOGICAL ORGANIZATION

The main memory of a computer is organized as a linear or 1 Dimensional address space consisting of sequence of bytes or words. At physical level, the secondary memory is similarly organized. **Please note that this organization closely mirrors the actual machine hardware but it does not correspond to the way in which programs are typically constructed.** Most programs are organized into modules some of which are modifiable and some are non-modifiable. If the OS and computer hardware can effectively deal with the user programs and data in the form of modules of some sort then a number of advantages can be realized.

2.8 PHYSICAL ORGANIZATION

As we known that a computer memory is organized atleast at 2 levels:

(*a*) Main Memory (MM)

(*b*) Secondary Memory (AUX).

Main Memory provides fast access at relatively high cost. Also, the main memory is volatile, that is, it does not provide permanent storage. Secondary memory (AUX) is slower and cheaper than main memory and is usually non-volatile. This, secondary memory of large capacity can be provided to allow for long-term storage of programs and data while a smaller main memory holds programs and data currently in use.

2.9 DYNAMIC LOADING AND DYNAMIC LINKING

Loading is the process of moving the program or a module from secondary storage devices (disk) to the main memory. It is of two types:—

(*a*) Compile-time loading

(*b*) Run-time loading.

When all routines are loaded in the main memory during compilation then it is called as static or compile-time loading. On the other hand, **if the routines are loaded in the main memory at the time of execution or running then it is called as dynamic loading.**

Say, a program in C/C++ occupies 1 KB in the secondary storage but it occupies hundreds of KB in the main memory because some routines and header files are also loaded in the main memory to execute that program. Generally, this loading is done at the time of execution of the program. **Please note that in case of dynamic loading, a routine is not loaded until it is called.** So, the advantage of dynamic loading is that an **unused routine is never loaded.** This saves memory space. This scheme is particularly useful when large amounts of code are needed to handle frequently occurring cases.

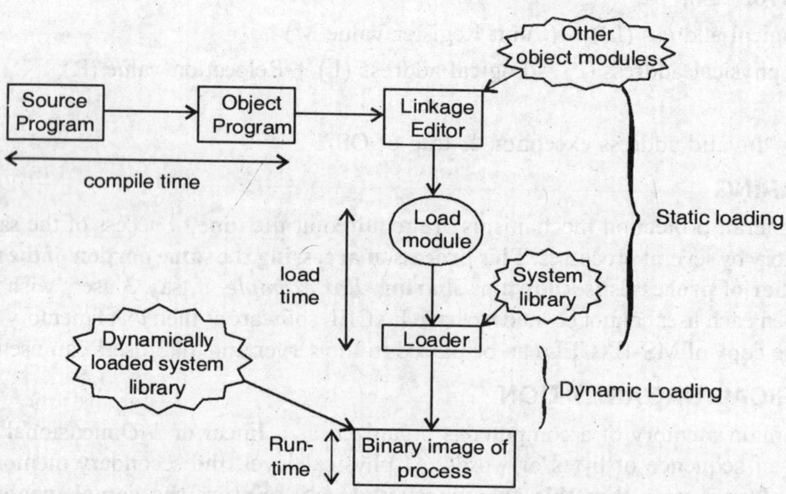

Fig. 2.6. Processing of a User Program

In this Figure 2.6, linking of the library files before the execution is called as **static linking.** And linking at the time of execution is known as **dynamic linking.** Most OS support static linking only. Dynamic linking is postponed till the execution time.

2.10 MEMORY ALLOCATION TECHNIQUES

Memory allocation is of two types:

(*a*) Contiguous storage allocation

(*b*) Non-contiguous storage allocation.

These are further categorized as follows:

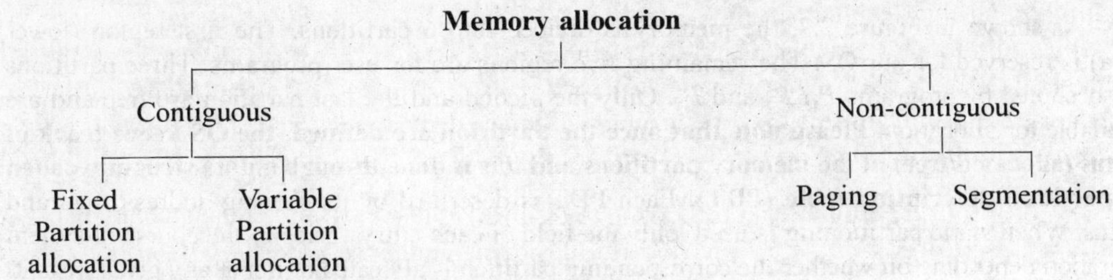

We will now study each of these techniques now.

2.10. 1 Contiguous Storage allocation

In contiguous memory (storage) allocation, a memory-resident program occupies a single contiguous block of physical memory. The memory is partitioned into blocks of different sizes to accomodate the programs. This partioning is of two types—

(*a*) Fixed-partition allocation (*b*) Variable-partition allocation

2.10.1.1 Fixed Partition allocation/Multiprogramming with fixed partition

In a multiprogramming environment, several programs reside in primary memory at a time and the CPU passes its control rapidly between these programs. One way to support multiprogramming is to divide the main memory into several partitions each of which is allocated to a single process. Depending on how and when partitions a created, there may be two types of memory partitioning:–

1. Static 2. Dynamic

Static partitioning implies that the division of memory into number of partitions and its size is made in the beginning prior to the execution of user programs and remains fixed thereafter.

In **Dynamic partitioning,** the size and the number of partitions are decided during the run time by the operating system.

Operation Principle

"We divide the memory into several fixed size partitions where each partition will accomodate only one program for execution. The number of programs (i.e., degree of multiprogramming) residing in the memory will be bound by the number of partition. When a program terminates, that partition is freed for another program waiting in a queue."

Example of fixed size partition

Figure 2.7 below shows an example of a fixed size partition.

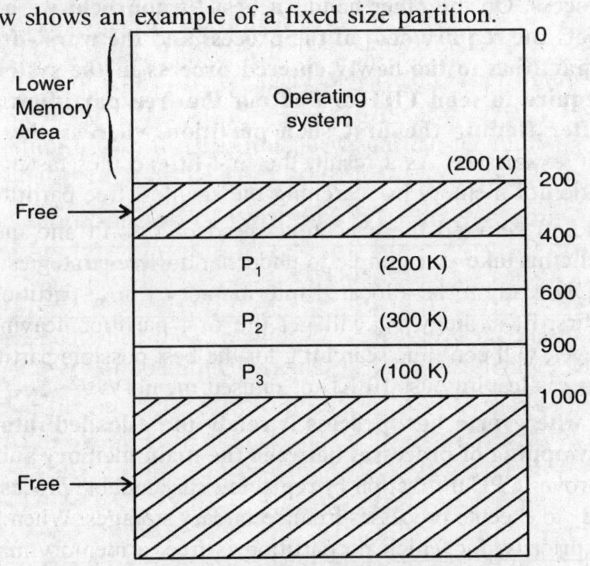

Fig. 2.7. Fixed size partition

As shown in Figure 2.7, the memory is divided into 6 partitions. The first region (lower area) is reserved for our OS. The remaining five regions are for user programs. Three partitions are occupied by programs P_1, P_2 and P_3. Only the second and the last partition are free and are available for allocation. **Please note that once the partition are defined, the OS keeps track of status (allocated/free) of the memory partitions and this is done through a data structure called as partition description table (PDT).** Each PDT is described by its starting address, size and status. When static partitioning is used, only the field of each entry varies in the course of system operation depending on whether the corresponding partition is allocated or not at any given instant. All other fields are static and contain the values defined at partition definition time.

So, we draw a PDT for figure 2.7.

Partition Number	Starting address of Partition	Size of Partition	Partition status
1	OK	200 K	Allocated
2	200 K	200 K	Free
3	400 K	200 K	Allocated
4	600 K	300 K	Allocated
5	900 K	100 K	Allocated
6	1000 K	100 K	Free

Fig. 2.8. PDT for figure 7

In order to load a new process, OS checks for the free memory partition with the help of PDT, if the search is found to be successful then the entry is marked as "Allocated". When the process terminates or is swapped-out, it is updated as "Free".

The three most common strategies to allocate free partitions to the new processes are—

1. First-fit
2. Best-fit
3. Worst-fit.

The approach followed in the **first-fit is to allocate the first free partition, large enough to accomodate the process.** On the other hand, **in best-fit approch, we allocate the smallest free partition that meets the requirement of the process and the worst-fit approach allocates the largest available partition to the newly entered process in the system. Please note that all these strategies require to scan PDT to find out the free partitions. Also note that the first-fit terminates after finding the first such partition whereas the best-fit continuous searching for the near exact size.** As a result, the first-fit executes faster whereas the best-fit achieves higher utilization of memory by searching the smallest free partition.

Therefore, a trade-off between the execution speed of first-fit and memory utilization of best-fit must be made. Let us take an example to understand these strategies. Say, a new process, P_4 with a size of 90 K is ready to be allocated into memory whose partition layout is given in Fig. 2.7. Now, using first-fit strategy, P_4 will get the first partition leaving 110 K of unused memory. Best-fit, however, will continue searching for the best possible partition and allocate the last partition to the process leaving just 10 KB of unused memory.

Please note that wherever a new process is ready to be loaded into memory and if no partition is free then swapping of processes between the main memory and secondary storage is done. Swapping improves CPU utilization by replacing suspendable processes but residing into main memory with ready to execute processes from secondary storages. When the scheduler admits a new process of high priority, for which no partition is free, a memory manager is invoked to make a partition free to accommodate the process. The memory manager performs this task by swapping out low priority processes suspended for a comparatively long time in order to load and execute the higher priority process. When the higher priority process is terminated, the lower priority process can be swapped back and continued.

Swapping requires secondary storage device such as a fast disk to store the suspended processes from the main memory. One problem with swapping process is that it takes lengthy time to access process from secondary storage device.

For example, to get an idea of total swap time, assume that a user program is 100K words and secondary storage device is a fixed head disk with an average latency of 8ms and a transfer rate of 250,000 words/second then a transfer of 100K words to or from memory takes : 8 ms + (100 K words/250,000 words/sec)

= 8ms + 100000 words/250,000 words/sec

= 8ms + 2/5 secs

= 8ms + 2000/5 ms

= 8 ms + 400 ms

= **408 ms** (approx.)

Since, we must both swap-in and swap-out, so the total swap time is about–

= 408 + 408

= **816 ms**

The overhead must be considered when deciding whether to swap a process in order to make room for another process. Now, the question is – **whether the process removed temporarily from any partition should be brought back to the same partition or any partition of adequate size?**

This depends upon the partitioning policy.

The binding of process to a specific partition **(static partitioning)** eliminates the overhead of run-time allocation of partition at the expense of lowest utilization of primary memory. On the other hand, systems where processes are not permanently bound to a specific partition **(dynamic partitioning)** are much more flexible and utilises memory more efficiently. The only drawback with dynamic partitioning approach is runtime overhead of partition allocation whenever a new process is swapped in. **The loading of a process into the same partition from where it was swapped out or into a different partition is dependent upon the relocation policy. Relocation refers to the ability to load and execute a given program into an arbitrary memory partition as opposed to fixed set of memory locations specified at program translation time.** Depending upon when and how the address translation from logical or virtual address to actual address or physical address of primary memory takes place, a process or program relocation may be regarded as—

(*a*) Static Relocation.

(*b*) Dynamic Relocation

If the relocation is performed before or during the loading of a program into memory by a relocating linker or a relocating loader, the relocation approach is called as static relocation. The static relocation is practically restricted to support only static binding of processes to partition.

Dynamic relocation refers to run-time mapping of virtual address into physical address with the support of some hardware mechanism such as base registers and limit registers. Relocation of memory references at run-time is shown in Figure 2.9.

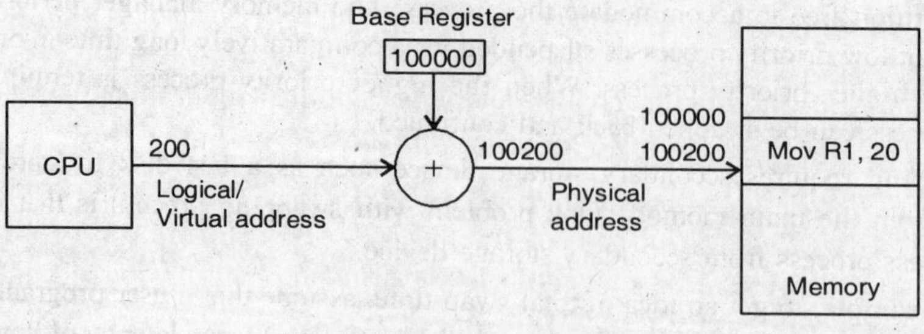

Fig. 2.9. Dynamic Relocation

When a process is scheduled, the base register is loaded with the starting address. Every memory address generated automatically has the base register contents added to it before being sent to the main memory. Thus, if the base register is 100000 (100 K), a MOVE R1, 20 which is supported to load the contents of virtual address 200 (relative to program beginning) into register, effectively turned into a MOV R1, 100000 + 200, without the instruction itself being modified. The hardware protects the base register to prevent user programs from modifying. Another use of base register for relocation is that a program can be moved anywhere in the memory after it has started execution.

Protection and Sharing

Multiprogramming introduces one essential problem of protection. Not only that the OS must be protected from user programs/processes but each user process/program should also be protected from maliciously accessing the areas of other processes.

In system that uses base register for relocation, a common approach is to use limit (bound) register for protection. **Please note that the primary function of a limit register is to detect attempts to access memory location beyong the boundary assigned by the operating system.** When a process is scheduled, the limit register is loaded with the highest virtual address in a program. This is shown in Fig. 2.10 below.

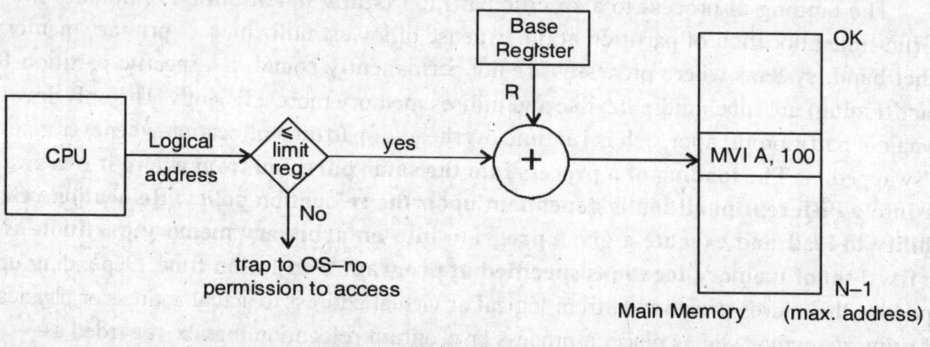

Fig. 2.10. Protection with Limit & Base Register

CPU generates a logical address. It is compared with the contents of limit register. If it (logical address) exceeds the value of limit register then no permission is given to the user process. In this way, any attempt to access a memory location beyond the boundary is trapped.

In addition to protection, a good memory management mechanism must also provide for controlled sharing of data and code between cooperating processes. One traditional approach to sharing is to place data and code in a dedicated common partition. However, any attempt by a participating process to access memory outside of its own participation is normally regarded as a protection violation. In systems with protection keys, this obstacle may be circumvented by charging the keys of all shared blocks upon every process switch in order to grant access rights to currently running process.

Disadvantages of fixed partitioning

Fixed partitioning imposes several restrictions. They are as follows:–

1. No single program (or process) may exceed the size of the largest partition in a given system.
2. It does not support a system having dynamic data structure such as stack, queue, heap etc.
3. It limits the degree of multiprogramming which in turn may reduce the effectiveness of short-term scheduling.
4. The main problem with fixed size partition is the wastage of memory by programs that are smaller than their partitions. **This is known as Internal fragmentation.**

   Let us understand Internal fragmentation in detail with an example. Say, we have a physical memory with the following fixed partitions.

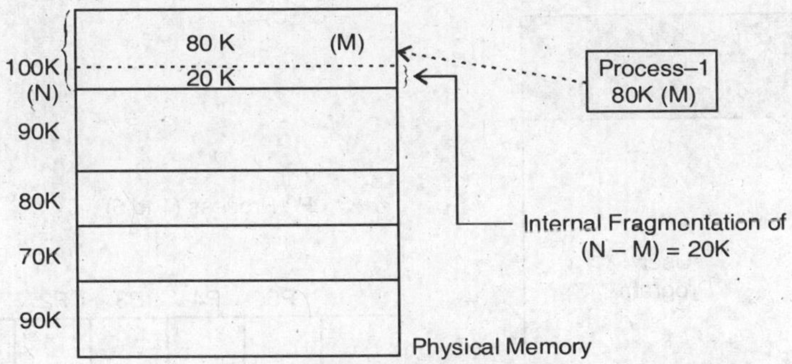

Fig. 2.11. Internal Fragmentation

As shown in Figure 2.11, a physical address space with fixed partitions. When a process or program of size, 80 K (M) arrives, it is accomodated in partition-1. But partition-1 is of 100K (N) size. So, M < N. Therefore, M can be given partition-1. **Please note that the leftover unused space is** (N – M) = (100 K – 80 K) = 20 K. **This causes internal fragmentation of 20 K here.** This scheme was used in **early batch systems** wherein the space requirement of a process could be easily known before hand. So, we list some advantages of this policy now.

Advantages of Fixed partition allocation

1. Implementation of this allocation scheme is simple.
2. The overhead of processing is also low.
3. It supports multiprogramming.
4. It requires no special costly hardware.
5. It makes efficient utilization of processor and I/O devices.

2.10.1.2 Variable-partition allocation/Multiprogramming with Dynamic Partitions

Another memory management approach is to create partitions dynamically to meet the requirements of each requesting process. This technique is called **dynamic partitioning or variable partitioning.** When a process terminates or is swapped-out then the memory manager can return the vacated space to the pool of free memory area from which partition allocations are made.

Comparison of fixed and dynamic partition schemes:

As compared to fixed partitions, in dynamic partition scheme, neither the size nor the number of dynamically allocated partition need be limited at any other time. **Please note that a memory manager continues creating and allocating partitions to the requesting processes until all physical memory is exhausted or maximum allowable degree of multiprogramming is reached.** The main difference between the fixed partition and dynamic (or variable) partitions is that the number, location and size of partitions vary dynamically in the latter as processes are created and terminated whereas in the former case, they are fixed. **Also note that the flexibility of not being tied to a fixed number of partitions that may be too large or too small for the requesting processes, improves memory utilization but it also complicates the process of allocation and de allocation of memory.** In variable partition, OS keeps track of which parts of memory are available and which are allocated.

Let us consider an example to understand this scheme. Say, we have a main memory of size = 650K out of which 50K is occupied by the OS program. Now, consider that there are 5 jobs waiting for memory allocation in a job queue. This is shown in Fig. 2.12 below.

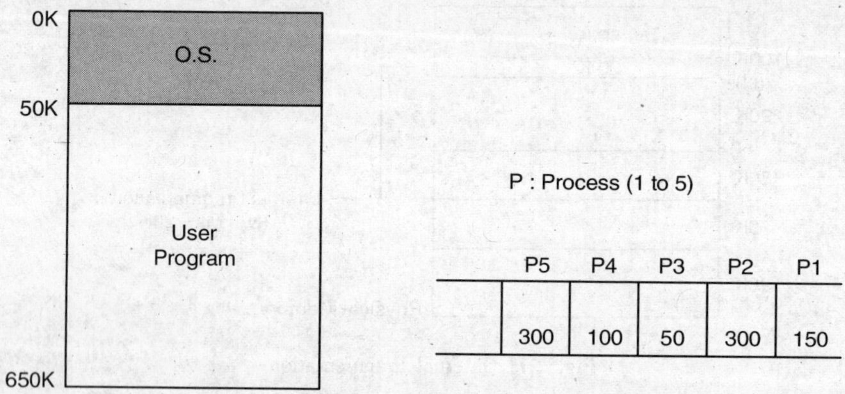

Fig. 2.12. Processes waiting in a queue for CPU

Applying FCFS scheduling policy, P1, P2 and P3 can be immediately allocated memory. Process-4 cannot be accomodated because there is only 600 – (150 + 300 + 50) = 600 – 500 = 100K left for it. That is,

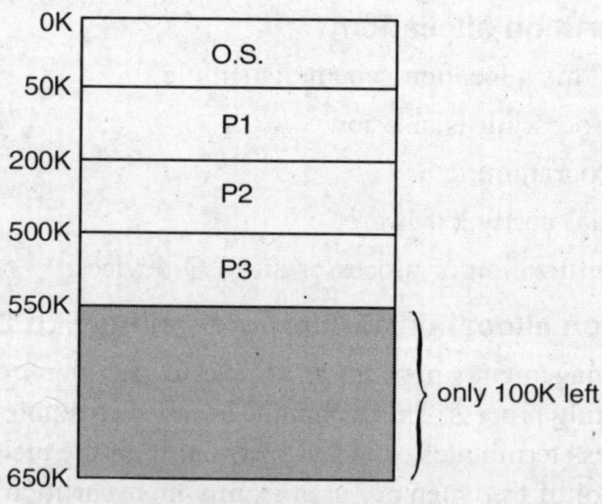

Fig. 2.13(*a*) P1, P2 & P3 allocation

Let us assume that after some time P1 terminates, releasing 150K memory space. This is shown in Fig. 2.13 (*b*).

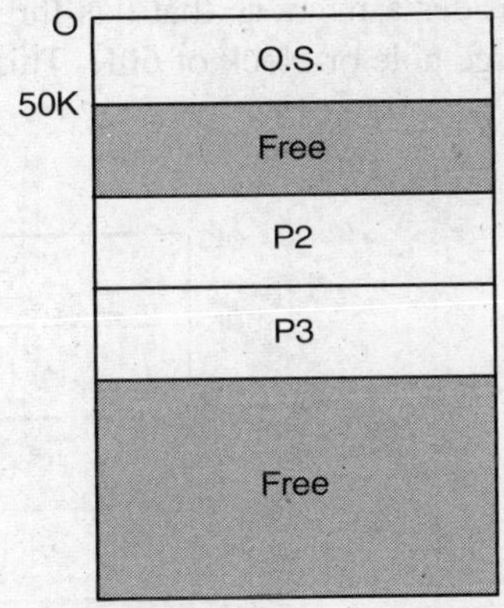

Fig. 2.13(*b*) P1 terminates

After that the control is returned to the process queue and the next process (P4) is swapped in the memory which is shown in Fig. 2.13 (*c*).

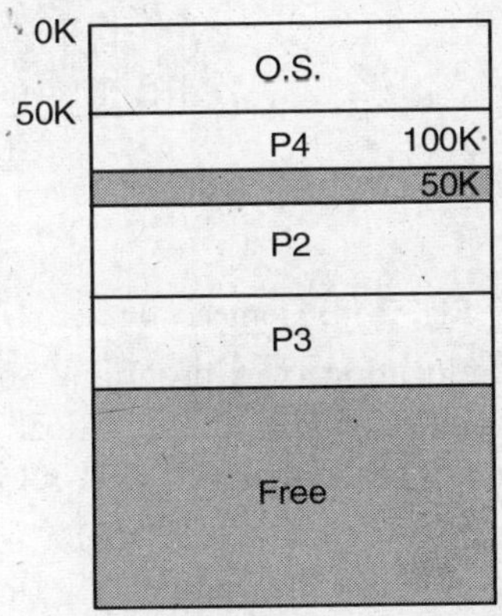

Fig. 2.13(*c*) P4 is swapped-in

However, we have 150K here and P4 is of 100K only. So, 50K is wasted. This is actually known as **external fragmentation** *i.e.*, when a free partition (say, 50K here) is too small to accomodate any process. The main problem with this approach is external fragmentation. **When the size of the memory is large enough for a requesting process, but if cannot satisfy a request because it is not contiguous then the storage is fragmented into a small number of holes (free spaces). This results in External Fragmentation.** It may be a minor or a major problem depending upon the total size of memory and the number and size of a program.

What is the solution to this problem?

One solution to this problem is **compaction. Compaction is a technique by which the resident programs are relocated in such a way that the small chunks of free memory are made contiguous to each other and clubbed together into a single free partition, that may be big enough to accommodate some more programs.** We need to move the processes in the memory in such a way that scattered pieces of unused (free) memory can be placed together so that any other process demanding contiguous memory for it can use it. **Please note that it is possible to combine all the holes (free spaces) into a large block by pushing all processes downward as far as possible.** As an example, consider a memory that has three holes of size 30K, 20K, 50K that have been compacted into one large hole or block of 60K. This is shown in Figure 2.14 below.

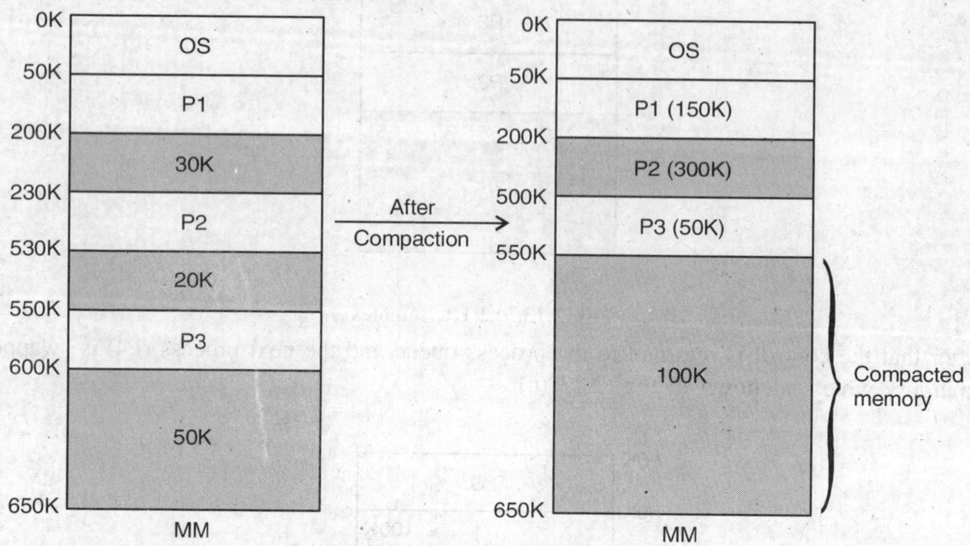

Fig. 2.14. Compaction

Compaction involves dynamic relocation of a program. So, we make use of a relocation register. Compaction is not possible if relocation is done statically i.e., at load time. So, we say, we need a dynamic relocation register. The contents of this relocation register as given by the formula:

[Relocation Register] = (Starting address of a process) – (load origin address of process).

The cost of compaction increases with the increase in the number of processes to be moved (relocated) in order to make use of the unused memory space.

Compaction is usually not done because it consumes a lot of CPU time. On a 1M microcomputer that has the capacity of copying at rate of 1 megabyte/sec., CPU takes one second (1s) to compact memory. Compaction is usually done on a large machine line mainframe or super computer because they are supported with a special hardware to perform this task at rate of 40 megabytes/sec or more. Actually, the solution of an optimal compaction strategy is quite difficult. Let us take an example and see how it happens?

If we simply move process 4 above 3, case-B, then we only move 300K. Or if we move Process-3 down below Process-4 (case-C) then we move only 200K. Whereas in case-A the total movement of P3 and P4 is 500K. This is shown in Fig. 2.15 on next page.

Please note that a large memory hole (block) is in the middle in case-C. Therefore, if we have a large number of processes then the selection of which process or processes for shifting downwards or upwards to meet the requirements for waiting process, is quite a difficult task.

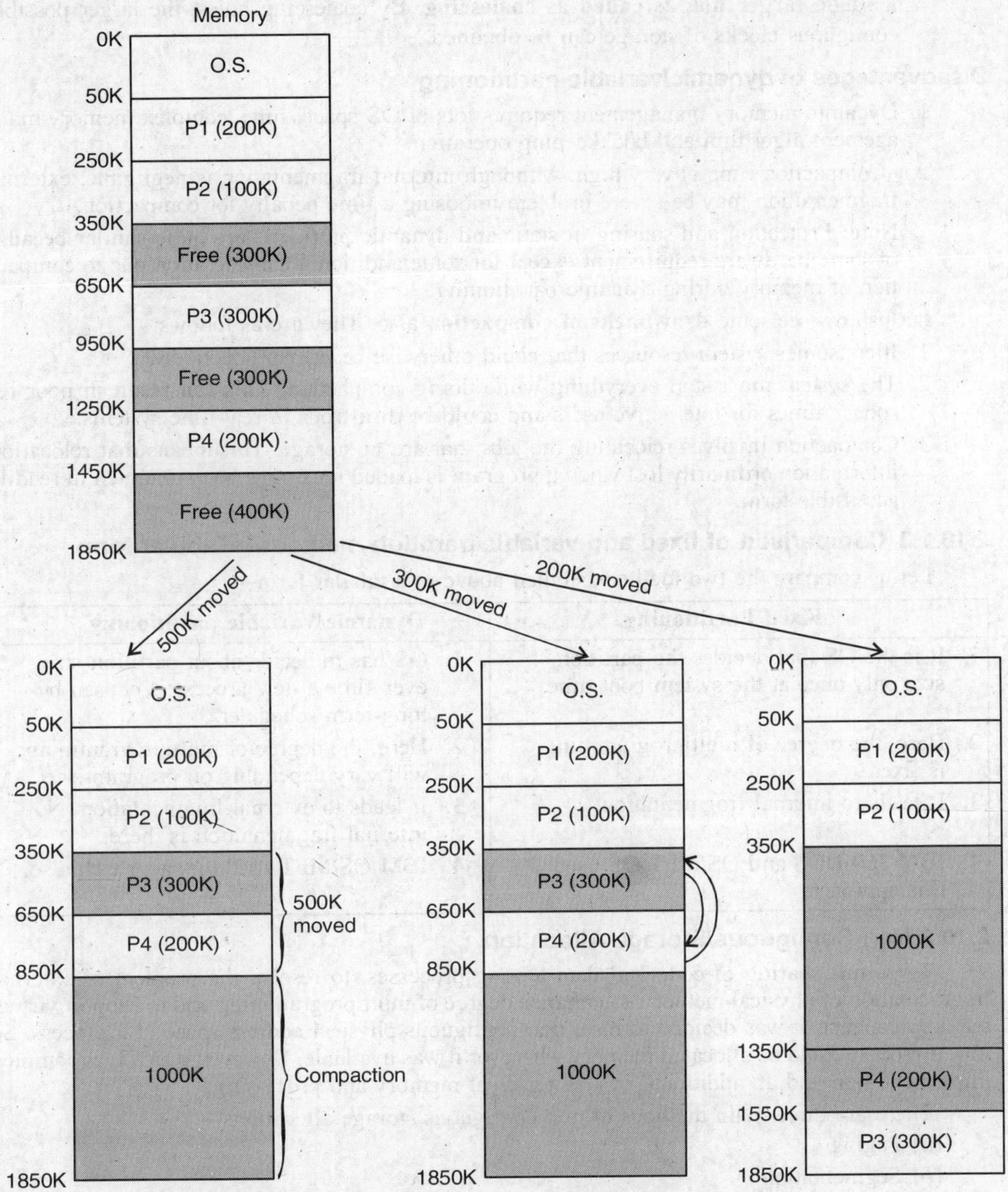

Fig. 2.15. Different ways of compaction

Advantages of dynamic partitioning

1. Memory utilization is generally better as partitions are created dynamically *i.e.*, partitions are created according to the size of the process.
2. No internal fragmentation as partitions are changed dynamically.
3. It supports those processes whose memory requirement increases during their execution. In that case, OS creates a larger partition and moves a process into it. If there is an adjacent free area, it simply expands it. **The process of merging adjacent holes to form**

a single larger hole is called as coalescing. By coalescing holes, the larger possible contiguous blocks of storage can be obtained.

Disadvantages of dynamic/variable partitioning

1. Dynamic memory management requires lots of OS space, time, complex memory management algorithm and bookkeeping operation.
2. Compaction time is very high. Although internal fragmentation is negligible, external fragmentation may be severe problem imposing a time penalty for compaction.

   Note: Protection and sharing in static and dynamic partitions are quite similar because of some hardware requirement except for some additional consideration due to compaction of memory during dynamic partitioning.

Let us now see some **drawbacks of compaction** also. They are as follows:–

1. It consumes system resources that could otherwise be used productively.
2. The system must stop everything while doing compaction. This can result in poor response times for interactive users and could be disastrous in real-time systems.
3. Compaction involves relocating the jobs that are in storage. This means that relocation information ordinarily lost when a program is loaded must now be maintained in readily accessible form.

2.10.1.3 Comparison of fixed and variable partition methods—Tabular form

Let us compare the two methods studied above in a tabular form—

Fixed Partitioning	Dynamic/Variable partitioning
1. It is the OS that decides the partition size only once at the system boot time.	1. OS has to decide about partition size, everytime a new process is chosen by long-term scheduler.
2. Here, the degree of multiprogramming is fixed.	2. Here, the degree of multiprogramming will vary depending on program size.
3. It leads to internal fragmentation.	3. It leads to external fragmentation. No internal fragmentation is there.
4. IBM-360 DOS and OS/MFT OS used this approach.	4. IBM OS/MFT used this approach also.

2.10.2 Non-Contiguous Storage Allocation

To permit sharing of code and data among processes, to resolve the problem of external fragmentation of physical memory, to enhance degree of multiprogramming and to support virtual memory concept, it was decided to have non-contiguous physical address space of a process. So now a process could be allocated memory wherever it was available. However, it involves complex implementation and an additional cost in terms of memory and processing.

There are three main methods of non-contiguous storage allocations—

(*a*) Paging
(*b*) Segmentation
(*c*) Segmentation with Paging

We discuss all these methods one by one now.

2.10.2.1 Paging

Paging is a memory management technique that permits a program's memory (contiguous) to be non-contiguous into the physical memory and thereby allowing a program to be allocated physical memory wherever it is possible. When a programmer wants to transfer data from one location to another, he might write an instruction, for example, MOV R1, 20A0 (*i.e.*, Contents of memory location, 20A0 are moved to register R1). Now, an address of memory location can be generated using indexing, base registers, segment registers and other ways. **These**

program generated address are called as logical or virtual addresses and they form the virtual address space. Please note here that there has to be a mapping between virtual address space and physical address space. This mapping is done through paging.

Address mapping in a Paging System (Key idea): The physical memory is conceptually divided into a number of fixed-size blocks called as frames (or page frames). The virtual address space or logical memory of a process is also broken into blocks of the same size called as pages. Whenever a program is to be executed, its pages are loaded into any frame from the disks. To show this paying concept, consider 2 processes—Process—A and Process-B. As shown in Figure 2.16 below is how the pages of process-A and process-B are loaded into the physical or main memory's frames.

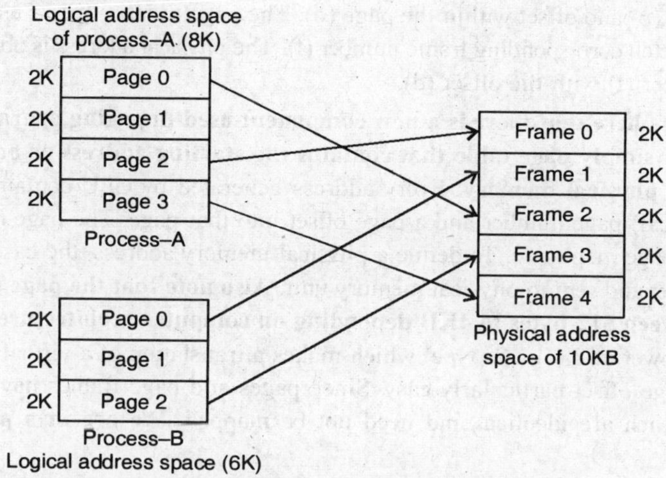

Fig. 2.16. Pages of Process-A and Process-B being loaded to physical memory.

Please note that the logical memory is divided into fixed size blocks called as pages whereas the physical (or main) memory is divided into fixed size blocks called as frames. And these pages are loaded into frames. This translation is done by **address mapping** in a paging system and is shown below in Figure 2.17.

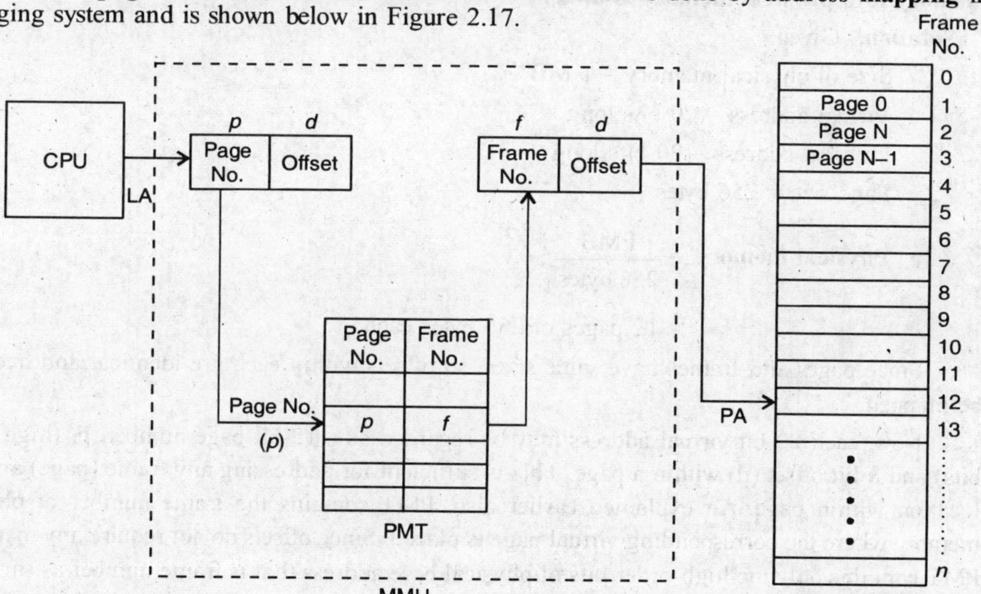

Fig. 2.17. Address mapping in Paging

Legends:

LA : Logical address

PA : Physical address

PMT : Page Map Table/Page Table

MMU : Memory Management Unit

Operation Principle

During the process execution, CPU generates a logical (or virtual) address, that comprises of page number (p) and offset within the page (d). The page number (p), is used to index into the page table and fetch corresponding frame number (f). The physical address is obtained by combining the frame number (f) with the offset (d).

Please note here that there is a new component used in paging operation i.e., page map table (PMT) or simply page table that contains the starting address or base address of each page stored in physical memory. Every address generated by CPU contains two components: Virtual (or logical) page number and a page offset into that page. The page number works as an index into the page map table. To define a physical memory address, the base address in PMT is added with offset and sent to physical memory unit. **Also note that the page size and frame size is defined between 512 bytes to 4KB depending on computer architecture.** The size of a page is typically a power of 2 (*i.e.*, 2^n type) which makes a translation of a virtual address into a page number and page offset particularly easy. Since pages and page frames have identical sizes, so offsets within each are identical and need not be mapped. **We are in a position to solve an example now.**

Example 1. Consider a paging system with a sample space of 1 MB physical storage where virtual and physical address is each 20 bits long. The page size is assumed to be 256 bytes. What will be the frame size of this physical memory? Show how mapping of user's view of memory into physical memory is done.

Solution. Given:

Size of physical memory = 1 MB

Virtual address = 20 bits long

Physical address = 20 bits long

Page size = 256 bytes

$$\therefore \textbf{ Physical memory} = \frac{1\text{ MB}}{256\text{ bytes}}$$

$$= 12 \text{ pages of } 256 \text{ bytes each.}$$

Since pages and frames have same sizes, so offsets within each are identical and need not be mapped.

Now, each 20 bit virtual address may be regarded as a 12-bit page number, p, (high order bits) and 8-bit offset (d) within a page. This is sufficient for addressing any frame (page) and any location within page. An explained earlier also, PMT contains the frame number of physical memory where the corresponding virtual page is placed. Since offsets do not require any mapping, PMT contains only the high-order bits of physical base address that is frame number as shown in Figure below.

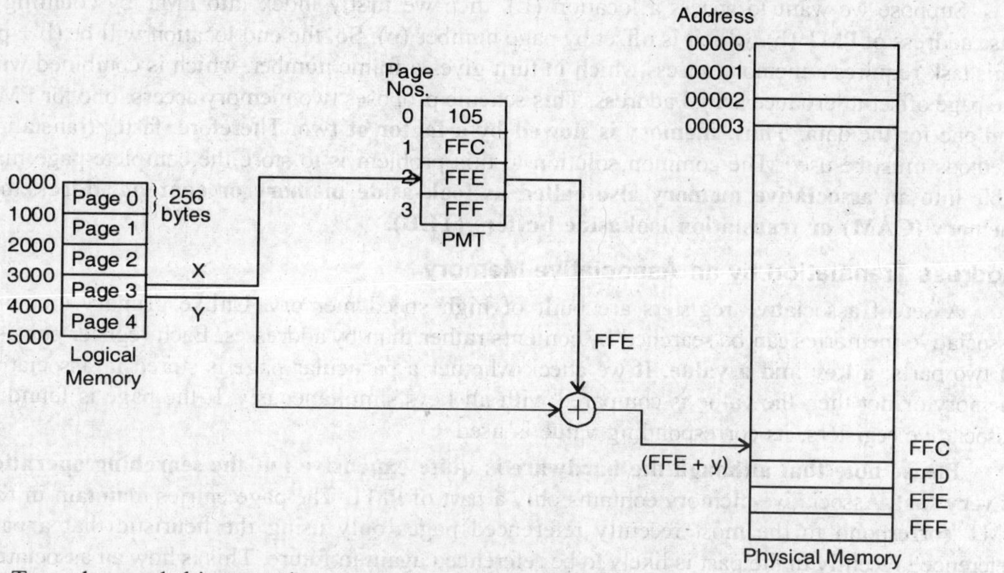

To understand this, say, there is an instruction, MOV R1, XY. Now, the virtual or logical address XY is split by the hardware mechanism as follows—

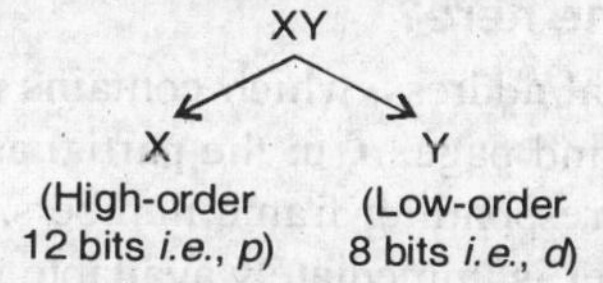

Remember that *p* is the page number and *d* is the offset. This page number (X, here) is used as an index into PMT and gets the corresponding physical address FFEH that is concatenated with the offset to produce the physical address of (FFE + y) H to refer to any data in the memory.

Hardware Support for Paging

The main objective for hardware support for paging is to store page map table and make virtual to physical address translation more efficient since every access to memory must go through the PMT. So, efficiency is the major consideration.

If the number of entries in PMT is quite small (around 256 entries) then registers can be used to reduce the access time. For keeping very large number of entries (say, 1,000,000 entries), **PMT is usually kept in primary memory because the use of registers for keeping such a large number of entries is not feasible.** Thus, PMT is usually kept in the primary memory and there is a Page Table Base Register (PTBR) pointer, pointing to the beginning of PMT.

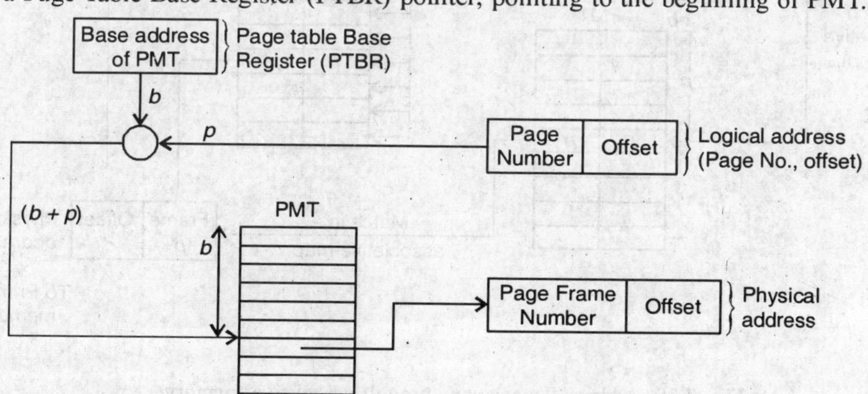

Fig. 2.18. Hardware Action for Paging Operation

Suppose we want to access a location (L), then we firstly index into PMT by counting a base address of PMT (b), which is offset by page number (p). So, the end location will be (b + p). This task requires a memory access which in turn gives a frame number, which is combined with the page offset to produce actual address. This scheme proposes two memory access, one for PMT and one for the data. **Thus, memory is slowed by a factor of two.** Therefore, faster translation methods must be used. The common solution to this problem is to store the complete page map table into an **associative memory also called as look-aside memory or content addressable memory (CAM) or translation lookaside buffers (TLB).**

Address Translation by an Associative Memory

A set of associative registers are built of high speed memory. Unlike primary memory, associative memories can be searched by contents rather than by addresses. Each register consists of two parts: **a key and a value.** If we check whether a particular page is stored in associative memory or not then the value is compared with all keys simultaneously. If the page is found in associative registers, its corresponding value is used.

Please note that although the hardware is quite expensive but the searching operation is very fast. Associative memory contains only a part of PMT. The page entries maintain in this PMT correspond to the most recently referenced pages only using the heuristic that a page referenced recently in the past is likely to be referenced again in future. This is how an associative memory and PMT works.

How dynamic translation is done here?

When a CPU generates a virtual address, which contains page no., *p* and offset *d*, address translation mechanism first tries to find page, *p*, in the partial associative page map table, which contains page number and their corresponding frame numbers. If the page number is found in associative registers, its frame number is immediately available which is combined with offset, *d*, to form the real address that corresponds to virtual address. This working is shown in Figure 2.19 below.

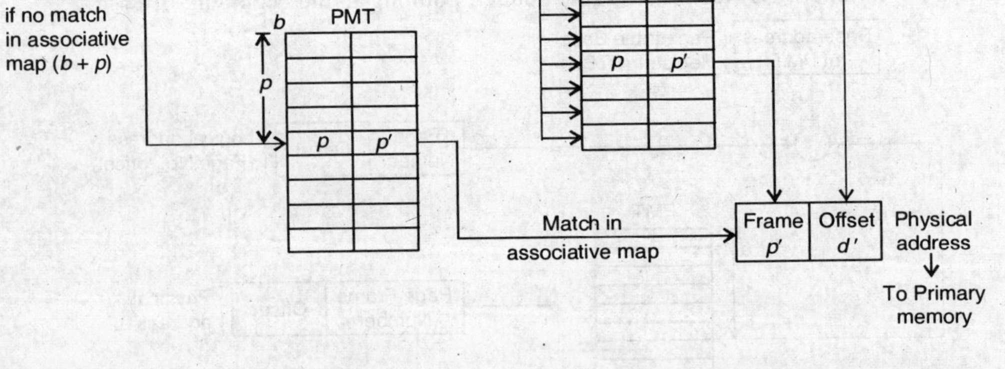

Fig. 2.19. Address Translation through associative memory

If the target page number is not in the associative registers, a reference to PMT in memory is made when the frame number is obtained. We can use it to access memory. In addition, we add the page number and frame number to the associative registers, so that they can be found very quickly on the next reference.

Please note that the percentage of times a page number is found in the associative registers is called as the hit ratio. A 70% hit ratio means that 70% of the time we find the desired page number in the associative registers. If it takes 60 nanoseconds to search the associative registers and 740 nanoseconds to access physical memory then total memory access time is (60 + 740) = 800 ns, *when the target page is in the associative registers.* If the target page (60 ns) is not found in the associative registers then we must first access primary memory (740 ns) for PMT for getting the corresponding frame number and then access the desired location in memory, another (740 ns) for a total of (60 + 740 + 740) = 1540 ns.

Please note have that the hit ratio is clearly related to the number of associative registers. With 8 or 16 associative registers, a hit ratio of 80% to 90% can be obtained.

Let the effective memory access time be 't_{eff}' in systems with run-time address translation equal to the sum of the address translation time t_{TR} and the subsequent access time needed to fetch the target from memory, t_M. Mathematically,

$$t_{eff} = t_{TR} + t_M \quad \text{... (1)}$$

with T_{LB} assisting t_{TR}, we get

$$t_{TR} = ht_{TLB} + (1 - h)(t_{TLB} + t_M) \quad \text{... (2)}$$

$$\therefore \quad t_{TR} = t_{TLB} + (1 - h)\, t_M$$

where 'h' is the TLB ratio

$$\therefore \quad \boxed{t_{eff} = t_{TLB} + (2-h)t_M} \quad \text{(from (1) and (2))}$$

Sharing and Protection in a Paging System Sharing: In a multiprogramming environment, where several users want to execute the same software, keeping a separate copy of the same for the individual users, will cause wastage of lot of primary memory. **For example,** consider a time-sharing system, which supports 20 terminals (users), each of which run a compiler. If 50 KB are required for compiler and 5Kbytes for data storage then the total amount of memory required to support 20 users will be–

(50 K * 20) + (5K * 20)

= 1100K (Slightly above 1 million byte)

The obvious solution to this problem is to share those pages among all users.

Sharing must be controlled to prevent one process from modifying data that another process is reading. In today's system that support sharing, programs consist of two separate parts, one for procedure code and another for data. **Please note that to be sharable, the code must be non-self-modifiable or reentrant or pure code.** The meaning of reentrant code is that it is read only. There should not be any attempt on part of users to modify this code. **Modifiable data or code cannot be shared.** Since reentrant code never changes while execution, two or more processes can execute the same code at the same time, without having a personal copy of it. But data for two different processes for the same code will of course be different. Each process has its own copy of registers and data storage to hold data for its own execution. So, only one copy of the compiler need to be kept in the primary memory. The page map table of each process maps onto the same physical copy of compiler but data pages are mapped into different frames. This is shown in Fig. 20.

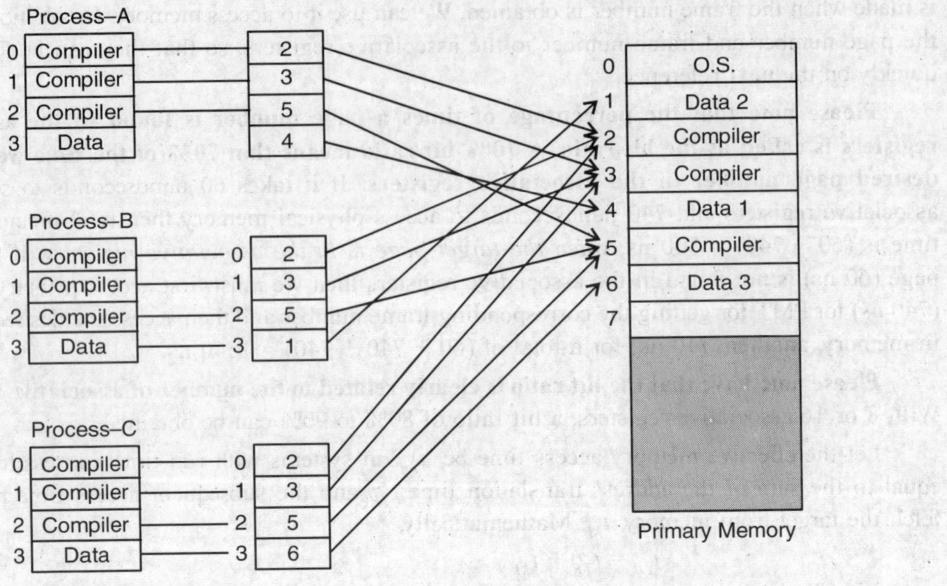

Fig. 2.20. Sharing in a Paging System

Therefore, to support, only one copy of the compiler (50K) plus 20 copies of 5K of data space per user is required. So, the total memory requirement will be now just 150 KB instead of 1 MB (mega byte) which is a significant saving.

To implement sharing, each page is identified as a sharable or non-sharable. As shown above in Fig. 2.20, pages 2, 3 and 5 are identified as sharing. By having PMT entries of different processes pointing to the same page frame, that page frame is shared among those processes. Sharing reduces the amount of primary storage needed for several users to run efficiently and make it possible for a given system to support more users.

Protection: Memory protection is usually done by protection bits associated with each page. These bits are usually kept in the page map table (PMT). One protection bit can define a page to be read/write or a read only. Since reference to each page is passed through the page map table (PMT) to find the correct frame number, protection bits can be checked to verify that no write operation is being used to read-only page. An attempt to do this type of operation is easily trapped.

Paging is normally transparent to the programmers, hence mechanical splitting of an address space into pages is performed irrespective of the possible logical relationships between the items under consideration. The protection in paging can also be obtained by means of protection keys.

Advantages and Disadvantages of Paging

Let us first of all see the advantages of paging. They are listed below:–

1. It supports time sharing systems.
2. It achieves a high degree of multiprogramming.
3. No external fragmentations.
4. Sharing of common code among the processes is now possible. Single copy of some standard programs like compilers, editors, Database systems can be kept in the physical memory and shared by many processes by making the page table of each of the processes such that it maps to frames having shared data or programs in the physical memory. **This means that many logical addresses will be mapped to one physical address.**

Disadvantages of Paging Scheme

There are some disadvantages of paging systems also. They are listed below:–

1. TLBs (Translation look-aside buffers) used during paging are limited in size.
2. Additional hardware costs of TLBs.
3. What if the size of page table gets very large? Either we can put the page table entries in *special registers* (done in PDP-11 minicomputer) or we put the page table in the **main memory.** Let another approach is to use an **inverted page table.** This scheme is shown in Fig. 2.21 below.

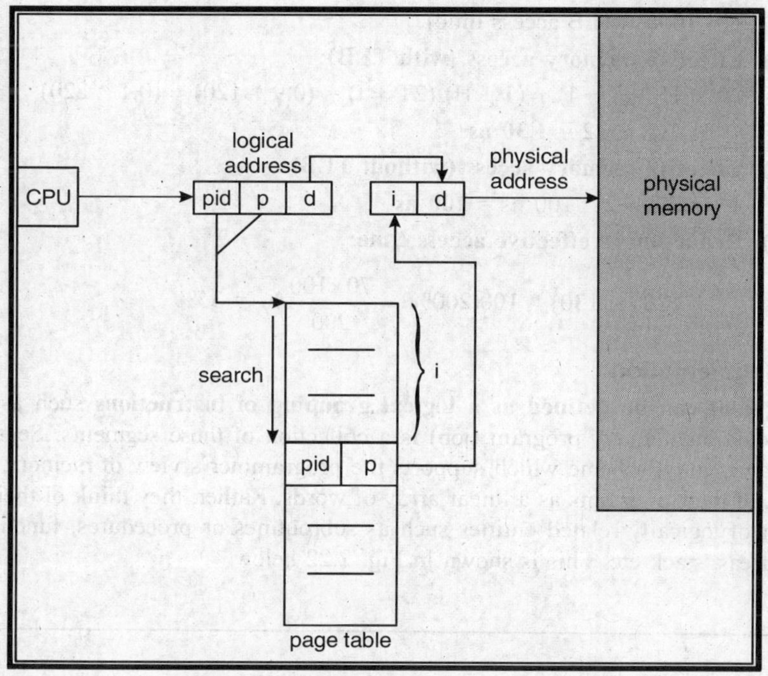

Fig. 2.21 Inverted Page Table Architecture

It's main features are given below:

- One entry for each real page of memory.
- Entry consists of the virtual address of the page stored in that real memory location, with information about the process that owns that page.
- Decreases memory needed to store each page table, but increases time needed to search the table when a page reference occurs.
- Use hash table to limit the search to one—or at most a few—page-table entries.

4. Paging also suffers from **Internal fragmentation.** Since, a program size may not be an exact multiple of the page size. Some space would remain unoccupied in the last page of a process. This results in internal fragmentation. The average memory loss due to internal fragmentation would be of the order of half page per process. **Please note that the larger is the page size, larger would be the loss of memory by internal fragmentation.** Say, a system supports a page-size of P bytes, then a program of size M bytes will have an internal fragmentation = P – (M % P) bytes.

We are in a position to solve a problem now.

Example 1: For a paged system, TLB hit ratio is 0.9. Let the RAM access time, t be 20ns and the TLB access time, T be 100ns. Find out–

(*a*) Effective memory access with TLB.

(*b*) Effective memory access withtout TLB.

(*c*) Reduction in effective access time?

Solution. Given :

H = 0.9 (Hit Ratio of TLB)

t = 20ns (RAM access time)

T = 100ns (TLB access time)

(*a*) Effective memory access (with TLB):

$= H * (T + t) + (1 - H)(2T + t) = (0.9 * 120) + (0.1 * 220)$

$= 108 + 22 =$ **1.30 ns**

(*b*) Effective memory access (without TLB):

$= 2T = 2 * 100$ ns = **200 ns**

(*c*) Reduction in effective access time:

$$= (200 - 130) * 100/200\% = \frac{70 \times 100}{200}\% = 35\%$$

2.10.2.2 Segmentation

A segment can be defined as a logical grouping of instructions such as a subroutine, array or a data area. Every program (job) is a collection of these segments. Segmentation is a memory management scheme which supports the programmer's view of memory. Programmers never think of their programs as a linear array of words. Rather, they think of their programs as a collection of logically related entities such as subroutines or procedures, functions, global or local data areas, stack etc. This is shown in Fig. 2.22 below.

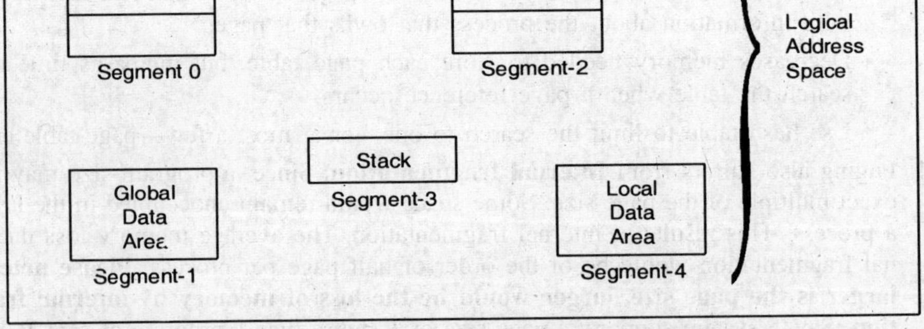

Fig. 2.22. Programmer's View of a Program

Segments are formed at program translation time by grouping together logically related entities. **Please note that the process of formation of these segments vary from one compiler to another.**

For example–

(1) **A PASCAL Compiler** might create separate segments for

(*a*) Code of each procedure

(*b*) Global data

(*c*) Local data or variable

(*d*) Stack for calling procedure and storing its parameter.

(2) **A FORTRAN Compiler** might create a separate segment for each common block, arrays might be formed as separate segments. To simplify the implementation procedures, each segments in a program is numbered and referred to by a segment number rather than a segment name. In segmented systems, components belonging to a single segment reside in one contiguous area but different segments belonging to the same process occupy non-contiguous area of physical memory because each segment is individually relocated.

Address Translation (Mapping) in a Segmented System

An important table that is used during address mapping is a **segment table.** A segment table is used by the memory management unit (MMU). It contains an entry for each segment of a process. A segment table contains the **base and segment size** columns. The *'base'* contains the starting physical address where the segment resides in momory and **'size'** gives the size of segment. Actually entries in the segment table contains many other vital informations like protection information indicating whether the process has permission to read, write or execute the segment.

The Fig. 2.23 given below shows how address mapping is done.

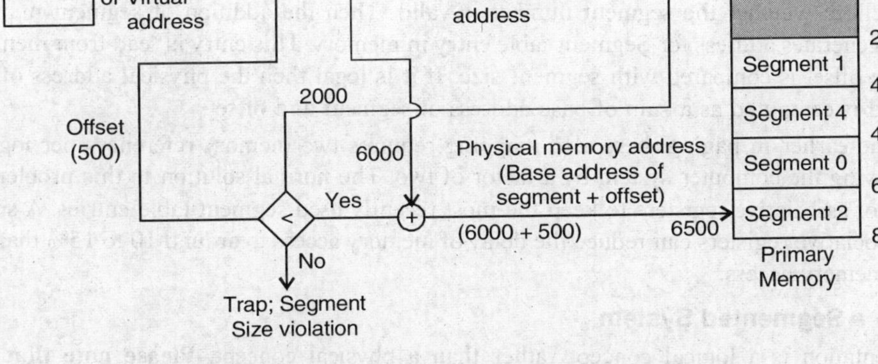

Fig. 2.23. Virtual to Physical mapping in a segmented system

A virtual (logical) address consists of two parts: a segment number and an offset into that segment. The segment number provided in the virtual address is used as an index into the segment table. Each row of the segment table contains a starting address (base address) of segment and a size of the segment. The offset of the virtual address must be within (less than or equal to) the size of the segment. If the offset of virtual address is not within the range, it is trapped by the operating system otherwise the offset is added to the base address of the segment to produce the physical address of the desired segment.

For example: Consider the five segments of Figure 21 that are numbered from 0 to 4. The segment table, in Figure 22, has a separate entry for each segment having the starting address (base address) of segment in physical memory and the size of that segment. It is clear from Figure 22 that segment-1 is 1500 words long, starting at location 2500. Thus, a reference word at 500 location within segment-1 is mapped onto location 2500 (base address) + 500 = 3000 *i.e.*, the actual physical address. Similarly, a reference to segment-2 at location 300 will be mapped to 6000 + 300 = 6300. **Please note, however that a reference to a word 900 of segment-4 would cause segment size violation and it will be trapped by the OS.** This is because now the physical address generated is 4000 (base address) + 900 = 4900 which is more than 4800, that happens to be the maximum limit of segment-4 in physical memory.

Implementation of Segment tables

Like the page map table, segment table can be stored either into fast registers or in primary memory. The main advantage to keep segment table in fast registers is that it can be accessed very fast because of simultaneous operations of comparison and addition of base address. **Please note that if a program consists of a large number of segments, it is not feasible to keep segment table in registers i.e., it must be kept in memory only. Also note that, in general, the size of a segment table is related to the size of virtual address space of a program. For example,** Intel 286 microprocessor is capable of supporting up to 16,000 segments of 64 KB each per process. So, it requires 16,000 entries per segment table. Given their long size, segment tables are kept in primary memory only. Being a collection of logically related items, segment tables are usually treated as special type segments. Their accessing is facilitated by a dedicated register called **segment table base register (STBR).** STBR points to the base of the running programs segment table. Since the number of segments used by programs may vary widely, another dedicated hardware register called as **Segment table limit register (STLR)** is used to mark the end of segment table pointed to by STBR. In this way, a segment table need contain only as many entries as there are segments actually defined in a given program. An attempt to access non-existent segment may be trapped by STLR.

For a virtual (or logical) address containing virtual segment number and offset, the first thing is to check whether the segment number is valid. Then the addition of segment number with STBR generates address for Segment table entry in memory. This entry is read from memory and then the offset is compared with segment size. If it is legal then the physical address of the desired word is computed as a sum of base address of segment and offset.

As done earlier in paging, here also mapping requires two memory references per logical address, slowing the computer system by a factor of two. The normal solution to this problem is to use a set of associative registers to keep the most recently used segment table entries. A small set of 16 associative registers can reduce the delay of memory access to around 10 to 15% than an unmapped memory access.

Sharing in a Segmented System

Segmentation is a logical concept rather than a physical concept. **Please note that the segments are not limited to a particular size as it is done with page size.** Rather segments are allowed to be as large as they require to be but with a reasonable limit. A segment for an arrray is as large as the array. A segment corresponding to a dynamic data structure such as stack, queue, binary tree etc. may increase and decrease in size as the data structure itself increases and decreases.

Sharing in a segmented system is simpler as compared to sharing in a paging system. Let us see how. For sharing a paging system there must be an entry for each page in page map table (PMT). Like, to share a stack in a paging system which is spread into 5 pages there will be 5 separate entries for each of the pages. Actually, it is a very difficult task to share dynamic data structure whose size keeps on changing during program execution. In a paging system, when a stack grows into a new page, information about this new page has to be adjusted at the execution time. **Please note, however, that in a segmented system, once a segment is declared as shared then the size of data structure may increase or decrease without changing the logical fact that they reside on a shared segment.** The sharing in a segmented system occurs only at the segment level.

Figure 23 below shows how sharing is done in a segmented system. Consider two users who will share a segment by simply having entries in their segment table that will be pointing to the same segment in the primary physical memory. This is shown below in Fig. 2.24.

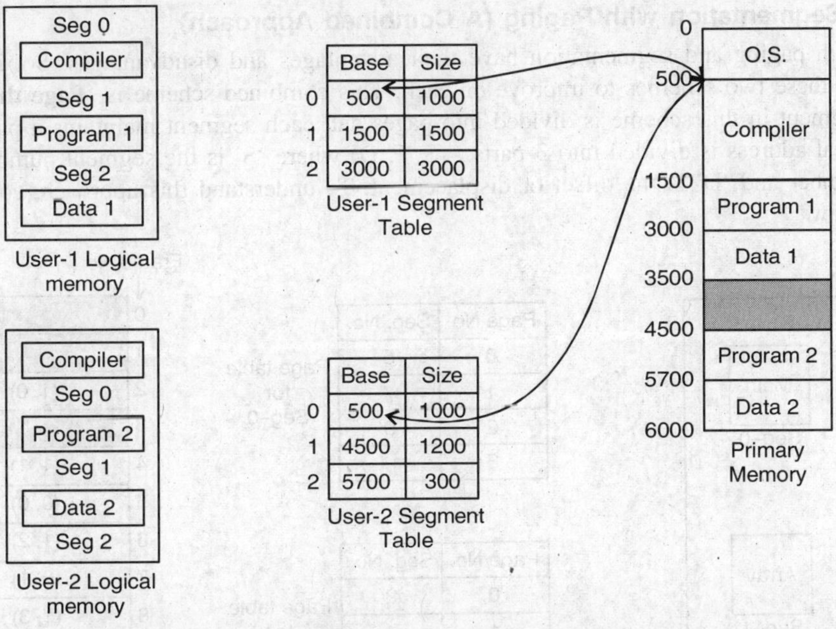

Fig. 2.24. Sharing in a segmented system

Protection in a segmented system

Protection of one segment from another segment is done through the protection bit. The memory mapping hardware checks the protection bit associated with each segment table entry to prevent illegal access to memory such as attempts to write into a read-only segment. By placing an array in its own segment, the memory management hardware will automatically check that array indexes are legal and do not stay outside the array boundaries. Thus, many common program errors will be detected by the hardware before they can cause serious damage.

Let us now discuss some advantages and disadvantages of segmentation.

Advantages of segmentation

1. Sharing of code or data is possible. So, there is no need of sharing the data or code twice in a physical memory.

2. Protection bits are associated with segments. It provides protection by not allowing to write to a segment that is read-only.
3. Segments can grow dynamically also.
4. Segmentation supports virtual memory also (which will be discussed in next chapter).
5. Dynamic linking and loading of segments is also possible.

Disadvantages of segmentation

1. As with paging, this mapping requires two memory references per logical address. This slows the system by a factor of two. Caching in the method used to solve this problem.
2. When the number of segments is large then the size of the segment table will also grow. So, it cannot be accommodated in any of the registers and has to be kept in memory. This, however, needs a good hardware support from the underlying architecture.
3. Segmentation is prone to external fragmentation. This may occur when all the blocks in the memory are too small to accommodate a segment. Compaction may, however, be used to solve the problem of external fragmentation.

2.10.3 Segmentation with Paging (A Combined Approach)

Both paging and segmentation have their advantages and disadvantages. So, it is better to combine these two schemes to improve on each. This combined scheme is **'Page the segments'.** Each segment in this scheme is divided into pages and each segment maintains a page table. So, the logical address is divided into 3 parts : (S, P, D) where 'S' is the segment number, 'P' is the page number and 'D' is the offset or displacement. To understand this approach, consider figure 2.25 below.

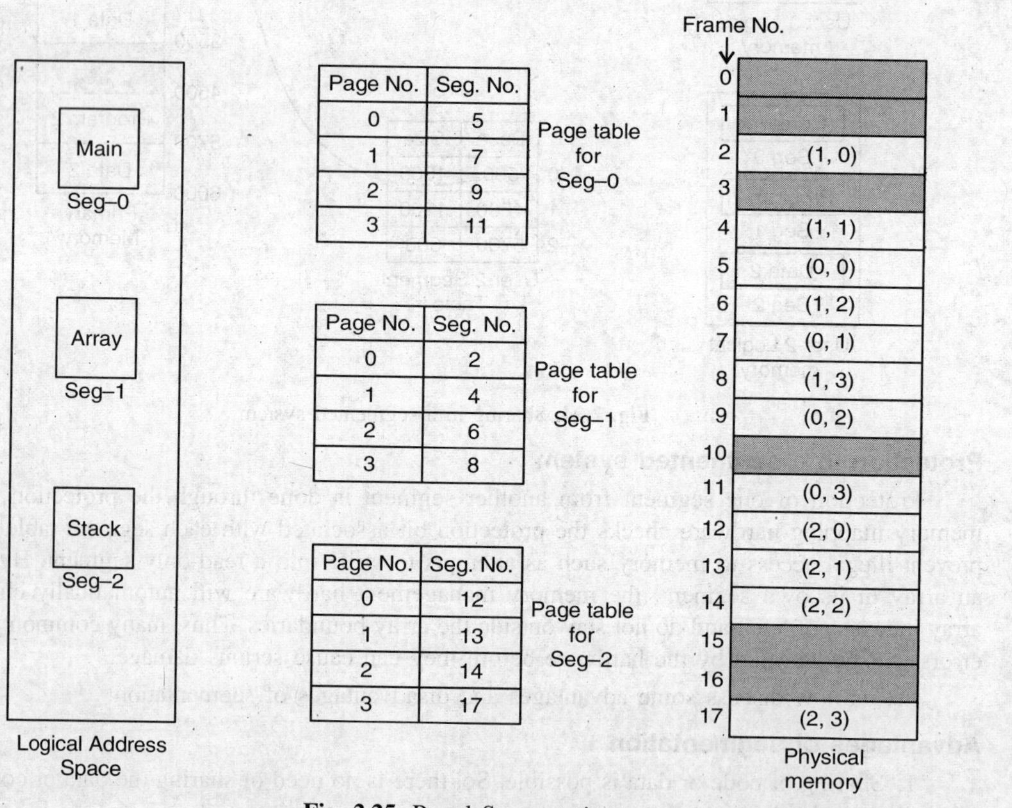

Fig. 2.25. Paged Segmentation

As shown in Fig. 24, the logical address space is divided into three (3) segments from 0 to 2. Each segment maintains a page table, which does mapping between pages and frames. **For example,** the frame number 6 shows the address (1, 2); '1' stands for segment number and '2' stands for the page number.

The main advantage of this scheme is to avoid fragmentation and that it supports user's view of memory.

2.10.4 Comparison of Paging and Segmentation—Tabular form

Let us tabulate the differences between paging and segmentation.

Paging	Segmentation
1. In paging scheme, the main memory is partitioned into frames (or blocks).	1. In segmentation scheme, the main memory is partitioned into segments.
2. The logical address space is divided into pages by the compiler or memory management unit (MMU)	2. The logical address space is divided into segments as specified by the programmer.
3. This scheme suffer from internal fragmentation or page breaks.	3. This scheme suffers from external fragmentation.
4. The Operating System maintains a free frames list; there is no need to search for free frame.	4. The operating system maintains the particulars of available memory.
5. The Operating System maintains a page map table for mapping between frames and pages.	5. The operating system maintains a segment map table for mapping purpose.
6. This scheme does not support the user's view of memory.	6. This scheme supports user view of memory.
7. Processor uses the page number and displacement to calculate absolute address (p, d).	7. Processor uses the segment number and displacement to calculate the absolute address (s, d).

Summary

In this chapter, we have studied various memory management schemes. Static and dynamic partitioning have been discussed. Both rely on identical hardware support for relocation and protection. Both the approches allow sharing in restricted manner. Paging and segmentation have also been discussed and compared.

2.10.5 Memory Management Techniques

Technique	Description	Strengths	Weaknesses
Fixed Partitioning	Main memory is divided into a number of static partitions at system generation time. A process may be loaded into a partition of equal or greater size.	Simple to implement little operating system overhead.	Inefficient use of memory due to internal fragmentation maximum number of active process is fixed.
Dynamic Partitioning	Partitions are created dynamically, so that each process is loaded into a partition of exactly the same size as that process.	No internal fragmentaiton; more efficient use of main memory.	Inefficient use of processor due to the need for compaction to counter external fragmentation.

Simple Paging	Main memory is divided into a number of equal-size frames. Each process is divided into a number of equal-size pages of the same length as frames. A process is loaded by loading all of its pages into available, not necessarily contiguous, frames.	No external fragmentation.	A small amount of internal fragmentation
Simple Segmentation	Each process is divided into a number of segments. A process loaded by loading all of its segments into dynamic partitions that need not be contiguous.	No internal fragmentation	Improved memory utilization and reduced overhead compared to dynamic partitioning.
Virtual Memory Paging	As with simple paging, except that it is not necessary to load all of the pages of a process. Nonresident pages that are needed are brought in later automatically.	No external fragmentation; higher. degree of multi programming; large virtual address space.	Overhead of complex memory management.
Virtual Memory Segmentation	As with simple segmentation except that it is not necessary to laod all of the segments of a process. Nonresident segments that are needed are brought in later automatically.	No internal fragmentation, higher degree of multi-programming; large virtual address space; protection and sharing support.	Overhead of complex memory management.

MULTIPLE-CHOICE QUESTIONS [MCQs]

1. Moving a process from main memory to the disk is called as—
   (a) Scheduling (b) Caching
   (c) Swapping (d) Spooling
2. A special purpose register that is set to the highest address occupied by the OS code is—
   (a) Fence Register (b) General Purpose Register
   (c) Protection Register (d) None of the above
3. Symbolic addresses are also known as—
   (a) Physical addresses. (b) Far addresses
   (c) Virtual addresses (d) None of the above
4. CPU generates—
   (a) Logical addresses (b) Physical addresses
   (c) Relocatable addresses (d) None of the above
5. The process of mapping of logical addresses to real physical addresses is known as—
   (a) Address Scheme (b) Addressing Modes
   (c) Address Binding (d) None of the above
6. The address binding for global variables occurs at—
   (a) Run-time (b) Load-time
   (c) Compile time (d) None of the above

7. An effective physical address is given by the formula—
   (*a*) Effective physical address = logical address / (contents of Relocation Register)
   (*b*) Effective Physical address = logical address * (contents of Relocation Register)
   (*c*) Effective Physical address = logical address + (contents of Relocation Register)
   (*d*) None of the above
8. MMU stands for—
   (*a*) Main Memory Unit (*b*) Memory Management Unit
   (*c*) Main Management Unit (*d*) None of the above
9. Logical memory is divided into—
   (*a*) Pages (*b*) Frames
   (*c*) Partitions (*d*) None of the above
10. The page size and frame size must be—
   (*a*) Equal (*b*) Unequal
   (*c*) Multiples of each other (*d*) None of the above
11. Sharing is possibe in which technique
   (*a*) Paging (*b*) Segmentation
   (*c*) Both '*a*' and '*b*' (*d*) None of the above
12. Which of the following statement is false—
   (*a*) A small page size causes large page tables
   (*b*) Internal fragmentation is increased with small pages.
   (*c*) A large page size causes instructions and data that will not be referenced.
   (*d*) I/O transfers are more efficient with large pages.
13. The problem of fragmentation arises in—
   (*a*) Static storage allocation (*b*) Stack allocation of storage
   (*c*) Stack allocation with dynamic binding (*d*) Heap allocation
14. Which of the following scheme suffers from External fragmentation—
   (*a*) Segmentation (*b*) Paging
   (*c*) Paged Segmentation (*d*) All of the above
15. The worst fit algorithm—
   (*a*) Is used only when nothing better is available.
   (*b*) Is to place program in largest available partition.
   (*c*) Should never be used.
   (*d*) Places a program in the smallest possible partition.

ANSWERS

1. *c*	**2.** *a*	**3.** *c*	**4.** *a*	**5.** *c*	**6.** *b*
7. *c*	**8.** *b*	**9.** *a*	**10.** *a*	**11.** *c*	**12.** *b*
13. *d*	**14.** *a*	**15.** *b*			

CONCEPTUAL SHORT QUESTIONS WITH ANSWERS

Q.1. Define the following terms—
   (*a*) Separation of Address
   (*b*) Wasted Memory
   (*c*) Time Complexity
   (*d*) Memory Access Overhead.

Ans. (*a*) The memory manager must manage distinct address spaces to prevent active process erroneously. A memory manager in a multiprogramming environment supports both memory protections by isolating disjoint address space and sharing of memory.

(*b*) It is a part of fraction of unused physical memory. Memory can be wasted due to internal fragmentation, external fragmentation and data structures.

(*c*) It is a combinational complexity of allocating and reallocating memory.

(*d*) It is defined as the duration of additional operations performed by a given memory management scheme in accessing memory.

Q.2. Can you suggest an algorithm to create a partition, P, under dynamic memory allocation?

Ans. Yes, the following algorithm can be used to create a partition, P, of size P_SIZE. We have used the following notations in this algorithm—

P_SIZE — Partition Size

F_SIZE — Free Size

P_BASE — Partition Base

F_BASE — Free Base

PDT — Partition Description Table

PCB — Process Control Block.

So, we write an algorithm now.

Step-(*a*) Search the free list for free area F with F_SIZE ≥ P_SIZE, if none found then algorithm terminates with error indication.

Step-(*b*) Calculate Difference = F_SIZE – P_SIZE, if difference ≤ *c* (a very small constant) then allocate the entire free area for creation of partition P by

P_SIZE = F_SIZE & P_BASE = F_BASE

Else

then allocate space for partition P from a block F with setting

P_BASE = F_BASE

F_SIZE = F_SIZE – P_SIZE

F_BASE = P_BASE + P_SIZE

Step-(*c*) Find the unused entry in PDT & record (P_BASE) & size (P_size) & set status to allocated.

Step-(*d*) Record the PDT's entry number in the PCB, for which the partition P is being created.

Q.3. Given a logical Address, L, low can you compute the corresponding physical address?

Ans. For a 'm' bit processor, the logical address will be m bits long.

Let the page size be 2^n bytes.

Then, the lower order n bits of a logical address, L will represent page offset (*d*) and the higher order (m – n) bits will represent the page number (p).

Then, page number, p = $L/2^n$

and page offset, d = $L\%2^n$

Let f be the frame number that holds the page referenced by logical address, L

Then, f can be obtained by indexing into page table, by using page number, p, as index i.e., f = page_table [p];

∴ Corresponding physical address = f * 2n + d.

This physical address is fed to the Memory Management Unit (MMU) to access the memory location, referenced by logical address, L. The maximum size of logical address space of a process can be 2^m bytes *i.e.*, upto 2^n pages.

Q.4. How can we reduce the memory overhead of a paged system?

Ans. There are three methods to reduce memory overhead of a paged system. They are as follows:–

1. By increasing the page size

This will correspondingly reduce the maximum number of pages in the logical address space, thus reducing the size of page table. But, increasing the page size would increase the loss of memory, due to internal fragmentation.

2. By creating a page table for the exact program size and using a Page Table Length Register (PTLR).

3. By using an inverted page table

The table is indexable by frame number, instead of page number. Each entry, in the table, contains page number, corresponding to the indexed frame number.

Q.5. How protection is done during paging?

Ans. Protection means security from unauthorized references from main memory. To provide protection, during paging, OS provides the **protection bits** that are associated with each frame. Generally, these bits are kept in page table. Sometimes these bits are said to be valid/not valid bits. Consider the figure given below—

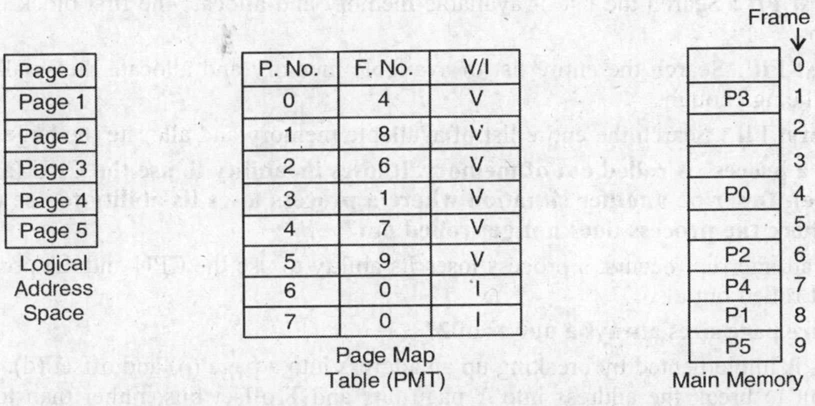

That is, page no. 0 is in frame number 4 of the main/physical memory. Also, page no. 5, is in frame number 9. This is true, hence the bit is set to 'V' *i.e.*, valid. But, page no. 6 is not in frame 0, as indicated by PMT above. So, we set it to 'I' *i.e.*, invalid. **Please note that it is our O.S. software only that sets/resets these bits.**

Q.6. Consider a logical address space of eight pages of 1024 words each, mapped onto a physical memory of 32 frames. How many bits are there in the logical address and in the physical address?

Ans. Logical address : 13 bits [∵ 1024 * 8 = 8192 = 2^{13}]

Physical address : 15 bits [∵ 32 * 8192 = 2^{15}]

Q.7. Given memory partitions of 100 K, 500 K, 200 K, 300 K and 600 K (in order), how would each of the algorithms (first-fit, best-fit, worst-fit) in parts a, b and c place processes of 212 K, 417 K, 112 K and 426 K (in order)? Which algorithm makes the best use of memory?

Ans. For the three allocation algorithms we have—

(1) First-fit Approach

212 K is put in 500 K partition

417 K is put in 600 K partition

112 K is put in 288 K partition (new partition = 500 K – 212 K = 288 K)

426 K must wait.

(2) Best-fit Approach

212 K is put in 300 K partition.

417 K is put in 500 K partition.

112 K is put in 200 K partition.

426 K is put in 600 K partition.

(3) Worst-fit Approach

212 K is put in 600 K partition.

417 K is put in 500 K partition.

112 K is put in 388 K partition.

426 K must wait.

In the example given here, the best-fit approach turns out to be the best.

Q.8. In one statement, how will you explain—

(*a*) First Fit

(*b*) Best Fit

(*c*) Worst Fit ?

Ans. **(*a*) First Fit :** Search the list of available memory and allocate the first block that is big enough.

(*b*) Best-Fit : Search the entire list of available memory and allocate the smallest block that is being enough.

(*c*) Worst Fit : Search the entire list of available memory and allocate the largest block.

Q.9. When a process is rolled out of memory, it loses its ability to use the CPU (atleast for a while). Describe another situation where a process loses its ability to use the CPU, but where the process does not get rolled out?

Ans. When an interrupt occurs, a process loses its ability to use the CPU and the process does not get rolled out also.

Q.10. Why are page sizes always a power of 2?

Ans. Paging is implemented by breaking up an address into a page (p) and offset (d). It is most efficient to break the address into *X* page bits and *Y* offset bits, rather than to perform arithematic on the address to calculate the page number and offset. **Because each bit position represents a power of 2, splitting an address between bits results in a page size that is power of 2.**

Q.11. Consider a paging system with the page table stored in memory.

(*a*) If a memory reference takes 200 ns, how long does a paged memory reference take?

(*b*) If we add associative registers and 75% of all page-table references are found in the associative registers, what is the effective memory reference time? (Assume that finding a page-table entry in the associative registers takes zero time, if the entry is there).

Ans. (*a*) It takes 200 ns to a access the page table and 200 ns to access the word in memory. So, a paged memory reference takes = 200 ns + 200 ns = **400ns.**

(*b*) The effective access time, EAT is

$= 0.75\ (200\ \text{ns}) + 0.25\ (400\ \text{ns})$
$= (150 + 100)\ \text{ns}$
$= \mathbf{250\ ns}$

Q.12 Paging and Segmentation are sometimes combined with one scheme. Why?

Ans. There are **two ways** to combine

(*a*) Segmented Paging

It is helpful when page table becomes very large. A large contiguous section of the page table that is unused can be collapsed into a single segment table entry with a page-table address of zero.

(*b*) Paged Segmentation

It is helpful when segments become very long that require a lot of time for allocation. By paging the segments, we reduce wasted memory due to external fragmentation as well as simplify the allocation.

Q.13. Consider the following segment table—

Segment No.	Base	Bound
0	219	600
1	2300	14
2	90	100
3	1327	580
4	1952	96

What are the physical addresses for the following logical addresses?

(*a*) 0, 430
(*b*) 0, 10
(*c*) 2, 500
(*d*) 3,400
(*e*) 4, 112

Where (0, 430) implies 430th instruction/data in 0th segment.

Ans. (*a*) *Given*—logical address = (0, 430)
i.e., (s, d) = (0, 430)
Now, d = 430 lies between 0 and 600 (*i.e.*, segment limit) and that d < bound or 430 < 600 is valid. So, the Physical address = d + base address
= 219 + 430
= **649**

(*b*) Now, L.A. = (1, 10) = (s, d)
∴ s = 1
d = 10
Now, d = 10 lies between 0 and segment-limit = 14
∴ Physical address = d + base address
= 10 + 2300
= **2310**

(*c*) Now, LA = (2, 500)
∴ (s, d) = (2, 500)
Now, d = 500 doesn't lie between 0 and segment – limit of 100. This will result in illegal reference and a trap to OS will be generated.

(*d*) Given now, L.A. = (3, 400)

∴ S = 3

d = 400

∴ d = 400 < 580 (i.e., d < bound)

∴ physical memory address = 1327 + 400

= 1727

(*e*) Now, L.A. = (4, 112)

∴ s = 4

d = 112

∴ d = 112 does not lie between 0 and 96.

∴ Invalid reference.

⇒ Trap to the O.S.

Q.14. In IBM-370 machine, memory protection is provided through the use of keys. A key is a 4-bit quantity. Each 2K block of memory has a key associated with it. The CPU also has a key (protection key) associated with it. A store operation is allowed only if both keys are equal or if either is zero. Which of the following memory-management schemes could be used successfully with this hardware?

(*a*) Bare machine

(*b*) Single-user program

(*c*) Multiprogramming with fixed number of processes

(*d*) Multiprogramming with a variable number of processes.

(*e*) Paging

(*f*) Segmentation

Ans. (*a*) Protection is not necessary, set system key to 0.

(*b*) Set system key to 0 when in supervisor mode.

(*c*) Region sizes must be fixed in the increments of 2KB. Allocate key with memory blocks.

(*d*) Same as above

(*e*) Frame size must be in increments of 2K bytes. Allocate key with pages.

(*f*) Segment size must be in increments of 2K bytes. Allocate key with segments.

Q.15. Consider an IBM-370 machine with 24-bit logical addresses. The page size is 2KB. What is the size of page. How many bits are adequate to address the bytes in pages. How many bits will be used as page number? Can you generalize your results.

Ans. When 2K byte pages are used,

Size of page = 2^{11} bytes

∴ 11 bits are required to address the bytes in the pages. The remaining (24 – 11) = 13 bits will be used as page number of specify the address of a particular page.

In general, if the size of logical address space is 2^l and size of each page is 2^p, then the high-order (l–p) bits of logical address specify the page number and the p, lower-order bits designate the page offset *i.e.,*

Page Number	Page Offset	Logical address
(l – p)	p	

The same holds true for the physical address space of size 2m and having the same frame-size as the page-size mentioned above *i.e.,*

Frame Number	Frame offset	Physical address
(m – p)	p	

EXERCISE QUESTIONS

Q.1. (*a*) Explain in detail:

(1) Paged segmentation

(2) Segmented Paging

(*b*) In a paged segmented system, a virtual address consists of 32 bits, of which 12 bits are used for displacement, 11 bits are a segment number and 9 bits are a page number. Calculate—

(1) Page size

(2) Maximum number of pages

(3) Maximum segmented size

(4) Maximum number of segments.

Ans. (*b*) **Hint:**

1. Page Size.

∴ 12 bits are allocated for displacement

∴ Page Size = 2^{12} = 4096 bytes.

2. Max. no. of pages:

Total pages = 512 ∗ Max. no. of segments

= 512 ∗ 2^{11} = 512 ∗ 2048

= 1048576

3. Max. Segment Size:

9 bits are available for page number per segment giving 2^9 = 512 pages / segments, each of 4KB.

∴ Max-segmcnt size = 512 ∗ 4K

= 2048 KB.

4. Max. Number of segments:

Max. no. of segments = 2^{11} = 2048

Q.2. What is the difference between virtual address space and physical address space?

Q.3. (*a*) What is paging? Explain with proper example.

(*b*) Explain the difference between internal and external fragmentation.

(*c*) A computer provides each process with 65,536 bytes of address space divided into pages of 4096 bytes. A particular program has a text size of 32,768 bytes, a data size of 16,386 bytes and a stack size of 15,870 bytes. Will this program fit in the address space? If the page size were 512 bytes, would it fit? Remember that a page may not contain parts of two different segments.

Q.4. (*a*) What is Internal fragmentation? Explain the basic method of implementing paging.

(*b*) Write short note on 'Segmentation'.

Q.5. Describe the paging scheme. Describe the working of the following under paging.

(*a*) Allocation of memory

(*b*) De-allocation of memory

(*c*) Memory sharing

(*d*) Memory protection

(*e*) Waste space management

Q.6. (*a*) Describe the segmented paging scheme of memory management and the hardware required to support the system.

(*b*) Suppose that a total of 64MB memory is available in a system. This memory space is partitioned into 8 fixed size slots of 8 MB each. Assume 8 processes are currently requesting memory usage with sizes indicated as below:—

[2MB, 4MB, 3MB, 7MB, 9MB, 6MB, 1MB, 8MB]

Calculate the size of memory wasted due to external and internal fragmentation. Derive the memory utilization ratio by dividing the total allocated memory by total requested memory.

Q.7. What is paging? What is the hardware support required for paging? Describe this with the help of a diagram. What are the security and protection mechanisms in paging?

Q.8. What are the functions of memory management in OS? List techniques used for memory managment.

Q.9. Describe single contiguous allocation method. List advantages and disadvantage of this method.

Q.10. Consider a paging system with the page table stored in memory.

(1) If a memory reference takes 1.2μs. How long does a paged memory reference take?

(2) If we add 8 associative registers and 75% of all base table references are found in the associative registers, what is the effective memory reference time?

(Assume that finding a page table entry in the associative registers table time, if it is there.)

Ans.

[Hint: (*a*) % of time that a passed memory reference time is 80% of the hit ratio with memory reference.

∴ Paged memory reference takes –

= memory reference ∗ 0.08

= 1.2 × 0.80 = **0.96 μ secs.**

(*b*) EAT = (0.75 ∗ 0.20) + 220

∴ [TLB search needs 20 ns, mem. access = 100 ns + byte access in memory = 100 ns]

= 90 + 44 = **134 ns.**

Q.11. Consider a system where a program can be separated into two parts: code and data. The CPU knows whether it wants an instruction (instruction fetch) or data (data fetch or store). Therefore, two base-limit register pairs are provided : one for instructions and one for data. The instruction base-limit pair is automatically read-only, so programs can be shared among different users. Discuss the advantages and disadvantages of this scheme.

[Hint: The major advantage of this scheme is that it is an effective mechanism for code and data sharing. For example, only one copy of an editor or a compiler needs to be kept in memory and this code can be shared by all processes needing access to the editor or complier code. Another advantage is protection of code against erroneous modification. The only disadvantage is that the code and data must be separated which is usually adhered to in a compiler-generated code.]

Q.12. On a system with paging, a process cannot access memory that it does not own, why? How could OS allow access to other memory? Why should it or should it not?

Q.13. Explain the difference between external and internal fragmentation. Which one occurs in a paging system and in pure segmentation.

Q.14. Consider a system that supports the strategies of contiguons, linked and indexed allocation. What cirteria should be used in deciding which strategy is best utilized for a particular file ?

CHAPTER

3

Virtual Memory

3.0 INTRODUCTION

Virtual memory is a technique of executing program instructions that may not fit entirely in the system memory. It is implemented with the help of a **secondary storage device.** Data is transferred from the secondary to main storage and vice versa, as and when required, according to some predetermined algorithm. So, it is a technique that permits the execution of processes, with their code and data only partially loaded into the physical memory.

Earlier the problem was how to fit large programs into the small memory. The solution was to break programs into small pieces called **overlays.** These overlays used to be on hard disk and were swapped in and out of memory by OS. But today, we use **the virtual memory management technique** which splits a program into a number of pieces and performs swapping. **Please note that the basic idea behind virtual memory is that the combined size of the program, data and stack may exceed the amount of physical memory. The O.S. keeps those parts of the program in the memory which are required during execution and the rest on the disk. For example,** a 1MB program can run on a 640K RAM machine by carefully choosing 640 K of program out of 1 MB to keep in memory at each instant and swapping pieces of a program between disk and memory as needed.

The **main objective** of this method was to support **multiprogramming** *i.e.*, to keep many processes in memory simultaneously. But this scheme requires that the entire process must be in the memory before the execution starts. Virtual memory is a memory management scheme that allows the execution of processes that may not be completely in the main memory. That is, virtual memory allows execution of partially loaded processes. As a result, user programs can be larger than the physical memory.

In virtual memory scheme, the programmers get an illusion of much larger memory than physical memory. So, the programmers are not concerned about fitting their programs into small physical memory. It has been observed that in many cases an entire program is not needed. Like in case of an assembler, 2 passes are required. In first pass, it scans the entire program and builds the symbol table and in the second pass it generated the object code. Therefore, only the program related to a particular pass should be in memory at a time but not an entire assembler program. This technique takes advantage of the fact that a program tends to have locality of reference and a process code is never required in its entirety, at the same time.

Advantages of Virtual Memory

There are some advantages of a partially loaded program in memory. They are discussed below:

1. The size of user's program would be no longer constrained by the available size of physical memory. Users would be able to write programs for very large virtual address space.
2. Since each user utilizes less physical memory, more users can keep their programs there simultaneously which will cause increase in CPU utilization and throughput.
3. Degree of programming can be varied over a large range.
4. Since a process may be loaded into a space of arbitrary size, which in turn reduces external fragmentation without the need to change the scheduled order of process execution. Moreover, the amount of space in use by a given process may be changing during its memory residence. As a result, the O.S. may speed up the execution of important processes by allocating more physical memory.

Table 3.1. Comparison between Simple Paging, Virtual Memory Paying, Simple Segmentation and Virtual Memory Segmentation

Simple Paging	*Virtual Memory Paging*	*Simple Segmentation*	*Vibral Memory Segmentation*
Main memory parttioned into small fixed size chunks called frames	Main memory parttioned into small fixed size chunks called frames	Main memory not not partitioned	Virtual Memory not partitioned
Programme broken into pages by the compiler or memory management system	Program broken into pages by the compiler or memory management system	Program segments specified by the programmer to the compiler (i.e., the decision is made by the programmer)	Program segments specified by the programmer to the compiler (i.e., the decision is made by the programmer)
Internal fragmentation within frames	Internal fragmentation within frames	No internal fragmentation	No internal fragmentation
No external fragmentation	No external fragmentation	External fragmentation	External fragmentation
Operating system must maintain a page table for each process showing which frame each page occupies	Operating system must maintain a page table for each process showing which frame each page occupies	Operating system must maintain a segment table for each process showing the load address and length of each segment	Operating system must maintain a segment table for each process showing the load address and length of each segment
Operating system must maintain a free frame list	Operating system must maintain a free frame list	Operating system must maintain a list of free holes in main memory	Operating system must maintain a list of free holes in main memory
Processor uses page number offset to calculate absolute address	Processor uses page number, offset to calculate absolute address	Processor uses segment number, offset to calculate absolute address	Processor uses segment number, offset to calculate absolute address
All the pages of a process must be in main memory for process to run unless overlays are used	Not all the pages of a process need be main memory frames for the process to run. Pages may be read in as needed.	All the segments of a process must be in main memory for process to run, unless overlays are used	Not all segments of a process need be in main memory frames for the process to run. Segments may be read in as needed
	Reading a page into main memory may require wirting a page out to disk		Reading a page into main memory require writing one or more segments out to disk.

Please note that the virtual memory can be implemented as an extension of paged or segmented memory scheme, also called as demand paging or demand segmentation respectively. Also note that the address translation is performed through page map table (PMT) or segment table (ST).

3.1 SWAPPING

As we already know, that an active program is one that is either executing or doing an I/O operation. Otherwise, it is an inactive program. **Swapping is the process of temporarily removing inactive programs from the main memory of a computer system.** Consider a practical scenario now.

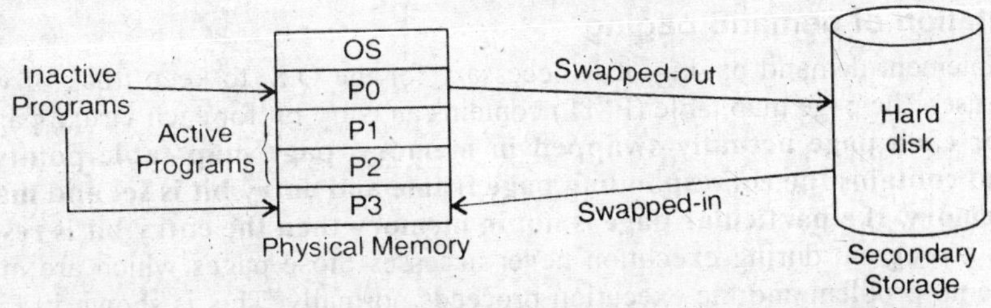

Fig. 3.1 P0 and P3 processes being swapped-out and swapped-in

As is clear from this Figure 3.1 that there is usually a set of active programs in memory. Out of these only one executes on the CPU while others perform I/O. Whenever an active program becomes inactive, the O.S. begins to swap it *i.e.*, when the system is falling short of main memory space. This involves writing program and data onto the secondary storage, typically a disk. **Please note that once a program is completely swapped out, the memory area allocated to it becomes free.** This happens in case of Round-Robin Scheduling (to be discussed later). A process is swapped out when its time quantum finishes and later it is brought into the memory for continued execution.

Many a times, a lower priority process may be swapped so that a higher priority process may be executed.

Let us now see how swapping is done in a virtual memory management scheme. Consider Fig. 3.2 now.

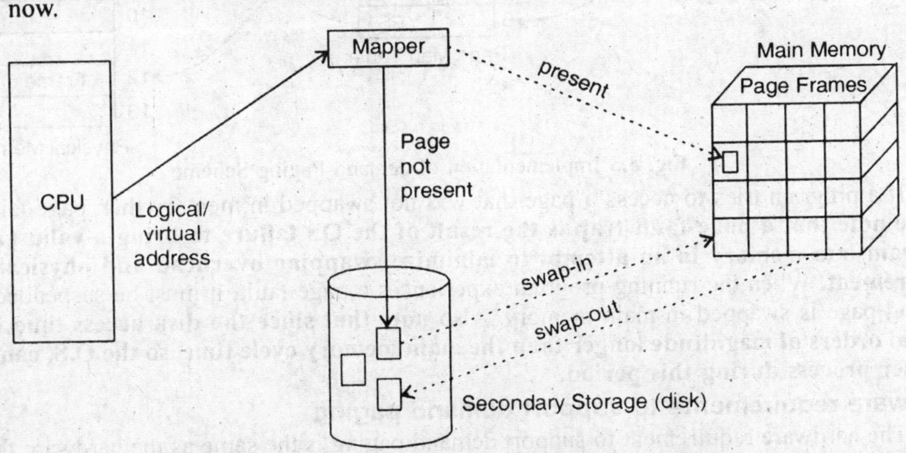

Fig. 3.2 Role of swapping in virtual memory management

From this Figure 3.2, we find that firstly the logical (or virtual) address generated by the CPU is converted to physical address. Then, it is checked whether the page is present in the main memory or not. If present then the mapper enters this page in the available frame where this page is accommodated in the main memory. But, if the mapper detects that the requested page is not present in the main memory then a page-fault occurs and the page must be read into a frame in the main memory from the secondary storage (*i.e.*, hard disk).

Swapping increase the O.S's overhead due to the need to perform swap-in and swap-out operations. **Please note that all OS do not perform swapping like DOS does not perform**

swapping but UNIX, WINDOWS and OS/2 perform swapping. Swapping increases CPU utilization and throughput.

3.2 DEMAND PAGING

It is a scheme in which a page is not loaded into the main memory from the secondary memory, until it is needed. So, in demand paging, pages are loaded only on demand and not in advance. The advantage here is that now lesser I/O is needed, less memory is needed, faster response and more users serviced now. **Please note that in this scheme, rather than swapping the entire program in memory, only those pages are swapped which are required currently by the system.**

Implementation of demand paging

To implement demand paging, it is necessary for the O.S. to keep track of which pages are currently in use. The page map table (PMT) contains an entry bit for each virtual page of the related process. **For each page actually swapped in memory, page map table points to the actual location that contains the corresponding page frame and entry bit is set and marked as 'YES' if it is in memory. If a particular page is not in memory then the entry bit is reset and marked as 'NO'.** If a program during execution never accesses those pages which are marked as 'NO', there will be no problem and the execution proceeds normally. This is shown in Fig. 3.3 below.

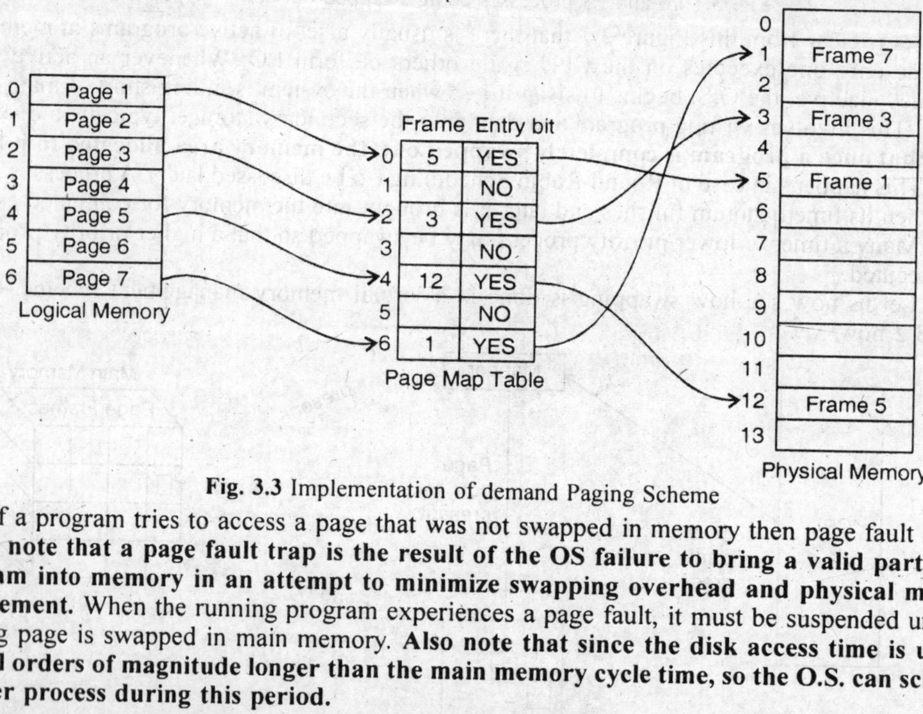

Fig. 3.3 Implementation of demand Paging Scheme

If a program tries to access a page that was not swapped in memory then page fault occurs. **Please note that a page fault trap is the result of the OS failure to bring a valid part of the program into memory in an attempt to minimize swapping overhead and physical memory requirement.** When the running program experiences a page fault, it must be suspended until the missing page is swapped in main memory. **Also note that since the disk access time is usually several orders of magnitude longer than the main memory cycle time, so the O.S. can schedule another process during this period.**

Hardware requirements to support demand paging

The hardware requirement to support demand paging is the same as the hardware for paging, that is,—

(*a*) A page map table (PMT) with the ability to mark YES and NO for page entry.

(*b*) A hard disk to hold those pages that are not in memory.

Performance of Demand Paging

1. Page fault rate, p, is given as–

   $0 \leq p \leq 1.0$

   i.e., if p = 0 then no page faults

if p = 1 then every reference is a fault

2. Effective Access Time (EAT) is given as follows—

EAT = $(1 - p)$ * memory access + p (page fault overhead) + (swap page out) + (swap page in) + (Restart overhead)

3.2.1 Pure Demand Paging

Pure demand paging is the form of demand paging in which not even a single page is loaded into memory initially. Therefore, the very first instruction causes a page fault in this case. This kind of demand paging may significantly decrease the performance of a computer system by generally increasing the effective access time of memory. If 'm_t' represents the memory access time and 'p' is the probability of occurrence of a page fault then the effective access time (EAT) is given by the formula–

$$EAT = (1 - p) * m_t + p * \text{page-fault time}$$

We are in a position to solve some problems now.

Example 1. Suppose we have a demand-paged memory. The page table is held in registers. It takes 8 milliseconds to service a page fault if an empty page is available or the replaced page is not modified and 20 milliseconds if the page replaced is modified. Memory access time is 100 nanoseconds.

Assume that the page to be replaced is modified 70 percent of the time. What is the maximum acceptable page-fault rate for an effective access time of no more than 200 nanoseconds?

Solution. From the given conditions, we get

$0.2\ \mu s = (1 - P) * 0.1\ \mu s + (0.3P) * 8$ millisec. $+ (0.7P) * 20$ millisec.

or $1 = - P + 2400\ P + 14000\ P$ [∵ 100 ns = 0.1 μ sec & 200 ns = 0.2 μ sec]

or $1 = 16399P$

or $\mathbf{P = 0.00006}$

Example 2. Consider a demand-paging system with a paging disk that has an average access and transfer time of 20 milliseconds.

Addresses are translated through a page table in main memory with an access time of 1 microsecond per memory access. Thus, each memory reference through the page table takes two accesses. To improve this time, we have added an associative memory that reduces access time to one memory reference, if the page-table entry is in the associative memory.

Assume that 80 percent of the accesses are in the associative memory and that, of the remaining 10 percent (or 2 percent of the total) causes page faults. What is the effective memory access time?

Solution. Effective Access Time (EAT) = (0.8) (1 sec) + (0.1) (2 sec) + (0.1) (5002 sec)

= 501.2 secs = **0.5 millisec.**

Example 3. On a system using demand paged memory, it takes 120 ns to satisfy a memory request if the page is in memory. If the page is not in memory, the request takes on an average 5ms. What would be the page fault to achieve an effective access time of | micro-second? Assume the system is running only a single process and the CPU is idle during page swaps. **[UPTU, B. Tech. (CSE) – 6th Sem, 2006-07]**

Solution. Now,

$120\text{ms} \times (1 - P) + P \times 5\text{ ms} = 1\text{ msec}$ ...(1)

But
$$\left.\begin{aligned} 5\text{ ms} &= 5 \times 10^{-3}\text{ sec} \\ 120\text{ ms} &= 120 \times 10^{-9}\text{ sec.} \\ 1\text{ msec} &= 1 \times 10^{-6}\text{ sec} \end{aligned}\right\}$$

$$\therefore \quad 120 \times 10^{-9} * (1 - P) + P * (5 \times 10^{-3}) = 1 \times 10^{-6}$$

$$120 \times 10^{-9} - P * 120 * 10^{-9} + 5P\, 10^{-3} = 1 \times 10^{-6}$$
$$= 1 \times 10^{-6} - P * 120 * 10^{-6} + 5P = 1 \times 10^{-3}$$
$$P\,[5 - 120 * 10^{-6}] = 1 \times 10^{-3} - 120 * 10^{-6}$$

or $$P * 4.999880 = 880 * 10^{-6}$$

or $$P = \frac{880 \times 10^{-6}}{4999880 \times 10^{-6}}$$
$$= 0.000176004$$
$$= 176.004 \times 10^{-6} \text{ sec}$$
$$\boxed{P = 176.004 \text{ M sec}}$$

3.3 PAGE FAULT

Whenever a processor needs to execute a particular page and that page is not available in main memory, this situation is said to be **"page fault"**. When the page fault occurs, the page replacement will be done. The word **"page replacement" means select a victim page in the main memory, replace that page with the required page from the backing store (Disk).** The students may have a doubt, how to select a victim page. **The answer is simple "Page replacement algorithms".** The page replacement algorithms select the victim pages.

Now a days the number of page replacement algorithms are available. Each operating system has its own page replacement policy. Now we consider some of the popular page replacement algorithms.

3.4 PAGE REPLACEMENT ALGORITHMS

3.4.1 FIFO algorithm: (First in First Out algorithm)

FIFO is the simplest page replacement algorithm, the idea behing this is **"Replace a page that page is the oldest page of all the pages of main memory" or "Replace the page that has been in memory longest".** FIFO focuses on the length of time a page has been in memory rather than how much the page is being used. To illustrate the page replacement algorithm, we shall use the reference string.

0 1 2 3 0 1 2 3 0 1 2 3 4 5 6 7

for a memory with 3 frames. This example incurs 16 page faults under FIFO, as shown in the table.

Table FIFO Behaviour

Frame	0	1	2	3	0	1	2	3	0	1	2	3	4	5	6	7
0	0*	0	0	3*	3	3	2*	2	2	1*	1	1	4*	4	4	7*
1		1*	1	1	0*	0	0	3*	3	3	2*	2	2	5*	5	5
2			2*	2	2	1*	1	1	0*	0	0	3*	3	3	6*	6
	√	√	√	√	√	√	√	√	√	√	√	√	√	√	√	√

This example incurs 16 pages faults. The symbol "*" indicates the new page in the memory. The symbol "√" indicates page fault. The performance of the page replacement algorithm is measured through the page fault rate.

∴ Page fault rate = Number of page faults/Number of bits in the reference string.

∴ PFR = 16/16 = 100%

An algorithm having the least page fault rate, will be the best one.

If the required page resides in the main memory, the page replacement is not required, in this situation we use the 'x', symbol. Consider the next example.

The reference string is 0, 1, 2, 3, 2, 5, 6, 3, 4, 6, 3, 7, 3, 1, 5, 3, 6, 3, 4, 2, 4, 3, 4, 5, 1. For a memory with 4 frames. This example incurs 12 page faults shown in the table.

Table FIFO behaviour

Frame	1	2	3	2	5	6	3	4	6	3	7	3	1
0	1*	1	1	1	1	6*	6	6	6*	6	6	6	1*
1	–	2*	2	2*	2	2	2	4*	4	4	4	4	4
2	–	–	3*	3	3	3	3*	3	3	3*	7*	7	7
3	–	–	–	–	5*	5	5	5	5	5	5	3*	3
	√	√	√	×	√	√	×	√	√	×	×	√	√

Frame	5	3	6	3	4	2	4	3	4	5	1
0	1	1	1	1	1	2*	2	2	2	2	2
1	5*	5	5	5	5	5	5	3*	3	3	3
2	7	7	6*	6	6	6	6	6	6	5*	5
3	3	3*	3	3*	4*	4	4*	4	4	4	1*
	√	×	√	×	√	√	×	√	×	√	√

Page fault rate = 16/24 = 75%

3.4.2 Optimal page replacement algorithm

The optimal page replacement algorithm has the lowest page fault rate of all algorithms. The criteria of this algorithm is **"Replace a page that will not be used for the longest period of time"**. To illustrate this algorithm, consider the reference string 1, 2, 3, 2, 5, 6, 3, 4, 6, 3, 4, 6, 3, 7, 3, 1, 5, 3, 6, 3, 4, 2, 4, 3, 4, 5, 1. Assume that the memory size is four frames. Consider the table below to calculate the page fault rate.

Table Optimal Behavior

Frame	1	2	3	2	5	6	3	4	6	3	7	3	1
0	1*	1	1	1	1	1	1	1	1	1	1	1	1*
1		2*	2	2*	2	6*	6	6	6*	6	6	6	6
2			3*	3	3	3	3*	3	3	3*	3	3*	3
3					5*	5	5	4*	4	4	7*	7	7
	√	√	√	×	√	√	×	√	×	×	√	×	×

Frame	5	3	6	3	4	2	4	3	4	5	1
0	1	1	1	1	1	2*	2	2	2	2	1*
1	6	6	6*	6	4*	4	4*	4	4*	4	4
2	3	3*	3	3*	3	3	3	3*	3	3	3
3	5*	5	5	5	5	5	5	5	5	5*	5
	√	×	×	×	√	√	×	×	×	×	√

∴ Page fault = 11/24

The optimal page replacement algorithm is difficult to implement, because it requires future knowledge of reference string, so this algorithm is used mainly for comparison studies.

3.4.3 Second chance page replacement algorithm

This algorithm searches for an old page that has not been referenced. If a page is oldest but has been referenced, it will not be considered for replacement. We simply modify the FIFO algorithm by introducing a **Referenced bit (R)**. We try to inspect the Referenced bit (R) of the oldest page.

If $R = 0$ then page is old and unused, so it is replaced immediately from memory and written to disk.

Else if R = 1 (clear bit) then the page is put at the end of list of pages and its load time is updated.

Then search is continued. So, what is happening is that the old page that has not been referenced in the previous clock is searched and depending upon R (set or clear) action is taken.

3.4.4 Clock Page Replacement Algorithm/Not Recently Used

This algorithm replaces a resident page which has not been accessed in the near past. This algorithm works as follows:

(1) The algorithm maintains a circular list of all resident pages. A **referenced bit (R)** is associated with each page, which is set whenever, a page is referenced.

(2) Either at regular intervals or whenever the number of free page-frame falls below a preset **threshold,** the algorithm sweeps the circular list. Sweeping works like this.

(*a*) It inspects the R bit of each page. If R = 1 (set) then it means that the page has been referenced in the near past.

So, R bit is now cleared and the algorithm proceeds to look at the next page.

(*b*) If R = 0 (clear) then it means that the page has not been referenced after the last sweep. Here, the modified bit (M) is inspected. If M = 0 then the page is declared non-resident and the frame is freed. Else if M = 1 then the page is scheduled for writing onto the disk.

(*c*) The algorithm continues the sweep, till the required number of frames has been freed.

(*d*) Next time, it commences from the point where it had left last time, as indicated by the pointer.

Please note that this algorithm differs from the second chance only in its implementation.

3.4.5 Least Recently used (LRU) algorithm and its' software implementation

LRU (Least Recently Used Algorithm)

The criteria of this algorithm is **"Replace a page that has not been used for the longest period of time"**. The strategy is **"Page replacement algorithm looking backward in time, rather than forward"**. To illustrate the algorithm consider the reference the string.

0, 1, 2, 3, 0, 1, 2, 3, 0, 1, 2, 3, 4, 5, 6, 7 with 3 main frames.

Frame	0	1	2	3	0	1	2	3	0	1	2	3	4	5	6	7
0	0*	0	0	3*	3	3	2*	2	2	1	1*	1	4*	4	4	7*
1		1*	1	1	0*	0	0	3*	3	3	2	2*	2	5*	5	5
2			2*	2	2	1*	1	1	0*	0	0	3	3	3	6*	6
	√	√	√	√	√	√	√	√	√	√	√	√	√	√	√	√

∴ Page fault rate = 16/16 = 100%

Software Implementation of LRU

A simple method to implement LRU in software is to use stack of page numbers. Whenever a page is referenced, its number is removed from the stack and put on the top. So, the top of stack is always the most recently used page number and the bottom is the LRU page number. It is time consuming to remove LRU page number from the stack. However, this algorithm does not suffer from Belady's anomaly (to be discussed later).

3.4.6 Least Frequently Used (LFU) algorithm

The Least Frequently used algorithm **"selects a page for replacement, if the page has not been used often in the past"** (or) **"Replace page that page has smallest count"**. For this algorithm each page maintains a counter, which counter value shows the least count, replace that page. The reason for this selection is that an actively used page should have a large reference count, so don't replace the activity used page. The frequency counter is reset each time a page is loaded. To illustrate this algorithm consider below reference string 0 1 2 3 0 1 2 3 0 1 2 3 4 5 6 7 with 3 memory frames.

Table LFU Algorithm

Frame	0	1	2	3	0	1	2	3	0	1	2	3	4	5	6	7
0	0*	0	0	0	0+	0	0	0	0+	01	0	3*	3	3	3	3
1		1*	1	1	1	1+	1	3*	3	1*	1	1	1	1	1	1
2			2	3*	3	3	2*	2	2	2	2+	2	4	5*	6*	7*
	√	√	√	√	×	×	√	√	×	√	×	√	√	√	√	√

∴ Page Fault Rate = 12/16

3.4.7 Most Frequently Used Algorithm (MFU)

The criteria of this algorithm is **replace a page that has the maximum frequency count of all pages.** The implementation of this algorithm is fairly expensive.

3.4.8 Belady's Anomaly

The general principle is if the number of frames is increased, the page fault rate will be decreased. For example, consider the following reference string.

7 0 1 2 0 3 0 4 2 3 0 3 2 1 2 0 1 7 0 1

if we apply the FIFO algorithm with 3 frames, there are 15 page faults occur, if we increase 4 frames, there are 12 page faults. Consider the reference string.

1, 2, 3, 4, 1, 2, 5, 1, 2, 3, 4, 5

The number of page faults for 4 frames (10) is greater than the number of faults for 3 frames (9). This result is most unexpected and is known as **"Belady's Anomaly"**.

Table 4 Frames

Frame	1	2	3	4	1	2	5	1	2	3	4	5
0	1	1	1	1	1+	1	5	5	5	5	4	4
1		2	2	2	2	2+	2	1*	1	1	1	5
2			3	3	3	3	3	3	2*	2	2	2
3					4	4	4	4	4	3	3	3
	√	√	√	√	×	×	√	√	√	√	√	√

∴ Page fault for 4 frames = 10/12

Frame	1	2	3	4	1	2	5	1	2	3	4	5
0	1*	1	1	4	4	4	5*	5	5	5	5	5+
1		2*	2	2*	1	1	1	1	1	3	3	3
2			3*	3	3*	2	2	2	2	2	4	4
	√	√	√	√	√	√	√	√	√	√	√	√

∴ Page fault for 3 frames = 9/12

Belady's Anomaly was not always true it is applicable only to FIFO algorithm.

3.4.9 Working Set Page Replacement Algorithm

The set of pages that a process is currently using is called its working set. Most processes exhibit a **locality of reference** meaning that during any phase of execution, the process references only a relatively small fraction of its pages. This model is based on the concept of current locality of reference of a process. **The working set principle states that:**

1. **A program should not be run, unless its working set is fully loaded in the memory.**
2. **No page of a process should be replaced, if it forms part of its working set.**

Ideally, the working set of a process should comprise its current locality. For this a working-set window (say Δ) is the set. The working set of a process comprises the set of pages referenced by it, during the most recent (Δ) references. The working set of a process at a time, t, is defined as:

$$W(t, \Delta) = \{\text{Set of pages } i \mid \text{page } i \text{ appears amongst } r_{t-\Delta+1} \ldots r_t\}$$

where r_t denotes a page referenced at time, t.

Now, Δ is the working set window *i.e.*, a fixed number of page references (say, 10000 instructions). This Δ must be carefully chosen, 3 cases arise

Case 1 : if Δ is too small then the working-set will not encompass entire locality.

Case 2 : if Δ is too large then the working set may encompass more than the current locality.

Case 3 : *if* $\Delta = \infty$ then it will encompass the entire program.

Please note here that the window size can be fine tuned by observing page fault frequency (PFF) of active processes. If PFF is found to be too high then the window size are increased else if PFF is found to be too low then the window size is reduced.

3.5 THRASHING

If the number of frames allocated to a low-priority process falls below the minimum number then we must suspend that process execution. We should then page out its remaining pages, freeing all its allocated frames. So, now swapping is required. We can find some process in a system that does not have "enough" frames. It is technically possible to reduce the number of allocated frames to the minimum, there is some (larger) number of pages in active use. If the process does not have this number of frames then it will quickly page fault. At this point, it must replace some page that will be needed again. Consequently, it quickly faults again and again. The process continues to fault, replacing pages for which it then faults and brings back in right away. Such a process would spend more time in paging than executing. **This high paging activity is called as thrashing. A process is said to be thrashing if it is spending more time in paging than in execution.** This results in a poor throughput of the system.

Cause of thrashing

Thrashing results in severe performance problems. Let us consider an example to understand this. We know that an OS monitors the CPU utilization. If CPU utilization is too low, we increase the degree of multiprogramming (DOM) by introducing a new process to the system. (A global page-replacement algorithm is used; it replaces pages with no regard to the process to which they belong. Now, say that a process enters a new phase in its execution and needs more frames. It starts faulting and taking frames away from other processes. These processes need those pages, however, and so they also fault, taking frames from other processes. These faulting processes must use the paging device to swap pages in and out. As they queue up for paging device, the ready queue empties. As processes wait, for the paging device, CPU utilization decreases. The CPU schedular sees the decreasing CPU utilization so it increases the degree of multiprogramming. The new process tries to get started by taking frames from running processes, causing more page faults, and a longer queue for the paging device. As a result, the CPU utilization drops even further. The CPU scheduler tries to increase the degree of multiprogramming even more. We say, thrashing has occurred and the system throughput plunges. The page fault rate (PFR) increases tremendously. As a result, the effective memory access time increases. No work is getting done because the processes are spending all their time in paging. This is shown in Figure 3.4.

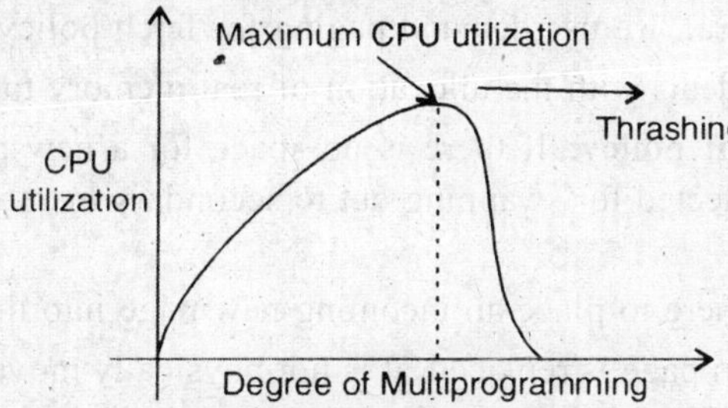

Fig. 3.4 Thrashing

3.6 PAGE REPLACEMENT POLICIES–LOCAL & GLOBAL

As we know that multiple processes compete for frames, so we can classify page replacement algorithms into 2 types—

(*a*) Local page replacement

(*b*) Global page replacement

Local page replacement

It means that when a process requests for a new page to be brought in and there are no free frames in the memory, we choose a frame allocated to only that process for replacement. Thus, this policy requires that each process selects from its own set of allocated frames only.

Global page replacement

It allows a process to select a replacement frame from the set of all frames, even if that frame is currently allocated to some other process. So, one process can take a frame from another. Thus, in this policy any frame from any other process can be replaced. Here the OS has to decide about the set of worst pages and then choose a page amongst them. In this case, process priorities also play a vital role. So, it is quite difficult to implement this policy.

3.7 DEMAND SEGMENTATION

Like demand paging, demand segmentation allocates segments rather than pages to processes. It keeps track of these segments in segment tables (like page tables) and store information about the segment size, location and protection. As in paging scheme, in segmentation also all segments do not have to be in memory to execute. The segment table contains a valid bit to show if the segment is in memory.

If the segment is in the main memory than the access continues else if it is not in memory then an OS trap occurs.

Remember that in demand paging we used a reference bit but here we use access bit that is used to select a segment to be replaced by another segment.

When a segment trap occurs, OS firstly determines whether there is sufficient free memory space to accommodate the segment. If there is no space in memory then the least recently used segment is chosen for replacement and is written to the disk.

Disadvantages of demand segmentation

1. It involves high overheads and is not an optimal means of making best use of the resources.

2. It suffers from the problem of external fragmentation.

3.8 O.S. SOFTWARE FACTORS

The O.S. software depends on certain factors. Since only some part of a program is to be loaded into a physical memory, so we need certain policies into the virtual memory management scheme. These policies are classified as follows:–

1. **Fetch policy:** It determines which page should be brought from secondary memory to the main memory. In general, we use demand paging for fetch policy.
2. **Allocation policy:** It deals with the allocation of real memory to each active process.
3. **Replacement/swap-out policy:** If there is no space for a new page in a physical memory which page is to be selected for swapping out to secondary memory in order to make a room for a new page?
4. **Placement policy:** Where to place an incoming new page into the physical memory?
5. **Page Buffering:** When page is replaced, it is not physically moved in main memory. Instead the entry in the page table for this page is removed and placed in either the free or modified page list. This is known as **page buffering.**

3.9 CASE STUDY OF WINDOWS-2000 MEMORY MANAGEMENT

The windows 2000 (or W2K) virtual memory manager controls how memory is allocated and how paging is done. The memory manager is desigend to operate over a variety of platforms and use page sizes ranging from 4 KB to 64 KB

Example Systems:

(*a*) Intel, PowerPC and MIPS platforms have 4096 bytes per page.

(*b*) DEC Alpha platforms have 8192 bytes/page.

Virtual address map of W2K

In W2K, every user process has its own virtual address space. Virtual address are 32-bits long. So, each process has 2^{32} = 4GB of virtual address space. Out of 4GB, 2GB is reserved for O.S. and remaining 2GB can be shared by processes. Fig. 3.5 shows that layout.

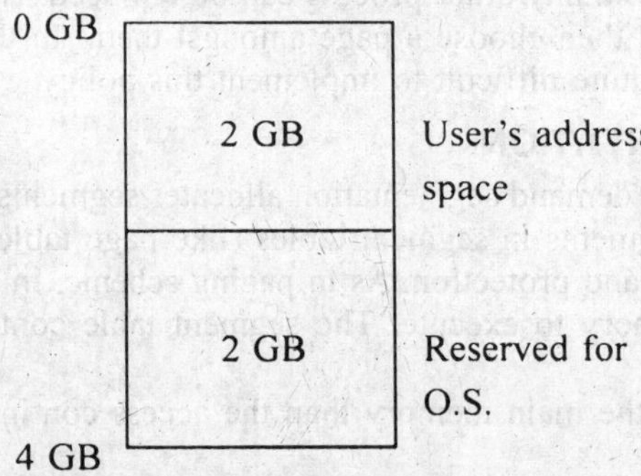

Fig. 3.5 Virtual address space of W2K.

However, there is an option of increasing this 2GB user's space to 3GB also. This is done so that large memory intensive applications can also be supported. This can improve the performance for applications like data mining.

Paging in W2K

When a process is created, it can make use of the entire 2GB user space. **Please note that this space is divided into fixed size pages, any of which can be brought into the main memory.**

In W2K, a page can be in one of the three states :–

(*a*) **Available:** Pages not currently used by this process.

(*b*) **Reserved :** A set of contiguous pages that the virtual memory manager (VMM) sets aside for a process but does not count against the process's memory quota until used. When a process needs to write to memory, some of the reserved memory is committed to the process.

(*c*) **Committed :** Pages for which VMM has set aside space in its paging file. **For example,** the disk file to which it writes pages when removing them from main memory.

Herein, the distinction between the reserved and committed memory is useful because—

1. It minimizes the amount of disk space set aside for a particular process, keeping that disk space free for other processes.
2. It enables a thread or process to declare an amount of memory that can be quickly allocated as needed.

Working sets in W2K

The working set management scheme used by W2K is a variable allocation and with a local scope. **When a process is first activated, it is assigned a certain number of page frames of main memory as its working set.** When a process, references a page not in memory, one of the resident pages of that process is swapped out and the new page is brought in. The working sets of active process are adjusted.

Conventions followed

There are two general rules followed here—

1. **When sufficient main memory is there,** the virtual memory manager allows the resident sets of active processes to grow. When a page fault occurs, a new page is brought into memory but no older page is swapped out, resulting in an increase of the resident set of that process by one page.
2. **When insufficient (scarce) memory is there,** the virtual memory manager (VMM) recovers memory for the system by moving less recently used pages out of the working sets of active processes, reducing the size of those resident sets.

Summary

We have studied about paging and segmentation in detail. A comparison of paging and segmentation has been given. Various page replacement algorithms have been discussed. We list these algorithms in table now.

	Algorithm	Comment
1.	Optimal	No use in practical systems.
2.	FIFO	Might throw out important pages.
3.	Second Chance	Better than FIFO above.
4.	Clock	Uses circular list, so realistic.
5.	LRU	Good but implementation difficult.
6.	NFU	An approximation to LRU.
7.	Working Set	Quite costly to implement.

MULTIPLE-CHOICE QUESTIONS [MCQs]

1. Virtual memory is—

(*a*) Simple to implement. (*b*) Used by all major commercial O.S.

(*c*) Less efficient memory utilization. (*d*) None of the above

2. Under virtual memory—
   (*a*) A single program is processed by two or more CPUs.
   (*b*) Two or more programs are stored in memory.
   (*c*) Only active pages are stored in memory.
   (*d*) None of the above.
3. Overlay is—
   (*a*) A system program.
   (*b*) A technique of allowing a program to be larger than the amount of memory allocated to it.
   (*c*) An O.S. itself
   (*d*) None of the above
4. Very high paging activity is known as
   (*a*) Demand Paging. (*b*) Demand Segmentation
   (*c*) Thrashing (*d*) None of the above
5. The process of temporarily removing inactive programs from the main memory of a computer system is known as—
   (*a*) Swapping (*b*) Compaction
   (*c*) Mapping (*d*) None of the above
6. The effective access time (EAT) of demand paging is given by the formula—
   (*a*) EAT = $(1 - p) * m_t + p *$ page fault time
   (*b*) EAT = $(1 + p) * m_t + p *$ page – fault time
   (*c*) EAT = $(1 * p * m_t) + p *$ page – fault time
   (*d*) None of the above
7. Page fault rate (PFR) is given by—
   (*a*) No. of page faults * No. of bits in the reference string.
   (*b*) No. of page faults/No. of bits in the reference string.
   (*c*) No. of page faults + No. of bits in the reference string.
   (*d*) None of the above.
8. Replace a page that has not been used for the longest period of time is the criteria of which of these algorithms—
   (*a*) FIFO (*b*) LRU
   (*c*) Optimal (*d*) None of the above
9. If the number of frames is increased, the page fault rate will decrease. This is known as—
   (*a*) Belady's Anomaly. (*b*) Working Set Theory.
   (*c*) Thrashing. (*d*) None of the above.
10. A high paging rate—
    (*a*) May cause high I/O rate. (*b*) Keeps the system well running.
    (*c*) Shows too much of processor activity. (*d*) None of the above.
11. The page fault frequency in virtual memory is reduced when—
    (*a*) the page size is reduced (*b*) Processes are unbound
    (*c*) Locality of reference is applicable to the process.
    (*d*) None of the above.
12. Loading the pages before letting processes run is known as—
    (*a*) Paging (*b*) Pre-paging
    (*c*) Thrashing (*d*) Compaction
13. A reference bit (R) is used in which of the following algorithms—
    (*a*) Second chance page replacement algorithm.
    (*b*) Clock page replacement algorithm.

(*c*) Both '*a*' and '*b*'. (*d*) None of the above.

14. One way to provide protection through hardware is—

(*a*) Using databases. (*b*) Using Fence Register

(*c*) Using counters. (*d*) None of the above.

15. The process of merging adjacent holes to form a single larger hole is called as—

(*a*) Fragmentation (*b*) Coalescing

(*c*) Swapping (*d*) None of the above

ANSWERS

1. *b*	**2.** *c*	**3.** *b*	**4.** *c*	**5.** *a*	**6.** *a*
7. *b*	**8.** *b*	**9.** *a*	**10.** *a*	**11.** *c*	**12.** *b*
13. *c*	**14.** *b*	**15.** *b*			

CONCEPTUAL SHORT QUESTIONS WITH ANSWERS

Q.1. Under what circumstances do page faults occur ? Describe the actions taken by the operating system when a page fault occurs.

Ans. A page fault occurs when an access to a page that has not been brought into main memory takes place. The steps followed by OS to handle a page fault are as follows—

Step-1: If a process refers to a page which is not in the physical memory then an internal table kept with a Process Control Block (PCB) is checked to verify whether a memory reference to a page was valid or invalid. **Please note that for every process, a PCB (mentioned above) is created.** This PCB contains vital informations about a process that will be discussed later.

Step-2: If the memory reference to a page was valid, but the page is missing, the process of bringing a page into the phyical memory starts.

Step-3: Free memory location is identified to bring a missing page.

Step-4: By reading the hard disk, the desired page is brought back into the free memory location.

Step-5: Once the page is in the physical memory, then both the page map table (PMT) and PCB are updated to indicate that the page is now in memory.

Step-6: Restart the instruction that was interrupted due to the missing page.

This can be shown diagrammatically also.

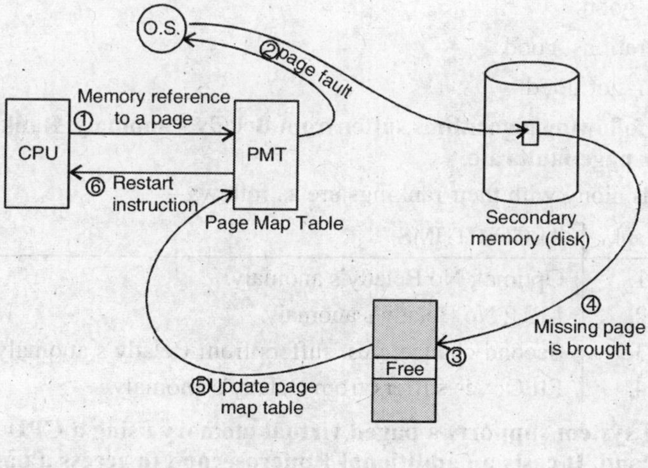

Q.2. Assume that you have a page reference string for a process with m frames (initially all empty). The page reference string has length p with n distinct page numbers occurring in it. For any page-replacement algorithms—

(*a*) What is a lower bound on the number of page faults?

(*b*) What is an upper bound on the number of page faults?

Ans. (*a*) n

(*b*) p

Q.3. A certain computer provides its users with a virtual memory space of 2^{32} bytes. The computer has 2^{18} bytes of physical memory. The virtual memory is implemented by paging and the page size is 4096 bytes. A user process generates the virtual address 11123456. Explain how the system establishes the corresponding physical location. Distinguish between sofware and hardware operations.

Ans. The virtual address in binary form is 0001 0001 0001 0010 0011 0100 0101 0110

Since the page size is 4096 bytes = 2^{12}, so the page table size is 2^{20}. Therefore, the low order 12 bits "0100 0101 0110" are used as the displacement into the page while the remaining 20 bits "0001 0001 0001 0010 0011" are used as the displacement in the page table.

Q.4. Which of the following programming techniques and structures are "good" for a demand paged environment? Which are "not good"? Explain your answers.

(*a*) Stack

(*b*) Hashed symbol table

(*c*) Sequential Search

(*d*) Binary Search

(*e*) Pure code

(*f*) Vector operations

(*g*) Indirection

Ans. (*a*) Stack-good

(*b*) Hashed symbol table–not good

(*c*) Sequential search–good

(*d*) Binary search–not good

(*e*) Pure code–good.

(*f*) Vector operations–good

(*g*) Indirection–not good

Q.5. Which of the following algorithms suffer from Belady's anomaly. Rank these algorithms based on their page-fault rate.

Ans. The algorithms along with their rankings are as follows—

Rank	ALGORITHMS
1.	Optimal; No Belady's anomaly.
2.	LRU; No Belady's anomaly.
3.	Second chance; yes, suffers from Belady's anomaly.
4.	FIFO; yes suffers from Belady's anomaly.

Q.6. An operating system supports a paged virtual memory using a CPU with a cycle time of 1 microsecond. It costs an additional 1 microsecond to access a page other than the

current one. Pages have 1000 words and the paging device is a drum that rotates at 3000 revolutions per minute and transfers 1 million words per second. The following statistical measurements were obtained from the system:

- **1 percent of all instructions executed accessed a page other than the current page.**
- **Of the instructions that accessed another page, 80 percent accessed a page already in memory.**
- **When a new page was required, the replaced page was modified 50 percent of the time.**

Calculate the effective instruction time on this system, assuming that the system is running one process only and that the processor is idle during drum transfers.

Ans. Effective access time, EAT

= 0.99 (1 sec) + 0.008 (2 sec) + 0.002 (10000 sec + 1000 sec)

+ 0.001 (10000 sec + 1000 sec)

= (0.99 + 0.016 + 22.0 + 11.0) sec

= **34.0 secs**

Q.7. Consider a demand paging system with the following time measured utilizations:–

CPU utilization	**20%**
Paging disk	**97.7%**
Other I/O devices	**5%**

Which (if any) of the following will probably improve CPU utilization? Explain your answer.

(*a*) Install a faster CPU.

(*b*) Install a bigger paging disk.

(*c*) Increase the degree of multiprogramming.

(*d*) Decrease the degree of multiprogramming.

(*e*) Install more main memory.

(*f*) Install a faster hard disk or multiple controllers with multiple hard disks.

(*g*) Add prepaging to the page fetch algorithms.

(*h*) Increase the page size.

(*i*) Install faster, other I/O devices?

Ans. The system is obviously spending most of its time paging, indicating over-allocation of memory. If the level of multiprogramming is reduced, resident processes would page fault less frequently and the CPU utilization would improve. Another way to improve performance would be to get more physical memory or a faster paging drum.

(*a*) **Getting a faster CPU**—NO

(*b*) **Getting a bigger paging drum**—NO

(*c*) **Increase the degree of multiprogramming**—NO

(*d*) **Decrease the degree of multiprogramming**—Yes

(*e*) **Install more main memory**—

Likely to improve CPU utilization as more pages can remain resident and not require and not require paging to or from the disks.

Install a faster hard disk or multiple controllers with multiple hard disks—

It is also an improvement as the disk bottleneck is removed by faster response and more throughput to the disks, the CPU will get more data, more quickly.

(*g*) **Add prepaging to the page fetch algorithms**—

Again, the CPU will get more data so it will be more in use. This is only the case if paging action is amenable to prefetching *i.e.*, some of the access is sequential.

(*h*) **Increase the page size—**

Increasing the page size will result in fewer page faults if data is being accessed sequentially. If data access is more or less random, more paging action could ensure because fewer pages can be kept in memory and more data is transferred per page fault. So, this change is as likely to decrease utilization as it is to increase it.

(*i*) **Install faster, other I/O devices—**

The answer is NO.

Q.8. Suppose that you want to use a paging algorithm that requires a reference bit (such as second-chance replacement or working-set model), but the hardware does not provide one. Sketch how you could simulate a reference bit even if one were not provided by the hardware or explain why it is not possible to do so. If it is possible, calculate what the cost would be.

Ans. We can use the valid/invalid bit supported in hardware to simulate the reference bit. Initially, set the bit to invalid. On first reference, a trap to the O.S. is generated. The O.S. will set a software bit to 1 and reset the valid/invalid bit to valid.

Q.9. Consider a demand-paged computer system that uses a paging drum, global LRU replacement and an allocation policy that shares frames equally among processes (that is, if there are m frames and n processes then each process gets m/n frames). The degree of multiprogramming is currenlty fixed at four. The system was recently measured to determine utilization of CPU and the paging drum. The results are one of the following alternatives. For each case, what is happening? Can the degree of multiprogramming be increased to increase the CPU utilization? Is the paging helping?

(*a*) CPU utilization 13 percent; disk utilization 97 percent.

(*b*) CPU utilization 87 percent; disk utilization 3 percent.

(*c*) CPU utilization 13 percent; disk utilization 3 percent.

Ans. (*a*) Thrashing is occurring.

(*b*) CPU utilization is sufficiently high to leave things alone. It can increase degree of multiprogramming.

(*c*) Increase the degree of multiprogramming.

Q. 10. Consider the following page reference string:

1, 2, 3, 4, 2, 1, 5, 6, 2, 1, 2, 3, 7, 6, 3, 2, 1, 2, 3, 6

How many pages faults would occur for the following replacement algorithms, assuming one, two, three, four, five, six or seven frames? Remember all frames are initially empty, so your first unique pages will all cost one fault each.

(*a*) LRU replacement

(*b*) FIFO replacement

(*c*) Optimal replacement.

Ans. The page faults are given below.

Number of frames	LRU	FIFO	OPTIMAL
1	20	20	20
2	17	18	15
3	15	16	11
4	10	14	8
5	8	10	7
6	7	9	7
7	7	7	7

Q.11. When virtual memory is implemented in a computing system, there are certain costs associated with the technique and certain benefits. List the costs and the benefits. It is possible for the costs to exceed the benefits. If it is, what measures can be taken to ensure that this does not happen?

Ans. The costs are additional hardware and slower access time. The benefits are good memory utilization and larger logical address space than physical address space.

Q.12. We have an O.S. for a machine that uses base and limit registers but we have modified the machine to provide a page table. Can the page tables be set up to simulate base and limit registers? How can they be or why can they not be?

Ans. The page table can be set up to simulate base and limit registers provided that the memory is allocated in fixed-size segments. In this way, the base of a segment can be entered into the page table and the valid/invalid bit used to indicate that portion of the segment as resident in the memory. There will be some problem with internal fragmentation.

Q.13. For a certain system, total number of frames is 64. The size of 2 processes, p_1 and p_2 are 10 and 127 respectively. How much is the allocation for each of these processes?

Ans. Given:

$m = 64$ (total no. of frames)

$S_1 = 10$ (size of process-1)

$S_2 = 127$ (size of process-2)

$$\therefore \sum_{i=1}^{2} S = S_1 + S_2 = 10 + 127 = 137 = S$$

$$\text{Allocation } (a_i) \text{ for } p_i = \frac{S_i}{S} * m \qquad (i \leftarrow 1 \text{ to } n \text{ processes})$$

$$\therefore a_1 = \frac{10}{137} * 64 \approx 5$$

$$a_2 = \frac{127}{137} * 64 \approx 59$$

Q.14. What happens if there is no free frame?

Ans. If there is no free frame then—

(*a*) Find some page in memory which is not really in use, swap it out.

(*b*) Same page may be brought into memory several times.

Q.15. What is the Optimal Page Replacement algorithm? Why is it difficult to implement it?

Ans. An optimal page-replacement algorithm has the lowest page fault rate of all the algorithms and will never suffer from the Belady's anomaly. This algorithm is based on the principle— **"Replace the page that will not be used for the longest period of time".**

But this algorithm is difficult to implement because it requires future knowledge of the reference string. Optimal algorithm is mainly used for comparison studies.

Q.16. Give a mathematical interpretation of the mapping process in a virtual memory.

Ans. The mapping process in a virtual memory is defined by virtual address space,

$$V = \{0, 1, ..., V-1\}$$

and the physical (real) memory space, M as

$$M = \{0, 1, ..., m-1\}$$

Now, $V > m$ in very large systems.

but $V < m$ in older mini and microcomputers

The O.S. dynamically allocates real memory to portions of the virtual address space. The mapping hardware must realize the function—

$f : V \to M$

such that

$$f(x) = \begin{cases} r \text{ if item } x \text{ is in real memory of} \\ \text{location-}r. \\ \text{missing item expection if term '}x\text{'} \\ \text{is not in real memory.} \end{cases}$$

Q.17. What is the page fault frequency (PFF)? Write down an algorithm for counting the page fault?

Ans. A process having inadequate frames will exhibit a high Page Fault Frequency (PFF). The actual page rate is calculated by a running process and is recorded in the Process Control Block (PCB). Two cases occur—

Case-1: When a process exceeds the upper page fault frequency threshold

More real pages may be allocated to it.

Case 2: When a process reaches lower page fault frequency threshold.

Stop allocation of new page frames.

This approach to page replacement is called *PFF*. The *PFF* parameter *P* is defined by—

$$P = \frac{1}{T}$$

Where 'T' : is the critical inter-page fault time.

'P' : is measured in number of page faults per millisecond.

The **PFF algorithm** is as follows—

Step-1: The O.S. defines a system wide (per process) critical page fault frequency (*P*).

Step-2: The O.S. measures virtual (process) time and stores the time of most recent page fault in the related PCB.

Step-3: When a page fault occurs, the O.S., acts as per following conditions:–

(*a*) If the last page fault occurred less than T = 1/P ms, the process is operating above PFF threshold and a new page fault is added from the pool to house the needed page.

(*b*) Otherwise process is operating below threshold, P and a page frame occupied by a page whose referenced bit is written into but are not set freed to accommodate the new page.

(*c*) The O.S. sweeps and reacts to referenced bits of all the resident pages. Unused pages are released and the freed page frames are returned to the pool for future allocations.

Q.18. Can you suggest a remedy for thrashing?

Ans. The OS has to swap-out some of the active processes, thus releasing some occupied frames, that can be made available to the other active processes, till PFF is brought within the thresholds (acceptable limits). When some of the active processes have completed, the swapped-out processes can be swapped-in and their execution resumed.

Q.19. Given a 4 GB ($\approx 4.3 \times 10^9$ bytes) of virtual space and typical page size of 4 kB. How many virtual pages would this imply? If each page table entry is 5 bytes, how much space is required for the whole page table?

Ans. Virtual space = 4 GB (4.3×10^9 bytes)

Page Size = 4 kB
Page table entry = 5 bytes
Size of page table = Page size × Page table entry
= $2^{12} \times 5$
= 20480 bytes
No. of virtual pages (virtual space/page size)
= $4.3 \times 10^9 / 4 \times 10^3$
= 107500 bytes

EXERCISE QUESTIONS

Q.1. When do page faults occur? Describe the actions taken by the O.S. when a page fault occurs.

Q.2. Write short notes on—
'Virtual Memory'.

Q.3. (*a*) Explain the static and dynamic memory allocation techniques with example.
(*b*) Consider the following page-reference string—
7, 0, 1, 2, 0, 3, 0, 4, 2, 3, 0, 3, 2, 1, 2, 0, 1, 7, 0, 1
How many page faults would occur for the following page replacement algorithms, assuming 3 frames:—
(1) FIFO, (2) Optimal (3) LRU.

Q.4. What is thrashing? What is the reason for it? How does working set theory solve the problem of thrashing?

Q. 5. What is Virtual memory? What hardware supports are needed to implement virtual memory? Illustrate with the help of an example that FIFO page replacement algorithm may encounter more number of page fault than the number of page fault encoutered by LRU page replacement algorithm.

Q. 6. If an instruction takes one microsecond and a page fault takes an additional 'n' microsecond, give a formula for the effective instruction time if page fault occurs every 'K' instructions.

Q. 7. (*a*) Explain the page replacement algorithms.
(*b*) What is thrashing? How does the system detect thrashing?

Q. 8. (*a*) Give some reasons as to why local page replacement is better than the global page replacement.

Q. 9. Compare the following Page Replacement algorithms using one example:
(*a*) FIFO (*b*) LRU (*c*) Optimal algorithms

Q.10. Consider the following page-reference string:—
1, 2, 3, 4, 2, 1, 5, 6, 1, 2, 2, 3, 7, 6, 3, 2, 1, 2, 3, 6
How many page faults would occur for the following replacement algorithms assuming one, two, three, four, six or even frames—
(*a*) LRU (*b*) FIFO (*c*) Optimal

Q.11. Write short notes on —'Demand Paging'

Q.12. (*a*) Compare the working set model to page fault frequency strategy to control thrashing.

(*b*) Write short notes on—
(1) Belady's anomaly
(2) Second chance algorithm.

Q.13. Consider the following sequence of memory references from a 4600 word program:
100, 110, 1040, 1700, 730, 3090, 1850, 2450, 2460, 4340, 4580, 3640

(*i*) Give the reference string assuming a page size of 100 words.

(*ii*) Find the page fault rate for this reference string, assuming 2000 words of memory available to the program and a FIFO replacement algorithm

(*iii*) What would be the page fault rate if LRU and optimal replacement algorithms are used?

Q.14. (*a*) Define and explain the use of "Dirty Bit" in demand paging.

(*b*) Define the term 'Virtual Memory' technique.

Explain with a neat diagram the steps involved in handling a page fault.

Q.15. Consider the following sequence of memory references from a 460 word program—
10, 11, 104, 170, 173, 73, 309, 185, 245, 246, 434, 498, 364

(*i*) Find the page fault rate, assuming "200" words of primary memory available, page of size "100" words and FIFO replacement algorithm.

(*ii*) What would be the page fault rate if we use an LRU replacement algorithms?

(*iii*) What is the page fault rate for the "Optimal replacement" algorithm?

(*iv*) What is the amount of "Internal Fragmentation"?

Q.16. How many page faults would occur for the following reference string for four page frames using LRU algorithm–
1, 2, 3, 4, 5, 3, 4, 1, 6, 7, 8, 7, 8, 9 7, 8, 9, 5, 4, 5, 4, 2.
[**Hints:** LRU for given data produces 11 faults]

Q.17. (*a*) What do you understand by Belady's anomaly? Which popular page replacement algorithm suffers form the Belady's anomaly ? Also give the name of the class of algorithms, which can never suffer from Belady's anomaly and why?

(*b*) A system using demand paged memory, takes 250 ns to satisfy a memory request if the page is in memory. If the page is not in memory, the request takes on an average 5 ms if a free frame is available or the page to be swapped out has not been modified or 12 ms if the page to be swapped out has been modified. What is the effective access time if the page fault rate is 2 % and 40% of the time the page to be replaced has been modified? Assume the system is running only a single process and the CPU is idle during page swaps.

Q.18. Consider the following page reference string –
1, 2, 3, 1, 4, 5, 6, 2, 1, 3, 2, 7, 6, 3, 4, 1, 2, 6
How many page faults would occur for the following replacement algorithms assuming six (6) frames. All frames are initially empty: (1) LRU (2) FIFO (3) OPT.

Q.19. Consider the following page reference string –
4, 3, 2, 1, 4, 3, 5, 4, 3, 2, 1, 5. How many pages fault would occur for the following page replacement algorithms for 3 page frames ? All frames are initially empty.
(i) FIFO replacement. (ii) LRU replacement.

UNIT - II

CHAPTER

4

Processes

4.0 PROCESS CONCEPT—AN INTRODUCTION

A process is an activity of some kind. It has a program code, input, output and a state. **We define the process as an instance of a program in execution.** It is the unit of work in a modern time-sharing operating system. **Please note that a process is more than the program code. It includes the current activity as represented by the value of the program counter (PC) and the contents of the processor's registers. Also remember that a process execution must progress in a sequential manner.** A process may generate many processes as it runs. A single processor may be shared among several processes with some scheduling policy being used by the CPU to allocate or deallocate a process.

4.1 COMPARISON OF A PROCESS AND A PROGRAM—TABULAR FORM

The differences between a program and a process are—

Program	Process
1. A program consists of a set of instructions in a programming language.	1. A process is a sequence of instruction execution.
2. A program is a static object that exists in a file.	2. A process is a dynamic object *i.e.*, a program in execution.
3. A program is loaded into the secondary storage devices.	3. A process is loaded into the main memory.
4. The time span of a program is unlimited.	4. The time span of a process is limited.
5. A program is a passive entity.	5. A process is an active entity.

4.2 PROCESS STATES

The lifecycle of a process can be divided into several states, each with its own characteristic to describe the process. It means that as a process starts executing, it goes through different states. Each process may be in one of the following states:–

1. **New:** The process has been created but not yet admitted to the pool of executable processes.
2. **Ready:** The process is ready for execution and is waiting to be allocated to a processor. All ready processes are kept in a queue and they keep waiting for CPU time to be allocated by the O.S. in order to run. A program called as scheduler, which is part of O.S., picks up one ready process for execution by passing a control to it.
3. **Running:** A process is now executing; actually using the CPU. The instructions within a process are executing. When a process gets a control from CPU plus other resources, it starts executing.

   The running process may require some I/O during execution. Depending on the particular scheduling policy of O.S., it may pass its control back to that process or O.S. may schedule another process if one is ready to run.

4. **Waiting blocked:** A process is waiting for some event to occur before it can continue execution. A waiting process lacks some resources other than the CPU. Such processes are normally not considered for execution until the related suspending conditions is fulfilled. The running process becomes suspended by invoking I/O routines whose result it needs in order to proceeds.
5. **Terminate:** When the process finally stops. A process terminates when it finishes executing its last statement. **Please note that at this point of time, the process may return some data to its parent process. Also note that the process can terminate during some other circumstances also.** A process can cause the termination of another process via an appropriate system call.

So, a process can be in one of these five states. This model is also known as a *five state model* and is shown below in Fig. 4.1.

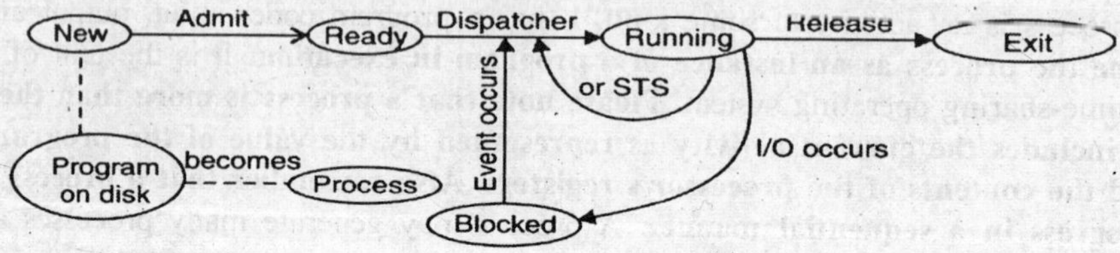

Fig. 4.1 Process State Diagram (PSD)

I. New State

Ist Step : I_1 + P_1 comes

2nd Step : Tables allocated built to manage process.

Program is in Hard disk and not in MM

II Exit State

Step 1 : P1 – aborts due to unrecoverable error

P1 termination moves it to Exit state

Step 2 : From tables, OR extracts required info terminates the proces (or debtes)

So, we find that as a process executes, it changes state. **The state is defined partly by the current activity of that process.**

4.3 PROCESS CONTROL BLOCK [PCB]/TASK CONTROL BLOCK

Another responsibility of an O.S. is to collect all information that it needs about a particular process into a data structure called as a **Process Control Block (PCB)/Task Control Block.** It acts as a repository (storage) for any information for processes. **Please note here that when a process is created, the O.S. creates a corresponding PCB and when it terminates, its PCB is released to the pool of free memory locations from which new PCBs are drawn. Also note that a process can compete for resources only when it has active PCB associated with it.** A PCB is implemented as a record containing vital information as shown below in Fig. 4.2.

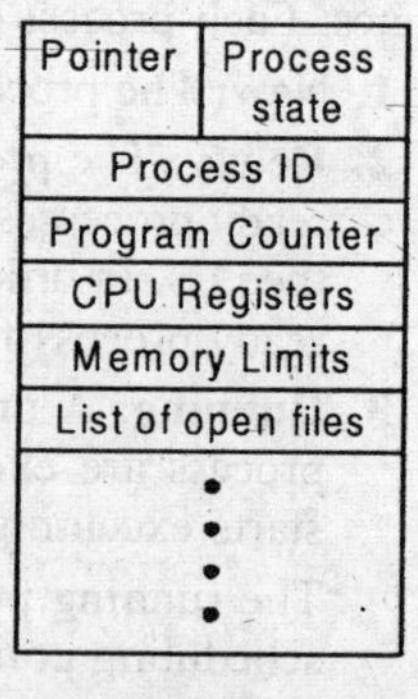

Fig. 4.2 Process Control Block/Task Control Block

Here, in this Figure, we have the following fields :–

1. **Process ID :** It is a unique process number or process identifier that identifies each process.
2. **Process State :** It indicates the current state of the process (that is, new, ready, running, waiting and terminated). Each process may be in any of these states.
3. **Program Counter :** It contains the address of the next instruction to be executed and thus is useful in indicating the status of a process.

4. **CPU Registers :** As we know that accumulator, general purpose registers, index registers are some of the CPU registers. Whenever, a processor switches over from one process to another process, information about the current status of the old process is saved in the register along with the program counter so that the process be allowed to continue correctly afterwards. This is shown below in Fig. 4.3.

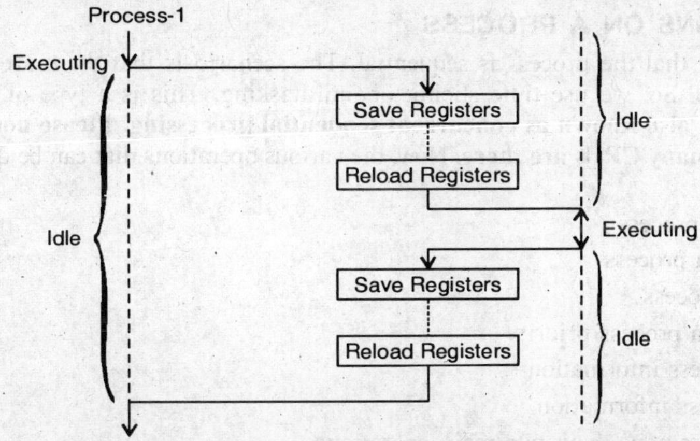

Fig. 4.3 Passing of CPU control from one process to another process

5. **Accounting information :** It includes the actual CPU time used in executing a process.
6. **I/O Status information :** It includes the names of I/O devices used by a process, list of open files information about allocation of peripheral devices to processes.
7. **Processor Scheduling details :** It includes a priority of a process, address to scheduling queues and so on.

4.4 PROCESS SCHEDULING—READY QUEUE V/S DEVICE QUEUE

Ready Queue—

It is a doubly linked list of processes which are ready to run. They are ordered by priority, the highest priority process is at the front of the queue. Because queue works on First-in First-out (FIFO) principle, so whenever the CPU takes up a new process, it actually selects the process with the highest priority. **Please note that when we say that the processes are listed together, we mean that actually their PCBs are linked together.** The header of the queue contains **two pointers.** The *first pointer* points to the first PCB and the **second points** to the last PCB in the list. **Also note that each PCB has a pointer to point to the next process in the ready queue.** This is shown in Fig. 4.4.

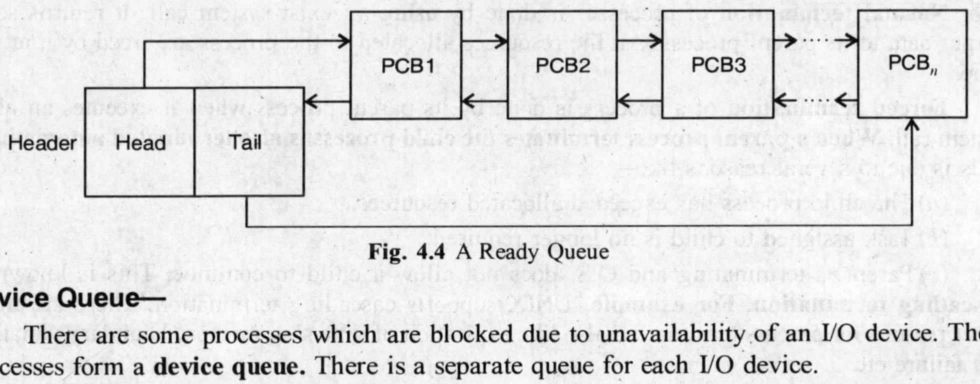

Fig. 4.4 A Ready Queue

Device Queue—

There are some processes which are blocked due to unavailability of an I/O device. These processes form a **device queue.** There is a separate queue for each I/O device.

Role of these two queues—

A process is created and is initially put in the **ready queue.** When CPU picks a process for its execution then a change in the state of the process occurs. If it's state is changed to block, it is added to the device queue of the device whose services are required by it. This task is done by the process scheduler.

4.5 OPERATIONS ON A PROCESS

As we know that the process is sequential. The scenario is that there are many processes and a single CPU. So, we use time slicing or multitasking. This is a type of **pseudo-parallel processing and is also known as concurrent sequential processing. Please note that in a true parallel system, many CPUs are there.** Now, the various operations that can be done on processes are as follows—

(*a*) Create a process

(*b*) Destroy a process

(*c*) Run a process

(*d*) Change a process priority

(*e*) Get process information

(*f*) Set process information

Let us discuss now about two main operations—

(*a*) Process creation

(*b*) Process termination.

4.5.1 Process Creation

It is the job of our O.S. to create processes. There are four ways of achieving it. They are as follows—

(*a*) For a **batch environment**, a process is created in response to the submission of a job.

(*b*) In an **interactive environment**, a process is created when a new user attempts to log on.

(*c*) The **operating system** can create a process to perform a function on behalf of a user program.

(*d*) A number of processes can be generated from the main process. For the purpose of **modularity** or to exploit **parallelism**, a user program can create a number of processes.

4.5.2 Process Termination

There are two types of terminations. They are as follows—

(*a*) Normal Termination

(*b*) Forced Termination

Normal termination of processes is done by using an exist system call. It returns some output data to its parent process. All the resources allocated to the process are freed by it at this time.

Forced termination of a process is done by its parent process when it executes an abort system call. **When a parent process terminates the child process is also terminated automatially.** This is due to several reasons like—

(*a*) The child process has exceeded allocated resources.

(*b*) Task assigned to child is no longer required.

(*c*) Parent is terminating and O.S. does not allow a child to continue. This is known as **cascading termination. For example**, UNIX supports cascading termination. There are many other reasons for process termination also like expiration of time slot, memory boundary violation, I/O failure etc.

4.6 COOPERATING PROCESSES

Two processes are said to be "Serial" if the execution of one must be complete before the execution of another process can start. While two processes are said to be "concurrent" if their execution can overlap in time. On the other hand, **the processes which execute concurrently (parallely) and affect or get affected by other processes executing in the system are known as cooperating processes.** A process gets affected by another process when data sharing or other resource sharing occurs. **Please note that any process which shares data with other processes is a cooperating process.** Such processes are required to speed up the computations, to allow sharing of information for user's ease and so on.

4.7 THREADS

A thread is similar to a sequential program like a thread also has a beginning, an end, a sequence etc. But a thread itself is not a program because it cannot run on its own. So, it runs within a program. **Please note that a thread is a single sequential flow of control within a program. A thread is also known as a light weight process.** This is so called because it runs within a program and thus it makes use of the resources that were actually allocated to the process (or program). A thread has some **similarities** to processes. A thread also has its lifecycle. They also share processor. Each thread has its own stack and a program counter (PC). A thread executes sequentially within a process.

But there are some **dissimilarities** between threads and processes. Threads are not independent of one another. Threads require lesser creation time as compared to a process. Thread requires lesser creation time. Switching between threads is faster. Threads enhance communication efficiencies.

4.7.1 Comparison of Process and Threads—in tabular form

Process	Thread
1. Processes cannot share the same memory.	1. Threads can share memory and files.
2. Process creation is time consuming	2. Thread creation is not time consuming.
3. Process execution is very slow.	3. Thread execution is very fast.
4. It takes more time to terminate a process.	4. It takes less time to terminate threads.
5. It takes more time to switch between two processes.	5. It takes less time to switch between two threads.
6. Process is loosely coupled *i.e.*, lesser resources sharing.	6. Threads are tightly coupled *i.e.*, more resource sharing.
7. Communication between processes is difficult.	7. Communication between threads is easy and efficient.
8. System calls are required for communication.	8. System calls are not required.
9. It is a **heavy weight** process as it requires more resources.	9. It is a **light weight** *process* as it requires fewer resources.
10. They are not suitable for exploiting parallelism.	10. They are suitable for exploiting parallelism.

4.7.2 Multithreading

A process is divided into the smaller tasks and each task is called as a **thread. The use of multiple threads in a single program, all running at the same time and performing different tasks is called as multithreading.**

For example, JAVA browser is a multithreaded application wherein you can scroll a page while it is downloading an applet or image, play animation and sound parallely, print a page in the background while you download a new page.

Based on the functionality, threads are put under four categories as shown below, in fig. 4.5.

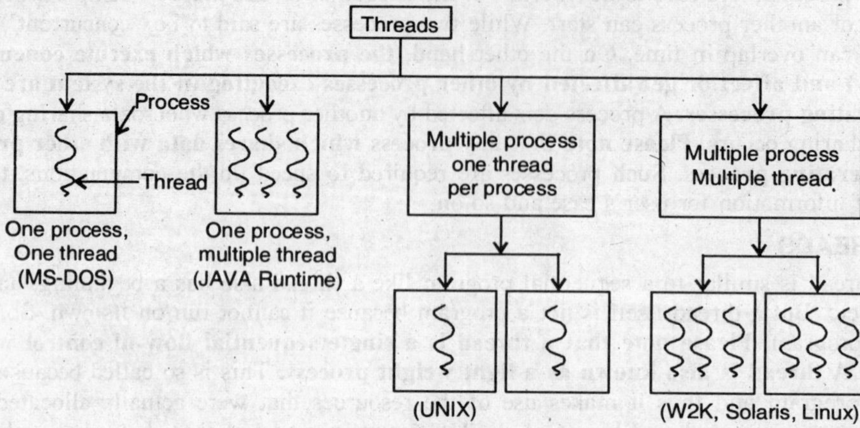

Fig. 4.5 Threads & Processes

Note from this Figure 4.5 that MS-DOS uses one process, one thread approach. JAVA Runtime uses one process, multiple thread approach. UNIX uses multiple processes but one thread per process. W2K, Solaris & Linux use multiple process. multiple threads approach.

Advantages of multithreading

1. **On single processor machines,** multithreading can help applications where :—
   (*a*) Some task take much longer to execute than others.
   (*b*) Some tasks need a better deterministic outcome than others.
   (*c*) Some user interface activity is to be run concurrently with hardware communications.
2. **On multiprocessor systems,** multithreading of an application will take the advantage of the additional hardware and it results in greatly improved overall performance.

4.7.3 User-level and Kernel-level threads

There are two ways of thread implementation. They are as follows:–

I User-Level threads

These type of threads are loaded in the user space only. So, the kernel does not know anything about them. **Please note that when threads are managed in the user space, each process must have its own private thread table.** This private table consists of the information of the program counter, stack pointer, registers etc. and is managed by the run-time system. This is shown in Fig. 4.6.

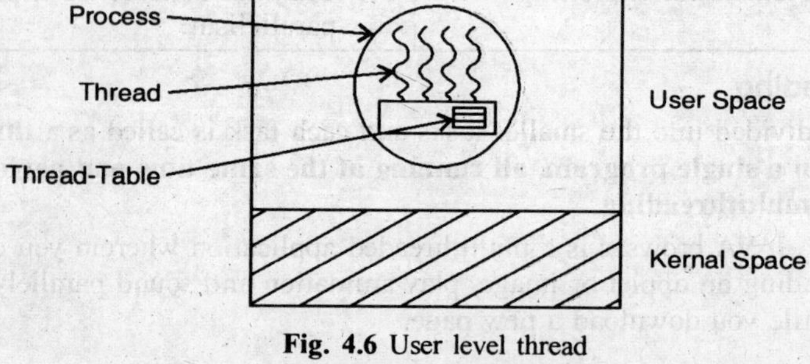

Fig. 4.6 User level thread

Let us discuss its advantages and disadvantages.

Advantages of User level threads

1. Each process can have its own scheduling algorithm.
2. User level threads can run on any O.S.
3. Faster switching among threads is possible.

Disadvantages of User-level threads

1. When a user level thread executes a system call, not only that thread is blocked but also all of the threads within the process are blocked. **Please note that this happens because the O.S. is unaware of the presence of threads and only knows about the existence of a process actually constituting these threads.**
2. Multithreaded application using user level threads cannot take the advantage of multiprocessing since Kernel assigns one process to only one processor at a time. This is because again the O.S. is unaware of the presence of threads and it schedules processes not threads.

II Kernel Level threads

In this method of thread implementation, the kernel does total work of thread movement. There is no thread table in each process. The kernel has a thread table. This table keeps track of all the threads in a system. Using Kernel calls only, a thread can create a new thread or destroy an existing thread. The kernel's thread table holds each thread registers, state and other information. **Please note that the information here is same as wlth the user level threads but it is now in the kernel instead of user space.** This is shown in Fig. 4.7.

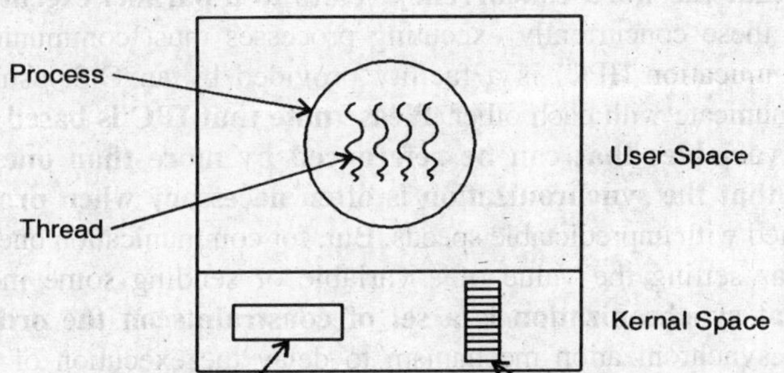

Fig. 4.7 Kernel Level Thread

Let us discuss its advantages and disadvantages now.

Advantages of Kernel Level threads

1. The O.S. is aware of the presence of threads in the processes. Hence, even if one thread of a process gets blocked, the O.S. chooses the next one to run, either from the same process or from the different one.
2. It supports multiprocessing also. It means that the Kernel can simultaneously schedule multiple threads from the same process on multiple processors.
3. Kernel routines themselves can be multithreaded.
4. If a thread within a process is blocked, then the kernel can schedule another thread of the same process.

Disadvantages of Kernel level threads

1. Switching between threads is time consuming because the kernel must do the switching.
2. Creation and destruction of the threads in the Kernel is costlier.

Combined/Hybrid approach

In this combined/hybrid approach, we combine both the user level and Kernel level approaches. In such a system, thread creation is done completely in the user space. Some O.S. provide this facility. **For example,** Solaris 2 (a UNIX version) is an example of such an O.S. It is shown in Fig. 4.8 below.

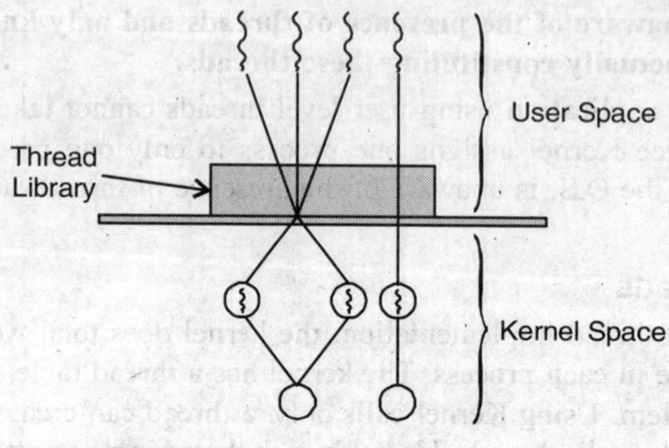

Fig. 4.8 A Combined Approach

4.8 INTERPROCESS COMMUNICATION (IPC)

As we know that the word concurrency refers to a parallel execution of a program. In order to cooperate, these concurrently executing processes must communicate and synchronize. Inter-process communication (IPC) is a facility provided by an O.S. using which cooperating processes can communicate with each other. **Please note that IPC is based on the use of shared variables i.e., the variables that can be referenced by more than one process or message passing. Also note that the synchronization is often necessary when processes communicate.** Processes are executed with unpredictable speeds. But, for communication one process must perform some action such as setting the value of a variable or sending some message that the other detects. **We say that synchronization is a set of constraints on the ordering of events.** The programmer uses a synchronization mechanism to delay the execution of a process in order to satisfy such constraints. **Please note that a concurrent process is the appearance of simultaneous execution of multiple processes.** It includes communication among processes, sharing and competing resources, synchronization of activities, allocation of process time, memory etc. It can be interleaved in time. In a single CPU, multiuser environment, overlapped, process execution can be done. In a multiprocessor, multiuser environment, the process can be independent and co-operating. It is our O.S. to keep track of various active processes. O.S. must protect data and physical resources. The result of a process must be independent of speed.

There are two ways of doing IPC and are discussed next.

4.8.1 Direct Communication Method (Inter-process Messages)

Consider two processes, P_0 and P_1. If a process P_0 sends a message to process P_1 by executing the O.S's system call **"send"** then the O.S. copies the message into a buffer and awaits execution of a **"receive"** call by process P_1. When P_1 executes a **"receive"**, the O.S. delivers the message to P_1. Process P_1 interprets the message and takes appropriate action determined by its contents. This may result in a reply being sent to P_0. If no message has been sent to P_1 by the time P_1 executes a receive call, the O.S. blocks P_1 till a message arrives for it. If many messages have been sent to P_1, the O.S. queues them and delivers them in FIFO order when P_1 executes "receive" calls. So, a direct communication occurs where the processes name each other. **Please note that such communication can be performed using shared variables.** Processes P_0 and P_1 can leave messages for each other in some shared variables. There are some implementation issues also to be considered here. They are as follows—

1. Naming of the sender and receiver processes

We need to consider some basic issues like how does the sender process know the name of the receiver process? And vice versa.

2. Message delivery protocols

Protocols determine the message data formats and the action of processes while sending and receiving messages.

3. O.S. responsibilities

We need to consider this issue also like buffering of messages, blocking and waking of processes etc.

In this method, 2 processes P_0 and P_1 will look as follows:

Process, P_0	**Process, P_1**
:	:
Send (P_1, < message >)	receive (P_0, < area addr >)
:	:

4.8.2 Indirect Communication Method (Mailboxes)

A mailbox or port is a repository for inter-process messages. It has a unique identity. A mailbox has an owner *i.e.*, nothing else but a process that created it. It is only the owner who can receive messages from a mailbox. Any process which knows the identity of a mailbox can send messages to it. These processes are called as the users of a mailbox.

Consider two processes, P_0 and P_1. P_0 is a creator process and it mentions a unique name to be given to the mailbox. P_1 uses the mailbox name, instead of a process-id, in its' send. That is,

Process, P_0	**Process, P_1**
:	:
Create-mailbox (sample);	Send (sample, <message>)
:	:

In this method, a sender need not know the name of the receiver. A process may own many mailboxes.

Apart from the creation and use of mailbox, the O.S., may permit the ownership of a mailbox to be transferred to another process. O.S. may also permit an owner to destroy a mailbox. In this case, the O.S. has the responsibility to inform all users of the mailbox accordingly.

4.9 CASE STUDY ON WINDOWS 2000 THREADS

Windows 2000 (2K) supports processes, jobs, threads and fibres.

Processes have virtual address spaces and are the containers for resources. **Threads** are the unit of execution that are scheduled, by the O.S. **Fibers** are light weight threads that are scheduled entirely in user space. **Please note here that jobs are collection of processes, processes are collection of threads and threads are collection of fibres.** So, we say,

$$\text{Fibers} \rightarrow \text{Threads} \rightarrow \text{Processes} \rightarrow \text{Jobs}$$

W2K processes have some important characteristics—

1. W2K processes are implemented as objects.
2. An executable process may contain one or more threads.
3. Both process and thread objects have built-in synchronization capabilities.

W2K makes use of two types of process-related objects—

(*a*) Processes

(*b*) Threads

A process is an entity corresponding to a user job or application that owns resources such as memory and open files. A thread is a dispatchable unit of work that executes sequentially and is interruptible, so that the processor can turn to another thread.

Each W2K process is represented by an object whose general structure is shown in Figure 4.9 (*a*).

Process	Object-type
• Process ID • Priority • Default Processor affinity • Quota limits • Execution time • I/O counters • Exit status • Exceptions/debugging ports	Object Attributes
• Create process • Open process • Query process information • Set process information • Current Process • Terminate Process	Services

Fig. 4.9 (*a*) Structure of process object

From the Figure 4.9 (*a*), it is clear that each process is defined by a number of attributes and encapsulates a number of actions or services, that it may perform. A process will perform a service upon receipt of the appropriate message. When W2K creates a new process, it uses the object class or type defined for the W2K process as a template to generate a new object instance. It is at the time of creation that the attribute values are assigned.

A W2K process must contain atleast one thread to execute. Those threads may then create other threads. In a multiprocessor system, multiple threads from the same process may execute in parallel. The object structure for a thread object is shown in Figure 4.9 (*b*).

Please note that some of the attributes of a thread resemble those of a process. Also note that in such cases, the thread attribute value is derived from the process attribute value. For example, the thread processor affinity is the set of processors in a multiprocessor system that may execute this thread. This set is equal to or a subset of the process processor affinity. This is shown in Fig. 4.9 (b).

Thread	Object-type
• Thread ID • Thread context • Dynamic Priority • Base Priority • Thread Processor affinity • Thread execution time • Alert Status • Suspension Count • Termination port • Thread Exit	Object Attributes
• Create thread • Suspend • Open thread • Resume • Query thread information • Terminate thread • Get & Set context	Services

Fig 4.9 ***(b)*** Thread object

Please note that one of the attributes of a thread object is context. This information enables threads to be suspended and resumed. Also note that it is possible to alter the behavior of a thread by altering its context when it is suspended.

W2K support concurrency among processes too. This is because threads in different processes may execute concurrently. Multiple (many) threads within the same process may be allocated to separate processors and thus executed concurrently. There are 2 cases—

Case-1 : Threads within the same process

Threads within the same process can exchange information through their common address space and have access to the shared resources of the process.

Case-2 : Threads in different processes

Threads in different processes can exchange information through shared memory that has been set up between the two processes. An object-oriented multithreaded process is an efficient means of implementing a server application. **For instance,** one server process can service a number of clients. Each client request, triggers the creation of a new thread within the server.

Thread states in Windows 2000

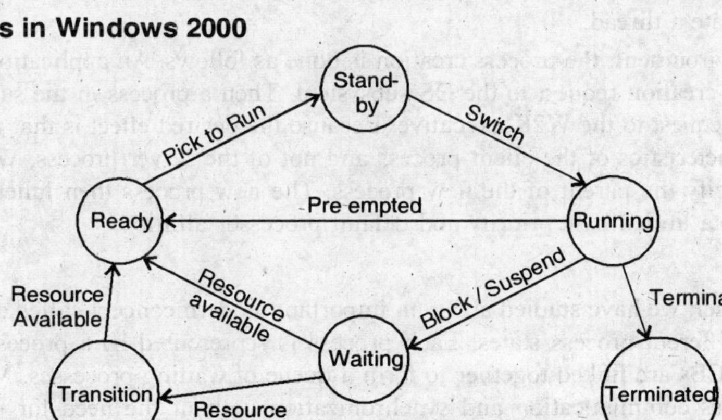

Fig. 4.10 States of thread in W2K

As shown in Fig. 4.10, an existing W2K thread is in one of the six states-

- **Ready:** Thread is ready to schedule for execution. The microkernel dispatcher keeps track of all ready threads and schedules in priority order.
- **Standby:** A standby thread has been selected to run next on a particular processor. The thread waits in this state until that processor is made available. If the standby thread's priority is high enough, the running thread on that processor may be preempted in favour of the standby thread. Otherwise, the standby thread waits until the running thread blocks or finishes its time slice.
- **Running:** Once the microkernel performs a thread or process switch, the standby thread enters the running state and begins execution and continues execution until it is preempted, exhaust its time slice, blocks or terminates. In the first two cases, it goes back to the ready state.
- **Waiting:** A thread enters the waiting state when—
  1. It is blocked on an event (e.g. I/O).
  2. It voluntarily waits for synchronization purpose, or
  3. An environment subsystem directs the threads to suspend itself. When the waiting condition is satisfied, the thread moves to the Ready State if all of its resources are available.
- **Transition:** A thread enters this state after waiting, if it is ready to run but the resources are not available. **For example,** the thread's stack may be paged out of memory when the resources are available, the thread goes to the Ready State.
- **Terminated:** A thread can be terminated by itself, by another thread or when its parent process terminates. Please note here that once housekeeping chores are completed, the thread is removed from the system or it may be retained by the executive for future reinitialization.

Please note that this general purpose process and thread facility must support the particular process and thread structures of the various O.S. clients. Also note that it is the job of each O.S. subsystem to exploit the W2K process and thread features to emulate the process and thread facilities of its corresponding O.S. This area of process/thread management is quite complex.

Actually, the process creation begins with a request for a new process from an O.S. application. The create process request is issued from an application to the corresponding protected subsytem. Then, the subsystem issues a process request to the W2K executive. W2K creates a process object and returns a handle to that object to the subsystem when W2K creates a process, it does not automatically create a thread.

In W2K environment, the process creation is done as follows. An application client process issues its process creation request to the OS subsystem. Then a process in the subsystem in turn issues a process request to the W2K executive. Because the desired effect is that the new process inherits the characteristics of the client process and not of the server process, W2K enables the subsystem to specify the parent of the new process. The new process then inherits the parent's access token, quota limits, base priority and default processor affinity.

Summary

In this chapter, we have studied about an important modern concept called as a process. We have also seen different process states. Each process is represented by a process control block (PCB). Several PCBs are linked together to form a queue of waiting processes. Message passing allows interprocess communication and synchronization without the need for global variables which is suitable for both centralized and distributed systems.

MULTIPLE-CHOICE QUESTIONS (MCQs)

1. The process is —
   (*a*) an instance of a program in execution
   (*b*) a program only.
   (*c*) A processor state.
   (*d*) None of the above
2. A program is passive while a process is —
   (*a*) inactive
   (*b*) spontaneous
   (*c*) active
   (*d*) None of the above
3. PCB stands for—
   (*a*) Process Control Board
   (*b*) Program Control Block
   (*c*) Process Control Block
   (*d*) None of the above
4. A process is created and is initially put in the
   (*a*) Ready queue
   (*b*) Device queue
   (*c*) Any of the above
   (*d*) None of the above
5. Exit ( ) systems call results in—
   (*a*) Forced termination
   (*b*) Normal termination
   (*c*) Abnormal termination
   (*d*) None of the above
6. A thread is a—
   (*a*) Task
   (*b*) Process
   (*c*) Program
   (*d*) Lightweight process
7. Generally, we have User-level threads and—
   (*a*) Programmer–level thread
   (*b*) Kernel–level thread
   (*c*) Program–level thread
   (*d*) None of the above
8. A null process has a process identifier of—
   (*a*) –1
   (*b*) 0
   (*c*) 1
   (*d*) Null
9. IPC stands for—
   (*a*) Internal Program Controller
   (*b*) Internal Process Control
   (*c*) Interprocess Communication
   (*d*) None of the above
10. IPCs can be done through—
    (*a*) Mails
    (*b*) Messages
    (*c*) System Cells
    (*d*) Traps

ANSWERS

1. *a*	**2.** *c*	**3.** *c*	**4.** *a*	**5.** *b*	**6.** *d*
7. *b*	**8.** *b*	**9.** *c*	**10.** *b*		

CONCEPTUAL SHORT QUESTIONS WITH ANSWERS

Q.1. What do you mean by Process hierarchies?

Ans. Operating system needs some way to create and kill processes. When a process is created, it creates another process which in turn creates some more processes and so on, thus forming a **process hierarchy or a process tree.**

Q.2. What are the two conditions under which a parent may terminate the execution of one of its children?

Ans. There are two conditions for a parent process to terminate the child process—

1. The task assigned to the child is no longer required.
2. The child has exceeded its usage of some of the resources it has been allocated.

Q.3. Several popular microcomputer operating systems provide little or no means of concurrent processing. Discuss the major complications that concurrent processing adds to an operating system.

Ans. A method of time sharing must be implemented to allow each of several processes to have access to the system. Involved in this are the pre-emption of processes that do not voluntarily give up the CPU (like by using a system call and Kernal being reentrant. So, more than one process may be executing Kernel code concurrently.

Processes and system resources must have protections and must be protected from each other. Any given processes must be limited in the amount of memory it can use and the operations it can perform on devices like disks.

Q.4. What two advantages do threads have over multiple processes? What major disadvantages do they have? Suggest one applications that would benefit from the use of threads and one that would not.

Ans. Threads are cheaper to create and destroy. They use very little resources while they exist. For example, they do use CPU time but they don't have totally separate memory spaces. Unfortunately, threads must "trust" each other to not to damage shared data.

For instance, one thread could destroy data that all the other threads rely on while the same could not happen between processes unless they used a system feature to allow them to share data. Any program that may do more than one task at one could benefit from multitasking. For instance, a program that reads input, processes it and outputs it could have three threads, one for each task. "Single minded" processes would not benefit from multiple threads like a program that displays the time of day.

Q.5. Provide two programming examples of multithreading giving improved performance over a single-threaded solution.

Ans. The two programming examples are as follows—

1. A web server that services each request in a separate thread.
2. A parallelized application such as matrix multiplication where different parts of the matrix may be worked on in parallel.
3. An interactive GUI program such as a debugger where a thread is used to monitor user input, another thread represents the running applications and a third thread monitors performance.

Q.6. Provide two programming examples of multithreading that would not improve performance over a single-threaded solution.

Ans. The two programming examples are as follows:—

1. Any kind of sequential program is not a good candidate to be threaded. **For example,** a program that calculates an individual tax return.
2. A "shell" program such as **C-shell or Korn shell.** Such a program must closely monitor its own working space such as open files, environment variables and current working directory.

Q.7. Describe the actions taken by—

(*a*) A Kernel to context switch between Kernel-level threads.

(*b*) A thread library to context switch between user-level threads.

Ans. (*a*) Context switching between kernel threads typically requires saving the value of the CPU registers from the thread being switched out and restoring the CPU registers of the new threads being scheduled.

(*b*) Context switching between user threads is quite similar to switching between kernel threads, althrough it is dependent on the threads library and how it maps user threads to kernel threads. In general, the context switching between user threads involves taking a user thread and replacing it with another thread. This act typically involves saving and restoring the state of the registers.

Q.8. What resources are used when a thread is created? How do they differ from those used when a process is created?

Ans. Thread creation typically uses fewer resources than process creation because a thread is smaller than a process. A process creation requires allocating a process control block (PCB), a rather large data structure. The PCB includes a memory map, list of open files and environment variables. Allocating and managing the memory map is typically the most time-consuming activity. Creating either a user or kernel thread involves allocating a small data structure to hold a register set, stack and priority.

Q.9. What services are to be provided by an OS for IPC?

Ans. There are two main services to be provided by OS for IPC and are as follows—

1. **Buffering:** The O.S. will buffer the messages in transit. So, it will create some buffers in the Systems Address Space.
2. **Synchronization of the sender and receiver process:**

   An O.S. will perform the following services for providing synchronization between the sender and the receiver—

   (*a*) The receiver process will be blocked, if it executes a **"receive"** call, when no message is pending delivery. The receiver process will be resumed on delivery of next message by the intended sender process.

   (*b*) The sender process will be blocked, if it executes a **"send"** call, when the allocated buffers are full, so pending delivery to the receiver. When the receiver process executes next "receive" call, it resmes the sender process.

Q.10. What are the three multithreading models? Give their main features.

Ans. There are three types of multithreading models. They are as follows—

I. Many-to-one model

The main features of this model are—

(*a*) Many user threads are mapped to one kernel thread.

(*b*) The entire process would block if a thread makes a blocking system call.

(*c*) Multiple threads are unable to run in parallel on multiprocessors.

II. One-to-one model

The main features are as follows—

(*a*) Each user thread is mapped to one kernel.

(*b*) It allows for parallel processing and does not fail if one thread blocks.

(*c*) Limits number of threads because the kernel threads are expensive.

III. Many-to-many model

The main features are as follows—

(*a*) Many user threads are mapped to the same or smaller number of kernel threads.

(*b*) Kernel threads can run in parallel and if one blocks, the kernel can schedule another for execution.

EXERCISE QUESTIONS

Q.1. Describe the actions taken by a Kernel to context switch among processes?

Q.2. (*a*) Suggest a method that ensures that the ready list of processes never become empty?

(*b*) Describe two uses of a Null process?

Q.3. (*a*) Define the term Process. Explain the different states of a process. List atleast six components of a Process Control Block.

(*b*) Define the term thread. Explain atleast three benefits of Multithreaded programming.

Q.4. Why is it expensive to switch between processes ? It is less expensive to switch between threads? Justify your answer.

Q.5. (*a*) What is a process? Explain different states of a process with the help of state diagram.

(*b*) What do you understand by concurrent processes? Show that O.S. works as a resource manager.

(*c*) Briefly describe the O.S. tasks involved in context switch.

Q.6. (*a*) Name four conditions which lead to the OS, terminating a process before the process has completed its computation.

(*b*) It is necessary for a Process Control Block (PCB) to be updated during the time that the running process has access to the CPU? Can a process execution priority be changed while it is running? Give reasons for your answer.

Q.7. How is the "process' defined in UNIX? How does the parent process control the child process in UNIX? Describe PCB with the help of a diagram.

[**Hint :** In UNIX O.S., a process is created by the "*fork*" system call and terminated by exit. When UNIX O.S., gets started, a special process "*init*" starts running. Then it creates (forks) one process per terminal. These processes wait for user to login. If login is correctly fed in, the login process executes a shall process to accept command. These commands may further create new processes and so on. Thus, all the processes in the system belong to a single tree with "*init*" at the root.]

Q.8. Describe the action taken by a thread library to context switch between user-level threads.

Q.9. Write short note on — 'Process Control Block'

Q.10. Explain the structure of a PCB and its significance when CPU switches from one user to another.

Q.11. What do you understand by Process? Explain various states of a process with suitable diagrams. Explain PCB.

Q.12. (*a*) Draw a state diagram of a process and label various transition. Explain the need of process suspension.

(*b*) Differentiate between used thread and kernel thread. What is thread cancellation. Explain its type.

(*c*) Explain various thread models with their relative advantages and disadvantages.

Q.13. What is PCB?

Q.14. What is a process? Describe the 7 states model for process.

CHAPTER 5

CPU Scheduling

5.0 INTRODUCTION

Scheduling refers to the set of policies and mechanisms that an OS supports for determining the order of execution of the pending jobs and processes. A **scheduler** is an operating system program (module) that selects the next job to be admitted for execution. **Please note that the main objective of scheduling is to increase CPU utilization and to increase the throughput. Throughput** means the amount of work accomplished in a given time interval. So, scheduling provides a priority mechanism for the process execution. It stream-lines the operation of processes. It optimizes the utilization of system resources. **Also note that the behavior of a process plays a key role in CPU Scheduling.** This is depicted by *CPU – I/O* **burst cycle**. A process will normally run for a while (known as a CPU burst), perform some I/O, (**known as I/O burst**) then run for a while more (the next **CPU burst**) and so on. The duration of interval between the CPU burst and I/O burst depends upon the following:

(*a*) **If the process is I/O bound:**

A process is I/O bound process if it performs lot of I/O operations as compared to other computation operations. Each I/O operation is followed by a short CPU burst to process the I/O. Thus, more I/O happens.

(*b*) **If the process is CPU bound:**

A process is CPU bound if it performs lot of computation and has very less I/O operations to do. There will be long CPU bursts with I/O bursts of very short duration.

Consider the process in Figure 5.1 below.

Load Store Add Store Read from file	CPU burst
Wait for I/O	I/O burst
Index Write to file	CPU burst
Wait for I/O	I/O burst
Load Store Add Store Read from file	CPU burst
• • •	

Fig 5.1 CPU – I/O burst cycle

As shown in Fig. 5.1, the process execution consists of a **cycle** of CPU execution and I/O wait. A process alternates between these two states. Process execution begins with **CPU burst** followed by an **I/O burst**, the last CPU burst will end with a system request to terminate the execution. The duration of each burst depends upon process to process.

5.1 SCHEDULERS

A Scheduler is an operating system program (module) that selects the next job to be admitted for execution. The OS has many schedulers but we shall discuss the three main types of schedulers next.

5.1.1 Long-term Scheduler

It is responsible for selecting the processes from secondary storage device like a disk and loads them into main memory for execution. It is also known as a **job scheduler**. The primary objective of a long-term scheduler is to provide a balanced mix of jobs. When the processor utilization is low then the scheduler admits more jobs to increase the number of processes in a ready queue. Similarly, when the utilization factor is very high then the long-term scheduler may reduce the rate of batch jobs.

Please note that it is known as a "long-term" scheduler because the time for which the scheduling is valid is long. That is, it executes less frequently as it takes from minutes to hours for the creation of new processes in the system. It's job is to ensure that there are always a fixed number of ready processes in the memory of the system. **Please note that if the average rate of number of processes arriving in memory is equal to that of departuring the system then the long-term scheduler may need to be invoked only when a process departs the system.** Because of the longer time taken by CPU during execution, the long-term scheduler can afford to take more time to decide which process should be selected for execution. **Also note that a long-term scheduler should take a careful selection of processes** *i.e.*, processes should be the combination of CPU and I/O bound types. This is because—

(*a*) **If all processes are I/O bound,** the ready queue will always be empty and

(*b*) **If all processes are CPU bound,** then no process will be waiting for I/O operation and again the system will be unbalanced.

Therefore, a long-term scheduler provides a good performance by selecting the combination of CPU bound and I/O bound processes.

Let us see this diagramatically.

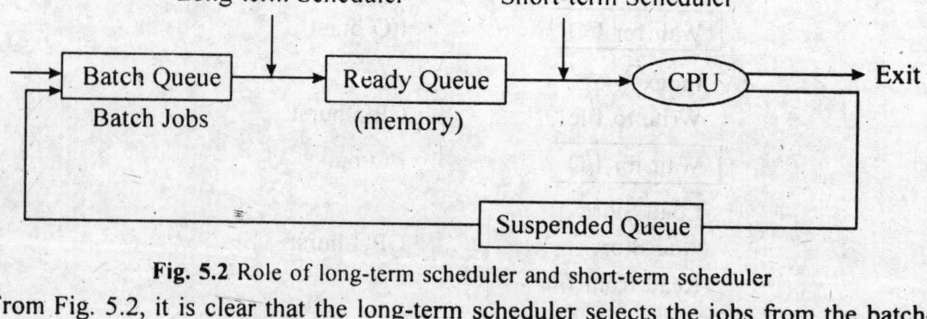

Fig. 5.2 Role of long-term scheduler and short-term scheduler

From Fig. 5.2, it is clear that the long-term scheduler selects the jobs from the batch-queue and loads them into memory. In memory these processes belong to a ready queue.

5.1.2 Short-term Scheduler

It allocates processes belonging to ready queue to CPU for immediate processing. Its main objective is to maximize CPU utilization. This scheduler has to work more frequently. It must select a new process for execution quite often because a CPU executes a process only for few millisecond before it goes for I/O operation. **Please note that a short-term scheduler executes atleast once every 10 millisecond.** If it takes 1 millisecond to decide to execute a process for 10 millisecond, then

$$\frac{1}{(10+1)} = \frac{1}{11} = 9\% \text{ of the CPU}$$

is being wasted simply for scheduling the work. Therefore, it must be very fast.

The process of assigning the CPU to a process is also called **Process Dispatching. A program responsible for assigning the CPU to the process that has been selected by the short-term scheduler is known as a dispatcher.** Assigning the CPU to a ready process involves three major steps:—

Step 1 : Context Switching

It implies the switching of CPU from one process to another. Switching the CPU to another process requires saving the state of the old process and loading the saved state for the new process. This task is performed by O.S. and is known as **Context switching.** The context of a process is represented in the PCB of a process. It includes the value of the CPU registers, the process state and memory management information. When a context switch occurs, the Kernel saves the context of the old process in its PCB and loads the saved context of the new process scheduled to run. **Please note that the context-switch time is a pure overhead because the system is not doing any useful work while switching.** The speed of this context-switching varies from machine to machine and it depends on the following factors—

(*a*) The speed of memory.

(*b*) The number of registers that must be copied.

(*c*) The existence of some special instructions.

Also note that the typical speeds range from 1 to 1000 microseconds.

For example: In Sun's UltraSPARC processor, the context-switch times are hardware dependent. It provides multiple sets of registers. Herein, a context switch simply includes changing the pointer to the current register set. **Please note that if active processes exceed register sets, the system resorts to copying register data to and from memory. Also note here that the more complex the operating system, the more work must be done during a context switch.** So, context switching is time consuming and thus an effort should be made to minimize the context switch time. It has become such a bottleneck that the programmers are using new structures (threads) to avoid it whenever possible.

Step 2 : Switching from monitor-mode to the user mode

As we know that our system works in two modes — a monitor mode and a user mode. A user process must be run in user mode; so changing of these modes is obvious.

Step 3 : Restart the execution of process

The execution of a process should be restarted by jumping to the instructions that was supposed to be executed when this process was last interrupted. **The time it takes by the dispatcher to stop one process and start another (running) is known as dispatch latency.** The degree of multiprogramming depends on the dispatch latency. **Please note here that if the dispatch latency increases then the degree of multiprogramming decreases. Also note that the overall time taken by the dispatcher is the sum of time consumed in all these operations.**

5.1.3 Medium term scheduler

Many a times, we need to remove a process from the main memory as this process may be in need of some I/O operation. So, such processes may be removed (or suspended) from the main memory to the hard disk. Later on, these processes can be reloaded into memory and continued from where it was left earlier. This saving of the suspended process is said to be swapped-out or rolled-out. And this swapping (in and out) is done by the medium-term scheduler. This is shown in Figure 5.3.

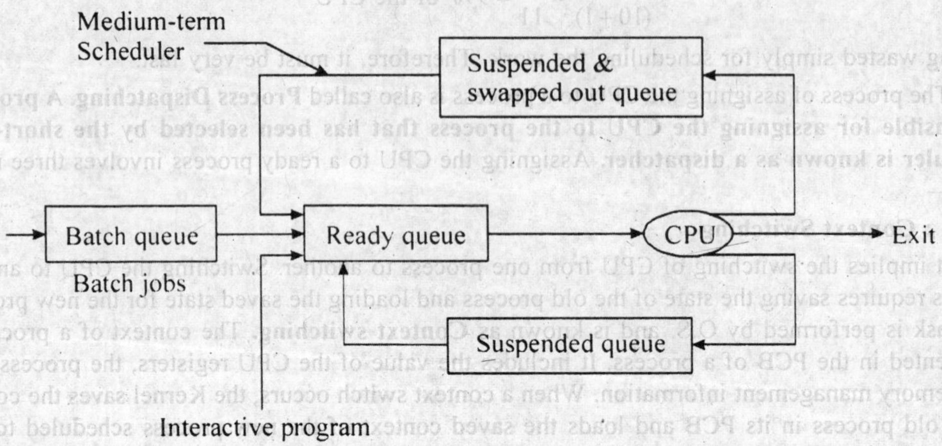

Fig. 5.3 Role of medium-term scheduler

Please note that the medium-term scheduler has nothing to do with the suspended processes. The moment the suspending condition is fulfilled, the medium term scheduler gets activated to allocate the memory and swap-in the process. For proper functioning, this scheduler must be provided with the information about the memory requirement of swapped-out processes which is usually recorded at the time of swapping.

Note: All versions of windows O.S. use swapping.

5.2 SCHEDULING CRITERIA

A Scheduler algorithm is evaluated against some widely accepted performance criteria. We need to consider the following five criteria—

1. CPU utilization.
2. Throughput.
3. Turn around time (TAT).
4. Waiting time (WT).
5. Response time (RT).

We shall now explain these criteria one by one.

1. **CPU utilization: It is defined as the average fraction of time during which CPU is busy, executing either user programs or system modules. The key idea is** that if the CPU is busy all the time then the utilization factor of all the components of the system will also be high. ***Please note that the higher is the CPU utilization, better it is.***
2. **Throughput: It is defined as the average amount of work completed per unit time.** One way to measure throughput is by means of the number of processes that are completed in a unit of time. **Please note here that the higher is the number of processes, the more work is apparently being done by the system. Also note that the higher is the throughput, better it is.** But this approach is not very useful for comparison because this is dependent on

the characteristics and the resource requirements of the process being executed. Thus, to compare the throughput of several scheduling algorithms it should feed the process with similar requirements.

3. **Turn around time (TAT): It is defined as the total time elapsed from the time the job is submitted (or process is created) to the time the job (or process) is completed.** It is the sum of periods spent waiting to get into memory, waiting in the ready queue, CPU time and I/O operations. So, we can write that—

   Turn arount time (TAT) = (Process finish time – Process arrival time) ...(1)

   Also, note that the lower is the average turnaround time, better it is.

4. **Waiting time (WT): It is defined as the total time spent by the job (or process) while waiting in suspended state or ready state, in a multiprogramming environment.** So, it may be given by a formula—

   Waiting time (WT) = (Turn around time – Processing time) ...(2)

   Please note here that the lower is the average waiting time, better it is.

5. **Response time (RT):** This parameter is usually considered for two systems — **time sharing and real-time operating system.** However, its characteristics differ in these two systems. **In time sharing system** it may be defined as the interval from the time the last character of a command line of a program or transaction is entered to the time the last result appears on the terminal.

   In real-time systems, it may be defined as the interval from the time an internal or external event is signaled to the time the first instruction of the respective interrupt service routine (ISR) is executed.

Note: Designing schedulers and selecting a set of its performance criterion, conflict with each other. For instance, the fastest response time in time sharing and real time system may result in low CPU utilization. Throughput and CPU utilization may be increased by executing the large number of processes, but then the response time may suffer. Hence, the design of a scheduler usually requires balance of all different requirements and constraints.

5.3 CPU SCHEDULING ALGORITHMS

CPU scheduling deals with the problem of deciding which of the processes in the ready queue be allocated to the CPU. Basically, there are two types of scheduling algorithms—

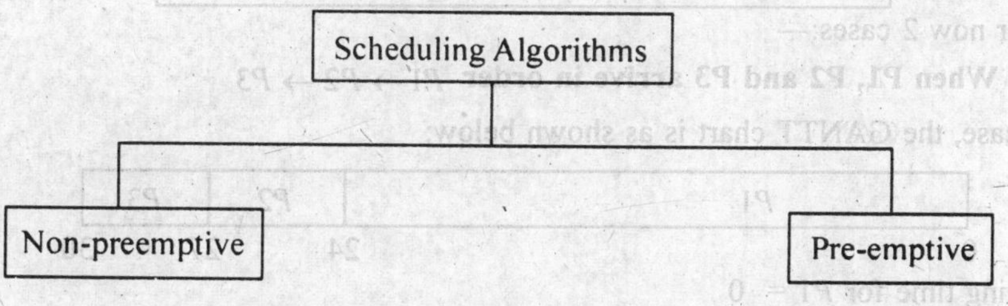

Fig. 5.4 Types of Scheduling algorithms

Which algorithm to select?

It depends on the environment and the type of application that will be supported by a given operating system. We will now discuss some CPU scheduling algorithms.

Let us compare the two in a tabular form.

Non-preemptive Scheduling	Pre-emptive Scheduling
1. In non-preemptive scheduling, if once a process has been allocated CPU then the CPU cannot be taken away from that process.	1. In pre-emptive scheduling, the CPU can be taken away before the completion of the process.
2. No preference is given when a higher priority job comes.	2. It is useful when a higher priority job comes as here the CPU can be snatched from a lower priority process.
3. The treatment of all processes is fairer.	3. The treatment of all processes is not fairer as CPU snatching is done either due to time constraints or due to a higher priority process request for its execution.
4. It is a cheaper scheduling method. **For example:** First-Come First-Served (FCFS) CPU scheduling algorithm is non-preemptive.	4. It is a costlier scheduling method. **For example:** Round-Robin (RR) CPU scheduling algorithm is preemptive.

5.3.1 First-Come, First-Served Scheduling (FCFS)

It is the simplest of all the scheduling algorithms. **The basic principle of this algorithm is to allocate the CPU in the order in which the processes arrive.** It's implementation involves a ready queue that works in First-in First-out order. When the CPU is free, it is assigned to a process which is in front of the ready queue. Once this process goes into a running state, its PCB is removed from the queue. A FCFS CPU scheduling algorithm is **non-preemptive** because the CPU has been allocated to a process that keeps the CPU busy until it is released. This usually results in poor performance. It is because of this non-preemption only that the component utilization rate is low and the system throughout is less. Also note here that the shorter jobs may suffer considerable turnaround delays and waiting times when CPU has been allocated to longer jobs.

For example: Consider the following set of processes — P1, P2 and P3 that arrive at time 0. That is,

Process	CPU Burst Time (ms)
$P1$	24
$P2$	3
$P3$	3

Consider now 2 cases:—

Case 1: When P1, P2 and P3 arrive in order $P1 \rightarrow P2 \rightarrow P3$

In this case, the GANTT chart is as shown below:

$P1$	$P2$	$P3$
0 – 24	24 – 27	27 – 30

$\therefore$ Waiting time for $P1$ = 0

Waiting tim^ for $P2$ = 24

Waiting time for $P3$ = 27

$$\therefore \text{Average Waiting Time (AWT)} = \frac{(0+24+27)}{3} = \mathbf{17\ ms}$$

and Average Turnaround Time (ATAT) = (24 + 27 + 30)/3 = **27 ms**

Case 2: When P1, P2 and P3 arrive in order $P2 \rightarrow P3 \rightarrow P1$.

In this case, the GANTT chart is as shown below:

P2	*P3*	*P1*
0 3	6	30

Waiting time for $P1$ = 6

Waiting time for P_2 = 0

Waiting time for P_3 = 3

Average waiting time (AWT) = (6 + 0 + 3)/3 = **3 ms**

Please note that in case-1 above, AWT = 17 ms **whereas in case-2,** AWT = 3 ms *only.* **So, case-2 is much better than case-1. This is because in case-1, the small processes (P_2 and P_3) had to wait longer for bigger processes to release the CPU. This effect is known as Convoy Effect.** This effect results in lower CPU utilization. Now, in case-2,

ATAT = (3 + 6 + 30)/3 = **13 ms**

whereas in case-1, ATAT = **27 ms**

So, in case-2, turnaround time also gets better.

The average waiting time under FCFS policy is generally not minimal. Under this scheme, the process that requests the CPU first is allocated the CPU first. When the process enters the ready queue, its Process Control Block (PCB) is linked which keeps the track of all the processes running and waiting. So, the average waiting time under the FCFS policy is very long.

Advantages of FCFS algorithm—

1. It is a simple algorithm and easy to implement.
2. It is suitable for Batch systems.

Disadvantages of FCFS algorithm—

1. The average waiting time is not minimal. (This has been explained above)
2. It is not suitable for time sharing systems like UNIX because in UNIX, each user should get the CPU for an equal amount of time interval and this algorithm does not follow this principle.
3. A proper mix of CPU bound and I/O bound jobs is required to achieve good results from FCFS scheduling.

We are in a position to solve some problems now.

Example 1. Consider the following Processes, *P1*, *P2* and *P3* with their CPU burst-time as shown below—

Process	CPU Burst Time (ms)
P1	10
P2	5
P3	5

Calculate the avearage waiting time if the processes arrive in order *P1* → *P2* → *P3* and that if they arrive in order *P2* → *P3* → *P1*.

Ans. If the processes arrive in order $P1 \rightarrow P2 \rightarrow P3$ then the GANTT chart is as shown below:

P1	*P2*	*P3*
0	10 15	20

$\therefore$ Waiting time for $P1$ = 0 ms

Waiting time for $P2$ = 10 ms

Waiting time for $P3$ = 15 ms

$\therefore$ Average Waiting Time (AWT) = (0 + 10 + 15)/3 = 25/3 = **8.33 ms**

But if the processes arrive in order $P2 \rightarrow P3 \rightarrow P1$ then the GANTT chart is as follows—

P2	P3	P1
0	5	10 20

$\therefore$ Waiting time for $P1$ = 0 ms

Waiting time for $P2$ = 5 ms

Waiting time for $P3$ = 10 ms

$\therefore$ Average Waiting Time (AWT) = $\frac{0+5+10}{3} = \frac{15}{3} = \mathbf{5\,ms}$

Thus, we can say that AWT will always depend upon the order in which processes arrive.

Note: CPU-burst time indicates that for how much time, the process needs the CPU. It is also called as **Run Time (RT) or Execution Time (ET).**

Example 2. Consider the following set of processes – *P*0, *P*1, *P*2 and *P*3. Their arrival time (in milliseconds) and their next burst times (in milliseconds) are also given. Find out—

(*a*) Average Turnaround Time (ATAT)

(*b*) Average Waiting Time (AWT)

(*c*) Waited TAT (WTAT)

(*d*) Average WTAT (AWTAT)

Process	Arrival Time (ms)	Next Burst (ms)
***P*0**	**0**	**10**
***P*1**	**1**	**6**
***P*2**	**3**	**2**
***P*3**	**5**	**4**

Ans. We draw its GANTT chart first.

P0	P1	P2	P3
0	10	16	18 22

This is because the arrival time is 0 (zero). So, we start with 0. The next burst is at 10 ms. The next burst is at (10 + 6) = 16 ms. Similarly, from column – 3, we get the next burst is at (16 + 2) = 18 ms. Final burst is at (18 + 4) = 22 ms. So, we get the GANTT chart above.

To compute it's WT, AWT, TAT, ATAT, WTAT & AWTAT, we draw another table—

Process	Arrival time (t_0)	Next burst (Δt)	Finish Time (T_1)	TAT ($= T_1 - t_0$)	WT = TAT – Δt
*P*0	0	10	10	10	0
*P*1	1	6	16	15	9
*P*2	3	2	18	15	13
*P*3	5	4	22	17	13

(*a*) $\therefore$ ATAT = (10 + 15 + 15 + 17)/4 = 57/4 = **14.25 ms** (*b*) $\therefore$ AWT = (0 + 9 + 13 + 13)/4 = 35/4 = **8.75 ms**

(*c*) $\therefore$ $\boxed{\text{WTAT}_i = \dfrac{\text{TAT}_i}{\text{RT}_i}}$ where $i \leftarrow 1$ to n (processes)

Now, from table above we know that TATs are 10, 15, 15, 17 for P_0 to P_3 respectively. What are their RT or ET or BT?

Now, RT = ET = BT = $T_1 = \Delta t$

$\therefore$ $RT_1 = T_1 - \Delta t = 10 - 10 = 0$

$RT_2 = T_2 - \Delta t = 16 - 6 = 10$

$RT_3 = T_3 - \Delta t = 18 - 2 = 16$

$RT_4 = T_4 - \Delta t = 22 - 4 = 18$

$$\therefore \text{WTAT}_i = \frac{10+15+15+17}{0+10+16+18} = \frac{57}{44} = \mathbf{1.295\,ms}$$

(*d*) $\because$ $$\text{AWTAT} = \frac{\text{WTAT}_i}{n} \qquad (i \leftarrow 1 \text{ to } n)$$

$$= \frac{10+15+15+17}{4} = \frac{57}{4} = \mathbf{14.25}\,\text{ms}$$

5.3.2 Shortest Job First Scheduling (SJF)

The basic principle of this algorithm is to allocate the CPU to the process with least CPU-burst time. The processes are available in the ready queue. CPU is always assigned to the process with least CPU burst time requirement. **Please note here that if the two processes have same CPU burst time then FCFS is used to break the tie.** This algorithm can be either preemptive or non-preemptive.

In SJF scheduling algorithm, the scheduling is done as follows. Consider a set of four processes — *P*1, *P*2, *P*3 and *P*4.

Process	CPU time
*P*1	5
*P*2	10
*P*3	8
*P*4	3

Since the process with smallest CPU burst time is executed first. So, these processes would be scheduled in $P4 \rightarrow P1 \rightarrow P3 \rightarrow P2$ order. So, Average Waiting Time, AWT

= (0 + 3 + 8 + 16)/4 = 27/4 = 6.75 ms

Whereas in FCFS scheduling algorithm,

AWT = (0 + 5 + 15 + 23)/4 = 43/4 = **10.75 ms**

SJF may be non-preemptive or preemptive SJF algorithm.

Case 1: Non-preemptive SJF

Consider four processes — *P*1, *P*2, *P*3 and *P*4 with their CPU burst-times given below—

Process	CPU time
*P*1	6
*P*2	8
*P*3	7
*P*4	3

Next we draw it's GANTT chart—

*P*4	*P*1	*P*3	*P*2

0 3 9 16 24

$\therefore$ Average Waiting Time (AWT) = (0 + 3 + 9 + 16)/4 = 7 ms

& Average Turnaround Time (ATAT) = (3 + 9 + 16 + 24)/4 = 13 ms

Case 2: Preemptive SJF (or Shortest-Remaining-Time-First)

Consider a set of four processes – *P*1, *P*2, *P*3 and *P*4 with their CPU burst times.

Process	Arrival Time	Burst Time
*P*1	0	8
*P*2	1	4
*P*3	2	9
*P*4	3	5

So, we draw it's GANTT chart now—

*P*1	*P*2	*P*4	*P*1	*P*3

0 1 5 10 17

When process, *P*2 arrives, the remaining time for *P*1 (*i.e.*, 7 ms) is larger than the time required for *P*2 (4 ms), so process, *P*1 is preempted and *P*2 is executed.

$$\therefore \text{AWT} = \frac{((10-1)+(1-1)+(17-2)+(5-3))}{4}$$

$$= \frac{9+0+15+2}{4} = \frac{26}{4} = \mathbf{6.5 ms}$$

In either case-1 or case-2 above, whenever the SJF scheduler is invoked, it searches the ready queue to find the job or the process with the shortest execution time. The difference between the two (preemptive and non-preemptive) SJF scheduler lies in the condition that lead to invocation of the scheduler and consequently the frequency of its execution.

We state two theorems now and give it's proof also.

Theorem 1. "Shortest Job First algorithm is optimal and gives minimum average waiting time."

Proof: Contradiction Method

Suppose SJF does not minimize the total waiting time.

That is, let $\alpha = J_1, J_2, J_3, J_4 \ldots J_n$ be the sequence that minimize the waiting time.

Let $\alpha' = J_1, J_2, \ldots J_{i-1}, J_j, J_{i+1}, \ldots J_{j-1}, J_i, J_{j+1} \ldots J_n$

i.e., α' is obtained from α by interchanging J_i & J_j.

$$W(\alpha) = \sum_{k=1}^{n-1} (n-k)t_k$$

$$= \sum_{\substack{k \neq i \\ k \neq j}}^{n-1} (n-k)t_k + (n-i)t_i + (n-j)t_j \qquad \ldots(1)$$

$$\text{So, } W(\alpha') = \sum_{\substack{k \neq i \\ k \neq j}}^{n-1} (n-k)t_k + (n-i)t_j + (n-j)t_i \qquad \ldots(2)$$

Subtracting equation 1 from equation 2 we get:

$$W(\alpha') - W(\alpha) = (n-i)[t_j - t_i] + (n-j)[t_i - t_j]$$

$$= -[t_i - t_j](n-i) + (n-j)[t_i - t_j]$$

$$= [t_i - t_j][-\cancel{n} + i + \cancel{n} - j]$$

$$= (i-j)(t_i - t_j) < 0$$

$\Rightarrow \quad W(\alpha') - W(\alpha) < 0$

$\Rightarrow \quad W(\alpha') < W(\alpha)$

$\Rightarrow \quad \alpha'$ is better minimum waiting time than α. α is an optimal solution waiting time.

Hence, SJF holds.

SJF is an optimal scheduling algorithm in terms of minimizing the average waiting time of a given set of processes.

SJF algorithm works optimally only when the exact future execution times of jobs or processes are known at the time of scheduling. **Please note that in case of short-term scheduling and pre-emption, more detailed knowledge of each individual CPU burst is required.**

In other words, the optimal performance of SJF scheduling is dependent upon future knowledge of the process/job behavior. We state another theorem now and give its proof.

Theorem 2. "The value of the next CPU burst can be predicted by using the Exponential Average of the previous measured values of CPU bursts."

Proof: We assume that the next CPU burst of a process will be similar to the previous ones.

Let τ_n be the length of the nth CPU burst.

t_n be the measured value of nth CPU burst.

Then, the predicted value of the next CPU burst, τ_{n+1} is given by—

$$\boxed{\tau_{n+1} = \alpha t_n + (1-\alpha)t_n}$$

This is a formula for the exponential average.

Where t_n = Most Recent Information

τ_n = Past History

α = Relative weights of recent and past history.

For $\alpha = 0$; $\tau_{n+1} = \tau_n$

& For $\alpha = 1$; $\tau_{n+1} = \tau_n$

However, the most common situation is $\alpha = \frac{1}{2}$. So recent and past history are equally weighted.

So, the new formula is—

$$\tau_{n+1} = \alpha t_n + (1-\alpha)\alpha t_{n-1} + \ldots + (1-\alpha)^j \alpha t_{n-j} + \ldots$$

Since, $\alpha << 1$ $[\because 0 < \alpha < 1]$

$$\therefore \boxed{\tau_{n+1} = \alpha t_n + (1-\alpha)\alpha t_{n-1}}$$

Note that $\alpha = 1$ means more weightage is assigned to the nearest history. And if $\alpha = 0$ then it implies that more weightage is assigned to distant history.

Actually, estimating future process behavior is not easy. This problem can be overcome by sorting the ready list of processes according to the increasing values of their remaining execution times. This will improve the Scheduler's performance.

Advantage of SJF Scheduling

Since this algorithm gives minimum average waiting time so it is an optimal algorithm.

Disadvantages of SJF Scheduling

1. It is difficult to know the length of next CPU burst time.
2. It cannot be implemented at the level of short-term CPU scheduling.
3. Big jobs are waiting for CPU. This results in **aging** problem.

We are in a position to solve some problems now.

Example 1. Consider the following set of processes having their CPU-burst time (in milliseconds) and having arrived almost at the same time.

Process	CPU Burst (ms)
*P*1	10
*P*2	5
*P*3	5

Find the average waiting time using—

(*a*) Non-preemptive SJF Scheduling.

(*b*) Preemptive SJF Scheduling.

Solution: (*a*) **Non-preemptive SJF Scheduling:**

Firstly, we draw its GANTT chart.

*P*3	*P*2	*P*1

0 2 7 17

$$\therefore \text{Average Waiting Time} = \frac{0+2+7}{3} = \frac{9}{3} = \mathbf{3\,ms}$$

(*b*) **Preemptive SJF Scheduling**

Assume that processes arrive in order $P1 \rightarrow P2 \rightarrow P3$. Then, using preemption we get the following GANTT chart—

*P*1	*P*2	*P*3	*P*2	*P*1

0 1 2 4 8 17

Please note that here, CPU will be taken away from the currently executing process whenever a process with less CPU burst time arrives. This is in comparison to the time remaining for the current process. In our example, the time when *P*2-process arrives, *P*1 needs 9ms to finish.

As $P2$'s CPU burst is 5ms < 9ms, therefore, $P1$'s execution will be preempted and $P2$ will be executed. Similarly, as $P3$ arrives, $P2$'s execution needs 3 ms whereas $P3$ needs only 2ms to execute, thus $P3$ takes over $P2$ and so on. Hence, we compute as follows—

Waiting time for $P1 = 0 + (8 - 1) = 7$ ms

Waiting time for $P2 = 1 + (4 - 2) = 3$ ms

Waiting time for $P3 = 2$ ms

$$\therefore \text{ Average Waiting Time (AWT)} = \frac{7+3+2}{3} = \frac{12}{3} = \mathbf{4\,ms}$$

Example 2. Consider the set of following processes, $P1 - P4$ as follows—

Process	Arrival Time	Burst Time
P1	**0**	**8**
P2	**1**	**4**
P3	**2**	**9**
P4	**3**	**5**

Find AWT using preemptive SJF algorithm?

Ans. If processes arrive in a ready queue according to their burst-time, then during the GANTT chart we get:

$P1$	$P2$	$P4$	$P1$	$P3$

0 1 5 10 17 26

Here, the process $P1$ started at time '0', since it is the only process in the queue. Process $P2$ arrives at time '1'. Note here that the remaining time for process $P1$ is larger than the time required by process $P2$. So, process $P1$ is preempted and process $P2$ is scheduled.

$$\therefore \text{ AWT} = \frac{[(10-1)+(1-1)+(17-2)+(5-3)]}{4}$$

$$= \frac{9+0+15+2}{4}$$

$$= \frac{11+15}{4} = \frac{26}{4} = \mathbf{6.5\,ms}$$

5.3.3 Shortest Remaining Time First (SRTF)

This algorithm is a preemptive scheduling algorithm. The short-term scheduler always chooses the process that has the shortest remaining processing time. When a new process joins the ready queue, the short-term scheduler compares the remaining time of executing process and new process. If the new process has the least CPU burst time, the scheduler selects that job and allocates CPU else it continues with the old process.

We are in a position to solve some problems now.

Example 1. Consider the set of processes, $P1$ to $P5$ with the following CPU-burst times—

Process	CPU burst time	Arrival Time
P1	**3**	**0**
P2	**6**	**2**
P3	**4**	**4**
P4	**5**	**6**
P5	**2**	**8**

Find average turn around time and relative delays?

Ans. We draw its' GANTT chart first—

$P1$	$P2$	$P3$	$P5$	$P2$	$P4$

0 3 4 8 10 15 20

As we know that process $P1$ arrives at time = 0 ms. So, $P1$ executes first. Now, $P2$ arrives at time 2 ms. So, $P1$'s remaining time is = 3 – 2 = 1 ms

And $P2$'s time is 6 ms

$\therefore$ 1 < 6

So, we continue with process $P1$ only. After the completion of $P1$, $P2$ is executed. At time 4 ms, $P3$ arrives.

$\therefore$ $P2$'s remaining time = 6 – 1 = 5 ms

and Burst time of $P3$ = 4 ms

And 4 < 5. So, $P3$ executes.

Now, at time = 6 ms, $P4$ arrives. Then, we compare the remaining time for $P3$ *i.e.*, 4 – 2 = 2 ms and CPU burst time of $P4$ is 5. Now, 2 < 5, so $P3$ continues executing. After the completion of $P3$, the ready queue consists of $P5$, $P2$ and $P4$. Since $P5$ is the least out of the three, so $P5$ executes first, then $P2$ and then $P4$.

$\because$ Turnaround time = FT – AT

$\therefore$ Turnaround time for $P1$ = 3 – 0 = 3

Turnaround time for $P2$ = 15 – 2 = 13

Turnaround time for $P3$ = 8 – 4 = 4

Turnaround time for $P4$ = 20 – 6 = 14

Turnaround time for $P5$ = 10 – 8 = 2

$$\therefore \text{ATAT} = \frac{36}{5} = \mathbf{7.2\,ms}$$

$$\text{Now, Relative delay} = \frac{\text{turnaround time}}{\text{service time}}$$

$\therefore$ Relative delay for $P1 = 3/3 = 1.00$

Relative delay for $P2 = 13/6 = 2.17$

Relative delay for $P3 = 4/4 = 1.00$

Relative delay for $P4 = 14/5 = 2.80$

Relative delay for $P5 = 2/2 = 1.00$

$$\therefore \text{Average relative delay} = \frac{(1 + 2.17 + 1 + 2.80 + 1)}{5}$$

$$= 7.97/5 = \mathbf{1.59\ ms}$$

Example 2. Assume you have the following jobs to execute with one processor.

Jobs	Burst Time	Arrival Time
1	9	0
2	5	2
3	6	3
4	4	5
5	8	6

(i) **Give a GANTT chart illustrating the execution of these jobs using SRTF algorithm.**

(ii) **Calculate the average TAT and WT.**

Ans. (*i*) We draw its GANTT chart first

*J*1	*J*4	*J*2	*J*3	*J*5	*J*1
0	5	9	14	28	37

$$\therefore \quad \text{AWT} = \frac{(5-5)+(9-2)+(14-3)+(20-6)+(28-0)}{5}$$

$$= \frac{(0+7+11+14+28)}{5} = \frac{60}{5} = \mathbf{12ms}$$

(*ii*)

$$\text{ATAT} = \frac{(J1+J2+J3+J4+J5)}{5} = \frac{9+14+20+28+37}{5}$$

$$= \frac{108}{5} = \mathbf{2.6\ ms}$$

Example 3. Consider the following set of processes in table below and the following scheduling algorithm –

(a) **SJF**

(b) **Shortest Remaining Job First**

Process id	Arrival Time	Execution Time
A	0	7
B	1	5
C	2	3
D	6	2
E	12	3

If there is a tie within the processes, the tie is broken in favour of the oldest process.

(i) **Draw Gantt Chart and find AWT & TAT for the two algorithms. Comment on your results, which one is better and why?**

(ii) **If the scheduler takes 0.2 units of CPU time in context switching for the completed job and 0.1 unit of additional CPU time for incomplete jobs for saving their context. Calculate the percentage of CPU time wasted in each case.**

Ans. Given:

Process id	**Arrival Time**	**Execution Time**
A	0	7
B	1	5
C	2	3
D	6	2
E	12	3

(*i*) **SJF:** It's GANTT chart is–

D	C	E	B	A

0 2 5 8 13 20

$$\therefore \quad AWT = \frac{2+5+8+13}{5} = 5.4 \text{ Units}$$

$$But\ TAT = WT + RT$$

∴

Pid	*WT*	*RT*	*TAT*
A	13	7	20
B	8	5	13
C	2	3	5
D	0	2	2
E	5	3	8

(*ii*) This algorithm is nothing else but preemptive SJF scheduling.
Its GANTT chart is–

A	B	C		A	D	A		E	A	B

0 1 2 5 6 8 12 15 16 20

∴

Process-id	*WT*
A	0 + 5 + 8 + 15 = 28
B	16
C	0
D	0
E	0

$$\therefore \quad AWT = \frac{(28+16)}{5} = 8.8 \text{ Units}$$

$$\therefore \quad TAT = WT + RT$$

∴

Pid	*WT*	*RT*	*TAT*
A	28	7	35
B	16	5	21
C	0	3	2
D	0	2	2
E	0	3	3

∴ *AWT* of SJF = 5.4 units

& *AWT* of SRJF = 8.8 units

And that 5.4 < 8.8 (of SJF of SRJF)

Also, TAT for processes C, D, E is zero (0) in SRJF.

5.3.4 Round Robin (RR) Scheduling algorithm

This is one of the oldest, simplest and widely used algorithms. The basic principle of this algorithm is as follows:—

Principle—"If there are n-processes in a ready queue and the time quantum is 'q' time intervals, then each process gets '1/n' of the CPU time in the chunks of at most 'q' units of time. Each process will have to wait for (n – 1) × q time units until its next time quantum comes in."

This algorithm is similar to FCFS algorithm but not it is a preemptive FCFS scheduling. The round robin scheduling algorithm is primarily used in time-sharing and a multi-user system where the primary requirement is to provide reasonably good response times and in general to share the system fairly among all system users. The preemption takes place after a fixed interval of time called **time quantum or time slice.** The CPU time is divided into slices. Each process is allocated a small time slice (usually 10 – 100 milliseconds) while it executes.

Please note that no process can run for more than one time slice because some other processes are waiting in the ready queue. If the time quantum expires then process goes to the end of the ready queue to wait for the next allocation. **Also note that if the running process releases a control to O.S. due to some I/O, then another process is scheduled to run.**

RR scheduling utilizes the system resources uniformly. Small process may be executed in a single time-slice giving good response time whereas long processes may require several time slices and thus be forced to pass through ready queue a few times before completion.

The performance of this **pure preemptive algorithm** depends on many factors—

1. **Size of time quantum (*q*):**

   If q is large then this algorithm becomes same as FCFS algorithm and thus performance degrades. **If q is small,** then the number of context switches increases and *q* almost equals the time taken to switch the CPU from one process to another. This wastes 50% of overall time.

   So, *q* should not be very large and should not be very small also so as to achieve good system performance.

2. **Number of context switches:**

   The number of context switches should not be too many as it slows down the overall execution of all the processes. **Please remember that the time quantum (q) should be large with respect to the context switch time.** This is done to ensure that a process keeps CPU for a considerable amount of time as compared to the time spent in context switching.

   Let us understand this with an example.

   Consider the set of three processes – *P*1, *P*2 and *P*3 with their CPU Burst times as shown below—

Process	Burst Time
*P*1	24
*P*2	3
*P*3	3

Say processes arrive at time *O* and the time quantum is 4ms. Find the average waiting time (AWT)?

We draw its' GANTT chart first.

*P*1	*P*2	*P*3	*P*1	*P*1	*P*1	*P*1	*P*1

0 4 7 10 14 18 22 26 30

If q = 4ms (given to us), then *P*1 gets the first 4 units of time. Since it requires another 20 units of time, it is preempted after the first time slice and the CPU is given to next process, *P*2. Since *P*2 just needs 3 units of time, it terminates as the time-slice expires. The CPU is then given to the next process, *P*3. It also needs 3 time units and hence terminates as the time-slice expires. **Please note that once each process has received one time slice, the CPU is returned to P1 for an additional time–slice.** It remains with *P*1 only as *P*2 and *P*3 are already completed.

We are in a position to solve some problems now.

Example 1. Consider a set of three processes, $P1$, $P2$ and $P3$ with their CPU burst times in milliseconds—

Process	CPU burst-time
P1	**10**
P2	**5**
P3	**2**

Assume time quantum, $q = 2$ ms. Find Average Waiting Time (AWT)?

Ans. We draw it's GANTT chart first as $q = 2$ms,

$P1$	$P2$	$P3$	$P1$	$P2$	$P1$	$P2$	$P1$	$P1$

0 2 4 6 8 10 12 13 15 17

$\therefore$ Waiting time for $P1 = 0 + (6 - 2) + (10 - 8) + (13 - 12)$

$= 4 + 2 + 1 = \mathbf{7\ ms}$

Waiting time for $P2 = 2 + (8 - 4) + (12 - 10)$

$= 2 + 4 + 2 = \mathbf{8\ ms}$

Waiting time for $P3 = \mathbf{4\ ms}$

$$\therefore \text{ Average Waiting Time (AWT)} = \frac{(7+8+4)}{3} = \frac{19}{3} = \mathbf{6.33\,ms}$$

As shown in GANTT chart above, $P1$ gets the CPU for $q = 2$ms. Then, context switching occurs and $P2$ gets CPU for 2ms and then again context switching occurs and $P3$ gets CPU for 2ms. Now, $P3$ terminates. So, $P3$ need not be given CPU again. $P1$ and $P2$ continue to share the CPU until they complete.

Example 2. Consider another set of three processes as $P1$, $P2$ and $P3$ with their CPU burst times (in ms) as given below—

Process	CPU burst-time (ms)
P1	**30**
P2	**6**
P3	**8**

Assume that time quantum, $q = 5$ms. Find average waiting time (AWT), Average Turnaround Time (TAT) and Average Response Time (ART)?

Ans. Firstly, $P1$ gets a time quantum of 5ms. But $P1$ still needs 25ms for its execution. As q has expired so, CPU switches from $P1$ to $P2$. When time quantum (q) of $P2$ expires, the CPU switches to process, $P3$. When all finish then CPU switches to $P1$ again as it still needs 25 ms. So, we draw a GANTT chart now.

$P1$	$P2$	$P3$	$P1$	$P2$	$P3$	$P1$	$P1$	$P1$	$P1$

0 5 10 15 20 21 24 29 34 39 44

$\therefore$ Waiting time for $P1 = 0 + (15 - 5) + (24 - 4) = 14$

Waiting time for $P2 = 5 + (20 - 10) = 15$

Waiting time for $P3 = 10 + (21 - 5) = 16$

$$\therefore \text{ Average Waiting Time (AWT)} = \frac{(14+15+16)}{3} = \frac{45}{3} = 15$$

Also, Turn around time for $P1$ = 44

Turn around time for $P2$ = 21

Turn around time for $P3$ = 24

$$\therefore \text{ Average TAT} = \frac{44+21+24}{3} = \frac{89}{3} = \mathbf{29.66\,ms}$$

We can also compute the response time for all these processes.

Response time for $P1$ = 0 ms

Response time for $P2$ = 5 ms

Response time for $P3$ = 10 ms

∴ Average response time = (0 + 5 + 10) = **5 ms**

5.3.5 Priority Scheduling (Preemptive and Non-preemptive)

In this algorithm, each process is given a priority. The scheduler always picks up the highest priority process for its execution from the ready queue. **Please note that the equal priority processes are scheduled on FCFS basis.** These priorities are generally some fixed range of numbers from 0 to 4095. The level of priority may be determined on the basis of resource requirements, process characteristics and its run-time behavior. **The basic principle used here is that priority scheduling is a form of preemptive scheduling where priority is the basis of preemption.** This type of scheduling may be of two types—

(*a*) Preemptive

(*b*) Non-preemptive

We have already seen preemptive scheduling. Some systems implement **non-preemptive scheduling** also where a higher priority job is added to the front of the ready queue so that it can be executed next, but it cannot preempt the currently executing process.

To understand preemptive and non-preemptive scheduling, let us consider two examples.

(*a*) **Preemptive (Priority-based) algorithm example**

Consider a set of three processes $P1$, $P2$ and $P3$ with their priorities and arrival times as given below—

Process	Burst time	Priority	Arrival time
$P1$	10	3	0
$P2$	5	2	1
$P3$	2	1	2

Where 1 – highest priority.

3 – least priority.

Now, we draw it's GANTT chart—

$P1$	$P2$	$P3$	$P2$	$P1$

0 1 2 4 8 17

$$\therefore \text{ Average Waiting Time (AWT)} = \frac{0+(8-1)+1+(4-2)+2}{3}$$

$$= \frac{7+1+2+2}{3} = \frac{12}{3} = \mathbf{4\,ms}$$

So, here preemption is based on the priority when $P1$ executes, $P2$ arrives with priority = 2 which is higher than priority of 3 of $P1$ and thus, $P1$ is preempted. This goes on.

Problems with preemptive priority scheduling

A major problem with a priority-based scheduling is indefinite blocking of a low priority process by a high priority process. This is called as **starvation. In general, the completion of a process within finite time cannot be guaranteed with this scheduling algorithm.**

A solution to this problem is **aging. Aging is a technique of gradually increasing the priority of processes that wait in the system for a long time.** Thus, the older processes attain high priority and are ensured of completion in a finite time.

(*b*) **Non-preemptive (Priority-based) algorithm example**

Herein, a higher priority job cannot preempt a low priority job as there is no preemption involved here. Consider a set of four processes – *P*0, *P*1, *P*2 and *P*3. There arrival times and burst times are given next—

Process	AT (ms)	Next Burst (ms)	Priority
*P*0	0	10	5
*P*1	1	6	4
*P*2	3	2	2
*P*3	5	4	0

Where 0 – highest priority
3 – least priority

∴ It's GANTT chart is—

*P*0	*P*3	*P*2	*P*1

0 10 14 16 22

Now, for each of these processes, we compute the finish time and waiting times from above.

Process	A.T. (T_0)	Next burst (Δt)	F.T. (T_1)	TAT = $T_1 - T_0$	WT = TAT – Δt
*P*0	0	10	10	10	00
*P*1	1	6	22	21	15
*P*2	3	2	16	13	11
*P*3	5	4	14	09	05

$$\therefore \text{ Average TAT} = \frac{(10+21+13+9)}{4} = \frac{53}{4} = \mathbf{13.25\,ms}$$

$$\& \text{ Average WT} = \frac{(0+15+11+5)}{4} = \frac{31}{4} = \mathbf{7.75\,ms}$$

Note here that the average TAT and average WT obtained with this algorithm are much worse than previous algorithms. But, these parameters are not very significant here as our main focus is to give higher priorities to critical processes.

5.3.6 Highest Response Ratio Next (HRRN)

This algorithm works on the **principle that execute that job first which has the highest response ratio.** We define response ratio as the ratio between turnaround time and response time.

That is, Response ratio = (W + S) / S

where W – Time spent waiting for the processor.
S – Service time.

This response ratio is also named as **normalized turnaround time.**

5.3.7 Multilevel Queue Scheduling

When processes can be easily classified into different groups then Multilevel Queue Scheduling (MLQ) is applied. MLQ Scheduling processes are classified into different groups. For eg., interactive processes (foreground) and batch processes (background) are two types of processes because of their different response time requirements, scheduling needs and priorities. A MLQ scheduling algorithm partitions the ready queue into separate queues. Processes are permanently assigned to each queue. This is done based upon the properties such as memory size or process type. Each queue has its own scheduling algorithm. **For example,** the interactive queue might be using Round-Robin algorithm for scheduling while batch queue follows FCFS. Different types of queues are also shown in fig. 5.5 below.

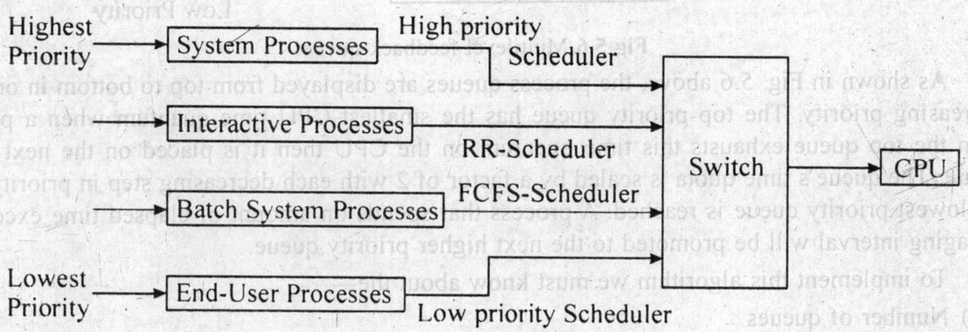

Fig. 5.5 Multiple queue scheduling

Now, there are different ways of managing queues.

Possibility I: We can assign a time slice to each queue which it can schedule among different processes in its queue. Interactive (or foreground) processes can be assigned 80% of CPU time whereas batch (or background) processes are given 20% of the CPU time.

Possibility II: We can execute the high priority queue first. It means that no process in the batch queue could run unless the queue for system processes and interactive processes were all empty. **Please note that if an interactive process entered the ready queue while a batch process is running, the batch process would be pre-empted.**

Advantages of MLQs—

The processes are permanently assigned to a queue when they enter the system. Since processes do not change their foreground or background nature, so there is **low scheduling overhead.**

Disadvantages of MLQs—

Starvation of processes for CPU occurs here as the processes are never allowed to change their queues (inflexibility) and that if one or the other higher priority queues never become empty.

5.3.8 Multilevel Feedback Queue Scheduling

It is an enhancement of multilevel queue scheduling. **The principle here is that processes can move between the queues now.** In this scheduling, the ready queue is partitioned into multiple queues of different priorities. The processes are assigned to the queues by the system based on their **CPU-burst characteristics**. This means that if a process consumes too much of a CPU time, it is placed into a lower priority queue. So, I/O-bound and interactive processes stay in the higher priority queues and CPU-bound processes move to the lower priority queues. However, these processes in lower priority queues should be promoted to the next higher priority queue after a suitable time interval. **This technique of moving lower priority processes to the next higher priority queue is known as aging.** This is shown in Fig. 5.6.

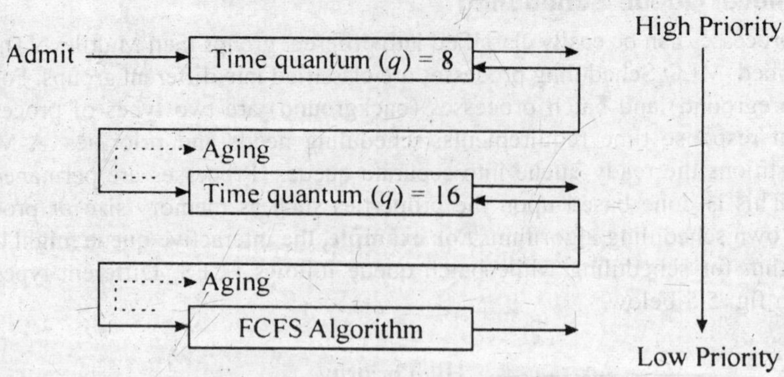

Fig 5.6 Multilevel feedback queues

As shown in Fig. 5.6 above, the process queues are displayed from top to bottom in order to decreasing priority. The top priority queue has the smallest CPU time quantum when a process from the top queue exhausts this time quantum on the CPU then it is placed on the next lower queue. The queue's time quota is scaled by a factor of 2 with each decreasing step in priority until the lowest priority queue is reached. A process that spends on amount of elapsed time exceeding the aging interval will be promoted to the next higher priority queue.

To implement this algorithm we must know about the—

(*a*) Number of queues
(*b*) Scheduling algorithm for each queue
(*c*) Method of moving a process to a higher priority queue
(*d*) Method of downgrading a process to a lower-priority queue
(*e*) Method of assigning a process to a queue initially

Advantages of MFQs—

1. It is a flexible scheduling algorithm as it allows the processes to move between the queues. So, I/O bound processes, do not have to wait long now.
2. Aging can be done. This form of aging prevents starvation.
3. It is the most general CPU scheduling algorithm and can be configured to match a specific system under design.

Disadvantages of MFQs—

1. It is a complex scheduling algorithm.
2. The best scheduler is required.
3. Moving the processes around the queues produces more CPU overheads.

5.4 MULTIPLE PROCESSOR SCHEDULING

We have already studied the CPU scheduling algorithms for single CPU systems. What if there are multiple (many) CPUs? Herein, the scheduling problem is more complex. If we consider **Homogeneous systems** *i.e.*, systems with identical processors then there are certain issues concerning multiprocessor scheduling. Some of these issues are given below—

(*a*) With identical processors, **load-sharing** can occur.
(*b*) With a separate queue for each processor, there could be a situation where one CPU could be idle with an empty queue while another processor is very busy.

To avoid this situation, we could use a **common ready queue.** All processes enter one queue and are scheduled onto any available processor. In such a scheme, one of the two scheduling approaches may be used:—

Case 1: Each processor is **self-scheduling.** Each processor executes after examining the ready queue and selects a process to be executed. **Please note that we have to take care so that no two processors should select the same process.**

Case 2: One processor is appointed as the scheduler for the other processors, thus creating a *master-slave structure*.

5.4.1 Static and Dynamic Scheduling

Static Scheduling requires prior knowledge of the program's behavior and resource requirements. It is an expensive procedure in terms of clock cycles. Because there were no general purpose O.S. for multiprocessors (super computers) so scheduling issues were resolved before run time only *i.e.*, during the program design phase. We use set theories, tasks graphs, mathematical proofs and other forms of numerical analysis to determine the optimum method of allocating processors and ordering events.

Dynamic Scheduling of tasks occur at the time of execution, so it seeks to minimize this overhead. Thus, dynamic scheduling differs from static scheduling in its objectives as well as its operations.

5.4.2 Dynamic Scheduling Goals

As we know that the primary focus of static scheduling is to minimize execution time while that of dynamic scheduling in a multiprocessor system is to—

(*a*) Minimize execution time.

(*b*) Minimize communication delays between processors.

(*c*) Maximize resource utilization.

Communication delays and resource utilization are primarily relevant in distributed systems. Most distributed systems are difficult to program due to the message passing that is required between processing elements (PEs). As a result, communication overhead can become a bottleneck.

Resource utilization becomes an issue in distributed heterogeneous systems where different processors may have sole access to specific hardware, software or data. The scheduler must keep track of all these resources and assign the tasks accordingly.

As we know that majority of multiprocessor systems are used for their high performance, fault tolerance (redundancy in case of failure) and scalability (increased performance with additional processors). **Please note here that each of these requires that the scheduler should maximize processor usage.**

And this is done through a procedure called **load balancing** where tasks are redistributed from heavily loaded to lightly loaded processors.

5.4.3 Performance Issues

In order for a multiprocessor system to run at all, a program must be divided into smaller steps that can run concurrently. Developing applications for multiprocessing computers require that a lot of thought be put into this process. **If the steps are small (fine grain tasks),** the overhead for CPU communication and O.S. intervention will severly degrade performance. However, **if the steps are large (coarse grain tasks),** parallelism is reduced. So, our goal is to find the right ratio for task granularity to maximize overall performance. As with static scheduling, there are many complex algorithms available to generate an ideal size of steps into which a process must be divided but the overhead of these operations makes it impractical for the O.S. to incorporate them.

5.4.4 Case Study on WINDOWS-NT

The simplest approach to dynamic scheduling balances the load across *n*-processors by running the **global scheduler** on an additional processor. The global scheduler dispatches tasks on a First-

In-First-Out (FIFO) basis to the other n-processors. Figure 5.6 shows a simple scheduler of WIN-NT.

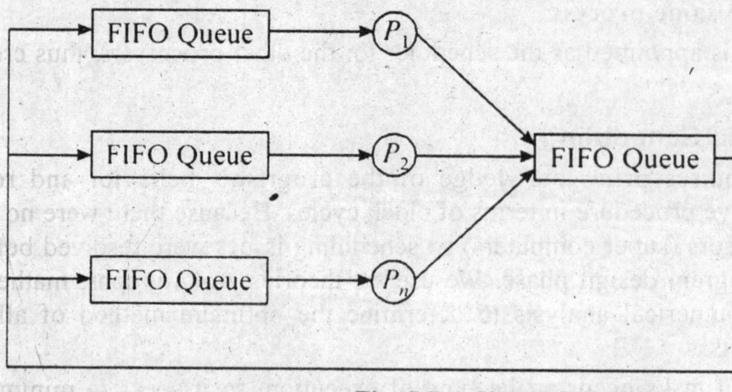

Fig. 5.7 A Simple Scheduler

As is clear from the above Figure 5.7, each of these processors maintains its own private waiting queue of tasks it has been assigned. When a task finishes execution, the processors $P1$, $P2$ and $P3$ gets the next one from the queue and runs it to completion. If a task needs the services of another task, it sends this request to the scheduler queue. The scheduler in turn uses FIFO principle to dispatch these requests to the processor with the currently shortest waiting queue, thereby balancing the load.

WIN-NT uses SMP version of this model to schedule threads on multiple processors. With this model approach, any thread can be assigned to any processor. Please note that scheduling threads on a computer with multiple processors is similar to scheduling threads on a computer with a single processor, however, the scheduler has a pool of available processors so it can schedule threads concurrently. In WIN-NT, the scheduling order is determined by thread priority.

5.5 REAL-TIME SCHEDULING

We have already studied in Chapter-1, regarding real-time systems and real-time O.S. Let us now discuss how processor scheduling is done in such systems.

Real-time systems may be hard or soft. Accordingly, the scheduling process will also differ. Like in hard real-time systems, its scheduler will have to ensure its completion within the prescribed time. On the other hand, in case of soft real-time systems, the scheduler can implement priority scheduling with real-time tasks having higher priority as compared to others.

5.5.1 Hard-Real Time Scheduling

Real-time scheduling is categorized as follows—

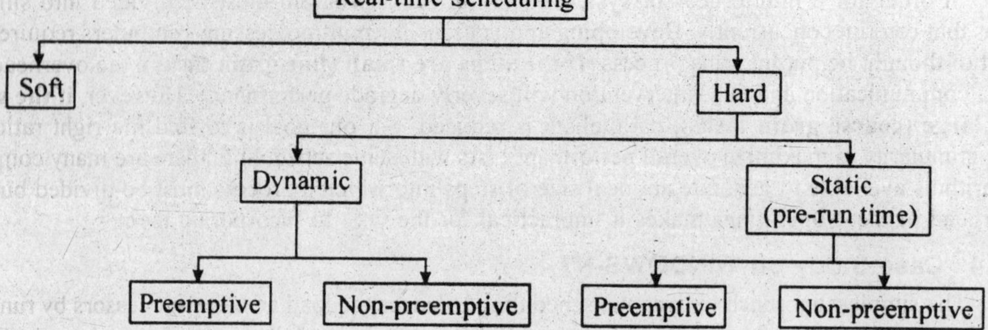

Fig. 5.8 Types of Real-Time Scheduling

A hard-real time system must execute a set of concurrent real-time task in such a way that all time-critical tasks meet their specified deadlines. Every task needs computational and data sources to complete the job. The scheduling problem is concerned with the allocation of the resources to satisfy the timing constraints.

So, hard real-time scheduling is put under two types — static and dynamic.

Static Scheduling: In this type of scheduling, the scheduling decisions are made at the compile time. A run-time schedule is generated off-line (statically) based on the prior knowledge of task-set parameters, e.g., maximum execution times, precedence constraints, mutual exclusion constraints and deadlines. So, run-time overhead is small.

Dynamic Scheduling: In this type of scheduling, the scheduling decisions are made at the run-time, selecting one out of the current set of ready tasks. **Please note that dynamic schedulers are flexible and adaptive. Also note that they can cause significant overheads because the time taken for scheduling adds to the time consumed in the run-time processing.**

This static and dynamic scheduling can be further classified as—either **preemptive or non-preemptive.**

In preemptive scheduling, the currently executing task will be preempted upon arrival of a higher priority task. **In non-preemptive scheduling,** the currently executing task will not be preempted until completion.

5.5.1.1 Dynamic Scheduling Algorithms

To determine whether a given set of ready tasks can be scheduled to meet their deadlines, a **schedulability test** is quite often used. We shall now discuss different scheduling algorithms and their schedulability criteria.

Rate Monotonic Algorithm (RMA): It is a **dynamic preemptive algorithm** based on *static priorities.* This RMA algorithm assigns **static priorities** based on task periods. **Please note that the task period is the time after which the tasks repeat. The inverse of a period is called the task arrival rate.** For example, a task with a period of 10ms repeats itself after every 10ms. The task with the shortest period gets the highest priority and the task with the longest period gets the lowest static priority. At run-time, the dispatcher selects the task with the highest priority for execution.

Earliest Deadline-First (EDF) algorithm: It is an **optimal dynamic** preemptive algorithm based on **dynamic priorities.** After any significant event, the task with the earliest deadline is assigned the highest dynamic priority. A significant event in a system can be blocking of a task, invocation of a task, completion of a task etc. The processor utilization can go upto 100% with EDF. The dispatcher operates in the same way as the dispatcher for the rate monotonic algorithm.

5.5.1.2 Static Scheduling Algorithms

Herein, the scheduling decisions are made during the compile time. This assumes parameters of all the tasks known as a priori and builds a schedule based on this. Once a schedule is made, it cannot be modified online. Static scheduling is generally not recommended for dynamic systems. There are no explicit static scheduling techniques except that a schedule is made to meet the deadline of the given application under known system configuration. There is no concept of priority in static scheduling. Based on task arrival pattern, a time line is built and embedded into the program and no change in schedules is possible during execution.

5.5.2 Soft Real-Time Scheduling

Herein, non-real, regular processes should be given less priority as compared to real-time processes. Real-time processes should never be overcome by any non-real time process whose priority has been increased by aging mechanism. For a real-time process, the dispatch latency *i.e.,* the time elapsed from the moment the process becomes runnable to the moment it actually begins to run, should be as small as possible. And this can be done by making the system calls used by the processes, preemptible. This can be achieved in two possible ways—

1. Preemptive points
2. Making kernal preemptive

What are preemptive points?

Preemptive point can be inserted in the system calls that take long time for execution. **Please remember that at this point, a checking can be done to see whether a higher priority real-time task needs to run or not.** If yes, the CPU can take up that higher priority job and leave this current job for sometime. After the completion of higher priority job, the interrupted process can continue with the system call. **Also note that the preemption points should be placed at those points where it is known that kernal data structures will not be modified.**

Kernel can be made preemptive to achieve low dispatch latency. This implies that now a non-real time process can always be preempted to make dispatch latency low for a real-time task. Some complex mechanism are needed to make a Kernal preemptive as its data structures need to be protected by incorporating various mechanisms. **For instance,** Solaris 2 is an O.S. that uses Kernel preemption to make dispatch latency low.

5.6 PERFORMANCE COMPARISON

The performance of the CPU scheduling algorithms depend on variety of features like the probability distribution of service times of various processes, the efficiency of scheduling and the content switching mechanisms and nature of I/O demand and the performance of the I/O subsystem.

5.6.1 Deterministic modelling

This method takes a particular predetermined work load and defines the performance of each algorithm for that work load. **For example,** assume that we have been given some workload. All four processes arrive at time = 0 ms. The length of CPU burst time is given in milliseconds as follows—

Process	CPU burst-time (ms)
*P*1	10
*P*2	1
*P*3	2
*P*4	5

We can apply FCFS, SJF or RR ($q = 2$) scheduling algorithms and find out the minimum average time out of all these results. Such an algorithm will be best. This type of algorithm execution is said to be **Deterministic Modelling.** It is simple and fast. It requires exact numbers for input and its answers apply to only those cases.

5.6.2 Queuing Analysis

It is an area of study that can be useful in comparing scheduling algorithms. Like, if we know the arrival rates and service rates then we can compute CPU utilization, average queue length, average wait time and so on. For example, if we consider Little's formula. *i.e.*,

$$N = \lambda * W$$

where N – Average queue length
λ – Average arrival rate in the queue
W – Waiting time of the process

We can use little formula to compute one of the three variables, if we know the other two.

5.6.3 Simulators

More accurate results or evaluations of scheduling algorithms can be done with simulations. Simulation involves programming a model of the computer system. Software data structures represent the major components of the system. When the simulation executes, statistics that indicate algorithm performance are gathered. The Figure 5.9 below shows the evaluation of CPU scheduling by simulation.

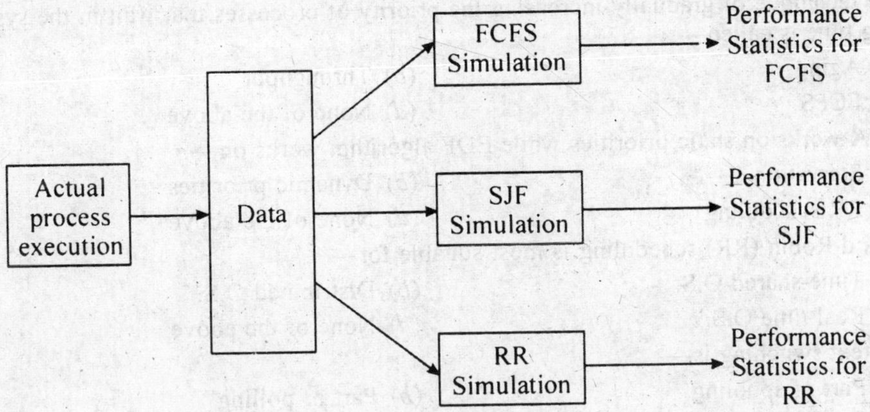

Fig. 5.9 Simulation — showing evaluation of CPU scheduling

Summary

In this chapter, we have studied different scheduling algorithms. We have discussed about uniprocessor and multiprocessor scheduling also. We have also taken a case study on WIN-NT. Also real-time scheduling has been discussed.

MULTIPLE CHOICE QUESTIONS (MCQs)

1. An O.S. program module that selects the next job to be admitted for execution is called as—

(*a*) Scheduler (*b*) Compiler
(*c*) Throughput (*d*) None of the above

2. A short-term scheduler executes atleast once every—

(*a*) 1 ms (*b*) 5 ms
(*c*) 10 ms (*d*) None of the above

3. A program responsible for assigning the CPU to the process that has been selected by the short-term scheduler is known as a—

(*a*) Scheduler (*b*) Dispatcher
(*c*) Debugger (*d*) None of the above

4. If dispatch latency increases then the degree of multiprogramming—

(*a*) increases (*b*) decreases
(*c*) Remains constant (*d*) None of the above

5. The average amount of work completed per unit time is called—

(*a*) CPU utilization (*b*) Bandwidth
(*c*) Turn around time (*d*) Throughput

6. The preemption of processes takes place after a fixed interval of time called—
   (*a*) Time slice (*b*) Time Quantum
   (*c*) Response time (*d*) None of the above
7. The indefinite blocking of low priority processes by a high priority processes is known as—
   (*a*) Starvation (*b*) Deadlock
   (*c*) Aging (*d*) None of the above
8. The technique of gradually increasing the priority of processes that wait in the system for a long time is called—
   (*a*) Aging (*b*) Throughput
   (*c*) FCFS (*d*) None of the above
9. RMA works on static priorities while EDF algorithm works on—
   (*a*) Starvation (*b*) Dynamic priorities
   (*c*) RR scheduling (*d*) None of the above
10. Round-Robin (RR) scheduling is most suitable for—
    (*a*) Time-shared O.S. (*b*) Distributed O.S.
    (*c*) Real-time O.S. (*d*) None of the above
11. Context switching is—
    (*a*) Part of spooling (*b*) Part of polling
    (*c*) Part of interrupt handling (*d*) None of the above
12. FIFO scheduling is—
    (*a*) Preemptive (*b*) Non-preemptive
    (*c*) Deadline scheduling (*d*) None of the above
13. In RR Scheduling, a ready queue is treated as a—
    (*a*) Circular queue (*b*) Doubly linked list
    (*c*) Stack (*d*) None of the above
14. A scheduling wherein the jobs are allowed to move between the queues—
    (*a*) Multilevel queue scheduling (*b*) RR Scheduling
    (*c*) Multilevel feedback scheduling (*d*) None of the above
15. RR Scheduling is a preemptive version of—
    (*a*) FIFO (*b*) SJF
    (*c*) MLQ (*d*) None of the above

ANSWERS

1. *a*	**2.** *c*	**3.** *b*	**4.** *b*	**5.** *d*	**6.** *b*
7. *a*	**8.** *a*	**9.** *c*	**10.** *a*	**11.** *c*	**12.** *b*
13. *a*	**14.** *c*	**15.** *a*			

CONCEPTUAL SHORT QUESTIONS (WITH ANSWERS)

Q.1. Define the term polling?

Ans. Polling is a technique in which one system checks the status of another independent system.

Q.2. How can you implement Round Robin Scheduling algorithm?

Ans. Implementation of RR scheduling algorithm needs a dedicated timer. The timer is usually set to interrupt the O.S. Whenever a time slice expires and thus force the scheduler to be involved. Processing the interrupt to switch the CPU to another process requires saving all the registers for the old process and then loading the registers for the new process. This task is known as **Context Switching.** The Scheduler itself simply stores the context of the running process, moves it to the end of the ready queue and dispatches the process at the head of the ready queue. Whenever the running process surrenders control to the O.S. before expiration of its time slice, the scheduler is again invoked to dispatch a new process to CPU.

Q.3. What advantage is there in having different time-quantum sizes on different levels of a multilevel queueing system?

Ans. The advantage is that the short jobs will have highest priority if they are shorter than the initial quantum. This services them fast and frees the CPU to concentrate on longer jobs. The jobs that are pushed to the next low level now can be given more time than the initial quantum time since the object is to run as many programs as fast as possible with minimum delays to other programs. Thus, by increasing the quantum with the level, shorter jobs will be allowed higher priority and longer jobs will be allowed to run simultaneously with minimal delays.

Q.4. Explain the differences in the degree to which the following scheduling algorithms discriminate in favor of short processes:

(*a*) FCFS

(*b*) RR

(*c*) Multilevel Feedback Queues.

Ans. (*a*) **FCFS:** It discriminates against short jobs since any short jobs arriving after long jobs will have a longer waiting time.

(*b*) **Round Robin:** It treats all jobs equally *i.e.*, giving them equal CPU burst times, so short jobs will be able to leave the system faster since they will finish first.

(*c*) **Multilevel Feedback Queues:** Discriminate very favourably toward short jobs since they work similar to the RR algorithm.

Q.5. Consider a variant of the RR scheduling algorithm where the entries in the ready queue are pointers to the PCBs—

(*a*) What would be the effect of putting two pointers to the same process in the ready queue?

(*b*) What would be the major advantages and disadvantages of this schemes?

(*c*) How would you modify the basic RR algorithm to achieve the same effect without duplicate pointers?

Ans. (*a*) In effect, that process will have increased its priority since by getting time more often; it is receiving preferential treatment.

(*b*) The advantage is that more important jobs could be given more time, in other words, higher priority in treatment. The consequence of course is that shorter jobs will suffer.

(*c*) Allot a longer amount of time to process deserving higher priority. In other words, have two or more quantums possible in the RR scheme.

Q.6. Suppose a scheduling algorithm (at the level of short term CPU scheduling) favors those processes that have used little processor time in the recent past. Why will this algorithm favor I/O-bound programs and yet not permanently starve CPU-bound programs?

Ans. It will favor the I/O bound programs because of the relatively short CPU burst request by them; however, the CPU bound programs will not starve because the I/O bound programs will relinquish the CPU relatively often to do their I/O.

Q.7. Consider the following preemptive priority scheduling algorithm based on dynamically changing priorities. Larger priority numbers imply higher priority. When a process is waiting for the CPU (in the ready queue, but not running), its priority changes at rate α; when it is running, its priority changes at rate β. All processes are given a priority of 0 when they enter the ready queue. The parameters α and β can be set to give many different scheduling algorithms.

(*a*) What is the algorithm that results from $\beta > \alpha > 0$?

(*b*) What is the algorithm that results from $\alpha < \beta < 0$?

Ans. (*a*) FCFS : First-Come First-Served.

(*b*) LIFO : Last-IN First-Out.

Q.8. A CPU Scheduling algorithm determines an order for the execution of its scheduled processes. Given *n* processes to be scheduled on one processor, how many possible different schedules are there? Give a formula in terms of *n*.

Ans. $n!\,(n! = n * n-1 * n-2 * \ldots * 2 * 1)$

Q.9. Assume you have the following jobs to execute with 1-processor:—

Job No.	Burst time (BT)	Priority
1	15	3
2	2	1
3	4	3
4	2	4
5	8	2

Jobs are assumed to have the order 1, 2, 3, 4 and 5. You have 1 CPU only.

(*a*) Give it's GANTT – chart and use

(1) FCFS

(2) RR, quantum (*q*) = 2

(3) SJF

(4) Non-preemptive algorithms

(*b*) Identify TAT, WAT, Waited TAT of each job and also find the ATAT and AWTAT of the above algorithm?

Ans. **(1) Using FCFS algorithm:**

We draw it's GANTT chart first.

J1	J2	J3	J4	J5
0–15	15–17	17–21	21–23	23–31

$\therefore$ TAT of J1 = 15 – 0 = 15

TAT of J2 = 17 – 0 = 17

TAT of J3 = 21 – 0 = 21

TAT of J4 = 23 – 0 = 23

TAT of J5 = 31 – 0 = 31

$$\therefore \text{ Average TAT} = \frac{15+17+21+23+31}{5} = 21.4$$

$$\text{and Average Waiting Time (AWT)} = \frac{0+15+17+21+23}{5} = 15.2$$

(2) **RR ($q = 2$):**

J1	J2	J3	J3	J4	J5	J5	J5	J5	J1	J1	J1	J1	J1	J1	J1

0 2 4 6 8 10 12 14 16 18 20 22 24 26 28 30 31

Now, J1 gets the first quantum of $q = 2$.

$\therefore$ J1 still needs = 15 – 2 = 13 units of time to execute properly.

Now, J2 needs 2 units only and it is less than J1's time left for execution.

$\therefore$ J2 is scheduled next. This goes on.

$\therefore$ TAT of J1 = 31 – 0 = 31

TAT of J2 = 4 – 0 = 4

TAT of J3 = 8 – 0 = 8

TAT of J4 = 10 – 0 = 10

TAT of J5 = 18 – 0 = 18

$$\therefore \text{ Average TAT (using RR)} = \frac{31+4+8+10+18}{5} = 14.2$$

Also, Waiting time of J1 = 16

Waiting time of J2 = 2

Waiting time of J3 = 4

Waiting time of J4 = 8

Waiting time of J5 = 10

$$\therefore \text{ Average W.T. (using RR)} = \frac{40}{5} = 8\,\text{ms}$$

(3) **SJF:** We draw it's GANTT chart first—

J2	J4	J3	J5	J1

0 2 4 8 16 31

$\therefore$ TAT of J5 = 16 – 0 = 16

TAT of J2 = 2 – 0 = 2

TAT of J3 = 8 – 0 = 8

TAT of J4 = 4 – 0 = 4

TAT of J1 = 31 – 0 = 31

$$\therefore \text{ Average TAT (using SJF)} = \frac{2+4+8+16+31}{5} = 12.2$$

$$\& \text{ Average Waiting Time} = \frac{0+2+4+8+16}{5} = 6.0$$

(4) **Priority (no preemption now):** It's GANTT chart is—

J2	J5	J1	J3	J4

0 2 10 25 29 31

$\therefore$ TAT of J1 = 2 – 0 = 2

TAT of J2 = 10 – 0 = 10

TAT of J3 = 25 – 0 = 25

TAT of J4 = 29 – 0 = 29

TAT of J5 = 31 – 0 = 31

$\therefore$ Average TAT (with priority & no preemption) = $\frac{2+10+25+29+31}{5}$ = **19.5**

& Waiting time of J1 = 10

Waiting time of J2 = 0

Waiting time of J3 = 25

Waiting time of J4 = 29

Waiting time of J5 = 2

$\therefore$ Average waiting time = $\frac{10+0+25+29+2}{5}$ = **13.2**

(5) $\because$ WTAT = $\frac{\text{TAT}}{\text{RT (or BT or ET)}}$

$\therefore$ **For FCFS:**

$$WTAT_1 = \frac{TAT_1}{RT_1} = \frac{15}{15} = 1$$

$$WTAT_2 = \frac{TAT_2}{RT_2} = \frac{17}{2} = 8.5$$

$$WTAT_3 = \frac{TAT_3}{RT_3} = \frac{21}{4} = 5.25$$

$$WTAT_4 = \frac{TAT_4}{RT_4} = \frac{23}{2} = 11.5$$

$$WTAT_5 = \frac{TAT_5}{RT_5} = \frac{31}{8} = 3.875$$

$\therefore$ WTAT (FCFS) = $\sum_{i=1}^{5} WTAT_i$

= 1 + 8.5 + 5.25 + 11.5 + 3.875 = **30.125**

& AWTAT (FCFS) = $\frac{30.125}{5}$ = **6.025**

Q.10. Assume that jobs arrive as follows—

Job No.	Arrival Time	Run Time
1	10.00	2.00 hrs
2	10.10	1.00 hrs
3	10.25	0.25 hrs

Using FCFS, calculate TAT of all three jobs above and hence ATAT?

Ans. $\because$ TAT = FT – AT

TAT : Turn around time

FT : Finish time

AT : Arrival time

$$\text{and ATAT} = \frac{\sum_{i=1}^{n} \text{TAT}_i}{n} \quad (n \text{ - processes/jobs})$$

So, we compute now.

Job No.	AT	ST	FT	TAT = FT – AT
1	10.00	10.00	12.00	12 – 10 = 2 hrs
2	10.10	12.00	13.00	13 – 10.10 = 2.90 hrs
3	10.25	13.00	13.25	13.25 – 10.25 = 3.00 hrs

$$\therefore \text{ ATAT} = \frac{2 + 2.90 + 3.00}{3}$$

$$= \frac{7.90}{3} = \mathbf{2.63\,hrs}$$

Also, WTAT of J1 = $2/2 = 1$

$$\text{WTAT of J2} = \frac{2.90}{1} = 2.90$$

$$\text{WTAT of J3} = \frac{3}{0.25} = 12$$

$$\therefore \text{ AWTAT} = \frac{15.90}{3} = \mathbf{5.3\,hrs}$$

Q.11. Find turn around times (TAT) and weighted TAT (WTAT) for the following—

Job No.	**AT**	**ST**	**FT**
1	**10.0**	**10**	**10.3**
2	**10.2**	**10.3**	**10.8**
3	**10.4**	**10.8**	**10.9**
4	**10.5**	**10.9**	**11.3**
5	**10.8**	**11.3**	**11.4**

Ans. $\because$ TAT = FT – AT

$\therefore$ TAT_1 of J1 = 10.3 – 10.0 = 0.3

TAT_2 of J2 = 10.8 – 10.2 = 0.6

TAT_3 of J3 = 10.9 – 10.4 = 0.5

TAT_4 of J4 = 11.3 – 10.5 = 0.8

TAT_5 of J5 = 11.4 – 10.8 = 0.6

$$\text{Now, ATAT} = \frac{0.3+0.6+0.5+0.8+0.6}{5} = \frac{2.8}{5} = 0.56$$

Also note that Run-Time (RT) is also named as Execution-Time (ET) or Burst-Time (BT) and is given as (FT – ST).

$$\text{Now, } WTAT_1 = \frac{TAT_1}{RT_1} = \frac{0.3}{0.3} = 1$$

$$WTAT_2 = \frac{TAT_2}{RT_2} = \frac{0.6}{0.5} = 1.2$$

$$WTAT_3 = \frac{TAT_3}{RT_3} = \frac{0.5}{0.1} = 5$$

$$WTAT_4 = \frac{TAT_4}{RT_4} = \frac{0.8}{0.4} = 2$$

$$WTAT_5 = \frac{TAT_5}{RT_5} = \frac{0.6}{0.1} = 6$$

$$\therefore \quad AWTAT = \frac{\sum_{i=1}^{5} WTAT_i}{n} = \frac{15.2}{5} = \mathbf{3.04}$$

Q.12. Find TAT, WTAT, ATAT and AWTAT of all 5-jobs given below—

Job No.	**RT**	**ST**	**FT**
1	**0.3**	**10.0**	**10.4**
2	**0.5**	**10.2**	**11.35**
3	**0.1**	**10.4**	**10.65**
4	**0.4**	**10.5**	**11.4**
5	**0.1**	**10.8**	**11.1**

Ans. We compute TAT and WTAT as follows—

Job No.	RT	ST	FT	TAT	WTAT
1	0.3	10.0	10.4	0.4	1.33
2	0.5	10.2	11.35	1.15	2.3
3	0.1	10.4	10.65	0.25	2.5
4	0.4	10.5	11.4	0.9	2.25
5	0.1	10.8	11.1	0.3	3.0
				3.00	11.38

$$\therefore \quad \text{ATAT} = \frac{3}{5} = 0.6$$

$$\text{and AWTAT} = \frac{11.38}{5} = \mathbf{2.276}$$

Q.13. Find TAT, ATAT, WTAT and AWTATs for the following—

Job No.	RT	ST	FT
1	0.3	10	13.0
2	0.5	10	13.5
3	0.25	10	13.75
4	0.25	10	14.0

Ans. We compute TAT and WTATs as follows—

Job No.	RT	ST	FT	TAT	WTAT
1	3.0	10	13.0	3.0	1.0
2	0.5	10	13.5	3.5	7.0
3	0.25	10	13.75	3.75	15.0
4	0.25	10	14.0	4.0	16.0
				14.25	39

$$\therefore \quad \text{ATAT} = \frac{14.25}{4} = \mathbf{3.56}$$

$$\text{and AWTAT} = \frac{39}{4} = \mathbf{10.0}$$

Q.14. Find TAT, WTAT, ATAT and AWTAT for the following—

Job No.	RT	ST	FT
1	0.3	10.0	10.356
2	0.5	10.2	11.05
3	0.1	10.4	10.581
4	0.4	10.5	11.158
5	0.1	10.8	11.025

Ans. We compute as follows—

Job No.	RT	ST	FT	TAT	WT
1	0.3	10.0	10.356	0.356	1.187
2	0.5	10.2	11.05	0.850	1.700
3	0.1	10.4	10.581	0.181	1.810
4	0.4	10.5	11.158	0.658	1.645
5	0.1	10.8	11.025	0.225	2.250
				2.270	8.592

$$\therefore \quad \text{ATAT} = \frac{2.270}{5} = \mathbf{0.454}$$

$$\text{and AWTAT} = \frac{8.592}{5} = \mathbf{1.718}$$

Q.15. Find TATs, ATATs, WTAT and AWTAT for the following—

Job No.	RT	AT	FT
1	**0.3**	**10.0**	**10.4**
2	**0.5**	**10.2**	**11.2**
3	**0.1**	**10.4**	**11.4**
4	**0.4**	**10.5**	**11.4**
5	**0.1**	**10.8**	**11.1**

Ans. We compute TAT and WTAT as follows—

Job No.	RT	AT	FT	TAT	WTAT
1	0.3	10.0	10.4	0.4	1.33
2	0.5	10.2	11.2	1.0	2.0
3	0.1	10.4	11.4	1.0	10.0
4	0.4	10.5	11.4	0.9	2.25
5	0.1	10.8	11.1	0.3	3.0
				3.6	18.58

$$\therefore \quad \text{ATAT} = \frac{3.6}{5} = \mathbf{0.72}$$

$$\text{and} \quad \text{AWTAT} = \frac{18.58}{5} = \mathbf{3.716}$$

Q. 16. Suppose that the following processes arrive for execution at time indicated –

Process	Arrival Time	Execution Time
***P*1**	**0.0**	**8**
***P*2**	**0.4**	**4**
***P*3**	**1.0**	**1**

(*i*) What is the average TAT for these processes with FCFS scheduling algorithm.

(*ii*) What is the AWT and ATAT for these processes with preemptive SJF algorithm?

Ans. (*i*) The GANTT chart is -

*P*1	*P*2	*P*3
0	8	12	13

$$\therefore \quad ATAT = \frac{(8 - 0.0) + (12 - 0.4) + (13 - 1.0)}{3}$$

$$= \frac{8 + 11.6 + 12}{3} = \frac{31.6}{3} = 10.533$$

***(ii)* The GANTT chart is–**

P3	*P2*	*P1*

0 1 5 13

$$\therefore \quad AWT = \frac{0+1+5}{3} = \frac{6}{3} = 2$$

$$\& \, ATAT = \frac{(1-1.0)+(5-0.4)+(13-0.0)}{3}$$

$$= \frac{0+4.6+13}{3} = \frac{17.6}{3} = 5.866$$

Q.17. Consider the set of processes as given in table 1 and the following scheduling algorithms–

(*i*) FCFS

(*ii*) RR (quantum = 2)

(*iii*) RR (quantum = 1)

Process id	**Arrival Time**	**Execution Time**
A	**0**	**4**
B	**2**	**7**
C	**3**	**3**
D	**3.5**	**3**
E	**4**	**5**

If there is a tie within the process, the tie is broken in favour of the oldest process.

(1) Draw the GANTT chart and find the average waiting time and response time for the algorithms. Comment on your result, which one is better and why ?

(2) If the scheduler takes 0.2 unit of CPU time, in context switching for completed job and 0.1 unit of additional CPU time for incomplete jobs for saving their context. Calculate the percentage of CPU time wasted in each case.

Ans. ***(i)* FCFS:** We draw the GANTT chart first by ignoring switching –

A	*B*	*C*	*D*	*E*

0 4 11 14 17 22

Pid	Arrival Time (AT/T_0)	Execution Time (Δt)	Start Time (T_1)	$RT = T_1 - T_0$	FT (T_2)	$TAT = T_2 - T_0$	$WT = TAT - \Delta t$
A	0	4	0	0	4	4	0
B	2	7	4	2	11	9	2
C	3	3	11	8	14	11	8
D	3.5	3	14	10.5	17	13.5	10.5
E	4	5	17	13	22	18	13

$\therefore \quad \Sigma RT = 33.5 \; \& \; \Sigma WT = 33.5$

$AWT = \Sigma WT/5 = 33.5/5 = 6.7$ units

Avg. Response Time = $\Sigma RT/5 = 33.5/5 = 6.7$ units

(ii) RR (q = 2)

A	B	A	C	D	E	B	C	D	E	B	E	B

0 2 4 6 8 10 12 14 15 16 18 20 21 22

Pid	Arrival (T_0)	Execution Time (Δt)	Start Time (T_1)	RT $= T_1 - T_0$	Finish Time (T_2)	TAT $= T_2 - T_0$	WT $=$ TAT$- \Delta t$
A	0	4	0	0	6	6	2
B	2	7	2	0	22	20	13
C	3	3	6	3	15	12	9
D	3.5	3	8	4.5	16	12.5	9.5
E	4	5	10	6	21	17	12

$\therefore \quad \Sigma RT = 13.5 \; \Sigma WT = 45.5$

$\therefore \quad 5 \times 10^6\, p - 120\, p = 1000 - 120$

$$(50{,}00{,}000 - 120)\, p = 880$$

$$4999880\, p = 850$$

$$p = \frac{880}{4999880} = 1.76 \times 10^{-4}$$

$\therefore$ To achieve the desired access time of I Msec $\boldsymbol{p \le 1.76 \times 10^{-4}}$

Q.18. Consider a variation of round -robin, we call it as progressive round robin. In progressive round robin each process has its own quantum. This starts out at 50 ms and increases by 50 ms each time it goes through the round robin queue. So long jobs keep getting longer and longer time slices. Give the advantages of this variant over ordinary round robin. You are also required to give disadvantages of this variant over ordinary RR algo?

Ans. 1. In normal RR algo, CPU scheduler goes around the ready queue, allocating the CPU to each process for a time interval of upto 1 time-quantum.

2. It is given that it start out at 50 ms and increases by 50 ms each time it goes to the ready queue
3. The increase of 50 ms each time would reduce context switching.
4. Avg. TAT in this case would not differ form normal RR algo.

EXERCISE QUESTIONS

Q.1. (*a*) What is CPU scheduling? Explain the long-term, medium-term and short-term scheduling?

(*b*) Given the following information—

Process	Arrival Time	Burst Time	Priority
A	0	3	3
B	1	6	5
C	2	1	2
D	3	4	1
E	4	2	4

Compute average waiting time and average turnaround time for the following scheduling algorithms:—

(1) Round Robin ($q = 1$).

(2) Priority preemptive.

(3) Preemptive SJF?

Q.2. Consider the following set of processes:—

Process	Burst Time (ms)	Arrival Time (ms)
P_0	75	0
P_1	40	10
P_2	25	10
P_3	20	80
P_4	45	85

Suppose a system uses Round-Robin Scheduling with $q = 15$ ms.

(1) Create a GANTT chart illustrating the execution of these processes.

(2) What is the turnaround time for process P_3.

(3) What is the average waiting and average turnaround time for these processes?

Q.3. Define preemptive scheduling algorithm.

Q.4. What is preemptive scheduling? Describe a preemptive scheduling algorithm that provides good response time.

Q.5. Explain the characteristics that are used to compare various CPU scheduling algorithms.

Q.6. Three batch jobs A, B, C arrive at a computer center at almost the same time. They have estimated running time 10, 4, 8 minutes. Their priorities are 3, 5, 4 respectively with 5 being the highest priority. For each of the following scheduling algorithms, determine the mean process turn around time. Ignore process switching overhead. All jobs are CPU bound—

(1) Round Robin.

(2) Preemptive multiprogramming.

Q.7. Five jobs are waiting to be run. Their expected run times are 9, 6, 3, 5 and X. In what order should they be run to minimize the average response time.

Q.8. (*a*) State why each of the following is incorrect—

1. The shorter the job, the better the service it should receive.
2. Because SJF gives performance for short jobs, it is useful in time sharing system.
3. SJF is fair.

(*b*) Assume that you have the following jobs to execute with one processor:

Job	Burst Time	Arrival Time
0	75	0
1	40	10
2	25	10
3	20	80
4	45	85

Say, RR algorithm is used with $q = 15$.

1. Draw a GANTT chart.
2. Find the average waiting and turnaround time.

Q.9. **(*a*)** One heuristic often used by CPU schedulers is that a process's past behavior is a good indicator of its future behavior. Give an example of a situation in which a CPU scheduler following this heuristic would make a bad decision.

(*b*) Assume you have the following jobs to execute with one processor:

Jobs	Arrival time	CPU burst	Priority
1	0	15	3
2	2	10	2
3	3	15	1
4	5	12	0
5	6	08	1

Priority is defined as $0 > 1 > 2 > 3 > \ldots$

1. Give a GANTT chart illustrating the execution of these jobs using preemptive priority algorithm.
2. Find out turnaround time and waiting time of each job.

Q.10. List four performance measures that schedulers use to maximize system performance. Write merits/demerits of the following scheduling algorithms with the help of an example:

1. Shortest remaining time next.
2. Time slice scheduling.
3. Priority based.

Q.11. Consider the following set of process, with the length of the CPU burst time given in milliseconds:

Process	Burst Time	Priority
P_1	10	3
P_2	1	1
P_3	2	3
P_4	1	4
P_5	5	2

The process are assumed to have arrived in the order P_1, P_2, P_3, P_4, P_5 all at time 0.

(*a*) Draw four Gantt charts that illustrate the execution of these processes using FCFS, SJF, a non-preemptive priority and RR ($q = 1$) scheduling.

(*b*) What is the turnaround time of each process for each of the scheduling algorithm in part-*a* ?

(*c*) What is the waiting time of each process for each of the scheduling algorithm in part-*a* ?

(*d*) Which of the schedules in part-*a* results in the minimal average waiting time (over all process) ?

[Hint:

(*a*) The four GANTT charts are:

Using SJF—

P2	P3	P4	P5	P1	P5	P1	P5	P1	P5	P1	P1	P3	P1	P5

UsingRR—

P1	P2	P4	P5	P3

Using FCFS—

P2	P4	P3	P5	P1

Using Priority—

P1	P3	P4	P5	P2

(*b*) **Turnaround times are as follows—**

	FCFS	RR	SJF	Priority
P_1	10	19	19	16
P_2	11	2	1	1
P_3	13	7	4	18
P_4	14	4	2	19
P_5	19	14	9	6

(*c*) **Waiting times are as follows—**

WT = TAT – BT

	FCFS	RR	SJF	Priority
P_1	0	9	9	6
P_2	10	1	0	0
P_3	11	5	2	16
P_4	13	3	1	18
P_5	14	9	4	1

(*d*) Shortest Job First (SJF).]

Q.12. (*a*) For the data given below, calculate the finish time for each job assuming that RR algorithm is used—

Job No.	Arrival Time	Burst Time
1	10.00	3 hr
2	10.50	2 hr
3	11.50	1 hr
4	11.50	1 hr

And also calculate the turn around time for each job.

(*b*) Briefly explain the characteristics used for the comparison of scheduling algorithms.

(*c*) Define and compare the multi-level feedback scheduling algorithm and multiqueue scheduling algorithm.

Q.13. Explain the priority scheduling algorithm and its major drawbacks.

Sol. Draw the GANTT chart and find AWT & RT of the process set given in the following table –

Process id	*AT*	*ET*	priority
A	0	10	3
B	0	2	1
C	1	3	3
D	2	1	5
E	2	4	2

Q.14. Calculate *TAT* & *AWT* for following set of processes, if the processes are scheduled using–
(1) SJF (2) Priority (both preemptive non-preemptive)

Process	*BT*	Priority	*AT*
*P*1	7	1	0
*P*2	3	2	4
*P*3	9	3	7

Consider the following processes with the arrival time and execution time as shown.

Process	*A.T*	*B.T*
A	0.0	8
B	0.4	4
C	1.0	1

Calculate AWT and ATAT using–

(1) FCFS

(2) SJF (non-preemptive)

(3) SJF (preemptive)

[Hint: (*ii*) Using FCFS: GANTT chart is

*P*1	*P*2	*P*3
0	8	12 – 13

0, 8, 12, 13

$$\text{AWT} = \frac{0 + (8 - .4) + (12 - 1)}{3} = \frac{7.6 + 11}{3} = \frac{18.6}{3} = 6.2$$

$$\&\ \text{ATAT} = \frac{8 + (12 - 4) + (13 - 1)}{3} = \frac{8 + 11.6 + 12}{3} = \frac{31.6}{3} = 10.53$$

(*ii*) SJF non-preemptive; GANTT chart is–

*P*1	*P*3	*P*2

0, 8, 9, 13

$$\therefore \quad AWT = \frac{0 + (9 - 0.4) + (8 - 1)}{3}$$

$$= \frac{8.6 + 7}{3} = \frac{15.6}{3} = 5.2$$

$$\& \ ATAT = \frac{8 + (13 - 0.4) + (9 - 1)}{3} = \frac{8 + 12.6 + 8}{3}$$

$$= \frac{28.6}{3} = 9.53$$

(*iii*) SJF Preemptive: It's GANTT chart is –

*P*1	*P*2	*P*3	*P*2	*P*1

0 0.4 1 2 5.4 13

$$\therefore \quad AWT = \frac{(0 + (5.4 - 0.4)) + (.4) +}{3} = \frac{5 + 1.4}{3}$$

$$= \frac{6.4}{3} = 2.133$$

$$\& \ ATAT = \frac{(0 + 13) + (5.4 - 0.4) + (2 - 1)}{3} = \frac{13 + 5 + 1}{3}$$

$$= \frac{19}{3} = 6.33$$

Q.15. What advantage is there in having different time–quantum sizes on different levels of a multilevel quering system ?

Q.16. Consider the table of processes shown below. Calculate the turn around time and waiting time for each process if RR scheduling is used with a time slice of 1 unit and 5 units.

Process	Arrival time	Processing time
A	0	1
B	1	5
C	2	1
D	3	5

CHAPTER 6

Process Synchronization

6.0 INTRODUCTION

As we know that the process of changing context from an executing program to an interrupt handler is called as **Context switching.** On the other hand, the method of changing context from an executing program to another process is called as **process switching.** Tasking may be implicit or explicit. **Implicit tasking** means processes are defined by the system whereas **explicit tasking** means processes are defined by the programmer in a single application. Suppose, C, L, S and R are four instructions each requiring 3 units, 4 units, 2 units, and 3 units of time, respectively. Then, there are 2 ways of executing them—

Way-I: Sequential processing

```
While (true)
   {
     C;
     L;
     S;
     R;
   }
```

So, one round takes 12 units of time.

Way II: Multitasking

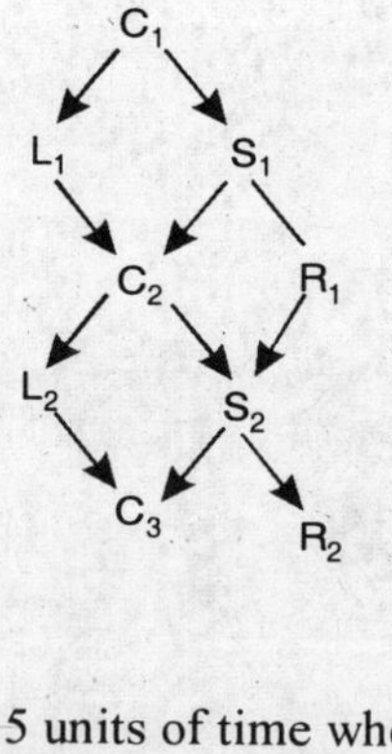

To complete two rounds, it takes 15 units of time whereas in the sequential case it takes 24 units of time. So, there is a performance gain.

However, process synchronization is needed here.

6.1 RACING PROBLEM

The situation where, two or more processes are reading or writing some shared data and the result depends on who runs precisely when, is called as a race condition. Our objective is - To avoid Race Condition.

6.2 HOW TO AVOID RACE CONDITION—A SOLUTION?

Firstly, we must define **what is critical section? A section of code or set of operations, in which process may be changing shared variables, updating a common file or a table etc., is known as critical section of that process.** For the processes that execute concurrently, it should be ensured that execution of critical section should be made atomic. **Atomic means that either an operation in the critical section should happen in it's entirety or not at all. It shouldn't be interrupted in the middle. Please note that the critical section of a process should not be executed concurrently with the critical section of another process.** This should be ensured by the **synchronization mechanism.**

The remainder section of code is called as the **remainder section.** Actually, the part of the program where a shared variable is a accessed is called as a **critical section.** To avoid **Race condition,** we must have the following:

"If one process is in critical section, other competing processes must be excluded to enter their critical sections i.e., a process must enter the critical section in a mutually exclusive way." This is called as the problem of Mutual Exclusion.

6.3 REQUIREMENTS FOR CS PROBLEM SOLUTIONS

There are **some fundamental requirements** to be met by concurrent processes in order to cooperate correctly and efficiently using the shared data. They are as follows:-

1. **Mutual Exclusion:** No two contending processes should be simultaneously executing inside their CS.
2. **Bounded Waiting:** No process should have to wait forever to enter its CS.
3. **Progress:** If no process is executing in its critical section and there exist some processes that wish to enter their critical sections, then only those processes that are not executing in their CS can participate in the decision of which will enter its CS next and this selection cannot be postponed indefinitely.
4. **No assumption:** No assumption should be made about relative speeds and priorities of contenting processes.

6.4 IDEAL SOLUTIONS TO RACE CONDITION PROBLEM

The basic protocol followed here is:

Basic protocol:

Negotiating protocol
CS
Release protocol

Now, we shall provide solutions to Race conditions from hardware and software point of view.

I Hardware solutions

The method is to **Disable Interrupt** (DI) while a process is modifying a shared variable. This ensures that no other process will make unexpected modifications to the shared variables. The structure of this solution is as follows:

```
Negotiating protocol : DI
                       CS
Release Protocol     : EI
                       RS
forever
```

where DI = Disable Interrupt.

CS = Critical Section.

EI = Enable Interrupt.

RS = Remainder Section

This solution is correct solution for a uniprocessor machine. It does not utilize multiprogramming. Thus, the performance of the system is degraded. **Also note that to disable interrupts, all processors will have to inter-communicate with each other which is a time consuming effort and will have a negative impact on system efficiency.**

Let us consider an example to understand this. As we know that many CPUs provide hardware instructions to read, modify and store a word atomically.

For example

(*a*) Motorola 68 K machine has Test-and-Set (TAS) instruction.

(*b*) IBM – 370 machine has Compare-and-swap (CAS) instruction.

(*c*) Intel 8086 machine has exchange (XCHG) instruction.

Please note that the basic idea is to be able to read out contents of a variable and set it to something else in one execution cycle atomically. So, a possible solution using Test-and-Set (TAS) instruction could be—

```
Repeat
    While Test-and-Set (lock)
        do nop;
    CS
    Lock : = false;
    RS
forever
```

Will this hardware solution satisfy the basic requirements? Let us see.

1. **Mutual Exclusion:** This requirement is met because if the first process is in critical section, it sets the value of lock true. Thus, the second process will always have a true value for Test-and-Set instruction. Therefore, it will not come out of the while loop till the lock is set to false by the first process currently executing its critical section.
2. **Progress:** This requirement is also met because if the second process does not want to enter its critical section now, the solution does not stop the first process to enter its critical section again.
3. **Efficiency:** It is an efficient solution because it is not biased with a particular process. Every process gets a fair chance to enter its critical section (CS) in a finite time.

II Software solution

We consider 2 cases here.

Case I : Two-process solution.

Case II : Multi-process solution (Bakery Algorithm).

Case-I : Two process solution

We discuss various algorithms here.

Algorithm 1:

```
Processes : P0 and P1
        Code for process i.
While (true)
    {
    While (turn ! = i) { };
    CS;        // critical section.
    turn = j;// turn - ON lock
    non CS; // Remainder Section
    }
```

But this algorithm has some drawbacks as it does not satisfy all requirements.

1. Mutual Exclusion is achieved.
2. No progress is seen.
3. Bounded wait is not achieved.

Algorithm 2:

```
Flag [ 0 . . 1] : Boolean
While (true)
    {
    flag [i] = true;
    While (flag [ j ] ) { };
        CS;
    flag [i] = false;
    non CS;    // Remainder Section
    }
```

Algorithm 3: Combination of Algorithm-1 and Algorithm-2

```
flag [0 . . 1] ;
turn : 0, 1;
while (true)
    {
    flag [i] = true;
    turn = j;
    while (flag [ j ] and turn = j ) { };
        CS;
    flag [ i ] = false;
    }
```

In Algorithm-3, we find that—

1. Mutual Exclusion is achieved.
2. Progress requirement is satisfied.
3. The bounded - waiting requirement is satisfied.

Case II: Multiple process Solution (Bakery Algorithm)

Data structures :

```
Choosing [ 0 ... n – 1]
Number    [ 0 ... n – 1]
While (true)
    {
    Choosing [i] = true ;
    number [ i ] = max × {number [0], number [1], ...... number [n – 1]} + 1:
    choosing [ i ] = false;
    for (j = 0; j < n; j++)
        {
        While [choosing [ j ] { };
        While (number [ j ] ! = 0 and (number [ j ], j) < number [ i ], i))
            { };
        }
        CS ; // critical section of Pi
        Number [ i ] = 0;
        RS ; // Remainder section of Pi
    }
```

Let us see whether this algorithm satisfies all four requirements or not.

1. Mutual Exclusion: If p_i is in the critical section, it implies that any other process, P_k, will have a number k! = 0 and number [k] will be greater than number [i]. Thus, at this time only P_i can execute its critical section. If P_k tries to enter its critical section, it will be looping in the second while loop as its number is greater than number of P_i.

2. Progress: Progress is there because a process after exiting from its cirtical section, makes its number 0 and it needs to take a new number to contest with other processes trying to enter their CS. Thus, every process will be fairly dealt with by being given an opportunity to enter its critical section after a finite time.

3. No assumption: In this algorithm, no assumptions have been made regarding the relative speed of processes.

4. Efficiency: As the processes are served on FCFS basis and that all processes are fairly dealt, so efficiency is also achieved here.

6.5 CRITICAL SECTION (CS) ALGORITHMS

An ideal algorithm to solve a CS problem should meet the four conditions of mutual exclusion, progress, Bounded waiting and no assumption. We shall now discuss some more algorithms related to CS.

6.5.1 Algorithm 1 : Peterson's Algorithm

```
int turn ;
boolean flag [2];
Process - 0 :
    do {flag [0] = true; // To enter CS
        turn = 1;
    While (flag [1] && true = = 1) // Entry section
        CS;
    flag [0] = false; // Exit from CS
        RS;
    } While (1) ;
Process - 1 :
    do { turn = 0; {flag [1] = true;
    While (flag [0] && turn = = 0) // Entry section
        CS;
    flag [1] = false; // Exit from CS
    turn = 0;
    RS;
    } While (1);
```

This algorithm meets all the three requirements of an ideal critical section solution. In case, both the processes set their flags to true almost simultaneously, the value of "turn" will break the tie, since it can assume only one value at a time either 0 or 1. If both the flags are set to true and the value of "turn" equals 0 then P_0 enters its CS and if the value of "turn" equals 1 then P_1 proceeds.

This is Peterson's Algorithm (1981).

6.5.2 Algorithm - 2 : Swap Algorithm

This algorithm is similar to the Test-and-Set algorithm and also suffers from the problem of starvation. The algorithm is given below:–

```
Void swap (boolean * key, boolean * flag)
    {
    boolean     temp = * flag;
                * flag = * key;
                * key = temp;
    }
// A process – Pi will access CS
boolean key;
do
    {
        key = true;
    While (key) swap (& key, & flag);
        CS; // As long as flag = true
                // Process is in CS
    flag = false;
        RS;
    }
    While (1);
```

The function "swap" is to be executed atomically otherwise Mutual Exclusion (ME) will not be ensured. The 'Progress' requirement is also satisfied. But it does not satisfy the Bounded-Waiting requirement. A process waiting to enter its critical section (CS) may have to wait for unduly long time or may have to wait forever. While a process is waiting, other cooperating processes may keep entering their CS repeatedly. So, this algorithm may cause starvation of waiting processes.

Modified Algorithm using TAS to Ensure Bounded Waiting

```
boolean lock;
boolean waiting [N];
boolean Test And Set (boolean * lock)
    {
    boolean      temp = * lock;
                 * lock = true;
                return  = termp;
    }
// Process-Pi will access CS as follows
do
    {
    Waiting [i] = true;
    While (waiting [i] && Test And Set (& lock));
    Waiting [i] = false;
    < Critical Section >
    J = (i + 1) % N;
    While ((j ! = i) && ! waiting [i])
          j = (j + 1) % N;
    if (j = = i) lock = false;
    else waiting [i] = false;
    < Remainder section >
    }
    While (1);
```

This algorithm meets the bounded waiting requirement because the waiting processes are serviced strictly in order of their process- *Id*. So, after a process requests entry into CS and before it enters, other cooperating processes can enter their respective CS at the most once.

6.6 OS TOOLS FOR PROCESS SYNCHRONIZATION

We have already discussed the hardware and software solutions for the critical section problem. Another way of providing solutions to this problem is by implementing synchronization tools in the software solutions.

Two such synchronization tools are—

Semaphores and monitors. We shall discuss semaphores first and monitors later in this chapter.

6.6.1 Semaphores - by Dijkstra

A semaphore is a variable which accepts non-negative integer values (ie., only positive values) and except for initialization may be accessed and manipulated only through two standard atomic operations Wait and Signal. The two primitives take only argument as the (*a*) *Wait* (*S*) : While (S < = 0)

```
{
// keep testing
}
S = S – 1;
```

(*b*) *Signal* (*S*): S = S + 1;

Please note here that the wait operation decrements the value of semaphore variable as soon as it would become non-negative. Also note that the signal operation increments the value of semaphore variable.

Remember that the modifications to the integer value of the semaphore in the wait and signal operations are **atomic,** *i.e.*, they are executed indivisibly. **It means that when one process modifies the semaphore, no other process can simultaneously modify the same semaphore value.** Furthermore, in case of wait (*s*), the testing of the integer value of S (S < 0) and its possible modifications (S = S – 1) must also be executed without any interruption.

Usage : For n processes CS

```
Wait (S);
   CS;
Signal (S);
Non CS;
```

This Semaphore structure above works to achieve mutual exclusion. Assume that one process A is already executing its CS then it implies that semaphore value at that time is zero as wait signal must have been executed for the process-A. If process-B now tries to enter its CS, it cannot enter the CS because it will have to wait before semaphore becomes greater than zero. This is possible only when process-A executes its signal operation, after executing its critical section. Thus, Semaphore is a powerful tool for interprocess synchronization and mutual exclusion. The simplicity and ease of implementation has made a semaphore a very popular tool that is usually found in the most of the O.S.

Mutual Exclusion : Software and Hardware Support

```
Const int n = /* No. of processes */
void P (int i)
    {
    while (true)
        {
        entercritical (i);
            // CS
        exit critical (i);
            // RS
        }
    }
void main ( )
    {
    parbegin (P(R1), P(R2) ..., P(Rn));
    }
```

Protocol Used:

```
while (true)
    {
        // DI
```

```
            CS      // Cannot be interrupted
            // EI
            // RS
        }
```

I Test & Set Instruction

```
boolean testset (int i)
        {
        if (i = = 0)
            {
            i = 1;
            return time;
            }
        else
            {
            return false;
            }
        }
```

// Program mutual Exclusion using TAS

```
Const int n = // no. of processes
        int bolt; // shared variable
        void P (int i)
            {
            while (true)
                {
                while (! testset (bolt))
                              // do nothing
                // Cs
                bolt = 0;
                // RS
                }
            }
        void main ( )
            {
            bolt = 0;    parbegin (P(1), P(2), ... P(n));
            }
```

say $n = 2$	$\text{bolt} = 0$
$\text{bolt} = 0$	$i = 2$
$i = 1$	$i = 1$
$\therefore p(1)$	$p(2)$

II. Exchange Instruction

```
void exchange (int register, int memory)
        {
          int temp;
          temp = memory;          // During this time access to
          memory = register;      // memory location is blocked
          register = temp;
        }
// program mutual excl using Exchange instr.
int const n = // no. of processes
int bolt; // shared variable
void P (int i)
```

```
        {
        int keyi;    // local var for each process
        while (true)
                {
                        keyi = 1;
                        while (keyi ! = 0)
                        exchange (keyi, bolt);
                        // CS
                        exchange (keyi, bolt);
                        // RS
        void main ( )
                {
                bolt = 0;   parbegin (P(1), P(2)...P(n));
                }
```

Dry Run:

```
    Say, n = 5
    bolt = 0 (shared var)
        outside CS
    For P1—
        i = 1
        keyi = 1
    exchange (1, 0)
    ∴   keyi = 0
        bolt = 1
    ⇒   P1 is in CS
    Now when P1 exits exchg. (0,1) is called
    ∴   keyi = 1
        bolt = 0
    ⇒   P1 is in RS now
        }   }
```

However, there are some drawbacks of semaphores also. They are as follows—

1. Semaphores are unstructured

They force programmers to follow strictly the synchronization protocols (WAIT) and SIGNAL. Any change in WAIT and SIGNAL operation sequence like forgetting either of them or simply jumping around them, may easily corrupt or block the entire system.

2. Semaphores do not support data abstraction

Data abstraction is a software model that specifies a set of data and operations that can be performed on the data. **Please note that even when used properly, semaphores can only protect access to CSs but cannot restrict the type of operations on shared resource performed by processes that have been granted permission.** Although these semaphores encourage interprocess communication via global variable yet it only protects from dangers of concurrency. Such global variables remain vulnerable to illegal on meaningless manipulation by processes legally allowed to modify them by executing correctly the semaphore operations themselves. Basically, the semaphores are of two types—

(1) Binary semaphores.

(2) Counting semaphores.

We will discuss Binary Semaphores first.

Binary Semaphore :

A Binary semaphore is an integer variable which can be accessed by a cooperating process through the use of two primitives i.e, Wait and Signal. A binary semaphore is initialized by the O.S. to 1 and it can assume only one of the two values *i.e.*, S = 0 or 1. **Please note that a semaphore may be provided in a programming as a language construct or as OS calls.**

Wait : The wait-primitive can be implemented as follows—

```
void wait (int * S)
    {
    While (* S = = 0); // keep looping as long as S = 0
    * S – – ;
    }
```

This wait-primitive is invoked by a cooperating process when it requests its entry into it's CS. The first process invoking will make the semaphore value = 0 and proceed to enter its critical section. If another process requests entry into its critical section then it is made to wait. This process will continuously check the value of semaphore, till it is found to be 1. Then, it will decrement the value to 0 and proceed to enter its critical section. **Please note that the two instructions that find out the value of semaphore** *i.e.*, while (* S = = 0) and the **other** * S – –, **that decrement the value to 0, have to be executed atomically, else it would be possible that more than one waiting process may find the value of semaphore to be 1, decrement it to 0 and proceed to enter their critical sections simultaneously. So, the requirement of mutual exclusion will be violated.**

Signal: The signal primitive can be implemented as follows:

```
void signal (int * S)
    {
    * S + + ;
    }
```

The signal-primitive is invoked by a cooperating process, when it is exiting from CS. We need to increment the value of semaphore to 1, to facilitate one of the waiting processes to enter it's CS.

In general, a process P_i can be synchronized for accessing it's CS as follows :–

```
do
    {
    Wait (& S);
      CS; // critical Section
    Signal (& S);
      RS; // Remainder section
    }
    While (1);
```

Will the use of these binary semaphores, satisfy the three requirements of an ideal solution? Let us see.

(*a*) **Mutual Exclusion:** If no process is executing in CS, then the semaphore value is 1. The first process that is executing "wait" operation will decrement the value to 0 and enter its critical section. The processes which execute "Wait" operation while a cooperating process is excuting in its CS, will find the semaphore value to be 0 and keep looping in the "while - loop" of "wait" operation. **Please note that due to this spinning of a waiting process in the while-loop, the binary semaphores are also known as spinlocks.**

When the process executing in the CS makes an exit (fom (CS), it will execute the "*signal*" operation and increment the semaphore value to 1. This goes on but note that **the wait operation is** to be executed atomically. **Please note here that at a time only one of the cooperating processes can enter critical section with the condition that the wait operation is executed atomically. Hence, the requirement of mutual exclusion is satisfied.**

(*b*) **Progress:** When no process is executing in the CS, the semaphore value will be 1. Then, one of the waiting processes looping in the while-loop of wait - operation will find the semaphere value to be 1, exit from the while-loop, decrement the semaphore value to 0 and enter CS. Thus, if no process is executing in CS and some are waiting to enter then one of the waiting processes will its CS immediately. **Thus, the requirement of progress is met.**

(*c*) **Bounded waiting:** Actually, one of the waiting processes will get entry into its CS, when a operating process executing in its CS exits. As this selection process is arbitrary, so a process waiting to enter its CS, is likely to face starvation. **So, the requirement of bounded waiting is not met.**

Advantages of Binary Semaphores–

1. The implementation of Binary semaphore is extremely simple.
2. A counting semaphore can be implemented using binary semaphores.

Disadvantages of Binary Semaphores

1. It does not meet the requirement of Bounded waiting.
2. A process, waiting to enter its CS, will perform Busy-waiting, thus wasting CPU cycles. That is why, the binary semaphores are called as **spinlocks.**

We shall discuss counting semaphore now.

Counting Semaphores.

The counting semphores are free of inherent disadvantages of binary semaphores discussed above. A counting semaphore comprises of—

1. An integer variable that is initialized to a value of K where K $\geq$ 0. During operation, it can assume any value $\leq$ K.
2. A **pointer** to a process queue. The queue will hold the process control Blocks (PCBs) of all those processes that are waiting to enter their CSs. This queue is implemented as a FCFS queue, so that the waiting processes are served in a FCFS order.

Queue Implementation of counting Semaphore

```
Struct semaphore
    {
    int val;
    int Q [MAX];
    } S;
Wait (s): S.Val : = S. Val – 1;      // wait for
                                     // semaphore to
                                     // become + ve &
                                     // then decrement
    if (S. val < 0)                  // by 1.
    {
    Add this pid to Q;
    Sleep; // Block it
    }
Signal (S) : S. Val + = 1;
    if (S. Val < = 0)
    {
```

```
Remove a process, P from Q;
Wake up (P);
}
```

Working: If a process-1 executes the wait operation and finds that the value of semaphore is currently not greater than 0 then instead of busy-waiting, it can be forced to change its state to "*blocked*". By a change in its state, it is automatically appended to a waiting queue associated with the semaphore. The CPU has full freedom to choose another process-2 to execute without being unnecessarily held by process-1.

Now, the blocked process-1 should be restarted when process-2 executes a signal operation. Operations like wakeup ( ) are used to change the state of process from blocked to ready state. The CPU scheduling algorithm should decide when a process has to get the CPU next.

Advantages of Counting Semaphore

1. Because the waiting processes will be permitted to enter their CS in a FCFS order, so the requirement of bounded waiting is fully met.
2. CPU cycles are saved here as a waiting process does not perform any busy waiting.

Disadvantages of Counting Semaphore

1. A counting semaphore is more complex to implement, since it involves implementation of FCFS queue.
2. Context switching is more, so more overheads are involved.

6.6.2 Semaphores (with C implementation)

Two or more processes can cooperate by means of simple signals, such that a process can be forced to stop at a specified place until it has received a specific signal. So, any complex coordination requirement can be satisfied by the appropriate structure of signals. And for signaling, special variables are used. These variables are called as **Semaphores**. Now 3 cases arise :–

(*a*) **To transmit a signal via** semaphores, S, a process executes the primitive, signal (S).

(*b*) **To receive a signal via** semaphore, S, a process executes the primitive, **wait (S)**.

(*c*) If the corresponding **signal has not been transmitted,** the process is suspended until the transmission takes place.

Thus, we can say that the **semaphore** (S) is a **variable** that is an integer (variable) value on which 3 operations are defined :–

1. A semaphore may be initialized to a **positive value.**
2. The **wait** operation decrements the semaphore value. If the value becomes **negative,** then the process executing the **wait** is **blocked**.
3. The **signal** operation increments the semaphore vaue. If the value is **not positive,** then a process blocked by a **wait** operation is **unblocked.**

Formal Definition of Semaphores

```
// Semaphore definition
    Struct semaphore {
                int count;
                queue Type queue;
                }
    void wait (semaphore S)
        {
```

```
                S. count – –;
                if (S. count < 0)   // if count is negative
                        {
                        // place this process in S. queue
                        // block it
                        }
        }
    void signal (semaphore S)
        {
        S. count ++;
        if (S. count < = 0)
                {
                // Remove process P from S. queue
                // place P on ready list.
                }
        }
```

Note here that the two primitives used are **wait** and **signal.** They are both assumed to be **atomic** *i.e.,* they cannot be interrupted and each routine can be treated as an individual step.

Binary Semaphores

A binary semaphore (bin_sema) may take on only 2 values 0 and 1.

Let us define it now.

```
// Binary Semaphore definition
struct bin_sema {
        enum (zero, one) value;
        queue Type queue;
        }
void wait B (bin_sema S)
    {
    if (S. value = = 1)
        S. value = 0);
    else
        {
        // place this process in S. queue
        // block it;
        }
    }
void signal B(bin_sema S)
    {
    if (S. queue. is_empty ( ))
        S. value = 1;
    else
        {
```

```
        // remove a process P from S. queue
        // place process P on ready list
        }
    }
```

Please note the following points regarding semaphores:–

1. For both semaphores defined here, a **queue** is used to hold processes waiting on the semaphore.
2. Policy used by this queue is FIFO *i.e.,* first-in-first-out. **It means that the process that has been blocked the longest is released from the queue first.** A Semaphore which uses this policy is called as a **strong semaphore.** On the other hand, **a semaphore that does not specify the order in which processes are removed from the queue is called as a weak semaphore.**
3. **Strong semaphores** prevent **starvation** and are more convenient and a very common semaphore used by all O.S.

Mutual Exclusion Problem Solution Using Semaphores

Consider '*n*' processes, stored in an array P(*i*). In each process, a wait (S) is executed just before its critical section. (*a*) **If the value of S becomes negative,** the process is suspended. (*b*) **If the value is 1,** then it is decremented. to 0 and the process immediately enters its critical section (CS) because 'S' is no longer positive, no other process will be able to enter its CS.

The semaphore is initialized to 1. Let us write its pseudocode first —

```
// ME using semaphores
    const int n = /* no. of processes*/
    semaphore S = 1;
    void P (int i)
        {
        while (true)
          {
          wait (S);
          /* CS */ ;
          signal (S);
                /* remainder/*;
          }
        }
    void main ( )
        {
        parbegin (P(1), P(2), ...P(n));
        }
```

Working:

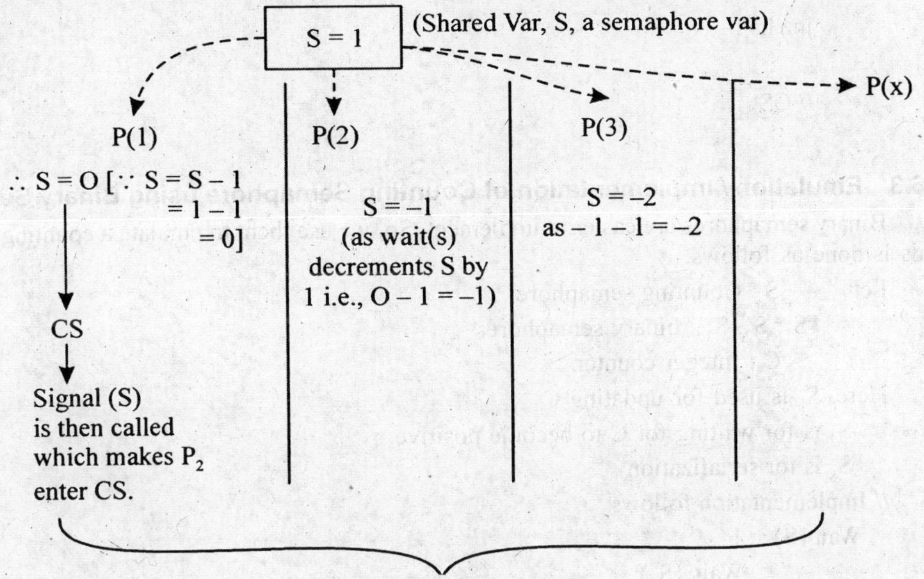

These are in rt.shift queue.

When P(1) finishes, $S \leftarrow S + 1$

Or

(P_1) or $S \leftarrow -1 + 1 = 0$

∴ P_2 is scheduled to enter its CS and this continues till P(n).

Note here that semaphore is initialized to 1.

Thus, the first process that executes a **wait** will be able to enter CS immediately, setting the value of S to O. **Please note that any other process trying to enter CS will find it busy and will be blocked, setting the value of S to –1. Also note that any number of processes may attempt entry; each such unsuccessful attempt results in a further decrement of the value of S.** When the process that initially entered its CS departs, S is incremented and one of the blocked processes (if any) is removed from the queue of blocked processes associated with the semaphore and put it in a ready state. When it is next scheduled by the OS, it may enter the CS.

The given pseudocode can equally well handle the requirement that more than one process be allowed in its CS at a time. To meet this requirement, we initialize the semaphore to a specified value. Thus,

(*a*) **S. Count ≥ 0 :** S. count is the number of processes that can execute wait (S) without suspension.

(*b*) **S. Count < 0 :** The magnitude of S. count is the number of processes suspended in S. queue.

Notes :

1. // Implementation of wait using XCNG

```
wait : mov al, 1
       xchg al, S
       cmp al, 0
       jnz wait
       ret.
```

2. // Implementation of exchange ALP

```
labl : Cmp keyi, bolt
       jnz labl
         :
       // CS
         :
```

6.6.3 Emulation / Implementation of Counting Semaphore using Binary Semaphores

Binary semaphores are easier to implement. So, we use them to emulate a counting semaphore. This is done as follows.

Let S : Counting semaphore

S_1, S_2, S_3 : binary semaphores

C : Integer counter.

Here, S_1 is used for updating C

S_2 is for waiting for C to become positive.

S_3 is for serialization

```
// Implementation follows
Wait (S) :  {
            Wait {S3);
            Wait (S1);
            C = C – 1;
            if (C < 0)
                {
                Signal (S1);
                Wait (S2);
                }
            else
                signal (S1);
            signal (S3);
            }
Signal (S) : {
            Wait (S1);
            C = C + 1;
            if (C <= 0)
            signal (S2);
            signal (S1);
            }
```

Herein, when a process exits its CS, one of the waiting processes at random will get enabled to enter its CS. So, this emulation fails to emulate the bounded - wait feature of a counting semaphore. Hence, this emulation does not emulate all the features of a counting semaphore.

6.7 INTERPROCESS COMMUNICATION

Concurrent cooperating processes must communicate to-

(*a*) Exchange data.

(*b*) Report progress.

(*c*) Access shared memory.

Synchronization is often necessary when processes communicate. Processes are executed with unpredictable speeds. To communicate, one process must perform some actions that the other can detect. This needs an order which is maintained by synchronization. Thus, synchronization means a set of constraints on the ordering of events. The programmer employs a synchronization mechnism to delay the execution of a process in order to satisfy such constraints.

6.7.1 Classical Synchronization Problems

We discuss some classical synchronization problems now.

6.7.1.1 The Producer - Consumer Problem / The Bounded (or finite) and Unbounded (or infinite) - Buffer Problem

Problem domain:

Given a set of cooperating processes, some of which "produce" data items (producers) to be "consumed" by others (consumers), with possible disparity between production and consumptions rates. Devise a synchronization protocol that allows both producers and consumers to operate concurrently at their respective service rates in such a way that produced items are consumed in the exact order in which they are produced (FIFO).

Semaphores Used : mutex = 1
Empty = N;
Full = 0;

Implementation using semaphores for this problem

Producer-Consumer Problem Implementations

Assume that the **buffer** is **infinite** and is a linear array of elements. Thus, **producer** and **consumer** functions in short can be defined as follows:

Producer:

```
While (true)
{
/* produce item V */
    b [in] = V;
    in ++;
}
```

Consumer:

```
While (true)
{
while (in < = out)
    /* do nothing */
w = b [out];
/* consume item w */
```

The contents of this infinite buffer (b) are —

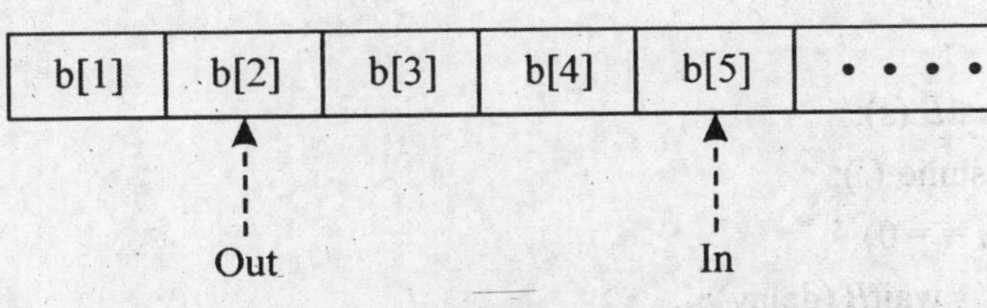

Working: The **producer** can generate items and store them in buffer at its own pace. Each time, an index (in) into the buffer is incremented. The **consumer** proceeds in a similar fashion but must make sure that it does not attempt to read from an empty buffer. Thus, the consumer makes sure that the producer has advanced beyond it (in > out) before proceeding.

Let us implement this using binary semaphores first.

Assumptions:

(*a*) Instead of maintaining indices **in** and **out,** we can simply keep track of the number of items (*n*) in the buffer (*b*) *i.e.,*

$$n = \text{in} - \text{out}$$

(*b*) Semaphore (*s*) is used to enforce *ME*.

(*c*) Semaphore **delay** is used to force the consumer to wait if buffer is empty. Thus, one possible implementation is:

```
// Producer – Consumer, C – Code
int n;
binary_Semaphore s = 1;
binary_Semaphore delay = 0;
void producer ( )
    {
        while (true)
            {
            produce ( );
            waitB (s);
            append ('c');
            n ++;
            if (n = = 1)
                signalB (delay);
            signalB (s);
            }
        }
Void consumer ( )
    {
        waitB (delay);
        while (true)
        {
        waitB (s);
        take ( );
        n – –;
        signalB (s);
        consume ( );
        if (n = = 0)
            waitB (delay);
        }
    }
void main ( )
    {
    n = 0;
```

```
parbegin (producer, consumer);
}
```

This code is simple as the producer is free to add to the buffer at any time. It performs **wait*B* (*s*)** before appending and **signal*B* (*s*)** after wards to prevent the consumer or any another producer from accessing the buffer during the append operation. **Also note that while in *CS*, the producer increments the value of *n*.** If $n = 1$, then the buffer was empty just prior to this append. So, the **producer** performs signal B (delay) to alert the consumer of this. The **consumer** begins by waiting for the first item to be produced, using wait$B$ (delay). Then, it takes an item and decrements n in its critical section. If the producer is able to stay ahead of the consumer then the consumer will rarely block on the semaphore **delay** because n will usually be positive. Hence, both producer and consumer will run correctly.

But this is an **incorrect solution.** A correct, simple, better and a general solution can be obtained if we use counting semaphores.

```
//Correct solution to infinite – buffer
//Producer or consumer problem (C – code).
//Var 'n' is now a semaphore
//n = no. of items in buffer
Semaphore n = 0;
Semaphore s = 1;
void producer ( )
    {
    while (true)
        {
        produce ( );
        wait (s);
        append ( );
        signal (s);
        signal (n);
        }
    }
void consumer ( )
    {
    while (true)
        {
        wait (n);
        wait (s);
        take ( );
        signal (s);
        consume ( );
        }
    }
```

```
        }
    }
    void main ( )
        {
            parbegin (producer, consumer);
        }
```

Two possibilities occur here:

Case-1: A mistake is made by interchanging the operations signal (*s*) and signal (*n*).

This would require that the signal (*n*) operation be performed in the producer's critical section (*CS*) without interruption by the consumer or another producer. **Please note that this would not affect the program because the consumer must wait on both semaphores before proceeding in any case.**

Case-2: A mistake is made by accidently reversing wait (*n*) and wait (*s*) operations.

Now, this produces a fatal error. If the consumer ever enters its CS when the buffer is empty (*n*. count = 0), then no producer can ever append to the buffer and the system is in deadlock state.

Now what will happen if **the buffer is finite or bounded?**

Note: Till now the buffer was infinite but now it is finite.

In such a case, a buffer is treated as a **circular storage.** So, it is a circular buffer and hence the pointer values must be as modulo the size of buffer. Thus, the producer and consumer functions will be:

```
// 'in' and 'out' are two limit-pointers
// Both are initialized to 0.
```

Producer:

```
While (true)
    {
    // produce item v
while ((in + 1) % n = = out)
    //do nothing

b [in] = v;
in = (in + 1) % n;
}
```

Consumer:

```
While (true)
    {
    while (in = = out)
        //do nothing
    w = b [out];
    out = (out + 1) % n;
    // consume item w
```

C – Code Solution for Bounded – Producer – Consumer Problem using Semaphore.

The 'wait' and 'signal' operations be implemented as atomic primitives. One method is to implement them in **hardware of firmware.** The problem is of mutual exchlusion (ME) *i.e.*, **"Only one process at a time may manipulate a semaphore with either a wait or signal operation."**

Thus, even Peterson's algorithm may be used here but this would entail a substantial processing overhead. A better alternative would be to use one of the hardware supported schemes for M.E.

```
// Bounded buffer program in C
const int size of buffer = / * buffer size * /
    semaphore s = 1;
```

```
    semaphore n = 0;
    semaphore e = size of buffer;
void producer ( )
    {
    while (true)
        {
        produce ( );
        wait (e);
        wait (s);
        append ( );
        signal (s);
        signal (n);
    }
}
void consumer ( )
    {
        while (true)
            {
            wait (n);
            wait (s);
            take ( );
            signal (s);
            signal (e);
            consume ( );
            }
    }
void main ( )
    {
    parbegin (producer, consumer);
    }
```

Two (2) possible solutions are there —

(*a*) Using Testset Instruction.

(*b*) Using Interrupts.

I Using Testset Instruction:

```
wait (s)
    {
    while (testset (s. flag))
        // do nothing
    s. count – –;
    if (s. count < 0)
```

```
        {
            place this process in s. queue;
            block this process and set integer s. flag to 0
        }
        else
            s. flag = 0;
        }

signal (s)
        {
        while (testset (s. flag))
            // do nothing
        s. count + +;
        if (s. count < = 0)
            {
                remove a process P from s. queue;
                place process P on reaedy list;
            }
            s. flag = 0;
        }
```

Using Interrupts:

A new integer variable is used here – s. flag. It involves a form of small amount of busy waiting. Thus, we write —

```
wait (s)
        {
            disable interrupts;
            s. count – –;
            if (s. count < 0)
            {
                place this process in s. queue;
                block this process and allow interrupts;
            }
            else
        }       enable interrupts;
signal (s)
        {
            disable interrupts;
            s. count + +;
            if (s. count < = 0)
            {
```

remove a process *P* from s. queue;

place process *P* on ready list;

}

enable interrupts;

}

6.7.1.2 The Dining Philosopher's Problem

Problem domain:

There are N philosophers, sitting around a round dining table. There are N plates placed on the table such that each plate is in front of a philosopher. There are N forks placed between the plates. There is a bowl of Noodles placed at the center of the table. Whenever a philosopher feels hungry, he tries to pick two forks/chopsticks which are shared with his nearest neighbours. If any of his neighbours happens to be eating at the time, the philosopher has to wait. Whenever a hungry philosopher gets two chopsticks, he pours Noodles in his plate and eats. After he finishes, he places the chopsticks back on to the table and starts thinking. Now, these chopsticks are available for his neighbours. This situation is shown below—

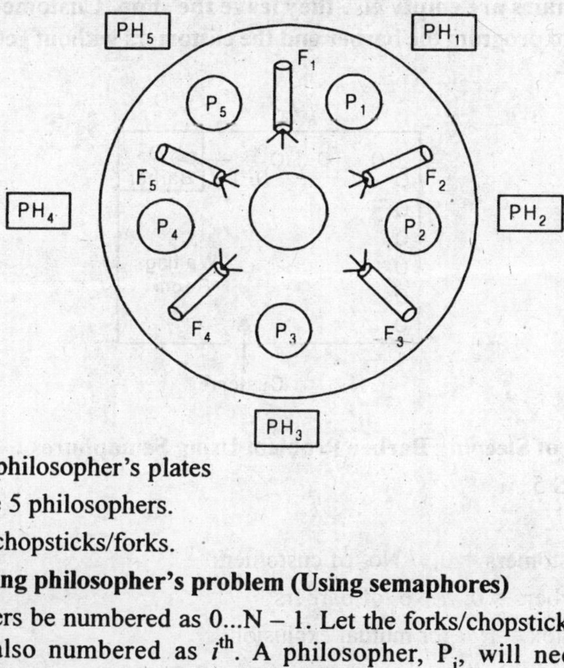

where P_1 ....P_5 are 5 philosopher's plates

PH_1 ....PH_5 are 5 philosophers.

F_1 ....F_5 are 5 chopsticks/forks.

Implementation of Dining philosopher's problem (Using semaphores)

Let the philosophers be numbered as 0...N – 1. Let the forks/chopsticks positioned at the left of philosopher *i*, be also numbered as i^{th}. A philosopher, P_i, will need chopsticks C_i and $C_{(i+1)\%N}$ and then only it can proceed to eat. So, we have–

```
Semaphore Chopstick [N];
do
        {
        wait (Chopstick [i]; // Pick left fork
        wait (Chopstick [i + 1] % N] ); // pick right fork
              < EAT >
        signal (Chopstick [i]); // Put back left chopstick
        signal (Chopstick [(i + 1) % N] ); // put back right chopstick
```

```
        <THINK>
    }
While (1);
```

However, this algorithm has certain limitations also. It is possible that all philosophers may feel hungry almost at the same time. They all will pick up their respective left forks (chopsticks) simultaneously. Now, all will keep waiting for their respective right forks forever. It is a deadlock condition. **Thus, the requirement of progress is not met.**

The algorithm given above can be modified such that **even numbered philosopher** [*ie.*, 0, 2, 4, 6, 8,...) attempts to pick the left chopstick (fork) first and then the right one. On the other hand, **an odd numbered philosopher** (*i.e*, 1, 3, 5, 7,...) attempts to pick the right fork first and then the left one.

6.7.1.3 The Sleeping Barber Problem

Problem domain:

A barber shop (saloon) has one barber, one barber chair and N chairs for waiting customers to sit. If there is no customer, the barber goes to sleep. When a customer arrives, he has to wake up the sleeping barber. If additional customers arrive while the barber is cutting a customer's hair then they sit if chairs are empty else they leave the shop. Customers are serviced in FCFS order. The problem is to program the barber and the customers without getting into race conditions. This is shown below:–

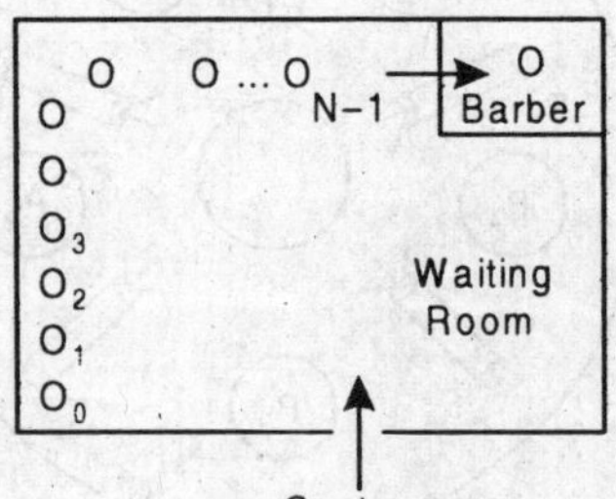

Implementation of Sleeping Barber Problem Using Semaphores

```
# define CHAIRS 5
typdef int sema;
        Sema customers = 0; // No. of customers
        Sema barbers = 0; // No. of barbers
        Sema mutex = 1; // for mutual exclusion
        int waiting = 0; // waiting customers
void barber (void)
        {
                while (true){
                down (& customers); // goto sleep if no. of cust = 0
                down (& mutex);
                waiting – – ;
                up (& barbers);     // Barber ready
                up (& mutex);
```

```
            cut-hair ( );
            }
        }
void customer (void)
        {
        down (& mutex);   // Enter CS
        if (waiting < CHAIRS)    // No free chairs
            {
            waiting + + ;
            up (& customers); // wakeup barber
            up (& mutex) ;
            down (& barbers) ;
            get-haircut ( );
            }
            else {
            up (& mutex) ; // shop is full, donot wait
            }
        }
```

6.7.1.4 Readers - Writers Problem

Problem domain:

Given a universe of readers that need a common data structure and a universe of writers that modify the same common data structure. Devise a synchronization protocol among the readers and writers that ensures consistency of common data while maintaining as high a degree of concurrency as possible.

Reader's priority:

1. **Arriving readers receive priority over waiting writers.**
2. **A waiting or arriving writer gains access to file only when there are no readers in the system.**
3. **When a writer is done with the file, all the waiting readers have priority over the waiting writers.**

Interchange the role of reader with writer to get the writer's priority version.

Semaphores used :

mutex : 1

R-mutex : 1

W-mutex : 1

RC : Readers count

```
Reader ( ) {
        While (true)
            {
            Wait (R - mutex);
            RC = RC + 1 ;
            if (RC = = 1)
            Wait (W - mutex);
            Signal (R - mutex);
```

```
                CS;     // Critical Section
                Wait (R - mutex);
                RC = RC – 1;
                if (RC = = 0)
                Signal (W - mutex);
                Signal (R - mutex);
                Non - CS;    // Remainder Section
                }
        }
Writer ( ) {
        While (true)
                {
                Wait (R - mutex);
                Wait (W - mutex);
                        Write;
                Signal (R - mutex);
                Signal (W - mutex);
                }
        }
```

6.7.2 Programming Errors in the Use of Semaphores

Use of semaphores have certain demerits also. They are as follows-

1. Leads to deadlock
2. A process can easily corrupt the shared resource.
3. Only for synchronization.
4. Violation of mutual exclusion.

Consider 2 cases here. **Case-I** shows violation of mutual exclusion whereas **Case-II** shows blocking critical section entry of cooperating processes forever.

Case - I	Case - II

P_1 :
Signal (& S); // Error
<CS>
	P_2 :
	Wait (& S); // Error
	<CS>
	// Signal (& S) missed out
	<RS>

Now, in case-I when P_1 performs signal on the semaphore (before its entry into cirtical section (CS)), it clears the path for two more cooperating processes to enter their CSs simultaneously. **Hence, this violates the requirement of mutual exclusion.**

In case-II, as shown above, since signal (& S) has not been performed while exiting from CS, the semaphore count has not been incremented. A waiting process has not been enabled to enter its CS. **Please note that the subsequent entry of the cooperating processes into their eritical sections will be blocked forever.** Even P_2 will not be permitted to re-enter its CS.

6.8 HIGH LEVEL SUPPORT FOR PROCESS SYNCHRONIZATION

One of the main problems with semaphore is that it is not syntactically related to the resources it protects. It does not warn the compiler that specific data structure/resources are being shared and its accesses need to be controlled. To remove this bottleneck, **Brinch - Harson** proposed two language's constructs, as follows—

1. Critical region.
2. Conditional critical region.

We shall explain these now in brief.

6.8.1 Critical Regions

A critical region is defined as a language construct that strictly enforces mutually exclusive use of a resource/data structure declared as shared. Critical regions enforce usage of shared variables and prevent potential errors resulting from improper use of ordinary semaphores. **Please note here that the critical region construct can be effectively used to solve critical section problem but it can not be used to solve some general synchronization problems.** For this purpose, *conditional critical region* must be used. It allows a process to wait till a certain condition is satisfied within a critical section without preventing other eligible processes from accessing the shared resource. **Also note that these mechanisms concern themselves on allowing only one process at a time to access a shared resource at any time.** The process permitted to access the resource may also corrupt it.

A **monitor** is a mechanism that helps here by safe sharing of resources among processes. Actually, a monitor allows access to shared resources through a set of well-defined public procedures so as to prevent illegal operations. This provides system integrity also. All the mechanisms discussed here are one outgrowth of semaphores. They all provide structured ways to control access to shared variable.

6.9 MONITORS

A monitor is defined as a collection of procedures, variables and data structures that are all grouped together in a special kind of module or package. It is a high level tool for process synchronization. Semaphores are primitive and flexible tools for mutual exclusion. The wait and signal operations may be scattered throughout a program. It is not easy to see the overall effect of these operations on the semaphores that they are affecting.

Monitors, however, are easier to control. In case of monitors, the functions to access the global variables are programmer defined. They are implemented in PASCAL, Modula-3 and JAVA language.

6.9.1 Characteristics of Monitors

1. Only one process may be executed in monitor at a time.
2. A process enters the monitor by invoking one of its procedures.
3. Local data variables are accessible only by monitor procedure and not by the external procedures.
4. Monitors are a programming language construct.
5. They control not only the time but also the nature of operations.

A monitor supports synchronization by the use of **Condition variables** that are accessible only within monitor. These variables support wait and signal operations.

C. wait - It will make the calling process wait on C's queue

C. signal - It will wake-up one process from the C's queue,

If no process is in C's queue, then the signal is lost unlike semaphores.

6.9.2 General Monitor Structure

The **general structure of a monitor** is as follows—

```
monitor < monitor name >
    {
    < global variable declarations >
    < functions to access global variables >
```

< initialization function of monitor >

}

So, we draw a structure of a monitor now.

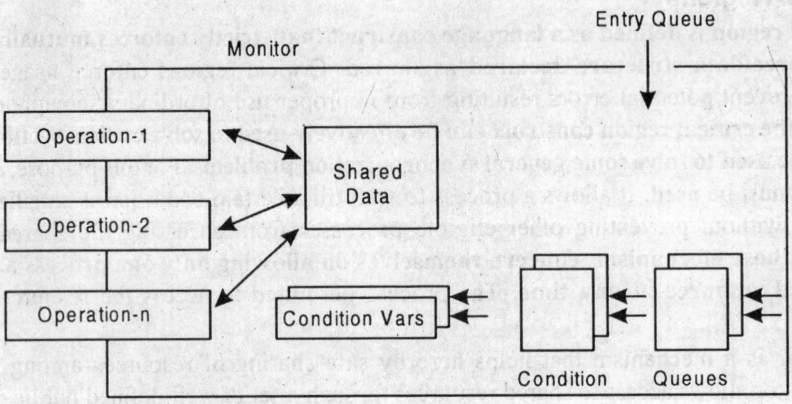

Fig 6.1 Structure of a Monitor

Working:

The monitor's wait/signal operations are different from that of semaphores. If a process is in a monitor signal and no task is waiting on the condition variable then the signal is lost. A process can enter the monitor by invoking any of its procedures through by single entry point that is guarded, so that only one process can be in the monitor at a time. Other processes that attempt to enter the monitor, join a queue of processes suspended, waiting for the monitor's availability. Once a process is in monitor, it may be temporarily suspended itself on condition, *t*, by issuing—

C. wait (*t*)

It is then placed in a queue of processes waiting to re-enter the monitor when the condition changes.

If a process that is executing in monitor detects a change in condition variable, *t*, it issues-

C. signal (*t*)

It alerts the corresponding condition queue that the condition has changed.

A condition variable is like a semaphore with two differences-

1. A *wait* on a condition variable always *blocks* the calling process. Thus, instead of busy waiting (as in case of semaphore), process will be blocked automatically
2. The signal operation resumes exactly one suspended process. If no process is suspended then the signal operation has no effect. Thus, the state of a condition variable is as though the operation was never executed. On the other hand, in case of semaphores, signal operation always affects the state of semaphore. Remember that this is done by incrementing its value by 1.

6.9.3 Algorithm-1 : Monitor-based Wait and Signal Operations

It's implementation is as follows—

Monitor wait-signal

```
{
Boolean busy;
Condition free;
Procedure mwait ( )
```

```
        {
        if (busy)
        free. wait;
        } busy = true;
Procedure msignal ( )
        {
        busy = false;
        free. signal;
        }
        busy = false;       // initialization
    }
```

6.9.4 Algorithm-2 : Monitor's implementation using semaphores

It's implementation is as follows—

```
Semaphore mutex = 1
void enter-monitor ( )
    {
    wait (mutex);
    }
void leave-normally ( )
    {
    signal (mutex);
    }
void leave–with–signal (sem C)
    {
    signal (C);
    }
void wait (sem C)  // goto sleep on a condition
    {
    signal (mutex);
    wait (C);
    }
```

6.10 INTERPROCESS COMMUNICATION (IPC)

6.10.1 Message Communication

Message passing is a simple mechanism suitable for both *Interprocess communication* and *synchronization* in the centralized as well as distributed environment. In this method, the processes send and receive messages instead of reading and writing shared variables. So, two primitives are used here-

1. Send (destination, & message);
2. Receive (source, & message);

6.10.2 Synchronous and Asynchronous Communication

Synchronous Communication

When the sender process executes a "send" call, it gets blocked (suspended) till the intended receiver executes a "receive" call and the message sent is delivered to the receiver process. It is only then that the sender process proceeds with further processing.

Asynchronous communication

Here, the sender is not blocked when there is no outstanding RECEIVE. Asynchronous, nonblocking SEND is implemented by having the OS accept and buffer outstanding messages until matching RECEIVEs are issued. So, the sending process may continue execution after sending a message and need not be suspended, regardless of the activity of receivers.

6.10.3 Merits and Demerits of Synchronous V/S Asynchronous Communication Merits of Synchronous Communication

1. It is a simpler mechanism to implement.
2. It does not require large amount of resources.
3. There is guaranteed delivery of message sent.

Demerits of synchronous Communication

1. The sender gets blocked after executing a "send" call till the intended receiver has got the message delivered.
2. Messages are sent by value or by reference. Each has its own disadvantages.

6.10.4 Naming Conventions

There are two types of naming—direct and indirect.

In direct message communication, process B and A are the identities of the receiver and the source of message respectively, *i.e.*,

```
process A;
..............
send (B, message)
.............
process B;
.............
receive (A, message)
```

The link is automatically established between the paths of processes that want to communicate. The link may be unidirectional, but is usually bidirectional.

In indirect massage communication, first process sends the message into the mailbox and the second process removes a message from the mailbox. This is as shown below:–

```
process A ;
...............
send (mailbox 1, message);
process B;
..............
receive (mailbox 1, message);
...............
```

Please note here that a link is established between a pair of processes only if they have a common mailbox. A link can be associated with more than two processes. A link can be either unidirectional or bidirectional.

Message exchange between two processes, transfers the contents of message from the sender's to the receiver's addressing space. This may be done by either copying the whole message into the receiver's addressing sapce or simply passing a pointer to the message between processes. The message is thus sent by value of by reference. In case of copying, the two processes remain fully decoupled.

6.10.5 OS role for IPC

The Operating System performs two main functions for IPC—

1. Buffering

The OS will buffer the messages into the buffers that are created in the System Address Space. A sender's message will be copied from the sender's address space to the next free slot in the system buffers. From this system buffer, the messages will be delivered to the receiver process in FCFS order when receiver process exccutes receive calls.

2. Synchronization

OS has to maintain proper synchronization between the sending and receiving processes.

6.11 ATOMIC TRANSACTIONS

A transaction is a unit of work that performs a single logical function. **Atomic transaction means that the transaction should be executed either in its entirety or not at all.** We have certain mechanisms to ensure the atomicity of transactions executed on volatile storage.

6.11.1 Log-Based Recovery

The actions performed by a transaction can be stored on a stable storage to ensure atomicity. The most commonly used method here is **write-ahead logging.** The following data is written-

- Transaction Name.
- Data-item Name.
- Old Value of data-item.
- New value of data-item.

Some other special log records are used to record significants events during transaction processing such as start of transaction, commit or abort of transaction and so on.

When a transaction gets aborted, it is this log that helps. The recovery algorithm uses two procedures:–

1. Undo.
2. Redo.

Here, **Undo (T)**— removes the impact of actions of a transaction, T.

and **Redo (T)**— repeats the actions of a transaction, T.

Which of the two procedures should be invoked for recovery?

Say that a transaction, T, starts executing and the system fails. In such a case, T should be undone if the log shows that T started but could not be committed whereas, if the log shows that T started and was also committed before the failure occurred then T should be redone.

There are two drawbacks of log-based recovery:-

1. Finding out that which transaction should be **undone** and which should be **redone** is very time consumig.
2. Recovery process is too slow.

To keep track of the database transactions, the DBMS maintains special files called *log-files* or **journals** that contain information about all updates.

To overcome these drawbacks, the concept of checkpoints is introduced.

6.11.2 Chekpoints

It is definded as a way of periodically committing the executed portions of transactions. Checkpoints are also called as syncpoints or save points. A checkpoint is a point of synchronization between the database and the transaction log file. **Please note here that all buffers are force-written to the secondary storage at the checkpoint. Also note that checkpoints are scheduled at predetermined interval** and involves operations like writing all log records in main memory to the secondary storage.

If the transactions are executed serially, when a failure occurs, we check the log file to find the transaction that started before the last checkpoint.

6.12 ATOMIC TRANSACTIONS—CONCURRENT EXECUTION

Achieving concurrent execution of atomic transactions is not easy. Many a times we say that serializability is achieved by interleaving atomic transaction. **But please remember that not all interleaved execution sequences will be serializable.** To ensure correct execution, certain concurrency control schemes should be used. These are discussed next.

6.12.1 Locking protocols

A transaction follows the two phase locking protocol, if all locking operations precede the first unlock operation in the transaction. This protocol ensures that each data item used by a transaction should be locked. These locks are of two types-

(*a*) Shared.
(*b*) Exclusive.

If a transaction T_1 has locked a data item which transaction T_2 also wants to lock then the following possibilities are there-

(1) If T_1 has a **shared lock** on a data-item, T_2 can also lock it in shared mode.
(2) If T_1 has **exclusive lock** on a data item, T_2 cannot lock it unless T_1 releases this data item.
(3) If T_1 unlocked the data item then T_2 can lock it either in shared or in exclusive mode, which ever is required.

Please note here that a transaction cannot unlock a data item as long as it access that data item. Even after the transaction has undergone last access of that data item, it may not release it to ensure serializability.

The two-phase locking protocol ensures serializability. This protocol requires that each transaction should issue *lock* and *unlock* requests in two phases—

1. Growing phase: In this phase, a transaction may **obtain locks** but may not release any lock. **Please note that in this phase the number of locks increases from zero to the maximum for the transaction.**

2. Shrinking phase : In this phase, a transaction may **release locks** but may not obtain any new locks. **Please note that in this phase, the number of locks decreases from maximum to zero.**

Initially, a transaction is in the growing phase. The transaction an acquire all the needed locks in this phase. Once the transaction releases a lock, it enters the shrinking phase in which no new locks can be obtained. This protocol ensures serializability but is not free from dead lock.

6.12.2 Time stamp based protocols

Time stamping is a concurrency control protocol in which the fundamental goal is to order transactions globally in such a way that older transactions get priority in the event of a conflict. This protocol requires that we must have prior knowledge about the order in which the transactions will be accessed. For ordering the transactions, we associate a **unique fixed timestamp.** These timestamps are **increasing numbers only.** And they are denoted by TS (T_i) for each transaction, T_i. This timestamp is assigned by the database system before the transaction, T_i, starts execution. If a transaction, T_i, has been assigned timestamp as TS (T_i) and a new transaction T_j enters system then

$$TS(T_i) < TS(T_j)$$

This timestamp may be implemented by using the value of a **system clock** *i.e.*, a transactions timestamp is equal to the value of the clock when the transaction enters the system. Or, one may use a **logical counter** that is incremented after a new timestamp has been assigned.

The timestamps of transactions determine the serializability order. Thus, if TS (T_i) < TS (T_j) then the system must ensure that the produced schedule is equivalent to a serial schedule in which transaction T_i appears before transaction T_j.

Implementation

To implement this scheme, we associate with each data item, *Q*, two timestamp values :–

(*a*) **W-timestamp (*Q*):** It denotes the largest timestamp of any transaction that executed write (*Q*) successfully.

(*b*) **R-timestamp (*Q*):** It denotes the largest timestamp of any transaction that executed read (*Q*) successfully.

These timestamps are updated whenever a new read (*Q*) or write (*Q*) instruction is executed.

The timestamp-ordering protocol

The timestamp-ordering protocol ensures that any conflicting read and write operations are executed in timestamp order. This protocol operates as follows—

1. Suppose that transaction, T_i issues read (*Q*).

(*a*) If TS (T_i) < W – timestamp (*Q*), then T_i needs to read a value of *Q* that was already over written. Hence, the read operation is rejected and T_i is rolled back.

(*b*) If TS (T_i) > = W – timestamp (*Q*), then the read operation is executed, and R-timestamp (*Q*) is set to the maximum of R–timestamp (Q) *i.e.*, TS (T_i).

2. Suppose that transaction T_i issues write (*Q*)

(*a*) If TS (T_i) < R – timestamp (*Q*) then the value of *Q* that T_i is producing was needed previously and the system assumed that value would never be produced. Hence, the write operation is rejected and T_i is rolled back.

(*b*) If TS (T_i) < W – timestamp (*Q*), then T_i is attempting to write an obsolete value of *Q*. Hence, this write operation is rejected and T_i is rolled back.

(*c*) Otherwise, the write operation is executed and W–timestamp (*Q*) is set to TS (T_i).

Note: A transaction, T_i, that is rolled back by the concurrency control scheme as a result of either a read or write operation being issued, is assigned a new timestamp and is restarted.

6.13 SYNCHRONIZATION IN SOLARIS 2—A CASE STUDY

Solaris supports the following thread synchronization methods–

(*a*) Mutual exclusion locks.

(*b*) Semaphores.

(*c*) Reader/Writers locks.

These primitives are implemented within the kernel for kernel threads.

We shall discuss them one by one-now.

Mutual Exclusion Lock

Mutual exclusion locks synchronize the threads by ensuring that only one thread at a time executes a CS of the code. A mutual exclusion lock consists of a variable of type mutex which can be manipulated by following routines-

(1) Mutex-Enter ( ) — to acquire the lock

(2) Mutex-Exit ( ) — to release the lock.

(3) Mutex-Tryenter ( ) — to acquire the lock, if it is not already held.

Semaphores

Solaris supports some counting semphores. The following are their primitives-

(1) Sema — P ( ) — Decrements the semaphore.

(2) Sema — V ( ) — Increments the semaphore

(3) Sema — Tryp ( ) — Decrement the semaphore if blocking is not required.

Condition Variables

They provide a logical abstraction for blocking a thread while waiting for a condition. Condition variables do not contain the actual condition to test, instead one locks the appropriate mutex, tests the condition and then blocks on the condition variable if the condition is not true. The primitives are—

(1) CV–waits ( ) : Blocks until the condition is signaled.

(2) CV–signal ( ) : Wakes up one of the threads blocked in CV—wait ( ).

(3) CV–Broad cast ( ) : Wakes up all threads blocked in CV—wait ( ).

Summary

In this chapter, we have studied that in order to cooperate, the concurrent executing processes must communicate and synchronize. Semaphores do help here. But some other outgrowths of semaphores are also helpful like critical regions, conditional critical regions and monitors. The study of concurrency is suitable in OS study because today the trend is towards multiprocessing and massive parallelism. Various OSs like solaris, WIN - XP and LINUX are proven examples of synchronization mechanism. Also we have seen how atomic transactions can be executed concurrently. **Interleaving is not a silver bullet**. So, we have various protocols to achieve that. These have been discussed here.

MULTIPLE CHOICE-QUESTIONS [MCQs]

1. The situation where, two or more processes are reading or writing some shared data and the result depends on who runs precisely when is called—

(*a*) Synchronization (*b*) Multitasking

(*c*) Race condition (*d*) None of the above

2. A section of code or set of operations in which process may be changing shared variables is known as a —

(*a*) Critical section (CS) (*b*) Atom

(*c*) Procedure (*d*) None of the above

3. DI stands for-

(*a*) Demand Input (*b*) Disable Interrupt

(*c*) Demand Interrupt (*d*) None of the above

4. 'Bakery Algorithm' will provide—

(*a*) Two-process solutions (*b*) Multi-process solutions

(*c*) Deadlock solutions (*d*) None of the above

5. Semaphores were given by

(*a*) Albrecht (*b*) Dijkstra

(*c*) Peterson (*d*) None of the above

6. 'Spinlocks' refer to—

(*a*) Binary semaphores (*b*) Counting semaphores

(*c*) Monitors (*d*) None of the above.

7. Critical region and conditional critical regions were proposed by-

(*a*) Dijkstra (*b*) Brinch-Harson.

(*c*) Peterson (*d*) None of the above

8. Critical region, conditional critical region and monitors are outgrowth of-

(*a*) Semaphores (*b*) Mutual Exclusion

(*c*) Synchronous communication (*d*) None of the above

9. Checkpoints are also named as—

(*a*) Syncpoints (*b*) Savepoints

(*c*) Both a and b (*d*) None of the above

10. A semaphore count of negative means that the queue contains—

(*a*) $(n + 1)$ waiting process (*b*) n waiting process

(*c*) $(n - 1)$ waiting process (*d*) None of the above

11. To avoid race condition, the number of processes that may be simultaneously inside their cirtical section is—

(*a*) 0 (*b*) 1

(*c*) 2 (*d*) 4

12. Solaris contains—

(*a*) an adaptive mutex. (*b*) Spinlocks.

(*c*) Dispatcher. (*d*) None of the above

ANSWERS

1. *c*	**2.** *a*	**3.** *b*	**4.** *b*	**5.** *b*	**6.** *a*
7. *b*	**8.** *a*	**9.** *c*	**10.** *b*	**11.** *b*	**12.** *a*

CONCEPTUAL SHORT QUESTIONS (WITH ANSWERS)

Q.1. "Spin locks are undesirable in a uni-processor environment but are useful in multiprocessor environment." Explain.

Ans. Spinlocks are undesirable in uniprocessor environment but are useful in a multiprocessor environment. This is because in a multiprocessor environment the ciritical section of the currently executing process is small. So, not much of the time is consumed in waiting as compared to the time consumed in context-switching.

Q. 2. Write a C-code to implement the classical dining philosophers problem.

Ans.

```
# include < prototypes. h >
# define n 8 // No. of philosophers
void philosopher (int j)    // j ← philosopher (0 to n – 1)
        {
        While (true)
            {
            think ( ) ; // philosopher thinking
            take-fork ( ); // take left fork
            take – fork (j + 1) % n); // take-right fork
            eat ( );
            put–fork ( j ); // put leftfork back on table
            put–fork (j + 1)%n) ; // put right fork on table
            }
        }
```

Q. 3. How can you implement semaphore using message?

Ans.

```
Mailbox : Semaphore
for (i = 0; i < n; i + +)
send (semaphore, Nullmsg);
wait (semaphore):
    Receive (Semaphore, msg);
Signal (Semaphore):
    Send (Semaphore, msg);
```

Q. 4. Show that if the wait and signal operations are not executed automatically, then mutual exclusion may be violated.

Ans. Suppose the value of semaphore, S = 1 and processes P_1 and P_2 execute wait (S) concurrently.

1. T_o : P_1 determines that value of S = 1. 2. T_1 : P_2 detrmines that value of S = 1.
3. T_2 : P_1 decrements S by 1 and enters critical section (CS).
4. T_3 : P_2 decrements S by 1 and enters CS.

Q.5 The Cigarette-Smokers problem. Consider a system with three smoker process and one agent process. Each smoker continuously makes a cigarette and smokes it. But to make a cigarette, the smoker needs three ingredients: tobacco, paper and matches. One of the smoker processes has paper, another has tobacco and the third has matches. The agent has an infinite supply of all three materials. The agent places two of the ingredients on the table. The smoker who has the remaining ingredient then makes and smokes a cigarette, signaling the agent on completion. The agent then puts out another two of the three ingredients and the cycle repeats. Write a program to synchronize the agent and the smokes.

Ans. The shared data structures are—

var a : array [0 ....2] of semaphore (Initially = 0)

agent : semaphore (Initially = 1)

(*a*) The **agent process** is coded as follows-

```
repeat
        Set i, j to a value between 0 and 2.
        Wait (agent);
        Signal (a [i] );
        Signal (a [j] ),
Until false;
```

(*b*) Each smoker process needs two ingredients represented by integers *r* and *s* each with value between 0 and 2.

```
repeat
    Wait (a [r] );
    Wait (a [s] );
    "smoke"
    signal (agent);
until false;
```

Q. 6 Write a monitor that implements an alarm clock that enables a calling program to delay itself for a specified number of time units (ticks). You may assume the existence of a real hardware clock which involves a procedure tick in your monitor at regular intervals.

Ans.
```
type alarm = monitor
    var X : condition,
procedure delay (T : integer);
    begin
            X. wait (T);
```

```
        X. signal;
    end
procedure tick;
    begin
        X. signal
    end
```

Q. 7 What is the meaning of the term busy waiting? What other kinds of waiting are there? Can busy waiting be avoided altogether?

Ans. A process is waiting for an event to occur and it does so by executing instructions. A process is waiting for an event to occur in some waiting queue (*e.g.*, I/O Semaphore) and it does so without having the CPU assigned to it.

Busy waiting cannot be avoided altogether.

Q. 8. In the Interprocess communication there are three explicit Interprocess interaction forms. What are they? Explain them.

Ans. The three forms are as follows-

1. Interprocess Synchronization

A set of protocols and mechanisms used to preserve system integrity and consistency in the concurrent process while sharing resources.

2. Interprocess Signals

The exchange of timing signals among concurrent process or threads used to coordinate their collective progress.

3. IPC

Concurrent cooperating processes must communicate for such purpose as exchanging of data, reporting progress and access of shared memory.

EXERCISE QUESTIONS

Q. 1. Show that if the wait and signal operations are not executed atomically then mutual exclusion may be violated?

Q. 2. (*a*) Consider a system consisting of processes $P_1, P_2, P_3 \ldots P_n$, each of which has a unique priority number. Write a monitor that allocates three identical line printers to these processes, using the priority numbers for deciding the order of allocation.

(*b*) Consider the IPC scheme where mailboxes are used.

(*i*) Suppose a process *P* wants to wait for two messages, one from mailbox *A* and other from mailbox *B*. What sequence of send and receive should it execute?

(*ii*) What sequence of send and receive should *P* execute if *P* wants to wait for one message either from mailbox *A* or from mailbox *B* or from both.

(*iii*) A receive operation makes a process wait until the mailbox is non empty. Either devise a scheme that allows a process to wait until a mailbox is empty or explain why such a situation can't exist.

Q. 3. (*a*) Explain the following terms with the help of examples-

(*i*) Race condition. (*ii*) Critical section. (*iii*) Mutual Exclusion with busy waiting.

(*b*) Explain the readers' and writers' classical IPC problem and its solution.

Q. 4. Write short notes on- "Semaphores."

Q. 5. Suggest a software solution for the problem of race condition for two processes. Show that your solution achieves mutual exclusion and progress requirement.

Q. 6. Implement semaphore using messages.

(*b*) Implement the wait operation using the X CNG instruction.

Hint :- WAIT : MOV Al, 1
XCHG AL, S
CMP AL, O
JNZ WAIT
RET

Q. 7. (*a*) Solve bounded buffer producer consumer problem using messages so that maximum concurrency is achieved.

(*b*) What is race condition? What criteria a solution to solve race condition should satisfy?

Q. 8. What is race condition? What criteria a solution to solve race condition should satisfy? Design a software solution to avoid race condition for 2 processes that satisfies all criteria that a solution to race condition should satisfy.

Q. 9. What is critical section? Explain atleast two classic problems of synchronization.

Q. 10. (*a*) What is mutual exclusion problem concerning to concurrent processes? Explain with suitable example.

(*b*) State the producer - consumer problem. Give a solution to the problem using semaphores.

(*c*) Describe critical section problem, in detail with suitable example.

(*d*) Explain semaphores. How can semaphore be used to enforce mutual exclusion? Give a suitable example.

Q. 11. What is a race condition? What are all the conditions that should hold good for its solution? Briefly explain various software and hardware solutions to it.

Q. 12. Explain what is meant by critical section and mutual exclusion with reference to multiprocess systems. Give the desirable properties of an acceptable solution to the mutual exclusion problem.

Q. 13. Explain critical section problem.

Q. 14. Write short notes on–

(*a*) Semaphores.

(*b*) Inter process communication.

Q. 15. Write a monitor that implements an alarm clock that enables a calling program to delay itself for a specified number of time units. You may assume the existence of a real hardware clock, which involves a procedure "tick" in your monitor at regular intervals.

Q. 16. What do you mean by a semaphore? State and solve the readers' writers' problem with the help of semaphore.

Q. 17. Describe IPC?

Q. 18. Define critical section problem and its solution using semaphore. Use this approach to solve producer consumer problem.

Q. 19. Define Mutual Exclusion and its need. One solution to it is TEST & LOCK instructions. Explain this approach and give its relative advantages and disadvantages.

Q. 20. Demonstrate process synchronization using producer– consumer problem.

Q. 21. Write short notes on Dining philosopher problem.

Q. 22. What is binary semaphore? Implement wait() and signal () without busy wait for binary semaphores. Write the help of binary semaphore, implement the counting semaphore.

Q. 23. Define Semaphores. How can it be used as a general synchronization tool ? What advantage does a semapore have as compared to a hardware test and set instruction ?

Q. 24. Define Critical Section problem. What are the necessary requirements for a solution to the critical section problem ? Explain.

UNIT - III

CHAPTER

7

Deadlocks

7.0 INTRODUCTION

Any computer system will support different number of resources like printers, plotters, tape drive, hard disks, files etc. Our operating systems have the ability to grant the exclusive access of a resource to a process temporarily. So, the set of processes become deadlocked. This permanent blocking of a set of processes that either compete for system resource or communicate with each other is a **deadlock.** So, we define now. **A deadlock is a situation where a process or a set of processes is blocked, waiting for some resource that is held by some other waiting processes.**

Examples of Deadlock

1. From our real-life situation, consider a four way crossings of traffic. It may result in a deadlock as no vehicle can be moved in this situation. This is shown in Fig. 7.1 below.

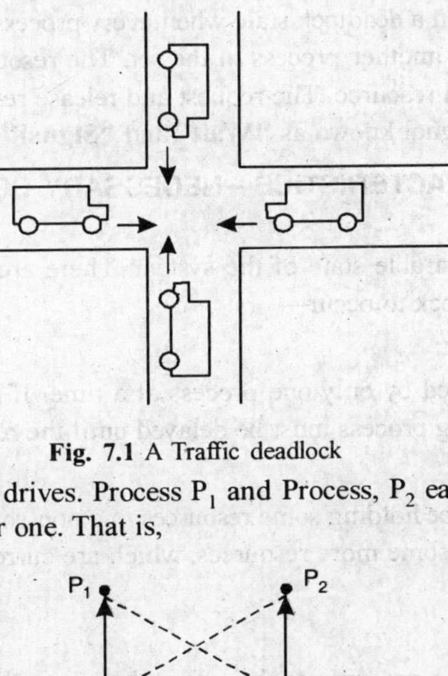

Fig. 7.1 A Traffic deadlock

2. A system has two tape drives. Process P_1 and Process, P_2 each hold one tape drive and now each needs another one. That is,

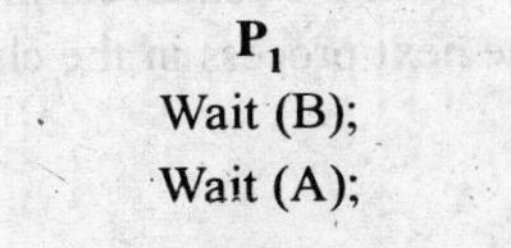

Fig. 7.2 A process printer deadlock

3. Semaphores A and B, both initialized to 1. That is,

P_0	P_1
Wait (A);	Wait (B);
Wait (B);	Wait (A);

This result in deadlock. As just wait is there but no signal is there.

Also note that if there are multiple resources of the same type, each is called an instance of that resource type. A **system table** records whether or not a resource is free. Whenever a request is made, a **look up operation** is done in the table. If a requested resource is being used by some other process then the requesting process is added to a queue for that resource. Thus, a **queue** is maintained for each resource.

7.1 SYSTEM MODEL

Let the resource types be R_1, R_2, ..., R_m (like CPU cycles, momory space, I/O devices etc.). Each resource type R_i has W_i instances. Each process utilizes a resource as follows—

1. **Request :** A process, needing a resource, will request the OS for assignment of the needed resource. Then the process waits, till OS assigns it an instance of the requested resource.
2. **Assignment :** The OS will assign to the requesting process an instance of the requested resource, whenever, it is available. Then, the process comes out of its waiting state.
3. **Use :** The process will use the assigned resource. In case, the resource is non-sharable, the process will have exclusive access to it.
4. **Release :** After the process finished with the use of assigned resource, it will return the resource to the system pool. The released resource can now be assigned to another waiting process.

A set of processes is in a deadlock state when every process in the set is waiting for an event that can be casued by only another process in the set. The resources are basically of two types—logical resource or physical resource. The request and release resources are system calls, it can be accomplished by special signal known as **"Wait"** and **"Signal"**.

7.2 DEADLOCK CHARACTERISTICS—NECESSARY CONDITIONS FOR DEADLOCK TO OCCUR.

Deadlock is an undesirable state of the system. There are **four conditions** that must hold simultaneously for a deadlock to occur—

1. Mutual Exclusion:

A resource can be used by only one process at a time. If another process requests for that resource then the requesting process must be delayed until the resource has been released.

2. Hold-and-Wait:

Some processes must be holding some resources in a non-sharable mode and at the same time must be waiting to acquire some more resources, which are currently held by other processes in a non-sharable mode.

3. No preemption

Resources granted to a process can be released back to the system only as a result of the voluntary action of that process, after the process has completed its task.

4. Circular wait

Deadlocked processes are involved in a circular chain such that each process holds one or more resources being requested by the next process in the chain. That is,

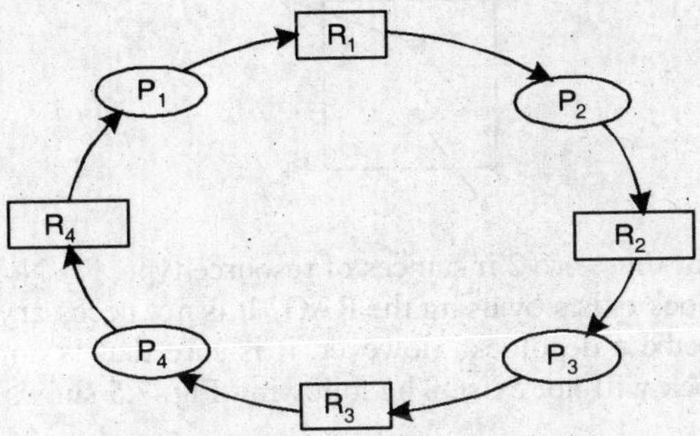

Fig. 7.3 Circular Wait

7.3 DEADLOCK DETECTION

7.3.1 Resource Allocation Graph (RAG)

A deadlock is described in terms of a **directed graph called as a system resource allocation graph.** The resource allocation graph (RAG) consists of two sets—

(*a*) a set of vertices, V.

(*b*) a set of edges, E.

The set of vertices is again divided into two categories— The set of all the active processes in the system i.e.,

$P = \{P_1, P_2, ... P_n\}$ and the set of all different type of resources i.e.,

$R = \{R_1, R_2, R_3, ... R_m\}$.

There are two types of edges in the resource allocation graph:—

1. A directed edge from the process P_i to resource type R_j and is denoted by—

   $P_i \rightarrow R_j$. It signifies that the ith process is requesting one unit of the resource type j. This edge is also called as a **request edge.**

2. A directed edge from the resouce R_i to process P_j denoted by $R_j \rightarrow P_j$. It signifies that one unit of ith resource is held by the process j. This edge is also called as an **allocation edge/assignment edge.**

Notations used in RAGs

We denote **a process by a circle** and each **resource by a rectangle.** *For example*—In the graph of Fig. 7.4 below—

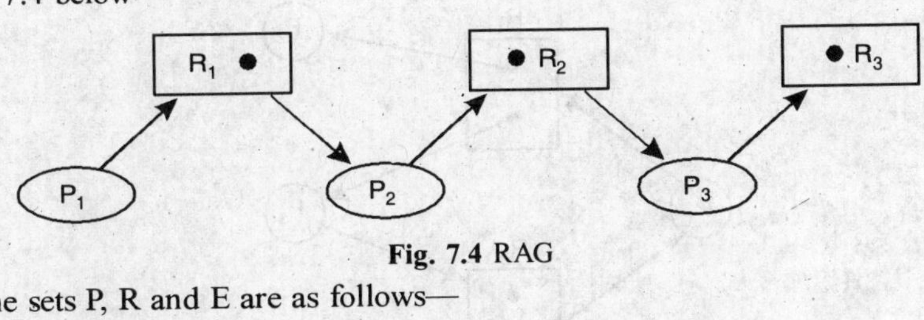

Fig. 7.4 RAG

Here, the sets P, R and E are as follows—

$P = \{P_1, P_2, P_3\}$

$R = \{R_1, R_2, R_3\}$

& $E = \{P_1 \rightarrow R_1,\ R_1 \rightarrow P_2,\ P_2 \rightarrow R_2,\ R_2 \rightarrow P_3,\ P_3 \rightarrow R_3\}$

However, if we have more number of instances of a Resource type then it is denoted by more dots. For e.g.:

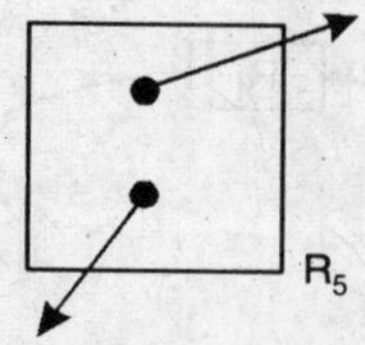

Here, 2-dots means that there are 2 instances of resource type, R_5. Now the question is—can we determine whether deadlock exists by using the RAG? It is not necessary. If a cycle exists in the RAG, there may or may not be a deadlock. However, it is sure that is no cycle exists *i.e.*, if the graph is acyclic then deadlock will not exist. The following Fig. 7.5 shows RAG with a deadlock.

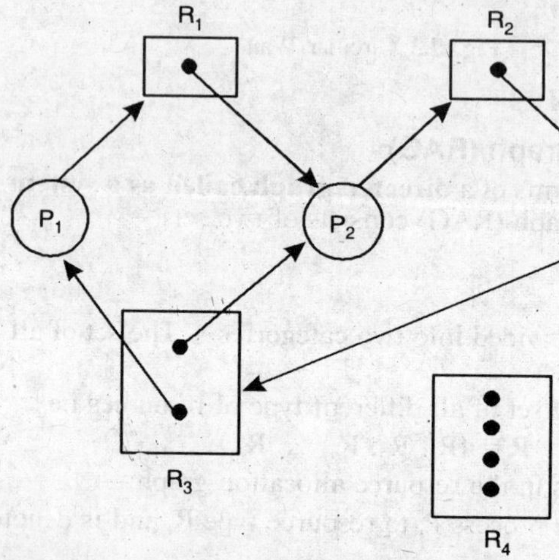

Fig. 7.5 RAG with deadlock

So, please remember that—

Acyclic RAG implies no deadlock. But the following is **not true—**

No deadlock implies Acyclic RAG

This means that cycles can be there even if there is no deadlock.

Now, consider a *RAG with* **a cycle but no deadlock.** This is shown in Fig. 7.6 below.

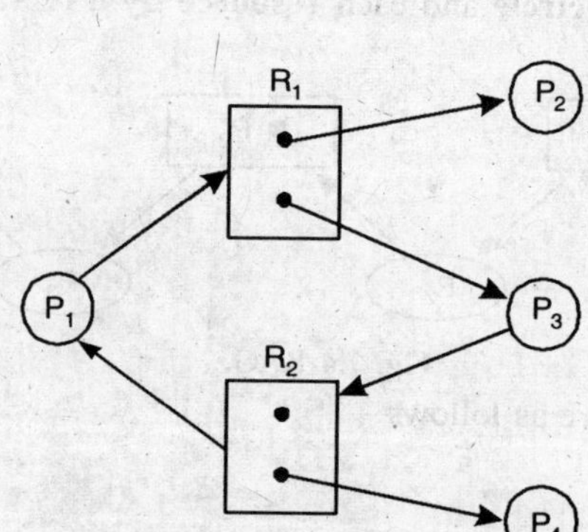

Fig. 7.6 RAG with a cycle but no Deadlock.

Please note that in Fig. 7.3 above, P_2 holds an instance of R_1 and P_4 holds an instance of R_2. Neither of these processes is waiting for a resource in the set R. P_2 and P_4 can release their resources. If they do then R_1 and R_2 will both have free instances. So, there will be no deadlock as those free instances can be assigned to P_1 and P_3 respectively and the arrows will be reversed. The request edges will turn into assignment edges. Then the graph will be acyclic and an acyclic RAG means no deadlock.

7.3.2 Methods of Deadlock Handling

Deadlocks can be handled by any of the following methods—

1. Deadlock prevention

Deadlock can be prevented from occurring by preventing one of the four necessary conditions to hold. If one of the conditions can be prevented from holding then deadlock will not occur.

2. Deadlock avoidance

Deadlocks can be avoided by maintaining the system in safe state. **A system is said to be in safe state, if all pending processes can be successfully executed in some sequence but satisfying their resource requirements completely. The sequence in which the pending processes can be executed is called as a safe sequence.**

A process is executed only if its maximum need of resources is within the system capacity. It is our OS that checks whether the systems will be in a safe or unsafe state after the allocation of requested resources. This can avoid deadlocks.

3. Deadlock recovery

Let the deadlock occur in the system and then try to recover the system from deadlock.

4. Allow deadlock to occur

Let the deadlocks occur in the system and deteriorate the system performance. When deadlock occurs, system will finally stop functioning. Just reboot the system. Thus, in summary the methods are

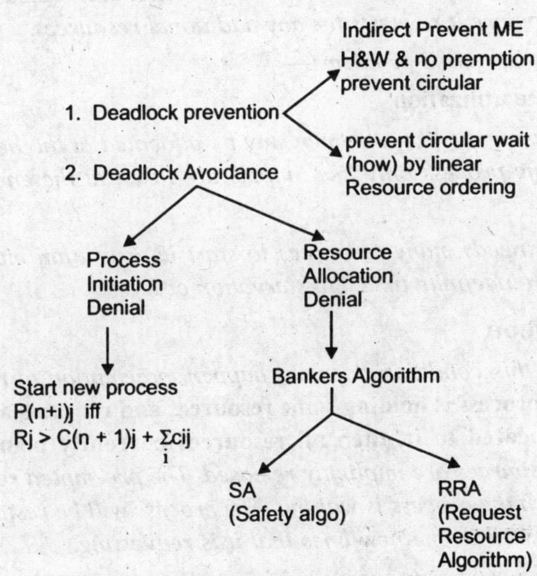

3. Deadlock Delection – periodically run this algorithm.

7.4 DEADLOCK PREVENTION

In this method, we design a system in such a way that the possibility of deadlock is excluded.

It can be done by two methods—

(a) Direct method

(b) Indirect method

In direct method, *we need to prevent the occurrence of a circular wait.*

In indirect method, *we need to prevent the occurrence of one of the three conditions—mutual exclusion, hold and wait and no preemption.*

Deadlock can be prevented by ensuring that atleast one of these conditions cannot hold. Let us discuss them one by one.

7.4.1 Mutual Exclusion

Mutual exclusion means only one process can use the resource at a time. *An effort should be made to prevent mutual exclusion.* **The rule followed here is to convert all non-sharable resource to sharable resource.** *Like if several processes would like to access a read-only file then allow that to happen. There is no need of mutual exclusion in such a case.* **But please note that few resources cannot be changed from non-sharable to sharable.** *For e.g., several processes cannot be allowed an update on a file simultaneously. Here, mutual exclusion is must. But we already know that mutual exclusion is one of the requirement of the critical section problem also.* **So, preventing it may sometimes lead to undesired results also.** *Thus, denying mutual exclusion can create more problems than it solves.* **In general, this condition cannot be disallowed.**

7.4.2 Hold-and-Wait

We need to ensure that hold-and-wait condition never occurs in the system. This means that we guarantee that whenever a process request for a resource, it does not hold any other resource. For this, we require that each process has to declare all its requirements in the beginning and before starting it has to be allocated all its required resources.

An alternative rule, allows a process to request resources only when the process has none: A process may request some resources and use them. It must release all the resources that it is currently allocated before it requests for any additional resources.

In either case there are 2 problems—

1. Low resource utilization

Many of the resources like a printer may be allocated at the beginning of the process but is used at the end of the process only like outputs are taken at the end of the process.

2. Starvation

A process that needs many resources to start its execution may be waiting for one or the other resource for an indefinite time. So, starvation occurs.

7.4.3 No preemption

To ensure that this condition does not happen, preemption of resources should be allowed. **The rule is — "If a process is holding some resources and requests another resource that cannot be immediately allocated to it, then all resources currently being held are preempted."** *In otherwords, these resources are implicitly released. The preempted resources are added to the list of resources for which the process is waiting. The process will be restarted only when it can regain its old resources, as well as the new ones that it is requesting.*

Alternative: *If a process requests some resources, we first check whether they are available. If they are available then we allocate them. If they are not available, we check whether they are allocated to some other process that is waiting for additional resources. If so, we preempt the desired resources from the waiting process and allocate them to the requesting process. If the* *resources are not either available or held by a waiting process, the requesting process must wait.*

7.4.4 Circular Wait

To ensure that this condition never holds, we impose **a total hierarchical ordering** *of all resource types. It is required that each process can only request the required resources in an increasing order to enumeration.*

Let $R = \{R_1, R_2 .... R_m\}$ *be the set of resource types. We assign a unique integer number (weight) to each resource type. By using these numbers, we can check using comparison whether one precedes another in our ordering. It can be given by a function.*

$$F\ (\text{resource-type}) \rightarrow N$$

Where N is any integer. Now consider that each process can request the resources only in an increasing order of enumeration. It simply means that the process can request instances of resource type, R_i*. After that, the process can request instances of resource type,* R_j*, if and only if* $F(R_j) > F(R_i)$*. Whenever a process requests an instance of resource type* R_j*, it has released any resources,* R_i *such that*

$$F(R_i) \geq F(R_j)$$

By using these rules, we can break the cyclic wait easily.

7.5 DEADLOCK AVOIDANCE

In this method, each process has to declare that which all resources are required and how many instances of each resource type it will require in its lifetime. If this information is available in advance, it is possible to construct an algorithm that ensures that the system will never load to deadlock. **Please note that a deadlock avoidance algorithm dynamically examines the resource allocation state to ensure that a circular wait condition can never exist. Also note here that the resource-allocation state is defined by the number of available and allocated resources and the maximum demands of the processes.**

The following are the requirements of Deadlock avoidance—

1. *The maximum resource requirement must be stated in advance.*
2. *The processes under consideration must be independent. There are no synchronization requirements.*
3. *There must be a fixed number of resources to allocate.*
4. *No process may exist till it releases the resources it is holding.*

Basically, this algorithm checks that after allocating resources, will the system be in a safe state or not?

A system is in safe state only if there exists a safe sequence. *A sequence of processes* $<P_1, P_2 ..., P_n>$ *is a safe sequence for the current allocation state if for each* P_i*, the resources that* P_i *can still request can be satisfied by the currently available resources plus the resources held by all the* P_j *such that* $j < i$*. In this situation, if the resources that process* P_i *needs are not immediately available then* P_i *can wait until all* P_j *have finished. When they have finished,* P_i *can obtain all of its needed resources, complete its designated task, return its allocated resources and terminate. When* P_i *terminates,* P_{i+1} *can obtain its needed resources and so on. If no such sequence exists, then the system state is said to be* **unsafe.** *A safe state is not a deadlock state. Unsafe state may be or may not be deadlock state.*

Consider the Fig. 7.7 below for better understanding.

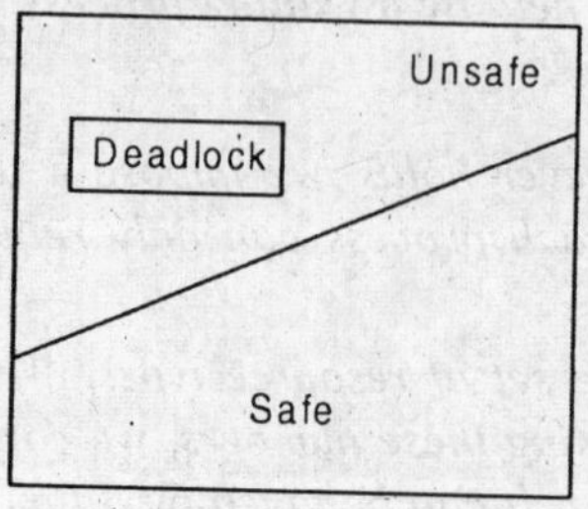

Fig. 7.7 *Safe, unsafe and deadlock state spaces.*

From Fig. 7.6, it is clear that **a safe state is not a deadlock state. Conversely, a deadlock state is an unsafe state.** *Not all unsafe states are deadlocks. However, an unsafe state may lead to a deadlock. As long as the state is safe, the OS can avoid unsafe states.*

We are in a position to generalize the process and resource relationship now. *Consider a system of 'n' processes and 'm' different types of resources. Then, this system can be defined by the following matrices—*

1. Resources = $(R_1, R_2, ... R_m)$

This matrix represents the total amount of resources in the system.

2. Available = $(V_1, V_2, V_3, ... V_m)$.

This matrix represents the total amount of each resource not allocated to a process.

3. Claim = $\begin{bmatrix} C_{11} & C_{12}..... & C_{1m} \\ C_{21} & C_{22}..... & C_{2m} \\ C_{n1} & C_{n2}..... & C_{nm} \end{bmatrix}$

This matrix represents the requirement of each process for each resource.

4. Allocation = $\begin{bmatrix} A_{11} & A_{12}..... & A_{1m} \\ A_{21} & A_{22}..... & A_{2m} \\ A_{n1} & A_{n2}..... & A_{nm} \end{bmatrix}$

This matrix represents the current allocation.

The matrix-3 (claim matrix) gives the maximum requirement of each process for each resource with one row dedicated to each process. **We need to prove now that a new process can be started only** *if* $R_i \geq C_{(n+1)i} + \sum_{k=1}^{n} C_{ki}$ **for all** ***i*****.**

To prove: $R_i \geq C_{(n+1)i} + \sum_{k=1}^{n} C_{ki}$ *(for all i)*

Proof: *Let us suppose that—*

C_{ij} — *Requirement of process–i for resource–j.*

A_{ij} — *Current allocation of resource–j to process–i.*

Now, the following relationship can be derived from all this—

1. $R_i = V_i + \sum_{k=1}^{n} A_{ki}$

That is, all resources are either available or allocated.

2. $C_{ki} \leq C_{ki}$ *for all k and i.*

It implies that no process can claim more than total amount of resource in the system.

3. $A_{ki} \leq C_{ki}$ *for all k and i.*

It means that no process is allocated resources of any type more than the process originally claimed to need.

From 1st, 2nd and 3rd observation, **we conclude that a new process can be started only if—**

$$R_i \geq C_{(n+1)i} + \sum_{k=1}^{n} C_{ki} \quad (\text{for all } i)$$

Hence, proved

We are in a position to solve a problem now.

Example 1. Consider that there are total 10 magnetic tapes. There are four (4) processes in the system, in which process P_1 may need maximum of 4-tapes, P_2 may need maximum of 3, P_3 may need maximum of 5 and P_4 may need maximum of 7 tape drives. The matrix is as follows—

Process	Max. Need	Allocated	Current Need
P_1	4	2	2
P_2	3	2	1
P_3	5	3	2
P_4	7	1	6

Is the system safe/unsafe?

Solution. *As we can see in the above table that the total number of tape drives that have been allocated are (2 + 2 + 3 + 1) = 8*

∴ Left-over tape drive are = 10 – 8 = 2

Thus, the system is in safe state. The sequence $< P_1, P_2, P_3, P_4 >$ *satisfies the safety condition, since process* P_1 *can be immediately granted all its required tape drives and then return them. The system will then have 4 available tape drives. Then, the process* P_2 *can get all its tape drives and return and this is continued till all processes are over.*

Given the concept of a safe state, we can define avoidance algorithms that ensure that the system will never deadlock. **The idea is simply to ensure that the system will always remain in a safe state.** *Initially, the system is in a safe state. Whenever, a process requests a resource that is currently available, the system must decide whether the resource can be allocated immediately or the process must wait.* **Please note here that the request is granted only if the allocation leaves the system in a safe state.**

Note: How do we know whether a state is safe or not?

We follow a **procedure** *here—*

1. **Start in the given state.**

2. **Simulate running each process to completion by allocating its maximum resources**

requirements and then releasing all resources.

3. **If all processes can complete, then the state is safe.**

7.5.1 RAG algorithm—One instance

The resource-allocation graph algorithm (RAG) is applicable to a resource allocation system with **single instance of each resource type.** *We get another variant of the RAG of Figure 7.3 which can be used for deadlock avoidance. What we do is that in addition to the* **request** *and the* **assignment edges,** *we introduce a new type of edge called as a* **claim edge.**

What is a claim edge?

A claim edge, $P_i \rightarrow R_j$ indicates that a process P_i may request resource R_j at sometime in the future. This edge resembles a request edge in direction but is represented by a **dashed line. Please note that when a process, P_i requests resource R_j, the claim edge $P_i \rightarrow R_j$ is converted to a request edge.** *Similarly, when a resource R_j is released by P_i, the assignment edge $R_j \rightarrow P_i$ is reconverted to a claim edge $P_i \rightarrow R_j$.* **Also note that the resources must be claimed a priori in the system, that is, before process P_i starts executing, all its claim edges must already appear in RAG.** *We can relax this condition by allowing a claim edge $P_i \rightarrow R_j$ to be added to the graph only if all the edges associated with process, P_i are claim edges.*

7.5.2 Banker's Algorithm—Multiple instances

The RAG algorithm discussed above is not applicable to a resource allocation system with multiple instances of each resource type. In such a situation, **Banker's Algorithm** *is used. This name was chosen because this algorithm could be used in a banking system to ensure that the bank never allocates its available cash such that it can no longer satisfy the needs of all its customers.*

When a new process enters the system, it must declare the maximum number of instances of each resource type that it may need. This number may not exceed the total number of resources in the system. When a user requests a set of resources, the system must determine whether the allocation of these resources will leave the system in a safe state. If so, then the resources are allocated else the process must wait until some other process releases enough resources.

Data structures used:

Let 'n' be the number of processes in the system and 'm' be the number of resource types. We need the following data structures to implement Banker's algorithm.

1. Available: *A vector of length 'm' indicates the number of available resources of each type. If Available [j] = k, there are k instances of resource type R_j available in the system.*

2. Max: *An (n * m) matrix defines the maximum demand of each process. If Max [i, j] = k, then process P_i may request at most k instances of resource type, R_j.*

3. Allocation: *An (n * m) matrix defines the number of resources of each type currently allocated to each process. If Allocation [i, j] = k, then process P_i is currently allocated k instances of resource type, R_j.*

4. Need: *An (n * m) matrix indicates the remaining resource need of each process. If Need [i, j] = k then process P_i may need k more instances of resource type R_j to complete its task.* **Please note that—**

$$\boxed{Need\ [i, j] = Max\ [i, j] - Allocation\ [i, j]}$$

Each row in the matrices— Allocation and Need is treated as a **vector.** *So, we can refer to them as* $Allocation_i$ *and* $Need_i$ *respectively. Herein,* **the vector, Allocation,** *specifies the resources currently allocated to process,* P_i. *Also the vector,* $Need_i$ *specifies the additional resources that process,* P_i *may still request to complete its task.*

Firstly, we need to write an algorithm that finds out whether or not a system is in a safe state. This algorithm is named as a **safety algorithm** *and is given below—*

Safety Algorithm

Step-1: *Let Work and Finish be the two vectors of length m and n, respectively. Initialize : Work = Available and Finish [i] = false*

for i = 1, 2, 3, ... n.

Step-2: *Find i such that both:*

(a) Finish [i] = false

(b) $Need_i \leq Work$

If no such i exists, go to step-4.

Step-3: $Work = Work + Allocation_i$

Finish [i] = true

go to step-2

Step-4: *If Finish [i] = true for all i, then the system is in a safe state else it is in unsafe state.*

This algorithm takes $0(m \times n^2)$ *operations to decide whether a state is safe.*

Next, we develop a **Resource-Request Algorithm.** *Let* $Request_i$ *be the request vector for process,* P_i. *If* $Request_i [j] = k$, *then process* P_i *wants k instances of resource type,* R_j. *When a request for resources is made by process,* P_i, *the following actions are taken:–*

Step-1: *If* $Request_i \leq Need_i$, *goto step-2. Else raise an exception (error) as the process has exceeded its maximum claim.*

Step-2: *If* $Request_i \leq Available$, *goto step-3. Else* P_i *must wait, since the resources are not available.*

Step-3: *Have the system pretend to have allocated the requested resources to process,* P_i, *by modifying the state as follows:*

$$Available = Available - Request_i;$$
$$Allocation_i = Allocation_i + Request_i;$$
$$Need_i = Need_i - Request_i;$$

If the resulting resource-allocation is safe, then the transaction is completed and process, P_i *is allocated its resources. However, if the new state is unsafe then* P_i *must wait for* $Request_i$ *and the old resource allocation state is restored.*

This algorithm is known as a Banker's algorithm and has good results. We are in a position to solve some problems now.

Example 1: **Let there be five processes (P_1 to P_5) and three resource types A, B, C.**

Resource type A has 10 instances.

Resource type B has 5 instances.

and Resource type C has 7 instances.

Suppose that at time, t_0, the following snapshot of the system has been taken:

	Allocation			Max			Available		
	A	B	C	A	B	C	A	B	C
P_1	0	1	0	7	5	3	3	3	2
P_2	2	0	0	3	2	2			
P_3	3	0	2	9	0	2			
P_4	2	1	1	2	2	2			
P_5	0	0	2	4	3	3			

Find the safe sequence? Is this system safe at time, t_0. If process, P_2 sends one additional request, can it be granted access? Say, P_2 sends the request of (1, 0, 2). What is the new content of matrix-Need? Is this state, a safe system state? Explain.

Solution. *Firstly, we need to find vector, need as follows—*

$\because$ $\boxed{Need = Max - Allocation}$

So, we get

Process	Allocation			Max			Available			Need		
	A	B	C	A	B	C	A	B	C	A	B	C
P_1	0	1	0	7	5	3	3	3	2	7	4	3
P_2	2	0	0	3	2	2				1	2	2
P_3	3	0	2	9	0	2				6	0	0
P_4	2	1	1	2	2	2				0	1	1
P_5	0	0	2	4	3	3				4	3	1

We can find a safe sequence as $< P_2, P_4, P_5, P_3, P_1 >$. So, we can say that the system is in safe state at time, t_0.

It is given that P_2 makes another request now—

A B C

$Request_2$ = (1, 0, 2)

This request is sent to OS. To decide whether this request can be immediately granted or not, we first check that $Request_i \leq Available$, which is true. We then pretend that this request has been fulfilled. We arrive at a new state as given below—

Process	Allocation			Max			Available			Need		
	A	B	C	A	B	C	A	B	C	A	B	C
P_1	0	1	0	7	5	3	2	3	0	7	4	3
P_2	3	0	2	3	2	2				0	2	0
P_3	3	0	2	9	0	2				6	0	0
P_4	2	1	1	2	2	2				0	1	1
P_5	0	0	2	4	3	3				4	3	1

Now, we check whether this new system is safe or not. For that, we execute our safety algorithm and find the sequence $< P_2, P_4, P_5, P_1, P_3 >$ satisfies our safety requirement. Hence, we can immediately grant the request of process, P_2. This is done as follows :

S1 : Request [1] = (1, 0, 2) given

$\leq$ (7, 4, 3)

Which is true

S2 : $\because$ $(1, 0, 2) \leq (3, 3, 2)$ *is true*

$Avail_1 = (3, 3, 2) - (1, 0, 2)$

$= (2, 3, 0)$

$Alloc_1 = (2, 0, 0) + (1, 0, 2)$

$= (3, 0, 2)$

$Need_1 = (1, 2, 2) - (1, 0, 2)$

$= (0, 2, 0)$

$\therefore$ P_2 *can be immediately granted resources.*

Please note that when the system is in this state, a request for (3, 3, 0) by process, P_5, cannot be granted since the resources are not available. Also note that a request for (0, 2, 0) by process, P_1 cannot be granted, even though the resources are available because after allocating the required resources by the process, P_1, there is no safe sequence available.

Example 2. Consider a system with five (5) process–P_0 to P_4 and three (3) resources A, B, C. Given that—

Resource type A has 10 instances.
Resource type B as 5 instances.
Resource type C has 7 instances.
Suppose that at time, t_0, the following snapshot of the system has been taken—

Process	Allocation			Max		
	R_1	R_2	R_3	R_1	R_2	R_3
P_0	0	1	0	7	5	3
P_1	2	0	0	3	2	2
P_2	3	0	2	9	0	2
P_3	2	1	1	2	2	2
P_4	0	0	2	4	3	3

Calculate the available matrix of resources. Find the need matrix. Find the safe sequence?

Solution. *The available matrix is calculated as follows—*

$\because$ $\boxed{Available = Total - Allocation}$

$\therefore R_1 = 10 - (2 + 3 + 2) = 3$

$R_2 = 5 - (1 + 1) = 3$

$R_3 = 7 - (2 + 1 + 2) = 2$

$\therefore$ *The available matrix is (3, 3, 2). Now, what is the Need matrix?*

$\because$ $\boxed{Need = Max - Allocation}$

So, we get

Process	R_1	R_2	R_3
P_0	(7–0)	(5–1)	(3–0)
P_1	(3–2)	(2–0)	(2–0)
P_2	(9–3)	(0–0)	(2–2)
P_3	(2–2)	(2–1)	(2–1)
P_4	(4–0)	(3–0)	(3–2)

which gives us the **Need matrix** *as follows—*

Process	Need		
	R_1	R_2	R_3
P_0	7	4	3
P_1	1	2	2
P_2	6	0	0
P_3	0	1	1
P_4	4	3	1

Applying Banker's algorithm, we now search the Need-matrix from P_0 to P_4 which is less than the available-matrix *i.e.*, (3, 3, 2). We find that (1, 2, 2) < (3, 3, 2). So, allocate the requesting resource to P_1. Now, the process, P_1's allocation is—

(2, 0, 0) + (1, 2, 2) = (3, 2, 2).

After the completion of job P_1, it releases the total resources. Then the available resource is—

(3, 3, 2) + (2, 0, 0) = (5, 3, 2)

We search the need matrix again, which is less than the available. Now, we find that—

(0, 1, 1) < (5, 3, 2)

So, allocate resources to P_3. After P_3 completes, it releases all its resources. Then,

Available = Available + Allocation

i.e., (5, 3, 2) + (2, 1, 1) = (7, 4, 3)

This process is continued till we find the safe state and is shown below :-

Banker's algorithm

Work = Available = (3, 3, 2)

P_0 : Finish [i] = false (i = 1)

$Need_1$ work

(7, 4, 3) (3, 3, 2)

Step 4 : ∴ Finish [1] = false × ∴ unsafe P_0

P_1 : Finish [i] = false [i = 2]

$Need_2$ work

(1, 2, 2) (3, 3, 2)

Step 3: Work = work + Allocation

∴ work (3, 3, 2) + (2, 0, 0)

work = (5, 3, 2)

Finsih [2] = true Safe P_1

P_2 Finish [i] = false [i = 3]

$Need_3$ work.

(6, 0, 0) (5, 3, 2)

Step 4: Finish [3] = true Unsafe P_2

P_3 : Finish [i] = false [i = 4]

$Need_4$ work

(0,1,1) (5, 3, 2)

Step 3: Work = work + Allocation

(5, 3, 2) = (5, 3, 2) + (2, 1, 1)

$(5,3,2,) = (7,4,3)$ work $= (7,4,3)$

Finish [4] = ture ∴ (Safe P_3)

P_4 : Finish [i] = false [i = 5]

$Need_5 = work$

$(4,3,1) \leq (7,4,5)$

work = Work + Allocation

$(7,4,5) = (7,4,3) + (0,0,2)$ (work = 7, 4, 5)

$(7,4,3) = (7,4,5)$ ∴ (safe P_4)

P_0 : Finish [1] = false [i = 1]

$need_1 \leq work$

$(7, 4, 3) \leq (7, 4, 5)$

work = Work + Allocation

$(7,4,5) = (7,4,5) + (0,1,0)$

$(7,4,5) = (7,5,5)$

work = (7, 5, 5)

(safe P_0)

P_2 : Finish [2] = false [i = 3]

$Need_3 \leq work$

$(6,0,0) \leq (7,5,5)$

Work = Work + Allocation

$(7,5,5) + (3,0,2)$ (7, 5, 5):

$(7,5,5) = 10, 5, 7$ (Safe P_2)

Safe sequence = $(P_1, P_3, P_4, P_0, P_2)$

7.6 DEADLOCK RECOVERY

We need mechanisms to detect whether deadlock exists in the system or not? If yes, methods to recover the system from such a state should be known.

7.6.1 Deadlock Detection Algorithm

Deadlock detection is used by employing an algorithm that tracks the circular waiting and killing one or more processes so that deadlock is removed. In deadlock detection technique, resources are granted to the requesting processes without any check. **The system state is examined periodically to determine if a set of processes is deadlocked. A deadlock is resolved by aborting and restarting a process, relinquishing all the resources that the process held.** There are two **algorithms** for deadlock detection and are discussed next.

7.6.1.1 For single instance of each resource type

1. If in the RAG, every resource has only one instance (or single instance) then we define a deadlock detection algorithm that uses a variant of the RAG and is called as a **Wait-for graph.** **How to get this graph from RAG?**

We can get this graph from Resource-allocation graph (RAG) **by removing the nodes of type resource and collapsing the appropriate edges.** In this situation, if the *wait-for graph* has any cycle then there is a deadlock in the system.

2. To detect deadlocks, the system needs to maintain the wait-for graph and to **periodically** invoke an algorithm that searches for a cycle in the graph. The complexity of this algorithm will be $O(n^2)$ where 'n' is the number of vertices in the graph.

Consider the following RAG—

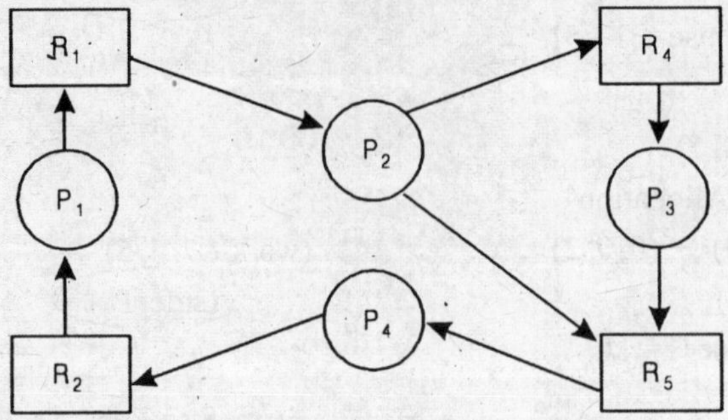

Fig. 7.8 *A RAG—Resource Allocation Graph*

We can draw its' corresponding wait for graph by removing all nodes that represents resources and collapsing their edges. Thus, we get a wait for graph as shown in Fig. 7.9 below:

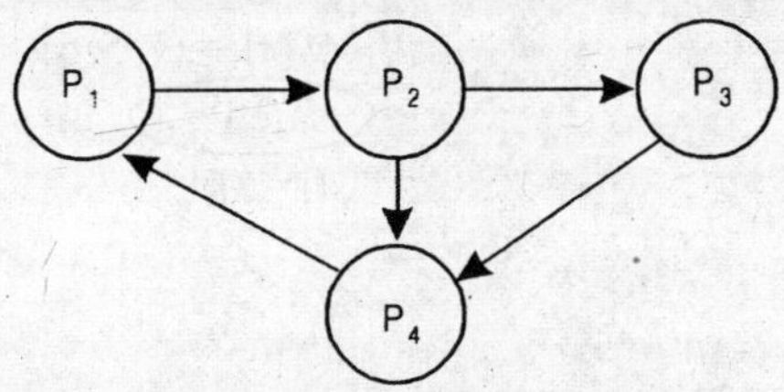

Fig. 7.9 *Corresponding wait for graph*

Observe carefully in Figure 7.9 that the system is in deadlock state as there exists a cycle between P_1, P_2 and P_4. Also, a cycle is found between P_1, P_2, P_3 and P_4. So, all processes P_1 to P_4 are deadlocked.

7.6.1.2 For Multiple Instances of each Resource Type

The wait-for graph discussed above is not applicable here because now we have multiple (many) instances of a resource type. In such a case of multiple instances, we use another algorithm that is similar to Banker's algorithm discussed earlier.

Data structures used:

1. **Available:** *A vector of length 'm' indicates the number of available resources of each type.*
2. **Allocation:** *An (n * m) matrix that defines the number of resources of each type currently allocated to each process.*
3. **Request:** *An (n * m) matrix that indicates the current request of each process. If Request [i, j] = k, then process P_i is requesting k more instances of resource type R_j.*

We now develop a deadlock detection algorithm. *This algorithm investigates every possible allocation sequence for processes that remain to be completed—*

Step-1: *Let Work and Finish be vectors of length m and n, respectively.*

Initialize Work = Available, for $i \leftarrow 1, 2, \ldots. n$. If Allocation $i \neq 0$, then Finish [i] = false; else Finish [i] = true.

Step-2: *Find an index i such that both:*

(a) Finish [i] = false.

(b) $Request_i \leq Work$

If no such i exists then go to step-4.

Step-3: *Work = Work + Allocation$_i$*

Finish [i] = true

goto step – 2

Step-4: *If Finish [i] = false, for some i, such that $1 \le i \le n$, then the system is in a deadlock state.*

Moreover, if Finish [i] = false, then process, P_i is deadlocked.

This algorithm requires an order of $(m * n^2)$ operations to detect whether the system is in a deadlocked state.

We are in a position to solve a problem now.

Example 1. Consider a system with five processes, P_0 to P_4 and there resource types A, B, C. Resource type A has 7 instances, resource type B has 2 instances and resource type C has 6 instances. Suppose that at time, t_0, we have the following resource-allocation state:—

	Allocation			**Request**			**Available**		
	A	*B*	*C*	*A*	*B*	*C*	*A*	*B*	*C*
P_0	0	1	0	0	0	0	0	0	0
P_1	2	0	0	2	0	2			
P_2	3	0	3	0	0	0			
P_3	2	1	1	1	0	0			
P_4	0	0	2	0	0	2			

We claim that the system is not in a deadlocked state. Indeed, if we execute our algorithm, we will find that the sequence < P_0, P_2, P_3, P_1, P_4 > will result in Finish [i] = true for all i. Suppose now process P_2 makes one additional request for an instance of type C. The Request matrix is modified as follows—

	Request		
	A	**B**	**C**
P_0	0	0	0
P_1	2	0	2
P_2	0	0	1
P_3	1	0	0
P_4	0	0	2

We claim that the system is deadlocked. Although we can reclaim that the resources held by process, P_0, the number of available resources is not sufficient to fulfill the requests of the other processes. Thus, a deadlock exists, consisting of processes P_1, P_2, P_3 and P_4.

7.7 OTHER METHODS OF DEADLOCK RECOVERY

When a detection algorithm determines that a deadlock exists then there are four (4) possible methods of recovery from deadlock. **Please note that if you will not free your system from deadlock then you may risk in degrading your system's performance.** *This may result in total system failure. In general, 4-methods can be used here—*

1. **Kill all** *deadlocked processes. This is quite simple and easy to implement.*
2. *Force all the deadlocked processes back to their last known state and restart them, if* **check pointing** *is done.*
3. *Kill processes* **one by one** *at a time until deadlock breaks.*
4. **Preempt** *resources until the deadlock is broken.*

Any process that loses a resource has to be restarted from a suitable earlier check-point.

Let us discuss, process termination and Resource preemption methods now.

7.7.1 Process Termination

There are two ways of process terminations—

1. Abort all deadlocked processes

This method will break the deadlock cycle but a great expense. This is because these processes may have computed for a long time and the results of these partial computations must be discarded and probably must be recomputed later.

2. Abort one process at a time until the deadlock cycle is eliminated

This method incurs considerable overhead since after each process is aborted, a deadlock detection algorithm must be invoked to determine whether any processes are still deadlocked.

However, aborting a process is not an easy job. **For instance,** if a process was in the midst of printing data on the printer, the system must reset the printer to a correct state before printing the next job.

Which process to select for its termination?

Many factors determine that which all processes must be chosen for abortion. Some of these factors are—

1. The priority of the process.
2. How long the process has computed?
3. How many resources have been used by it?
4. What type of resources have been used?
5. How many more resources are required?

7.7.2 Resource preemption

We may preempt (snatch) some of the resources for recovery from the deadlock state and allocate these resources to other processes until the deadlock cycle is broken.

There are three issues pertaining to resource preemption—

1. Selecting a victim

Which resource and which process needs to be preempted? As in process termination, we must determine the order of preemption to minimize cost. Cost factors may include such parameters as the number of resources a deadlock process is holding and the amount of time a deadlocked process has thus for consumed during its execution.

2. Rollback

If we preempt a resource from a process, what should be done with that process? Obviously, it cannot continue with its normal execution as it is missing some needed resource. We must roll back the process to some safe state and restart it from that state.

3. Starvation

How to ensure that starvation will not occur? This means that a particular process must not be deprived of resources again and again.

7.8 CASE STUDY ON SOLARIS METHOD OF HANDLING DEADLOCKS

This has already been given in section 6.13 of previous chapter-6.

Summary

We must invoke deadlock detection algorithm once a deadlock occurs. But it is very expensive to invoke this algorithm for every request. So, a simple solution is to invoke this algorithm at less frequent intervals like once per hour or whenever CPU utilization falls below 40%. We have various *approaches like detection, prevention and avoidance in OS for deadlock handling. Let us summarize in a tabular form—*

Method	Policy of Resource allocations	Schemes	Advantages	Disadvantages
1. Detection	*Requested resources are possible*	*Invoke periodically to test for.*	*Never delays process initiation and facilitates on-line.*	*Inherent preemption losses.*
2. Prevention	*Conservative under commits resources*	*(a) Requesting all resources at once.*	*(1) Works well for processes that perform a single burst of activity.* *(2) No preemption necessary*	*(1) Inefficient* *(2) Delays process initiation*
		(b) Preemption	*(3) Convenient when applied to resources whose state can be saved.*	*(3) Preempts more often then necessary.* *(4) Subject to cyclic restart.*
		(c) Resource ordering	*(4) Feasible to enforce* *(5) Need no run-time computation as problem is solved in system design.*	*(5) Preempts without much use.* *(6) Disallows incremental resource requests.*
3. Avoidance	*Selects midway between that of detection and prevention.*	*Manipulate to find atleast one safe path.*	*No preemption is necessary.*	*(1) Future resource requirements must be known* *(2) Processes can be blocked for long periods.*

MULTIPLE CHOICE QUESTIONS [MCQs]

1. *A situation where a process or a set of processes is blocked, waiting for some resource that is held by some other waiting processes:*

(a) Mutual Exclusion *(b) Semaphore*

(c) Deadlock *(d) None of the above*

2. *A resource type, R is represented by 3-dots, it has—*

(a) 2 instances. *(b) 3 instances.*

(c) 4 instances. *(d) 6 instances.*

3. *Acyclic RAG implies—*
   (a) *No deadlock* (b) *Deadlock*
   (c) *Starvation* (d) *None of the above*
4. *A safe state is—*
   (a) *Deadlock state* (b) *Non-deadlocked state.*
   (c) *Polling state* (d) *None of the above*
5. *A new process can be started only if—*

   (a) $R_i < C_{(n+1)i} + \sum_{k=1}^{n} C_{ki}$ *(for all i)*

   (b) $R_i = C_{(n+1)i} + \sum_{k=1}^{n} C_{ki}$ *(for all i)*

   (c) $R_i \geq C_{(n+1)i} + \sum_{k=1}^{n} C_{ki}$ *(for all i)*

   (d) *None of the above*
6. *RAG stands for—*
   (a) *Resource and Graph.* (b) *Resource Allocation Graph*
   (c) *Resource After Graph* (d) *None of the above*
7. *A claim edge is represented, usually, by a—*
   (a) *Solid line* (b) *Thin line*
   (c) *Dashed line* (d) *None of the above*
8. *For multiple instances of a resource type which algorithm is used—*
   (a) *Divide and Conquer algorithm* (b) *Banker's Algorithm*
   (c) *Sorting Algorithm* (d) *None of the above*
9. *The Need-matrix is given by the formula*
   (a) *Need = Max – Allocation*
   (b) *Need = Max + Allocation*
   (c) *Need = Max * Allocation*
   (d) *None of the above*
10. *The safety-algorithm takes—*
    (a) *0 (mn)* (b) *0 (mn²)*
    (c) *0 (m + n)* (d) *None of the above*
11. *Another variant of RAG is—*
    (a) *Call graph* (b) *Wait-for graph*
    (c) *Shortest path graph* (d) *None of the above*
12. *Banker's algorithm for resource allocation deals with—*
    (a) *Deadlock prevention* (b) *Deadlock avoidance*
    (c) *Deadlock recovery* (d) *None of the above*

13. *In Resource Allocation Graph (RAG), circles represent—*

(a) Processes *(b) Resources*

(c) Both 'a' and 'b' *(d) None of the above*

14. *A set of resource allocations such that the system can allocate resources to each process in some order and still avoid deadlock is—*

(a) Unsafe state *(b) Safe state*

(c) Starvation *(d) None of the above*

15. *To recover from deadlock, the method used is—*

(a) Process termination *(b) Resource preemption*

(c) Both 'a' and 'b' *(d) None of the above*

ANSWERS

1. *c*	**2.** *b*	**3.** *a*	**4.** *b*	**5.** *c*	**6.** *b*
7. *c*	**8.** *b*	**9.** *a*	**10.** *b*	**11.** *b*	**12.** *b*
13. *a*	**14.** *b*	**15.** *c*			

CONCEPTUAL SHORT QUESTIONS WITH ANSWERS

Q. 1. Distinguish between one instance of Resource type and Multiple instances of Resource type?

Ans. *We tabulate the differences as follows.*

Single Instances	**Multiple Instances**
1. Cyclic RAG implies a deadlock.	*1. Cyclic RAG need not always imply deadlock*
2. If a cycle in RAG involves only a set of resource type S, each of which has a single instance then deadlock must have occurred.	*2. If there is a cycle in RAG, it does not necessarily imply that a deadlock has occurred.*
3. If every resource has only a single instances then we define a wait-for graph to prevent deadlocks.	*3. When we have multiple instances of a resource type then wait-for graph is not applicable.*
4. A single instance of a resource type is represented by a single dot in a rectangle, i.e., 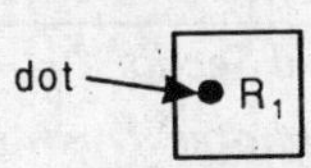 *It shows single instance of resource type,* R_1.	*4. Multiple instances of a resource type are represented by many dots, Like, 2 dots shows 2-instances of the resource types, 3 dots show 3-instances and so on, i.e.,* 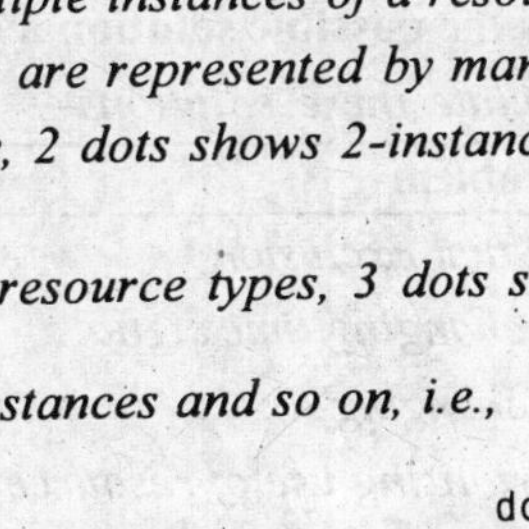

5. An algorithm to detect a cycle in a graph requires an order of n^2 operations, 'n' being the number of vertices.	*5. An algorithm to detect whether a system is in a deadlocked state requires an order of (mn^2) operations.*

Q. 2. Consider the classic Dining Philosophers problem. How will you check to see if the algorithm can prevent deadlock?

Ans. *Problem domain for classic Dining Philosophers problem is as follows—*

"Five philosophers, with five plates and five forks. A philosopher needs two forks (one on his left and one on his right) in order to eat. Deadlock occurs if all philosophers (each of them) picks up one fork and then waits indefinitely for his neighbour to release the other one and as a consequence all starve."

4 Conditions for deadlock are there. How will they apply here? Let us see.

(1) Mutual Exclusion: *Only one philosopher can use a fork at any one time.*

(2) Hold and Wait: *Deadlock only occurs when philosophers hold one fork and are waiting for the second.*

(3) No preemption: *If one philosopher could take a fork from his neighbour then the problem is sorted out.*

4. Circular Wait: *The circular table shows how the philosopher chain has double back on itself to form the circular chain.*

Is there a known safe solution?

There are two cases.

Case I : Odd number of philosophers (n is odd)

If 'n' is **odd** *then there is no way in which to specify the order of each philosopher to pick up the forks, so that deadlock can never occur. Thus, there is no correct way to solve this problem.*

Case II: Even number of philosophers (n is even)

If 'n' is **even** *then the problem can be solved by writing two different methods. If all the* **odd philosophers** *were to pick up the fork on their left and then one on their right and all* **even philosophers** *were to pick up the fork on their right and then the one on their left, then no deadlock would occur.*

Q. 3. The following are the problems in concurrent processing—

1. Mutual Exclusion 2. Exchanging time signals

3. Exchanging data 4. Serializing use of resource

5. Controlling access to Critical Section (buffers)

What is the possible solution available with you for the above mentioned problems?

Ans. *We tabulate there solutions—*

Problem	**Solution**
1. Mutual Exclusion	*1. Critical Section*
2. Exchanging time signals	*2. Semaphores*
3. Exchanging	*3. Message Buffers*
4. Serializing use of resource	*4. Mutual Exclusion*
5. Controlling access to CS	*5. Semaphores*

Q. 4. List examples of deadlocks that are not related to a computer-system environment.

Ans. 1. Two trains moving on a single track in opposite directions.

2. A person going down a ladder while another person is climbing up the ladder.

3. Two cars travelling on the same lane from opposite directions

Q. 5. Is it possible to have a deadlock involving only one single process? Explain your answer.

Ans. No, deadlock is not possible in only single process. This follows directly from the hold-and-wait condition.

Q. 6. Consider a system consisting of four resources of the same type that are shared by three processes, each of which needs atmost two resources. Show that the system is deadlock-free.

Ans. Suppose that the system is deadlocked. This implies that each process is holding one resource and is waiting for one more. Since there are three processes and four resources, one process must be able to obtain two resources. This process requires no more resources and therefore it will return its resources when done.

Q. 7. Can a system detect that some of its processes are starving? If you answer yes, explain how it can. If you answer no, explain how the system can deal with the starvation problem.

Ans. Detection of starvation in effect requires future knowledge since no amount of record-keeping statistics on processes can determine if it is making "progress" or not. However, starvation can be prevented by *aging* a process. This means maintaining a rollback count for each process and including this is a part of the cost factor in the selection process for a victim for preemption/roll back.

Q. 8. Consider the following snapshot of a system:

	Allocation				**Max**				**Available**			
	A	**B**	**C**	**D**	**A**	**B**	**C**	**D**	**A**	**B**	**C**	**D**
P_0	**0**	**0**	**1**	**2**	**0**	**0**	**1**	**2**	**1**	**5**	**2**	**0**
P_1	**1**	**0**	**0**	**0**	**1**	**7**	**5**	**0**				
P_2	**1**	**3**	**5**	**4**	**2**	**3**	**5**	**6**				
P_3	**0**	**6**	**3**	**2**	**0**	**6**	**5**	**2**				
P_4	**0**	**0**	**1**	**4**	**0**	**6**	**5**	**6**				

Answer the following questions using Banker's algorithm:—

(*a*) What is the content of the matrix Need? **(*b*) Is the system in a safe state?**

(*c*) If a request from process P_1 arrives for (0, 4, 2, 0), can the request be granted immediately?

Ans. (*a*) Need = Max – Allocation

∴ The contents of Need-matrix are—

	Need			
	A	B	C	D
P_0	0	0	0	0
P_1	0	7	5	0
P_2	1	0	0	2
P_3	0	0	2	0
P_4	0	6	4	2

(*b*) **Yes,** the sequence < P_0, P_2, P_1, P_3, P_4 > satisfies the safety requirement.

(*c*) **Yes,** since

(1) (0, 4, 2, 0) ≤ Available (i.e., 1, 5, 2, 0).

(2) (0, 4, 2, 0) ≤ Max_i; (i.e., 1, 7, 5, 0) for P_1.

(3) The **new system state** after allocation has been made is—

	Allocation				Max				Need				Available			
	A	B	C	D	A	B	C	D	A	B	C	D	A	B	C	D
P_0	0	0	1	2	0	0	1	2	0	0	0	0	1	1	0	0
P_1	1	4	2	0	1	7	5	0	0	3	3	0				
P_2	1	3	5	4	2	3	5	6	1	0	0	2				
P_3	0	6	3	2	0	6	5	2	0	0	2	0				
P_4	0	0	1	4	0	6	5	6	0	6	4	2				

∵ New allocation for P_1 = [Previous allocation + New request for allocation]
= (1, 0, 0, 0) + (0, 4, 2, 0)
= (1, 4, 2, 0) for P_1.

Also, Need = Max – Allocation (shown in table)

and Available = Available – Request
= (1, 5, 2, 0) – (0, 4, 2, 0)
= (1, 1, 0, 0) (shown in table above)

The sequence < P_0, P_2, P_1, P_3, P_4 > satisfies the safety requirement.

Q. 9. Consider the following snapshot of a system—

Process	Allocation			Max		
	A	B	C	A	B	C
P_0	0	1	0	7	5	3
P_1	2	0	0	3	2	2
P_2	3	0	2	9	0	2
P_3	2	1	1	2	2	2
P_4	0	0	2	4	3	3

Let the available number of resources be given by avail vector as (3, 3, 2). Use Banker's algorithm and answer—

1. **Find the contents of the matrix 'Need'?**
2. **Is the system in a safe-state?**
3. **If a request from process P4 for (3, 3, 0) arrives, can it be granted immediately?**

Ans. 1. The contents of the **Need-matrix** are—

∵ Need = Max – Allocation

∴

Process	Need		
	A	B	C
P_0	7	4	3
P_1	1	2	2
P_2	6	0	0
P_3	0	1	1
P_4	4	3	1

2. A **safe sequence** < P_1, P_3, P_0, P_2, P_4 > exists after applying the Banker's algorithm.

3. P_4 requests for (3, 3, 2). A safe sequence < P_1, P_3, P_2, P_4, P_0 > exists after applying the Banker's algorithm. Thus, the request can be granted immediately as it will not cause deadlock in the system.

Q. 10. Define what is a livelock?

Ans. Livelock (or indefinite postponement) is a situation in which some processes are making progress towards completion but one or more other processes are locked out of the resource.

To prevent this situation, some semaphore implementations are helpful to service the waiting processes.

EXERCISE QUESTIONS

Q. 1. (*a*) Writc four necessary conditions for Deadlock.

(*b*) What constitute a state of a system? What is a safe state? Describe an algorithm to check whether a given state is safe or not?

Q. 2. Define the term Deadlock. Under what conditions does a Deadlock occur? Explain them.

Q. 3. What are the necessary conditions for a deadlock? Explain the deadlock avoidance algorithm by means of two dimensional matrices?

Q. 4. Explain briefly "Banker's Algorithm". Consider a system which runs 5000 jobs per month with no deadlock prevention or avoidance scheme. Deadlock occur about twice a month and require the operator to terminate and rerun about 10 jobs per deadlock. Each job is worth about Rs. 65.00 (in CPU time) and the jobs terminated tend to be about half done when they are killed.

A system programmer has estimated that a deadlock avoidance algorithm would be installed in the system with an increase in average execution time per job of about 10%. Since the machine currently has 10% idle time, all 5000 jobs per month could still be run, although turnaround time would increase by about 20% on average.

1. What are the arguments for installing deadlock avoidance algorithm?
2. What are the arguments against installing the deadlock avoidance algorithm?

Q. 5. Write short notes on—

Deadlock Recovery.

Q. 6. It is proposed to use a multi-resource Banker's algorithm in an OS containing 3 resource classes. The number of resource units available for allocation is (7, 7) and 10 respectively. The current resource state is as given below –

(1) Is the current allocation state safe?

(2) Would the following requests be granted in the current state?

Process	Allocated Resources			Maximum Requirements			Available Resources		
	R1	R2	R3	R1	R2	R3	R1	R2	R3
P1	2	2	3	3	6	8	7	7	10
P2	2	0	3	4	3	3			
P3	1	2	4	3	4	4			

- Process P1 requests (1, 1, 0)
- Process P2 requests (0, 1, 0)
- Process P3 request (0, 1, 0)

Ans. (*a*) The max need is defined to the maximum requirement allocated resource and is–

∴

Process	Need		
	R1	R2	R3
P1	1	4	5
P2	2	3	0
P3	2	2	0

(*b*) **yes,** Current allocation in a safe state because sequence < P1, P2, P3 > or < P2, P3, P1> or <P3, P2, P1> satisfies the safety criteria.

(*c*) The process P1 requests (1, 1, 0) will grant the request. The process P2 requests (0,1,0) will also grant the request. But the process P3 requests (0, 1, 0) will not grant the request. So, the above requests are not granted in the current state.

Q. 7. What are the necessary conditions to hold a deadlock in a system? Explain the Resource allocation graph algorithm to deal with deadlock problem. What are the limitations of this approach?

Q. 8. What is deadlock and its conditions? How deadlock can be avoided?

Q. 9. (a) Explain the four necessary conditions that must be in effect for a deadlock to exist. Explain two methods for handling deadlocks.

(b) Explain deadlock detection in centralized and fully distributed approach. Why deadlock detection is much more expensive in a distributed environment than it is in a centralized environment ?

CHAPTER

8

Device Management

8.0 INTRODUCTION

The operating system has an important role in managing the I/O operations. Some of these roles are—

(1) To track the status of each device *i.e.*, all Input/Output devices.

(2) To decide that which process will get a device and for how long.

(3) To allocate and deallocate devices.

I/O devices can be roughly grouped under three categories-

(*a*) **Human readable** : Those devices that establish the communication between computer and user. **For example** : Keyboard, mouse printer, VDU etc.

(*b*) **Machine readable** : Those device that are suitable for communicating with electronic equipment. **For example** : disk, tape drives, sensors, controllers etc.

(*c*) **Communication:** Those devices that are suitable for communicating with remote devices. **For example** : Digital line drivers and moderns.

8.1 TYPES OF ALLOCATING DEVICES

The devices can be managed and allocated by an OS in three possible ways-

(*a*) Dedicated.

(*b*) Shared.

(*c*) Virtual.

8.1.1 Dedicated devices

An OS can use a device in a dedicated manner by assigning it to only one process till that process terminates.

For example : Tape drives, plotters etc.

It is difficult to share these devices.

This scheme has some other disadvantages also. It can be a very inefficient scheme particularly when the device is not used 100% of time. System may not always get full utilization of that device.

8.1.2 Shared devices

Herein, the OS can assign a device in such a way that it can be **shared** among several processes.

For example: Printers, Hard disks etc.

Sharing is possible by **interleaved** execution of requests of processes for devices. The device manager is responsible for the same. When two processes request for a device at the same time, **contentions** may arise. So, some policy is required. One such policy can be prioritization of processes. The advantage of sharing is that the device utilization reaches almost 100% if it is shared among several processes.

8.1.3 Virtual devices

SPOOLING (Simultaneous Peripheral Operation On Line) technique can be used to convert dedicated devices to shared devices. This technique is applicable to a large number of peripheral devices like printers.

For example: Printers are converted to sharable device through a SPOOLING program that re-routes all printing requests to the disk. The disk sends the output to the printer only when all other requests have been linked up before this request have been finished. But to the user, who has just given a request for printer, it appears that this system has its own dedicated printer attached to it. This is because when he/she gives a printing command, SPOOLING occurs and he/she can resume the work. **Please note that this technique can convert one printer into several "virtual" printers.** This improves its performance as well as its use.

8.2 DEVICE MANAGEMENT TECHNIQUES

The status of channels, control units and devices must be checked by the device management routines. Channels and control units frequently create a serious bottleneck. We discuss various techniques to mitigate this problem and are discussed next.

8.2.1 Independent Device Operation

Some devices are capable of doing an I/O operation without any support from the channel or control unit (CU).

For example: Seek operation on a disk may require 50 ms, needs a channel only to do this operation. The seek can be completed by the device alone. Similarly, there are operations that may require both the device and CU but not the channel for completion.

8.2.2 Buffering

To avoid overheads and inefficiencies, it is sometimes convenient to perform input transfers in advance of requests being made and to perform output transfers sometime after the request is made. This technique is known as Buffering. A Buffer is a temporary storage area. **There are three reasons for Buffering**

(1) If the producer device is high speed, the consumer device is low speed at that time buffering is required.

For example: A hard disk (a producer) and a printer (a consumer).

(2) If two devices have different data-block sizes then also buffering is required.

For example : During packets transmission over the network, the sender sends the packets which are initially stored in buffer and then sent to the receiver. This is because the format of packet at the two ends is different. Receiver's packet format is obtained by the conversion process.

(3) Buffering supports copy semantics for application I/O.

For example: Copying data between kernel buffers and application data space.

There are **three buffering techniques—**

I. Single Buffering (or Anticipated Buffering).

II. Double Buffering (or Buffer swapping).

III. Circular Buffering.

Let us discuss these techniques now.

I Single Buffering / Anticipated Buffering

The simplest type of support that OS can provide is single buffering. In this method, when a user process issues an I/O request, the OS assigns a buffer in the system portion of main memory to the operation.

In a non-buffered system, as shown in Fig 8.1 (*a*), OS does not assign any buffer.

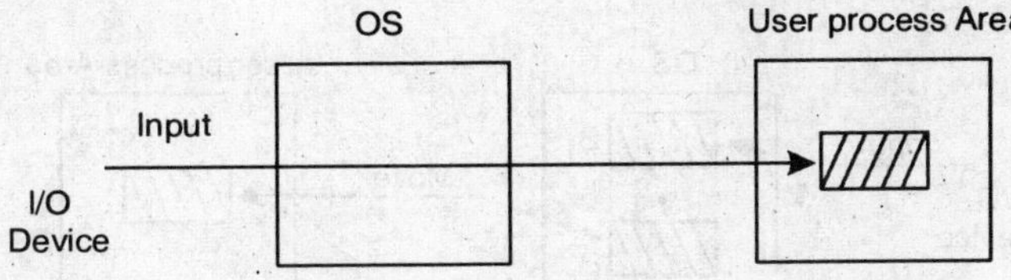

Fig. 8.1 (*a*) Non-buffered system

Whereas, in a buffered system, as shown in Fig. 8.1 (*b*) OS assigins a buffer, *i.e*,

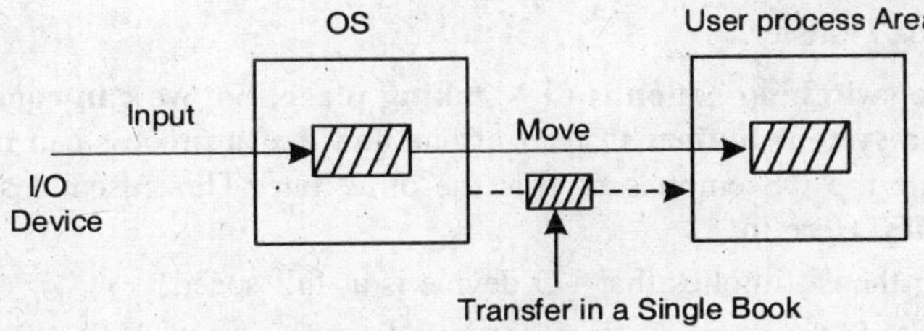

Fig. 8.1 (*b*) Buffered system

In single Buffering,

(*a*) OS assigns a buffer in the main memory for I/O request.

(*b*) Input transfers are made to buffer.

(*c*) Block is moved to user space when needed.

(*d*) User process can process one block of data while another block is moved into the buffer.

(*e*) Swapping of user process is allowed since input is taking place in the system memory and not the user memory.

When the transfer is complete, the process moves the block into user space and requests another block. This technique is also called as *anticipated buffering.* This speeds up the process.

We can compare the two systems in Fig. 8.1 (*a*) and Fig 8.1 (*b*).

Let T - Time required to input one block.

C - Computation time that intervenes between the input request.

M - Time to move the data in to user space.

Then with **no buffering method,** the execution time per block is given by-

$$\text{Time} = T + C$$

Whereas with buffering (single) method, the execution time per plock is given by

$$\text{Time} = \text{Max}\ (C, T) + M$$

Herein, we can overlap I/O with computation. **Please note that generally, the latter quantity is less than the former quantitiy.**

II Double Buffering / Fuffer Swapping-

We can further improve the single buffering method by assigning two system buffers to the operation. Now, **a process can transfer data to (or form) one buffer while the O.S. empties (or fills) the other. This technique is known as double buffering or buffer swapping.**

This is shown in Fig. 8.2

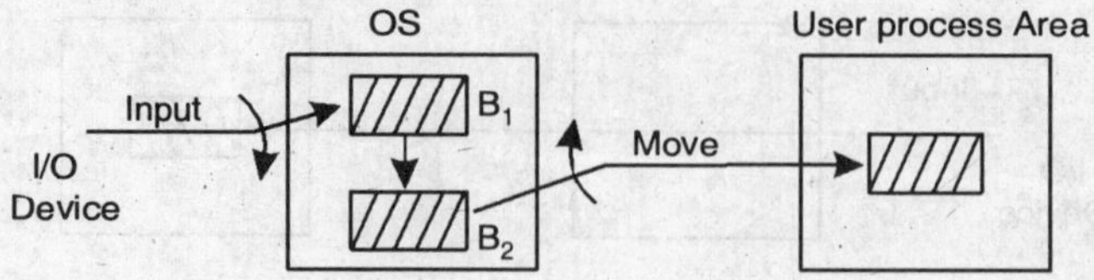

Fig 8.2 Double Buffering.

B_1 : Buffer - I for I/O.

B_2 : Buffer II for Transfer.

Please note the switching action is (⮍) taking place. So, we can conclude that in this technique we use **two system buffers** instead of one and that a process can transfer data to or from one buffer while the OS empties or fills the other one. This resembles to a **producer - consumer relationship.** Here in,

if $(C + M) < T$; then it implies that I/O device is at full speed.

and if $(C + M) > T$; then process does not wait for I/O.

III Circular Buffering

Double buffering is inadequate if the process performs rapid bursts of I/O. In this case, the problem is solved by using more than two buffers. When more than two buffers are used, the collection of buffers is itself referred to as a **circular buffer.**

As shown in Fig. 8.3, circular buffers are provided for the delay in I/O side and transmission side.

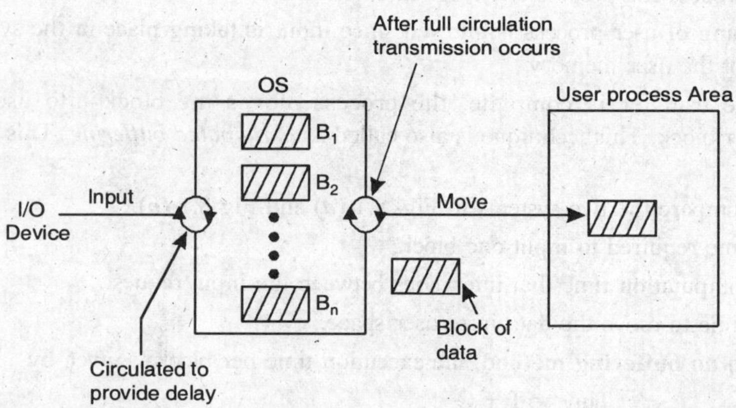

Fig 8.3 Circular Buffering

So, we conclude that in circular buffering—

(*a*) More than two buffers are used.

(*b*) Each individual buffer is one unit in a circular buffer.

(*c*) Used when I/O operation must keep up with process.

Uses of Buffering techniques

The following are the uses of Buffering techniques :-

(1) Buffering is a technique that smoothes out peaks in I/O demand.

(2) No amount of buffering will allow an I/O device to keep pace indefinitely with a process when the average demand of the process is greater than the I/O device can service.

(3) All buffers will eventually fill up and the process will have to wait after processing each block of data.

(4) In a multiprogramming environment, when there is a variety of I/O activity and a variety of process activity to service, buffering is one of the tool that can increase the efficiency of the OS and the performance of individual processes.

8.2.3 Multiple paths

The channel and CU bottlenecks can be mitigated by buying more channels and CUs. This is, however, quite costly. So, we use channels and CUs in a more flexible manner. This results in **multiple paths** to each device.

For example: Consider Fig. 8.4 below that shows I/O configuration with multiple paths.

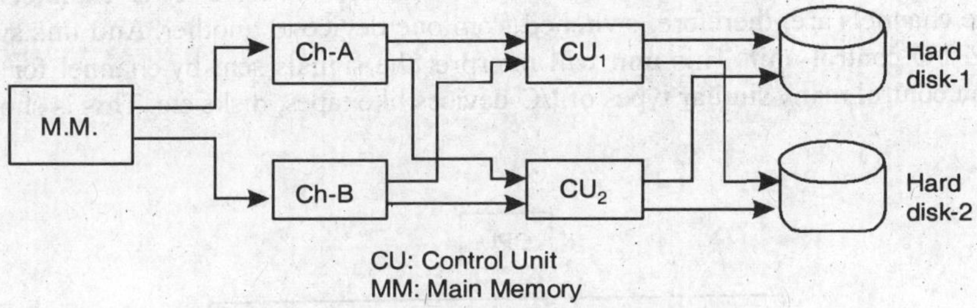

Fig. 8.4 Multiple path System.

As shown in Fig. 8.4, there are two paths to move from channel–A to Hard-disk–1. That is,

path-1: Ch – A → CU_1 → Hard disk – 1

path-2: Ch – A → CU_2 → Hard disk – 1

If path -1 is busy, then path – 2 can be followed to access hard disk –1. This is not only flexible but reliable too.

8.3 I/O CHANNELS

To provide a path for the data to flow between I/O devices and the main memory, *I/O* **channels** are used. I/O **channels** use **channel programs** that specify the action to be performed by the devices and to control data transmission between main memory and CUs. **Channels are specialized processing units** used to operate the I/O devices. They are cheaper too. They free CPU from slow operations such as reading cards. Also, the CPU can operate several channels simultaneously. So, many devices can function at the same time. Naturally, an OS has to supervise these operations.

I/O channels are of three types—

(*a*) Selector channel.

(*b*) Multiplexor channel.

(*c*) Block multiplexor channel.

We shall explain each of these one by one.

I Selector channel

This channel is used to select one device for service at a time. This channel is basically used for high speed I/O devices such as magnetic disks and drums. Thus, each I/O request is usually completed quickly and then another device is selected for I/O.

II Multiplexor channel

This channel is capable of servicing many devices simultaneously. It is able to accomplish this only for slow I/O devices like card readers, card punches and printers.

III Block Multiplexor Channel

A compromise solution that allows multiple channel pograms for high speed devices to be active on the same I/O channel is a Block Multiplexor channel. This channel performs one channel instruction for one device and then automatically switches to perform an instruction for another device and so on. **Please note that this block multiplexor channel resembles the selector as it services only one device at any given time and it also resembles the multiplexor as it does not have to wait until the entire channel program is completed before it can service another device.**

8.4 I/O CONTROL UNITS

We should remember that channels are costlier. Hence, we have fewer channels and more devices. The channels are, therefore, switched from one device to another. And this switching is done by and I/O control unit. This unit will interpret the signals sent by channel for switching. Each CU can control many similar types of I/O devices like tapes, disks etc. This is shown in Fig. 8.5 below.

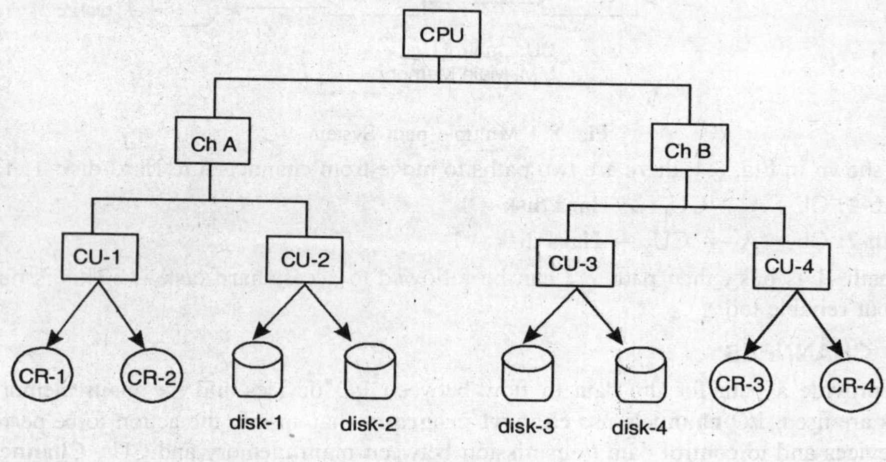

Fig 8.5 I/O subsystem

Legends : Ch – Channel
CU – Control Unit
CR – Card Reader

Note that in Fig 8.5, there is one CU for controlling Card - Readers, one for disks and so on. The device management routines must keep track of the status of these channels, CUs and devices. For proper functioning of channels and CUs, techniques like buffering, multiple paths and block multiplexing are used and have been discussed earlier.

8.5 I/O TRAFFIC CONTROLLER

The I/O traffic controller is concerned with the mechanics and not policies. By mechanics, I mean the following — Is it possible to assign the device? The traffic controller maintains the status information of a device. This I/O traffic controller becomes quite complex in its working because of the interdependencies introduced due to scarcity of channels and CUs.

Functions of I/O traffic controller

There are three main functions of I/O traffic controller—

(1) It must determine if there is atleast one path available.

(2) If more than one path is available then it must determine which one to select.

(3) If all paths are busy, it must determine when one will become available.

To accomplish these three functions, I/O traffic controller maintains a database that stores the status and connections between channels, CUs etc. All this is achieved by means of various control blocks like Unit Control Blocks (UCB), Control Unit Control Block (CUCB) and Channel Control Block (CCB). A UCB has the following srtucture—

Device Unit Identification
Status of the device
List of CUs connected to this device
List of processes waiting for this device

Fig 8.6 Unit Control Block (UCB)

Similarly, the other two control blocks store channel related information.

The **first function** is achieved by starting at the desired UCB and working back through the connected CUs and channels to find a combination that is available. In similer fashion, it is possible to determine all available paths. The **second function** is important when I/O configuration is asymmetric. This is because in this configuration, selection of one path may block out other I/O requests.

8.6 I/O DEVICE HANDLER

For each type of I/O device, usually there is a different device handler algorithm. The main functions of I/O device handler are as follows—

(1) Setting up the channel command words.

(2) Handing error conditions.

(3) Processing I/O interrupts.

(4) Providing device dependent scheduling algorithms.

We will discuss about disk scheduling algorithms in next chapter.

8.7 DEVICE ALLOCATION CONSIDERATIONS

Device allocation involves three major techniques—

(*a*) Dedicated

(*b*) Shared

(*c*) Virtual

We shall describe each of these now.

I Dedicated devices

These are the devices that are dedicated to one program at a time and are not reassigned until that program releases the device, usually at the termination of the program. This assignment of a device to a program is done by using the CPU scheduling algorithms.

For example: Positioning a magnetic tape to the desired data record is quite time consuming. We need to **switch** the use of such a device among several programs which is quite tedious. Thus, these devices are dedicated to one program and are released only at the termination of the program.

II Shared devices

Direct access memory devices like disks, drums etc. can be repositioned easily. So, it is possible to share it among several programs running concurrently. **Please note that a shared device is logically treated as if it were a group of dedicated devices.** Each porgram using a shared device logically has a separate area to itself. **Also note that it is the direct access property of the device that makes it economical to switch back and forth among these areas.** This is decided by the device management routines.

For both **dedicated** and **shared** devices, static and dynamic allocation decisions must be made. Please note that, in general, the device management tries to spread the **allocation among devices so as to minimize channel and control unit bottlenecks.** But channels and CUs are not permanently assigned to a program. This is because they are scarce. When I/O request is finished, these units are deallocated for next usage.

III Virtual devices

A virtual technique transforms a dedicated device into a shared device. Thus, it is a special case of dedicated and shared allocation.

Summary

In this chapter, we have seen that I/O places a large amount of stress on system efficiency and performance. To improve efficiency, we try to reduce context switches, reduce interrupts and balance utilization of system resources.

MULTIPLE CHOICE QUESTIONS [MCQs]

1. Keyboard, mouse and printer are–

(*a*) Human readable devices. (*b*) Machine readable devices.

(*c*) Communication devices. (*d*) None of the above.

2. SPOOLING stands for—

(*a*) Spontaneous Peripheral operation online

(*b*) Small peripheral operation online

(*c*) Simultaneous peripheral operation online

(*d*) None of the above.

3. Input transfers are done in advance and output transfers after sometime, in which of these technique-

(*a*) SPOOLING (*b*) Buffering

(*c*) Swapping (*d*) None of the above.

4. Double buffering is also known as-

(*a*) Anticipated Buffering (*b*) Buffer Swapping

(*c*) Circular Buffering (*d*) None of the above

5. With no buffering method, the execution time per block is given by–

(*a*) Time = T + C (*b*) Time = T – C

(*c*) Time = T/C (*d*) Time = T * C

6. In double buffering, an I/O device is at full speed implies-

(*a*) (C + M) > T (*b*) (C + M) = T

(*c*) (C + M) < T (*d*) None of the above

7. A virtual device is–

(*a*) Dedicated for one purpose

(*b*) A shared device converted to a dedicated device

(*c*) A dedicated device converted to a shared device

(*d*) None of the above

8. A technique that smoothes out peaks in I/O demand is-

(*a*) Spooling (*b*) Buffering

(*c*) Swapping (*d*) None of the above

9. UCB stands for-

(*a*) Unified Control Block (*b*) Unit Control Block

(*c*) Universal Control Block (*d*) None of the above

10. Error handling and I/O interrupt handling are the functions of-

(*a*) I/O Device Handler (*b*) I/O Traffic Controller

(*c*) I/O Scheduler (*d*) None of the above

ANSWERS

1. *a*	**2.** *c*	**3.** *b*	**4.** *b*	**5.** *a*	**6.** *c*
7. *b*	**8.** *b*	**9.** *b*	**10.** *a*		

CONCEPTUAL SHORT QUESTIONS WITH ANSWERS

Q. 1. Distinguish between Block-oriented and stream-oriented I/O devices?

Ans. Let us tabulate the differences in a tabular form-

Block-oriented	Stream oriented
1. These devices store information in **blocks.**	1. These devices have **no block** structures.
2. Blocks are of fixed size.	2. Data is transfered in and out as a stream of bytes.
3. Different device drivers are used. **For example:** Disks and tapes.	3. Here, also the device drivers are different. **For example:** Terminals, printers, ports, mouse etc.

Q. 2. There are two main OS design objectives - Explain them.

Ans. There are two types of OS design objectives-

1. Efficiency: Most I/O devices are extremely slow compared to the main memory. I/O cannot keep up with processor speed. The use of multiprogramming allows for some processes to be waiting for I/O while another process executes. Swapping is used to bring in additional ready processes.

2. Generality: It is desirable to handle all I/O devices in a uniform manner. We need to hide the details of device I/O in lower-level routines. Processes and upper levels see the devices in general terms such as read, write, open, close etc.

Q. 3. State three advantages of placing functionality in a device controller rather than in the Kernel. State three disadvantages.

Ans. The three **advantages** are as follows—

(1) Bugs are less likely to cause an OS crash.

(2) Performance can be improved by utilizing dedicated hardware and hard-coded algorithms.

(3) The kernel is simplified by moving algorithms out of it.

The three **disadvantages** are as follows—

(1) Bugs are harder to fix. A new firmware version or new hardware is needed.

(2) Improving algorithms likewise require a hardware update rather than first kernel or device driver update.

(3) Embedded algorithms could conflict with application's use of the device causing decreased performance.

Q. 4. Consider the following I/O scenarios on a single-user PC-

(*a*) A mouse used with a graphical user interface.

(*b*) A tape drive on a multitasking OS.

(*c*) A disk drive containing user files.

(*d*) A graphics card with direct bus connection, accessible through memory-mapped I/O. For each of these I/O scenarios would you design the OS to use buffering, spooling, caching or a combination? Would you use polled I/O or interrupt driven I/O? Give reasons for your choices.

Ans.

(*a*) **Buffering** may be needed to record the mouse movement during times when higher priority operations are taking place, **spooling** and **caching** are inappropriate. Interrupt driven I/O is most appropriate.

(*b*) **Buffering** may be needed to manage throughput difference between the tape drive and the source or destination of the I/O. **Caching** can be used to hold copies of data that resides on the tape for faster access. **Spooling** could be used to stage data to the device when multiple users desire to read from or write to it. Interrupt driven I/O is likely to allow the best performance.

(*c*) **Buffering** can be used to hold data while in transit from user space to the disk and vice versa. **Caching** can be used to hold disk resident data for improved performance.

Spooling is not necessary because disks are shared-access devices. Interrupt driven I/O is best for devices such as disks that transfer data at slow rates.

(*d*) **Buffering** may be needed to control multiple access and for performance **double buffering** can be used to hold the next screen image while displaying the current one **caching** and **spooling** are not necessary due to fast and shared-access nature of devices. Polling and interrupts are only useful for input and for I/O completion detection, neither of which is needed for a memory-mapped device.

Q. 5. Describe three circumstances under which blocking I/O should be used. Describe three circumstances under which non-blocking I/O should be used. Why not just implement nonblocking I/O and have processes busy-wait until their device is ready?

Ans. Generally, **blocking I/O** is appropriate when the process will only be waiting for one specific event. **For example,** a disk, tape or keyboard read by an application program.

Non-blocking I/O is useful when I/O may come from more than one source and the order of the I/O arrival is not predetermined. **For example,** Network demons listening to more than one network socket, window managers that accept mouse movement as well as keyboard input and I/O management programs such as a copy command that copies data between I/O devices. In the last case, the program could optimize its performance by buffering the input and output and using non-blocking I/O to keep both devices fully occupied.

Non-blocking I/O is more complicated for programmers because of the asynchronous rendezvous that is needed when an I/O occurs. Also, busy waiting is less efficient than interrupt-driven I/O, so the overall system performance would decrease.

Q. 6. Why might a system use interrupt-driven I/O to manage a single serial port but polling I/O to manage a front-end processor, such as a terminal concentrator?

Ans. Polling can be more efficient than the interrupt-driven I/O. This is the case when the I/O is frequent and of short duration. Even though a single serial port will perform I/O relatively infrequently and should thus, use interrupts, a collection of serial ports such as those in a terminal concentrator can produce a lot of short I/O operations and interrupting for each one could create a heavy load on the system. A well-timed polling loop could alleviate that load without wasting many resources through looping with no I/O needed.

Q. 7. Why is it important to scale up system bus and device speeds as the CPU speed increases?

Ans. Consider a system which perfoms 50% I/O and 50% computers. Doubling the CPU performance on this system would increase the total system performance by only 50%. Doubling both system aspects would increase performance by 100%. Generally, it is important to remove the current system bottleneck and to increase overall system performance rather than blindly increasing the performance of individual system components.

Q. 8. Distinguish between a STREAMS driver and a STREAMS module.

Ans. The *STREAMS driver* controls a physical device that could be involved in a STREAMS operation. The STREAMS module modifies the flow of data between the head (the user interface) and the driver.

Q. 9. How does DMA increase system concurrency? How does it complicate hardware design?

Ans. DMA increases system concurrency by allowing the CPU to perform tasks while the DMA system transfers data via the system and memory buses. Hardware design is complicated because the DMA controller must be integrated into the system and the system must allow the DMA controller to be a bus master. Cycle stealing may also be necessary to allow the CPU and DMA controller to share use of the memory bus.

EXERCISE QUESTIONS

Q. 1. Discuss the following operations /terms with suitable examples-

(*a*) Buffering (*b*) Block multiplexing.

(*c*) Virtual devices. (*d*) Device allocation considerations.

Q. 2. Explain single buffering and double buffering.

Q. 3. State the difference between SPOOLING and BUFFERING.

Q. 4. State the advantages and disadvantages of placing functionality in a device controller rather than in the kernel.

Q. 5. Comment about blocking and non-blocking I/O.

Q. 6. Distinguish between–

(*a*) Block and character devices.

(*b*) Blocking and non-blocking I/O.

CHAPTER
9
Secondary Storage Structure

9.0 INTRODUCTION

Magnetic tapes were used in olden days for data storage. Now-a-days disks are used as they require lesser access time. However, tapes today may be used for backup storages where infrequently used information is used. In multiprogramming environment, several different processes may want to use the system's resources simultaneously.

For example, processes will contend to access an auxiliary storage device like a disk. The disk drive needs some mechanism to resolve this contention, sharing the resource between the processes efficiently.

9.1 HARD DISK STRUCTURE

A magnetic hard disk consists of a collection of **platters** which rotate about a central **spindle. These platters are flat and circular in shape. They are metal disks covered with magnetic recording material on both sides.** Each disk's platter has a diameter ranging from 1.8 to 5.25 inches. Each disk surface is divided into concentric circles called as **tracks.** Each track is divided into **sectors** where the information is stored. **Please note that the information stored is not volatile.** This means that the information on hard disk is permanent. The reading and writing device is called as the **head** which moves over the surface of the platters until it finds the track and sector it requires. This situation is similar to a person finding someone else's house. Firstly, he/she finds the street number (track) and then the particular house number (sector). There is one head for each surface on which information is stored each on its own arm. **Please note that the arms are usually connected together so that the head moves in unison.** This is so because then each head is over the same track on each surface. **Also note that the collection of all tracks (t) which are under the heads at any time forms a cyclinder.** This is shown in Fig. 9.1.

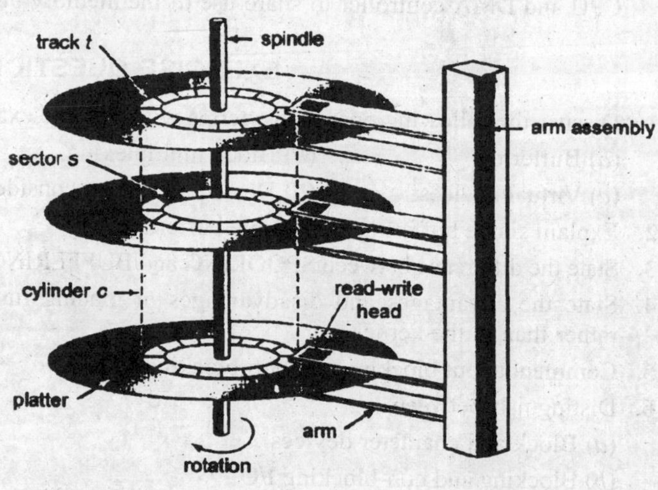

Fig 9.1 Hard disk structure.

Please note here that the number of disk cylinders will be equal to the number of tracks on each platter.

A hard disk drive records data on the surfaces of platter that is coated with a substance containing grouped up iron or other substances that allows zeros and ones to be recorded as tiny spots of magnetization. When the disk drive is ON, the spindle rotates at a high speed of 12,000 r.p.m.

Steps involved for read/write operation

To read/write a bit of data on the disk, the head has to be right over the spot where data is stored. It involves the following steps-

Step-1 : The correct head /correct surface must be selected. This operation is very fast (a few microseconds) as it is done electronically.

Step-2 : The head has to move to the correct distance from the center of the disk. This movement is called as a **seek operation** and it involves physical movement of arm–in or out. As this arm has mass (inertia), so it must be accelerated and decelerated. When it is completed then the disk has to wait a bit for vibrations that are caused by the jerky movement to die out. This process of seeking takes several milliseconds, depending on how for the head to move.

Step-3 : The disk has to rotate until the correct spot is under the selected disk. Since the disk is constantly spinning, all the drive has to do is waiting for the correct spot to come around.

Step-4 : Finally, the actual data has to be transferred. **Please note that during a read operation, the data is usually transferred to a RAM buffer in the device and then copied (by DMA) to the main memory of the system. Similarly, during write operation, the data is transferred by DMA to a buffer in the disk and then copied onto the surface of a platter.**

This results in latencies that will be discussed in next section of this chapter.

How access to data is made?

The data on a disk is divided up into **blocks /disk blocks** which are of fixed size. **Please remember that the hardware will support only reading or writing of the whole of the block at a time. Also note that if a program has to change one bit or one byte on the disk then it has to read in an entire disk block, make required changes and then write it back out.**

Each block has a location that is called as a **disk address.** This address will consist of **three** numbers

(*Cylinder number*, *track number* and *sector number*)

Actually, the part of the disk swept out by a head while it is not moving is a ring shaped region on the surface called as a **track.** The **track number indicates how far the data is from the centre of the disk, called as axle.** Each track is divided up into some number of **sectors. Please note that on some disks, the outer tracks have more sectors than the inner ones because the outer tracks are longer but all sectors are of the same size.** The set of tracks swept out by all the heads while the arm is not moving is called as a **cylinder.** Thus, a seek operation moves to a new cylinder, positioning each on one track of the cylinder.

9.2 HARD DISK PERFORMANCE PARAMETERS–TERMINOLOGIES

Whether the particular algorithm of disk scheduling is better for the given situation or not will depend on certain parameters. We define some of these parameters now.

1. **Seek time: It is defined as the time required to move the disk arm to the required track.** It consists of two key components-
   (*a*) The initial startup time.
   (*b*) The time taken to traverse the tracks that have to be crossed once the access arm is up to speed.

Please note that the traversal time is not a linear function of the number of tracks but includes a start up time and a settling time i.e., the time after positioning the head over the target track until track identification is confirmed. The linear formula for the seek-time is given below:

$$\boxed{T_S = m * n + S}$$

where T_S : Estimated Seek time

n : Number of tracks traversed.

m : Constant that depends on the disk drive

S : Start up time

Today, the average seek time has greatly been reduced due to the reduction in the disk size. It is about 5 to 10 ms.

2. **Rotational Delay:** It is defined as the time required to reach the desired sector by the read/write head. **Magnetic disks** have rotational speeds in the range-5400 to 10,000 r.p.m. Thus, at 100,000 rpm, the average rotational delay will be 3ms. However, our floppy disks typically rotates between 300 and 600 rpm. Thus, now the average delay will be between 100 and 200 ms.
3. **Transfer Time:** The transfer time to or from the disk depends on the speed of the disk given by the relationship—

$$\boxed{T = \frac{b}{rN}}$$

Where T = transfer time.

b = number of bytes to be transferred.

N = number of bytes on a track.

r = rotation speed in revolutions/second.

The total average access time is expressed as

$$\boxed{T_a = T_S + \frac{1}{2r} + \frac{b}{rN}}$$

where T_S is the average seek time.

9.3 HARD-DISK SCHEDULING ALGORITHMS

When a process wants to do disk I/O, an O.S. call is made. This may take some time. The process is put in a blocked state and the I/O request is sent to the device driver. If the disk is idle, the operation is started else if the disk is busy, servicing another request then it is added to a queue of requests. Using FCFS here in not advisable. This is because the requests from different processes may be scattered all over the disk and if FCFS scheduling is done here then lot of jumping around the disk is involved. This will result in excessive rotational latency and seek time, for all processes or for the entire system. So, better algorithms are needed now. We discuss them one by one now.

9.3.1 First-in First-out (FIFO) / First-come First-served (FCFS) algorithm

The **principle** used here is as follows **"The disk controller processes the I/O requests in the order in which they arrive, thereby moving backwards and forwards across the surface of the disk to get to the next requested location each time."** Since no reordering of request takes place so the head may move almost randomly across the surface of the disk. This algorithm minimizes the response time.

Consider an example to understand this. A disk queue has the following requests to read tracks—

87, 170, 40, 150, 36, 72, 66, 15

If the disk head is initially at cylinder 60. Then it will first move from 60 to 87, then 87 to 170, 170 to 40, 40 to 150, 150 to 36, 36 to 72, 72 to 66 and 66 to 15. This is shown in Fig. 9.2 below—

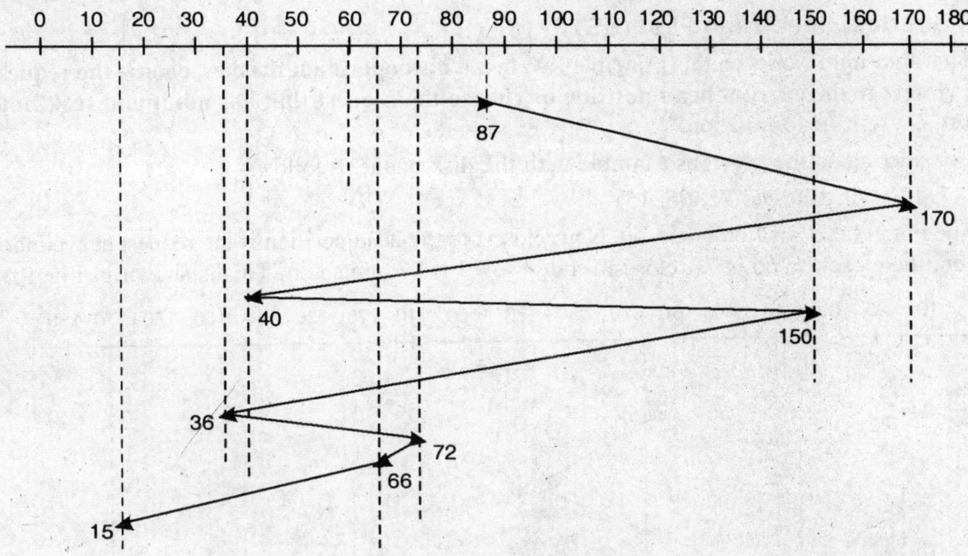

Fig 9.2 FCFS Scheduling

∴ Total head movement is given by—

(60 to 87) + (87 to 170) + (170 to 40) + (40 to 150) + (150 to 36) + (36 to 72) + (72 to 66) + (66 to 15).

$= (87 - 60) + (170 - 87) + (170 - 40) + (150 - 40) + (150 - 36) + (72 - 36) + (72 - 66) + (66 - 15)$

$= (27 + 83 + 130 + 110 + 114 + 36 + 6 + 51)$

= 557 cylinders

∴ Average head movement $= \frac{557}{8}$

= 69.6 cylinders.

∴ *Movement of disk head is as follows—*

60 → 87 → 170 → 40 → 150 → 36 → 72 → 66 → 15

↑

Starting head position

Advantages of FCFS disk scheduling

(1) It is a very simple algorithm to implement.

(2) Improved response time as a request gets response in fair amount of time.

Disadvantages of FCFS disk scheduling

(1) It inolves a lot of random head movements and disk rotations.

(2) Throughput is not efficient.

(3) It is used in small systems only where I/O efficiency is not very important.

(4) FCFS is acceptable when the load on a disk is light. As the load grows, FCFS tends to saturate the device and the response time becomes longer.

9.3.2 Shortest Seek Time First (SSTF)

This algorithm works on this principle- **"When a disk operation finishes, choose the request that is closest to the current head position or choose the request that has minimum seek time from the current head position."**

Consider again the previous example with the disk queue as follows-

(87, 170, 40, 150, 36, 72, 66, 15)

The initial head position is say, 60. Now, closest to the head position is the request at cyclinder 66. Then, the closest to 66 is 72, closest request to 72 is 87 and so on. This is shown in Fig. 9.3.

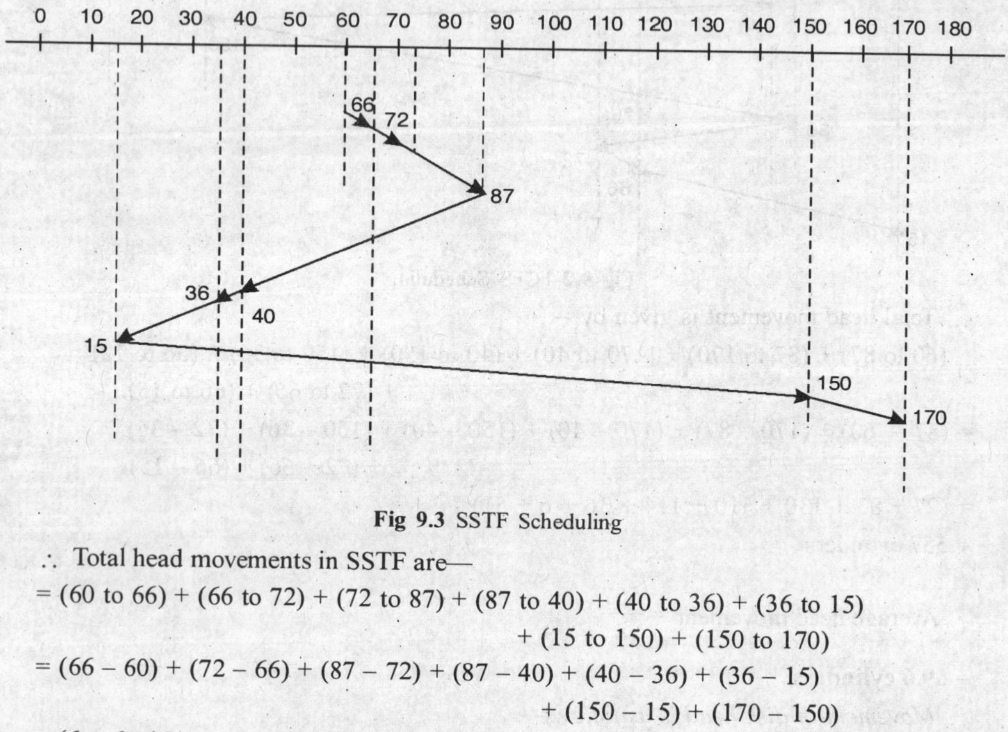

Fig 9.3 SSTF Scheduling

∴ Total head movements in SSTF are—

= (60 to 66) + (66 to 72) + (72 to 87) + (87 to 40) + (40 to 36) + (36 to 15) + (15 to 150) + (150 to 170)

= (66 – 60) + (72 – 66) + (87 – 72) + (87 – 40) + (40 – 36) + (36 – 15) + (150 – 15) + (170 – 150)

= (6 + 6 +15 + 37 + 4 + 21 + 135 + 20)

= **244 cylinders**

∴ Average head movements are $= \frac{244}{8} = 30.5$ cylinders

Please note that the average head movement in FCFS was 69.6 cylinders whereas in this (SSTF) algorithm is 30.5 cylinders, which is less than half of the distance required for FCFS. Thus, there is substantial improvement in disk throughput.

Advantages of SSTF scheduling

(1) It minimizes latency.

(2) Better throughput than FIFO method.

Disadvantages of SSTF Scheduling

(1) **Starvation** may occur here. As we know that requests arrive at random in a real system. Some process may have to wait for a long time until its requests are satisfied, if new requests with shorter seek time keep arriving. This may cause starvation of some requests.

(2) SSTF services requests for those tracks which are highly localized. So, the innermost and outermost tracks receive poor service as compared to the midrange tracks.

9.3.3 SCAN/Elevator algorithm

The **principle** used in this algorithm is as follows:

"The disk head constantly moves from the most inner cylinder to the outer cylinder and then it changes its direction back towards the center. As the head moves, if there is a request for the current disk position then it is satisfied."

This algorithm is sometimes called as the **elevator algorithm** because the disk arm behaves just like an elevator of a building, firstly it services all the request of going up and then reaching at the top, it goes downward. The disk head progresses in a **single direction** *i.e.*, from the center of the disk to the edge or vice versa, serving the closest request in that direction. When it runs out of requests in the direction it is currently moving, it switches to the opposite direction. This algorithm usually gives more equitable service to all requests. In worst case, it can still lead to **starvation.** While it is satisfying requests on one cylinder, other requests for the same cylinder could arrive. If enough requests for the same cylinder keep coming, the heads would stay at that cylinder forever, starving all other requests. To solve this problem, we put an upper limit on how long the heads will stay at any one cylinder. One simple scheme is to serve those requests only that are already there when the heads gets there. So, any new requests for that cylinder, while existing requests are being served will have to wait for the next pass.

Consider the previous disk queue again. That is,

(87, 170, 40, 150, 36, 72, 66, 15)

The head movement starts from 60th cylinder.

Scan algorithm needs two informations—

(*a*) Direction of head movement.

(*b*) Last position of the disk-head (say, 180th cylinder here).

From starting cylinder, say 60, the request goes to 87 in the queue. But before servicing cylinder 87, it will also check to see if there are any cylinders inbetween 60 and 87 then they will also be serviced. We find that cylinder 66, 72 are inbetween, so the Disk movement is from (60 to 66), (66 to 72), (72 to 87), (87 to 150), (150 to 170), (170 to 180), (180 to 36) and (36 to 15). This is shown in Fig. 9.4.

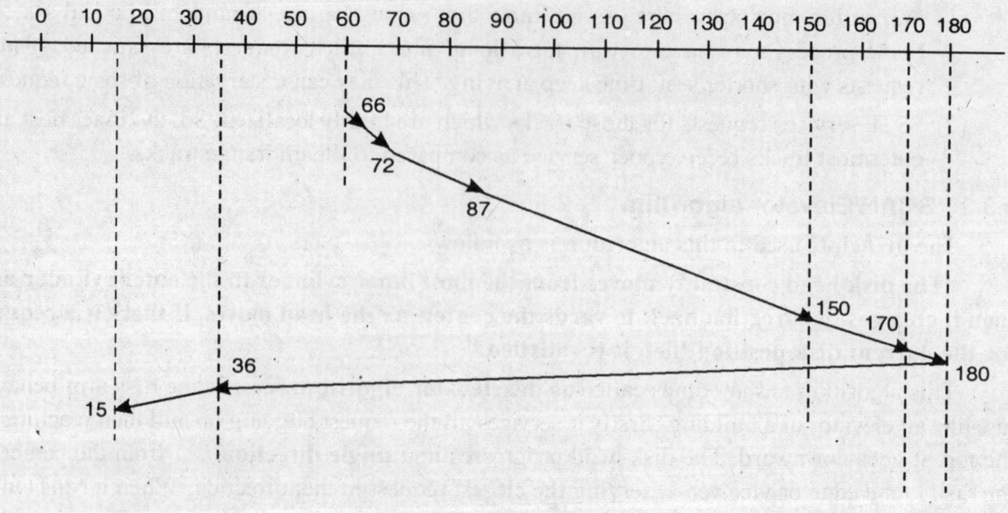

Fig 9.4 SCAN Scheduling

$\therefore$ Total Head Movement = | (66 – 60) | + | (72 – 66) | + | (87 – 72) | + | (150 – 87) | + | (170 – 150) | + | (180 – 170) | + | (180 – 36) | + | (36 – 15) |
= 6 + 6 + 15 + 63 + 20 + 10 + 144 + 21
= **285 cylinders**

Also, the average movements = $\dfrac{\text{Total number of head movements}}{\text{number of requests}}$

$= \dfrac{285}{8}$ = **35.6 cylinders**

So, we observe here that if any request comes on its way, it will be serviced immediately while the request arriving just behind the head will have to wait until disk head moves to the end of the disk, reverses direction and returns before being serviced.

Advantages of SCAN algorithm

(1) The throughput is better then FIFO.

(2) It has been the basis of most disk scheduling strategies.

(3) It eliminates the discrimination inherent in SSTF Schemes.

(4) No starvation problems.

Disadvantages of SCAN algorithm

(1) Because of the continuous scanning of disk from end to end, the outer tracks are visited less often than the mid range tracks.

(2) Also, as the disk arm keeps scanning between two extremes, this may result in wear and tear of the disk assembly.

(3) Certain requests arriving ahead of the arm position would get immediate service but some other requests that arrive behind the arm position will have to wait for the arm to return back. So, this algorithm is not fair.

9.3.4 C–SCAN algorithm / One-way Elevator algorithm

C-SCAN stands for circular-SCAN and is so called **because this algorithm treats the cylinder as a circular list.** C-SCAN is similar to SCAN but I/O requests are only satisfied when the drive head is moving in one direction across the surface of the disk. **Principle: The head sweeps from the innermost cylinder to the outermost cylinder satisfying the waiting requests in order of their locations. When it reaches the outermost cylinder, it sweeps back to the innermost cylinder without satisfying any requests and then starts again.**

Why one-way elevator algorithm?

The two-way elevator algorithm discussed earlier gives poorer service to requests near the center and edges of the disk than to requests inbetween. Suppose, it takes time, t, for a pass from center to the edge or vice versa. A request at the either end of a pass *i.e.*, near the hub or the edge of the disk, may have to wait up to time = 2t for the heads to travel to the other end and back. So, on the average the delay will be 't'. A request near the middle *ie.*, half way between the hub and the edge, will get twice as good service.

$\therefore$ Worst case delay = t and average delay = $t/2$, in this case.

If this bias is a problem, it can be solved **by making the elevator run in one direction only,** say, from hub to edge. When it finishes the request closed to the edge, it seeks all the way back to the first request *i.e.*, the one close to the hub and starts another pass from hub to edge. **Please note that, in general, this technique will increase the total amount of seek time because of the long seek from the edge back to the hub, but on a heavily loaded disk, that seek will be so infrequent as not make much difference. Let us consider an example to understand C-SCAN algorithm.**

Say, Queue is our previous queue only but now the cylinders will be treated as a **circular list-** (87, 170, 40, 150, 36, 72, 66, 15)

Say, that the starting cylinder = 60th. Since head moves from outermost cylinder to the innermost and vice-versa, so we get this graph as shown in Fig. 9.5. **But please remember that it does not satisfy any requests when it moves back.**

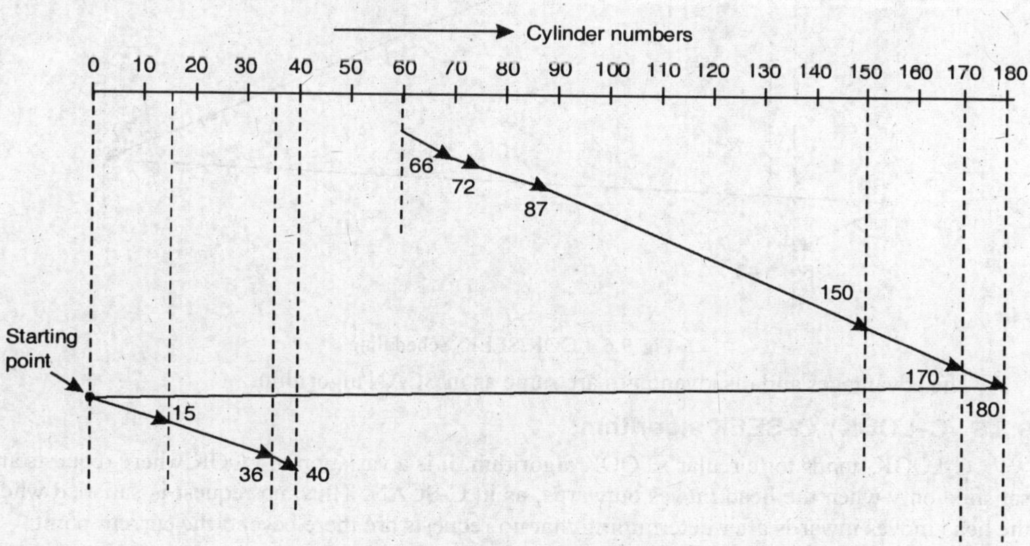

Fig. 9.5 C-SCAN Scheduling.

Advantages of C-SCAN algorithm

(1) It is more fair as compared to SCAN.

(2) It provides more uniform waiting time

Disadvantages of C-SCAN algorithm

(1) The time taken for the back swing has been ignored.

(2) The average head movements in this algorithm is more as compared to SCAN algorithm.

(3) This method increases the total seek time because of the long seek from the edge back to the hub.

9.3.5 LOOK/SEEK algorithm

The **pinciple** of this algorithm is as follows-

"The drive sweeps across the surface of the disk in alternating directions, satisfying requests. But now, the drive makes use of the information it has about the locations requested by the waiting requests."

For instance, a sweep out, towards the outer edge of the disk will be reversed when there are no waiting requests for locations beyond the current cylinder. This improves both, throughput and the response time.

Consider an example to understand it. Say, disk queue has this request-
(87, 170, 40, 150, 36, 72, 66, 15) and starting cylinder = 60th (again).

Then, we get the graph as shown in Fig. 9.6 below. It is observed in Fig. 9.6 that the disk arm will not go to the extremes now although it will alternate in both the directions.

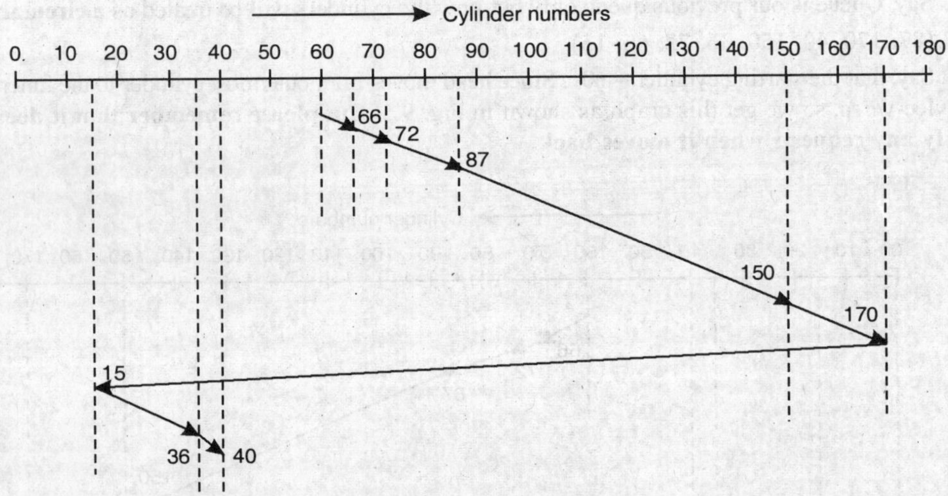

Fig 9.6 LOOK/SEEK Scheduling

The advantages and disadvantages are same as in SCAN algorithm.

9.3.6 C–LOOK / C–SEEK algorithm

C-LOOK stands for circular - LOOK algorithm. It is a variation of LOOK where requests are satisfied only when the head moves outwards, as in C-SCAN. Thus, no request is satisfied when the head moves inwards after determining that no requests are there beyond the current point.

Consider an example to understand this. Say, the I/O request queue is-

(23, 89, 132, 42, 187).

The disk head starts at number 100. So, disk movement will be from 100 to 89 (as 89 comes on its way while moving to the other end), (89 to 42), (42 to 23), (23 to 187) and (187 to 132). So, we draw a graph of Fig. 9.7.

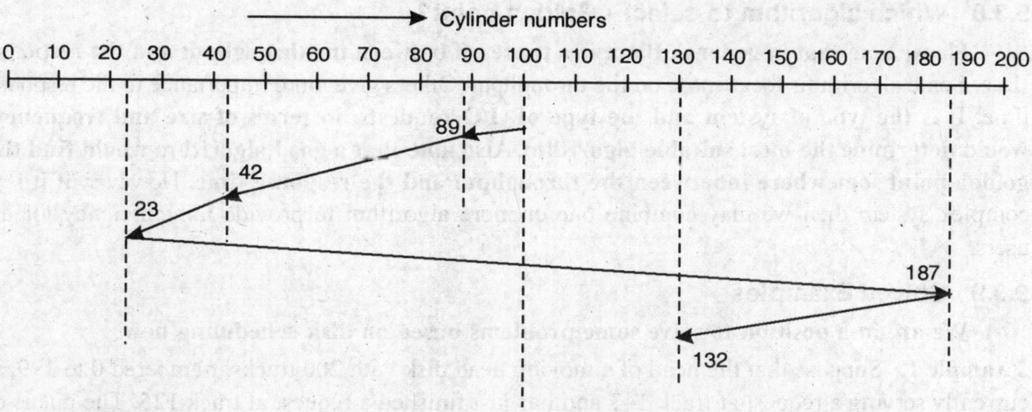

Fig. 9.7 C-LOOK/C-SEEK Scheduling

∴ Total head movements are-

$$| (100 - 89) | + | (89 - 42) | + | (42 - 23) | + | (23 - 187) | + | (187 - 132) |$$

$$= 11 + 47 + 19 + 164 + 55$$

$$= \textbf{296 cylinders}$$

$$\therefore \text{ Average head movements} = \frac{296}{5}$$

$$= \textbf{59.2 cylinders}$$

It is based on C-SCAN only.

9.3.7 N–STEP SACN and FSCAN algorithm

With SSTF, SCAN and C-SCAN algorithms, it is possible that the arm may not move for a considerable period of time.

For example, if one process or more than one processes have high access rates to one track then they can monopolize the entire device by repeated requests to that track. This feature will affect high-density multi surface disks more than the lower density disks. To avoid this problem, the disk request queue can be **segmented,** with one segment at a time being processed completely. Based on this approach, we have two algorithms-

(*a*) N-STEP SCAN algorithm.

(*b*) F SCAN algorithm.

We shall explain each of these one by one.

N-STEP SCAN algorithm

This policy segments the disk request queue into the sub-queues of length, N. These sub-queues are then processed one at a time using SCAN. While a queue is being processed, now requests must be added to some other queue. If fewer than N requests are available at the end of a scan, then all of them are processed with the next scan. Here, when N = 1, the FIFO policy is adopted and for large values of N, the performance of this N-STEP-SCAN algorithm approaches to that of SCAN.

FSCAN algorithm

It uses two subqueues. When a Scan begins, all of the requests are in one of the queues, with the other empty. During the scan, all new requests are put into the other queue. Thus, the service of new requests is deferred until all of the old requests have been processed.

9.3.8 Which algorithm to select - Golden point?

Please note that in general, there is a trade off between the throughput and the response time. Some algorithms focus more on the throughput. Others give more importance to the response time. **It is the type of system and the type of I/O requests, in terms of size and frequency, would determine the most suitable algorithm. Also note that a good algorithm would find the golden point somewhere inbetween the throughput and the response time.** However, if it is a complex system then we may combine one or more algorithm to provide fair efficiency for all users.

9.3.9 Solved Examples

We are in a position to solve some problems based on disk scheduling now.

Example 1. Suppose that the head of a moving head disk with 200 tracks, numbered 0 to 199, is currently serving a request at track 143 and has just finished a request at track 125. The queue of requests is kept in the FIFO order—

86, 147, 91, 177, 94, 150, 102, 175, 130.

What is the total number of head movements needed to satisfy these requests for the following disk-scheduling algorithms—

(*a*) FCFS (*b*) SSTF (*c*) SCAN

(*d*) LOOK (*e*) C-SCAN. ?

Solution. (*a*) FCFS Scheduling:

Here, the head will move in the following order-

$143 \rightarrow 86 \rightarrow 147 \rightarrow 91 \rightarrow 177 \rightarrow 94 \rightarrow 150 \rightarrow 102 \rightarrow 175 \rightarrow 130$

$\therefore$ Total number of head movements are:-

$$|86-143| + |147-86| + |91-147| + |177-91| + |94-177| + |150-94| + |102-150| + |175-102| + |130-175|$$

$$= \textbf{565 cylinders}$$

and average head movements $= \dfrac{565}{9} = \textbf{62.77 cylinders}$

(*b*) SSTF Scheduling :

The head will move in the following order-

$143 \rightarrow 147 \rightarrow 150 \rightarrow 130 \rightarrow 102 \rightarrow 94 \rightarrow 91 \rightarrow 86 \rightarrow 175 \rightarrow 177$

$\therefore$ Total number of head movements are :—

$$|143-147| + |150-147| + |130-150| + |102-130| + |94-102| + |91-94| + |86-91| + |175-86| + |177-175|$$

$$= \textbf{162 cylinders}$$

$\therefore$ Average head movement $= \dfrac{162}{9} = \textbf{18 cylinders}$

(c) SCAN algorithm

The head moves in this order:–

143 → 147 → 150 → 175 → 177 → 199 → 130 → 102 → 94 → 91 → 86

∴ Total number of head movements are :—

$$|147-143|+|150-147|+|175-150|+|177-175|+|199-177|+|130-199| + |102-130|+|94-102|+|91-94|+|86-91$$

= **169 cylinders**

$$\therefore \text{ Average head movement} = \frac{169}{9} = \mathbf{18.77 \text{ cylinders}}$$

(d) LOOK algorithm

The head will move in the following order:-

143 → 147 → 150 → 175 → 177 → 130 → 102 → 94 → 91 → 86

∴ Total number of head movements

$$|147-143|+|150-147|+|175-150|+|177-175|+|130-177|+|102-130| + |94-102|+|91-94|+|86-91|$$

= **125 cylinders**

$$\therefore \text{ Average head movement} = \frac{125}{9} \text{ cylinders}$$

= **13.88 cylinders**

(e) C– SCAN algorithm

The head will move in the following order:-

143 → 147 → 150 → 175 → 177 → 199 → 0 → 86 → 91 → 94 → 102 → 130|

∴ Total number of head movements are-

$$|147-143|+|150-147|+|175-150|+|177-175|+|199-177|+|0-199| + |86-0|+|91-86|+|94-91|+|102-94|+|130-102|$$

= **385 cylinders.**

$$\therefore \text{ Average head movement} = \frac{385}{9} = \mathbf{42.77 \text{ cylinders}}$$

Example 2. Suppose that a disk drive has 5000 cylinders, numbered 0 to 4999. The drive is currently serving a request at cylinder 143, and the previous request was at cylinder 125. The queue of pending requests, in FIFO order is-

(86, 1470, 913, 1774, 948, 1509, 1022, 1750, 130)

Starting from the current head position, what is the total distance (in cylinders) that the disk arm moves to satisfy all pending requests for each of the following disk scheduling algorithms

(a) FCFS (b) SSTF
(c) SCAN (d) LOOK
(e) C-SCAN (f) C-LOOK

Solution.

(*a*) **The FCFS Schedule is-**

(143, 86, 1470, 913, 1774, 948, 1509, 1022, 1750, 130)

∴ Total seek distance is **7081**

(*b*) **The SSTF Schedule is-**

(143, 130, 86, 913, 948, 1022, 1470, 1509, 1750, 1774)

∴ Total seek distance is **1745**

(*c*) **The SCAN Schedule is-**

(143, 913, 948, 1022 1470, 1509, 1750, 1774, 4999, 130, 86)

∴ Total seek distance is **9769**

(*d*) **The LOOK Schelule is-**

(143, 913, 948, 1022, 1470, 1509, 1750, 1774, 130, 86)

∴ Total seek distance is **3319**

(*e*) **The C-SACN Schedule is-**

(143, 913, 948, 1022, 1470, 1509, 1750, 1774, 4999, 86, 130)

∴ Total seek distance = **9813**

(*f*) **The C-LOOK Schedule is-**

(143, 913, 948, 1022, 1470, 1509, 1750, 1774, 86, 130)

∴ Total seek distance = **3363**

9.4 SWAP-SPACE MANAGEMENT

It is one of the functions of an OS to do swap-space management on the disk. Swap space may be a **normal file or a separate disk partition,** 2-cases arise:-

Case-1: ***If the swap space is a large file*** within the file system, we can use all the file operations like create, rename etc. to manipulate it. This is easy but suffers from external fragmentation as it may leave unused space holes on the disk that cannot be further used by a single process or a page.

Case 2: If swap space is created in a separate disk partition, then a separate swap-space manager can be used to allocate or de-allocate the blocks. It uses certain algorithms to optimize speed. This, however, creates a fixed amount of swap space during disk partition.

The size of the swap space depends upon the extent of its usage. Some systems may use swap space to hold entire process image whereas others may use it to hold pages that have been pushed out of the main memory.

9.5 RAID (REDUNDANT ARRAY OF INDEPENDENT DISKS)

We have heard many-a-times about the hard disk failure /crash which means that the O.S. cannot read the stored data and instructions from the disk. Now, recovering from a disk crash may take hours. So, the disk should be made more reliable.

We can overcome such problems with the help of *RAID*. It was first introduced by David A. Patterson and Garth Gibson at the University of California in 1988.

Basic idea: "To combine multiple, small, inexpensive disk drives into an array to accomplish performance goals that are not attainable with one large expensive drive." An array, here, means a collection of hard disks that work cooperatively. Please note here that this array of drives will appear to the computer as a single logical storage unit or a drive.

Advantages of RAID technology

(1) High data transfer rates.

(2) Increased system throughput.

(3) Rate of read request *i.e.*, number of reads per unit time, is also doubled as read requests can be sent to any of the multiple disks in parallel.

Disadvantages of RAID technology

1. Having more disks, reduces overall system reliability.

The performance improvement can be done by two methods-

(*a*) Data stripping (or parallelism).

(*b*) Using Redundancy.

Data Stripping: It is defined as the process of splitting of data into equal-size partitions over multiple disks to make them appear as a single large, fast disk. These multiple disks are also called as disk arrays. The process is transparent. The size of the partition is called as a stripping unit. Furthermore, it uses Round-Robin (RR) algorithm in the disk arrays. Please note that the disk array gives the user the abstraction of having a single, very large disk.

However, this technique has lower reliability. To overcome this problem we have another technique called as **Redundancy** and is discussed next.

Redundancy: It is defined as the process of storing extra or duplicate information which is used for rebuilding the lost information only in the event of disk failure of disk crashes. It is introduced using **mirroring or shadowing technique in which data is duplicated on every disk.**

RAID Lavels

RAID Supports 7-levels *i.e.*, from RAID – 0 to RAID – 6. We shall discuss each of these one by one now.

Level–0: RAID–0 (Stripping /Span).

The RAID level 0 scheme uses data stripping at the block level to increase the maximum bandwidth available. At this level, no redundant information like mirroring or parity bits is maintained.

At this level, the data that is to be stored is divided into number of parts called as **strips.** These strips are then loaded across the members of disk-array as shown in Fig. 9.8.

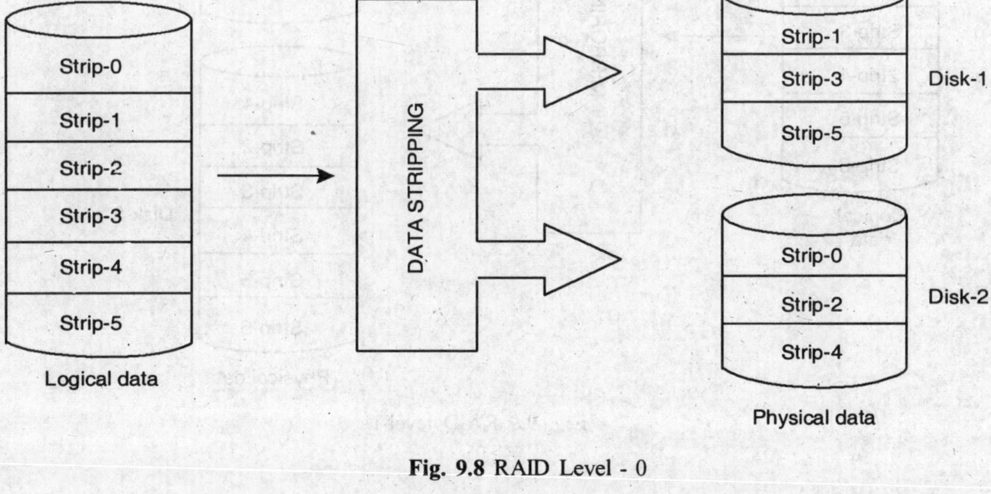

Fig. 9.8 RAID Level - 0

Advantages of level - 0

Following are the advantages of RAID, level–0:-

(1) The block transfer time is reduced as parallel block transfers can be done now.

(2) It is a very fast technique.

(3) Balanced workload among disk-array members.

(4) It is useful for high performance systems.

(5) It is performance oriented disk mapping method.

Disadvantages of level - 0

Following are the disadvantages of RAID, level–0:-

(1) No Redundancy of data.

(2) No fault tolerance.

(3) Even if one disk member fails, it affects the entire array.

Please note, however, that the effective disk space utilization for a RAID level-0 system is always 100%.

Level 1 : RAID-1 (Mirroring)

Disk mirroring is defined as the process of writing data to the duplicate disks simultaneously. If one of the disk drive fails, the system can instantly switch to the other disk without any loss of data or service. Disk mirroring is commonly used in ONLINE database systems where it is critical that the data should be a accessible at all times.

For example, in airline reservation system, the existing database should be mirrored to recover from disk crash.

This is shown in Fig. 9.9 below.

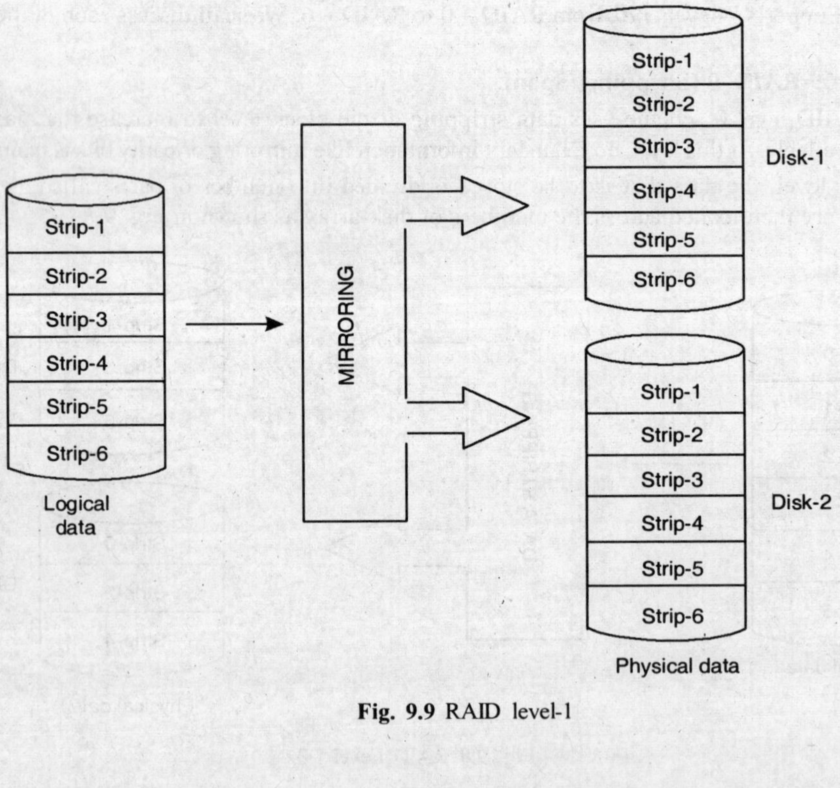

Fig. 9.9 RAID level-1

Advantages of level -1 : Following are the advantages of level-1:

1. Greater reliability as if Disk-1 fails, Disk-2 sill retains same copy of data.
2. Fault tolerance is more.
3. Failure recovery is simple.
4. It has better performance.

Disadvantages of level-1

Following are the disadvantages of level-1:–

(1) It is a costly technique as duplicate data is to be maintained.

(2) The minimum number of drives needed at this level are 2.

Please note, however, that the effective disk space utilization for a RAID Level-1 system is 50%.

Level-2 : RAID 2 (Error Correcting Code)

This level uses single bit stripping unit and employs parity bits for error correction. It is also known as **memory-style error correcting codes** (ECC) organization. It uses **hamming codes.** So, the strips are very small at this level, usually, as a single byte or word. *The* **hamming code** is calculated across corresponding bit positions on each disk and the bits of the code are stored in the corresponding bit positions on multiple disks. But this level is rarely implemented.

Also note that the effective disk space utilization for a RAID level -2 system is upto 53%. This effective space utilization increases with an increase in the number of data disks.

Level-3: RAID - 3 (Bit interleaved Parity)

It was a parallel access. The data is distributed in small strips. In this technique, a simple parity bit is computed for the set of individual bits in the same position on all of the data disks. All this requires is a single redundant disk. In case of a disk crash, the parity drive is accessed and data is reconstructed from the remaining devices.

Advantages of level-3

Following are the advantages of RAID -3:

(1) It needs a single disk only. So, it is less expensive than level-2.

(2) Very high data transfer rates because the data are stripped in very small strips.

(3) Any I/O request will involve the parallel transfer of data from all the data disks.

Disadvantages of level-3

Following are the disadvantages of RAID-3:-

(1) It is rarely used.

(2) It processes only one I/O at a time.

Please note that the effective storage space utilization is 80%. Also note that the effective space utilization increases with the number of data disks.

Level-4: RAID-4 (Block - interleaved parity)

It uses a dedicated disk to store a parity block. The parity information is calculated for each **stripe** of stripped data and stored on a parity disk. If one of the disk fails then the information is rebuilt on a separate disk using the parity information. If the parity disk fails, the parity informaton is recalculated on a spare disk.

Advantages (s) of Level-4

Following are the advantages of level-4:-

(1) It uses block-level stripping which has the advantage that the read requests of the size of a disk block can be served entirely by the disk where the request block resides.

(2) It is better suited to transaction I/O rather than large file transfers.

Disadvantages of level-4

(1) The parity drive can be a bottle-neck during write operations.

(2) The data transfer rate for each access is slower.

At this level, for many data disks only one check disk is needed **Please note here that the effective storage space utilization is therefore 80%. Also note that the effective space utilization increases with the number of data disks.**

Level-5: RAID–5 (Block-interleaved Distributed Parity)

In this method, the parity strips are distributed across all n disks. It eliminates the write bottle necks. The only botte neck here is the parity calculation process. But, today even this is not a bottleneck. RAID-5 requires atleast 3 disks to implement.

Advantages of level–5

Following are the advantages of level-5:–

(1) Several write requests can be done in parallel.

(2) Highest data transmission rate.

(3) Low ECC (parity) disks to the data disks- this implies a high efficiency.

(4) Since data is distributed over all disks, so read requests involve all disks. So, requests have a higher level of parallelism.

(5) Best redundancy performance for small and large read and large write requests.

Disadvantages of level–5

Following are the disadvantages of level–5:

(1) Most complex controller design.

(2) Difficult to rebuild in case of disk failure.

(3) It involves high overhead for small writes because to change 1-byte in a file, the entire stripe must be read, the byte changed, the parity information recalculated and the entire strip is rewritten.

(4) Disk failure has a medium impact on the throughput.

Please note here that the effective space utilisation of RAID level -5 system is 80% as in level-3 and level-4 systems.

Level-6: RAID-6 (P + Q Redundancy)

This level uses (P + Q) redundancy scheme. It uses error-correcting codes (ECC) called as **Reed-Solomon codes,** instead of using parity. It is similar to level-5 but stores **extra redundant information to guard** against multiple disk failures.

Advantage (s) of level-6

Following are the advantages-

(1) It provides extremely good recoveries. It can recover from upto two simultaneous disk failures.

(2) More reliability and data safety.

(3) High performance for large as well as small requests.

Disadvantages of level-6

Following are the disadvantages-

(1) Higher time overheads for write.

(2) Stores extra redundant information to guard against multiple disk failures.

Please note that here the effective storage space utilisation is only 66%.

9.6 DISK SPACE ALLOCATION METHODS

As we know that files are stored on disk, so the management of disk space is a major problem for the designers. If we wish to allocate space to file we have to know what blocks on the disk are available. So, we need a disk allocation table (DAT) in addition to Fat Allocation Table (FAT).

Please note that the OS maintains a list of free disk spaces to keep track of all disk blocks which are not being used by any file. When ever a file has to be created, the list of free disk space is searched for and then allocated to the new file. The amount of space allocated to this file is then removed from the space list. When a file is deleted, its disks space is added to the free space list.

How to manage free disk blocks?

To manage free disk blocks two main techniques are used-

(*a*) Bit vector or Bit table or Bit map.

(*b*) Linked free space list or chain free points. We discuss both these techniques first.

I Bit vector or Bit table or Bit map

The list of free disk spaces is implemented as a **bit map or bit vector.** Each block is represented by a single bit. '0' (zero) is marked as a **free block** whereas '1' is for **allocated block.**

For example, consider a disk of figure 9.10 where blocks 1, 3, 5, 7, 9, 11 and 13 are free blocks (marked as 0s) and other blocks are allocated (marked as 1s).

Blocks→	0	1	2	3	4	5	6	7	8	9	10	11	12	13
Bits→	1	0	1	0	1	0	1	0	1	0	1	0	1	0

Fig 9.10 Bit map

0 ≡ free block

1 ≡ allocated block

Please note that this bit-map is stored on specific place on the disk. Like a 90 MB disk requires 90,000 bits for the map where 1 block = 1KB.

Advantages of Bit vector /Bit table/Bit map

The following are the advantages of this technique

(1) It is simple and efficient method to find the first free block or n-consecutive free blocks on the disk.

(2) A bit map requires lesser space as it uses 1-bit per block.

Disadvantages of Bit vector/Bit table/Bit map

The following are the disadvantages of this technique—

(1) Extra disk space is required to store bit map. **Note that a disk with n-blocks require a bitmap of n-bits.**

(2) It may require a special hardware support to do bit-operations *i.e*, finding out which bit is 1 and which bit is 0.

(3) Bit maps are inefficient unless they are kept in main memory and are written to disk occasionally for recovery needs.

For example:

Say, disk size = 1 GB (2^{30} bytes)

block size = 2^{12} bytes.

$$\text{Then, number of blocks} = \frac{2^{30}}{2^{12}}$$

$$= 2^{30-12} = 2^{18} \text{ (blocks)}$$

Now, corresponding to each block, a bit will be there in the bit map.

∴ Size of bit map = 2^{18} bits (or 256 KB) *i.e.*, **if disk size is large then bit map will also be large.** And storing this map in memory is not feasible.

II Linked free space list/Chain free points

In this method, all free blocks are linked together. **Each free block points to the next free block. The first free block is pointed by a head pointer** which is kept in a special location on the disk. This first free block will point to the second free block, second free block will point to third free block and so on. This is shown in Fig. 9.11 below.

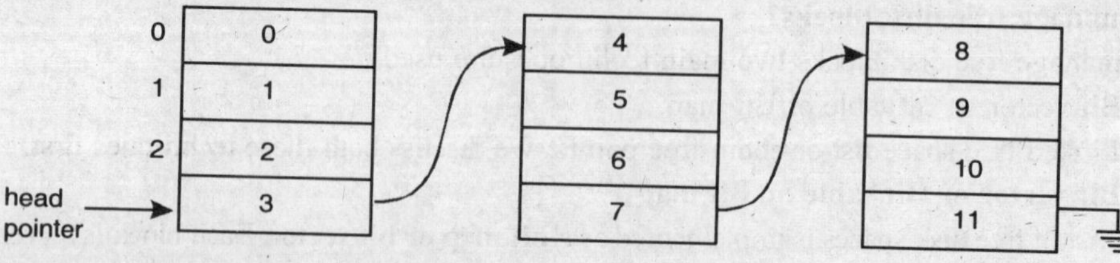

Fig. 9.11 Linked list of free blocks

Here, in this figure, block-3 (*i.e.*, first free block) of the linked list is pointed by a head pointer. Block-3 contains the address of next free block 4, and block-4 will contain the address of block-6 and so on. The last free block in the chain is block-8 which is not pointing to any free block.

Advantages of linked free space list

(1) If a file is to be allocated a free block, the OS can simply allocate the first block in the free space list-and move the head-pointer to the next free block in the list.

(2) No disk fragmentations as every block is utilized.

Disadvantages of linked free space list

(1) It is not very efficient scheme as to traverse the list, we must read each block requiring substantial time.

(2) Pointers used here will also consume disk space. Additional memory is, therefore, required.

For example, a 20 MB hard disk needs a free list of maximum 40 blocks to hold all 20,000 disk block numbers.

Comparison of these two approaches

As compared to linked list, the bit-map requires less space since it uses 1 bit per block. Only if the disk is nearly full with the linked list, it requires fewer blocks than the bit-map. If there is enough main memory to hold bit-map then this method is better than the linked list method. However, if only one block of memory can be spared for keeping track of free disk blocks and the disk is nearly full then the linked list method is preferred.

9.6.1 Contiguous Allocation

In this method, the files are assigned to contiguous areas of secondary storage. The file size area of the file to be created is specified by the user in advance. If the desired amount of contiguous space is not available then the file cannot be created. In this method, all successive records of a file are normally physically adjacent to each other. This increases the accessing speed of records. So, the scattered records (throughout the disk) are accessed slowly. This scheme of contiguous allocation is simple. For sequential access, the file system remembers the disk address of the last block and when access reads the next block. Say, for direct access to block, b, of a file that starts at location, C, we can immediately access block (C + b). Thus, contiguous allocation supports both sequential and direct accessing.

The file directories in contiguous allocation systems are easy to implement. **Please note that for each file, it is necessary to retain the starting address of the file and the files size. Also note that if the size of the file is N blocks long and starts at location, L, then it occupies blocks L, L + 1, …, L + N – 1. As shown in Fig. 9.12 (a), the directory entry for each file indicates the address of the starting block and the size of the length for this file.**

File	Start	Size
F1	1	3
F2	10	2
F3	7	1
F4	5	2

Directory

Fig. 9.12 (*a*) Directory

For this directory, the block allocation is done as follows—

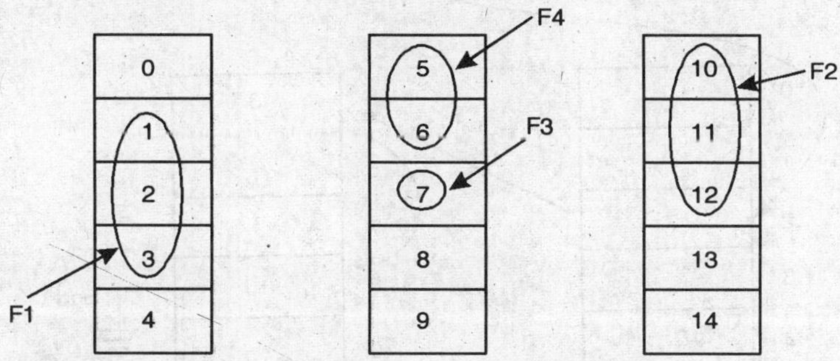

Fig. 9.12 (*b*) Contiguous allocation of files, F1 - F4

The problem, here, is that how to find the space for a new file if the implementation of a free space list is done through a bit-map method. It is so because then for the creation of a n-bytes long file, we need to find n, 0-bits a row.

Advantages of contiguous allocations

(1) It is simple to implement.

(2) Due to contiguous (or continous) allocations, the performance is good.

Disadvantages of contiguous allocations

(1) It is not feasible unless the maximum file size is known at the time of file creation.

(2) Disk Fragmentation may occur here. Compaction cannot be done as Disk's compaction is quite costlier.

(3) It suffers from dynamic storage allocation problem *i.e.*, how to satisfy a request of size, N, from a list of free holes (or unallocated, free segment).

(4) Major problem is how to determine the space needed for a file. This is not a problem during file-copy task but for other applications, this is quite difficult and unreliable.

We may have to make an initial guess also, many a times. If the file turns out to be larger than the guessed size then its extension can be placed in some other disk area. This is called as **file overflow.**

9.6.2 Non-contiguous allocation

As we know that files tend to either grow or shrink overtime. So, contiguous storage allocations are being replaced by more dynamic non-contiguous storage allocation systems.

We have two schemes to study

(*a*) Linked allocation.

(*b*) Indexed allocation

We explain each of these now.

9.6.2.1 Linked Allocation

This method of allocation is a disk-based version of the linked list. Here, each file is the linked list of disk blocks. **Please note that these disk blocks may be scattered throughout the disk.** A few bytes of each disk-block contains the address of the next block. **Also note that the directory contains a pointer to the first and last blocks of the file.**

Consider an example to understand this. Say, that directory is—

File	Start	End
F5	2	8

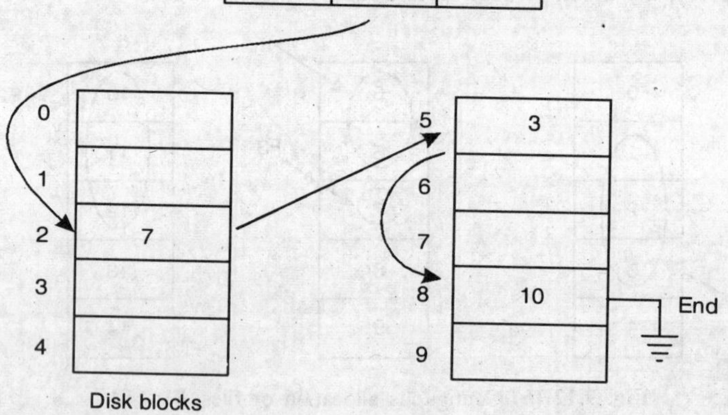

Fig. 9.13 Linked list allocation of disk blocks

As shown in Fig. 9.13, there is a file of 2 disk blocks, which starts at block-2 and ends at block-8.

Advantages of linked allocation

(1) Blocks are completely utilized here. So, no disk fragmentations.

(2) The disk address of first block can be used to locate the rest of the blocks.

Disadvantages of linked allocation

(1) It is not an efficient scheme because the list traversal needs to read each block which is quite time consuming.

(2) Pointers also consume more memory.

(3) No support for direct accessing as blocks are scattered all over the disk.

9.6.2.2 Indexed Allocation

In this scheme, each file is provided with its own **index block,** which is an array of disk block pointers *i.e.*, addresses. **The Nth entry in the index block points to the Nth disk block of the**

file. The directory contains the address of the index block. **Please note that to read the Nth disk block, the pointer in the Nth index block entry is used to find the desired block and then read. Also note that these index blocks are just like the page map tables in our paged memory systems.**

For example, Say disk blocks are of size 512 bytes, pointers take 4 bytes, then the index block can contain upto 128 pointers to disk blocks. **This means that the largest file in such a system cannot exceed 128 blocks of 512 bytes each.**

Please note that if file size exceeds 64 KB then we may use two-level indexing as shown in Fig. 9.14 below—

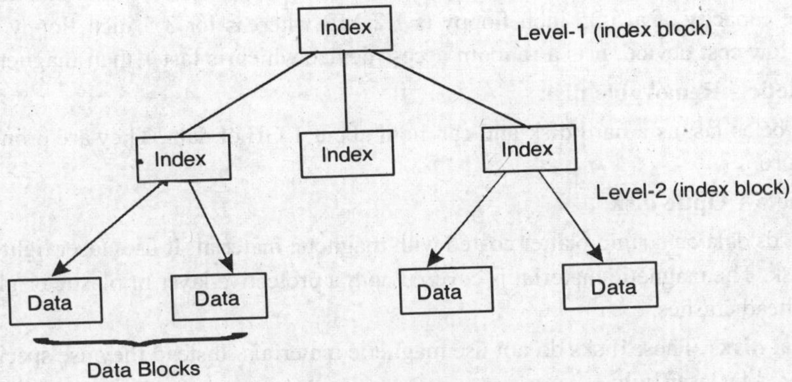

Fig. 9.14 Two-level indexing

If we want to search for a disk block in this scheme, the O.S. uses the first level index to find the second level index which in turn contains pointers to the disk blocks. This can continue till level-3 or level-4 also but usually two-levels are sufficient. This increases our addressing capacity to almost double, thereby supporting file sizes upto 8MB and 1GB of file spaces.

Advantages of Indexed /Grouped allocation

The following are the advantages of indexed allocation-

(') It supports both sequential and direct access. So, they are very popular.

(2) These block indexes are not physically stored as the part of FAT (File Allocation Table).

(3) No external fragmentation.

(4) Indexing of free space can be done by means of the bit map.

(5) Entire block is available for data as no space is occupied by pointers.

Disadvantages of Indexed/Grouped allocation

The following are the disadvantages of Indexed allocation-

(1) Large number of disk accesses is necessary to retrieve the address of the target block on disk. So, we have to keep some index blocks in memory which is dangerous if disk is large.

(2) It requires lot of space for keeping pointers. Here, pointer overhead is more as compared to the pointer overhead of linked - list allocation.

(3) Most files are generally small. If we use linked allocation for these files of one or two blocks then we only need a space for one pointer per block whereas in an indexed allocation, an entire index block must be allocated even if one or more pointers are null.

(4) Indexed allocation is more complex and time consuming.

Please note that it is also possible to combine contiguous allocation with the indexed allocation by using contiguous allocation for small files (upto 3 to 4 blocks) and then automatically switching to the indexed allocation, if the file grows. Also note that contiguous allocation is efficient for small files and most of our files are usually small. The average performance can also be quite good.

9.7 STABLE STORAGE IMPLEMENTATIONS

There are various types of storage devices used for tertiary storage. We discuss some of them.

Floppy disks: It is a thin flexible disk coated with magnetic material and is enclosed in a protective plastic case. They are 5.25 inch or 3.5 inch in diameter. They come in single or double density. The capacity of a 5.25 inch floppy is 1.2 MB whereas for 3.5 inch floppy is 1.44 MB. Floppy is a low cost device. It is a random access device which is faster than magnetic tape.

Magnetic – Removable disk

It can be as fast as a hard disk and can hold about 1 GB of data. They are prone to damage from exposure.

Magneto – Optic disk

It records data on a rigid platter coated with magnetic material. It uses laser light to read data from this disk. The magnetic material is covered with a protective layer of plastic or glass. So, it is resistant to head crashes.

Optical disks. These disks do not use magnetic materials. Instead they use special materials that are altered by laser light.

WORM (Write - Once, Read-Many) disks

As the name suggests, these disks are written once but read many times. They are made of thin aluminium film sandwiched between two glass or plastic platters. During bit writing process, a laser light is used to burn a small hole through the aluminium, this hole cannot be reversed, so sectors can be written once only. These disks are reliable and durable. It can store vast amount of data in gigabytes (10^9 bytes). The access time is less than 30 seconds.

CD-ROM and DVDS

Compact disks (CDs) can store more than 1 GB of data. Digital Video Disks (DVDs) can store more than 20 gigabytes (GB) of data on both sides of the disk. These optical device have many advantages—

(*a*) Large storage device

(*b*) Reliable

(*c*) Non-Volatile

But a special care is required for its handling.

Magnetic tapes

A magnetic tape is a ferrite coated magnetic strips of plastics wounded on reels on which data is encoded. It is kept in a spool and takes seconds or minutes for moving to the correct spot. Data or information on tapes is stored character by character. Tapes have high storage capacity-40GB to 300GB. They also have a read/write head which is an electromagnet. This read/write head reads magnetized areas, converts them to electrical signals and sends them to main memory for further processing. Tapes are cheaper than disks and are non-volatile. However, the data access is sequential and slower.

9.8 CASE STUDY ON WIN-2000 I/O

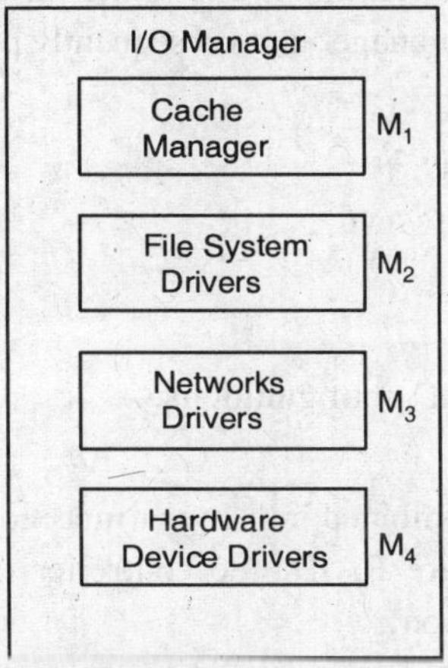

Fig 9.15 W2K I/O Manager

As shown in Fig. 9.15 above is a windows 2000 (W2K) I/O Manager. The I/O manager consists of four modules, $M_1 - M_4$. They are as follows—

1. Cache Manager

It provides a caching facility in the main memory to all file systems and network components. **The cache can be dynamically increased or decreased depending on a particular activity as the amount of available physical memory varies.** It includes two services to improve overall performance-

(*a*) **Lazy write:** The updates are recorded in the cache by the system. They are not recorded on the disk. Later on, when the demand on the processor is low, the cache manager writes the changes to disk. However, say if a particular cache block is updated in the meantime then there will be net savings.

(*b*) **Lazy commit :** This is similar to lazy write for transaction processing. Here, they system caches the committed information and later writes it to the file system log by a background process.

2. File system Drivers

The I/O manager treats a file system driver as just another device driver and routes message for certain volumes to the appropriate software driver for that device adapter.

3. Network Drivers

It includes integrated networking capabilities and support distributed applications.

4. Hardware Device Drivers

These drivers access the hardware registers of the peripheral devices through the entry points in W2K Executive DLL (Dynamic Link Libraries). A set of routines exists for every platform that WIN-2000 supports. The routine names are the same for all platforms so that the source code of W2K device drivers is portable across different processor types.

Actually, W2K offers two modes of I/O operation. They are-

(*a*) Asynchronous mode.

(*b*) Synchronous mode.

In asynchronous I/O, an application initiates an I/O operation and then can continue processing while the I/O request is fulfilled.

In synchronous I/O, an application is blocked until the I/O operation completes.

Asynchronous I/O is more efficient as it allows the thread to continue execution while the I/O operation is queued by the I/O manager and subsequently performed. WIN- 2000 provides four ways of signalling I/O completion:—

(*a*) *Signaling device kernel object.*

(*b*) *Signaling an event kernel object.*

(*c*) *Alterable I/O.*

(*d*) *I/O completion ports.*

W2K supports 2 types of RAID configurations:—

(*a*) Hardware RAID:

Separate physical disks are combined into one or more logical disks by the disk controller or disk storage hardware. In hardware RAID, the controller interface handles the creation and regeneration of redundant information.

(*b*) Software RAID:

Non-contiguous disk space is combined into one or more logical partitions by the fault-tolerant software disk driver, FTDISK. W2K server implements this RAID facility within its O.S. It can be used with any set of multiple disks.

MULTIPLE-CHOICE QUESTIONS [MCQs]

1. In a hard disk, what rotates about a central spindle—

(*a*) Disk (*b*) Platter

(*c*) Sector (*d*) None of the above

2. The collection of tracks under the head at any time is known as—

(*a*) Cylinder (*b*) Sector

(*c*) Spindle (*d*) None of the above.

3. Disk address consists of—

(*a*) (Cylinder number, track number)

(*b*) (Cylinder number, track number, sector number)

(*c*) (Cylinder number, sector number)

(*d*) None of the above

4. The time required to move the disk arm to the required track is known as—

(*a*) Latency time (*b*) Access time

(*c*) Seek time (*d*) None of the above

5. Seek-time is given by the equation—

(*a*) $T_s = mn + S$ (*b*) $T_s = m + nS$

(*c*) $T_s = m - nS$ (*d*) $T_s = m * S$

6. Transfer time, T, is given by the formula—

(*a*) $T = b * rN$ (*b*) $T = b + rN$

(*c*) $T = b / rN$ (*d*) None of the above

7. The total average access time is given by—

(*a*) $T_a = T_s + \frac{1}{2r} + \frac{b}{rN}$ (*b*) $T_a = T_s + \frac{1}{2r} - \frac{b}{rN}$

(*c*) $T_a = T_s + \frac{1}{2r} + \frac{b}{N}$ (*d*) None of the above

8. SSTF stands for-

(*a*) Small Seek time first. (*b*) Simple Seek time first.

(*c*) Shortest Seek time first. (*d*) None of the above.

9. Elevator algorithm is another name for-

(*a*) SACN (*b*) SSTF

(*c*) SCFS (*d*) None of the above

10. C-SCAN, 'C' stands for—

(*a*) Common (*b*) Circular

(*c*) Commit (*d*) None of the above

11. RAID stands for-

(*a*) Retrieval Array of Independent disks.

(*b*) Redundant Array of Independent disks.

(*c*) Round Allocation of Independent disks

(*d*) None of the above

12. The process of splitting of data into equal size partitions over multiple disks is known as-

(*a*) Data stripping (*b*) Arrays of disks.

(*c*) RAID (*d*) None of the above

13. The process of storing extra or duplicate information used for rebuilding the lost information in event of disk failure is known as-

(*a*) Stripping. (*b*) Redundancy.

(*c*) Disk Array. (*d*) None of the above

14. RAID supports—

(*a*) 5 - levels. (*b*) 6 - levels.

(*c*) 7 - levels. (*d*) None of the above

15. Mirroring refers to—

(*a*) RAID - 1 (*b*) RAID - 2

(*c*) RAID - 3 (*d*) None of the above.

16. ECC stands for—

(*a*) Error Correcting codes. (*b*) Error Common codes.

(*c*) Error cost codes (*d*) None of the above.

17. A disk with n-blocks requires a bit-map of—

(*a*) (n + 1) bits. (*b*) n bits.

(*c*) (n – 1) bits (*d*) None of the above

18. WORM stands for—

(*a*) Write-only, Read-many. (*b*) Write-once, Read -many

(*c*) Write-once, Read-memory (*d*) None of the above

19. DVD stands for—

(*a*) Digital very Digital.
(*b*) Direct video Digital.
(*c*) Digital video Disks.
(*d*) None of the above.

20. WIN-2000 (W2K) Support—

(*a*) 2 types of RAID.
(*b*) 3 types of RAID.
(*c*) 4 types of RAID.
(*d*) None of the above

ANSWERS

1. *b*	**2.** *a*	**3.** *b*	**4.** *c*	**5.** *a*	**6.** *c*
7. *a*	**8.** *c*	**9.** *a*	**10.** *b*	**11.** *b*	**12.** *a*
13. *b*	**14.** *c*	**15.** *a*	**16.** *a*	**17.** *b*	**18.** *b*
19. *c*	**20.** *a*				

CONCEPTUAL SHORT QUESTIONS WITH ANSWERS

Q. 1. None of the disk-scheduling disciplines, except FCFS, is truly fair (starvations may occur).

(a) Explain why this assertion is true.

(b) Describe a way to modify algorithms such as SCAN to ensure fairness.

(c) Explain why fairness is an important goal in a time-sharing system.

(d) Give three or more examples of circumstances in which it is important that O.S. be unfair in servicing I/O requests.

Ans. (*a*) New requests for the track over which the head currently resides can theoretically arrive as quickly as these requests are being serviced.

(*b*) All older requests could be forced to the top of the queue. An associated bit for each could be set to indicate that no new request could be moved ahead of these requests. For SSTF, the rest of the queue would have to be reorganized with respect to the last of these old requests.

(*c*) To prevent unusually long response times.

(*d*) Paying and swapping should take priority over user requests. Kernel-initiated I/O (Like writing of file system metadata) can take priority over user I/O. And, if the kernel supports real-time process priorities, the I/O requests of those processes should be preferred.

Q. 2. Requests are not usually uniformly distributed. For example, the cylinders on which the file directory structures reside are accessed more frequently than are most files. Suppose that you know that 50% of the requests are for a small fixed number of cylinders.

(a) Which of the scheduling algorithm would be best?

(b) Can you suggest a new scheduling algorithm for this case? If you can, describe your algorithm.

Ans. (*a*) SSTF algorithm would be best under such circumstances. Because 50% of the requests are for a fixed number of cylinders, when we encounter a series of requests, half of them will be in a small fixed number of cylinders and using SSTF scheduling, we can make sure that this half of requests can be serviced by requiring the least number of head movements. For the other half of requests, using SSTF scheduling gives us a sub-optimal solution.

(*b*) We know that 50% of the requests are for a small fixed number of cylinders and suppose that these cylinders are a round cylinder, X. Given a series of requests, we can determine which one to service next according to which one is closest to the cylinder, X. First, we select the cylinders from the one side of cylinder, X, after servicing all the requests from one side of cylinder X, we proceed to serve the other requests from the other side of cylinder, X. It's performance will be better than SSTF scheduling.

Q. 3. How UNIX uses addressing in order to save space ?

Ans. UNIX combines direct and indexed addressing in order to save space and to provide faster access to small files. In UNIX OS, the first 15 pointers of the index block are kept in device directory. The first 10 pointers contain direct address of 10 data blocks on the disks. The next 3 pointers point to indirect blocks.

Q. 4. The performance of indexed allocation depends upon the index structure, the size of file and the position of block desired. Explain.

Ans. Indexed allocation is more complex. If the index block is already in memory, then the access can be made directly. However, it requires lot of memory space. If the memory space is not available then we may have to read the index block first and then the desired data block. For a two level index, two index block reads may be required. For larger files, accessing a block at the EOF would require the reading of all of the index blocks to follow the **pointer chain** before the data block could be read finally.

Q. 5. What is disk duplexing?

Ans. In WIN - 2000, in software RAID facility, it uses RAID-1 and RAID-5. In case of RAID-1 (disk mirroring), the two disks containing the primary and mirrored partitions may be on the same disk controller or different disk controllers. This configuration is known as **disk duplexing.**

Q. 6. Suppose that the disk rotates at 7200 rpm.

(*a*) What is the average rotational latency of this disk drive?

(*b*) What seek distance can be covered in the time that you found for part-a?

Ans. (*a*) 7200 rpm gives 120 rotations per second.

$\therefore$ Full rotation takes 8.33 ms & Average rotational latency (a half rotation) takes **4.167 ms.**

(*b*) $t = 4.167$ ms (from above)

$\therefore\ t = 0.7561 + 0.2439\ L$

$\therefore\ 4.167 = 0.7561 + 0.2439\ L$

or $L = 195.58$

$\therefore$ We can seek over 195 tracks (about 4% of the disk) during an average rotational latency.

Q. 7. The reliability of a hard-disk drive is typically described in terms of a quantity called mean time between failures (MTBF). Although this quantity is called a "time," the MTBF actually is measured in drive-hours per failure.

(*a*) If a disk farm contains 1000 drives, each of which has a 750,000 hour MTBF, which of the following best describes how often a drive failure will occur in that disk farm: once per thousand years, once per century, once per decade, once per year, or once per month, once per week, once per day, once per hour, once per minute, or once per second?

(*b*) Mortality statistics indicate that, on the average, a U.S. resident has about 1 chance in 1000 of dying between ages 20 and 21 years. Deduce the MTBF hours for 20 year olds. Convert this figure from hours to years. What does this MTBF tell you about the expected lifetime of a 20 year old ?

(c) The manufacturer claims a 1-million hour MTBF for a certain model of disk drive. What can you say about the number of years that one of those drives can be expected to last ?

Ans. (*a*) 750,000 drive-hours per failure divided by 1000 drives gives 750 hours per failure about 31 days or once per month.

(*b*) The human-hours per failure is 8760 (hours in a year) divided by 0.001 failure, giving a value of 8,760,000 "hours" for the MTBF. 8760,000 hours equals 1000 years. This tells us nothing about the expected lifetime of a person of age 20.

(*c*) The MTBF tells nothing about the expected lifetime. Hard disk drives are generally designed to have a lifetime of 5 years. If such a drive truly has a million-hour MTBF, it is very unlikely that the drive will fail during its expected lifetime.

Q. 8. The term "fastwide SCSI-II" denotes a SCSI bus that operates at a data rate of 20 megabytes per second when it moves a packet of bytes between the host and a device. Suppose that a fast wide SCSI-II disk drive spins at 7200 RPM, has a sector size of 512 bytes, and holds 160 sectors per track.

(a) Estimate the sustained transfer rate of this drive in megabytes per second.

(b) Suppose that the drive has 7000 cylinders, 20 tracks per cylinder, a head switch time (from one platter to another) of 0.5 millisecond, and an adjacent cylinder seek time of 2 milliseconds. Use this additional information to give an accurate estimate of the sustained transfer rate for a huge transfer.

(c) Suppose that the average seek time for the drive is 8 milliseonds. Estimate the I/Os per second and the effective transfer rate for a random-access workload that reads individual sectors that are scattered across the disk.

(d) Calculate the random-access I/Os per second and transfer rate for I/O sizes of 4 kilobytes, 8 kilobytes, and 64 kilobytes.

(e) If multiple requests are in the queue, a scheduling algorithm such as SCAN should be able to reduce the average seek distance. Suppose that a random-access workload is reading 8-kilobyte pages, the average queue length is 10, and the scheduling algorithm reduces the average seek time to 3 milliseconds. Now calculate the I/Os per second and the effective transfer rate of the drive.

Ans. (*a*) The disk spins 120 times per second, and each spin transfers a track of 80 KB. Thus, the sustained transfer rate can be approximated as 9600 KB/s.

(*b*) Suppose that 100 cylinders is a huge transfer. The transfer rate is total bytes divided by total time. Bytes: 100 cyl* 10 trk/cyk,*80 kB/trk, *i.e.*, 160,000 KB. Time: rotation time + track switch time + cylinder switch time. Rotation time is 2000 trks / 120 trks per sec, *i.e.*, 16.667 s. Track switch time is 19 switch per cyl* 100 cyl* 0.5 ms, *i.e.*, 950 ms. Cylinder switch time is 99* 2 ms, *i.e.*, 198ms. Thus, the total time is 16.667 + 0.950 + 0.198, *i.e.*, 17.815 s. (We are ignoring any initial seek and rotational latency, which might add about 12 ms to the schedule, *i.e.* 0.1%.) Thus the transfer rate is 8981.2 KB/s. The overhead of track and cylinder switching is about 6.5%.

(*c*) The time per transfer is 8 ms to seek + 4.167 ms average rotational latency + 0.052 ms (calculated from 1 / (120 trk per second * 160 sector per trk)) to rotate one sector past the disk head during reading. We calculate the transfers per second as 1 / (0.012219), *i.e.*, 81.8. Since each transfer is 0.5 KB, the transfer rate is 40.9 KB/s.

(*d*) We ignore track and cylinder crossings for simplicity. For reads of size 4 KB, 8 KB, and 64 KB, the corresponding I/Os per second are calculated from the seek, rotational latency, and rotational transfer time as in the previous item, giving (respectively) 1/(0.0126),

1/(0.013) and 1 / (0.019). Thus we get 79.4, 76.9, and 52.6 transfers per second, respectively. Transfer rates are obtained from 4, 8, and 64 times these I/O r s, giving 318 KB/s, 615 KB/s and 3366 KB/s, respectively.

(*e*) From 1 / (3 + 4.167 + 0.83) we obtain 125 I/Os per second. From 8 KB per I/O we obtain 1000 KB/s.

Q. 9. You can use simple estimates to compare the cost and performa ce of a terabyte storage system made entirely from disks with one that incorporates tertiary storage. Suppose that magnetic disks each hold 10 gigabytes, cost $ 1000, transfer 5 megabytes per second, and have an average access latency of 15 milliseconds. Suppose that a tape library costs $10 per gigabyte, transfers 10 megabytes per second, and has an average access latency of 20 seconds. Compute the total cost, the maximum total data rate, and the average waiting time for a pure disk system. If you make any assumptions about the workload, describe and justify them. Now, suppose that 5 percent of the data are frequently used, so they must reside on disk, but the other 95 percent are archived in the tape library. Further suppose that 95 percent of the requests are handled by the disk system and the other 5 percent are handled by the library. What are the total cost, the maximum total data rate, and the average waiting time for this herarchical storage system?

Ans. First let's consider the pure disk system. One terabyte is 1024 GB. To be correct, we need 103 disks at 10 GB each. But since this question is about approximations, we will simplify the arithmetic by rounding off the numbers. The pure disk system will have 100 drives. The cost of the disk drives would be $100,000, plus about 20% for cables, power supplies, and enclosures, *i.e.*, around $120,000. The aggregate data rate would be 100 5 MB/s, or 500 MB/s. The average waiting time depends on the workload. Suppose that the requests are for transfers of size 8 KB, and suppose that the requests are randomly distributed over the disk drives. If the system is lightly loaded, a typical request will arrive at an idle disk, so the response time will be 15 ms access time plus about 2 ms transfer time. If the system is heavily loaded, the delay will increase, roughly in proportion to the queue length.

Now let's consder the hierarchical storage system. The total disk space required is 5% of 1 TB, which is 50 GB. Consequently, we need 5 disks, so the cost of the disk storage is $5,000 (plus 20%, *i.e.* $6,000). The cost of the 950 GB tape library is $9500. Thus the total storage cost is $15,500. The maximum total data rate depends on the number of drives in the tape library. We suppose there is only 1 drive. Then the aggregate data rate is 6 10 MB/s *i.e.*, 60 MB/s. For a lightly loaded system, 95% of the requests will be satisfied by the disks with a delay of about 17ms. The other 5% of the requests will be satisfied by the tape library, with a delay of slightly more than 20 seconds. Thus the average delay will be (950.017 + 520)/100, or about 1 second. Even with an empty request queue at the tape library, the latency of the tape drive is responsible for almost all of the system's response latency, because 1/20th of the workload is sent to a device that has a 20 second latency. If the system is more heavily loaded, the average delay will increase in proportion to the length of the queue of requests waiting for service form the tape drive.

The hierarchical system is much cheaper. For the 95% of the requests that are served by the disks, the performance is as a pure-disk system. But the maximum data rate of the hierarchical system is much worse than for the pure-disk system, as is the average response time.

Q. 10. Suppose that a one-sided 5.25 inch optical-disk cartridge has an areal density of 1 gigabit per square inch. Suppose that a magnetic tape has an areal density of 20

megabits per square inch, and is 1/2 inch wide and 1800 feet long. Calculate an estimate of the storage capacities of these two kinds of storage cartridges. Suppose that an optical tape exists that has the same physical size as the tape, but the same storage density as the optical disk. What volume of data could the optical tape hold? What would be a marketable price for the optical tape if the magnetic tape cost $25?

Ans. The area of a 5.25 inch disk is about 19.625 square inches. If suppose that the diameter of the spindle hub is 1.5 inches, the hub occupies an area of about 1.77 squre inches, leaving 17.86 square inches for data storage. Therefore, we estimate the storage capacity of the optical disk to be 2.2 gigabytes.

The surface area of the tape is 10,800 square inches, so its storage capacity is about 26 gigabytes.

If the 10,800 square inches of tape had a storage density of 1 gigabit per square inch, the capacity of the tape would be about 1,350 gigabytes, or 1.3 terabytes. If we charge the same price per gigabyte for the optical tape as for magnetic tape, the optiacal tape cartridge would cost about 50 times more than the magnetic tape, *i.e.*, $1250.

Q. 11. Suppose that we agree that 1 kilobyte is 1,024 bytes, 1 megabyte is 1, 024_2 bytes and 1 gigabyte is $1{,}024_3$ bytes. This progression contginues through terabytes, petabytes, and exabytes ($1{,}024_6$). There are currently several newproposed scientific projects that plan to record and store a few exabytes of data during the next dacade. To answer the following questions, you will need to make a few reasonable assumptions; state the assumptions that you make.

(*a*) How many disk drives would be required to hold 4 exabytes of data?

(*b*) How many magnetic tapes would be required to hold 4 exabytes of data?

(*c*) How many optical tapes would be required to hold 4 exabytes of data?

(*d*) How many holographic storage cartridges would be required to hold 4 exabytes of data?

(*e*) How many cubic feet of storage space would each option require?

Ans. (*a*) Assume that a disk drive holds 10 GB. Then 100 disks hold 1 TB, 100,000 disks hold 1 PB, and 100,000 disks hold 1 EB. To store 4 EB would require about 400 million disks. If a magnetic tape holds 40 GB, only 100 million tapes would be required. If an optical tape holds 50 times more data than a magnetic tape, 2 million optical tapes would suffice. If a holographic cartridge can store 180 GB, about 22.2 million cartridges would be required.

(*b*) A 3.5" disk drive is about 1" high, 4" wide, and 6" deep. In feet, this is 1/12 by 1/3 by 1/2, or 1/72 cubic feet. Packed densely, the 400 million disks would occupy 5.6 million cubic feet. If we allow a factor of 2 for air space and space for power supplies, the required capacity is about 11 million cubic feet.

(*c*) A 1/ 2" tape cartridge is about 1" high and 4.5" square. The volume is about 1/85 cubic feet. For 100 million magnetic tapes packed densely, the volume is about 1-2 million cubic feet. For 2 million optical tapes, the volume is 23,400 cubic feet.

(*d*) A CD-ROM is 4.75" in diameter and about 1/16" thick. If we assume that a holostore disk is stored in a library slot that is 5" square and 1/8" wide, we calculate the volume of 22.2 million disks to be about 40,000 cubic feet.

Q. 12. Is disk scheduling other than FCFS scheduling, useful in a single-user environment? Explain your answer.

Ans. In a single-user environment, the I/O queue usually is empty. Requests generally arrive from a single process for one block or for a sequence of consecutive blocks. In these cases,

FCFS is an economical method of disk scheduling. But LOOK is nearly as easy to program and will give much better performance when multiple processes are performing concurrent I/O, such as when a Web browser retrieves data in the background while the operating system is paging and another application is active in the foreground.

Q.13 Explain why SSTF scheduling tends to favor middle cylinders over the innermost and outermost cylinders.

Ans. The center of the disk is the location having the smallest average distance to all other tracks. Thus the disk head tends to move away from the edges of the disk. Here is another way to think of it. The current location of the head divides the cylinders into two groups. If the head is not in the center of the disk and a new request arrives, the new request is more likely to be in the group that includes the centre of the disk; thus, the head is more likely to move in that direction.

Q. 14. Requests are not usually uniformly distributed. For example, a cylinder containing the file system FAT or inodes can be expected to be accessed more frequently than a cylinder that only contains files. Suppose you know that 50 percent of the requests are for a small, fixed number of cylinders.

(*a*) Would any of the scheduling algorithms discussed in this chapter be particularly good for this case? Explain your answer.

(*b*) Propose a disk-scheduling algorithm that gives even better performance by taking advantage of this "hot spot" on the disk.

(*c*) File systems typically find data blocks via an indirection table, such as a FAT in DOS or Inodes in UNIX. Describe one or more ways to take advantage of this indirection to improve the disk performance.

Ans. (*a*) SSTF would take greatest advantage of the situation. FCFS could cause unnecessary head movement if references to the "high-demand" cylinders were interspersed with references to cylinders far away.

(*b*) Here are some ideas. Place the hot data near the middle of the disk. Modify SSTF to prevent starvation. Add the policy that if the disk becomes idle for more than, say 50 ms, the operating system generates an **anticipatory seek** to the hot region, since the next request is more likely to be there.

(*c*) Cache the metadata in primary memory, and locate a file's data and metadata in close physical proximity on the disk. (UNIX accomplishes the latter goal by allocating data and metadata in regions called **cylinder groups.**)

Q. 15. Why is rotational latency usually not considered in disk scheduling? How would you modify SSTF, SCAN, and C-SCAN to include latency optimization?

Ans. Most disks do not export their rotational position information to the host. Even if they did, the time for this information to reach the scheduler would be subject to imprecision and the time consumed by the scheduler is variable, so the rotational position information would become incorrect. Further, the disk requests are usually given in terms of logical block numbers, and the mapping between logical blocks and physical locations is very complex.

Q. 16. How would use of a RAM disk affect your selection of a disk-scheduling algorithm? What factors would you need to consider? Do the same considerations apply to hard-disk scheduling, given that the file system stores recently used blocks in a buffer cache in main memory?

Ans. Disk scheduling attempts to reduce the overhead time of disk head positioning. Since a RAM disk has uniform access times, scheduling is largely unnecessary. The comparison between RAM disk and the main memory disk-cache has no implications for hard-disk scheduling because we only schedule the buffer cache misses, not the requests that find their data in main memory.

Q. 17. Why is it important to balance file system I/O among the disks and controllers on a system in a multitasking environment?

Ans. A system can only perform at the speed of its slowest bottleneck. Disks or disk controllers are frequently the bottleneck in modern systems as their individual performance cannot keep up with that of the CPU and system bus. By balancing I/O among disks and controllers, neither an individual disk nor a controller is overwhelmed, so that bottleneck is avoided.

Q. 18. What are the tradeoffs involved in rereading code pages from the file system versus using swap space to store them?

Ans. If code pages are stored in swap space, they can be transferred more quickly to main memory (because swap space allocation is tuned for faster performance than general file system allocation). Using swap space can require startup time if the pages are copied there at process invocation rather than just being paged out to swap space on demand. Also, more swap space must be allocated if it is used for both code and data pages.

Q. 19. Is there any way to implement truly stable storage? Explain your answer.

Ans. Truly stable storage would never lose data. The fundamental technique for stable storage is to maintain multiple copies of the data, so that if one copy is destroyed, some other copy is still available for use. But for any scheme, we can imagine a large enough disaster that all copies are destroyed.

Q. 20. Remapping of bad blocks by sector sparing or sector slipping could influence performance. Suppose that the drive has a total of 100 bad sectors at randon locations and that each bad sector is mapped to a spare that is located on a different track, but within the same cylinder. Estimate the number of I/Os per second and the effective transfer rate for a random-access workload consisting of 8-kilobyte reads, with a queue length of 1 (that is, the choice of scheduling algorithm is not a factor). What is the effect of a bad sector on performance?

Ans. Since the disk holds 22,400,000 sectors, the probability of requesting one of the 100 remapped sectors is very small, An example of a worst-case event is that we attempt to read, say, an 8 KB page, but one sector from the middle is defective and has been remapped to the worst possible location on another track in that cylinder. In this case, the time for the retrieval could be 8 ms to seek, plus two track switches and two full rotational latencies. It is likely that a modern controller would read all the requested good sectors from the original track before switching to the spare track to retrieve the remapped sector and thus would incur only one track switch and rotational latency. So the time would be 8 ms seek + 4.17 ms average rotational latency + 0.05 ms track switch + 8.3 ms rotational latency + 0.83 ms read time (8 KB is 16 sectors, 1/10 of a track rotation). Thus, the time to service this request would be 21.8 ms, giving an I/O rate of 45.9 requests per second and an effective bandwidth of 367 KB/s. For a severely time-constrained application this might matter, but the overall impact in the weighted average of 100 remapped sectors and 22.4 million good sectors is nil.

Q. 21. Discuss the relative advantages and disadvantages of sector sparing and sector slipping.

Ans. Sector sparing can cause an extra track switch and rotational latency, causing an unlucky request to require an extra 8 ms of time. Sector slipping has less impact during future reading, but at sector remapping time it can require the reading and writing of an entire track's worth of data to slip the sectors past the bad spot.

Q. 22. The operating system generally treats removable disks as shared file systems but assigns a tape drive to only one application at time. Give three reasons that could explain this difference in treatment of disks and tapes. Describe additional features that would be required of the operating system to support shared file-system access to a tape jukebox. Would the applications sharing the tape jukebox need any special properties, or could they use the files as though the files were disk-resident? Explain your answer.

Ans. (*a*) Disks have fast random-access times, so they give good performance for interleaved access streams. By contrast, tapes have high positioning times. Consequently, if two users attempt to share a tape drive for reading, the drive will spend most of its time switching tapes and positioning to the desired data, and relatively little time performing data transfers. This performance problem is similar to the thrashing of a virtual memory system that has insufficient physical memory.

(*b*) Tape cartridges are removable. The owner of the data may wish to store the cartridge off-site (far away from the computer) to keep a copy of the data safe from a fire at the location of the computer.

(*c*) Tape cartridges are often used to send large volumes of data from a producer of data to the consumer. Such a tape cartridge is reserved for that particular data transfer and cannot be used for general-purpose shared storage space.

To support shared file-system access to a tape jukebox, the operating system would need to perform the usual file-system duties, including

Manage a file-system name space over the collection of tapes

Perform space allocation

Schedule the I/O operations

The applications that access a tape-resident file system would need to be tolerant of lengthy delays. For improved performance, it would be desirable for the application to be able to disclose a large number of I/O operations so that the tape-scheduling algorithms could generate efficient schedules.

Q. 23. In a disk jukebox, what would be the effect of having more open files than the number of drives in the jukebox?

Ans. Two bad outcomes could result. One possibility is starvation of the applications that issue blocking I/Os to tapes that are not mounted in drives. Another possibility is thrashing, as the jukebox is commanded to switch tapes after every I/O operation.

Q. 24. What would be the effect on cost and perfomance if tape storage were to achive the same areal density as disk storage?

Ans. To achieve the same areal density as a magnetic disk, the areal density of a tape would need to improve by two orders of magnitude. This would cause tape storage to be much cheaper than disk storage. The storage capacity of a tape would increase to more than 1 terabyte, which could enable a single tape to replace a jukebox of tapes in today's technology, further reducing the cost. The areal density has no direct bearing on the data transfer rate, but the higher capacity per tape might reduce the overhead of tape switching.

Q. 25. If magnetic hard disks eventually have the same cost per gigbyte as do tapes, will tapes become obsolete, or will they still be needed? Explain your answer.

Ans. Tapes are easily removable, so they are useful for off-site backups and for bulk transfer of data (by sending cartridges). As a rule, a magnetic hard disk is not a removable medium.

Q. 26. Suppose you had immediate access (through memory cell) to the current cylinder and sector of a disk. Suppose the disk has 400 cylinders and it takes 1 ms to seek over a cylinder. Suppose disk has 32 sectors/track and it takes 0.5 ms to spin over one sector. Write a unified shortest access time first scheduling algorithm for this disk. The algorithm should choose the closest request, taking both cylinder and sector into account. Assume you have a queue of requests, each with a cylinder and sector number.

Ans. 1. It is given that the disk has 400 cylinders and it takes/ms to seek over a cylinder. Also it is given that the disk has 32 sectors / track and it takes 0.5 ms to spin over one sector.

2. The Shortest Service Time 'First (SSTF) scheduling algorithm can be used in this case. Because this polling requires the least movement of the disk arm from its current position.

3. So, we will have minimum seek time. **But please note that minimum seek time doesn't always guarantee that the average seek time over a number of arm movement will be minimum.**

4. Another algorithm is N step-SCAN. In this algorithm, the disk request is queued into sub queues of length V. Subsequently it reprocessed one at a time using SCAN.

5. While a queue is being processed, now request must be added to some other queue. If fewer than N request are available of the and of a scan, then all of them are processed with the next scan.

EXERCISE QUESTIONS

Q. 1. (*a*) Describe various disk space allocation strategies with their merits and demerits. And discuss also the criteria that have to decide which strategy is to be adopted for a particular file.

(*b*) A disk drive has 50 cylinders, numbered 0 to 49. The drive is currently serving a request at cylinder 15, and the previous request was at cylinder 9. The queue of pending requests, in FIFO order is 4, 40, 11, 35, 7, 14,.

(*i*) SSTF (*ii*) SCAN

(*iii*) LOOK (*iv*) C-SCAN

Q. 2. (*a*) Is SSTF disk scheduling algorithm fair *i.e.*, no request is starved? If yes, prove it. If no, modify the SSTF algorithm so that it is fair.

(*b*) Discuss (1) the Linked and

(2) Indexed disk block allocation methods. Discuss their merits and demerits.

Q. 3. Describe the FCFS, SCAN and C-SCAN disk scheduling algorithms. Construct a disk request string for which C-SCAN will be better than the other three.

Q. 4. Discuss the

(1) Contiguous (2) Linked, and (3) Indexed disk

block allocation methods. Discuss their merits and demerits.

Q. 5. What are the different ways of implementing a free space list? Explain them.

Q. 6. Disk request come into the disk drive for cylinders 10, 22, 20, 2, 40, 6 and 38 in that order. A seek takes 6ms/cylinder moved. How much seek time is needed for "elevator algorithm."

Q. 7. (*a*) Suppose that a disk has 5000 cylinders. The drive is currently serving a request at cylinder 143 and the previous request was at cylinder 125. The queue of pending request in FIFO order is 80, 1470, 913, 1774, 948, 1509, 1022, 1750, 130.

What is the total distance that the disk arm moves for the following algorithms:-

(*i*) FCFS (*ii*) SSTF (*iii*) LOOK (*iv*) C-SCAN.

(*b*) State the advantages and disadvantages of placing functionality in a device controller rather than in the kernel.

Q. 8. Suppose you had immediate access (through a memory cell) to the current cylinder and a sector of a disk. Suppose the disk has 400 cylinder and it takes one millisecond to seek over a cylinder. Suppose disk has 32 sectors per track and it takes 0.5 millisecond to spin over one sector. Write a unified shortest access-time-first scheduling algorithm for this disk. The algorithm should choose closest request taking both cylinder and sector into account. Assume you have a queue of requests, each with a cylinder and sector number.

Q. 9. Consider a system where free-space is kept in a free-space list.

(*i*) Suppose that the pointer to the free space list is lost. Can the system reconstruct the free-space list? Explain.

(*ii*) Suggest a scheme to ensure that the pointer is never lost as a result of memory failure.

(*iii*) Describe indexed allocation method of file on disk in detail. Give its merits and demerits over other methods.

Q. 10. What are different methods of disk storage addressing?

Q. 11. Write short notes on–Disk structure.

Q. 12. A disk with 1000 cylinders, numbered 0 to 999, compute the number of tracks the disk arm must move to satisfy all the requests in the disk queue. Assume the last request serviced was at track 345 and the head is moving towards track 0. The queue in FIFO order contains request for the following tracks:

123,874, 692, 475, 105, 376

Perform the computation for the following scheduling algorithms—

(1) FIFO (2) SSTF (3) SCAN

Q. 13. Explain indexed allocation method of disk.

Q. 14. The head of a moving head disk with 100 tracks numbered 0 to 99 is currently serving a request 55. If queue of request is 10, 70, 75, 23, 65 which of the two disk scheduling algorithms FCFS and SSTF will require less head movement ? Find the total head movement for each of the algorithm ?

UNIT - IV

CHAPTER

10

Information Management

10.0 INTRODUCTION

We wish to store information for a **long term** and to make it **sharable** among various processes. OS provides a uniform logical view of information storage on various secondary storage media like disks and tapes. This uniform logical storage unit is called as a **File. A file is a collection of related information defined by its user.** It is abstracted from physical properties of the device on which it is stored.

Please note that an OS maps the files onto secondary storage devices. Also note that these secondary media are non-volatile i.e., the contents persist even when power is turned off. A file may contain a source code, an object code, an executable code, text, numeric data, graphics, set of library functions, etc.

10.1 A SIMPLE FILE SYSTEM

Physically, a file is the smallest allocation on a secondary storage (disks). On the other hand, **logically** a file is a sequence of logical records i.e., a sequence of bits and bytes.

Some systems support a single uniform set of file manipulation features for both file management and I/O device management. This feature is known as **device independence. It simply means that all I/O devices must appear as a set of files only to the users.** However, some OS are better at device independence than others. *For example*, in UNIX OS, a file system (e.g. of disk) can be mounted anywhere in the file *tree*, allowing any file to be accessible by its path name, without regard to which device it is on.

A file has various attributes which are discussed next.

10.1.1 File Attributes

A file has various attributes from the user's point of view. They are as follows–

(1) **Name:** A string of alphanumeric characters and some special characters like underscore. Some of the systems are case sensitive. All OS allow strings of length of 1 to 8 letters as legal filenames. So, "Rajiv", "Chopra", "Senior-Lecturer" are some possible examples of filenames. Every file is given an extension also like •doc, •xls, •c, •cpp, •z, •asm and so on.

(2) **Identifier:** It is a unique identification of a file. It is internal to the system. OS makes references to the related file using these identifiers.

(3) **Type:** As mentioned above, '**type**' attribute indicates the type of the file. For example, T• doc indicates that it is a WORD file, A• cpp indicates it is a C++ source code file, rajiv• cpp• z indicates that the file has been compressed or zipped.

(4) **Location:** It indicates the complete access path of the file for locating it on the device like C:/Windows/tc/tl.cpp.

(5) **Size:** It indicates the current size of the file in bytes or blocks.

(6) **Protection:** It refers to the access control information. *For example* – owner of the file, read/write permissions etc.

(7) **Time, Date, User Identification:** Records of information pertaining to creation, update and last use of the file.

(8) **Version Number:** This field shows the version number of a file, along with the creation/update date/time.

10.2 FILE ACCESS METHODS

File organization refers to the logical structuring of the record determined by the sequence in which they are accessed. As discussed earlier, *logical definition* of a file is that it is a set of logical records. It is allocated storage space on a disk in terms of physical blocks. Normally, the block size of 512 bytes. All basic read/write operations are in terms of blocks. Last block of a file may not be fully occupied. This results in loss of some storage space. This is known as *Internal Fragmentation.*

Please note here that the average disk space lost due to internal fragmentation is of the order of half block per file. Hence, larger is the block size, larger will be the disk space lost. This is due to internal fragmentation.

The File Management System (FMS) has certain functions. Some of the main functions are as follows–

(1) Mapping of logical file address to physical disk address

(2) Management of disk space allocation and deallocation

(3) Keeping track of all files in the system

(4) Support for protection and sharing of files recovery

These are the basic functions performed by the FMS module of any OS.

We discuss some file access methods now.

10.2.1 Pile

It is defined as an arrangement of record in a sequence in which they arrive. Each record consists of one burst of data. Each field in these records should be **self–describing.** The length of each field is indicated by delimiters known as **default**. Pile files are used when the data are not easy to organize. When the stored data varies in size and structure then this arrangement is best. A pile structure is shown in Fig. 10.1.

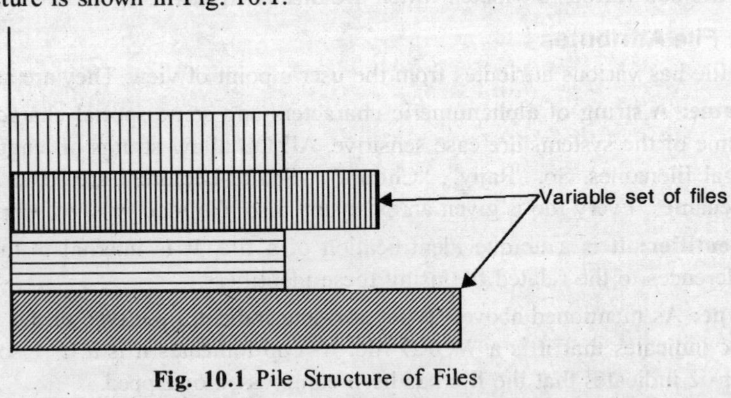

Fig. 10.1 Pile Structure of Files

10.2.2 Sequential File Access

A Sequential file is an ordered file. It is a set of contiguously stored records on a physical storage device such as a magnetic disk, tape or CD–ROM. In a sequential file organization, reords are stored in sequential (ascending or descending) order onto the secondary storage media. To locate a particular record, a program scans the file from the beginning until the desired record is located. In general, to locate *n*th record, we need to go through all (*n*–1) records first.

Advantages of a sequential file

The following are some of it's advantages–

(1) Simplicity of organization
(2) Ease of access to the next record
(3) Sequential retrieval of records on a primary key is very fast
(4) Absence of auxiliary data structure
(5) Creation of an automatic backup copy

Disadvantages of a sequential file

The following are some of it's disadvantages—

(1) Sequential access is not efficient
(2) Record deletion creates a waste space and requires some type of record reorganization
(3) Average access time of a record is equal to the time to access half of the file
(4) Simple queries are time consuming for large files
(5) Insertion and deletion of records is expensive as the records must remain physically ordered

Applications of Sequential files

Some of the main applications of sequential files are as follows–

(1) These files are typically used in batch applications and payroll applications
(2) These files can also be organized in form of a linked list. Each block of file has a pointer pointing towards a new block

10.2.3 Direct Access/Hash files/Random Access/Relative Access

In a direct or hash file organization, **mapping or transformation** of the search key value of a record is made directly to the address of the storage location at which that record is to reside in the file. One way of doing it is *hashing.* **Hashing is defined as the process of direct mapping by performing some arithmetic manipulation with the help of faster algorithms called as the hash functions.**

In a hash file, the data is scattered throughout the disk in a random order. The processing of a hash file is dependent on how the search key set for the records is transformed into the addresses of secondary storage device, like a hard disk, to locate the desired record. This is shown in Fig. 10.2.

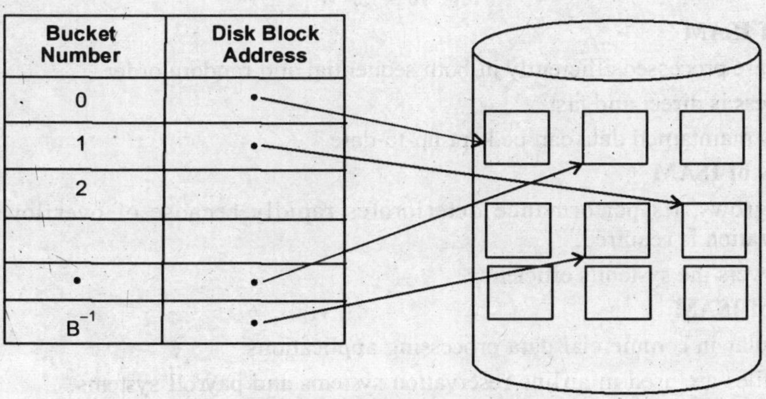

Fig 10.2 Direct/Hashing access

Advantages of a direct file

(1) Data access is direct and fast

(2) Centrally maintained data can be kept up-to-date

Disadvantages of a direct file

(1) As the entire data is to be stored on disk but disk (hardware) is expensive

(2) There is no back up if a file gets destroyed. This is so because files are updated directly and no transaction files are maintained.

Applications of a direct file

This access method is most suitable for DBMS files.

10.2.4 Indexed Sequential File

It is a direct processing method that combines the features of both sequential and direct access of records.

A sequential file (sorted on primary key) that is indexed is called as an indexed sequential file.

IBM also developed **Indexed Sequential Access Method** (ISAM). It uses a small master index that points to disk blocks of a secondary index. The secondary disk blocks will further point to the actual disk blocks allocated to a file. The file is kept sorted on a defined key. To find a match for a key, we first make a binary search in the master index table which provides a block number of the secondary index. The secondary block is read into the memory and a binary is made in the secondary index to determine the address of the file block containing the key value. Finally, the block is searched sequentially to determine the record containing the key value. This is shown in Figure 10.3.

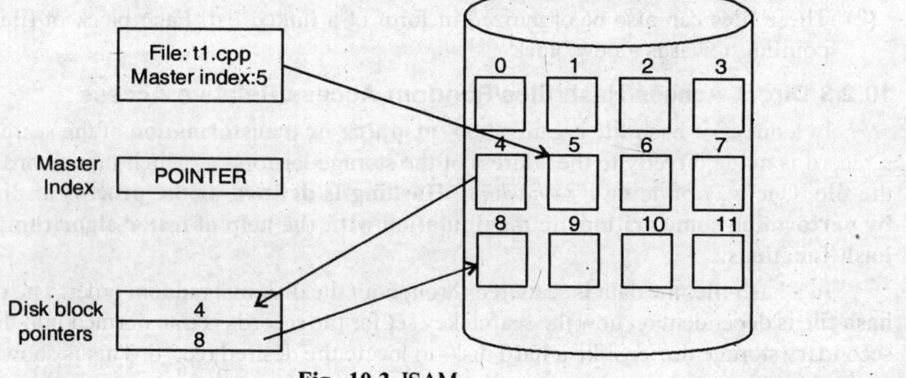

Fig. 10.3 ISAM

Advantages of ISAM

(1) Records are processed efficiently in both sequential and random order.

(2) Data access is direct and fast.

(3) Centrally maintained data can be kept up-to-date.

Disadvantages of ISAM

(1) As file grows, its performance deteriorates rapidly because of overflows and thus reorganization is required.

(2) ISAM lowers the system's efficiency.

Applications of ISAM

(1) Very popular in commercial data processing applications.

(2) Indexed files are used in airline reservation systems and payroll systems.

(3) Used where rate of insertion is very high.

10.3 DIRECTORY STRUCTURE

A directory groups the files owned by a user. It contains information about files and thus is **central** to the functioning of the file system. It contains information like file attributes, it's location and it's ownership. It can be viewed as a symbol table that translates the filenames into their directory entries.

10.3.1 Hierarchical Directory Systems

Typically, a directory contains a number of entries, one per file. In many systems, directories are treated as files which keep track for all other files. **A Single flat directory** can contain a list of all files in a system. **Please note that flat directories are those directories in which the root directory contains all system files and there is no other subdirectory.** On the other hand, when **hierarchical directories** are used, the collection of all directory and subdirectory entries define the totality of system files. This is a better way to organize files. This is shown in Fig 10.4.

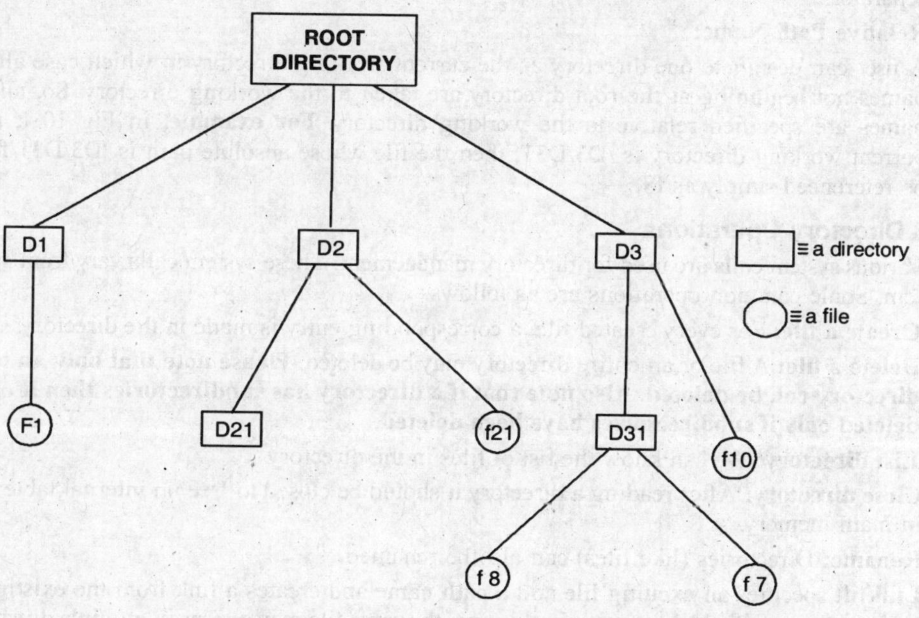

Fig. 10.4 Hierarchical Directory

Where are the directories stored?

If directories are stored in the main memory then they take lot of memory but searching of a file will be faster. **While if they are kept on secondary storage device** then searching will be slower.

So, the **solution** is as follows. Most systems resolve this problem by keeping directories on secondary storage system and by copying to the main memory only the actively used entries. The identities of the actively used entries are made known to the system when files are opened.

Please note that these directories are stored on disks, so the efficiency of directory operations is affected by the number of disk accesses required to complete a search, to append or to remove an entry.

Hence, directories are organized in a way that minimize the search, addition and deletion time.

A single flat directory is not very suitable for searching as it takes O(n) comparisons to locate a given entry. Here, 'n' is the number of all entries in a directory. In worst case scenario, even hashing is not good.

10.3.2 Access paths

When a file system is organized as a directory tree/hierarchical form then there are two ways to specify the filenames uniquely. They are as follows–

I. Absolute Path Name:

In this method, **each file is given an absolute pathname consisting of the path from the root directory to the files. For example,** in figure 10.4, the path C:/D3/D31/f8 means that the root directory contains a subdirectory, D3, which in turn contains a subdirectory D31, which contains file, f8.

Please note that the absolute path name always starts at the root directory and are unique. Also note that '/' has been used as a separator. Some 'OS' use '/' or '>' also as separators.

II. Relative Path Name:

A user can designate one directory as the current working directory in which case all pεth names not beginning at the root directory are taken to the working directory. So, all path names are specified relative to the working directory. **For example,** in Fig 10.4, if the current working directory is /D3/D31, then the file whose absolute path is /D3/D31/f8 can be referenced simply as f8.

10.3.3 Directory Operations

Various system calls are used for directory management. These system calls vary from system to system. Some common operations are as follows–

(1) **Create a file:** For every created file, a corresponding entry is made in the directory.

(2) **Delete a file:** A file or an entire directory may be deleted. **Please note that only an empty directory can be deleted. Also note that if a directory has subdirectories then it can be deleted only if subdirectories have been deleted.**

(3) **List directory:** We can know the list of files in the directory.

(4) **Close directory:** After reading a directory it should be closed to free up internal table space in main memory.

(5) **Rename:** Directories (like files) can also be renamed.

(6) **Link:** It specifies an exciting file and a path name and creates a link from the existing file to the name specified by the path. In this way, the same file may appear in multiple directories.

(7) **Unlink:** A directory entry is removed. If the file that is to be unlinked is present in one directory only, it is removed from the file system else if it is present in multiple directories then only the path name specified is removed.

10.4 FILE PROTECTION

Security of files has always been a prime concern to us. We now discuss the issues related to file protection.

10.4.1 Access Control

We can perform various operations on files. Some of them are–

(*a*) Read – Read a file
(*b*) Write – Write to the file
(*c*) Append – Append to the file
(*d*) Delete – Delete a file
(*e*) List – List the name and attributes of a file

(*f*) Rename – Rename a file

(*g*) Edit – Changing the contents of a file

(*h*) Copy – Make a copy of a file

These operations can be controlled through **access control lists** (*ACLs*) and groups. This list may contain the user name and their access types. **An ACL may be associated with each file and directory.**

There are some other protection mechanisms also. Files can be protected by a **password.** It is better to give a password to a subdirectory rather than an individual file.

10.5 I–NODES–AN ARRAY OF DISK ADDRESSES

In this scheme, each file is associated with a little table called as an **i–node or index–node.** It lists the attributes and disk addresses of the file's blocks. An i–node is shown in Fig. 10.5.

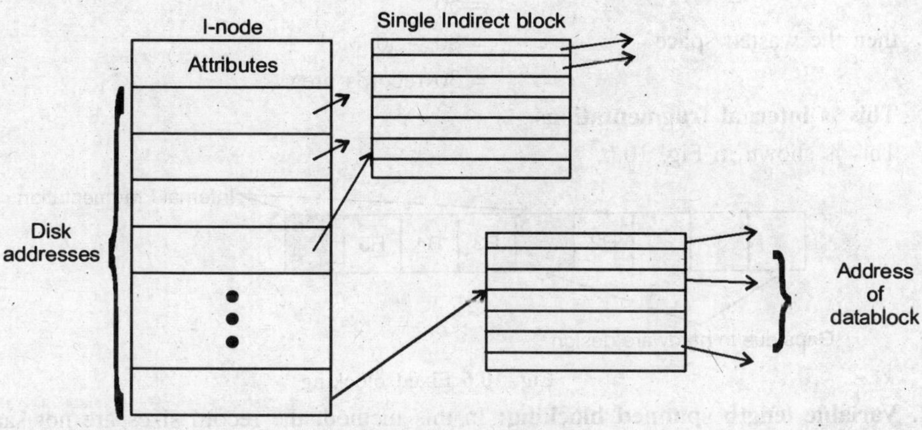

Fig. 10.5 I– NODE

Three Cases arise—

Case I: For smaller files, the first few disk addresses and all the necessary information are stored in the i–node itself. Whenever a file is opened, all this information is fetched from disk to the main memory.

Case II: For larger files, one of the addresses in the i–node is the address of a disk block called as single indirect block. This block contains additional disk addresses.

Case III: For more larger files, the i–node may contain another address which is the address of a disk block called a **double indirect block.** This block contains the addresses of the blocks containing the lists of single indirect blocks. Each of these single indirect blocks point to a few hundred data blocks. Similarly, a triple indirect block can also be used.

10.6 OTHER FREE SPACE MANAGEMENT TECHNIQUE

We have already studied in chapter–9, various free space management techniques. One another approach is **Counting.** We discuss this scheme now.

In general, several contiguous blocks may be allocated or freed simultaneously, particularly when contiguous allocation algorithm has been used for allocating disk space. So, instead of keeping a list of addresses of n–free blocks, it is more convenient to keep the address of the first free block and the number, n, of free contiguous blocks that follow the first block. **Please note that each entry in the free space list will consist of a disk address and a count.** So, this will make the overall list shorter in size.

10.7 RECORD BLOCKING

Records are the logical unit of access of a file. **Blocks** are units of I/O with secondary storage. For I/O to be performed, records must be organized as blocks. **Please note that, in general, the I/O transfer time is reduced by using larger blocks.** Also note that larger blocks require larger I/O buffers. This blocking can be done in three ways–

1. Fixed blocking
2. Variable length spanned blocking
3. Variable length unspanned blocking

We shall discuss each of these now.

1. **Fixed blocking:** In this method, the record lengths are fixed. The prescribed number of records are stored in a block.

   For example: If the block capacity = 80 records and the number of record in the block = 50

   then the wasted space = 80 – 50

   = 30 records area

   This is internal fragmentations.

   This is shown in Fig. 10.6.

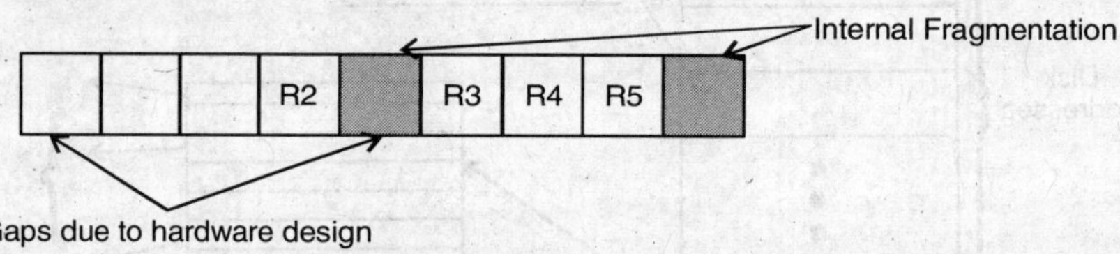

Fig. 10.6 Fixed blocking

2. **Variable length spanned blocking:** In this method, the record sizes are not same. Here, the variable length records are packed into blocks with no unused space. So, some records may divide into two blocks. In this situation, a pointer is passed from one block to another block. This is shown in Fig. 10.7 below.

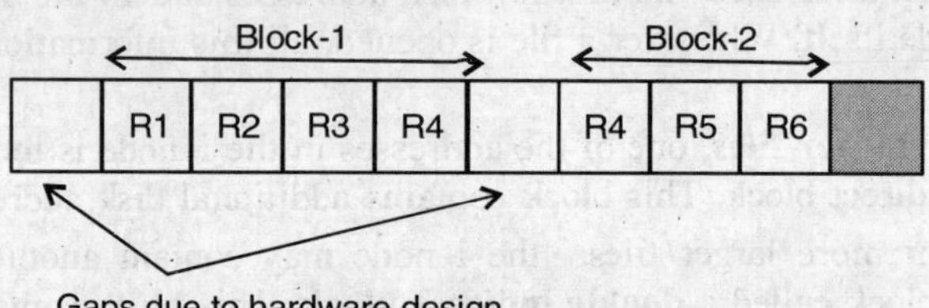

Fig. 10.7 Variable length blocking spanned

3. **Variable length unspanned blocking:** In this method, the records are of variable length but the records are not spanned between the blocks. Here, the wasted area is a serious problem as the remainder of a block cannot be used if the next record is larger than the remaining unused space. This is shown in Fig. 10.8.

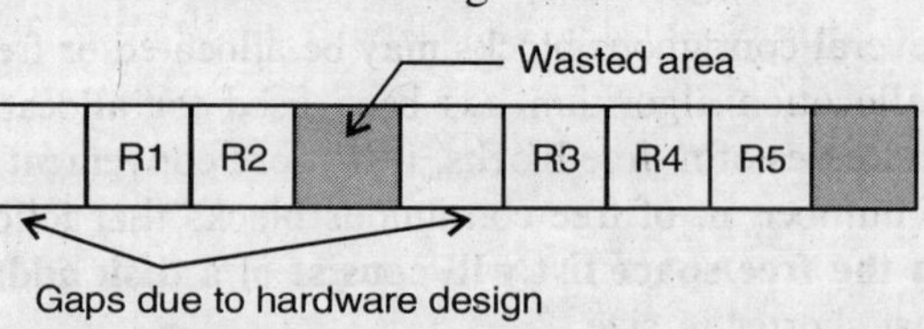

Fig. 10.8 Variable length blocking unspanned

10.8 CASE STUDY ON WIN–2000 FILE SYSTEM

Windows 2000/W2K supports a number of file systems like file allocation table (FAT) that runs on WIN–95, MS–DOS and OS/2. To meet high-end requirements for workstations and servers, the W2K developers also developed the W2K File System (NTFS). High-end applications means client/server applications, Engineering and scientific applications and some network applications.

NTFS uses 64–bit disk addresses and can support disk partitions up to 2^{64} bytes.

Features of NTFS

(1) NTFS can easily recover from system crashes and disk failures. Also, it uses redundant storage for critical file system data.

(2) NTFS uses W2K object model to enforce security. An open file is implemented as a file object with a security descriptor that defines its security attributes.

(3) In NTFS, it is possible to define multiple data streams for a single file.

(4) NTFS associates a collection of attributes with each file. The set of file descriptions is organized as a relational database so that files can be indexed by any attribute.

Actually, cluster is the basic unit of allocation in NTFS (1 cluster = 1 KB). This cluster allocation makes NTFS independent of the physical sector size. The individual filename in NTFS are limited to 255 characters. And NTFS is not case sensitive.

NTFS uses a powerful approach of organizing information on a disk. **Please note that every element on disk volume is a file and every file consists of a collection of attributes. Also note that the data contents of a file are treated as an attribute.** NTFS volume has the first few sectors as **boot–sector.** It contains information about the volume layout. Then there is a Master file table (MFT). MFT is a list of all contents on this NTFS volume and is or relational database structure. **MFT is the heart of WIN–2000 (2K) file system.** It is organized as a table of variable length rows known as **records. Please remember that each row describes a file or a folder on this volume,** including the MFT itself, which is treated as a file. **If the file size is small,** then the entire file is located in a row of the MFT. **Else if the file size is large,** then the row for that file contains partial information and the rest of the file spills over other available clusters on the volume. There are pointers to those clusters in the MFT row of that file.

The key elements of NTFS that support recoverability are–

(*a*) I/O Manager.

(*b*) Log File Service.

(*c*) Cache Manager.

(*d*) Virtual memory manager.

Please note here that the recovery procedures used by NTFS are designed to recover file system data and not the file contents. NTFS uses **logging** for recovery. Each operation is called as a **transaction.** Each suboperation of a transaction that alters a file system is recorded in a **log file** before being recorded on the disk.

Using this log file, a partially completed transaction at the time of a crash can later be redone or undone when the system recovers.

SUMMARY

In this chapter, we have learned that the file system is the most visible part of any OS. For many users, the convenience and usability of the OS. is determined by the interface, structure and the reliability of the file system. We have also studied the various ways to organise files and the ways to map files onto devices.

MULTIPLE-CHOICE QUESTIONS [MCQs]

1. A collection of related information defined by its user is known as–
   (*a*) File (*b*) Directory
   (*c*) Disk (*d*) None of the above
2. The secondary media is–
   (*a*) Volatile (*b*) Non-Volatile
   (*c*) Large (*d*) None of the above
3. Larger is the block size, larger will be the–
   (*a*) Directory size (*b*) Disk space lost
   (*c*) Disk space gained (*d*) None of the above
4. An arrangement of record in a sequence in which they arrive is known as a–
   (*a*) Pile (*b*) File
   (*c*) Disk (*d*) None of the above
5. For batch and payroll applications, which file is better–
   (*a*) Random file (*b*) Sequential File
   (*c*) Indexed file (*d*) None of the above
6. The process of direct mapping by using some faster algorithms is called as–
   (*a*) Hashing (*b*) Searching
   (*c*) Sorting (*d*) None of the above
7. ISAM stands for–
   (*a*) Indian Standard Access Method (*b*) Indexed Simple Access Method
   (*c*) Indexed Sequential Access Method (*d*) None of the above
8. ISAM was developed by–
   (*a*) HCL (*b*) TCS
   (*c*) IBM (*d*) None of the above
9. Those directories in which the root directory has all system files and no other subdirectory is known as–
   (*a*) Flat directory (*b*) Single directory
   (*c*) Hierarchical directory (*d*) None of the above
10. Searching on a single flat directory requires–
    (*a*) $O(n^2)$ comparisons (*b*) $O(n \log n)$ comparisons
    (*c*) $O(n)$ comparisons (*d*) $O(n^3)$ comparisons
11. A pathname that starts at root directory is–
    (*a*) Absolute (*b*) Relative
    (*c*) Hybrid (*d*) None of the above
12. All pathnames are specified relative to the working directory–
    (*a*) Absolute pathname (*b*) Relative pathname
    (*c*) Hybrid pathname (*d*) None of the above
13. ACL stands for–
    (*a*) Absolute Control List (*b*) Access Control List
    (*c*) Abrupt Control List (*d*) None of the above

14. i–node stands for–

(*a*) Indian–node
(*b*) Index–node
(*c*) Internal–node
(*d*) Internet–node

15. The heart of NTFS is–

(*a*) MVT
(*b*) MFT
(*c*) MMS
(*d*) None of the above

ANSWERS

1. *a*	**2.** *b*	**3.** *b*	**4.** *a*	**5.** *b*	**6.** *a*
7. *c*	**8.** *c*	**9.** *a*	**10.** *c*	**11.** *a*	**12.** *b*
13. *b*	**14.** *b*	**15.** *b*			

CONCEPTUAL SHORT QUESTIONS (WITH ANSWERS)

Q.1. How can you make authentication very effective?

Ans. There are two primary measures to make authentication very effective–

(1) **False Acceptance Ratio**

It is the percentage of illegitimate user enormously admitted

(2) **False Rejection Ratio**

It is the percentage of legitimate users who are denied access due to failure of authentication.

Please note that our objective is to minimize both false acceptance and false rejection ratios.

Q.2. Consider a system that supports 5000 users. Suppose that you want to allow 4990 of these users to be able to access one file.

(*a*) How would you specify this protection scheme in UNIX?

(*b*) Could you suggest another protection scheme that can be used more effectively for this purpose than the scheme provided by UNIX?

Ans. (*a*) There are two methods of achieving this—

(1) Create an access control list (ACL) with the names of all 4990 users.

(2) Put these 4990 users in one group and set the group access accordingly. This scheme cannot always be implemented since user groups are restricted by the system.

(*b*) The universe access information applies to all users unless their name appears in the access control list (ACL) with different access permission. With this scheme, you simply put the names of the remaining ten users in ACL but with no access privileges allowed.

Q.3. Can a direct access file be read sequentially? Explain

Ans. Yes, keep a counter, c. Set it initially to 0. After reading record c, increment c.

Q.4. Consider a file currently consisting of 100 blocks. Assume that the file control block (and the index block, in case of indexed allocation) is already in memory. Calculate how many disk I/O operationsare required for contiguous, linked and indexed (single-level) allocation strategies, if, for one block, the following conditions hold. In the contiguous allocation case, assume that there is no room to grow in the beginning but there is a room to grow in the end. Assume that the block information to be added is stored in memory.

(*a*) **The block is added at the beginning**
(*b*) **The block is added in the middle**
(*c*) **The block is added at the end**
(*d*) **The block is removed from the beginning**
(*e*) **The block is removed from the middle**
(*f*) **The block is removed from the end**

Ans. The disk I/O operations required for Contiguous, Linked and Indexed allocations are as follows–

	Contiguous	Linked	Indexed
(*a*)	201	1	1
(*b*)	101	52	1
(*c*)	1	3	1
(*d*)	198	1	0
(*e*)	98	52	0
(*f*)	0	100	0

Q.5. Consider a file system on a disk that has both logical and physical block sizes of 512 bytes. Assume that the information about each file is already in memory. For each of the three allocation strategies (contiguous, linked and indexed), answer these questions:–

(*a*) **How is the logical-to-physical address mapping accomplished in this system? (For the indexed allocation; assume that a file is always less than 512 blocks long).**

(*b*) **If we are currently at logical block 10 and want to access logical block 4, how many physical blocks must be read from the disk?**

Ans. Let *Z* be the starting file address (block number).

(*a*) **Contiguous:** Divide the logical address by 512 with *X* and *Y* as the resulting quotient and remainder respectively.

(1) Add *X* to *Z* to obtain the physical block number. *Y* is the displacement into that block

(2) 1

(*b*) **Linked:** Divide the logical physical address by 511 with *X* and *Y* as the resulting quotient and remainder respectively.

(1) Chase down the linked list getting $(X + 1)$ blocks. $(Y + 1)$ is the displacement into the last physical block.

(2) 4.

(*c*) **Indexed:** Divide the logical address by 512 with *X* and *Y* as the resulting quotient and remainder respectively.

(1) Get the index block into memory. The physical block address is contained in the index book at location *X*. *Y* is the displacement into the desired physical block.

(2) 2.

Q.6. What is an access control matrix?

Ans. Suppose that we have '*n*' users and '*m*' files. Then certain users use a user matrix of order name to implement control over access of certain files. If the entry $a\ (i, j) = 1$ then the user U_i can access file F_j.

Q.7. Fragmentation on a disk could be eliminated by compaction. But disks do not have relocation or base registers, so how can files be relocated?

Ans. Relocation of files on secondary storage involves considerable overhead as data blocks would have to be read into main memory and written back out to their new locations. That is, relocation can be done by bringing different data blocks into memory, relocate them and store them on the disk again. Also, relocation registers apply only to sequential files and many disk files are not sequential. Even sequential files can be allocated non-contiguous blocks if links between logically sequential blocks are maintained by the disk system. So, there may not be any need for relocation at all.

Q.8. Can there be inconsistency between the bit map loaded into the main memory and that on the disk?

Ans. Yes, there is a possibility of inconsistency between the bit map loaded into the main memory and that on the disk. To avoid such a situation, set bit for block *i* to 1 on the disk, allocate this block *i* and set bit for block-*i* to 1 in memory.

Q.9. What criteria should be used to decide which strategy contiguous, linked, indexed allocation) is best utilized for a particular file?

Ans. The criteria is as follows–

(1) **Contiguous allocation strategy** should be used if file is usually accessed sequentially and is relatively small.

(2) **Linked allocation strategy** should be used if file is large and usually accessed sequentially.

(3) **Indexed allocation strategy** should be used if file is large and usually accessed randomly.

Q.10 Consider a file system where a file can be deleted and its disk space reclaimed while links to that file still exist. What problems may occur if a new file is created in the same storage area or with the same absolute path name? How can these problems be avoided?

Ans. Let F1 be the old file and F2 be the new file. A user wishing to access F1 through an existing link will actually access F2. **Note that the access protection for file F1 is used rather than the one associated with F2.** This problem can be avoided by insuring that all links to a deleted file are also deleted. This can be done in many ways–

(*a*) Maintain a list of all links to a file, removing each of them when the file is deleted.

(*b*) Retain the links.

(*c*) Maintain a file reference list or counter, deleting the file only after all links or references to that file have been deleted.

EXERCISE QUESTIONS

Q.1. Discuss the linked allocation and index allocation schemes for a file allocation. Compare the index allocation scheme with the contiguous allocation scheme.

Q.2. Describe various file allocation strategies. Also discuss the criteria that have to decide which strategy is to be adopted for a particular file.

Q.3. Describe the layout of the UNIX file system. What is the structure of *i*–node? How does the pathname get translated to *i*–node number?

Q.4. What is FAT?

Q.5. (*a*) Explain the six basic file operations
(*b*) What are the different ways of implementing a free space list? Explain them.

Q.6. Consider a system where free–space is kept in a free–space list.
(1) Suppose that the pointer to the free space list is lost. Can the system reconstruct the free-space list? Explain.
(2) Suggest a scheme to ensure that the pointer is never lost as a result of memory failure.
(3) Describe the indexed allocation method of file on disk in detail. Give its merits and demerits over other methods.

Q.7. What are the basic functions of a file system? Briefly explain the three levels of device abstraction and disk storage addressing in implementation of a file management system.

Q.8. (*a*) Explain the purpose of the open and close operation.
(*b*) What problem could occur if a system allowed a file system to be mounted simultaneously at more than one location.

Q.9. Explain different methods for allocating disk spaces to files.

Q.10. Write short notes on—
(*a*) I–nodes
(*b*) I/O system of UNIX

Q.11. Discuss contiguous Linked, Index and multilevel indexing file allocation schemes. Which allocation scheme will minimize the amount of space required in directory structure and why?

Q.12. (*a*) What are the functions of a file system.
(*b*) Draw the file structure of UNIX OS or DOS OS.
(*c*) List five system calls related to file system.

Q.13. Discuss various file allocation and access methods. Compare their advantages and disadvantages.

Q.14. (*a*) Explain File Concept, access method and directory implementation.
(*b*) Explain file types and file access (sequential and random access)

CHAPTER 11

Assembly Language Programming Overview

11.0 INTERNAL ARCHITECTURE OF 8086

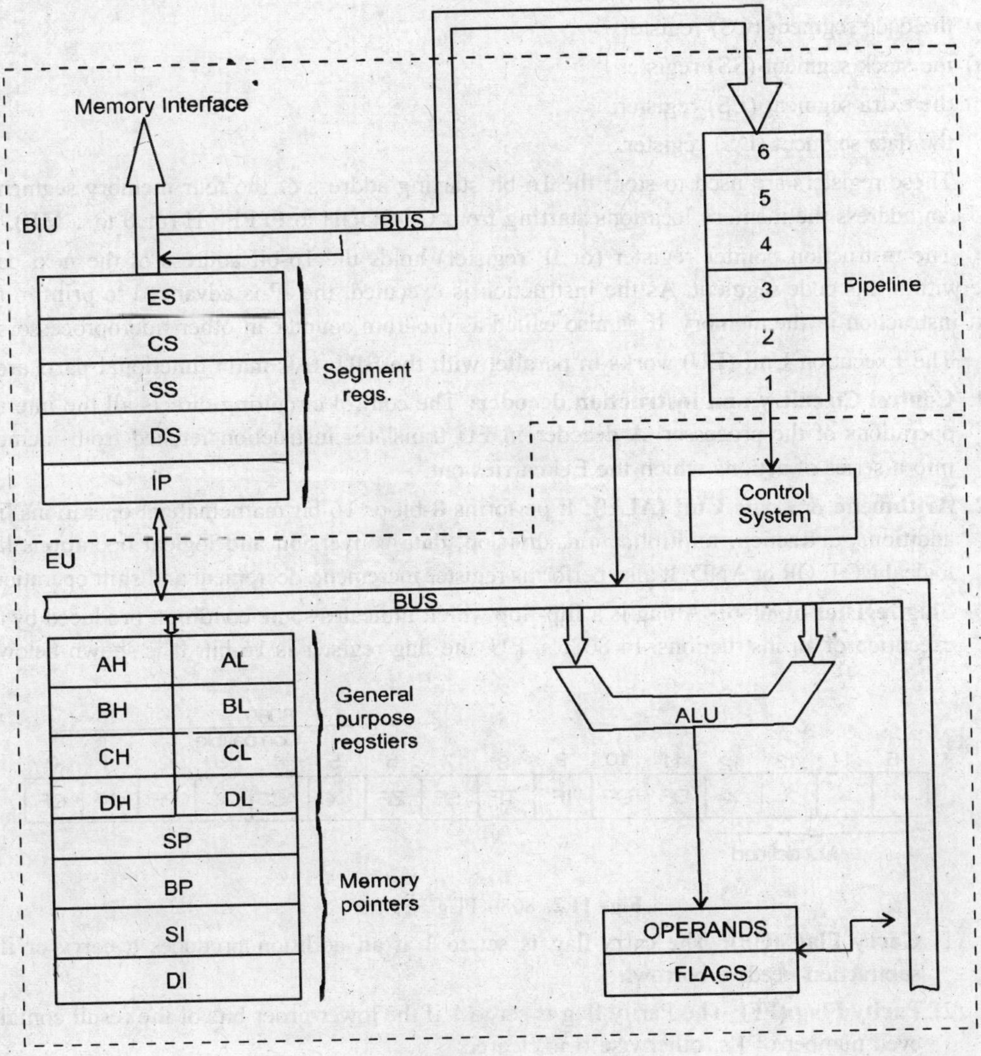

Fig. 11.1 8086 Internal Schema (architecture)

The 8086 CPU is divided into two independent functional parts:

(*a*) Bus Interface Unit (BIU)

(*b*) Execution Unit (EU)

This is done to divide the work between these two units and hence increase the processing speed.

The Bus Interface Unit (BIU) sends out addresses, fetches instructions from memory, reads data from ports and memory and writes data to ports and memory. To speed up the program execution, BIU fetches as many as six instruction bytes ahead of time from memory. The prefetched instruction bytes are held for the EU in a FIFO group of registered called a **queue.** This is done to increase processing speeds. This is also known as **pipelining.**

The BIU contains four segment registers, that is,

(*a*) the code segment (CS) register.

(*b*) the stack segment (SS) register.

(*c*) the extra segment (ES) register.

(*d*) the data segment (DS) register.

These registers are used to store the 16-bit starting address of the four memory segments. BIU can address the memory locations starting from OOOOOH to FFFFF H (or 0 to 1 MB).

The instruction pointer register (or IP register) holds the 16-bit address of the next code byte within this code segment. As the instruction is executed, the IP is advanced to print to the next instruction in the memory. IP is also called as program counter in other microprocessors.

The Execution Unit (EU) works in parallel with the BIU. IA's main functional parts are :

1. **Control Circuitry and instruction decoder:** The control circuiting directs all the internal operations of the processor. A decoder in EU translates instruction fetched from memory into a series of actions which the EU carries out.
2. **Arithmetic & Logic Unit (ALU):** It performs 8-bit or 16-bit mathematical operations like addition, subtraction, multiplication, division, data conversion and logical operations like logical NOT, OR or AND. It also performs register increment, decrement and shift operations.
3. **Flag register of 8086:-** A flag is a flip-flop which indicates some condition produced by the execution of an instructions. In 8086's, EU, the flag-register is 16-bit. It is shown below:-

Bit	15	14	13	12	11	10	9	8	7	6	5	4	3	2	1	0
	X	X	X	X	DF	DF	IF	TF	SF	ZF	X	ACF	X	PF	X	CF

(Bits 15–12: Not defined; Bits 7–0: 8085 Compatible)

Fig. 11.2. 8086 Flag Register

(1) **Carry Flag (CF):** The carry-flag is set to 1 if an addition produces a carry or if a subtraction needs a borrow.

(2) **Parity Flag (PF):** The Parity flag is set to 1 if the lower-order bits of the result contains even number of 1's; otherwise if is cleared.

(3) **Auxilliary Carry Flag (ACF):** The Auxilliary Flag is set to 1 if there is a carry out of 3rd bit during an addition process or a borrow by the third bit during subtraction.

(4) **Zero Flag (ZF):** The zero flag is set to 1, if an addition or a subtraction produces a zero result.

(5) **Sign Flag (SF):** The Sign Flag is set to 1 , if the MSB is one; else sign flag is reset.

(6) **Trap Flag (TF):** If the Trap Flag is set to 1, a trap interrupt type is executed after instruction. The CPU resets this Flag while transferring control to the interrupts handler.

(7) **Interrupt Flag (IF):** If the interrupt enable flag is set, a markable interrupt type can be recognized by the CPU else those interrupts are ignored.

(8) **Direction Flag (DF):** Certain instructions such as STD, CLD etc. can modify this flag. If DF = 0, then the string is processed from the beginning with lowest address and moving towards highest address. If DF = 1, the string is processed from higher address towards the lower address. It increments/decrements the index pointers based on the status of the DF.

(9) **Overflow Flag (OF):** This flag is set to 1, if an addition produces a carry out of the MSB or when MSB needs a borrow during subtraction.

4. **General Purpose Registers (GPRs):** These registers are of 16-bit size. They are used as a source or destination register during data transfer, as pointers to memory and as counters. Like, AX-register (16-bit) is composed of two 8-bit registes, namely, AH and AL *i.e.*, A-higher and A-lower registers. This AX-registers is also known as **Accumulator.**

5. **Pointer and Index Registers:** The 8086 processor has two pointer registers - SP and BP and two index registers - SI and DI. The pointer registers are used for storing the offset address of data elements stored in the stack. The index registers are used for storing offset of array elements.

11.1 ADDRESSING MODES IN 8086

It is a method of specifying the effective address of the operends in the memory. These are of various kinds:

1. **Immediate Addressing Mode:-** In this mode, data is the part of the instruction.

   For example: MOV AX, 100; AX ← 100

   It will move the value 100 into register, AX.

2. **Implicit Addressing Mode — In this mode,** the instruction assumes that data is in a predefined register.

   For example: CMC; complement carry-flag: Here, the data is in the flag-register and is thus complemented. These instructions are also called as **zero address instructions.**

3. **Direct Addressing Mode:-** In this mode, the address of the data is a part of the instruction.

   For example: MOV AX, (1050H)

   It means that the data is in the memory location pointed to by the address 1050H.

4. **Indirect Adressing Mode:-** In this mode, the address of the operand is in the register.

   For example: MOV AX, (BX)

   Here, the data in the memory pointed to by the register BX is copied to the register AX.

5. **Register Addressing Mode:-** In this mode, the operands on which instruction operate are stored in the specified registers.

   For e.g.,
   ```
   MOV AX, DX ; AX ← DX
   ADD BX, AX  ; BX ← BX + AX
   ```

   These instructions use only registers and hence it is known as the **register addressing mode.**

11.2 INSTRUCTION-SET OF 8086:

LOOP INSTRUCTION: This instruction is used to repeat a series of instructions some number of times.

Example:
```
       mov ch, 00L
       mov cl, 08L
       mov al, 10 L
next:  add al, 07L
       inc al
       loop next     ; if CX ≠ 0 then go to
       sub al, 07L   ; label next and decrement
       sub al, 07L   ; CX reg. by 1. else go to
       sub al, 07L   ; next statement (s).
```

MOV Instruction:

Syntax: MOV destination, source

Example: MOV CX, 037AH; Put immediate no. 037AH in CX-reg.

Example 2: MOV AX, BX

Example 3: MOV BL, [4000 H] ; copy byte from 4000H to BL reg.

MOVS/MOVSB/MOVSW:

Syntax: MOVS destination, source

Example:
```
mov si, 2000L    ; SI points to start of source string
mov di, 2400 L   ; DI points to desti. string
mov cx, 04h      ; Length of string in CX-reg
cld              ; autoincrement SI & DI
Rep MOVSB        ; Decre-CX & move bytes till CX = 0
```

MUL Instruction: Multiplies 2 bytes or words.

Syntax: MUL Source

Example: MUL BH; AL times BH, result in AX

Example 2:
```
MOV AX, MULTIPLICAND-16; 16-bit multiplicand
MOV CL, MULTIPLIER-8; 8 bit multiplier incl
MOV CH, 00H ; set upper-byte of CX to O's.
MUL CX ; AX times CX, 32-bit result ; in DX and AX.
```

NEG Instruction: Form 2's complement

Syntax: NEG destination

Example:
```
NEG AL ; Replace number in AL with
       ; its 2s-complement.
```

Example 2:
```
NEG BX ; Replace word in BX with
       ; its 2s-complement.
```

NOP instruction: Can be used to increase the delay of a delay loop.

Example:
```
MOV CX, N
KILL_TIME : NOP; Perform no operation
    NOP
    LOOP KILL-TIME
```

NOT instruction: Invert each bit of operand.

Syntax: NOT destination

Example: NOT BX ; complement contents of BX-
; register

OR Instruction: It ORs (+) each bit source byte or word with corresponding bit in destination byte or word.

Syntax: OR destination, Source

Example: OR AH, CL ; CL ORed with AH
; result in AH. CL
; not changed

Example 2: OR BL, 80H ; BL ORed with immediate
; data 80 H

OUT Instruction: Output a byte or word to a port

Syntax: OUT port, accumulator

Example: OUT 3BH, AL
; copy contents of AL to
; port 3BH

RCL instruction: Rotate operand to left through CF

Syntax: RCL destination, count

Example: RCL DX ; Word in DX, 1 bit left
; MSB to CF
; CF to LSB

Example 2: MOV CL, 2
RCL AX, CL ; Rotate AX two bit positions

RCR instruction: Rotate operand to right through CF

Syntax: RCR destination, count

Example: RCR BX, 1 ; Word in BX, right 1-bit
; CF to MSB, LSB to CF

ROL Instruction: Rotate all bits of operand Left, MSB to LSB.

Syntax: ROL destination, count

Example: ROL AX, 1 ; word in AX one bit position
; Left, MSB to LSB.

Example 2: MOVCL, OHL
ROL BL, CL ; rotate bl, 4-times, to left

ROR Instruction: Rotate all bits of operand Right, LSB to MSB.

Syntax: ROR destination, count

Example: ROR BL, 1 ; Rotate all bits in BL,
; right one bit, LSB to MSB

SAL/SHL Instruction: Shift operand bits left, put zero in LSB (s).

Syntax: SAL/SHL destination, count

Example: SAL BX, 1; shift word in BX, 1 bit position left, 0 in LSB
CF ← MSB ← LSB ← O

Example 2: MOV CL, 02H

SAL BP, CL ; Shift byte in BP, 2 bit.

; positions Left, 0 in LSB

SHR Instruction: Shift operand bits right, put zero in MSB (s). i.e.,

O → MSB → LSB → CF

Syntax: SHR destination, count

Example: SHR BP, 1 ; shift word in BP, one

; bit position right, 0 in ; MSB

STC Instruction: Set carry flag to one.

TEST Instruction: It ANDs the contents of a source byte or word with destination byte or word.

Syntax: TEST destination, source

Example: TEST AL, BH; AND BH with AL but no result is stored. It updates flags.

XCHG Instruction: It exchanges contents of a register with contents of another register.

Syntax: XCHG destination, Source

Example: XCHG AX, BX; exchange word in BX with word in AX.

XOR Instruction: Exclusive OR corresponding bits of two operands.

Syntax: XOR desination, source

Example: XOR CL, BH ; Byte in BH, exclusive-ORed with byte in CL. Result in CL, BH not changed.

11.3 SOLVED PROGRAMMING EXAMPLES

Example 11.1 Write an assembly language program (8086 based) to find the factorial of a number?

Solution:

```
data-here segment
    m1 db "Enter your number : "," "$"
    m2 db "Its factorial is: ","$"
    m3 db "Its factorial is 1 ","$"
    m4 db "Its factorial is 0 ","$"
data-here ends
code-here segment
    assume CS : code_here,
            ds : data_here
start:      mov ax, data_here       ; Initialize ds,
            mov ds, ax              ; since you are
                                    ; using memory
            mov dx, offset m1       ; display m1
            mov ah, 09L
            nif 21L
            mov  ah, 01L            ; read n
            int 21h
            mov al, dl
            mov bl, al
```

```
          cmp al, OAh
          ja table
          sub al, 30h
          jmp chair
table:    sub al, 07h
          mov bl, al
          sub bl, 30h
          mov al, bl
chair:    cmp al, OOh
          je l1
          cmp al, 01h
          je l2
          call facto
          jnp l3
l1:       call cr-lf
          mov dx, offset m3
          move ah, 09h
          int 21h
          mov ah, 4ch; exit to DOS
          int 21h
l2:       call cr-lf
          mov dx, offset m4
          mov ah, 09h
          int 21h
          mov ah, 4ch
          int 21h
l3:       call cr-lf
          mov dx, offset m2
          mov ah, 09h
          int 21h
          call display
          mov ah, 4ch
          int 21h
facto proc near
          mov bl, al
l1A:      dec bl
          mul bl              ; (al) ← (al) * (bl)
          cmp bl, 01h
          ja l1A
          mov dl, al
          ret
```

```
facto endp
cr-lf      proc near           ; This procedure introduces
           mov ah, 02h         ; newlines
           mov dl, 0d h        ; 0dh and OAL are newline
           int 21h             ; characters
           mov ah, 02h
           mov dl, OAh
           int 21h
           ret
cr-lf endp
display proc near              ; HEX to decimal conversion
           mov bh, 00
           sub ah, ah          ; ah ← 00
again_1:   cmp ax, 03E8h
           jl sub_hund
           inc bh
           jmp again_1
sub-hund:  mov cx, ax
           add bh, 30h
           mov dl, bh
           mov ah, 02h         ; display it
           int 21h
           mov bh, 00
           mov ax, cx
again_2:   cmp ax, 0064 h
           jl sub-ten
           sub ax, 0064h
           inc bh
           jmp again_2
sub-ten:   mov cx, ax
           add bh, 30h
           mov dl, bh
           mov ah, 02h
           int 21h
           mov bh, 00
           mov ax, cx
again_3:   cmp ax, 10h
           jl print
           sub ax, 10h
           inc bh
           jmp again_3
```

```
print:    mov cx, ax
          add bh, 30h
          mov dl, bh
          mov ah, 02
          int 21h
          add cx, 30h
          mov dh, 00
          mov dx, cx
          mov ah, 02h
          int 21h
          ret
display end p
```

Example 11.2 Write an assembly language program (8086 based) to multiply two matrices. Try to give keboard entry?

Solution:

```
data-here segment
          m1 db "Enter matrix - 1 : "," $"
          m2 db "Enter matrix-2 : ","$"
          m3 db "Resultant matrix is : ","$"
data-here ends
code-here segment
          assume cs: code-here, ds: data-here
start:    mov ax, data-here
          mov ds, ax
          mov si, 0000h
          mov dx, offset ml
          mov ah, 09h
          int 21h
l1:       mov ah, 01h           ; accept elements
          dec cl                ; Read 10-elements
          jnz l1
          mov dx, offset m2
          mov ah, 09h
          int 21h
          mov bl, 09h
l2:       mov ah, 01h
          dec bl
          jnz l2
          jmp l3
l3:       mov dx, offset m3
          mov ah, 09h
          int 21h
          mov al, 00h
```

```
            mov al, A [si]
            add al, B [si]
            mov c[si], al
l4:         mov dl, c [si]
            mov ah, 02h
            dec cx
            jnz l1
            int 21h
            mov ah, 4ch
            int 21h
code-here ends
            end start
```

Example 11.3 Write an Assembly language program (8086 base(d) to multiply two 16 bit binary numbers. Assume that your result can be as high as 32-bits?

Solution:

```
data_here segment
        Muliplicand dw 2000H; first word
        Multiplier dw 20AOH; second word
        product dw 2 Dup(0); result here
data_here ends
code-here segment
        assume cs:code_here, ds:data_here
main: mov ax, data_here
        mov ds, ax
        mov ax, multiplicand; get one word in Accumulator
        mul multiplier; multiply
        mov product, ax
        mov product +2, dx
        mov ah, 4ch
        int 2lh
code-here ends
end main
```

Example 11.4 Write an assembly language program (8086 based) to find average of two numbers?

Solution:

```
data-here segment
        high db 92 H ; high & low
        low db 55H   ; are 2 nos.
        avg db ? ; store result
date_here ends
code_here segment
        assume cs; code-here, ds:data_here.
main: mov ax, data_here; Initialize ds reg.
```

```
        mov ds, ax
        mov al, high ; get first no.
        add al, low; add the two nos.
        mov ah, ooh; clear ah-reg.
        adc ah, 00h ; [ah] ← [ah] +1
        mov al, 02h; bl gets divisor
        div bl
        mov avg, al; store result
        code-here ends
end main
```

PROGRAMS FOR PRACTICE

Q.1. Write an assembly language program to sum the following series:-

(*a*) 1+ 2+ 3+ ..... 100 (*b*) 2 + 4 + 6 + ...100

(*c*) 1 + 2 + 3 + ...N (*d*) 2 + 4 + 6 + ...2 N

(*e*) $1^2 + 2^2 + 3^2 + 4^2 + \ldots\ldots N^2$?

Q.2. Write a complete ALP to read the temperature in Fahrenheit & to print it's centigrade equivalent. Use the formula given below:

$$C = \frac{5}{9}\,(F-32)?$$

Q.3. Write an 8086 based assembly language program to compute the following:-

$$V = (a * b) + c\ ?$$

Q.4. Write an assembly language program to find the square root of a number. Read your number from the keyboard?

Q.5. Write an ALP to generate Fibonacci Series till n?

Q.6. Write an ALP to check whether

(*a*) a given string is a palindrome or not.

(*b*) given integer is a palindrome or not?

[**Hint:** TOOT, ROOR etc are palindromes; 121, 111, etc are also palindromes]?

Q.7. WAP to sort an array using bubble-sort. Read the array & its's size from the keyboard?

Q.8. Write an 8086-based ALP to reverse a string?

Q.9. Write an ALP to check whether the given number is even or not?

Q.10. Write an ALP to check whether the given number is positive or negative?

Q.11. Write an ALP to search for an element in an array?

Q.12. Write an ALP find the GCD of 2 numbers, U & V?

Q.13. Write an ALP to calculate the roots of a given quadratic equation:

$ax^2 + bx + c = 0$, where $D = b^2 - 4ac$

if $D > 0$ the root 1 $= \dfrac{-b + \sqrt{D}}{2a}$

& root 2 $= \dfrac{-b - \sqrt{D}}{2a}$

If $D = 0$ then,

$$\text{root 1} = \text{root 2} = \frac{-b}{2a}$$

else if $D < 0$ then print the message and roots are complex & imaginary?

Q.14. Define the following terms with examples:

(*a*) Assemblers (*b*) Compilers
(*c*) Interpreters (*d*) Loaders
(*e*) Open Subroutine (or Macros) (*f*) Closed Subroutine
(*g*) a Formal system (*h*) MFT
(*i*) MVT (*j*) Fragmentation
(*k*) Traffic controller (l) Scheduler
(*m*) I/O processor (n) I/O programming
(*o*) Segment (p) Operating Systems
(*q*) Batch System.

Q.15. How does the CPU know whether a given location represents an instruction or data in memory?

Q.16. Write a short note on "Evolution of O.S."?

Q.17. Discuss in detail the brief architecture of 8086 CPU?

Q.18. Explain the Flag-register of 8086 machine?

Q.19. What are the different types of addressing modes in 8086?

Q.20. Write a short note on segmentation in 8086?

Q.21. Explain what is instruction pipeling in 8086?

Q.22. When will queue store wrong opcodes?

Q.23. How are registers more useful than memories?

Q.24. Define:

(*a*) Nibble (*b*) Byte
(*c*) Word (*d*) Masking
(*e*) Unmasking (*f*) Re-entrant procedures
(*g*) Recursive procedures

Q.25. Explain the following instructions in 8086:

(*a*) RCL (*b*) RCR
(*c*) ROL (*d*) ROR

Q.26. Explain in detail the pin configuration of 8086 CPU?

Q.27. What is the difference between 8086 operating in Minimum mode & 8086 in maximum mode?

Q.28. Why is 8086 memory set up as two byte wide bank?

11.4 ASSEMBLERS

RISC versus CISC processors:

RISC is an acronym for Reduced Instruction Set Computer. The main features of RISC processors are:

- Few Powerful Instructions.
- Single clock cycle Execution for most instruction

- Register-based execution .
- Highly Pipelines Architecture
- Highly Integrated Architecture
- Carefully designed memory hierarchy including processor register and caches.
- Can be made to work upto 70% faster than CISC processors.

Examples of RISC processor: i860, SPARC, POWER PCs, RISC processors are used to build.

Supercomputers for high performance computing. For e.g., i860 family of processors are used to build PARAM (Parallel Machine) Supercomputer at C-DAC, India.

"CISC is an acronym for Complex Instruction Set Computer. The main features of CISC processors are:

- Rich and Wide variety of powerful Instructions.
- Design of CISC processors is complex.

Examples of CISC processors: Intel x86 family processors and Motorola MC 68000.

11.5 ASSEMBLER—AN INTRODUCTION

An assembler is a program that accepts as input an assembly language program and produces its machine language equivalent along with the information for the loader.

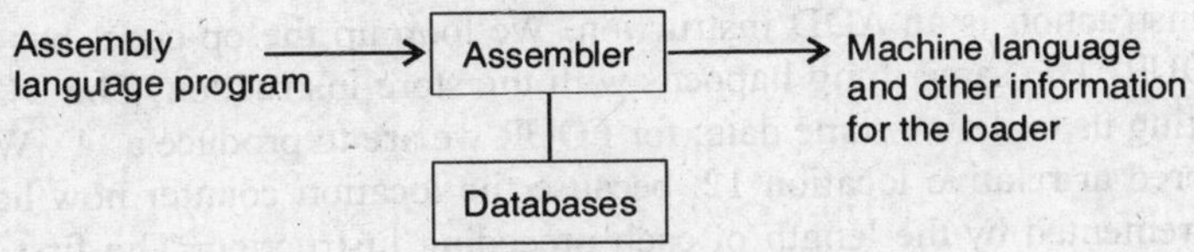

Fig. 11.3. An Assembler

What this other information is? The externally defined symbols are passed on the loader. The assembler does not know the address (value) of these symbols and it is up to the loader to find the programs containing them, load then into core and place the values of these symbols in the calling program.

11.6 GENERAL DESIGN PROCEDURE

There are six (6) steps to be followed for designing an assembler by the software designer:

1. Specify the problem.
2. Specify data structure.
3. Define format of data structures
4. Specify algorithm
5. Look for modularity
6. Repeat 1 through 5 on modules.

Now we shall apply these steps one by one.

11.7 DESIGN OF ASSEMBLER – A CASE STUDY

Step 1 :- Problem: Let us pretend that we are the assembler varying to translate the program, given below:

Source Program

```
RAJ     START   0
        USING   *, 15
        L       1, FIVE
```

	A	1, FOUR
	ST	1, TEMP
FOUR	DC	F'4'
FIVE	DC	F'5'
TEMP	DS	1F
END		

We read the start-instruction end note that is a pseudo-op instruction (to the assembler) giving RAJ as the name of this program; the assembler must pass the name on to the loader. The next instruction is the USING pseudo-op. This tells the assembler (us) that reg-15 is the base register and at execution time will contain the address of the first instruction of the program. Next comes a Load instruction: L 1, FIVE. We put the corresponding bit-configuration for L (mnemonic) in appropriate place in the machine language instruction. Now we need the address of FIVE. At this point, however, we do not know, where FIVE is, so we cannot supply its address. Because no index register is being used, we put in 0 for the index register. We know that reg-15 is being used as the base register, but we cannot calculate the offset. The base reg-15 is pointing to the beginning of this program and the offset is going to be the difference between the location FIVE and the location of the beginning of the program, which is not known at this time. We maintain a location counter indicating the relative address of the instruction being processed; this counter is incremented by 4 (length of load instruction).

The next instruction is an ADD instruction. We loop up the op-code, but we do not know the offset for FOUR. The same thing happens with the store instruction. The DC instruction is a pseudo-op directing us to define some data; for FOUR we are to produce a '4'. We know that this word will be stored at relative location 12, because the location counter now has the value, 12, having been incremented by the length of each preceding instruction. The first instruction, four bytes long, is at relative address 0. The next two instructions are also four bytes long.

We say that the symbol 'FOUR' has the value 12 (*i.e.*, value of LC). The next instruction has a label FIVE and an associated LC value of 16. the label, TEMP, has an associated value of 20. We, thus, have produced the code in the center column below:

First Pass

Relative address	**Mnemonic instruction**
0	L 1, -(0, 15)
4	A 1, -(0,15)
8	ST 1, -(0,15)
12	4
16	5
20	-

As a assembler, we can now go back through the program and fill the offsets, as calculated above.

Second Pass

Relative address	**Mnemonic instruction**
0	L 1, 16 (0, 15)
4	A 1, 12 (0,15)
8	ST 1, 20 (0,15)
12	4
16	5
20	-

Because symbols can appear before they are defined, it is convenient to make two passes over the input. The first pass has only to define the symbols, the second pass can then generate the instructions and addresses.

We can group these tasks into two passes or sequential scans over the input.

Pass 1: Purpose – define symbols and literals

Pass 2: Purpose – generate object program

Step 2:- **Data Structure:** The 2nd step in our design procedure is to establish the databases that we have to work with.

Pass 1 databases are:

1. Input Source Program.
2. A Location Counter (LC), used to keep track of each instruction's location.
3. A table, the Machine-operation Table (MOTT) that indicates the symbolic mnemonic for each instruction and its length (two, four, or six bytes).
4. A table, the Pseudo-Operation Table (POTT) that indicates the symbolic mnemonic and action to be taken for each pseudo-op in pass-1.
5. A table, the Symbol Table (ST) that is used to store each label and its corresponding value.
6. A table, the literal table (LT), that is used to store each literal encountered and its corresponding assigned location.
7. A copy of input to be used later by pass 2. This may be stored in a secondary storage device such as magnetic tape, disk or drum or the original source deck may be read by assembler a second time for pass 2.

The **overview of Pass 1** is given below:-

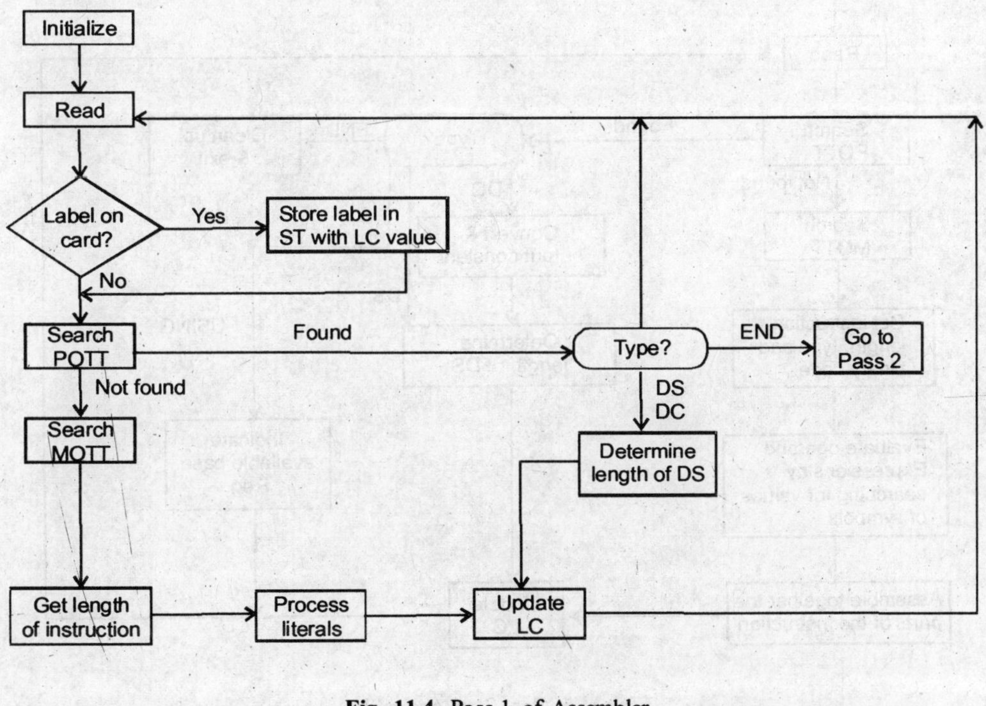

Fig. 11.4. Pass-1 of Assembler

Pass 2 databases:

1. Copy of source program input to pass 1.
2. Location Counter (LC).
3. A table, **the Machine Operation Table (MOTT)** that indicates for each instruction:
   (*a*) symbolic mnemonic
   (*b*) length
   (*c*) binary machine of code and
   (*d*) format
4. A table, the **Pseudo Operation Table (POTT)**, that indicates for each Pseudo-op the symbolic mnemonic and the action to be taken in pass 2.
5. The **symbol table** (ST), prepared in pass 1, containing each label and its corresponding value.
6. A table, the **Base Table (BT)**, that indicates which registers are currently specified as base registers by USING pseudo-ops and what are the specified contents of these registers.
7. **A work-space, INST,** that is used to hold each instruction as its various parts (e.g., binary op code, register fields, length fields) are being assembled together.
8. A workspace, PRINT LINE, used to produce a printed listing.

   A workspace, PUNCH CARD, used prior to actual outputting for converting the assembled instructions into the format needed by loader. An output deck of assembled instructions in the format needed by the loader.

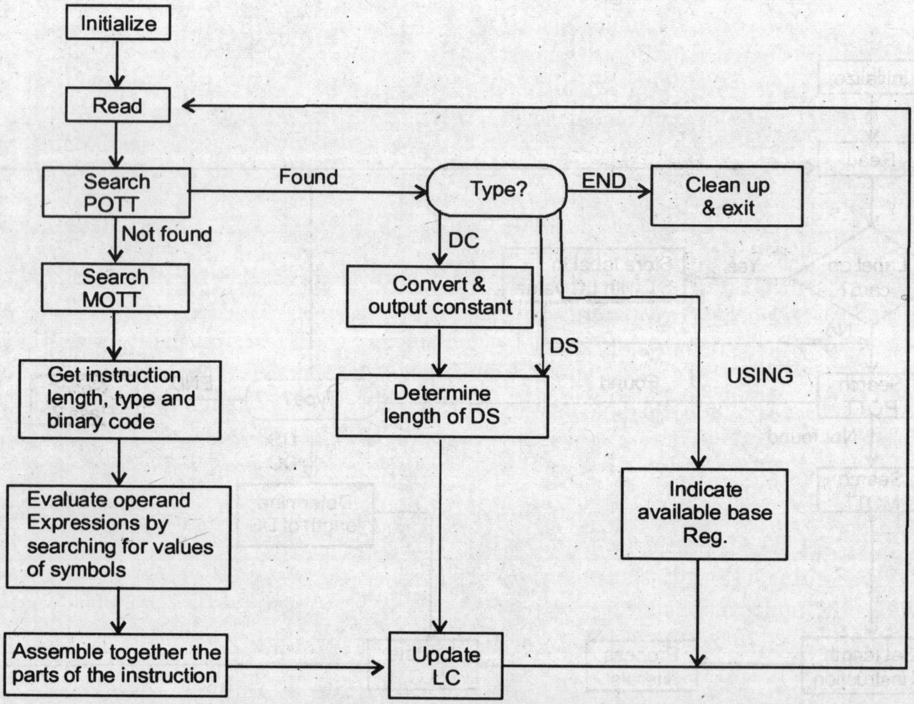

Fig. 11.5. Pass-2 of Assembler

Pseudo-ops and Machine-ops

A pseudo-op is an assembly language instruction that specifies an operation of the assembler. A machine-op represents to the assembler, a machine instruction. Consider the following IBM-360 based ALP:-

```
TEST     START                  ; Identifies name of program
         BALR 15,0              ; Set reg. -15 to the address of next instruction
         USING BEGIN +2, 15     ; Pseudo-op indicating to assembles register 15 is
                                  base register and its content is address of next
                                  instruction.
           :
           :
TEN      DC      F'10'          ; constant 10
FOUR     DC      F'4'           ; constant 4
FTY9     DC      F'49'
DATA     DC      F'1,3,3,4'     ; Words to be processed.
END
```

Explanation:- In this program,

1. **USING is a pseudo-op** that indicates to the assembler which general register to use as a base and what its contents will be. This is necessary because no special registers are set aside for addressing, thus the programmer must inform the assembler which register to use and how to use them.
2. **BALR** is an instruction to the computer to Load a register with the address of next instruction. When the second operand is register 0, as in program above, execution proceeds with the next instruction. It is important to see the distinction between BALR, which loads the base register and the USING, which informs the assembler what is in the base register.
3. **START is a pseudo-op** that tells the assembler where the beginning of program is and allows the user to give a name to the program. In this case the name is TEST.
4. **END is a pseudo-op** that tells the assembler that the last card of the program has been reached.
5. **The Define Constant (DC) and Define Storage (DS) instructions are pseudo-ops** that instructs the assembler to place a 10, a 4 and a 49 in 3 consecutive full words ("F") in memory and 4 move for data.

Micro flow chart showing execution of an instruction within CPU:

Consider the following instruction

ADD 2, 176

It would cause the data stored in memory location 176 to be added to the current contents of general register-2. The resulting sum would be left as new contents of register-2. It's micro flow chart is:

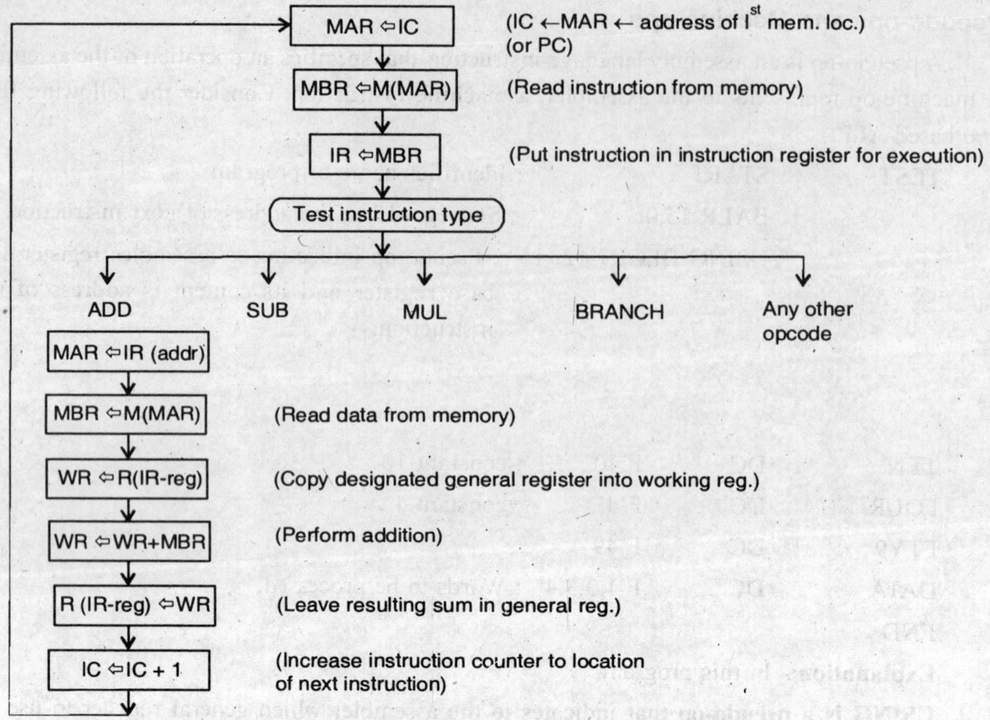

Fig. 11.6. A Micro flow chart

General machine Structure

Almost all conventional modern computer are based upon the **"stored program computer"** concept, generally credited to the mathematician **John Von Newmann (1903-1957)**

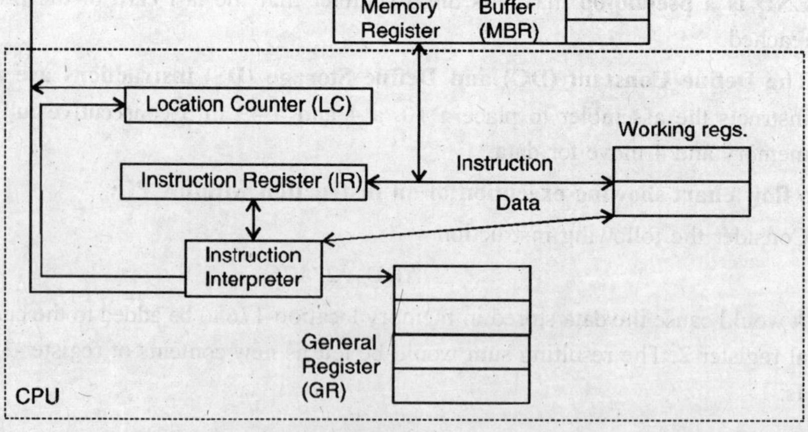

Fig. 11.7. Structure of the CPU for typical Newmann machine such as IBM-360.

Memory Buffer Register (MBR) contains a copy of the designated memory location specified by MAR, after a read or write.

Memory controller is a hardware that transfers data between MBR and the core memory location, the address of which is in the MAR.

General Approach to a **New machine.**

It consists of finding answers to a series of questions:-

1. **Memory:** What is the memory's basic unit, size and addressing scheme?
2. **Registers:** How many registers are there? What are their size, function & interrelationship?
3. **Data:** What types of data can be handled by the computer? Can it handle characters, numbers, logical data? How is this data stored?
4. **Instructions:** What are the classes of instructions on the machine? Are there arithmetic instructions, logical instructions, symbol manipulation instructions? What are their formats? How are they stored in memory?

   I/O channels may be thought of as separate computer which interpret special instructions for inputting and outputting information from the memory.

   The CPU consists of an instruction interpreter, a location counter, an instruction register and various working and general registers. The **instruction interpreter** is a group of electrical circuits (hardware), that performs the intent of instructions fetched from memory.

   The Location Counter (LC), also called Program Counter (PC) or Instruction Counter (IC), is a hardware memory device which denotes the location of the current instruction being executed.

   A copy of the current instruction is stored in the **Instruction Register (IR).**

   The working registers are memory devices that serve as **"scratch pads"** for the instruction interpreter while the general registers are used by the programmer as storage locations and for special functions.

   Memory Address Register (MAR) contains the address of the memory location that is to be read from or stored into.
5. **Special features:** What is the interrupt structure of the machine? What sort of protection mechanisms is available to the user?

All these questions have been answered in context of IBM-360 too.

1. **Memory: The basic unit of memory in IBM-360 is a byte – 8 bits of information. That is, each addressable position in memory can contain 8-bits of information.** There are facilities to operate on contiguous bytes. The basic units are as follows:

Unit of memory	Bytes	Length of Bits
Byte	1	8
Half word	2	16
Word	4	32
Double word	8	64

   A unit of memory consisting of four bits is sometimes referred to as a nibble. The size of the 360 memory is up to 2^{24} bytes.
2. **Registers: The 360 has 16 general-purpose registers consisting of 32 bits each.** There are 4 floating-point registers consisting of 64 bits each. It has 16 bit Program Status Word (PSW) that contains the value of the location counter, protection, information and interrupt status.

   The general purpose registers may be used for various arithmetic and logical operations and as base registers. When the programmer uses them in arithmetic or logical operations, he thinks of these registers as scratch pads to which numbers are added, subtracted, compared and so forth. Take for example the instruction

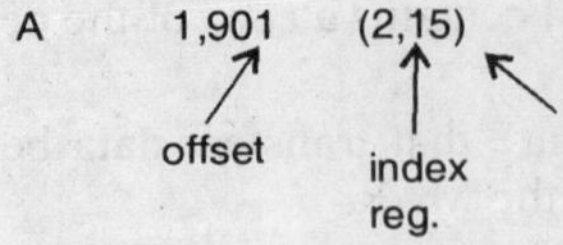

It is interpreted as an add instruction. A number is to be added to the contents of register 1. The location of the number is 901 (offset) plus the contents of register 2 (index) plus the contents of register-15 (base).

3. **DATA:**360 may store several different types of data. If 360 interprets the contents of 2-bytes as an integer i.e.,

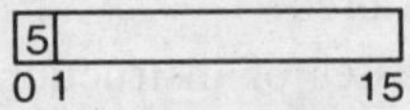

then it interprets the first bit as sign and the remaining 15 as a binary number.

All data and instructions are physically stored as sequences of binary ones and zeros. For convenience, binary numbers are usually written in HEX-form.

Note: Our computers, basically, works on hexadecimal (HEX) numbers. When binary numbers become too big then they are compressed to HEX form.

The 360 allows the storage of numbers in decimal form. For e.g., the number 12 could appear in one-byte, as, 1 in BCD will be 0001 and 2 would 0010. Decimal forms are useful in business data processing.

4. **INSTRUCTIONS**- The 360 has a arithmetic, logical, control or transfer and special interrupt instructions. There are many formats of instructions. These formats differ basically in types of operands they use.

Register operands refer to data stored in one of the 16 general registers (32 bits long). Since registers are usually constructed of high-speed circuitry, they provide faster access to data than does core storage.

Storage operands refer to data stored in core memory.

Immediate operands are a single byte of data and are stored as part of the instruction.

Special features- IBM-360 has got its own interrupts and hardware protections.

Step-3. Format of Data Bases: The 3rd step in our design procedure is to specify the format and content of each of the databases. Pass 2 requires a MOT containing name, length, binary code & format; Pass 1 requires only name and length.

The Machine-OP Table (MOTT) and Pseudo OP Tables (POTT) are examples of fixed tables.

MOTT 6-bytes per Entry.

Mnemonic Op code (4 bytes) (characters)	**Binary op code (1-byte) (HEX)**	**Instruction length (2-bits) (binary**	**Instruction format (3 bits) (binary**	**Not used in this design (3-bits)**
"Abbb"	5A	10	001	
"AHbb"	4A	10	001	
"ALbb"	5E	10	001	
⋮	⋮		⋮	
⋮	⋮		⋮	
"MVCb"	D2	11	100	

b~ represents the character "blank"

Codes: Instruction length – 01 = 1 HW = 2 bytes

10 = 2 HW = 4 bytes

11 = 3HW = 6 bytes

Instruction format - 000 = RR

001 = RX

010 = RS

011 = SI

100 = SS

RR format is :

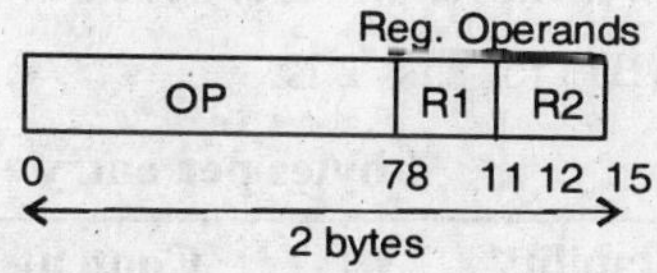

RX format is:

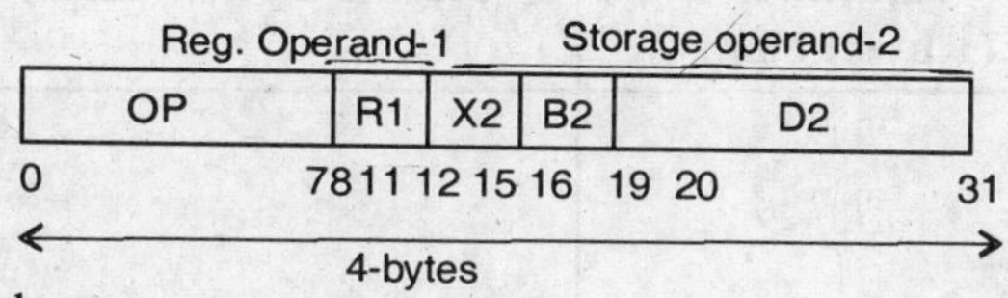

OP ~ operation code

Ri ~ contents of GPR used as operand

Xi ~ contents of GPR used as index

Bi ~ contents of GPR used as base

Di ~ displacement

and POTT for Pass 1 and Pass 2 is :

8 bytes / entry

Pseudo-oP (5-bytes) (character)	Address of routine to process pseudo-op (3 bytes)
"DROP b"	P1 DROP
"END bb"	P1 END
"EQUbb"	P1 EQU Those are labels of routines in Pass 2
"START"	P1 START
"USING"	P1 USING

Format of Symbol – Table (ST) for pass 1 & 2:

Symbol (8-bytes) (characters)	Value (4-bytes) (HEX)	Length (1-byte) (HEX)	Relocation (1-byte) (character)
"RAJ bbbb"	0000	01	"R"
"FOUR bbbb"	000C	04	"R"
"FIVE bbbb"	0010	04	"R"
"TEN pbbbb"	0014	04	"R"

The symbol table includes not only the name and assembly-time value fields but also a length field and a relative-location indicator. The length-field indicates the length (in bytes) of the instruction or datum to which the symbol is attached. For example:

COMMA	DC	C ','
F	DS	F

Here, symbol COMMA has length 1, F has length 4. The symbol * (current value of LC) always has a length of 1. The 'length field' is used by the assembler to calculate length codes used with certain instruction types.

The relative location indicator tells the assembler whether the value of symbol is absolute (does not change of the program is moved in core) or relative to the base of the program.

Similarly, the Base Table (BT) for pass 2 is:

4-bytes per entry

	Availability Indicator (1 byte) char.	**Contents of Base Reg. (3-bytes) (HEX)**	
1.	"N"	–	↑
2.	"N"	–	
"	"	"	15 entries
"	"	"	
"	"	"	
"	"	"	
"	"	"	
"	"	"	
"	"	"	
14.	"N"	-	
15.	"Y"	00 00 00	↓

Code: y ~ Base register specified in USING pseudo-op.

N ~ Means Base register never specified in USING pseudo-op

This base table is used by the assembler to generate the proper base register reference in machine instructions and to compute the correct offsets. Basically, the assembler must generate an address (offset, a base-register number and an index register number) for most symbolic references. The symbol table contains the address of the symbol relative to the beginning of the program. When generating an address the assembler may use the base-register table to choose a base-register. The address is then formulated.

Step 4: Specify algorithm:

Pass 1 : DEFINE SYMBOLS

The purpose of the first pass is to assign a location to each instruction and data-defining pseudo-instruction and thus to define values for symbols appearing in the label fields of the source program. Initially, the Location Counter (LC) is set to the first location in the program (relative address 0). Then a source statement is read. The op-code field is examined to determine if it is a pseudo-op; if it is not, the table of machine op-codes (MOTT) is searched to find a match for the source statement's op code field. The matched MOTT entry specifies the length (2, 4 or 6 bytes) of the instruction. The operand field is scanned for the pressure of a literal, (literal creates data areas for the programs e.g., = F'10', = F'49', = F'4' are literals which will result in the creation of a data area containing 10, 49 & 4 resp.). If a new literal is found, it is entered in the literal table (LT) for later processing. Format of LT is same as that for ST. If there is a label, the symbol is saved in the ST along with the current value of LC. Finally, the current value of the location counter is incremented by the length of the instruction and a copy of the source and is saved for use by pass-2. The above sequence is then repeated for the next instruction.

We now consider what must be done to access a pseudo-op. The simplest procedure occurs for USING and DROP. Pass-1 is only concerned with Pseudo-ops that define symbols (labels) or affect the LC; using & DROP do neither. The assembler need only save the USING and DROP cards for pass-2. The DS and DC pseudo-ops can affect both the DC and the definition of symbols in pass-1. The operand field must be examined to determine the number of bytes of storage required. When the END pseudo-op is encountered, pass-1 is terminated. Before transferring control to pass-2, there are various "housekeeping" operations that must be performed. These include assigning locations to literals that have been collected during Pass-1, a procedure that is very similar to that for the DC pseudo-op. Then we go for pass-2.

Pass 2: GENERATE CODE

After all the symbols have been defined by Pass-1, it is possible to finish the assembly by processing each card and determining values for its operation code and its operand field. Also, a pass-2 must structure the generated code into the appropriate format for later processing by the loader, and print an assembly listing containing the original sources and the HEX equivalent of the bytes generated. The LC is initialized as in Pass-1 and the processing continues.

A card is read from the source file left by pass-1. As in pass-1, the opcode field is examine to determine if it is a pseudo-op; if it is not, the table of (MOTT) machine opcodes is searched to find a match for the card's opcode field. The matching MOTT entry specifies the length, binary op code and the format-type of the instruction. The operand fields of the different instruction format types requre somewhat different processing.

The USING and DROP pseudo-ops, which were largely ignored in pass-1, require additional processing in pass-2. The operand fields of pseudo-ops are evaluated; then the corresponding BT entry is either marked as available, if USING or unavailable if DROP. The BT is used extensively in Pass-2 to compute the base and displacement fields for machine instructions with storage operands.

The DS and DC pseudo-ops are processed essentially as in pass-1. In pass-2, however, active code must be generated for the DC pseudo-op. Depending upon the data-types specified, this involve various conversions and symbol evaluations.

The END pseudo-op indicates the end of source program and terminates the assembly. Various "housekeeping" tasks must now be performed.

For example: Code must be generated for any literal remaining in the LT.

Step 5: LOOK FOR MODULARITY

We now review our design, looking for functions that can be isolated. Each of these functions should independently go through the entire design process. Thus, these functions can be implemented in the respective sections of Pass-1 and Pass-2. So, rather than viewing the assembler as a single program, we view it as a coordinated collection of routines each of relatively minor size and complexity. Various functions that we can write are:

Pass-1: READ 1 Function to Read next source card

POTTGET 1 Search function to search the pass-POTT for a match with the operation of the current source card.

MOTTGET 1 Search the MOTT for a match with the operation of the currents source card.

Similarly, STSTO, LTSTO, WRITE1, DLENGTH, STSRCH functions can be written.

& in Pass-2

READ 2 Read the next assembly source card from the copy.

POTTGET 2 Similar to POTGET 1 (Search POTT)

MOTTGET 2 Similar to pass 1 (Search MOTT)

BTSTO Insert data into BT

LTGEN Generate code for literals.

SUMMARY

We have seen how assemblers, compilers, macro processors and loaders can be designed.

QUESTIONS FOR PRACTICE:

Q.1. What are the different steps that you will follows to design an assembler?

Q.2. Given a source Program, how will you translate this program as done by assembler?

Q.3. List down and explain the various databases that are required during PASS-1 & PASS-2 of an assembler?

Q.4. Draw a complete flowchart to show the PASS-1 of a two pass assembler?

Q.5. Draw a complete flowchart to show the PASS-2 of a two pass assembler?

Q.6. Clearly explain as to why we need two passes in an assembler?

Q.7. Distinguish between a pseudo-op and machine-op with examples?

Q.8. Define what is a micro flowchart? Given an instruction, ADD 2, 176; Draw its complete micro flowchart and explain.

Q.9. Explain clearly with figures, Von Neumann's architecture?

Q.10. What is the general approach to a new machine?

Q.11. Explain the format of MOT & POT as used during PASS-1 & PASS-2 of an assembler?

Q.12. Explain the role of symbol table (ST) for pass-1 & pass-2?

Q.13. Distinguish between RISC and CISC processors?

11.8 INTRODUCTION TO LOADERS

The loaders is a program which accepts the object program decks, prepares these programs for execution by the computer and initiates the execution. In particular, the loader must perform.

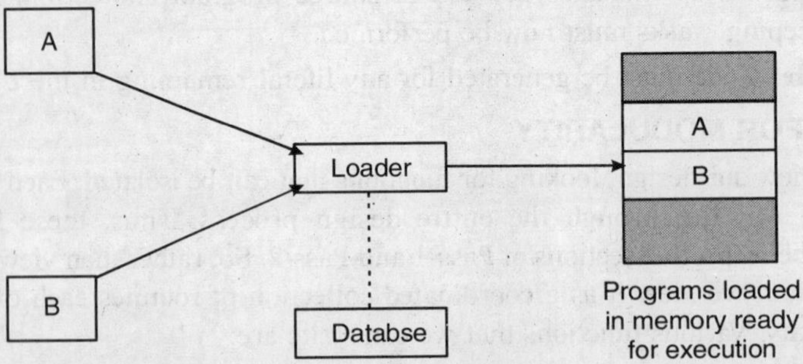

Fig. 11.8 A loader

Four functions:
1. Allocate space in memory for the programs, **(allocation).**
2. Resolve symbolic references between object decks **(linking).**
3. Adjust all address dependent locations, such as address constants, to correspond to the allocated space **(relocation).**
4. Physically place the machine instructions and data into memory **(loading).**

11.9 DIFFERENT LOADER SCHEMES

I. "Compile-and-go" Loaders – One method of performing the loader functions is to have the assembler run in one part of memory and place the assembled machine instructions and data, as they are assembled directly into their assigned memory locations. When the assembly is completed, the assembler causes a transfer to the starting instruction of the program. This is a simple solution, involving no extra procedures. It is used by the WATFOR, FORTRAN compiler.

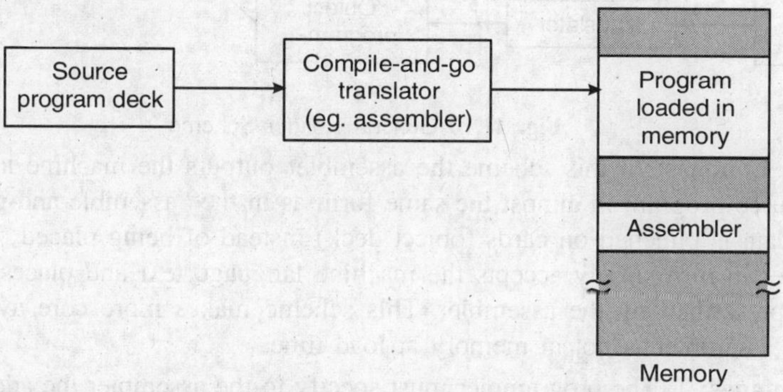

Fig. 11.9 "Compile-and-go" loader scheme.

Such a loading scheme is commonly called **"compile-and-go"** or **"assembler-and-go"**. It is relatively easy to implement. The assembler simply places the code into core and the "loader" consists of one instruction that transfer to the starting instruction of the newly assembled program.

Disadvantages –
1. A portion of memory is wasted because the core occupied by the assembler is unavailable to the object program.
2. It is necessary to retranslate (assemble) the user's program deck every time it is run.
3. It is very difficult to handle multiple segments, especially if the source programs are in different languages (eg. one subroutine in assembly language and another subroutine in FORTRAN).

II. General Loader Scheme – Outputting the instructions data as they are assembled circumvents the problem of wasting core for the assembler. Such an output could be saved and loaded whenever the code was to be executed. The assembled programs could be loaded into the same area in core that the assembler occupied. **This output form, which may be on cards containing a coded form of the instructions, is called an object deck.**

The use of an object deck as intermediate data to avoid one disadvantage of the preceding "compile-and-go" scheme requires the addition of a new program to the system a loader. The loader accepts the assembled machine instructions, data and other information present in the object format and places machine instructions and data in core in an executable computer form. The loader is assumed to be smaller than the assembler, so that more memory is available to the user. A further advantage is that reassembly is no longer necessary to run the program at a later date.

Finally, if all the source program translators (assemblers, and compilers) produce compatible object-deck-program formats and use compatible linkage conventions, it is possible to write subroutines in several different languages since the object decks to be processed by the loader will be in the same "**language**" (machine language).

The **General loader scheme** is shown below:-

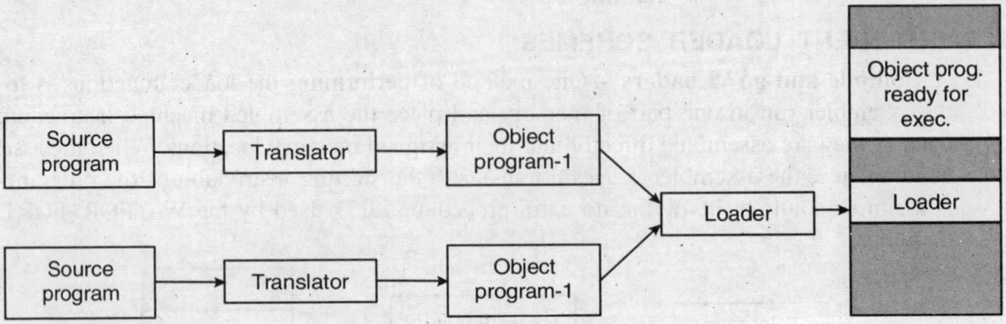

Fig. 11.10 General Loader Scheme

III. Absolute Loaders: In this scheme the assembler outputs the machine language translation of the source program in almost the same form as in the "assemble-and-go" scheme, except that the data is punched on cards (object deck) instead of being placed directly in memory. The loader in turn simply accepts the machine language text and places it into core at the location prescribed by the assembler. This scheme makes more core available to the user since the assembler is not in memory at load time.

Disadvantages: 1. The programmer must specify to the assembler the address in core where the program is to be loaded.

2. If there are multiple subroutines, the programmer must remember the address of each and use that absolute address explicitly in his other subroutines to perform subroutine linkage.

The Fig. 11.11 below illustrates the operation of an absolute assembler and an absolute loader. The programmer must be careful not to assign two subroutines to the same or overlapping locations.

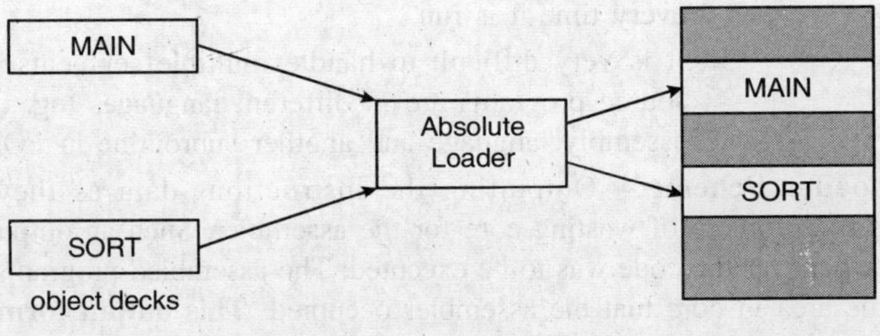

Fig. 11.11 Role of an absolute loader

The MAIN program is assigned to locations 100247 and the sqrt-subroutine is assigned locations 400477. If changes were made to MAIN that increased its length to more than 300-bytes, the end of MAIN (at 100 + 300 = 400) would overlap the start of SQRT (at 400). It would then be necessary to assign SQRT to a new location by changing its START pseudo-op card and reassembling it. Furthermore, it would also be necessary to modify all other subroutines that referred to the address of SQRT. In situations where dozens of subroutines are being used, this manual "shuffling" can get very complex, tedious and wasteful of core. The four loader functions are accomplished as follows in Absolute loading scheme:

1. Allocation – by programmer
2. Linking – by programmer
3. Relocation – by assembler
4. Loading – by loader

IV. **Relocating Loader: To avoid possible reassembling of all subroutines when a single subroutine is changed and to perform the tasks of allocation and linking for the programmer, the general class of relocating loaders was introduced. For eg: Binary Symbolic Subroutine (BSS) loader which was used in IBM-7094, IBM 1130, GE 635 machines.** The BSS loader allows many procedure segments yet only one data segment. The assembler assembles each procedure segment independently and passes onto the loader the text and information as to relocation and intersegment references. The output of a relocating assembler using a BSS scheme is the object program and information about all other programs it references. In addition, there is information (relocation information) as to locations in this program that need to be changed if it is to be loaded in an arbitrary place in core *i.e.*, the locations which are dependent on the core allocation.

For each source program the assembler outputs a text (machine translation of the program) prefixed by a transfer-vector that consists of addresses containing names of the subroutines referenced by the source program. For e.g., If a Square Root Routine (SQRT) was referenced and was the first subroutine called, the first location in the transfer vector would contain the symbolic name SQRT. The statement calling SQRT would be translated into a transfer instruction indicating a branch to the location of the transfer vector associated with SQRT. The assembler would also provide the loader with additional information such as the length of the entire program and the length of the transfer vector portion. After loading the text and the transfer vector into core, the loader would load each subroutine identified in the transfer vector. It would then place a transfer instruction to the corresponding subroutine in each entry in the transfer vector. Thus, the execution of the call SQRT statement would result in a branch to the first location in the transfer vector, which would contain a transfer instruction to the location of SQRT. Since it is necessary to relocate the address portion of every instruction, in case of absence of 360–type base registers, this problem is often solved by the use of **"relocation bits".** The assembler associates a bit with each instruction or address field. If this bit equals one, then the corresponding address field must be relocated; otherwise the field is not relocated. **These relocation indicators are known as relocation bits and are included in the object deck. So, relocation bits are used to solve the problem of relocation; transfer vector is used to solve the problem of linking and the program length information is used to solve the problem of allocation.**

11.10 DESIGN OF AN ABSOLUTE LOADER

With an absolute loading scheme the programmer and the assembler perform the tasks of allocation, relocation and linking. Therefore, it is only necessary for the loader to read cards of the object deck and move the text on the cards into the absolute locations specified by the assembler.

There are **two types of information** that the object deck must communicate from the assembler to the loader. **First,** it must convey the machine instructions that the assembler has created along with the assigned core location. **Second,** it must convey the entry point of the program, which is where the loader is to transfer control when all instructions are loaded. Assuming that this information is transmitted on cards, a possible format is shown below:-

Text cards (for instructions and data)

Card column	**contents**
1	card type = 0 (for text card identifier)
2	count of number of bytes (1 byte per column) of information on card
3-5	Address at which data on card is to be put
6-7	Empty
8-72	Instructions & data to be loaded
73-80	card sequence number

Transfer cards (to hold entry point to program)

Card column	**contents**
1	card type = 1 (card-id)
2	count = 0
3-5	address of entry point
6-72	Empty
73-80	card sequence number

Please note that in the card format shown, the instructions are stored on the card as one core byte per column. When a card is read, it is stored in core as 80 contiguous bytes.

ALGORITHMS – Algorithm and flowchart of an Absolute loader:

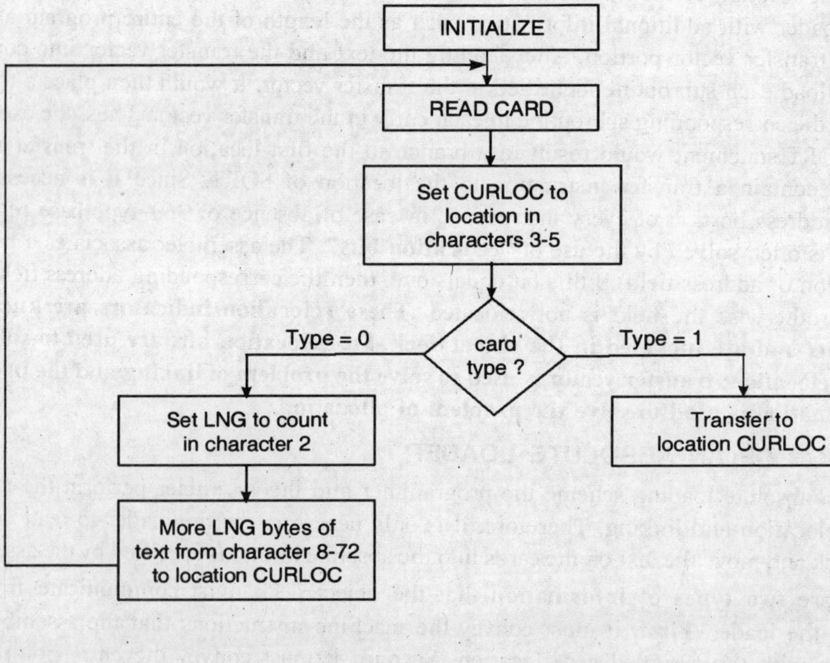

Fig. 11.12 Absolute loader algorithm

Explaination – The object deck for this loader consists of a series of text cards terminated by a transfer card. Therefore, the loader should read one card at a time moving the text to the location specified on the card, until the transfer card is reached. At this point the assembled instructions are in core and it is only necessary to transfer to entry point specified on the transfer card.

11.11 BOOTSTRAP LOADERS

Still we have neglected to answer one important question. **How is the loader itself loaded into memory?** Of course we could say that the O.S. loads the loader. **A bootstrap loader is a loader that is added to the beginning of all object programs that are to be loaded into an empty and idle system. This includes, for example, the O.S. itself.** To overcome the problems of Absolute loader, we go for a built-in hardware function that reads a fixed-length record from some device into memory at fixed location. After the read operation is complete, control is automatically transferred to the address in memory where the record was stored. This record contains machine instructions that load the absolute program that follows. If the loading process requires more instructions than can be read in a single record, this first record causes the reading of others and these in turn can cause the reading of still more records – hence the term bootstrap

Disadvantages of BSS-loader scheme-

1. The transfer vector linkage is only useful for transfer and is not well suited for loading or storing external data (data located in another procedure segment).
2. The transfer vector increases the size of the object program in memory.
3. Finally, BSS loader processes procedure segments but does not facilitate access to data segments that can be shared. This last shortcoming is overcome in many BSS loaders by allowing one common data segment, often called COMMON.

V Direct-Linking Loader: A DLL is a general re-locatable loader and is perhaps the most popular scheme. It has the advantage of allowing the programmer multiple procedure segments and multiple data segments and of giving him complete freedom in referencing data or instructions contained in other segments.

The assembler (translator) must give the loader the following information with each procedure or data segment:

1. The length of segment
2. A list of all the symbols in the segment that may be referenced by other segments and their relative location within the segment.
3. A list of all symbols not defined in the segment but referenced in the segment.
4. Information as to where address constants are located in the segment and a description of four to revise their values.
5. The machine code translation of the source program and the relative addresses assigned.

The assembler produces four types of cards in the object deck: ESD, TXT, RLD and END.

1. **ESD or External Symbol Dictionary Cards** contain information about all symbols that are defined in this program but that may be referenced elsewhere and all symbols referenced in this program but defined elsewhere.
2. **Text (TXT) cards** contain the actual object code translated version of the source program.
3. **Relocation and Linkage Directory (RLD)** cards contain information about those locations in program whose contents depend on the address at which the program is placed. For such locations the assembler must supply information enabling the loader to correct their contents.
4. The **END card** indicates the end of object deck.

Consider the following program:

```
RAJIV     START
          ENTRY   RESULT
          EXTXN   SUM
          BALR    12,0
          USING   *, 12
          ST      14, SAVE
          L       1, POINTER
          L       15, ASUM
          BALR    14, 15
          ST      1, RESULT
          L       14, SAVE
          BR      14
TABLE     DC      F' 1. 7, 9, 10, 3'
POINTER   DC      A (TABLE)
RESULT    DS      F
SAVE      DS      F
ASUM      DC      A(SUM)
          END
```

In such a case what will be the contents of ESD, TXT, RLD card?

Contents of ESD cards: Three ESD cards are needed for the program RAJIV. The first card contains the name of program RAJIV, which may be referenced externally. The "type" mnemonic we have used is SD which implies that the symbol is a Segment Definition. The relative address of RAJIV is 0 and the length of program is 64. The Second ESD card his the symbol RESULT, which is a Local Definition (LD); its relative address is 52. The third ESD card specifies that the symbol SUM is an External Reference (ER). So, we draw the table below:

ESD Cards:

Reference No	Symbol	Type	Relative Location	Length
1	RAJIV	SD	0	64
2	RESULT	LD	52	-
3	SUM	ER	-	-

Contents of TXT cards: The TXT card contains the actual assembled program. So, we draw the table below:

TXT cards:

Reference No	Relative Location	Object Code	
4	0	BALR	12, 0
6	2	ST	14,54 (0,12)
7	6	L	1, 46 (0, 12)
8	10	L	15, 58 (0,12)
9	14	BALR	14,15

10	16	ST	1, 50 (0, 12)
11	20	L	14,54 (0, 12)
12	24	BCR	15,14
13	28	1	
13	32	7	
13	36	9	
13	40	10	
13	44	3	
14	48	28	
17	60	0	

Contents of RLD cards: The RLD cards contain the following information:

1. The location of each constant that needs to be changed due to relocation
2. By what it has to be changed
3. The operation to be performed

So, we draw the table below:

RLD cards:

Reference no.	symbol	Flag	Length	Relative Location
14	RAJIV	+	4	48
17	SUM	+	4	60

Here, 48 denotes the relative location of a constant that must be changed; a plus sign denotes that something must be added to the constant and the symbol field indicating that the value of external symbol RAJIV must be added to be relative location 48. The relative value of RAJIV is 0. When the program is loaded, the loader will determine its absolute value. Similarly, the second RLD card contains 60, denoting the relative location of a constant that must be changed. The symbol field indicates that the value of external symbol SUM must be added to relative location 60. Although the assembler does not know the absolute address of sum, the loader will later be able to fill in the correct value.

"The process of adjusting the address constant of an internal symbol, such as TABLE, is normally called relocation". And the process of supplying the contents of an address constant for an external symbol, such as SUM, is known as linking.

Disadvantage of D.L.L.—

(1) It's demerit is that it is necessary to allocate, relocate, link and load all of the subroutines each time in order to execute a program. Since there may be tens and hundreds of subroutines involved such as SQRT utility, this loading process can be extremely time consuming.

(2) Furthermore, even though the loader program may be smaller than the assembler, it does absorb a considerable amount of space.

11.12 BINDERS AND A MODULE LOADER

A binder is a program that performs the same functions as the direct-linking loader. That is, **it binds subroutines together.** Rather than placing the relocated and linked text directly into memory, it outputs the text as a file or card deck. This cutput file is in a format ready to be loaded and is typically called as a **load module.**

The **module loader** has to physically load the module into the core. So, we can say that the **loading process** is divided into **two** separate programs-

(a) a **binder**

(b) and a **module loader**

The **binder** performs the functions of **allocation, relocation** and **linking** whereas the **module loader** merely performs the function of loading.

Categories of binders-

There are two major classes of binders. They are as follows-

(a) Core image builder

(b) Linkage Editor

Core-image builder is a simple binder. It produces a load module that looks very much like a single absolute loader deck. This means that the specific core allocation of the program is performed at the time that the subroutines are bound together. Since this kind of module looks like an actual **"Snapshot"** or **"image"** of a section of core, it is called as a **core image module** and the corresponding binder is called as a **core image builder**.

Linkage editor is more complex. It can keep track of the relocation information so that the resulting load module can be further relocated and thereby loaded anywhere in core. In this case the module loader must perform additional allocation and relocation as well as loading but it does not have to worry about the complex problems of linking.

In both cases, a program that is to be used repeatedly need only be bound once and then can be loaded whenever required. **The core image builder binder is relatively simple and fast. The linkage editor binder is somewhat more complex but allows a more flexible allocation and loading scheme.**

Dynamic loading and dynamic linking

Usually the functions (or sub routines) of a program are called at different times. **For example, the pass 1 and pass2 of an assembler are mutually exclusive.** We try to draw an overlay structure that shows which module calls which other module.

Consider a program consisting of five sub programs – A, B, C, D and E that require 100 KB of core, i.e.,

	A	20 K
	B	20 K
100K	C	30 K
	D	10 K
	E	20 K

We draw its overlay structure now—

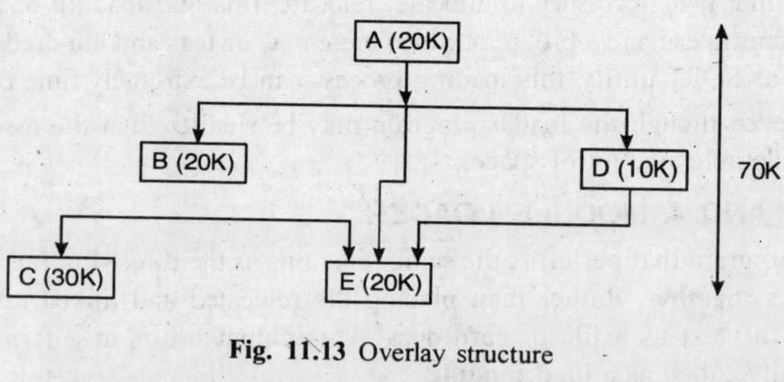

Fig. 11.13 Overlay structure

It shows that module A, calls B, D and E, module B calls C and E, D only calls E. But C and E do not call any other routines. **Please note that procedures B and D are never in use at the sometime.** Similarly, C and E are not in use at sometime. **So, if we load only those procedures that are actually to be used at any particular time than the amount of core needed is equal to the longest path of the overlay structure.** From Fig. above, it happens to be 70 K.

Dynamic Linking: It is a mechanism by which loading and linking of external references are postponed until execution time. It is our assembler that produces text, binding and the relocation information. The loader loads the main program.

11.13 MACROS AND MACRO PROCESSORS

Macro instructions (or Macros) are single-line abbreviations for groups of instructions. In employing a macro, the programmer essentially defines a single **"instruction"** to represent a block of code. For every occurrence of this one-line macro instruction in his program, the macro processing assembler will substitute the entire block.

11.13.1 Macro Instructions – In its simplest form, a macro is an abbreviation for a sequence of operations. Consider the following program:

Example 1:

```
            :
        A   1, DATA        ; Add contents of DATA to reg. -1
        A   2, DATA
        A   3, DATA
            :
        A   1, DATA
        A   2, DATA
        A   3, DATA
            :
DATA    DC       F'5'
            :
```

In the above program the sequence

```
        A   1, DATA
        A   2, DATA
        A   3, DATA
```

occurs twice. A macro facility permits us to attach a name to this sequence and to use this name in its place.

A macro processor effectively constitutes a separate language processor with its own language.

It's **syntax** is:

```
MACRO  <——————— Start of definition
[    ] <——————— Macro name
 ____ 
 ____  } <————— Sequence to be abbreviation
 ____ 
MEND   <——————— End of definition.
```

The MACRO pseudo-op is the first line of the definition and identifies the following line as the macro-instruction name. Following the name line is the sequence of instructions being abbreviated – the instructions comprising the 'macro' instruction. The definition is terminated by a line with the **MEND ('macro end') pseudo op.**

Once the macro has been defined, the use of the macro name as an operation mnemonic in an assembly program is equivalent to the use of the corresponding instruction sequence.

So, our example might be rewritten as follows—

```
        Source-code                     Expanded source
          MACRO              |
          INCR               |
        A       1, DATA      |
        A       2, DATA      |
        A       3, DATA      |
        MEND                 |
          :                  |              :
          :                  |              :
        INCR                 |  { A        1, DATA
          :                  |  { A        2, DATA
          :                  |  { A        3, DATA
        INCR                 |  { A        1, DATA
          :                  |  { A        2, DATA
          :                  |  { A        3, DATA
DATA    DC      F'5'            DATA  DC        F'5"
```

i.e., in this case the macro processor replaces each macro call with the lines—

```
A       1, DATA
A       2, DATA
A       3, DATA
```

This process of replacement is called expanding the macro. Please note that the macro definition itself does not appear in the expanded source code. The definition is saved by the macro processor. **The occurrence of the macro name in the source program is called as macro call.**

11.13.2 Four Features of a Macro Facility

1. Macro Instruction Arguments: The macro facility presented thus far is capable of inserting blocks of instructions in place of macro calls. All of the calls to any given macro will be replaced by identical blocks. This macro lacks flexibility: there is no way for a specific macro call to modify the coding that replaces it. An important extension of this facility consists of providing for arguments or parameters, in macro calls

Example:

```
                :
        A       1, DATA1
        A       2, DATA1
        A       3, DATA1
                :
        A       1, DATA2
        A       2, DATA2
        A       3, DATA2
                :
DATA1   DC      F'5'
DATA2   DC      F'10'
```

Here, the instruction sequences are very similar but not identical. First sequence operates on DATA1 as operand and second using DATA2. They perform same operation with a variable parameter or argument. **Such a parameter is called a macro instruction argument or "*dummy argument*".** It is specified on the macro name line and distinguished by ampersand (&) which is always its first character. So, preceding program could be written as:

Source

```
        MACRO                  ; Macro INCR
        INCR & ARG             ; has 1-arg.
          A      1, & ARG
          A      2, & ARG
          A      3, &ARG
        MEND
          :
        INCR    DATA 1         ;Use DATA 1 as      { A    1, DATA 1
          :                       Operand          { A    2, DATA1
          :                                        { A    3, DATA 1
        INCR    DATA 2         ;Use DATA2 as         A    1, DATA 2
          :                       Operand            A    1, DATA 2
          :                                          A    2, DATA 2
          :                                          A    3, DATA 2
DATA 1  DC      F'5'
DATA 2  DC      F'10'
          :
```

It is possible to supply more than one argument in a macro call. Each argument must correspond to a definition ("dummy") argument on the macro name line of macro definition. When a macro call is processed, the arguments supplied are substituted for the respective dummy arguments in the macro definition.

Here, we have specified 4-arguments, including a label argument. Label arguments are treated just like those written as "operands" of a macro instructs. The argument appearing in the label field on the macro name line & in call to the macro, differs from other arguments only in its location. Label arguments are convenient but non essential features that enhance the similarity between macro instructions and ordinary assembly language instructions.

This can be useful when a macro has arguments – labels for example – that are passed.

There are generally 2 ways of specifying arguments to a macro call:

(a) **Positional argument** – As used in previous example, Arguments are matched with dummy arguments according to the order in which they appear. Like in a macro call 'INCR A, B, C' A, B and C replaces the first, second and third dummy arguments.

(b) **Keyword arguments** – allows reference to dummy arguments by name as well as by position.

Referring to the dummy arguments appearing in the definition of INCR, we might write:

'INCR & ARG1 = A, & ARG 3 = C, & ARG 2 = B'

or INCR & ARG1 = A, & ARG 2 = & ARG 3 = C'

Any arguments not supplied are assumed blank by the macro processor.

Consider the following program:

```
                :
LOOP1       A       1, DATA 1
            A       1, DATA 2
            A       1, DATA 3
                :
LOOP 2      A       1, DATA 3  )
            A       2, DATA 2  }  Sequence of operands differs.
            A       3, DATA 1  )
                :
DATA 1      DC      F'5'
DATA 2      DC      F'10'
DATA 3      DC      F'15'
```

This program could be written as:

Source

```
:     MACRO
&LAB  INCR          &ARG1, & ARG 2, & ARG 3
&LAB    A           1, & ARG 1
        A           2, & ARG 2
        A           3, & ARG 3
      MEND
        :                                                   :
LOOP1 INCR          DATA1, DATA2, DATA 3       {  LOOP 1 A      1, DATA 1
        :                                                A      2, DATA 2
                                                         A      3, DATA 3
LOOP 2  INCR        DATA3, DATA 2, DATA 1
        :                                      {  LOOP 2 A      1, DATA 3
        :                                                A      2, DATA 2
        :                                                A      3, DATA 1
DATA 1 DC      F'5'                                             :
DATA 2 DC      F'10'                                            :
DATA 3 DC      F'15'
```

2. Conditional Macro Expansion: Two important macro processor pseudo–ops, AIF and AGO, permit conditional reordering of the sequence of macro expansion, consider the following program:-

```
                        :
LOOP1           A       1, DATA 1
                A       2, DATA 2
                A       3, DATA 3
                        :
```

```
LOOP2     A     1, DATA 3
          A     2, DATA 2
          :
LOOP3     A     1, DATA 1
          :
DATA1     DC    F'5'
DATA2     DC    F'10'
DATA3     DC    F'15'
          :
```

In this example, the operands labels and the number of instructions generated change in each sequence. This program could be written as follows:

```
          :
          MACRO
&ARGO     VARY       & COUNT, & ARG1, & ARG2, & ARG3
&ARGO     A          1, & ARG 1
          AIF        (& COUNT EQ 1). FINI          ; Test if
                                                   ; &COUNT = 1
          A          2, & ARG 2
          AIF        (& COUNT EQ 2).FINI  ;Test if & COUNT = 2
          A          3, &ARG 3
.FINI     MEND
```

```
                                             Expanded source
          :                                          :
                                             LOOP 1  A   1, DATA 1
LOOP1     VARY  3, DATA1, DATA 2, DATA 3             A   2, DATA 2
                                                     A   3, DATA 3
LOOP2     VARY  2, DATA 3, DATA2                     :
                                             LOOP 2  A   1, DATA 3
          :                                          A   2, DATA 2
          :                                              :
LOOP 3    VARY  1, DATA1                     LOOP3   A   1, DATA 1
          :
DATA 1    DC    F'5'
DATA 2    DC    F'10'
DATA 3    DC    F'15'
```

Explanation: Labels starting with a period (.), such as, .FINI, are macro labels and do not appear in the output of the macro processor. The statement AIF (& COUNT EQ 1) .FINI directs the macro processor to skip to statement labeled . FINI if the parameter corresponding to &COUNT is a 1; otherwise, the macro processor is to continue with the statement following AIF pseudo-op.

AIF is a conditional branch pseudo-op; it performs an arithmetic test and branches only if the tested condition is true. The HGO is an unconditional branch pseudo-op or 'go to' statement. It specifics a label appearing on some other statement in macro instruction definition; the macro processor continues sequential processing of instructions with the indicated statement. These statements are directives to macro process and do not appear in macro expansions. Just as conditional and unconditional branch instructions in an assembly lang. program direct the order of program flow, AIF and AGO control the sequence in which macro processor expands the statements in macro instruction. Branches and tests in the macro instruction language permit the use of highly general macros that assemble selectively and it is this facility of macros that is one of the systems programmer's most powerful programming tools.

3. Macro calls within Macros: Since macro calls are "abbreviations" of instruction sequences, it seems reasonable that such "abbreviations" should be available within other macro definitions. For example,

```
MACRO
ADD1      &ARG
  L       1, &ARG
  A       1, = F'1'
 ST       1, & ARG
MEND
MACRO
ADDS      &ARG1, & ARG2, & ARG3
ADD1      & ARG1
ADD1      & ARG2
ADD1      & ARG3
MEND
```

Here, within the macro "ADS", there are three separate calls to a previously defined macro ADD1'. **Such use of macros results in macro expansion on multiple 'levels'.** Thus,

Source	**Expanded source** (level-1)	**Expanded source** (level-2)
⋮		
⋮		
MACRO		
ADD1 & ARG		
L 1, & ARG		
A 1, = F'1'		
ST 1, & ARG		
MEND		
MACRO		
ADDS &ARG1, &ARG2, & ARG3	Expansion of ADDS	Expansion of ADD1
ADD1 & ARG1	⋮	⋮
ADD1 &ARG2	ADD1 DATA1 →	L1, DATA1
ADD1 &ARG3	ADD1 DATA2	A1, = F'1'
MEND	ADD1 DATA3 →	ST 1, DATA1
⋮		
ADDS DATA1, DATA2, DATA3		L1, DATA2
		A1, = F'1'
		ST 1, DATA2

Macro calls within macros can involve several levels. For example, the macro ADDS might be called within the definition of another macro. In fact, conditional macro facilities (such as AIF and AG) make it possible for a macro to call itself. So long as this does not cause an infinite loop-So long as at some point, the macro, having being called for the nth-time, decides not to call itself again – it makes perfectly good sense.

4. Macro Instructions defining Macros: Consider the following program-

```
                                   MACRO
                                   DEFINE & SUBR      ; Macro name : DEFINE
                                   MACRO
Definition          Definition     & SUBR &y          ; Dummy macro name
of                      of            :
macro                 macro           :
DEFINE                & SUB           :
                                   MEND
                                   MEND
```

Here, we have defined a macro named DEFINE, which when called with a subroutine name defines a macro with the same name as the subroutine. **It is important to note that inner macro definition is not callable until outer macro has been called.** This is because of the method by which definitions are implemented.

The user might then call this macro with the statement

DEFINE COS

defining a new macro named COS: the statement expands into a new macro definition. User might subsequently call the COS macro as follows:

COS AR

And the macroprocessor will call inner macro with & y = AR.

These macro definitions within macros are sometimes called **"macro definitions within macro definitions"**.

11.13.3 Four basic tasks that any microprocessor must perform

1. Recognize macro definitions: A macroprocessor must recognize macro definitions identified by the MACRO and MEND pseudo-ops. This task becomes complicated when macro definitions appear within macros. When MACROs and MENDs are nested, the macroprocessor must recognize the nesting and must correctly match the last or outer MEND with the first MACRO. All of the intervening text, including nested MACROs and MENDs, defines a single macro instruction.

2. Save the definitions: The processor must store the macro instruction definitions, which it will need for expanding macro calls.

3. Recognize calls: The processor must recognize macro calls that appear as operation mnemonics. This suggests that macro names be handled as a type of opcode.

4. Expand calls and substitute arguments: The processor must substitute for dummy or macro definition arguments, the corresponding arguments from a macro call; the resulting symbolic text is then substituted for the macro call. This text, of course, may contain additional macro definitions or calls.

Summary: The macroprocessor must recognize and process macro definitions and macro calls.

Macroprocessors design steps

Step-1 Problem definition. A macroprocessor, like an assembler, scans and processes lines of a text. Our macroprocessor algorithm, will make two systematic scans or passes over the input text, searching first for macro definitions and then for macro calls. Just as our assembler cannot process a reference to a symbol before its definition, so the macroprocessor cannot expend a macro call before having found and saved the corresponding macro definition. Thus we need two passes over the input text one to handle definitions and one to handle calls. **The first pass,** examining every operation code, will save all macro definitions in a Macro Definition Table (MDT) and save a copy of input text on secondary storage (e.g. magnetic tape) for use in pass-2. **The 1st pass** will also prepare a **Macro Name Table (MNT)** along with MDT.

The 2nd pass will then examine every operation mnemonic and replace each macro name with the appropriate text from the macro definitions.

Step-2 Specification of Database:

Pass 1 data bases are:

1. The **input macro source deck**
2. The **output macro source deck** copy for use by pass 2
3. The **Macro Definition Table (MDT)** used to store the body of the macro definitions.
4. The **Macro Name Table (MNT),** used to store the names of defined macros.
5. The **Macro Definition Table Counter (MDTC),** used to indicate the next available entry in MDT.
6. The **Macro Name Table Counter (MNTC),** used to indicate the next available entry in MNT.
7. The **Argument List Array (ALA),** used to substitute index markers (#) for dummy arguments before storing a macro definition.

Pass 2 databases:

1. The copy of the **input macro source deck.**
2. The **output expanded source deck** to be used as input to the assembler.
3. The **Macro Definition Table (MDT),** created by Pass 1.
4. The **Macro Name Table,** created by Pass 1.
5. The **Macro Definition Table Pointer (MDTP),** used to indicate the next line of text to be used during macro expansion.
6. The **Argument List Array (ALA),** used to substitute macro call arguments for the index markers in the stored macro definition.

Step-3 specification of database format:

ARGUMENT LIST ARRAY: The Argument List Array (ALA) is used during both pass 1 and pass 2 but for somewhat reverse functions. During pass 1, in order to simplify later argument replacement during macro expansion, dummy arguments in the macro definition are replaced with positional indicators when the definition is stored. The ith dummy argument on the macro name card is represented in the body of the macro by the index marker symbol # where # *i* is a symbol reserved for the use of the macroprocessor (i.e., not available to programmer. These symbols are used in conjunction with the argument list prepared before expansion of a macro call. Consider the macro INCR defined earlier. The stored macro definition would be:

Macro Definition Table (MDT)

```
        :
& Lab INCR & ARG1, &ARG2, &ARG3; Dummy arg.
# 0         A     1, #1         ; Index marker's substituted for dummy arguments.
            A     2, # 2
            A     3, # 3
        MEND
        :
```

During pass 2, it is necessary to substitute macro call arguments for the index markers stored in the macro definition. Thus, on encountering the call

LOOP1 INCR DATA1, DATA2, DATA3

The macro call expander would prepare an ALA:

ALA

Index	(8 bytes/entry) Argument	
0	"LOOP1bbb"	
1	"DATA1bbb"	; Arg(s) of macro
2	"DATA2bbb"	call are substituted
3	"DATA3bbb"	in Pass 2.

MACRO DEFINITION TABLE: is a table of next lines; it's-input is from 80-column cards, the MDT can be a table with 80-byte strings as entries. Every line of each macro definition, except MACRO line, is stored in MDT. For eg: An INCR macro can be stored as follows:

MDT

	Index	80 bytes per entry Card
	⋮	⋮
MDTC →	15	& LAB INCR & ARG1, &ARG2, & ARG3
or MDTP	16	# 0 A 1, # 1
	17	A 2, # 2
	18	A 3, # 3
	19	MEND
	⋮	⋮

Macro Name Table (MNT): It has the following format:

	Index	(8 bytes) Name	(4 bytes) MDT index
	⋮	⋮	⋮
MNTC →	3	"INCRbbbb"	15
	⋮	⋮	⋮

Each MNT entry consists of a character string (i.e, macro name) and a pointer (index) to the entry in MDT that corresponds to the beginning of the macro definition.

Step 4 – Algorithm: Each of the algorithms makes a line-by-line scan over its input.

PASS 1 – MACRO DEFINITION: The algorithm for pass 1 tests each input line. If it is a MACRO pseudo-op, the entire macro definition that follows it, is saved in the next available locations in MDT. The 1st line of the definition is the macro name line. The name is entered into MNT, along with a pointer to the first location of the MDT entry of the definition. When the END pseudo-op is encountered, all of the macro-definitions have been processed, so control transfers to pass 2 in order to process macro calls.

The **flowchart for pass-1** is given below:

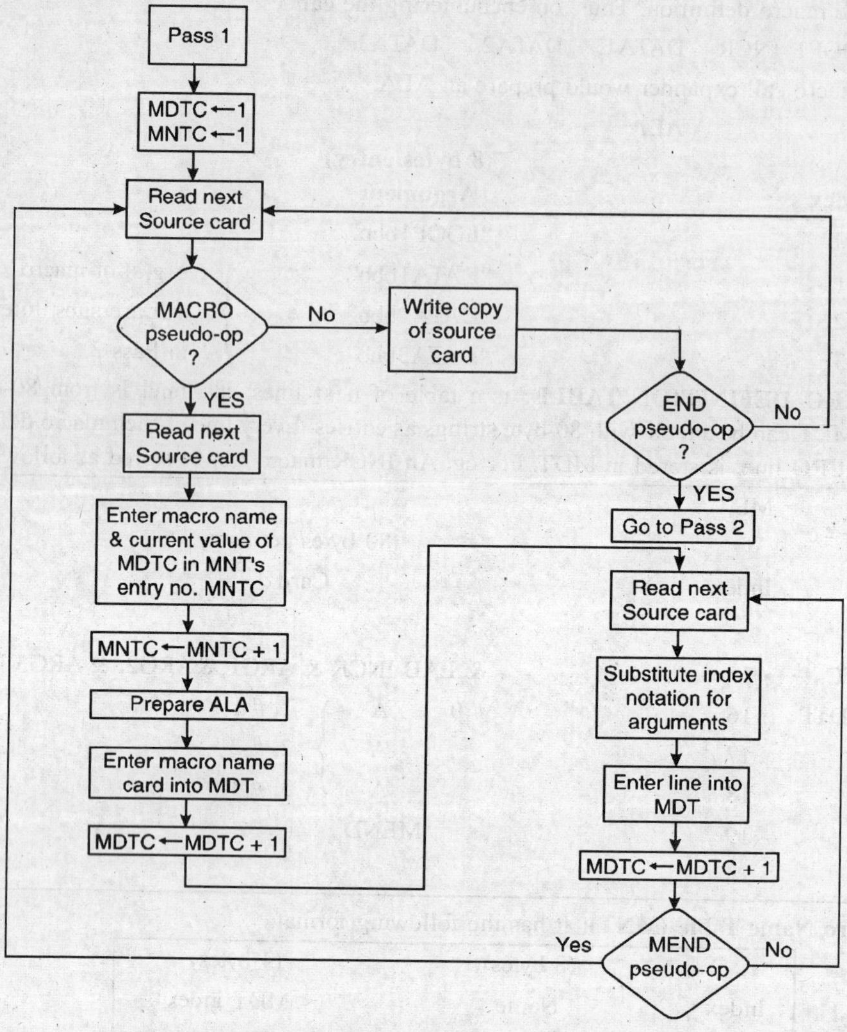

Fig. 11.14 Shows Pass 1 – processing macro definitions

PASS 2 – MACRO CALLS & EXPANSION: The algorithm for pass 2, tests the operation mnemonic of each input line to see if it is a name in the MNT. When a call is found, the call processor sets a pointer, MDTP, to the corresponding macro definition stored in the MDT. The initial value of MDTP is obtained from the "MDT index" field of the MNT entry. The macro expander prepares ALA consisting of a table of dummy argument indices and the corresponding arguments to the call. This list is simply a succession of symbols ordered to match the dummy arguments on the name card. (The first is the label argument which is considered to have an index of zero).

Reading proceeds from the MDT; as each successive line is read, the values from the argument list are substituted for dummy argument indices in the macro definition. Reading of MEND line in MDT, terminates expansion of macro and scanning continues from the input file. When the END pseudo-op is encountered, the expanded source deck is transferred to the assembler for further processing.

The purpose of pass 2 is to process macro calls & expansion. It's **flowchart is** given below:

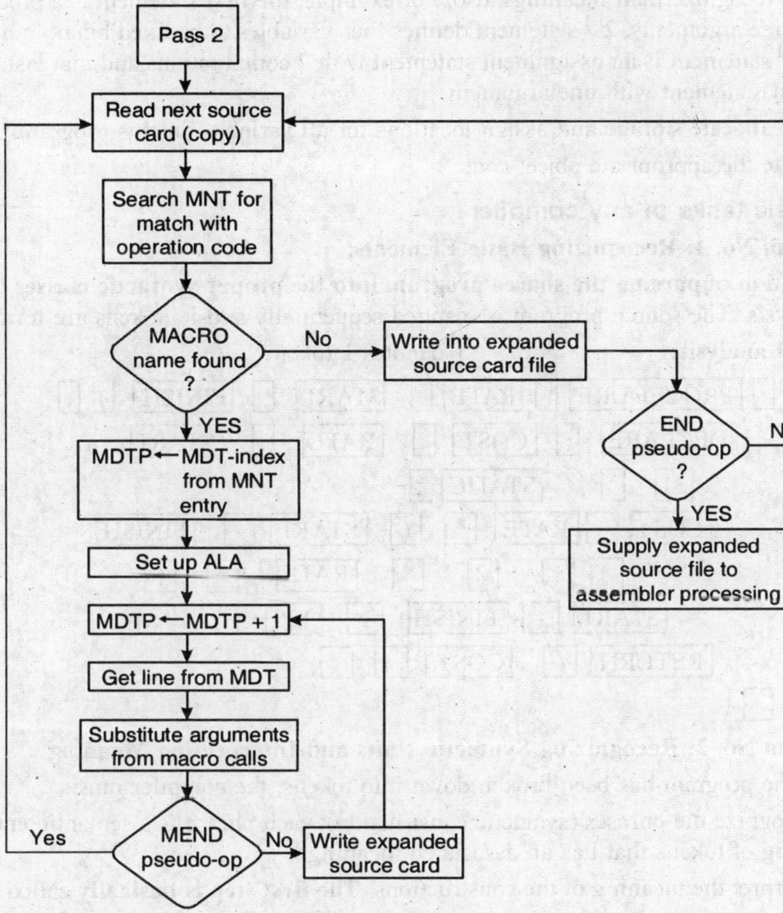

Fig. 11.15 Pass 2 showing macrocall processing and expansion

11.14 COMPILERS

11.14.1 Introduction

What is a compiler? A compiler accepts a program written in a higher level language as input and produces its machine language equivalent as output. Consider following PL-program:

```
WCM: PROCEDURE CRATE, START, FINISH)
        DECLARE (COST, RATE, START, FINISH) FIXED BINARY (31) STATIC
        COST = RATE * (START-FINISH) + 2 * RATE *  (START-FNISH-100).
        RETURN (COST);
END;
```

11.14.2 What must a compiler do to compile this program?

1. It must recognize certain strings as basic element eg. Recognize that COST is a variable, WCM is a label, PROCEDURE is a key word and "=" is an operator.
2. It must recognize their meanings also. For example, the first statement is a procedure name with three arguments. 2nd statement defines four variables to be fixed binary numbers of 31-bits. 3rd statement is an assignment statement with 7 computations and that last statement is a return statement with one argument.
3. It must allocate storage and assign locations for all variables in this program.
4. Generate the appropriate object code.

11.14.3 Basic tasks of any compiler

Problem No. 1: Recognizing Basic Elements:

The action of parsing the source program into the proper syntactic classes is known as lexical analysis. The source program is scanned sequentially and its tokens are formed:

Lexical analysis: [ ] denotes 1 token

WCM | : | PROCEDURE | (| RATE | , | START | , | FINISH |) | :

DECLARE | (| COST | , | RATE | , | START | ...

31 |) | STATIC | ;

COST | = | RATE | * | (| START | – | FINISH

) | + | 2 | * | RATE | * | (

START | – | FINISH | – | 100 |) | ;

RETURN | (| COST |) | ;

END | ;

Problem No. 2: Recognizing Syntactic Units and Interpreting Meaning

Once the program has been broken down into tokens, the compiler must:

(*a*) Recognize the phrases (syntactic construction); each phrase is a semantic entity and is a string of tokens that has an associated meaning.

(*b*) Interpret the meaning of the constructions. **The first step is basically** called as syntactic syntax analysis. It also notes syntactic errors if any. **The second step** is to interpret the meaning (semantics). Associated with each syntactic construction is a defined meaning.

For eg: [ ] ← Basic syntactic constructs

| | ← Tokens

| WCM | : | PROCEDURE | (| RATE | , | START | , | FINISH |) | ; |

—valid procedure statement

eg. 2 | RETURN | (| COST |) | ; | —valid return statement

INTERMEDIATE FORM – The compiler now creates an intermediate form of the source program. It has **2-advantages** – 1. It facilitates optimization of object code

2. It allows a logical separation between machine-independent phases (lexical, syntax etc) and machine dependent phases (code generation and assembly).

One intermediate form of an arithmetic statement is a parse tree. Consider arithmetic statement: COST = RATE * (START – FINISH) + 2 * Rate * (START – FINISH – 100);

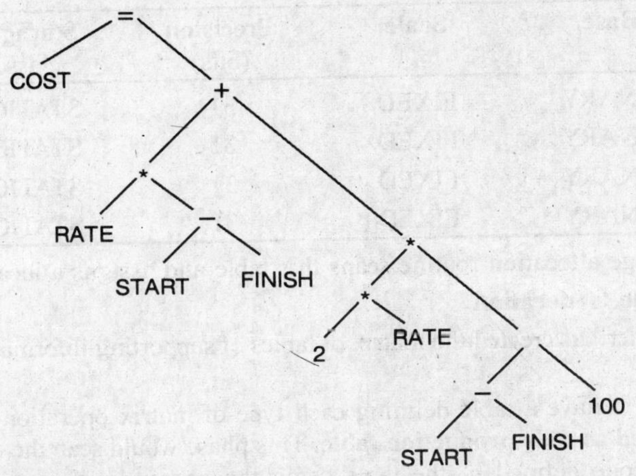

Rules are followed here:

1. Any variable is a terminal node of the tree.
2. For every operator, construct a binary tree whose left branch is a tree for operand-1 and whose right branch is the tree for operand-2.

Similarly arithmetic & non-arithmetic statements are stored in matrix form, as shown:

Matrix line no.	Operator	Operand1	Operand2	
1	-	START	FINISH	
2	*	RATE	M1	(Inter result)
3	*	2	RATE	
4	-	START	FINISH	
5	-	M4	100	
6	*	M3	M5	(intermediate result)
7	+	M2	M6	
8	=	COST	M7	

The above table is the matrix form representation of arithmetic statements. Similarly, for non-arithmetic statements, example matrix is:

Matrix

Source		Operator	Operand1	Operand2
RETURN (COST);	→	Return	Cost	
END;	→	End		

Similarly, non-executable statements like DECLARE are also entered into tables, to be used by other parts of the compiler.

Problem No. 3: Storage Allocation

In Declare statement given below:

DECLARE (COST, RATE, START, FINISH) FIXED BINARY (31) STATIC

The interpretation phase constructs the identifier table as shown below:

Name	Base	Scale	Precision (bits)	Storage class	Location
COST	BINARY	FIXED	31	STATIC	0
RATE	BINARY	FIXED	31	STATIC	4
START	BINARY	FIXED	31	STATIC	8
FINISH	BINARY	FIXED	31	STATIC	12

Then, the storage allocation routine scans this table and assigns a location to each scaler.

Problem No. 4: Code Generation

Once the compiler has created the matrix of tables of supporting information, it may generate the object code.

One scheme is to have a table defining each type of matrix operation with the associated object code. **It is called as code production table.** This phase would scan the matrix and generate, for each entry, the code defined in the table using the operands of matrix entries to further specialize the code. **"One way to view this scheme is that we are treating operators in matrix as macro-calls, operands as arguments and the production table as macro definitions.** Say, standard code definitions for -, *, +, = are as follows

```
-  L    1, & OPERAND1
   S    1, & OPERAND2
   ST   1, M & N
-----------------------
*  L    1, & OPERAND1
   M    0, & OPERAND2
   ST   1, M & N
-----------------------
+  L    1, & OPERAND1
   A    1, & OPERAND2
   ST   1, M & N
-----------------------
=  L    1, & OPERAND2
   ST   1, & OPERAND1
```

where, & OPERAND1 is the first operand of matrix & OPERAND2 is the second operand, & N is line number of matrix entry being examined.

For eg:

MATRIX:		**Generated code**	
1.	– START FINISH	L	1, START
		S	1, FINISH
		ST	1, M1
2.	* RATE M1	L	1, RATE
		M	0, M1
		ST	1, M2
3.	* 2 RATE	L	1, F'2'
		M	0, RATE
		ST	1, M3
4.	– START FINISH	L	1, START
		S	1, FINISH
		ST	1, M4

5.	– M4 100	L	1, M4
		S	1, = F' 100'
		ST	1, M5
6.	* M3 M5	L	1, M3
		M	0, M5
		ST	1, M6
7.	+ M2 M6	L	1, M2
		A	1, M6
		ST	1, M7
8.	= COST M7	L	1, M7
		ST	1, COST

But these are certain problems with above code. Aren't lines 1 and 4 redundant code. So, to solve this we try to do optimization — Elimination of common subexpressions. So, we now get:.

1.	–	Start	FINISH
2.	*	RATE	M1
3.	*	2	RATE
4.			
5.	–	M1	100
6.	*	M3	M5
7.	*	M2	M6
8.	=	COST	M7

Fig: Matrix after elimination of common subexpression.

This is **machine independent optimization,** which is done before we use the matrix as a basis for code generation. **Such a process is called optimization phase and is logically separated from code generation.**

11.14.4 General Model of Compiler

As shown in Figure 11.16 following are the phases of compiler

1. **Lexical analysis** – recognition of basic elements and creation of uniform symbols.
2. **Syntax analysis** – recognition of basic syntactic constructs through reductions.
3. **Interpretation** – definition of exact meaning, creation of matrix and tables by action routines.
4. **Machine Independent optimization** – creation of more optimal matrix.
5. **Storage assignment** – modification of identifier and literal tables. It makes entries in the matrix that allow code generation to create code that allocates dynamic storage and also allow the assembly phase to reserve the proper amounts of static storage.
6. **Code generation** – use of microprocessor to produce more optimal assembly code.
7. **Assembly and output-resolving symbolic address** (labels) and generating machine language.

Also, **following databases are used by the compiler:**

1. **Source code** – forms lines of communication between phase.
2. **Uniform symbol table** – consists of a full or partial list of tokens as they appear in program created by lexical analysis and used for syntax analysis.
3. **Terminal table** – a permanent table which lists all keywords and special symbols of language in symbolic form.

4. **Identifier table** – contains all variables in the program, temporary storages, if any, and any information needed to allocate storage for them.
5. **Literal tables**- contains all constants in the program.
6. **Reductions** – permanent table of decision rules in form of patterns for matching to discover syntactic structure.
7. **Matrix** – intermediate form of the program which is created by the action routines, optimized and then used for code generation.
8. **Code productions** – permanent table of definition. There is one entry defining code for each possible matrix operator.
9. **Assembly code** – assembly language version of the program which is created by the code generation phase and is input to the assembly phase.
10. **Relocatable object code-final** output of the assembly phase, ready to be used as input to loader.

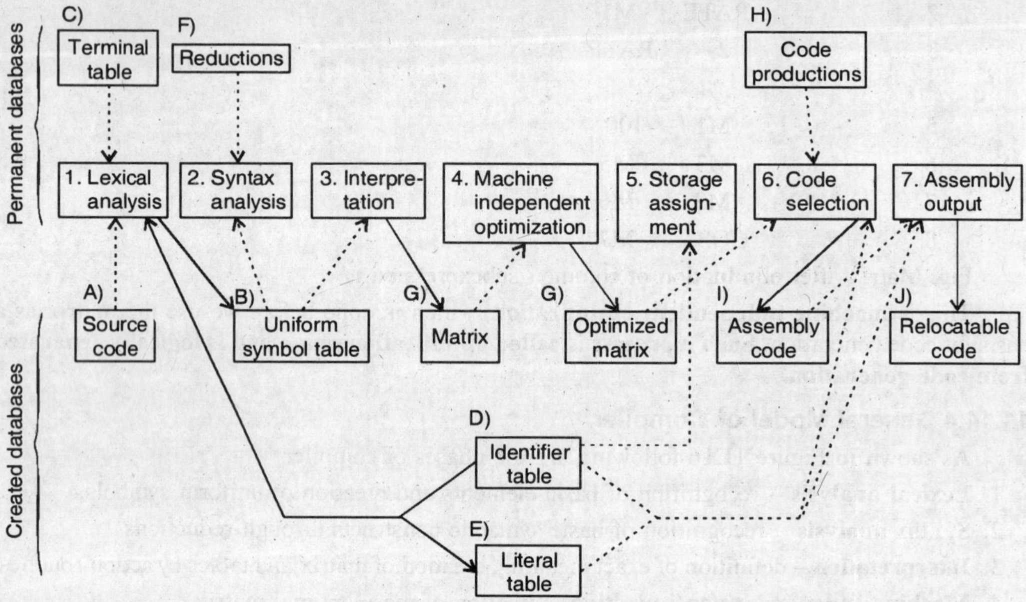

Fig. 11.16 Structure of a compiler

- Solid lines indicate creation of data.
- Dashed lines indicate references.
- Phases of compiler communicate by databases.

11.14.5 Phases of the compiler

Phase I. Lexical:

Tasks: The three tasks of the lexical analysis phase are:

1. To parse the source program into the basic element or tokens of the language.
2. To build a literal table and an identifier table.
3. To build a uniform symbol table.

Databases: These tasks involve manipulations of five databases. Possible forms for these are:

1. **Source program** – original form of program; appears to the compiler as a string of characters.

2. **Terminal table** – a permanent database that has an entry for each terminal symbol eg. Arithmetic operators, keywords, non-alphameric symbols. Each entry consists of the terminal symbol, an indication of its classification (like operator, break character) and its precedence.

Symbol	Indicator	Precedence

Fig. 11.17 Terminal table entry

3. **Literal table** – created by lexical analysis to describe all literals used in the source program.

Literal	Base	Scale	Precision	Other information	Address

Fig. 11.18 Literal table entry

The attributes of this table such as data type or precision, can be deduced from the literal itself and filled in by lexical analysis.

4. **Identifier table** – created by lexical analysis to describe all identifiers used in the source program. It creates the entry and places the name of identifier into that entry.

Name	Data attributes	Address

Identifier table entry

5. **Uniform symbol table** – created by lexical analysis to represent the program as a string of tokens rather than of individual characters.

Table	Index

Fig. 11.19 Uniform symbol table entry

ALGORITHM: The first task of lexical analysis algorithm is to phase the input character string into tokens. The second is to make the appropriate entries in the tables. **A "token" is a substring of the input string that represents a basic element of the language.** Lexical analysis recognizes three types of tokens: terminal symbols, possible identifiers and literals; and puts them accordingly in the tables.

Phase II. Syntax: The function of this phase is to recognize the major constructs of the language and to call the appropriate action routines that will generate the intermediate form or matrix for these constructs.

Databases: Uniform symbol table – created by phase-I and containing the source program in the form of uniform symbols. It is used by the syntax and interpretation phases as the source of input to stack. Each symbol from the US-table enters the stack only once.

Stack – is a collection of uniform symbols that is currently being worked on by the syntax analysis and interpretation phases.

Reductions – the syntax rules of the source language are contained in the reduction table. The syntax analysis phase is an interpreter driven by the reductions.

Phase III. Interpretation: It is typically a collection of routines that are called when a construct is recognized in the syntactic phase. The purpose of these routines (called **action routines)** is to create an intermediate form of the source program and add information to the identifier table.

The syntactic phase actually recognizes syntactic constructs while this phase interprets the precise meaning into the matrix or identifier table.

Databases:

- Uniform symbol table is used
- **Stack** – contains the tokens currently being parsed by the syntax and interpretation phases.
- **Identifier table** – Previous phase enters the identifiers in name field while this phase enters all the attributes. This information is used later for generating appropriate code.
- **Matrix** – the primary intermediate form of program. There are **two reasons** for having a matrix:

(1) It allows the first four phases of the compiler to be machine-independent.

(2) It allows machine – independent optimization of the program to occur before the code generation phase.

ALGORITHM:

There is no one algorithm for this phase since it is a collection of individual action routines that accomplish specific tasks when involved by syntax analysis phase. In particular these routines may:

(1) Do any necessary additional parsing.

(2) Create new entries in the matrix.

Phase-IV: Optimization phase

Databases used:

Matrix – is the major database used by the optimization phase. To facilitate the elimination or insertion of entries into the matrix, we add to each entry, forward and backward pointers. It helps in easy addition or deletion of duplicate entries as the order is maintained. A matrix entry new looks like:

Operator	Operand 1	Operand 2	Forward pointer	Backward pointer

Algorithm: These are 4 algorithms for 4 optimization techniques:

1. Elimination of common sub expressions.
2. Compile time compute: Doing computations involving constants at compile time saves both space execution time for the object program.
3. Boolean expression optimization:

eg. If *a* OR *b* OR *c* THEN

End if

Rather than testing each part of operator OR, we just test only one condition, say *a*, then *b* or *c* are not computed.

4. More invariant computations outside the loops.

If a computation within a loop depends on a variable that does not change within that loop, the computation may be moved outside the loop.

Phase V: Storage Assignment phase-

The purpose of this phase is to:

1. Assign storage to all variables referenced in the source program.
2. Assign storage to all temporary locations that are necessary for intermediate results.
3. Assign storage to literals.
4. Ensure that the storage is allocated and appropriate locations are initialized.

Databases:

Identifier table – created by lexical analysis and furnished with all attribute entries by interpretation phase. Storage assignment designates locations to all identifiers that denote data. The next two phases will use this information.

Temporary storage table – created by the interpretation phase to describe the temporary results of computations in the matrix.

Literal table – This phase assigns all literal addresses and places an entry in the matrix to denote that code generation should allocate this storage.

Matrix – Storage assignment places entries into the matrix to ensure that code generation creates enough storage for identifiers, temporary storage and literals. It also ensures that the appropriate ones are initialized.

IBM-360 machine uses a register pointing to the beginning of each storage block.

Register-1	→	Static storage area & literals

This requires storage assignment to calculate only the offsets for all static storage. The code generate phase will 1) Use these offsets to generate the address used in instructions and 2) generate appropriate code that will load a register with a pointer to appropriate storage block at execution time and before that storage is accessed.

The storage allocation phase first scans through the identifier table, assigning locations to each entry with a storage class of static. It uses a LC, initialized at zero, to keep track of how much storage it has assigned.

This allows code generation to generate the proper amount of storage. For each variable that requires initialization, the storage allocation phase generates a matrix entry:

Initialize	Variable	

This tells code generation to put into the proper storage location the initial value that the action routines saved in the identifier table.

A similar scan of the identifier table is made for automatic storage and controlled storage. The scan enters relative locations for each entry code generation than uses the relative location entry to generate the address part of instructions. No storage is generated at the compile time.

Phase VI: Code Generation

Purpose of the code generation phase is to produce the appropriate code (assembly or machine lang.)

Databases:

Matrix – each entry has its operator defined in the code pattern database. In other words, the operator of each entry serves as a macro with the operand as arguments.

Identifier table, literal table – are used to determine the data type and locations of the variables (operand of the matrix) so that proper accessing code with the correct address is generated.

Code productions (macro definition) – a permanent database defining all possible matrix operators. We have already drawn the code production table for the operators -, *, +, =. We will redefine the + operator using an enhanced code production language to allow some machine-dependent optimization.

Algorithm: We implement code generation process in same way as that for the assembler macroprocessor.

Phase-VII: Assembly Phase

The task of the assembly phase depends on how much has been done in code generation. If lot of work has been done in code generation, then the assembly phase must resolve label references in the object program, format the object deck and format the appropriate information for the loader. This phase must (1) resolve label references (2) calculate addresses (3) generate binary machine instructions and (4) generate storage.

Databases: (1) Identifier table – This phase uses this database to enter the value of all labels into the identifier table **(2) Literal table** – To place the literals on appropriate TXT card. **(3) Object code** – The output of the code – generation.

ALGORITHM: This phase scans the object code, resolving all label references and producing the TXT cards. It then scans the identifier table to create the ESD cards. The RLD cards are created using the object code, ESD cards and the identifier table.

Summary

System Software Support the operation of the computers. For example: Compilers, assemblers, loaders, linkers, O.S. are system softwares. This chapter discusses about these system softwares about their design and data structures used.

MULTIPLE-CHOICE QUESTIONS (MCQs)

1. BIU stands for-
(*a*) Bus Internal Unit (*b*) Bus Interface Unit
(*c*) Bus Idea Unit (*d*) None of the above

2. ACF is a
(*a*) Register (*b*) Flag
(*c*)Accumulator (*d*) None of the above

3. MOV AX, 200 represents:-
(*a*) Immediate Addressing Mode (*b*) Implicit Addressing Mode
(*c*) Direct Addressing Mode (*d*) None of the above

4. RISC stands for-
(*a*) Real Instruction Set Computer (*b*) Reduced Instruction Set Computer
(*c*) Reduced Internal Set Computer (*d*) None of the above

5. *i*860 is a-
(*a*) RISC (*b*) CISC
(*c*) Supercomputer (*d*) None of the above

6. USING is a
(*a*) Macro (*b*) Microinstruction
(*c*) Pseudo-op (*d*) None of the above

7. POT stands for-
(*a*) Parent Operation Table (*b*) Pseudo Operation Table
(*c*) Preliminary Opcode Table (*d*) None of the above

8. IBM-360 has-
(*a*) 16 GPRs (*b*) 17 GPRs
(*c*) 18 GPRs (*d*) 19 GPRs

9. "Compile-and-go" is an-
(*a*) Assembler (*b*) Linker
(*c*) Loading Scheme (*d*) None of the above

10. A simple binder is-
(*a*) Core-image builder (*b*) C-compiler
(*c*) JAVA-compiler (*d*) None of the above

11. Arguments to a macro call can be ______
(*a*) Positional only (*b*) Keyword only
(*c*) Both '*a*' and '*b*' (*d*) None of the above

12. MDTP stands for ______
(*a*) Macro domain Table pointer (*b*) Macro definition Table pointer
(*c*) Macro defined Table pointer (*d*) None of the above

13. Compiler's design involves ______
(*a*) 7 phases (*b*) 8 phases
(*c*) 6 phases (*d*) None of the above

14. Compilers use ______
(*a*) Databases (*b*) Lists
(*c*) op-codes (*d*) None of the above

15. Parsing is the job of ______
(*a*) Syntax phase (*b*) Lexical phase
(*c*) Assembly phase (*d*) None of the above

ANSWERS

1. *b*	**2.** *b*	**3.** *a*	**4.** *b*	**5.** *a*	**6.** *c*
7. *b*	**8.** *a*	**9.** *c*	**10.** *a*	**11.** *c*	**12.** *b*
13. *a*	**14.** *a*	**15.** *b*			

CONCEPTUAL SHORT QUESTIONS WITH ANSWERS

Q.1. Compare the compiler and an interpreter ?

Ans. The comparison between a compiler and an interpreter is given below:-

Compiler	Interpreter
1. It converts the whole program into the machine code and then executes into one.	1. It converts the program into the machine code one step at a time and then runs only that very step
2. All errors are listed together after compilation	2. If there is any error at any line of the program then it will be displayed immediately after the translation of the line.
3 Execution time is less.	3. Execution time is more.
4. It is slow for debugging.	4. It is good for fast debugging
5. Only one .EXE file is created.	5. No .EXE file is created
For example: C/C++ compilers, TC compiler COBOL compilers etc.	**For example:** VB 6.0 interpreter.

Q.2. Compare a linker and linkage editor in a tabular form.

Ans.

Linker	Linkage Editor
1. Linking of object modules and necessary libraries are done and immediately loaded into main memory.	1. Linking of object modules and necessary libraries are done and stored in a file or library. The output is called is a **linked program.**
2. It is used only once.	2. It can be used many a times.
3. Library search and resolution of external reference is done each time once.	3. Library Search and resolution of external reference must be done only once.
4. This type of linking is not suitable for program which is executed repeatedly.	4. This is very much suitable for program which is executed repeatedly.

Q.3. Define what is a flipper?

Ans. The portion of the loader that actually intercepts the "calls" and loads the necessary procedure is called as an **Overlay Supervisor or flipper.**

Q.4. Name some commonly used assemblers?

Ans. (*a*) Intel 8086 macro assembler (ASM 86)

(*b*) Borland Turbo Assembler (TASM)

(*c*) IBM Macro Assembler (MASM)

Q.5. Compare machine language, assembly language and high level languages.

Ans.

Machine language	Assembly language	High level language
1. Programs written in machine language are difficult to write, debug and understand.	1. Programs in assembly language are less difficult than machine language.	1. Programs in high level language are easy to write, debug and understand.
2. Programs are not portable.	2. Programs are not portable	2. Programs are portable.
3. Programmer has to keep track of memory addresses.	3. Programmer has to keep track of the memory addresses	3. No need to keep track of memory addresses
4. No translator is required to convert into machine code.	4. No translator is required to convert into machine code	4. Compiler or interpreter is required.
5. The execution of programs is very fast.	5. The execution of programs is slower than machine language programs.	5. The execution of program is slower than high level language programs.

EXERCISE QUESTIONS

Q.1. Describe the usage of the following commands:

(a) mov (b) add (c) sub (d) and (e) cmp

(f) jmp (g) or (h) je and jne (i) brk (j) get

Q.2. (a) Compare and contrast RISC and CISC machines on their architecture, programming facilities and memory management.

(b) Describe the working of a single pass assembler.

Q.3. (a) Write a Intel 8086 assembly code (for an assembler of your choice, specify the assembler) to write the message "Hello World" to the screen.

(b) Write an assembly subroutine/macro to multiply two integers by repetitive addition.

Q.4. What do you understand by the following terms (explain in brief)
(a) Re-locatable code (b) Boot strap loader
(c) Static and Dynamic linking

Q.5. Explain the following terms (in brief) in context to macro-processors:
(a) Concatenation of macro parameter. (b) Unique label generation
(c) Recursive macro expansion

Q.6. Explain the following terms with examples:
(a) Terminal symbols (b) Alphabet Set
(c) The null string (d) Production Rules
(e) Regular languages

Q.7. Describe the architecture of a compiler with a brief explanation of the working at every stage of compilation

Q.8. Write notes on **any three** of the following:
(a) Code optimization (b) 8086 optimization
(c) Interpreters (d) LEX & YACC
(e) Multi-pass Assembler

Q.9. Explain Any Ten of the following:-
(a) Features of RISC machine (b) Features of CISC machine
(c) Compiler and Interpreter (d) Top down Parsing
(e) Label as an argument to macro (f) Conditional Macro expansion
(g) Macro calls within macros (h) Macro instructions defining macros
(i) Absolute loaders (j) Relocating loaders
(k) Dynamic loading (l) Dynamic linking

Q.10. Explain the different tasks performed by a two pass assembler, with the help of a flow-chart.

Q.11. Write notes on lex and yacc utilities.

Q.12. Generate IBM-360 assembly code corresponding to the following statement and perform all possible optimization over it.
Result = ((A–C) * C) / 10 + E* (C–A)–(A–C+B)
Assume that registers 1-6 are available for computation

Q.13. Write with examples all the addressing modes in 8086.

Q.14. (a) Draw a finite automata for a C language identifier.
(b) Generate the parse-tree for the C statement
$$a = (b + c) \times 5 - c/d$$

Q.15. Write the meaning of the mnemories
(a) MOVS (b) SCAS (c) SAR
(d) STOS (e) SAHF

Q.16. Write an assembly language program (8086 codes)
(a) To read a character from the keyboard and to print it.
(b) To read a two digited integer from keyboard and to print it's square.

Q.17. (a) Define the following:-
(i) Assembler (ii) Loader
(iii) Macro (iv) Formal system
(b) Draw the micro flowchart for *ADD* instruction ADD 8, 101. Where 8 is a register number and 101 is the memory location?
(c) Explain the different instruction formats of IBM 360 machine.

Q.18. (a) Write a IBM 360 Assembly Language program to compute the function
$$A = 2 * B + 2 * C - 1$$
(b) What is the difference between :

(i) INDEX EQU 5 and
INDEX DC F'5'.
(ii) CR and CLR instruction.

(c) What is the difference between:
(i) Processor, Procedure (ii) Procedure, Program
(iii) Processor, I/O channel (iv) Multiprocessing, Multiprogramming

Q.19. (a) Give the over view flowchart and explain Pass-2 of a Two pass Assembler
(b) For the following program give the assembled output and relevant entries in the database tables:

```
MORE      START
          BALE 15,0
          USING *,15
          L4, = F'3'
IN        L R1, CONST 1
          A R1, CONST 1
          ST R1, CONST 2
          CLI CONST 2 + 4, 8
          BNE IN
          BCT4, IN
R1        EQU 1
CONST 1   DC R'4'
CONST 2   DS F
          END
```

Q.20 (a) What is Hashing? What are the advantages of Hashing? Explain in brief, the different algorithms used to resolve address conflicts during insertion.
(b) Explain with examples, the different ways of defining MACROS.

Q.21. (a) Why are MACROS processed in two passes, usually? Explain in brief the different functions carried out by Pass-1 and Pass-2 of a Macro-processor, separately.
(b) What is the difference between MACRO and subroutines w.r.t execution speed, memory and program efficiency?
(c) Explain the importance of using index markers in the creation of a Macro definition table.

Q.22. (a) List the different functions of a, general Loading Scheme. Explain with an example, how these functions are implemented in a Relocatable loader.
(b) What are the advantages of incorporating:
(i) Dynamic Loading; and (ii) Dynamic Linking
(c) What relevant information do the four types of cards in Direct Linking Loader convey?

Q.23. (a) Consider the following segments of a program:

```
        SEGMENT 1                      SEGMENT 2
SLN     START 0              GRADER    START 0
        EXTRN A, C2                    ENTRY C2
        BALR 15, 0                     BALR 15, 0
        USING *, 15                    USING *, 15
        SR 4, 4                        SR 4,4
        SLL 1,2                        L 6, C3
        L0, ANS (1)                    ST 1, C3 + 4
        BR 14                          LA 1, C3
        DC A (A + 10)                  L2, JOHNSON
CODE    DC 2C' JJ'           JOHNSON   BR 14
        DC AC (2)            C2        DC A (GRADER)
```

```
        DC 12C'2'        C3        DC8F'3'
ANS     DC 5H'0'                   END
        END
```

Prepare ESD, TXT, RLD and END cards for the above program segments in a DLL scheme.

(b) List the different phases of a compiler and explain their functions

Q24. Write short notes on (any *four*) :

(i) Subroutine Linkages. (ii) Absolute Loader.
(iii) Optimization in Compiler Design. (iv) Intermediate Code.
(v) Databases used by compiler.

Q.25. (a) What do you understand by the term "systems programming"? Explain in brief the activities of a system programmer.

(b) Distinguish between the following:-
(i) Processor and procedure. (ii) Pure procedures and impure procedures.

(c) What is job control language? Explain in brief its usage.

Q.26. (a) What are the advantages of the IBM 360's multiple register scheme over machines with fewer or specialized registers? Explain in brief.

(b) List the different IMB 360 instruction formats and explain in brief the way of computing effective memory address in each case.

(c) Give the usage of following operations in programming an IBM 360 machine:
(i) USING (ii) BALR; (iii) BCT; and (iv) CD.

Q.27. (a) What feature of assembly language requires a two pass assembler? Compare single pass and two pass assemblers.

(b) List tables of information maintained by an assembler during pass 1 and pass 2. Give the structure of each table.

(c) What is pseudo operation? Clearly bring their need in the design of assembler.

Q.28. (a) Define the following terms:
(i) Searching; (ii) Sorting; and (iii) Hashing.

(b) What is the difference between searching and sorting ? List few good searching and sorting techniques that are widely used and compare them.

(c) Why must the operand field of the EQU pseudo-op be evaluated in pass 1?

Q.29. (a) Why does an assembly language programmer used macros? Explain the definition and usage of macros.

(b) Explain the following-
(i) Macro instructions defining macros
(ii) Macro calls within macros

(c) Is the design of macroprocessor dependent on assembler source code format? Justify your answer.

Q.30. (a) What is a loader? Enumerate different types of loaders.

(b) List the advantages of the following:-
(i) binding at load time over assembly time.
(ii) binding at load time over execution time.

(c) Describe the function of each of the RLD, ESD, TXT and END cards.

Q.31. (a) What is the purpose of the ID number in ESD cards? Why is it not needed for locally defined symbols? Explain in brief.

(b) Is there a difference between binder and DLL? Justify your answer.

(c) Enumerate different phases of compiler. Explain what do you understand by code optimization.

Q.32. Write adequate notes on:

(a) Different data formats on IBM 360. (b) Use of DS and DC pseudo-ops.
(c) Macro name and Definition tables. (d) Subroutine linkages.

CHAPTER

12

Protection

12.0 INTRODUCTION

Organizations must be concerned with the inherent security threats associated with the systems and the business that are done on web. The unauthorized user access, data tampering and eaves dropping are very common. The solution is to provide user authentication, encryption of data and access control to all information. Today, millions of persons are using networks for banking, shopping to handle their financial and personal data, so security is mandatory. With the advent of distributed systems, security became another challenge.

12.1 GOAL OF PROTECTION

The main goal of protection is to prevent accidental and intentional destructive behaviour in multiprogramming systems. In these systems, the OS should enable the users to safely share a common logical address space like files as well as a common physical address space like memory.

Another goal of protection is to ensure fair and reliable resource usage i.e., each program component active in a system should use the system resources only in accordance with certain policies. Now the policies for a resource usage may vary. So, the protection mechanisms should be provided as tools for the enforcement of these varying policies.

12.2 MECHANISMS AND POLICIES

Mechanisms determine how to do something whereas **policies** decide what will be done and not how it will be done. The processes are subjected to policies that govern the use of resources so as to ensure orderly and efficient operation of a system. The role of protection in a system is to provide a mechanism for the enforcement of the policies. Policies are likely to change from place to place or time to time.

12.3 DOMAIN OF PROTECTION

The concept of protection domain specifies a set of objects and types of operations that may be performed on each object. A protection domain is a collection of access rights and each is a pair of (object identifier, right set). Domain need not be static. Elements of the domain can change because objects are deleted or created and the access rights are modified. **Please remember that domains may overlap; meaning that a single object can participate in multiple domains with different access rights given there.** A process executes in a protection domain at a point in time. **This binding is not static.** The process may switch between different protection domains during execution.

12.4 ACCESS MATRIX

The protection mechanism is different for primary and secondary memory. A computer system consists of a set of processes that operate on and manipulate a set of objects. Like, file is a software object.

From the software point of view, each object is an abstract data type. The operations on an object may transform the state of object. The protection procedure should ensure that–

(1) No process is allowed to apply a function in appropriate to a given object type.

(2) Each process is permitted to apply only those functions that are explicitly authorized for a specific object.

The authority to execute an operation on an object is called as access rights. We use the concept of **protection domain** which specifies a set of objects and types of operations that may be performed on each object. A protection domain is a collection of access rights and each is a pair of (object identifier, right set).

There is a concept of **access matrix** which represents all access right of all the objects in computer system. It is shown by a 2D–Matrix. It includes both hardware and software objects.

Domain \ Object	F1	F2	F3	Printer
D1	Read Write		Execute	Output
D2		Read		
D3			Read Write	Output

F:File

Fig. 12.1 Access Matrix Control technique

In Fig. 12.1, the blank entries are indicating no access rights. A process is executing in domain D1 and D2 can only read the object File–2 (F2). File–3 (F3) is sharing in domain D3 and is also executable in domain D1.

It is a useful model. But this matrix is not sufficient to store all access rights, captured and expressed in it. There are some access control mechanisms. They are discussed below.

12.5 IMPLEMENTATION OF ACCESS MATRIX

I. Access Hierarchies

When a user program needs to perform an operation outside of its protection domain then it calls for the OS. **Please note that at the control transfer point, (like the supervisor call instruction) the OS can check the user's authority and grant or deny execution accordingly.**

There are some protection rings that are used to define a domain of access. **Please note that at any given time, each process runs in a specific protection ring.** The range is $(0, r–1)$. These are used in multics. **Also note that the access privilege of ring–*j* are a subject of ring–*i* for**

$$0 \leq i \leq j \leq r-1$$

This is shown in Fig 12.2

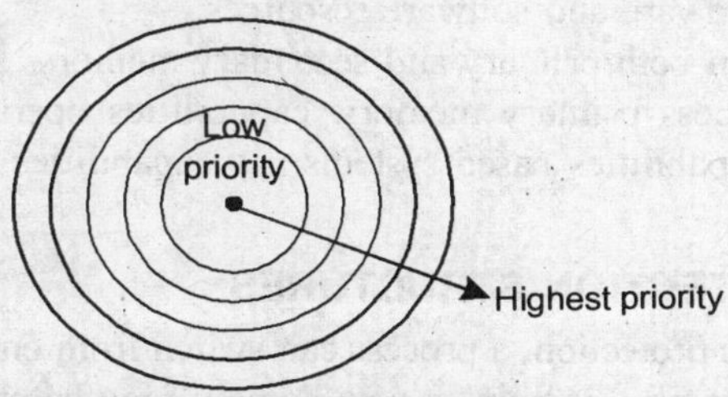

Fig. 12.2 Protection Rings

Here, inner rings have higher access rights protection barriers. Some calls are invoked by hardware when a lesser privileged outer ring needs to call on a service running in an inner/more privileged ring.

This concept of access hierarchy is not unique. It is used in software also. A block of structured language is shown below in Fig. 12.3

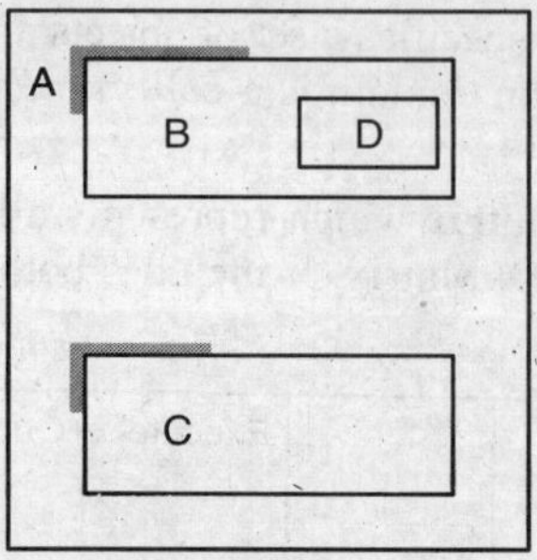

Fig. 12.3 Blocked structure Language

Herein, the identifiers declared in block A are accessible in all of A's nested blocks. A statement contained in inner block D may legally reference all identifiers declared in D's outer blocks A and B but not to the disjoint block C. Statements in block A don't have access to variable declared in blocks B and D. Also, the variables declared in block D can't be accessed from block B.

II. Access Lists

An access list is an exhaustive enumeration of the specific access rights of all entities (domains) that are authorized access to a given object.

What is an access List?

An access list for a specific object is a list that contains all nonempty cells of a column of access matrix associated with a given object. Many variations of the access list scheme are used to store access information in file systems. Access lists may be combined with other schemes also in order to strengthen the protection. When the number of authorized users are large then some systems divide lesers into group and store only the aggregate group access rights. This saves storage space.

III. Capability Lists

Instead of storing and maintaining access lists per object, the system can also maintain access rights list per subject. These systems combine addressing and protection functions in a single mechanism that is used to access all system objects. It is a token (or ticket) that gives permission to access a specific object in a specified manner. Various capability mechanisms are–

(1) Address both primary and secondary memory.

(2) Access both hardware and software resources.

(3) Protect objects in both primary and secondary memory.

When used to access primary memory, capabilities operate in a manner similar to the segmentation. These capabilities based systems use capabilities stored in a capability lists with access rights.

12.6 DYNAMIC PROTECTION STRUCTURES

In case of dynamic protection, a process can switch from one domain to another. So, instead of changing the contents of a domain, a new domain may be created with the changed content and the process may be switched to this new domain.

12.7 PROTECTION AND SECURITY ISSUES

Various processes must be protected from one other's activities. The **protection** mechanisms deal with controlling the access of programs, processes or users to the resources of a computer system.

Security is an issue that requires a control over the external environment within which the system operates. Mechanisms are needed to protect the external environment of a system. Security violations of a system may be either accidental or intentional. Accidental misuse is easier to protect rather than intentional misuse.

Newer OSs like WIN–NT, 2000 provide the needed security issues.

12.8 CRYPTOGRAPHIC TECHNIQUES

What is Cryptography?

Cryptography is defined as an art of achieving security by enclosing messages to make them non-readable.

For example, Encryption is a cryptography technique. **Encryption is defined as the process of conversion of the plaintext (original message) into the ciphertext (coded message).** It is also named as **enciphering. The reverse process of conversion of ciphertext to the plaintext is known as decryption or deciphering. The art of devising the ciphers is called as cryptography and the art of breaking the cipher is known as Cryptoanalysis.**

Also note that–

Cryptography + Cryptoanalysis = Cryptology

There are **two types** of crypto-systems—**Secret-key and public-key.**

In **secret-key cryptography** or **symmetric cryptography,** the same key is used for both **encryption** and **decryption. For example,** IBM in 1970 developed a secret-key cryptosystem named as **DES-Data Encryption Standard.**

In **public-key cryptography** or **asymmetric crytography,** each user has a public key and a private key.

The public key is made public while the private key remains secret. **Encryption is done with the public key while decryption is done with the private key. For example,** RSA–Rivest, Shamir and Adleman (after inventors names) is a public key cryptosystem.

How encryption works?

Encryption or encoding of the information helps prevent it by unauthorized user. Both the sender and the receiver have to know what set of rules (called cipher) was used to transform original information into its cipher text (code) form–cipher text.

A simple cipher might be to add an arbitrary number of characters to all the characters in the message.

For example, Say,

"Udupa" – is the original name

"Irida" – is the cipher text

(arbitrary no. chosen is "12")

1 2 3 4 5 6 7 8 9 10 11 12

A B C D E F G H I J K L M N O P Q R S T U V W X Y Z

Now, to decrypt (decode) "Irida" first start counting from letter "I" and replace the letter "I" in the coded text with the letter which comes after the count 12. So, "I" is replaced by "U". Similarly, for other letters this process is repeated and finally we get the original text as Udupa. **Please note here that both the sender and the receiver has to know the arbitrary number chosen in order to encrypt and decrypt the original message.**

Asymmetric cryptographic algorithms are computationally slow. One **way hash functions** or **fast cryptographic algorithms** are used to convert a message of any length into a **single string of digits** called as a **message digest.** This **message digest** is then **encrypted** with a **private key** to form **digital signature**. So, the overall process is–

$$\text{(Hash function} \rightarrow \text{Message Digest)} \xrightarrow[\text{with private key}]{\text{Encrypted}} \text{Digital signature.}$$

12.9 INTRODUCTION TO DISTRIBUTED SYSTEMS

The distributed system is a system which looks like an ordinary centralized OS but runs on multiple CPUs. It consists of several computers that **do not share** the memory or a clock. All computers communicate with each other by a **common communication network. Each computer contains its own memory and CPU.** It seems to be a uniprocessor only to a user but is actually a collection of distinct machines. Each computer owns its own local resources. They have access to resources of other machine also i.e., remote resources. **Please note that the distributed OS allows a program to run on several CPUs at the same time.** So, effective CPU scheduling is needed. **Also note that the basic idea behind the development of these distributed system was the development of cost effective powerful microprocessors useful for significant communications.**

Features of a distributed system

Some common features of a distributed systems are as follows–

(1) Resource sharing (local and Remote)
(2) Quick response time
(3) High throughputs
(4) High reliability
(5) Easily expandable (or Modular expansion)

All this is possible due to simultaneous execution of many processes at different computers. The failure of one components of the system will not affect the entire system.

The Distributed Systems are put under three categories–

(1) Mini Computer Model
(2) Workstation Model
(3) Processor Pool Model

A Minicomputer Model of distributed system architecture consists of several Mini computers (like VAX). Each minicomputer supports the handling of multiple users and provides an easy access to all the resources present in the communication network. Remote access to other computer resources is also possible. Many processors process the same job concurrently on different machines.

A workstation model consists of many workstations interconnected together (several thousands). Each workstation is provided to one user. A user can access the data of any workstation present in the Distributed System environment.

Please note that the number of processors (CPU) and the number of users in the architecture environment are normally equal. Also note that each workstation has its own processor, memory, coprocessor and disk storage.

For example: Athena, Andrew are common distributed OS using this model.

A processor-pool model is used to allocate one or more processor to a single user. Herein, **the number of processors is greater than the number of users.** A user can request more than one CPU also at a time. When a user task is over, the CPU is free now to work with another user. This creates a **Pool for the processors.** The user has complete access to the processor pool. This increases the running speed of the application.

For example, Amoeba (a distributed OS) uses this approach.

Design issues of Distributed OS

Knowledge, naming, compatibility, scalability, synchronization, resource management and security are some of the design issues to be considered when we design a distributed system.

SUMMARY

Various protection and Security Mechanisms have been dealt in this Chapter. Cryptography has been explained. A distributed OS is an ordinary, centralized OS but it can run on multiple independent CPUs.

MULTIPLE CHOICE QUESTIONS (MCQs)

(1) The main goal of protection is to–
   (*a*) Prevent accidental and intentional behaviour
   (*b*) Implement multiprogramming
   (*c*) Protect deadlocks
   (*d*) None of the above

(2) The process of conversion of plaintext to ciphertext is known as–
   (*a*) Encryption (*b*) Decryption
   (*c*) Hash function (*d*) None of the above

(3) The art of devising ciphers is called as–
   (*a*) Message digest (*b*) Hash functions
   (*c*) Cryptography (*d*) None of the above

(4) DES stands for–
   (*a*) Digital Equipment Standard (*b*) Data Encryption Standard
   (*c*) Domain Encryption Security (*d*) None of the above

(5) Hash functions are used to produce the message digests which are then encrypted with a private key to get–
   (*a*) Cipher text (*b*) Digital Signature
   (*c*) Public Key (*d*) None of the above

ANSWERS

1. *a* **2.** *a* **3.** *c* **4.** *b* **5.** *b*

CONCEPTUAL SHORT QUESTIONS WITH ANSWERS

Q.1 Consider a computing environment where a process is given the privilege of accessing an object only n–times. Suggest a scheme for implementing this policy.

Ans. Add an integer counter with the capability.

Q.2 Consider a computing environment where a unique number is associated with each process and each object in the system. Suppose that we allow a process with number n to access an object with number m only if n > m. What type of protection structure do we have?

Ans. Hierarchical structure.

Q.3. Capability lists are usually kept within the address space of the user. How does the system ensure that the user cannot modify the contents of the list?

Ans. A capability list is considered a **protected object** and is accessed only indirectly by the user. The OS ensures the user cannot access the capability list directly.

Q.4. Compare Access Lists and Capabilities Lists.

Ans. The differences between the Access Lists and the Capabilities list are given below

Access Lists	Capabilities Lists
(1) Each object (resource) has a list of pairs of the form– (Subject, access rights).	(1) Each Subject (user, process or procedure) has a list of pairs of the form– (object, access rights).
(2) They are grouped into classes.	(2) Capabilities are the names of the objects. The objects not referred to in a capability list cannot be even named.
(3) The default is that everyone should be able to access a file.	(3) The default is that no one should be able to access a file unless they have been given a capability.
(4) Access lists are simple and are used in almost all file systems.	(4) Capabilities are used in systems that need to be very secure.
(5) Access lists are one of the ways of recording access rights in a system.	(5) Capability based systems combine the addressing and protection functions in a single mechanism that is used to access all system objects.

Q.4. What is biometric authentication? What are its advantages and disadvantages?

Ans. Some user characteristics can be established by means of biometric techniques–

(*a*) **Physiological characteristics**

Like fingerprints, hand geometry, patterns in retina etc.

(*b*) **Behavioural characteristics**

Like voice pattern, signature dynamics and timing of keystrokes.

Please note that in general, behavioural characteristics can vary with a user's state. For example, signature dynamics and keystroke patterns may vary with user's stress level and fatigue.

The biometrics detection devices are self-contained and independent of the systen.

Advantages of biometrics authentication are–

(1) Increased accuracy of user authentication.

(2) Reduction of errors in security conscious environments.

Disadvantages of biometrics authentication are–

(1) Increased cost.

(2) Potential invasion of privacy.

(3) Reluctance of some users.

Q.5. Suppose that you share a file on a network with your friend so that he can copy this file from your system. What rights should be given on this file? What will be the contents of cell of access matrix corresponding to this grant?

Ans. **"Read–only"** right should be given to him. The access matrix cell will contain.

	File–1
Rahul	r

Where 'Rahul' is the name of your friend and file–1 is to be shared.

EXERCISE QUESTIONS

Q.1. Write short notes on – File protection and security.

Q.2. Explain different protection methods for file system in UNIX OS.

Q.3. What is an Access Control Matrix? What is Bell–La Padula access control model?

Q.4. How does distributed system ensure mutual exclusion. Explain with the help of a diagram.

Q.5. How can protection and security be achieved in an OS? Explain

Q.6. List and interpret the security policies and mechanisms involved in a computer system.

Q.7. The list of passwords is kept within the OS. If a user manages to read this list, password protection is no longer provided. Suggest a scheme that will avoid this problem.

[**Hint**: Encrypt the passwords internally so that they can only be accessed in the coded form. The only person with access or knowledge of decoding should be the system operator]

Q.8. Write the steps of RSA algorithm with example.

[**Hint:** RSA algorithm is based on number theory. Here, we have to calculate 'e' in the range [0, n–1] and again have to find a unique integer d in [0, n–1], like $e^d \bmod n = 1$

The algorithm is as follows–

S1: Consider two large primes p & q.

S2: Calculate $n = pq$ and $\phi(n) = (p-1)(q-1)$.

S3: Consider a number ϕ to be a large, random integer, that is relatively prime to $\phi(n)$ such that $gcd(d, d(n)) = 1$

S4: Find e such that $e^d \bmod (\phi(n)) = 1$

These parameters may be used to encipher plaintext, P, where $o < d < n$. If plaintext is longer, it must be broken into strings, smaller than n. Ciphertext is obtained as $C = P^e \bmod(n)$. C may be decrypted as $P = C^d \bmod(n)$. This algorithm shows that encryption and decryption are inverses of each other.

For example: Consider $p = 7$ and $q = 17$

$\therefore$ n = p.q = 7 * 17 = 119

$\therefore$ ϕ(n) = (p–1) (q–1)
= (7–1) (17–1)
= 6 * 16
= 96

e = 5

d = ?

Now, de = 1 mod 96

But ed = k ϕ (n) + 1 = M mod n

[From mod arithematic]

ed = k(96) + 1

Now, we need to select d such that we get it in form of equation–1, above i.e,

77 * 5 = 385 = 4 * 96 + 1

↑ $\phi(n)$ ↑ remainder

$\therefore$ d must be 77]

CHAPTER

13

Symbian OS – A CASE STUDY

ABSTRACT

Symbian OS is designed for the mobile phone environment. It addresses constraints of mobile phones by providing a framework to handle low memory situations, a power management model, and a rich software layer implementing industry standards for communications, telephony and data rendering. Even with these abundant features, Symbian OS puts no constraints on the integration of other peripheral hardware. This flexibility allows handset manufacturers to pursue innovative and original designs.

Symbian OS is proven on several platforms. It started life as the operating system for the Psion series of consumer PDA products (including Series 5mx, Revo and netBook), and various adaptations by Diamond, Oregon Scientific and Ericsson. The first dedicated mobile phone incorporating Symbian OS was the Ericsson R380 Smartphone, which incorporated a flip-open keypad to reveal a touch screen display and several connected applications. Most recently available is the Nokia 9210 Communicator, a mobile phone that has a QWERTY keyboard and color display, and is fully open to third-party applications written in Java or C++.

The five key points - small mobile devices, mass-market, intermittent wireless connectivity, diversity of products and an open platform for independent software developers - are the premises on which Symbian OS was designed and developed. This makes it distinct from any desktop, workstation or server operating system. This also makes Symbian OS different from embedded operating systems, or any of its competitors, which weren't designed with all these key points in mind.

Symbian is committed to open standards. Symbian OS has a POSIX-compliant interface and a Sun-approved JVM, and the company is actively working with emerging standards, such as J2ME, Bluetooth, MMS, SyncML, IPv6 and WCDMA. As well as its own developer support organization, books, papers and courses, Symbian delivers a global network of third-party competency and training centers - the Symbian Competence Centers and Symbian Training Centers. These are specifically directed at enabling other organizations and developers to take part in this new economy. Symbian has announced and implemented a strategy that will see Symbian OS running on many advanced open mobile phones.

INTRODUCTION

Small devices come in many shapes and sizes, each addressing distinct target markets that have different requirements. The market segment we are interested in is that of the mobile phone. The primary requirement of this market segment is that all products are great phones. This segment spans voice-centric phones with information capability to information-centric devices with voice capability. These advanced mobile phones integrate fully-featured personal digital assistant (PDA) capabilities with those of a traditional mobile phone in a single unit. There are several critical factors for the need of operating systems in this market. It is important to look at the mobile phone market in isolation. It has specific needs that make it unlike markets for PCs or fixed domestic appliances. Scaling down a PC operating system, or bolting communication capabilities onto a small and basic operating system, results in too many fundamental compromises. Symbian believes that the mobile phone market has five key characteristics that make it unique, and result in the need for a specifically designed operating system:

1. mobile phones are both small and mobile.
2. mobile phones are ubiquitous - they target a mass-market of consumer, enterprise and professional users.
3. mobile phones are occasionally connected - they can be used when connected to the wireless phone network, locally to other devices, or on their own.
4. manufacturers need to differentiate their products in order to innovate and compete in a fast-evolving market
5. the platform has to be open to enable independent technology and software vendors to develop third-party applications, technologies and services.

The way to grow the mobile phone market is to create good products - and the only way to create good products is to address each of these characteristics and ensure that technology doesn't limit functionality. Meeting the impressive growth forecast by analysts in a reasonable time frame is only possible with the right operating system.

Symbian and its licensees aim to create a mass market for advanced open mobile phones. To deliver products that *satisfy* mobile phone users, an operating system must be engineered to take into account key functional demands of advanced communications on 2.5G and 3G networks.

To fit into the limited amount of memory a mobile phone may have, the operating system must be compact. However, it must still provide a rich set of functionality. What is needed to power a mobile phone is not a mini-operating system but a different operating system - one that is tailored. Symbian is dedicated to mobile phones and Symbian OS has been designed to meet the sophisticated requirements of the mobile phone market that mini-operating systems can't. They simply run out of stream.

The five key points - small mobile devices, mass-market, intermittent wireless connectivity, diversity of products and an open platform for independent software developers - are the premises on which Symbian OS was designed and developed. This makes it distinct from any desktop, workstation or server operating system. This also makes Symbian OS different from embedded operating systems, or any of its competitors, which weren't designed with all these key points in mind.

Symbian is committed to open standards. Symbian OS has a POS1X-compliant interface and a Sun-approved JVM, and the company is actively working with emerging standards, such as J2ME, Bluetooth, MMS, SyncML, IPv6 and WCDMA. As well as its own developer support organization, books, papers and courses, Symbian delivers a global network of third-party competency and training centers - the Symbian Competence Centers and Symbian Training Centers. These are specifically directed at enabling other organizations and developers to take part in this new economy. Symbian has announced and implemented a strategy that will see Symbian OS running on many advanced open mobile phones. Products launched, such as the Sony Ericsson P800 smartphone, the Nokia 9200 Communicator series and the NTT DoCoMo Fujitsu 2102V [2], show the diversity of mobile phones that can be created with Symbian OS. Other Symbian OS licensees include BenQ Motorola, Panasonic, Samsung, Sendo and Siemens. Over the next year, we can look forward to an even wider range of mobile phones.

NEED FOR SYMBIAN OS

This describes the key characteristics required of an operating system designed for mobile phones and explains why Symbian OS is the best-in-class mobile operating system.

1. Small and mobile, but always available

Mobile phones are both small and, by definition, mobile. This creates high user expectations. For instance, if you have your agenda on a phone that you also use to make calls and exchange data, you expect to be able to carry it with you at all times and to be instantly available whenever you want to use it. Fulfilling these expectations makes considerable demands on power management. The device needs to be responsive in all situations and cannot afford to go through a long boot sequence when it is turned on. In fact, the device should never be powered down completely since it needs to activate timed alarms or handle incoming calls. At the same time, a mobile phone must provide many hours of operation on a single charge or set of batteries. Meeting these contradictory requirements can only be done if the whole operating system is designed for efficiency.

2. Addressing the mass-market

Reliability is a major issue for mass-market phones. Data loss in a personal mobile phone causes a loss of trust between the user and the phone. A mobile phone therefore must be at least as resilient as paper diaries and agendas. Recalling phones to install service packs is a commercial and practical last resort - a mobile phone should never lock up or come with a major software defect. In fact, to use a PC term, it should never ever need a "reboot"! This is a far cry from desktop computers where bugs, crashes and reboots are expected. It may come as a surprise to many computer users that a robust and reliable operating system is perfectly achievable. Even though nobody can guarantee bug-free software, a good operating system can make it much easier to write robust and reliable applications. Reliability requires good software engineering (including object-orientation) and a good error-handling framework. Engineering best practice greatly helps reduce the number and severity of bugs while the error-handling framework enables graceful recovery from run-time errors, such as running out of memory, low battery power or dropping a communication link.

Reducing the possibility of user code making the whole system unstable goes a long way towards achieving robustness. Ideally, the kernel, with its privileged code, should be small. System servers running without special privilege should handle much of the functionality conventionally handled by device drivers.

An effective memory management system is needed to prevent memory leaks. System resources should be released as soon as they are no longer needed and an effective, easy-to-use error-handling framework should manage out-of-memory errors properly. For systems that are never completely shut down and cannot be rebooted, keeping an accurate track of resources makes the difference between peak performance at all times and slow degradation to partial, or total, lack of usability. Applications and system modules that allocate blocks of memory should cater for the possibility that none might be available. Defensive programming has to be applied from the operating system through the application level.

However, reliability alone is not enough to make good products. Sound consumer design is also necessary, where:

1. Product applications take advantage of the mobile phone's unique characteristics as well as its environment
2. Products should be designed to meet current usability and future developments in wireless technology

3. Consistency of style is paramount - if a feature is too complex to use, then it cannot justify either the time it took to develop or the space it takes in the device.

An operating system targeted at mobile phones must support these design principals by offering a high level of integration with communication and personal information management (PIM) functionality. Symbian OS combines high functionality middleware with superior wireless communications through an integrated mailbox and the integration of Java and PIM functionality (agenda and contacts).

3. Handling occasional connectivity

Accessing remote data, sending email or synchronizing calendars requires some type of connection. Mobility constraints generally make a wireless connection preferable whether wide area (using wireless telephony) or personal area (such as infrared or bluetooth). Wireless connectivity is patchy, caused by different protocols around the world, fade-outs while moving and incomplete coverage "a€" especially in remote areas, in some buildings or while airborne. It is unwise to rely on a permanent mobile connection - it is very frustrating for the user if such a connection is assumed. Wide area wireless networks are - and always will be - much slower than wired networks. An operating system must take this into account by delivering rich applications that are designed to manipulate the user's data while it is on the phone even when no connection is established. In short, the mobile phone must function as an advanced client, not a thin client, and the operating system must support this. There must be a smooth transition between being a window on the network and a self-sufficient device. Connectivity requires an operating system with genuine multi-tasking, communications-capable real-time performance and a rich suite of communications protocols. In addition to the real-time requirements to maintain connections, the operating system must provide mechanisms to handle dropped connections gracefully and inform the user appropriately. To provide a smooth transition to the user and to be able to support forthcoming standards (such as third-generation W-CDMA and its evolution), network stacks must be abstracted in such a way that the application-level interface remains consistent no matter what type of protocol stack is used. The operating system has to provide a rich set of APIs to ensure that applications can benefit fully from current connectivity possibilities and be easily adapted to take advantage of new protocols as they are implemented.

4. Product diversity

There is an apparent contradiction between software developers who want to develop for just one popular platform and manufacturers who each want to have a range of distinctive and innovative products. The circle can be squared by separating the user interface from the core operating system. Advanced mobile phones or "'Smartphones" will come in all sorts of shapes - from traditional designs resembling today's mobile phones with main input via the phone keypad, to a tablet form factor operated with a stylus, to phones with larger screens and small keyboards.

The different input mechanisms and form factors strongly influence the intended primary use of devices. With a very small screen and just a keypad, the main use tends to be voice calls. With pen input, browsing is quite convenient, but data entry is not. A keyboard is obviously the most practical mechanism to enter a large amount of data. These distinctions imply that user interfaces are ultimately both device and market dependent. Product differentiation isn't just a matter of operating system design. The operating system vendor must allow its licensees freedom to innovate and develop new product lines. Whether or not a vendor allows this is a key feature of its commercial model.

To support distinct phone families and yet maximize code reuse, Symbian focuses on the common code:Symbian OS, which includes a multi-tasking multithreaded core, a user interface framework, data services enablers, application engines and integrated PIM functionality and wireless communications. Licensees are active participants in software development, creating a large development organization to extend Symbian OS. This results in thousands of developers among licensees and partners having access to source code and ensuring that Symbian OS remains an "open standard" - open and advanced. This strategy ensures that Symbian OS phone manufacturers can create highly differentiated products while sharing a technology platform and keeping the learning curve to a minimum.

5. Open platform

An operating system for the mass-market must be open for third-party development - by independent software vendors, enterprise IT departments, network operators and Symbian OS licensees. In turn, this implies a manageable learning curve, standard languages such as C++ and Java, along with SDKs, tools, documentation, books, technical support and training. Symbian OS has a rich set of APIs for independent software developers, partners and licensees to write their applications.

Even though mobile phones are small and mobile, they can offer facilities as rich as those on desktop computers, in addition to basic functions such as voice and data communication. The operating system has to support both conventional and mobile computing paradigms, and developers need knowledge of both.

To reduce the time-to-market, developers should become proficient in as short a time as possible. Supporting standards that they may already know or can easily learn from a multitude of sources is necessary. Standards also make the platform more open and hence attract more developers.

Traditional standards such as Unicode for internationalization, a POSIX API, and Java are a must, but for an operating system to take its place in the connected world, open standards such as TCP/IP, POP3, IMAP4, SMTP, SMS, MMS, Bluetooth, OBEX, WAP, i-mode, Java and SyncML should also be supported.

Symbian has trusted leading partners in the mobile phone market and actively participates in standards organizations (such as the Open Mobile Alliance and the Java Community Process). Through these, Symbian has advance knowledge of future technologies and can test Symbian OS with many different phone systems. This ensures the stability and the future place of Symbian OS. Furthermore, a user interface framework, data service enablers and application engines provide a solid base for application developers to target.

SYMBIAN HISTORY

Symbian OS started life as EPOC - the operating system used for many years in Psion handheld devices. When Symbian was formed in 1998, Psion contributed EPOC into the group. EPOC was renamed Symbian OS and has been progressively updated, incorporating both voice and data telephony technologies of ever greater sophistication with every product release.

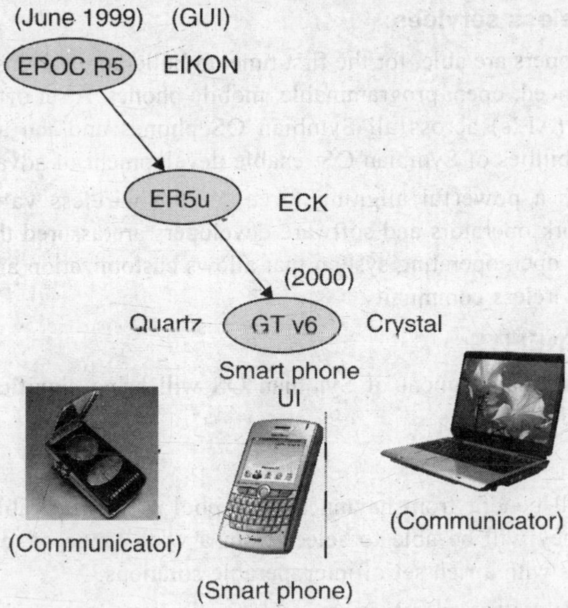

THE COMPANY:

Headquartered in London, Symbian Ltd. is owned by Ericsson, Nokia, Panasonic, Psion, Siemens and Sony-Ericsson.

CUSTOMERS:

Symbian's customers include all of its shareholders, but any company is free to license the product - Symbian OS is open to all on equal terms. So far, in addition to the shareholders, Sony, Sanyo, Kenwood and Fujitsu have all taken licenses.

BASIC PRINCIPLES:

The cornerstone of Symbian's modus operandi is to use open -agreed - standards wherever possible. Symbian is focused squarely on one part of the value chain - providing the base operating system for mobile internet devices. This enables manufacturers, networks and application developers to work together on a common platform.

SYMBIAN OS:

By setting the standard for wireless value computing and telephony, Symbian brings together the wireless value chain. Symbian OS drives standards for the interoperation of data-enabled mobile phones with mobile networks, content applications and services:

1. A platform for wireless services:

Symbian delivers an advanced, open, standard operating system to its licensees. Symbian OS is flexible and scalable enough to be used in the variety of mobile phones needed to meet a wide range of user requirements. Symbian OS supports complex requirements of network protocols worldwide and enables a broad, international community.

2. Providing wireless services:

Open standards ensure global network interoperability, allowing mobile phones users to communicate with anyone, anyway, at anytime. The compelling advanced data services that operators can provide on Symbian OS phones will help minimize churn and maximize revenue.

3. Developing wireless services:

Software developers are able, for the first time, to build applications and services for a global mass market of advanced, open, programmable, mobile phones. A set of standard application programming interfaces (APIs) across all Symbian OS phones and the advanced computing and communication capabilities of Symbian OS, enable development of advanced services.

Symbian OS is a powerful aligning force for the wireless value chain. Mobile phone manufacturers, network operators and software developers are assured that they are working with an industry standard, open operating system that allows customization and is focused on the mass market, driving the wireless community.

COMMERCIAL BENEFITS

The widespread establishment of Symbian OS will bring significant commercial benefits, both direct and indirect.

Operators:

1. Operators will benefit from having a wide pool of interoperable devices, built on open standards. They will be able to select from a wide range of terminal and infrastructure manufacturers with a rich set of interoperable solutions.
2. In terms of value that operators can add, applications and content can all be made more cost effectively supplied - given the common OS shared across phones.

Developers:

1. Developers will benefit from being able to target a greater number of consumers across one platform. Their porting and development costs will dramatically decline as the common OS means that applications will need to be developed once.
2. Applications can be written virtually by anybody. This software could be stand-alone, used only by the user of the device. However. Just as easily, the software could be a networking application, enabling users to communicate with other users, or to access a resource somewhere in the internet.
3. Equally, whilst the cost are reduced, potential returns are increased as a wider pool of users is accessible - a win-win situation for all concerned.

Indirect benefits for the whole industry:

1. The above benefits assume that the number of users stays constant. In establishing Symbian OS, Nokia and the other industry players believe that there will be a **Metcalfe effec-whereby the value of a network is the square of the number of users**. As users proliferate, they will attract more, attracting even more users and consequently, more application developers, and content. This will benefit the whole industry.
2. Symbian OS is the key to creation of this virtuous circle.

SYMBIAN OS: FUNDAMENTAL REQUIREMENTS

There are some fundamental requirements which are very much essential for an OS for mobile phones.

1. It must work on stand alone portable devices.
2. It must work on different sorts of devices.
3. It must be future proof.
4. It must be open to all to licence on fair and equal terms.

5. It must be open to all to develop applications - again with a level playing field for all.
6. It mist be based on open standards.

Perhaps the most important requirement is to work on a stand alone device. Symbian OS is fundamentally designed for mobile phones -with highly advanced features - but they must still function primarily as mobile phones. This means that expectations are already set - for a user to consider buying Symbian OS based phones, they must outperform the user's current model in some areas and be at least equal in all others. The performance benchmark for Symbian OS is not the PC or portable computing devices but the phones that around one billion people already have in their pockets.

SYMBIAN OS: ARCHITECTURE

Symbian OS architecture is designed to meet a number of requirements. It must be hardware independent so it can be used on a variety of phone types, it must be extendable so it can cope with future developments, and it must be open to all to develop for.

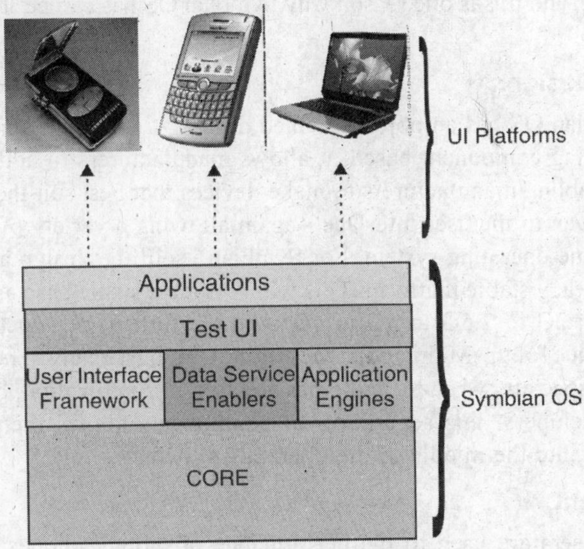

Architectural Overview

1. **Core** - Symbian OS core is common to all devices, i.e. kernel, file server, memory management and device drivers. Above this core, components can be added or removed depending on the product requirements.
2. **System Layer** - The system layer provides communication and computing services such as TCP/IP, IMAP4, SMS and database management.
3. **Application Engines** - Above the System Layer sits the Application Engines, enabling software developers (be they either employed by the phone manufacturer or independent) to create user interface to data.
4. **User Interface Software** - USI can be made or licensed by manufacturers.
5. **Applications** - Applications are slotted in above the user interface.

FEATURES OF SYMBIAN OS

There are many features that makes Symbian OS ideal for mobile devices. Some of these are briefly explained below.

Client-Server Architecture:

The power of the client-server framework is widely acknowledged in the software community. In Symbian OS, clients are programs that have user interfaces, and servers are programs that can only be accessed via a well defined interface from other programs. The role of a client is to serve the user, while servers ensure timely response to all the clients while controlling the access to the resources of the actual system. Additionally, in practice, one server will often have many extra servers relying on the original server.

Event Management:

Event management has long been considered a core strength of Symbian OS - reflecting the fact that Symbian OS was designed from the start to have event based time sharing in a single thread. Rather than more conventional methods of having multi threaded applications. Symbian OS enables the developer to think in terms of interactions and behaviors as the main artifacts. Enabling this shift from procedural to interactive designs have been one of the main challenges of modern software engineering, and this is one reason why Symbian OS has earned its reputation for advanced design.

Object Oriented Design:

Because Symbian OS has an object oriented design, it is easy to configure for different sorts of hardware, and being component based, it allows manufacturers to add or remove components. This is crucial in enabling manufacturers to make devices that best suit their customers needs. This flexibility extends even to the user interface - again allowing a variety of different device designs to work from the same operating system. For Symbian itself, the design allows new technology to be slotted into an already stable platform. This will provide a stable base as the telecommunications industry moves from 2G to 2.5G to 3G to 4G, with the further introduction of new technologies such as SyncML, BlueTooth, Multimedia Messaging amongst many. The picture will grow ever more complicated, especially when technologies are used in combination, but Symbian OS is ready! For application developers, this separation of components allows them to program far richer applications -getting into the middle of the operating system.

Power Management:

Symbian OS users are used to the performance of mobile phones -and so demand similar performance in terms of weight and operating times when they adopt new devices. Power management is built into the kernel of Symbian OS and is designed to make efficient use of the processors and peripherals and so minimize power usage. When peripherals are not being used they are switched off by the system. This lowers battery consumption, prolonging usage and allows for smaller batteries. This meets the requirement to work on stand alone portable devices, enabling manufacturers to make phones that capture the **optimum combination of size and weight for their target market.**

Robust and Dependable:

Symbian OS users will have experienced the performance levels achieved in this area by mobile phones. Devices should not lose user data, crash or require rebooting.

Symbian achieves this in two ways:

1. Each process runs in a protected address space, thus it is not possible for one application to overwrite another's address space.
2. The kernel also runs in a protected address space, so that a bug in one application cannot overwrite the kernel's stack or heap.

The client-server architecture of Symbian OS allows applications to exchange data without compromising overall system integrity. This meets the requirement to work on stand alone portable devices, even though Symbian devices offer greatly enhanced functionality over standard mobile phones

Memory Management:

For stand alone portable devices, memory management is important. The need to minimize weight, device size and cost means the amount of memory available on a Symbian OS device is often quite limited. Symbian OS always assumes that the memory available is limited, and minimizes consumption at every turn. Consequently, less memory is actually required by the system. Also having less memory helps to keep down power consumption.

Full Multitasking:

Symbian OS runs each application as a separate process, allowing multiple applications to run concurrently. For instance, if a user is checking the calendar, and receives a call, the system must allow the user to switch between applications instantaneously. Equally, should the phone call result in an appointment, the user must be able to check the calendar -and still maintain the phone call. As phones become more data enabled, this ability will become ever more important.

An Open Operating System:

Symbian OS is an open OS. The different aspects of this statement is explained below.

1. Open to anyone to license:

All manufacturers are treated equally - licensing Symbian OS is open to all on fair and equal terms.

2. Open to anyone to develop applications:

The even-handed approach adopted towards manufacturers extends towards developers. API's are made available as a matter of course. Support for 3rd party developers is a key tenet of Symbian OS so full of SDKs and support are available for all products. Anyone can build an application for Symbian OS and again there is fair and equal access for all.

3. Based on open standards:

Symbian focuses on one clear part of the value chain - providing a platform for all to build upon. Consequently Symbian avoids proprietary standards. It is an active participant in many standards forums - often drawing on the expertise of its shareholders and licensees. The components of Symbian OS are based on agreed open standards.

WRITING APPLICATIONS FOR SYMBIAN OS

Symbian OS is written in C++, so it is natural fit to develop applications also in C++. This provides the developer with the most flexibility and scope. However, this flexibility brings with it complexity, and in some cases it may be more appropriate to develop an application in Java, which is also well supported Symbian OS devices.

Symbian's use of C++ is efficient and thoroughly object-oriented. The design of the OS focuses on getting the most out of the limited hardware resources of mobile devices and this affects the way that code is written throughout the system including at the application level. This requires developers to get used to a few programming idioms that aren't common in other systems. However, these idioms help in making efficient use of the hardware resources, especially the very limited amount of memory. They also help simplify some of the more difficult tasks in application development.

Some of the idioms are:

1. The cleanup stack - A straightforward method for claiming back memory if a memory allocation fails partway through a function.
2. The rule that a C++ constructor cannot leave (*i.e.* cause an exception). This results in a two-phase construction system for object, (*i.e.* make a empty new object first, then allocate the memory in a second step) which makes the cleanup stack system keep working even for complicated class constructions.
3. Various naming conventions. eg. C, T and R type classes, L (leaving) and non-L functions. The conventions quickly tell the developer useful information about the class or method without having to look up the definition.

Multitasking:

One of the major design decisions taken in developing Symbian OS was to optimize the system for efficient event handling from the ground up. Native Symbian OS programs are written from the viewpoint of the events that occur rather than the traditional programming model of a main control program that regularly polls for events and then performs the appropriate actions. This traditional model often requires multiple threads to be used to perform these actions and this results in the complicated problem of synchronizing access to resources.

Symbian OS multitasking system eliminates this problem by having only a single thread that responds to events as they happen. An Active Scheduler implements non-preemptive multitasking within the context of this single thread. The Active Scheduler catches the events as they occur and then runs the appropriate Active Object for that event. The Active Object does the processing for that event and then returns control to the Active Scheduler. If several events occur in quick succession, they are stored and each Active Object is run in turn. There is a priority system to determine which Active Object should be run first, but if there is an Active Object is already running it will run to completion before the next one can be run, even if the next one is of a higher priority. Thus we have multitasking that is non-preemptive. Since an Active Object function can't be preempted there is no need to use mutexers, semaphores, critical sections or any kind of synchronization to protect against the activities of other Active Objects in the thread. However, to keep the system responsive, the processing of each event must be quick so that control is returned in order for the next event to be processed. Traditional multithreading is also implemented in Symbian OS. Multiple application and servers can be run simultaneously. Threads implement preemptive multitasking, so one thread can preempt another if it has to handle an event - for instance, the window server can handle a key - press event while an application is running, by preempting the running application thread. The ability of one thread to preempt another depends on thread priority. The most critical threads in the system are given the highest priorities - with the kernel, including device drivers, the highest priority of all.

Application Architecture:

Symbian OS has an application architecture that helps developers manage the complexity of graphical user interface based applications. A Symbian OS application is made up of several parts. An Application Engine that contains all the non-UI parts of an application, an Application UI that handles the application events coming from the user and calls the Engine, and then there is the Application View (or several views) which contains the actual windows and controls (eg. buttons, text and graphics) that show on the screen of a Symbian OS device. The Application Architecture has a built in Active Scheduler so that developers don't need to understand the ins and outs of the Active Object system when writing normal applications.

The tools that come with Symbian OS SDK can be used to generate an application with this basic structure. This provides the developer with a good guide for how to continue the development of the application.

Java:

All Symbian OS devices have Java available on them. The higher end devices tend to have Personal Java and the more popular devices have MIDP Java.

Development environment (SDKs):

The main part of an SDK are a device emulator that runs on a PC, a cross compiler for compiling software for the device and assorted tools that are required for application development. There is also a large amount of documentation and plenty of example applications in the SDK that help a developer get started with using the system.

CONCLUSION

Symbian OS is a robust multi-tasking operating system, designed specifically for real-world wireless environments and the constraints of mobile phones (including limited amount of memory). Symbian OS is natively IP-based, with fully integrated communications and messaging. It supports all the leading industry standards that will be essential for this generation of data-enabled mobile phones. Symbian OS enables a large community of developers. The open platform allows the installation of third party software to further enhance the platform.

BIBLIOGRAPHY

- http://www.techalone.com/symbian-os.php http://ezinearticles.com/7Latest-Technology-in-Computer-Hardware&id= 1672812
- http://www.college-seminars..com/Forum-Computer-Science-Seminar-Topics?page=12
- http://techalone.com/index.php/tag/latest-seminar-topics-in-computer-science/symbian/
- http://www.blogcatalog.com/blogs/latest-seminar-topic-for-students/posts/tag/computer+science/
- http://www.college-seminars.com/Forum-Computer-Science-Seminar-Topics
- http://www.college-seminars.com/Thread-HTAM-Download-Full-Seminar-Report
- Morris, Ben (June 22, 2007), *The Symbian OS architecture sourcebook : design and evolution of a mobile phone OS,* John Wiley & Sons, pp. 630, ISBN 0470018461

CHAPTER 14

Case Study on UNIX

UNIX History

1. In 1960s and 1970s, every computer manufacturer supplied O.S. as a **proprietary** (its own right) **software**. These O.Ss were written for their own **specific machine.**
2. Each machine had an instruction set and the O.S. was written in an **intermediate assembly language.** Thus, no two O.S. were alike in features. So, whenever a user moved to another new machine, he would be expected to learn a new O.S. **Also note that no two machines could even exchange information.**
3. Dennis Richie (Bell Labs., USA) thus developed UNICS (i.e., Uniplexed Information and Computing System). It provided an interpreted common (uniplexed) command language environment across platforms.
4. Then Ken Thompson changed UNICS to UNIX. Modern UNIX O.S provide an extensive suit of tools.

UNIX Features

1. UNIX provides a rich set of generic tools too. **For eg.** UNIX provides generic string matching tools. These tools enhance a user's productivity.
2. Users have access to the same tools which are also used by UNIX as an O.S. UNIX is thus an open system.
3. X-Windows helped in development of GUI for current/newer applications.
4. UNIX supports Client Server architecture, Thus, it forms a backbone support for communication networks.
5. TCP/IP protocol was first developed on UNIX only.

Summary of History

First UNIX at Bell Labs (1969; ALP $\xrightarrow{\text{then in}}$ C)

↓

Bell Labs makes UNIX freeware

↓

Berkeley UNIX (in 1978)

↓

TCP/IP on UNIX & X–WINDOWS (1980s)

↓

Web & LINUX (in 1990s)

UNIX Architecture

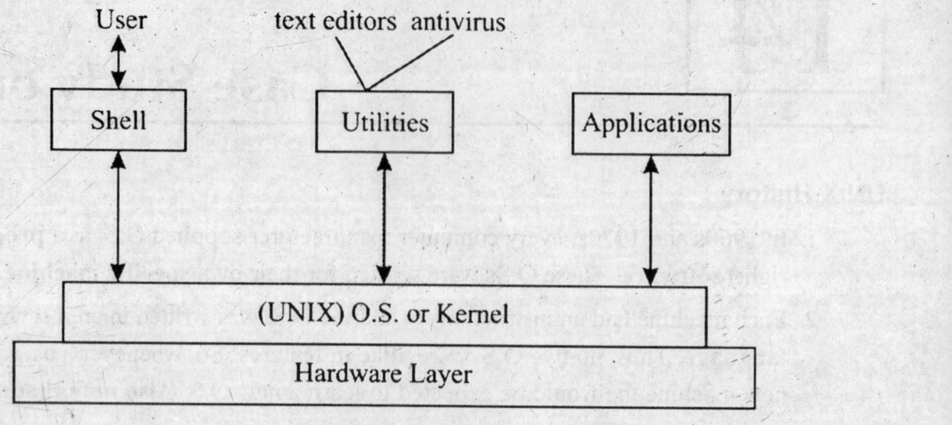

Fig. 1: *UNIX Architecture*

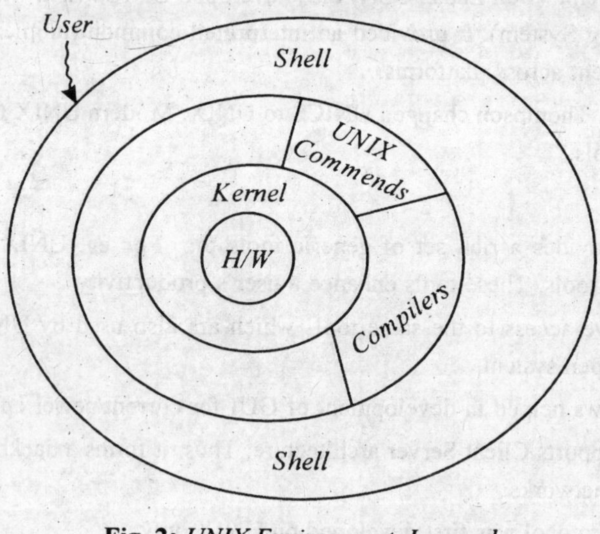

Fig. 2: *UNIX Environment–Layered*

Kernel–*Controls hardware, creates processes and implements multitasking.*

Shell–*Interprets user commands and sends them to Kernel via command prompt.*

Dialects of UNIX

- *HP/UX from HP*
- *Sun OS or Solaris from SUN.*

A UNIX environment is basically a command–driven environment i.e., commands can be given on each window. User can thus run multiple applications–one in each window. From Fig.1 and Fig. 2., it may be observed that UNIX provides a user–friendly shell. It hides the system kernel beneath the **shell.** *The* **shell** *interface accepts user commands. The user command is interpreted by the shell. Then shell seeks the desired service from the kernel on behalf of the user.* **Please understand that in UNIX, everything works on 2 basic concepts:**

(a) **Files**

(b) **Processes**

Users organize applications using files and processes. **A program text is a file.** A program in execution is a process. One application may use several files also. Files may be a text file or an image file too.

File System in UNIX

UNIX allows users to group related files within a directory *i.e.,* a doc file and an image file may be grouped differently within same directory. Even other directory may be created. UNIX also allows the creation of sub–directories to organize files hierarchically so, such a file organization creates a tree of directories with files as leaves.

> **Note:** When you log into a UNIX system, you always do it in your login directory. Starting from the login directory, you make create files as well as sub–directories too.

Practical Creations

1. Create a directory–Courses under HOME DIRECTORY.
2. Now, Create directories called OS, SE and COMPILERS *i.e.,*

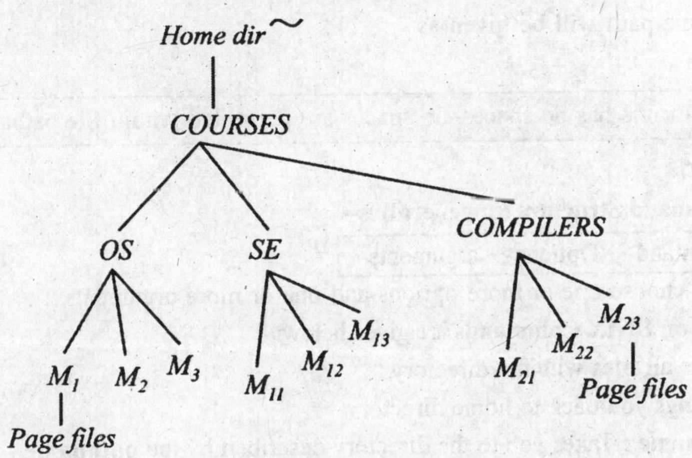

Fig. 3: Hireracical UNIX file System.

From fig. 3, it is crystal clear that the COURSES directory has 3 sub-directories named as OS, SE and COMPILERS. Within these subdirectories, there are **modules.** At the leaf node, there are individual **page files**–*i.e.,* links that help us to navigate. **Please note that a home directory is usually denoted by a tilde (~). Also note that it is very** vital to understand how to reach a particular file in such a file hierarchy.

For. eg. To reach a particular file (in such a file hierarchy) in OS course then we need to traverse down from the home to COURSES to OS to a particular module. **This is called as path traversal.** So, in this eg. the path would be–

/COURSES/OS/ module M_1.

Please note here how each step in the path hierarchy is seperated by a for ward slash. Thus, we say that directory COURSES has a sub-directory or a child directory as OS. **We can also** say that COURSES is parent directory of OS.

In UNIX, all paths emanate from a directory called as **root.** The **root** directory has **no parent.** A user's **login directory** is usually a child of a directory named home which is a child of "/" *i.e.,* **root.** It is under home, user's home directories are created with the user's login name. Thus,

/ (root directory)

↓

HOME (dir)

↓

Login (dir)

The directory where you may be currently located is denoted by a **period (.) symbol.** The parent of current directory is denoted by two periods (. .). These two are special **symbols.** These symbols are used when the user has to make a reference **relative** to the present postion in the file sytem. An **abolute path name** would trace the file path starting with root as in

/home/rajiv/COURSES/OS/module M_1.

Say, We are in directory COURSES

then the same path will be given as–

./OS/M_1.

> **Note:** File pathname has no spaces–no spaces are permitted within file pathnames.

UNIX Commands

UNIX Command Structure (in general) is–

<Unix Command> <Options> <arguments>

A user may choose one or more options and one or more arguments.

Some **common UNIX Commands** are given below:

1. **ls :** It hits all files within a directory.
2. **cd :** Brings you back to home directory.
3. **cd pathname :** Takes you to the directory described by the **pathname.**
4. **rm filename :** Removes file filename from the current directory.
5. **pwd : Prints** the name of current working directory.
6. **mkdir subdirname : Creates** a subdirectory under the current directory with the name **subdirname.**
7. **rmdir subdirname : Removes** a subdirectory under the current directory with the name **subdirname.**
8. **touch filename :** Creates a file in the current directory with the name filename.

Note: This file on creation has O chracters and O lines.

In general, keep in mind that files have 3 basic operations on them–

(*a*) You **create and write** to a file.

(*b*) You **read** a file.

(*c*) You **execute** a file.

Actually, UNIX supports four types of files:–

(*a*) **Ordinary Files :** Are text files. Programs written in specific languages may have specific extensions like ·C, ·Cpp, ·txt, ·docx, ·pptx, ·dll etc. Use editors to create files.

(*b*) **Directory Files :** Subdirectories are treated as files by UNIX.

(c) **Binary Files :** *Are executable files.*

(d) **Special Files :** *These files provide I/o capability for UNIX. UNIX treats the device IO as file communication.*

Other UNIX Commands

1. **bc :** *Gives you a basic Calculator.*
2. **cal :** *Shows calender for current month.*
3. **clear :** *Clears screen.*
4. *cp f1 f2 : Creates a copy of file f1 in f2.*
5. **date :** *Shows current date and time.*
6. **echo <text> :** *Echos back <text> onto the screen.*
7. **history :** *Shows previously given command history.*
8. **More filename :** *Shows file 'filename' one page at a time.* **Less** *command also does the same except that it gives* **scrolling also.**
9. **Cat file name :** *Displays the file filename on the screen.*
10. **Cat filename (s) > new file:** *It combines all files in filename (s) and outputs to create a file–newfile. It* **redirects** *(>) to a newfile.*
11. **exit :** *Exits the current shell.*
12. **man AUnix Cmd :** *It describes the use of a command with all its possible options and arguments.*

Summary

UNIX is not very portable but two of its standards–X/open and POSIX are portable. UNIX architecture, history and commands have been discussed here.

MULTIPLE CHOICE-QUESTIONS [MCQs]

1. *UNIX was initially named as—*

(a) SIMICS *(b) MIMICS*

(c) UNICS *(d) None of the above*

2. *Group of related files is called as—*

(a) Directory *(b) Sub-directory*

(c) Images *(d) None of the above*

3. *All paths emanate from a directory called as a—*

(a) File *(b) Root*

(c) Parent *(d) Home*

4. *Executables are—*

(a) Binaries *(b) Directories*

(c) Special files *(d) Ordinary files.*

5. *Cal command in UNIX—*

(a) Clears screen *(b) Shows calculator*

(c) Shows calender. *(d) Shows date*

ANSWERS

1. *c* **2.** *a* **3.** *b* **4.** *a* **5.** *c*

CONCEPTUAL SHORT QUESTIONS (WITH ANSWERS)

Q.1. What are different file operations based on—

(*a*) Editor–based operations

(*b*) OS terminology?

Ans. Different file operations are–

Usage	Editor based	OS terminology based
1. Create	Under file menu New.	A create command is available with explicit read/write option
2. Read	Open to read	Specified at the time of open.
3. Write	Save to write.	Specified at time of open.

Q.2. What are different file oriented services?

Ans.

USAGE	Unix Shell Command
1. copy a file.	cp
2. Rename a file.	mv
3. Delete a file	nn
4. List files	ls
5. Make a directory	mkdir
6. Change current directory	cd

EXERCISE QUESTIONS

Q.1. Do as directed:–

(*a*) Create a directory called '*l1*' in your directory.

(*b*) Create a directory called '*l2*' under '*l1*' and change dir to '*lz*'.

(*c*) Create a file called 'temp' under '*l2*'.

(*d*) Copy the file 'temp' in dir. '*l1*'.

(*e*) While you are still in dir. '*l2*', List the contents of directory '*l1*'.

Q.2. What does the character tilde (~) represent?

Q.3. What is the short cut to move up one level from current directory.

Q.4. List all ·h files under the root directory and display it page by page.

[Hint: [cd··/ls*·h/move]

Q.5. Why

(*a*) UNIX has so many tools.

(*b*) UNIX is an open system.

APPENDIX

Appendix A

CASE–STUDY on LEX and YACC tools

lex is a software tools designed to solve a wide class of problems drawn from text processing, code enciphering, compiler writing, and other areas. It can be used to check the spelling of words for errors in text processing, to translate certain patterns of characters into others in code enciphering, and to determine what the tokens (smallest meaningful sequences of characters) are in the program being compiled in compiler writing. The problem common to all of these tasks is recognizing different strings of characters that satisfy certain characteristics. In the compiler writing case, creating the ability to solve the problem requires implementing the compiler's lexical analyzer. Hence the name **lex**.

A.1. Overview

It is not essential to use **lex** to handle problems of this kind, which can be handled by a standard language like C too. In fact, what **lex** does is produce such C progrms. (**lex** is therefore called a program generator.) What **lex** offers is typically a faster, easier way to create programs that perform these tasks. Its weakness is that it often produces C programs that are longer than necessary for the task at hand and that execute more slowly than they otherwise might. In many applications this is a minor consideration, and the advantages of usig **lex** considerably outweight it.

The diagram in Figure 2.1 shows what **lex** does. The **lex** source consists of a list of rules specifying sequences of characters (expressions) to be searched for in an input text, and he actions to be taken when an expression is found. The source is read by the **lex** program generator. The output of the program generator is a C program that, in turn, must be compiled by a host language C compiler to generate the executable object program that does the lexical analysis. Note that this procedure is not typically automatic; user intervention is required. Finally, the lexical analyser program produced by this process takes as input any source file and produces the desired output, such as altered text or a list of tokens.

lex can also be used to collect statistical data on features of the input, such as character count, word length, number of occurences of a word, and so forth. In later sectioins of this chapter, the following are explained.

- how to write **lex** source to do some of these tasks ?
- how to translate **lex** source ?
- how to compile, link, and execute the lexical analyzer in C ?
- how to run the lexical analyzer program ?

```
lex source  →  lex  →  lex Analyzer in C
                            ↓
                        C Compiler
                            ↓
               Input  →  lex Analyzer  →  Output
               Text      Program          Tokens
                                          Text, etc.
```

Figure 1: Creation and Use of a Lexical Analyzer with text

A.2. Writing lex programs

A lex specification or program consists of **at most three sections:** definitions, rules, and user subroutines. The rules section is mandatory. Sections for definitions and user subroutines are optional, but if present, must appear in the indicated order.

A.2.1. The Fundamentals of lex Rules

The mandatory rules section opens with the delimiter %%. If a subroutines section follows, another %% delimiter ends the rules section. If there is no second delimiter, the rules section is presumed to continue to the end of the program.

Each rule consists of (1) a **specification of the pattern sought** and (2) **the action(s) to take on finding it.** (Note the dual meaning of the term specification - it may mean either the entire lex source itself or, within it, a representation of a particular pattern to be recognized). Whenever the input consists of patterns not sought, lex writes out the input exactly as it funds it. So, the simplest lex program is just the beginning rules delimiter, %%. It writes out the entire input to the output with no changes at all. Typically, the rules are more elaborate than that.

A.2.2. Specifications

The patterns of interest may be specified with a notation called **regular expressions.** A regular expression is formed by stringing together characters with or without operators. The simplest regular expressions are strings of text characters with no operators at all. For example,

apple
orange
pluto

These three regular expressions match any occurrences of those character strings in an input text. If the lexical analyzer **a.out** is to remove every occurrence of **orange**, from the input text, the rule is:

orange;

Since an action was not specified on the right (before the semicolon), **lex** does nothing but print out the original input text with every occurrence of this regular expression removed, that is, without any occurrence of the string **orange** at all.

Unlike **orange** above, most of the expressions to be searched for, cannot be specified so easily. The expression itself might simply be too long. More commonly, the class of desired expressions is too large; it may, in fact, be infinite. Using operators regular expressions can be formed, signifying any expression of a certain class. **The + operator, for instance, means one or more occurrences of the preceding expression, the means 0 or 1 occurrence(s) of the preceding expression (this is equivalent to saying that the preceding expression is optional), and * means 0 or more occurrences of the preceding expression.** (It may at first seem odd to speak of 0 occurrences of an expression and to need an operator to capture the idea, but it is often quite helpful). So m+ is a regular expression matching any string of ms such as each of the following:

mmm

m

mmmmm

mm

and 7* is a regular expression matching any string of zero or more 7s:

77
77777
777

The string of blanks on the third line matches simply because it has no 7s in it at all.

Brackets, [], indicate anyone character from the string of characters specified between the brackets. Thus, **[dgka]** matches a single **d, g, k,** or **a**. **Note that commas are not included within the brackets.** Any comma here would be taken as a character to be recognized in the input text. Ranges within a standard alphabetic or numeric order are indicated with a hyphen, - The sequence [**a-z**], for instance, indicates any lowercase letter. Somewhat more interestingly,

[A-Za-z0-9*&#]

is a regular expression that matches any letter (whether upper- or lowercase), any digit, an asterisk, an ampersand, or a sharp character. Given the input text

$$$$?? ????!!!*$$ $$$$$$&+====r~~#((

the lexical analyzer with the previous specification in one of its rules will recognize the *, &, is no action

The operators become especially powerful in combination. For example, the regular expression to recognize an identifier in many programming languages is

[a-zA-Z] [0-9a-zA-Z]*

An identifier in these languages is defined to be a letter followed by zero or more letters or digits, and that is just what the regular expression says. The first pair of brackets matches any letter. The second, if it were not followed by a * , would match any digit or letter. The two pairs of brackets with their enclosed characters would then match any letter followed by a digit or a letter. But with the asterisk, *, the example matches any letter followed by any number of letters or digits. In particular, it would recognize the following as identifiers.

e

pay

distance

pH

EngineNo99

R2D2

would not recognize the following as identifiers:

not_idenTIFER

5 times

$hello

because **not_idenTIFER** has an embedded underscore; **5 times** starts with a digit, not a letter, and **$hello** starts with a special character. Of course, you may want to write the specifications for these three example as an exercise.

A potential problem with operator characters is how one can refer to them as characters to look for in our search pattern. The last example, for instance, will not recognize text with an * in it. **lex** solves the problem in one of two ways: a character enclosed in quotation marks or a character preceded by a \ is taken literally, that is, as part of the text to be searched for. To use the backslash method to recognize, say, an * followed by any number of digits, one can use the pattern

[1–9]

To recognize a \itself, two backslashes can be used: \\.

A.2.3. Actions

Once **lex** recognizes a string matching the regular expression at the start of a rule, it looks to the right of the rule for the action to be performed. Kinds of actions include recording the token type found and its value, if any; replacing one token with another; and counting the number of instances of a token or token type. These actions are to be written as program fragments in the host language C. An action may consist of as many statements as are needed for the job at hand. A message may be printed noting that the text has been found or a message transforming the text in some way. Thus, to recognize the expression Amelia Earhart and to note such recognition, the rule

```
"Amelia Earhart"
printf("found Amelia");
```

would do. And to replace in a text lengthy medical terms with their equivalent acronyms, a rule such as

```
Electroencephalogram printf("EEG" ;
```

would be called for. To count the lines in a text, one needs to recognize end-of-lines and increment a linecounter, **lex** uses the standard escape sequences from **C** like **\n** for end-of-line.

To count lines one can have

```
\n lineno++;
```

where **lineno**, like other C variables, is declared in the definitions section that we discuss later.

Lex stores every character string that it recognizes in a character array called yytext[]. This arrray can be printed or the contents of this array can be manipulated as one needs. Sometimes the action may consist of two or more C statements and one must (or for style and clarity, choose to) write it on several lines. To inform lex that the action is for one rule only, the C code can simply be enclosed in braces. For example, to count the total number of all digit strings in an input text, print the running total of the number of digit strings (not their sum) and print out each one as soon as it is found, the lex code for this might

```
+? [1–9] + { digstrngcount++;
printf ("%d", digstrngcount);
printf ("%s", yytext); }
```

This specification matches digit strings whether they are preceded by a plus sign or not, because the? indicates that the preceding plus sign is optional. In addition, it will catch negative digit strings because that portion following the minus sign, -, will match the specification. The next section explains how to distinguish negative from positive integers.

A.3. Advanced lex Usage

lex provides a suite of features that lets you process input text riddled with quite complicated patterns. These include rules that decide what specification is relevant, when more than one seems so at first; functions that transform one matching pattern into another; and the use of definitions and subroutines. Before considering these features, you may want to affirm your understanding so far by examining an example drawing together several of the points already covered.

```
%%
-[0-9]+        printf ("negative integer");
+?[0-9]+       printf ("positive integer");
-0.[0-9]+      printf ("negative fraction, no whole number part");
rail[ ] + road printf("railroad is one word");
crook          printf("Here's a crook");
function       subprogcount++;
```

```
G[a-zA-Z]*    printf("may have a G word here:" , yytext)
              Gstringcount++; }
```

The first, three rules recognize, negative integers, positive integers, and negative fractions between 0 and -1. The use of the terminating + in each specification ensures that one or more digits compose the number in question. Each of the next three rules recognize a specific pattern. The specification for **railroad** matches cases where one or more blanks intervene between the two syllables of the word. In the cases of **railroad and crook**, a synonym could have been printed rather than the messages stated.

The rule recognizing a **function** simply increments a counter. The last rule illustrates several points:

- The braces specify an action sequence extending over several lines.
- Its action uses the **lex** array **yytext[ ]**, which stores the recognized character string.
- Its specification uses the * to indicate that zero or more letters may follow **G**.

A.3.1 Some Special Features

Besides storing the recognized character string in yytext[], **lex** automatically counts the number of characters in a match and stores it in the variable **yyleng**. This variable may be used to refer to any specific character just placed in the array **yytext[]**. Since **C numbers locations in an array starting with 0, to print out the third digit (if there is one) in a just recognized integer, one might write**

```
[1–9]+   {if (yyleng > 2)
         printf ("%c", yytext[2]);}
```

lex follows a number of high-level rules to resolve ambiguities that may arise from the set of rules written. *Prima facie*, any reserved word, for instance, could match two rules. In the lexical analyzer example developed later in the section on lex and yacc, the reserved word end could match the second rule as well as the seventh, the one for identifiers.

> **NOTE**
>
> **lex** follows the rule that where there is a match with two or more rules in a specification, the first rule is the one whose action will be executed

By placing the rule for end and the other reserved words before the rule for identifiers, it can be ensured that the reserved words will be duly recognized.

Another potential problem arises from cases where one pattern being searched for is the prefix of another. For instance, the last two rules in the lexical analyzer example above are designed to recognize > and > =. If the text has the string > = at one point, one might worry that the lexical analyzer would stop as soon as it recognized > character to execute the rule for > rather than read the next character and execute the rule for >=.

> **NOTE**
>
> **lex** follows the rule that it matches the longest character string possible and executes the rule for that.

Here it would recognize the >= and act accordingly. As .a further example, the rule would enable distinguishing + from ++ in a program in C.

Yet another potential problem exists when the analyzer must read characters beyond the string being looked for because it cannot be sure it has in fact found it until it reads the additional characters.These cases reveal the irnportannce of trailing context. The classic example here is the DO statement in FORTRAN. In this statement

DO 50 k = 1, 20, 1

one cannot be sure that the first 1 is the initial value of the index **k** until the first comma is read. Unil then, one might have the assignment statement

DO50k = 1

(Remember that FORTRAN ignores all blanks,) The way to handle this is to use the forward looking slash, / (not the backslash, \), which signifies that what follows is trailing context, something not to be stored in **yytext[],** because it is not part of the token itself. So the rule to recognize the FORTRAN DO statement could be.

30/[ ] *[0-9] [ ] *[a-zA-Z0-9]+=[a-zA-Z0-9]+, printf("found DO");

Different versions of FORTRAN have limits on the size of identifiers, here the index name. To simplify the example, the rule accepts an index name of any length.

lex uses the $ as an operator to mark a special trailing context-the end of line. (It is therefore equivalent to **\n.**) An example would be a rule to ignore all blanks and tabs at the end of a line:

[\t]+$;

On the other hand, if a pattern is to be matched only when it starts a line, **lex** offers the circumflex ^, as the operator. The formatter **nroff**, for example, demands that a line is never started with a blank, so one might want to check input to nroff with some such rule as:

^[ ] printf("error: remove leading blank");

Finally, some of the user-specified action statements themselves may require reading another character, putting one back to be read again a moment later, or writing a character on an out-put device. **lex** supplies three functions to handle these tasks - **input**(), **unput**(c), and **output**(c), respectively. One way to ignore all characters between two special characters, say between a pair of double quotation marks, would be to use **input**(), thus:

\" while (input() != '"');

Upon finding the first double quotation mark, the generated **a.out** will simply continue reading all subsequent characters so long as none is a quotation mark, and not again look for a match until it finds a second double quotation mark.

To handle special **I/O** needs, such as writing to several files, standard I/O routines in C can be used to rewrite functions **input**(), **unput**(c), and **output**(c). These and other programrner defined functions should be placed in the subroutines sections. The new routines will then replace the standard ones. The standard **input**(), in fact, is equivalent to **getchar**(), and the standard **output**(c) is equivalent to **putchar**(c).

There are a number of **lex** routines that enable handling sequences of characters to be processed in more than one way. These include **yymore**(), **yyless**(*n*), and **REJECT**. The text matching a specification is stored in the array **yytext**[]. In general, once the action is performed for the specification, the characters in **ytext**[] are overwritten with succeeding characters in the input stream to form the next match. The function **yymore**(), by contrast, ensures that the succeeding characters recognized are appended to those already in **yytext**[]. This lets the user do one thing and then another, when one string of characters is significant and a longer one including the first is significant as well. Consider a character string bound by **B**'s and interspersed with one at an arbitrary location.

B...B...B

In a simple code deciphering situation, the count of the number of characters between the first and second **B**'s may be obtained and then added to the number of characters between the second and third **B**. (Only the last **B** is not to be counted.) The code to do this is

```
B(^B]*{         if (flag = 0)
                      save = yyleng;
                      flag = 1;
                      yymore();
                else   {
                      importantno = save + yyleng;
                      flag = 0; }
        }
```

where **flag**, **save**, and **importantno** are declared (and at least **flag** initialized to 0) in the definitions section. The **flag** distinguishes the character sequence terminating just before the second **B** from that terminating just before the third.

The function **yylcss**(*n*) enables reset of the end point of the string to be considered to the *n*th character in the original **yytext**[]. Suppose in the code deciphering business, the gimmick is to work with only half the characters in a sequence ending with a certain one, say upper- or lowercase **Z**. The code might be

```
[a-yA-Y] + [Zz]      { yyless(yyleng/2);,
                     ... process first half of string ... }
```

Finally, the function REJECT lets one process strings of characters more easily even when they overlap or contain one another as parts. REJECT docs this by immediately jumping to the next rule and its specification without changing the contents of **yytext**[]. If the number of occurrences both of the regular expression **snapdragon** and of its subexpression dragon in an input text are to be counted; the following will do:

```
snapdragon
dragan                {" countflowers++; REJECT;}
countmonsters++;
```

As an example of one pattern overlapping another, the following counts the number of occurrences of the expressions **comedian** and **diana**, even where the input text has sequences such as **comediana**...

```
comedian              {comiccount++;. REJECT;}
diana                 princesscount++;
```

The actions here may be considerably more complicated than simply incrementing a counter. In all cases, the counters and other necessary variables are declared in the definitions section commencing the **lex** specification.

A.3.2. Definitions

The **lex** definitions section may contain any of several classes of items. The most critical are external definitions, #**include** statements, and abbreviations. For legal **lex** source this section is optional, but in most cases some of these items are necessary. External definitions have the form and function that they do in C. They declare that variables globally defined elsewhere (perhaps in another source file) will be accessed in your **lex**-generated **a.out**. Consider a declaration from an example to be developed later.

```
extern int tokval;
```

When an integer value is stored in a variable declared in this way, it will be accessible in the routine, say a parser, that calls it. If, on the other hand, a local variable is to be defined for use within the action sequence of one rule (as for the index variable for a loop), the variable can be declared at the start of the action itself right after the left brace, {.

The purpose of the **#include** statement is the same as in C: to include files of importance for the program. Some variable declarations and **lex** definitions might be needed in more than one **lex** source file. It is then advantageous to place them all in one file to be included in every file that needs them. One example occurs in using **lex** with **yacc**, which generates parsers that call a lexical analyzer. In this context, the file **y.tab.h,** which may contain #**define's** for token names should be included. Like the declarations, **#include** statements should come between %{ and }%, thus:

```
%{
#include "y.tab.h"
extern int tokval;
int lineno;
%}
```

In the definitions section, after the %} that ends the **#include's** and declarations, the abbreviations for regular expressions to be used in the rules section can be placed. The abbreviation appears on the left of the line and, separated by one or more spaces, its definition or translation appears on the right. When later abbreviations are used in the rules, they should be enclosed within braces.

NOTE

The purpose of abbreviations is to avoid needless repetition in writing the specifications and to provide clarity in reading them.

As an example, consider the **lex** source reviewed at the beginning of this section on advanced **lex** usage. The usage of definitions simplifies the later reference to digits, letters, and blanks. This is especially true if the specifications appear several times:

```
D               [0-9]
L               [a-zA-Z]
B               []
%%
-{D}+           printf ("negative integer");
+?{D}+          printf ("positive integer");
-0 {D}+         printf ("negative fraction")
G{L}*           printf ("may have a G word here");
rail {B}+road   printf ("railroad is one word");
crook           printf("criminal");
\" \/ {B}+      printf (".\"");
```

The last rule, newly added to the example is somewhat more complex than the others. **The rule ensures that a period always precedes a quotation mark at the end of a sentence**. It would change example" . to example." This . (dot) matches every character.

A.3.3. Subroutines

One may want to use subroutines in **lex** for much the same reason that one does in other programming languages. Action code that is to be used for several rules can be written once and called when needed. As with definitions, this can simplify the writing and reading of programs. The function **put_in_tabl()**, to be discussed in the next section on **lex** and **yacc**, is a good candidate for a subroutine.

Another reason to place a routine in this section is to highlight some code of interest or to simplify the rules section, even if the code is to be used for one rule only. As an example, consider the following routine to ignore comments in a language like C where comments occur between * and */:

```
"/*"      skipcmnts ();
.
.         /* rest of rules */
%%
skipcmnts ()
{
          for(;;)
          {
                    while (input () ! = '*');
                    if (input () ! = '/')
                    unput(yytext[yyleng 1]);
                    else return;
          }
}
```

There are three points of interest in this example. **First,** the **unput**(*c*) function (putting back the last character read) is necessary to avoid missing the final / if the comment ends unusually with a '**/. In this case, eventually having read an *, the analyzer finds that the next character is not the terminal / and must read some more. **Second,** the expression **yytext[yyleng-1]** picks out that last character read. **Third,** this routine assumes that the comments are not nested. (This is indeed the case with the C language). If, unlike C, they are nested in the source text, after **input**( )ing the first */ ending the inner group of comments, the **a.out** will read the rest of the comments as if they were part of the input to be searched for patterns.

Other examples of subroutines would be programmer-defined versions of the I/O routines **input**( ), **unput**(c), and **output**( ), discussed above. Subroutines such as these that may be exploited by many different programs would probably do best to be stored in their own individual file or library to be called as needed. The appropriate #**include** statements would then be necessary in the definitions section.

A.3.4. Using lex with yacc

If one works on a compiler project or develops a program to check the validity of an input language, he may want to use the system program tool **yacc**. **yacc** generates parsers, programs that analyze input to ensure that it is syntactically correct. **lex** often forms a fruitful union with **yacc** in the compiler development context. Whether or not one plans to use **lex** with **yacc**, this section can be read because it covers information of interest to all **lex** programmers.

The lexical analyzer that **lex** generates (not the file that stores it) takes the name **yylex**( ). This name is convenient because **yacc** calls its lexical analyzer by this very name. To use **lex** to create the lexical analyzer for the parser of a compiler, each **lex** action should be ended with the statement **return** *token*, where *token* is a defined term whose value is an integer. The integer value of the token returned indicates to the parser what the lexical analyzer has found. The parser, whose file is called **y.tab.c** by **yacc**, then resumes control and makes another call to the lexical analyzer when it needs another token.

In a compiler, the different values of the token indicate what, if any, reserved word of the language has been found or whether an identifier, constant, arithmetic operand, or relational operator has been found. In the latter cases, the analyzer must also specify the exact value of the token: what the identifier is, whether the constant, say, is 9 or 888, whether the operand is + or * (multiply), and whether the relational operator is = or>. Consider the following portion of **lex** source for a lexical analyzer for some programming language perhaps slightly reminiscent of Ada:

```
begin                 return (BEGIN);
end                   return (END);
while                 return (WHILE);
if                    return (IF);
package               return (PACKAGE);
reverse               return (REVERSE);
loop                  return (LOOP);
[a–zA–Z] [a–zA-Z0-9]*      {      tokval = put_in_tab( ); return (identifier); }
[0–9]+               {      tokval = put_in_tab ( ); return (INTEGER); }
\+         {          tokval = PLUS; return (ARITHOP);}
\-         {          tokval = MINUS; return (ARITHOP); }
>          {          tokval = GREATER; return (RELOP); }
> =        {      tokval = GREATEREQL; return (RELOP);}
```

Despite appearances, the tokens returned, and the values assigned to **tokval**, are indeed integers. Good programming style dictates that we use informative terms such as **BEGIN**, **END**, **WHILE**, and so forth to signify the integers the parser understands; rather than use the integers themselves. You establish the association by using **#define** statements in your parser calling routine in C. For example,

```
#define    BEGIN  1
#define    END    2
#define    PLUS   7
```

If the need arises to change the integer for some token type, then the **#define** statement in the parser can be changed rather than hunting through the entire program, changing every occurrence of the particulr integer. In using **yacc** to generate the parser, it is helpful to insert the statement

```
#include y.tab.h
```

into the definitions section of the **lex** source. The file **y.tab.h** provides **#define** statements that associate token names such as **BEGIN**, **END**, and so on with the integers of significance to the generated parser.

To indicate the reserved words in the example, the returned integer values suffice. For the other token types, the integer value of the token type is stored in the programmer-defined variable **tokval**. This variable, whose definition was an example in the definitions section, is globally defined so that the parser as well as the lexical analyzer can access it. **yacc** provides the variable **yyival** for the same purpose.

The example shows two ways to assign a value to **tokval**. First, a function **put_in_tabl( )** places the name and type of the identifier or constant in a symbol table so that the compiler can refer to it in this or a later stage of the compilation process. More to the present point, **put_in_table( )** assigns a type value to **tokval** so that the parser can use the information immediately to determine the syntactic correctness of the input text. The function **put_in_tab ( )** would be a routine that the compiler writer might place in the subroutines section discussed later.

Second, in the last few actions of the example, tokval is assigned a specific integer indicating which operand or relational operator the analyzer recognized. If the variable PLUS, for instance, is associated with the interger 7 by means of the **#define** statement above, then when a + sign is recognized, the action assigns to **tokval** the value 7, which indicates the +. The analyzer indicates the general class of operator by the value it returns to the parser (in the example, the integer signified by ARITHOP or RELOP).

A.4. Running lex Under the UNIX System

As the following few steps are reviewed, the Figure 1 at the start of the chapter may be recalled. To produce the lexical analyzer in C,

lex lex.*l*

can be used, where **lex.*l*** is the file containing the **lex** specification. The name **lex.*l*** is conventionally the favourite, but in general any name can be used. The output file that **lex** produces is automatically called **lex.yy.c;** this is the lexical analyzer program that is created with **lex**. This can be compiled and linked as any C program, making sure that the **lex** library is invoked with the ***-ll*** option.

cc lex.yy.c *-ll*

The **lex** library provides a default **main**() program that calls the lexical analyzer under the name **yylex**(), so a local **main**() need not be supplied.

If the **lex** specification is spread across several files, **lex** can be run with each of them individually, but each **lex.yy.c** file should be renamed (with **mv**) before running **lex** on the next one. Otherwise, each will overwrite the previous one. Once all the generated **.c** files are ready, they can be compiled in one command line.

With the executable **a.out** produced, any desired input text can be analyzed. Suppose that the text is stored under the filename **textin** (this name is also arbitrary). The lexical analyzer **a.out** by default takes input from the terminal. To have it take the file **textin** as input, simple redirection can be used, thus:

a.out < textin

By default, output will appear on the tenminal, but can be redirected as well:

a.out < textin > textout

In running **lex** with **yacc**, either may be run first.

yacc -d grammar.y

lex lex.*l*

spawns a parser in the file **y.tab.c.** (The **.d** option creates the file **y.tab.h,** which contains the **#define** statements that associate the **yacc** assigned integer token values with the user-defined token names.) To compile and link the output files produced,

cc lex.yy.c y.tab.c -ly *-ll*

can be used. The **yacc** library is loaded (with tho **-ly** option) before the **lex** library (with the ***-ll*** option) to ensure that the **main**() program supplied will call the **yacc** parser.

There are several options available with the **lex** command. If one or more of them are used, they should be placed between the command name **lex** and the filename argument. To see the C program, **lex.yy.c,** that **lex** generates on the terminal (the default output device), the **-t** option can be used.

lex -t lex.*l*

The **-v** option prints out a small set of statistics describing the so-called finite automata that **lex** produces with the C program **lex.yy.c.**

lex uses a table (a two-dimensional array in C) to represent its finite automaton. The maximum number of states that the finite automaton requires is set by default to 500. If the **lex** source has a large number of rules or the rules are very complex, this default value may be too small. The value can be enlarged by placing another entry in the definitions section of the **lex** source, as follows:

%n 700

This entry tells **lex** to make the table large enough to handle as many as 700 states. (The –v option will indicate how large a number one should choose). If the maximum number of state transitions needs to be increased beyond 2000, the designated parameter is **a**, thus:

%a 2800

The *Programmer's Reference Manual* page on **lex** contains a list of all the options available with the **lex** command.

This tutorial has tried to introduce the concepts of **lex** programming. As with any programming language, the way to master it is to write programs and then write some more.

APPENDIX B: SYLLABUS (GGSIPU) 2015

GGSIPU, (NEW SYLLABUS – 2015)

OPERATING SYSTEMS

Paper Code: ETCS–304	**L**	**T/P**	**C**
Paper : Operating Systems	**3**	**1**	**4**

INSTRUCTIONS TO PAPER SETTERS: **Maximum Marks : 75**

1. Question No. 1 should be compulsory and cover the entire syllabus. This question should have objective or short answer type questions. It should be of 25 marks.
2. Apart from Question No. 1, rest of the paper shall consist of four units as per the syllabus. Every unit should have two questions. However, student may be asked to attempt only 1 question from each unit. Each question should be of 12.5 marks.

Objective: *The goal of this course is to provide an introduction to the internal operation of modern operating systems. The course will cover processes and threads, mutual exclusion, CPU scheduling, deadlock, memory management, and file systems.*

UNIT I

Introduction: What is an Operating System, Simple Batch Systems, Multiprogrammed Batches systems, Time-sharing Systems, Personal-computer systems, Parallel systems, Distributed Systems, Real-Time Systems, OS – A Resource Manager.

Memory Organization & Management: Memory Organization, Memory Hierarchy, Memory Management Strategies, Contiguous versus non-Contiguous memory allocation, Partition Management Techniques, Logical versus Physical Address space, swapping, Paging, Segmentation, Segmentation with Paging.

Virtual Memory: Demand Paging, Page Replacement, Page-replacement Algorithms, Performance of Demand Paging, Thrashing, Demand Segmentation, and Overlay Concepts.

[T1] [T2] [R2] [R3] [No. of hrs. 10]

UNIT II

Processes: Introduction, Process states, process management, Interrupts, Interprocess Communication

Threads: Introduction, Thread states, Thread Operation, Threading Models.

Processor Scheduling: Scheduling levels, pre emptive vs no pre emptive scheduling, priorities, scheduling objective, scheduling criteria, scheduling algorithms, demand scheduling, real time scheduling.

Process Synchronization: Mutual exclusion, software solution to Mutual exclusion problem; hardware solution to Mutual exclusion problem, semaphores, Critical section problems. Case study on Dining philosopher problem, Barber shop problem etc.

[T1] [T2] [R3] [No. of hrs. 10]

UNIT III

Deadlocks: Examples of deadlock, resource concepts necessary conditions for deadlock, deadlock solution, deadlock prevention, deadloack avoidance with Bankers algorithms, deadock detection, deadlock recovery.

Device Management: Disk Sheduling Strategies, Rotational Optimization, System Consideration, Caching and Buffering.

[T1] [T2] [R1] [No. of hrs. 10]

UNIT IV

File System: Introduction, File Organization, Logical File System, Physical File System, File Allocation strategy, Free Space Management, File Access Control, Data Access Techniques, Data Integrity Protection, Case study on file system viz FAT32, NTFS, Ext2/Ext3 etc.

[T1] [T2] [R4] [R5] [No. of hrs. 10]

GGSIPU, New Revised Syllabus 2015

OPERATING SYSTEMS (LINUX PROGRAMMING AND ADMINISTRATION) LAB

	L	T/P	C
Paper Code: ETCS–352			
Paper : Operating Systems (Linux Programming and Administration) Lab	**0**	**2**	**I**

List of Experiments:

1. Write a program to implement CPU scheduling for first come first serve.
2. Write a program to implement CPU scheduling for shortest job first.
3. Write a program to perform priority scheduling.
4. Write a program to implement CPU scheduling for Round Robin.
5. Write a program for page replacement policy using (*a*) LRU (*b*) FIFO (*c*) Optimal.
6. Write a program to implement first fit, best fit and worst fit algorithm for memory management.
7. Write a program to implement reader/writer problem using semaphore.
8. Write a program to implement Banker's algorithm for deadlock avoidance.

NOTE:– At least 8 Experiment out of the list must be done in the semester.

Appendix C

Glossary

1. **Address:** The number of a particular memory or peripheral storage location.
2. **Address Binding:** The binding of instructions and data for a process to physical memory or absolute addresses at the compile time, load time or execution time.
3. **Address space:** It is the total amount of memory that can be addressed by the computer. For instance, Pentium (or 586) machine can address upto 4GB of physical memory and 64TB of virtual memory.
4. **Allocation:** It means reservation of resources like memory or disk.
5. **Base:** It is a starting or reference point.
6. **Batch:** A group of jobs.
7. **Block:** A group of disk records that is stored and transferred as a single unit.
8. **Buffer:** A separate, small memory area for some specialized functions.
9. **Consistency:** It means keeping the same data in several copies of the same file through processes that might be altering one or other of the copies.
10. **Context Switch:** CPU Switching from one process to another. Typical range is from 1–1000 microseconds.
11. **Contiguous:** Side by side or adjacent to each other.
12. **Directory:** A data structure on a secondary storage device like FDD, HDD etc.
13. **Effective Access Time (EAT):** How long it takes for a data byte in memory to be transferred to or from the CPU. It can be increased by page faulting which occurs in demand paging.
14. **Fault rate:** The rate of occurrences of faults which occurs when the CPU requests code which is not currently stored in the memory.
15. **GANTT chart:** A type of floating bar chart usually used in project management to show the use of resources/tasks over time.
16. **Hardware:** The physical portion of the computer.
17. **Interrupt:** A signal that is generated when some I/O is required.
18. **Memory Mapping:** The location of instructions and data in memory.
19. **Time slice:** A short interval of time allotted to each user or program in a multitasking or timesharing system.
20. **Transaction:** An atomic unit of work.
21. **Volatile:** A memory is said to be volatile if its contents are lost if the power is turned off.
22. **Word:** 1 word = 2 bytes
23. **Wormhole Routing:** It is a way of pipelining packet transmission in a multihop network.

Appendix D

EXPERIMENTS (PROGRAMS) FOR O.S. LAB. WITH SOLUTIONS

Expt.1: WAP in C to implement Multipath Routing.

Expt.2: WAP in C to implement Best–fit and first-fit allocation algorithms.

Expt.3: WAP in C to implement different page replacement algorithms.

Expt.4: WAP in C to implement and compare various CPU scheduling algorithms.

Expt.5: WAP in C to implement data compression and decompression using HUFFMAN Coding algorithm.

Expt.6: WAP in C to implement Banker's algorithm.

Expt.7: WAP in C to implement shortest path algorithm.

Expt.8: WAP in C to implement encryption and decryption algorithms.

Expt.9: WAP using Shell programming to list the number of files created by a user and to list the total files created by the user.

Expt.10: WAP in C to transfer a file between two stations.

Expt.11: WAP in C to implement Djikstra's algorithm of shortest path.

Expt.12: WAP in C to create MOT and POT tables.

Expt.13: WAP in C to find the length of given ALP. Also find the number of machine opcodes and pseudo–opcodes.

Expt.14: Write a shell program to count number of files.

Expt.15: WAP in C to sequence n–jobs through two machines.

Expt.16: WAP in C to create symbol Table (ST), Base Table (BT) and Literal Table (LT) of a given ALP.

Expt.17: WAP in C to search for a symbol in ST in experiment–16 (above) and to print the line number, if NOT FOUND.

Expt.18: WAP in C to process RR–type of instruction.

Expt.19: WAP in C to create MDT, MNT and ALA (for MACROS–Pass 1) for a given source program.

Expt.20: WAP in C (Linux based) to simulate on producer–consumer problem in bounded buffer using counting semaphores and mutex.

Expt.21: WAP in C(Linux-based) to implement your own Linux-shall. Also rewrite the same program using DOS intermpys.

Experiments in OS Lab

Experiment No.1

MULTIPATH ROUTING

```
# include <stdio.h>
# include<bios.h>
# define     true 1
# define     false 0
typedef struct
    {
        int vnode;
        float wt;
    } make;
typedef struct
        {
            int dnode;
            make class1;
            make class 2;
            make class 3;
        } form;
form table[10][10];
int m[10][10], n; /* n = no. of nodes */
void readmat ( ) /* read matrix–m */
{ int i, j;
for (i = 1; i < = n; i ++)
    for (j = i + 1; j < = n; j ++)
        {
            printf ("\n enter element %d %d", i, j):
            scanf ("%d", &m[i] [j]);
            m[j][i] = m[i]][j];
        }
            return;
}
void printmat ( ) /* print the matrix–m */
{ int i, j;
    for (i = 1; i < = n; i ++)
```

```
        {
            for (j = 1; j < = n; j ++)
            printf ("%d    ",m[i][j]);
            printf ("\n");
        }
        return;
}
int connect (a, b)
int a,b;
{   if (m[a][b]==1)
        return (true):
        else
            return (false):
}
void print_tables( )
{   int i,j,k;
    for (i = 1; i < = n; i++)
    {   printf ("\n\n\n press any number to continue\n");
        k = getch();/* scanf ("%d", &k); */
printf ("\n\n\n table source node \n\n", i);
for (j = 1; j < = n; j ++)
if (i ! = j)
{printf ("%d\t %d\t %1.2f\t %d \t %1.2f\t%d\t%1.2f\n",
table[i][j]. dnode, table [i][j].class1.vnode, table[i][j]. class1.wt,
table [i] [j]. class2. vnode, table [i][j]. class2.wt,table [i][j]. class 3. vnode, table[i][j]. class3.wt);
    }
    }
    return;
    }
    float random ( )
    {
        long L;
        float F;
        t = biostime (0, t)
        t = t% 100;
        if (t <  0)
            t+=100;
            r = L/100.0;
            return (r);
}
void path( )
{
    int x,y,a,b;
    float rdm;
```

```
printf ("\n\n\n enter the source node: \n");
scanf ("%d", & x);
printf ("\n enter the destination node:");
scanf ("%d", &y);
rdm = random( );
printf ("the random no is %f", rdm);
if ((rdm > 0) & & (rdm < = 0.6))
{
    printf ("\n the next node taken = % d", table [x] [y]. class 1. vnode);
}
else
    if ((rdm > 0.6) & & (rdm < = 0.85))
    {
        printf ("\n the next node taken =%d", table [x][y]. class2. vnode);
    }
else
    if ((rdm>0.85) && (rdm < 1))
    {
        a = table [x][y]. class3.vnode;
        b = table[x][y]. class2.vnode;
        printf ("\n\n\n the path taken=%d %d %d %d; x, a, b, y);
    }
        return;
}
/*  float random ( )
    {
        long t;
        float r;
            t = biostime (0, t);
        t = t% 100;
        if (t < 0)
            t = t + 100;
            r = t/100.0;
        return (r);
}
*/
void main ( )
{   int i,j,h,x,y,z;
    int ch = 0;
printf ("\n enter the no of nodes \n");
scanf ("%d", & n);
readmat ( );
print.f ("\n\n adjacency matrix\n\n");
printmat ( );
printf ("\n\n");
```

```
while (ch! = 27)
{
for (i = 1; i < = n; i++)
    {    for (j = 1; j < = n; j++)
              {
                   if (i! = j)
                   {
                   table [i][j]. dnode = j;
/* finding path for 1 hop*/
if (connect(i,j) = = true)
{table [i][j]. class1. vnode=j;
table[i][j]. class1. wt=0.6;
}
/* finding path for 2 hop*/
for (k = 1; k < = n; k++)
if (K! = i && k! = j)
if ((connect(i,k) = = true) && (connect(k, j) = done))
{
table[i][j].class2.vnode = k;
table[i][j].class2.wt = 0.25;
break;
}
/* finding path of 3 hop*/
for (x = 1; x < = n;x++)
for (y = 1; y < = n; y ++)
if ((x! = i && x! = j) && (y! = i && y! = j)
if ((connect (i, x) = = true) && (connect (x,y) = = true) && (conneet(y,j) = = true))
{
table [i][j].class3.vnode = x;
table[i][j].class3. wt = 0.15;
break;
}
} /* if*/
} /* for*/
} /*for*/
print_tables ( );
path ( );
printf ("\n press < Enter > to continue & <ESC> to exit\n");
ch = getch( );
}
}
```

Experiment No. 2

Program–2

Comparison of Best–fit and first–fit allocation algorithms:–

These 2–algorithms, are for allocation of memory for Jobs. Memory in contiguous and in the form of blocks of fixed size. The problem of OS is to allocate memory to the requesting jobs in such a way that the wastage (of space) is minimum.

In a multiuser system, not all jobs are brought into main memory because if that happens then user will be kept with very little memory.

To avoid this the above two algorithms are used, the jobs which are currently being modified, or processed are allowed to stay in the memory & rest will be put in a locking store. When that particular jobs turn of execution comes then it is wrapped into main memory from the locking store.

Example :

No. of partition = 5

Partitions are :- 100, 200, 400, 300, 500

JOB - ID:- 1 2 3 4 5

Size:- 150 250 450 50 350

First-fit

P. No.	Part-size	Status	JOB-ID	Wastage
1	100	1	4	50
2	200	1	1	50
3	400	1	2	150
4	300	0		0
5	500	1	3	50

JOB-5 WAITS IN QUEUE AND IS PUT IN PARTITION 3 OR 5 IF EITHER JOB-2 OR 3 IS REMOVED

BEST-FIT

P. No.	Part-size	Status	JOB-ID	Wastage
1	100	1	4	50
2	200	1	1	50
3	400	1	5	50
4	300	1	2	50
5	500	1	3	50

SINCE ALL JOBS ARE PUT IN PARTITIONS, QUEUE REMAINS EMPTY.

Algorithm for First-fit:-

1. Read the number of partitions.
2. Read the size of the partitions.
3. Read the job-ID & size of the job.
4. If the partition is empty & if the job fits into the partition put the job.
5. Make status as 1 & calculate wastage of memory.
6. If the job does not fit into partition or if the partition is occupied put the job in a queue. This job must wait until a job is removed.
7. Repeat the same process for all jobs & display the wastage status & job-id.

Algorithm for Best-fit:-

1. Read the number of partitions.
2. Read the size of the partitions.

3. Read the job size & its ID.
4. Find an index such that its partition is free & the wastage in minimum when the job is put.
5. If found the job is put into the partition & the status of partition is made 1.
   If NOT found, put the job in a queue to be processed later when another job completes.
6. If a job finishes processing, check the first job in the queue whether it can be allocated memory.

```
# include <stdio.h>
int        Par-size [20], status [20], wastage [20],
           bstatus [20], bwastage[20];
char       j, id [10] [50], bj, id [10] [50];
int        i, j, k, l, m, n;
main ( )
{
           int d, p, i;
           char job f[15];
           int  size;
printf ("\t Enter no. of partitions : \n");
scanf ("%d", &n);
printf ("Enter the size of the partition :\n");
           for (i = 0; i < n; i++)
                  {
                  printf ("Enter size of partition: % d \n"; i +1);
                  scanf ("%d", & Par_size [i};
           }
do
           {
                  clrscr ( );
printf ("\n\n-ADD A JOB \n");
printf ("\n\n 2. REMOVE A JOB \n");
printf ("\n\n 3. EXIT \n");
printf ("Enter your choice:);
scanf ("%d", & choice);
switch (choice)
           {
Case 1:
printf ("Enter the job: \n");
scanf ("%s", jobf);
printf ("Enter the size: \n");
scanf ("%d", & size);
first-fit (jobf, size);
printf ("\n");
Best-fit (job f, size);
break;
```

```
Case-2:
      printf ("Enter job to be removed: \n");
      scanf ("%s", jobf);
      firstft_fn (jobf);
      printf ("\n");
      bestfit-fn (jobf);
      break;
Case 3:
                  break;
            }
      } while (toupper (getchar ( ))== 'y');
      }
      void first-ft ( )
            {
                  int x;
      printf ("FIRST FIT \n");
      for (x = 0; x<n; x++)
      if (size [x] < = Par-size[n] && status [x] = = 0)
            {
                  status[x] = 1;
                  wastage [x] : par-size[x].size [x];
      ]
            i++;
      for (i = 0 ; i<n ; i++)
            {
      printf ("%d %d %d %s %d \n, i+1,
            par-size [i], status [i],
            j-id[i], wastage [i]);
            }
            return;
      }
      void first-ff( )
            {
                  int j;
      for (j = 0; j<n; j++)
            if (strcpy (job, job_id[j] ==0)
      {
      strcpy (j-id[j], "");
      wastage {j] = 0;
      status [j] = 0;
      }
      for (i = 0; i<n; i++)
      printf ("%d %d %d %s %d \n", i+1, par-size [i], status [i], wastage [i]);
      return;
```

```
}
printf ("Job not found \n");
return;
}
void      Best-fit (jobf, size)
char      jobf [ ];
int       size;
{
int a, x, y;
for (x = 0; x < n; x ++)
{
if (size < =par-size [x] && bstatus [x] ==0)
{
temp [a] = Par-size [x];
temp 1 [a] = x;
          a ++;
          }
     }
if (x = = n)
     {
     [m] = size ;
strcpy (ba [m], bj-id);
          m++;
}
min = temp [0];
for (y = 1; y < n; y++)
     {
          if (min > temp [y])
          {
          min = temp [y];
               d = y;
          }
}
bstatus [temp1[d]]=1;
bwastage [temp1[d]] = min-size;
strcpy (bj-id [temp1[d]], job);
for (i =0 ; i< n ; i++)
printf ("%d %d %d %s %d \n", i+1, par-size [i], bstatus [i], bj–id [i], bwastage [i]);
return;
}
```

Experiment No. 3

```
#include<stdio.h>
int fsize, nopages, page [25], frame[15], fifoc = 0, 1ruc = 0, optc = 0, op, af;
void print frame (t)
int t;
{
    int i;
    if (frame [i]! = – 1)
    {
            printf ("frames are:");
            for (i = 1, i< =fsize; i ++)
            if (frame[i] ==-1)
            print f (" ");
            else
                    printf ("%d", frame [i]);
                    printf("\n");
    }
}
            int. present (tpage)
            int tpage;
            {
                    int. i;
                    for (i = 1; i< = fsize; i++)
                        if (frame[i] == tpage)
                    return (1);
                    else return (0);
            }
                    void fifo ( )
                    {
                            int i = 0, j = 1;
                            for (i = 1; i < = fsize; i ++)
                            frame [i] = –1;
                            for (i = 1; i < = no pages; i++)
                            {
                                    if (!present (page [i]))
                                    {
                                    if (j <=fsize)
                                    {
                                    frame [j] = page[i];
                                    j++;
                                    }
                                    else
                                    {
```

```
                                        j = 1;
                                        frame [j] = page[i];
                                        j++;
                                        }
                                        printf ("received page %d", page[i]);
                                        printframe (page[i]);
                                        } /*outer-if closes */
                                        else
                                        fifoc++;
                        } /* for closes*/
                        } /* fifo closes */
int isoptimal ( )
{
int. i, j, count[25], temp=0;
for (i = 1; i < = nopages; i++)
count[i] = 0;
for (i = 1; i< = fsize; i++)
{
for (j = cp+1; j < = nopages;j++)
if (frame[i]! = page[j])
count [i]++;
else
break;
}
for (i = 1; i < = fsize; i++)
{
if (count[i] > temp)
{
af = i;
temp = count [i];
}
}
return (af);
}
void optimal ( )
{
int i, j =1;
af = 0,
for (i = 1; i < = fsize; i++)
frame[i] = -1;
for (i = 1, i; < = nopages; i++)
{
cp = i;
```

```
if (!present(page[i]))
{
if (j < = fsize)
{
frame[j] = page[i];
j++;
}
else
{
isoptimal ( );
frame [af] = page [i];
/* j++; */
}
printf ("received page %d", page [i]);
printframe (page[i]);
}
else
optc++;
}
}
int islru ( )
{
int i, j, count[25], temp = 0;
for (i =1; i < = nopages; i++)
count[i] = 0;
for (i = 1; i< = fsize; i++)
{
for (j=cp–1; j > = 1; j– –)
if (frame[i]! = page [j])
count [i]++;
else break;
}
for (i =1; i < = fsize; i++)
{
if (count[i]>temp)
{
af = i;
temp = count[i];
}
}
return (af);
}
```

```
void lru( )
{
int i, j =1;
for (i =1; i < = fsize; i++)    /*Repeat*/
frame[i] = –1;
for (i = 1; i < = nopages; i++)
{
cp = i;
af = 0;
if (!present(page[i]))
{
if (j<=fsize)
{
frame[j] = page[i];
j++;
}
else
{
islru ( );
frame[af] = page[i];
j++;
}
printf ("received page %d", page[i]);
printframe(page [i]);
}
else
lruc++;
}
}
void main
{
int i, j;
char ch[2];
printf ("enter the size of frame(m);");
scanf ("%d", &fsize);
printf ("enter the no of pages:");
scanf ("%d", &nopages);
printf ("enter the sequence of page no.'s \n");
for (i = 1; i < = nopages; i++)
scanf ("%d", &page[i]);
printf ("allocation of frames in fifo method \n");
fifo( );
```

```
printf ("\npress any ket to continue...");
scanf ("%s", ch);
printf ("allocation of frames in opt method \n");
optimal ( );
printf("\n press any key to continue");
scanf ("%s", ch);
printf ("\n allocation of frames lru method \n");
lru ( );
printf ("\n press any key to continue...");
scanf ("%s", ch);
printf ("SUCCESS\tFAILURE\n"); /*follows below*/
printf ("fifo %d\t%d\n", fifoc, nopages – fifoc);       /*
printf ("opt %d\t%d\n", optc, nopages–optc); .:
printf ("lru %d\t%d\\n\n", lruc, nopages–lruc);
printf ("SUCCESS RATE \t FAILURE RATE\n");
printf ("fifo  % f\t\t%f\n", (fifoc*1.0/nopages)*100.0;
(nopages – fifoc) *1.0/nopages*100.0);
printf("opt%f \t%f\n", (optc*1.0/nopages)*100.0,
(no pages – optc) * 1.0/nopages * 100.0); }
printf ("lru %f\t\t%f\n; lruc *1.0/nopages) *100.0;
}
```

EXPERIMENT NO.4

Comparison of CPU scheduling Algorithms:–

(pre-emptive & non-preemptive)

(1) FCFS (Non–pre–emptive).
2) SJF (Non–pre–emptive).
3) Priority (Non–pre–emptive).
4) SRJF (preemptive).
5) Priority (preemptive).
6) Round Robin (pre–emptive).

Description:–

FCFS: – The first come first serve algorithm is a non-premptive algorithms. The jobs arrive and the CPU goes on executing them without any check for any priority or run–time.

As it does not check for any conditions it has many disadvantages.

For eg: if a lower priority job is being executed and if a job of higher priority arrives then it has to wait till the job of lower priority completes.

SJF: The shortest job first is an algorithm which checks for the condition of shortest job i.e., suppose if it finds a shortest job or a job which has less runtime then that is selected for execution. Afer its execution, CPU scheduler then again repeats the search for the next job which is the shortest. This is the non-preemptive part of SJF algorithm.

In pre-emptive algorithm while one job is executing if there is any other job waiting in the ready queue with less burst time then the CPU puts the current job into ready queue without terminating and quits up that job from the ready queue. If there is no job in the ready queue then the current job will be executed till completion and then checks in the queue. This algorithm is also called the shortest remaining job First (SRJF) algorithm.

Priority – Based Algorithms

In the non-preemptive algorithm the CPU scheduler checks for the job which has the highest priority and the CPU scheduler picks up that job for execution. After the execution of this job the scheduler then gets the job which has the highest priority among the jobs in the ready queue.

In the pre-emptive part of the algorithm if a job is being executed and before the completion of this job if a job of higher priority arrives at the queue, then the current job is put into the queue without termination and the job with the highest priority is picked up for execution.

Round Robin

This is a pre-emptive algorithm so here one job can force the other to stop execution. Here a time quantum will be fixed for every job in the queue which will be equal for all the jobs. Each job has to execute for the specified period of time and go back to the ready queue and make way for the next job in the queue. When the job is completed it will not enter the queue. This is to be repeated until all the jobs are completed.

Example

JOB	ARRIVAL	BURST–TIME	PRIORITY
J1	10.0	0.3	2
J2	10.2	0.1	5
J3	10.3	0.4	7
J4	10.5	0..3	2
J5	10.7	0.2	1

FIFO

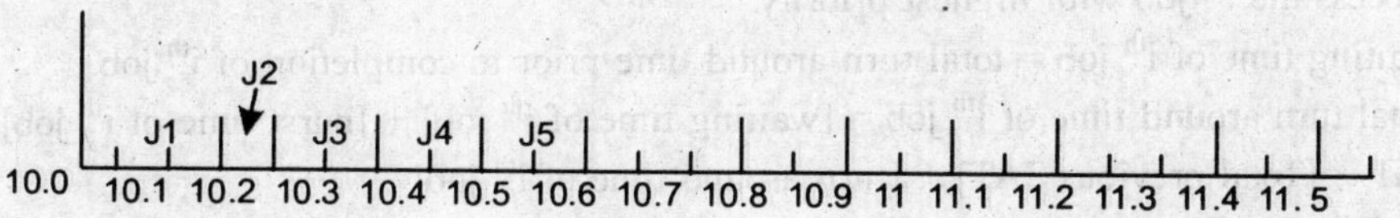

SJF:-

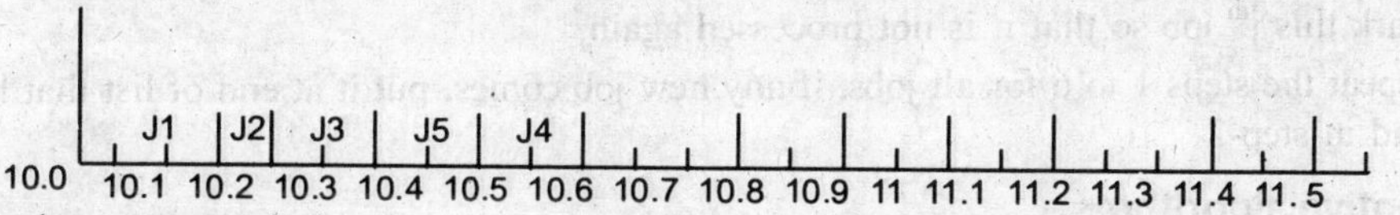

Priority:- (non-preemptive)

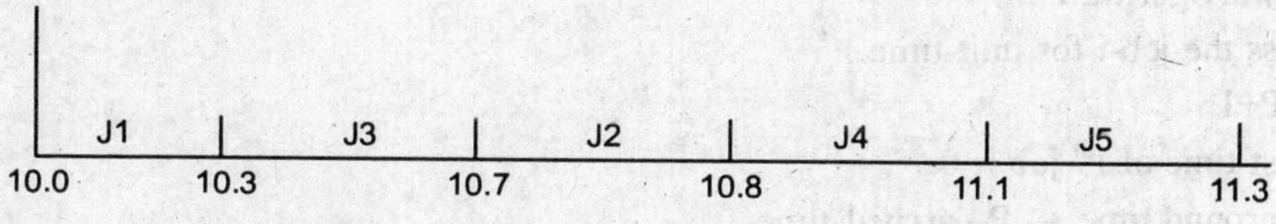

SJRF :

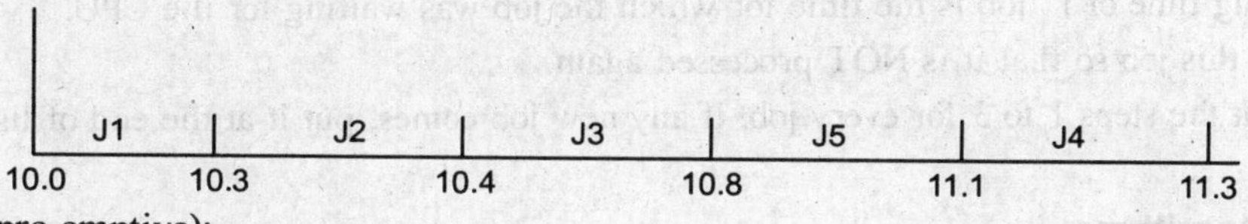

Priority (pre-emptive):-

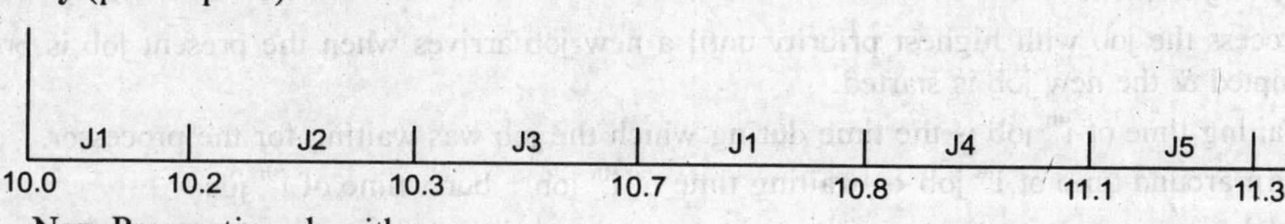

Non–Preemptive algorithms:–

FCFS algorithms:–

(1) Process the incoming job.

(2) Waiting time of ith–job is total turn around time of prior to completion of ith job, if i = 1 then witing time of job is 0.

(3) Turn around time of ith job is completion time — arriving time.

(4) Total turn around time = [previous total turn around time] + [i^{th} jobs turn around time]

(5) Total waiting time = [previous total turn around time] + [waiting time of ith job]

(6) Repeat steps 1 through 6 for all jobs and if any new job has come, put it at the end of the list that has been read in step 1.

SJF algorithm:-

(1) Process the job with shortest burst time.

(2) Waiting time of ith job is total turn around time prior to completion of ith job.

(3) Turn around time of ith job = [waiting time of ith job] + [burst time of ith job]

(4) Total turn around time = [Precious total turn around time] + [turn around time of ith job]

(5) Total waiting time = Previous total waiting time + Waiting time of ith job

(6) Repeat steps 1 to 5 for all jobs and if any new job, put it at the end of the list that has been read in step-1.

Priority Algorithms-

(1) Process the ith job with highest priority.

(2) Waiting time of ith job = total turn around time prior to completion of ith job.

(3) Total turn around time of ith job = [waiting time of ith job] + [burst time of ith job]

(4) TAT = [Total previous TAT] + [turn around time of ith job]

(5) TWT = [Total previous waiting time] + [waiting time of job]

(6) Mark this i^{th} job so that it is not processed again.

(7) Repeat the steps 1 to 6 for all jobs, if any new job comes, put it at end of list that has been read in step-2

Pre-emptive algorithms:-

Round *Robin* Algorithm:-

(1) Process the job-i for unit time.

(2) P ← P+1

(3) If burst time of ith job = 0.

Turn around time ← P– arrival time

Waiting time of ith job is the time for which the job was waiting for the CPU.

(4) Mark this job so that it is NOT processed again.

(5) Repeat the steps 1 to 3 for every job, if any new job comes, put it at the end of list read in step-1.

Priority Algorithm:-

(1) Process the job with highest priority until a new job arrives when the present job is pre-empted & the new job is started.

(2) Waiting time of ith job is the time during which the job was waiting for the processor.

(3) Turn around time of ith job ← waiting time of ith job + burst time of ith job.

(4) Total turn around time ← previous total turn around time + turn around time of ith job.

(5) Total waiting time ← [Previous total waiting time] + [Waiting time of ith job]

(6) Repeat steps 1 to 5 for all jobs & if any new job comes, put it at the end of list that has been read in step-1.

SJRF Algorithm:-

(1) Process the job with shortest time until a new job arrives when the present job is pre-empted and new job is started.

(2) Waiting time of ith job = time during which job was waiting for the CPU.

(3) Turn around time of ith job ← waiting time of ith job + burst time of ith job.

(4) Total turn around time ← previous total waiting time + turn around time of the ith job.

(5) Total waiting time → Previous total waiting time + waiting time of ith job.

(6) Repeat steps 1 to 5 for all jobs and if any new job comes, put it at the end of the list that has been read in step 1.

Program:

```
void FCFS ( )
{
  int i ;
for (i = 0; i< = No-jobs; i++)
```

```
finish-time [1][i] = 0
ATAT[1] = 0;
AWT [1] = 0;
current-time = arrival-time [1];
for (i = 1; i < = No-jobs; i++)
  {
if (current-time < arrival-time [i])
  current-time = arrival-time [i] + burst-time[i];
else
current-time = current-time + Burst-time [i];
finish-time [1] [i] = finish-time [1] [i–i1] + burst-time [i];
TAT [1] [i] = finish-time [1] [i] - arrival time [i];
wt [1] [i] = TAT [1] [i] - burst-time [i];
ATAT [1] = ATAT [1] + TAT [1] [i];
AWT [1] = AWT [1] + WT [1] [i];
}
}
int SJF-F (t)
int t;
  {
int i, sjob = 0;
short-time = 1000;
for (i = 1; i < = No-jobs; i++)
if (! finished-job [i])
if (arrival-time [i] < = t && burst-time [i] < short-time)
{
short-time = burst-time [i];
  sjob = i;
}
  return (sjob);
}
int priority 1-F (t)
int t;
{
int i, hjob, priority- no = 0;
for (i = 1; i < = no-jobs; i++)
if (! finished-job [i])
if (arrival-time [i] < = t && priority-of-job [1] > priority-No)
{
Priority-no. = Priority-of-job [i];
hjob = i;
}
```

```
return (hjob);
}
void SJF-priority (K)
    int K;
    {
int i, j = 0, SJ, PJ;
for (i = 0; i< = no. of jobs; i++)
    {
finish-time [K] [i] = 0;
    finished-Job [1] = 0;
}
ATAT [K] = 0;
AWT [K] = 0;
Current-time = arrival-time [1];
i = 1;
SJ = arrival-time [1];
While (i < = No-jobs)
    {
            PJ =J;
if (K = = 2)
    J = SJF-F (SJ);
else
    J = Priority 1-F (SJ);
SJ = Finish-time [K] [J] = current-time;
TAT [K] [J] = finish-time [K] [J]-arrival-time [J];
WT [K] [J] = TAT [K] [J] - burst-time [J];
ATAT[K] = ATAT [K] + TAT [K] [J];
AWT [K] = AWT [K] + WT [K] [J];
finished-job [J] = 1;
i++;
}
}
```

EXPERIMENT NO.5

WACP to implement data compression & decompression using HUFFMAN coding alorithms.

Algorithms:-

(1) Read the input text.
(2) Count the number of characters in the text.
(3) Given a count of total number of any given characters.
(4) Calculate count value for all characters which appear in the text.
(5) Find probability of the characters.
(6) Sort these probabilities in descending order and take the lowest two values and create a tree.
(7) When 2 nodes are joined insert the parent node, whose count is equal to the sum of the children node.
(8) Repeat steps (6) & (7) till there is only one probability left.
(9) Travers binary tree with left child as 0 & right child as 1.
(10) Store the code in a file and count the equivalent number for that and print the compressed part.

```
#include <ctype.h>
#include <stdio.h>
#include<graphics.h>
struct node {
    int prob;
    char chr;
    struct node *left;
    struct node *right;
    int visit;
};
struct node *tree [100];
struct oput
    {
    char c;
    char no [100];
    }
    codes [100];
FILE *out;
# define nullptr (struct node*) 0
    int tree-p = 0;
    int no-char = 0;
    struct node *root;
void leaf-node (x)
    char x;
    {
            int i, j;
            int present = 0;
```

```
no-char ++;
if (tree-p >0)
{
for (j = 0; j < tree-p && !present; j++)
{
if (tree [j]  → chr = = x)
{
tree [j] → prob ++;
present = 1;
}
}
}
if (! present)
{
tree [tree-p] = (struct node *) malloc (size of (struct node));
tree [tree-p] → chr = x;
tree [tree-p] → prob = 1;
tree [tree-p] → left = 0;
tree [tree-p] → right = 0;
tree [tree-p] → visit =  0;
        tree-p++;
    }
return;
}
void descend-order ( )
{
int i, j;
struct node *t;
for (i = 0; i < tree-p-1; i++)
for (j = i+1; j <tree-p; j++)
}
root = tree [0];
}
int gen (root, input)
char input [80];
struct node *root;
{
char code [100];
int i = 0, k, j, l = 0;
struct node *t;
t = root;
code [0] = '\0';
```

```
while (1)
        {
        if (t → visit ==1)
        {
        return (i);
        }
        if (t → left = = 0 & & t → right = = 0)
        {
        t → visit = 1;
        {
        codes [i].c = t → chr;
        codes [l].no[l] = '\0';
        codes [l] = '\o';
  strcpy [codes [i]. no, code);
  }
  l = 0;
  t = root;
  i++;
}
else
if (tree [i] → prob < tree [j] → prob.)
  {
  t = tree [i];
  tree [i] = tree [j];
  tree [j] = t;
  }
  return;
}
void connect ( )
  {
  int i;
  struct node *t;
  root = (struct node *) malloc (size of (struct node));
  while (tree-p > 1)
  {
  no-char ++;
  t = (struct node *) malloc (size of (struct node));
  t → left = tree [tree–p–1];
  t → right = tree [tree–p–2];
  t → prob = tree [tree–p–1] → prob + tree [tree–p–2] → prob;
  t → chr = '#';
  t → visit = 0;
  tree-p – = 2;
```

```
    tree [tree-p] = t;
    tree - p ++ ;
    descend-order ( );
    if (t → left ! = 0 && t → left → visit == 0)
    {
    t = t → left;
    code [l] = '0';
    l ++;
    }
    else
    if (t → right! = 0 && t → right → visit = = 0 )
    {
    t = t → right;
    code [l] = '1';
    l ++;
}
if [t → left → visit = = 1 & & t → right → visit = = 1)
{
t → visit = 1;
    l = 0;
    code [0] = '\0';
    t = root;
}
}
}
void disp (input, i)
char input [80];
int i;
{
int j = 0, k;
printf ("\n Input =%s\n", input);
out = fopen ("out.dat", "w");
printf ("\n generated code for each character \n \n");
while (input [j]! = '\0')
    {
    for (k = 0; k<i; k++)
    {
    if (codes [k].c == input [j])
    {
    printf ("%s \t %c \n", codes [k]. no., codes [K]. c);
    fprintf (out, "%s", codes [k].no);
    }
```

```
}
j ++;
}
fprintf (out, "\n");
getchar();
}
decompress ( )
{
int j;
struct node *t;
char new-str [80];
fclose (out);
out = fopen ("out.dat", "r");
printf ("\n code to be transmitted\n");
fgets (new-str, 80, out);
t = root;
printf ("%s \n", new-str);
j = 0;
printf ("\n\n Recovered original text \n")
while (new-str [j] ! = '\0')
{
if (t → left = =  0 & & t → right = = 0)
{
printf ("%c", t → chr);
t = root;
}
if (new-str [j] = = '0')
t = t → left;
if (new-str [j] = = '1')
t = t → right;
j + +;
}
}
main ( )
{
char input [80];
int i, n;
system ("cls");
printf ("\n\t Enter the text");
fflush(stdin);
gets (input);
scarf ("% [^\n]", input);
```

```
print ("%s", input);
printf ("\n");
n = strlen (input);
for (i = 0; i < n; i++)
leaf – node (input [i]);
descend-order ( ) ;
connect ( );
i = gen (root, input);
disp (input, i);
printf ("\n press any key to continue \n");
getchar ( );
decompress ( );
no_char--;
getchar ( );
}
```

INPUT:–

Left traversal $\rightarrow 0$

& right traversal $\rightarrow 1$

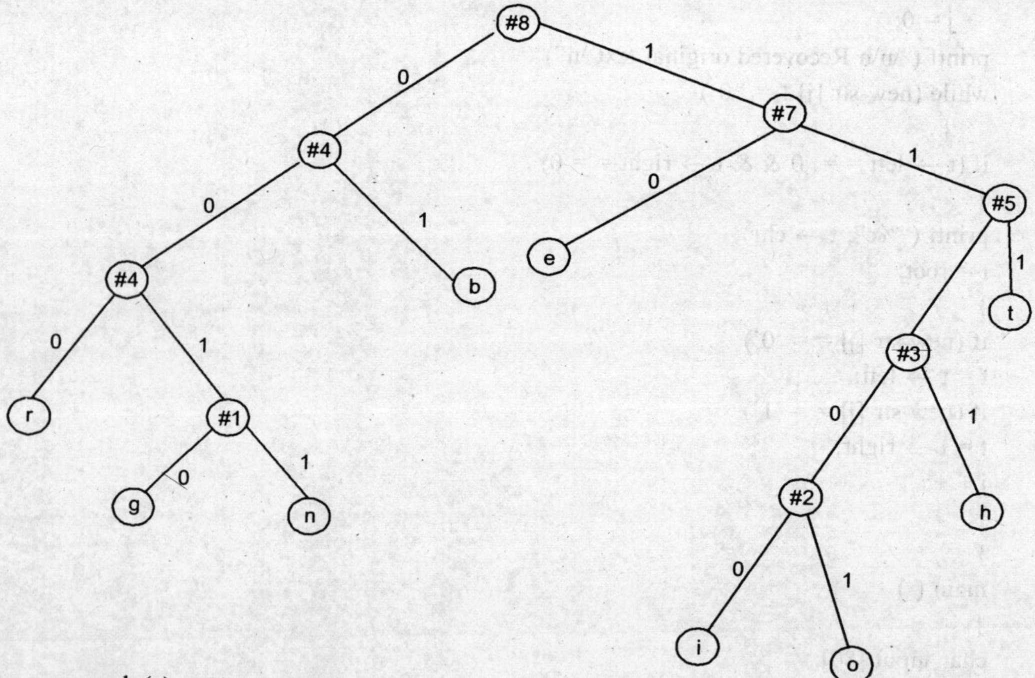

$\therefore$ prob (e) = 5/17 prob(t) = 2/17

prob (p) = 3/17 prob(r) = 2/17

prob (h) = 1/17 prob (i) = 1/17

prob (s) = 1/17 prob (n) = 1/17

prob (g) = $\frac{1}{17}$

∴ code for e ≡ 10

code for b ≡ 01

code for t ≡ 111

code for r ≡ 000

code for h ≡ 1101

code for i ≡ 11000

code for s ≡ 11001

code for g ≡ 0010

code for n ≡ 0011

∴ Total no. of bits $= (17 \times 8) + 50$

$= 136 + 50$

= **186** bits

EXPERIMENT NO.6

DEADLOCKS

```
#include <stdio.h>
int. n,m, req[20][20], alloc[20][20], max [20][20], avail[20], need [20][20], p[25], x = 1;
int flag, f = 0, dead [20], ins[10];
void inputs (t)
int t;
{
int i, j;
clrcsr ( );
printf ("\nEnter the no of processes:");
scanf ("%d", &n);
printf ("Enter the no of resource types:");
scanf("%d", &m);
for (i = 1; i < = m; i ++)
{
printf ("Enter the instances of resource %d:", i);
scanf ("%d", &ins[i]);
avail[i] = ins[i];
}
/* printf ("Enter the allocation matrix.\n");
for (i = 1; i < = n; i++)
for (j = 1; j< = m; j++) {
scanf ("%d", alloc[i][j]);
avail[j]-=alloc[i][j];
}
*/
if (t==1)
{
printf ("Enter the max matrix\n");
for (i = 1; i < = n; i++)
for (j = 1; j < = m; j++)
{
scanf ("%d", &max [i][j]);
/* need [i][j] = max[i][j]-alloc[i][j];*/
}
}
printf ("Enter the allocation matrix.\n");
for (i = 1; i<=n; i++)
for (j = 1; j < = m; j++)
{scanf ("%d", &alloc [i][j]);
avail[j]-=alloc[i][j];
}
```

```
if (t ==1)
{for (i=1;i<=n;i++)
for (j = 1; j < = m; j++)
{need [i][j] = max[i][j]-alloc[i][j];
}
}
if (t ==2)
{
printf ("Enter the request matrix.\n");
for (i = 1; ı<=n; i++)
for (j = 1; j < = m; j++)
scanf("%d", &req[i][j]);
}
/* printf("Enter the available vector\n");
for (i=1; i<=n;i++)
scanf ("%d", &avail[i]);*/ }
void print(t)
int t;
{
int i, j;
clrscr ( );
if (t ==1)
printf ("\n\tAllocation\t Need\t\tAvailable\n");
else
printf ("\n\tAllocation\t Request\tAvailable\n");
for (i=1; i<=n;i++)
{
printf ("\n\t");
for (j = 1; j < = m; j++)
printf ("%d", &alloc[i][j]);
printf ("\t\t");
for (j = 1; j < = m; j++)
if (t ==1)
printf ("%d", need[i][j]);
else
printf ("%d", req[i][j]);
printf ("\t\t");
if (i ==1)
for (j = 1; j < = m; j++)
printf ("%d", avail[j]));
}
```

```
}
void bank ( );
{
int i, j, k;
printf ("\n bankers algo to avoid deadlock\n");
getch ( );
do
{
print(1);
printf ("\n any requests (y/n)");
if (toupper (getch( )) ! = 'Y')
break;
printf ("\n enter the request no\n");
scanf ("%d", &k);
printf("\n enter the corresponding requests\n");
for (i = 1; i< = m;i++);
{printf ("request for resource %d", i);
scanf ("%d", &req[k][i];
if (req[k][i]> need[k][i]);     /*step-1*/
{printf ("\n invalid entry (request exceedsmax claim) enter again\n");
i --;
}
}
flag = 0
for  (i = 1; i< = m;i++);
if (req[k][i]> avail[i])
flag=1;     /* step - 2*/
if (flage ==1)
{printf ("process%d must wait, since resource not available\n", k);
}
else
{
for (i = 1; i < = n; i++)
(avail[i]-=req[k][i];
alloc[k][i] += req[k][i];
need [k][i] - = req[k][i];
}
If (!rj) /*rj → safety algoithm*/
{
for (i = 1; i < = n; i++)
{avail[i] + =req[k][i];
alloc[k][i] - =req[k][i];
```

```
need[k][i] + =req[k][i];
}
printf ("process%d has to wait since deadlock may arise\n", k);
}
else
{printf ("the resource has been successfully allotted to the process\n");
printf("\n the safe sequence is: \n");
for (i = 1; i < n; i++)
printf ("%d-->", p[i]);
printf ("%d", p[n]);
} }
x = 1;
printf ("\npress ENTER key to continue...\n");
getchar ( );
getchar ( );
}while (1):
}

int compare (s,t)
int s[20], t[20];
{
int p, boolean = 0;
for (p=1; p < = m && !boolean; p++)
if (s[p] > t[p])
boolean = 1;
return (boolean);
}
int rj( )     /* safety algorithm */
{
int i, work [20], a, b, finish [20], 1, safe over;
for (i = 1; i < = m; i++)
                    work [i] = avail[i];
for (i = 1; i < = n; i ++)
                    finish [i] = 0;
for (i = 1; i < = n; i ++)
{
if (!finish[i] && !compare(need[i], work))
{
for (b = 1; b < = m, b++)
                    work [b] = work [b] + alloc[i][b];
finish[i]=1;
p[x] = i;
x++;
```

```
if (i==n)
i = 0;
}
}
for (i = 1; i< = n; i++)
if (finish[i] == 0)
                return (0);
return (1);
}
int menu ( )
{
int choice;
clrscr ( );
printf ("\n\n\n\n\n\n");
printf ("\t\t\t---\n");
printf ("\t\t\t Menu \n");
printf ("\t\t\t---\n);
printf ("\t\t\t 1. Avoidance\n");
printf ("\t\t\t 2. Detection\n");
printf ("\t\t\t 3. exit\n");
printf ("\t\t\t ----\n");
printf ("\n\n\n\n\n\n\n Enter choice:");
scanf ("%d", &choice);
return (choice);
}
int detection ( )
{
int work [20], finish[20], i, j,1, flag1 = 0;
for (i = 1; i< = m; i++)
                work[i] = avail[i];
for (i = 1; i < = n; i++)
{
flag1 = 0;
for (j =1; j < = m; j ++)
If (alloc[i][j]! = 0)
                flag1 = 1;
if (flag1 ==1)
                finish[i] = 0;
else
                finish[i] = 1;
}
for (i = 1; i < = n; i ++)
```

```
{
if (!finish[i] && !compare (req[i], work))
{
for (j = 1; j < = m; j++)
work[j]+ = alloc[i][j];
finish[i] = 1;
i = 0;
}
}
l = 1;
for (i = 1; i < = n; i++)
if (finish [i] = =0)
{dead[1] = i;
1++;
}
if(1 ==1)
                    return (99);
else
                    return (l);
}
main ( )
{
int i, j, k;
char c;
do
{ i = menu ( );
switch (i)
{
case 1: inputs (1);
                    bank ( );
                    break;
case 2: inputs (2);
                    getch ( );
do
{
print (2);
j = detection( );
printf ("\n\n");
if(j! = 99) {
getch ( );
printf ("\n deadlock exists, consisting of process\n");
for (i = 1; i < = (j – 1); i ++)
```

```
{
printf ("%d", dead[i]);
printf (",");
}
/*printf ("%d", dead(j-1]);"/
printf ("\n");
}
else
printf ("\nthere is no deadlock\n");    /* if j = 99 */
printf ("\nany additional request by any process (y/n)\n");
c = getch( );
if (toupper (c) = = 'Y')
{
printf ("\nenter the process no which wants to make additional requests\n");
scanf ("%d", &k);
printf ("\n enter the request vector for process %d\n", k);
for (j = 1; j < = m; j++)
                    scanf ("%d, &req [k][j]);
}
else
{
break;
}
}while(1);
break:
case 3:
                    /*default;*/
                    exit (1);
}
} while (1);
}
```

Experiment No.7

To implement shortest path algorithm

```
#include <stdio.h>
# define INFINITY 2000 /* (n–1) M is better than infinity */
main ( )
{
int a[20] [20], b[20][20];
int i, j, n, k; /* n is no. of vertices or nodes */
/* a[i][j] is weight–matrix */
printf ("Enter no. of vertices (n): \n");
scanf ("%d", &n);
printf ("%d \n", n);
printf ("Enter weight matrix: \n");
for (i = 0; i < n; i++)
for (j = 0; j < n; j++)
scanf ("%d", &a[i][j]);
for (i = 0; i < n; ++i)
a [i] [i] = 0;            /* set weight-matrix to all zeros*/
for (i = 0; i < n; i++)
{
for (j = 0; j < n; j++)
printf ("%d", a[i][j]);
printf ("\n");
}
/* Initially set b[i][j] = a[i][j]*/
for (i = 0; i < n; i++)
for (j = 0; j < n; j++)
{
b[i][j] = a[i][j];
if (!a[i][j] && (i! = j)\b [i][j] = INFINITY;
}
for (k = 0; k < n; k++)
for (i = 0; i < n; i++)
for (i = 0; j < n; j++)
if (b[i][k] && b[k][j])
if (b[i][k] + b[k][j] < b[i][j])
b[i] [j] = b[i][k] + b[k] [j];
printf ("\n shortest path matrix: \n");
for (i = 0; i < n; ++i)
{
for (j = 0; j < n; ++j)
printf ("%d", b[i][j]);printf ("\n");
}
}
```

OUTPUT–

Enter n (no. of vertices): 4

Enter weight matrix:–

0	0	7	2
0	0	0	0
3	0	0	3
3	0	2	0

Shortest path matrix is:–

0	2000	4	2
2000	0	2000	2000
3	2000	0	3
3	2000	2	0

Experiment No.8

```
# include<stdio.h>
# include<conio.h>
# include<string.h>
char txt [10][10][10], txt [10][10][10], key [10], key1 [10], text[200];
int val[10], len. len1, nblk;
sort ( )
{
int i, j;
char temp;
for (i = 0; i < len–1; i++)      /* len is size of array */
for (j = i + 1; j < len; j++)
                    if (key [i]> key [j]){
                    temp = key[i];
                    key [i] = key [j];
                    key [j] = temp;
}
printf ("\nsorted keyword --> %s\n", key);
}
int search (c)
char c:
{
int i = 0;
while (i < len) {
if (c==key [i])
return (i);  /* search successful */
else
i++;
}
}
```

```
int form ( )
{
int i, j;
for (i = 0; i < len; i++) {
                    j = search (key1 [i]);
                    val[i] = j;
}
printf ("code word --> \n");
for (i = 0; i <len; i++)
                    printf ("%d", val[i]);
printf ("\n");
return;
}
int fblk ( )
{
int i, j, k, l;
i = len*len;
j = len/i;
k = len1%i;
if (k>0)
                    j = j +1;
nblk = j;
1 = 0;
k = 0;
while (1 < nblk) {
for (i = 0; i < len; i++)
for (j = 0, j < len; j++) {
if (k < lenl)
txt [1] [i] [j] = text [k];
else
txt [1][i][j] = '#';
k++;
} /* for loop closes*/
l++;
} /* while closes*/
printf ("simple blocks formed → \n");
for (i = 0; i < nblk; i++) {
for (j = 0; j < len; j++){
for (k = 0; k < len; k++)
                    printf ("%c", txt [i][j][k]);
printf ("\n");
}
```

```
printf ("\n\n\n");
getche ( );
}
}
int search1 (t)
int t;
{
int. i = 0;
while (i < len) {
if (t ==val[i])
                    return (i);
else
                    i++;
}
}
int fenblk( )/* print encrypted text*/
{
int i, j, k, p;
for (i =o; i < nblk; i++)
                    for (j = 0; j<len; j++)
                    for (k =0; k<len; k++) {
p = search1 (k) ;
txt 1[i] [j] [k] = txt [i] [j] [p];
}
printf ("encrypted text --->\n");
for (i = 0, i < nblk; i++){
for (j = 0; j<len; j++){
                    for (k = 0; k<len;k++)
printf("%c",txt[i][j][k];
printf("\n");
}
printf("n\n\n");
getche( );
}
}
int dckblk( ) /* print decrypted text */
{
int i, j, k, l, p;
for (i = 0, i < nblk; i++)
                    for (j = 0; j < len; j++)
                    for (k = 0; k < len; k++) {
p = val [k];
```

```
if (txt1 [i] [j] [p]! = '#')
                    printf ("%c"; txt1 [i] [i] [p]);
  }
getche( );
return;
]
main ( )
{
  printf ("\n enter the keyword--->\n");
  scanf("%s", key);
  strcpy (key1, key);
Len = str len (key);
sort();
  form( );
  printf ("\n enter the text ---->\n");
  fflush (stdin);
  scanf ("%[^\n]", text);
  lenl = strlen (text);
  fblk( );
  fenblk( );
  dckblk ( ) ;
}
```

Experiment No. 9

SHELL PROGRAMMING

(a) List the 'no. of files' created by a user on a particular day.

(b) List the total files created by the user along with the disk usage. If the disk space exceeds 2000, display the message "EXCESS USAGE".

(a)
```
mon = 'date | cut – c5 – 7'
dat = 'date | cut – c9 – 10'
echo "The date is : \t $ mon \t $ date
i = 701
while test {i} - lc 778
do
echo "7 sem $ i"
id/user 2/7sem $i
res =' ls-al | grep $ mon | grep $ dat | wc-
echo "no. of files = \c"
ech $ res
echo "The file names are: \n");
i = ' expr $ i + 1'
done
```

(b)
```
i = 701
mess = "excess usage"
while test {i} – lc 778
do
id /user 2/7sem$i
t-files = 'ls-al | 'wc-l'
t-usage = 'du – s | cut – d " ".fl'
no = 'du-s | cut-d ".fl"
if [sno-gt 200]
then
echo "\t 7 sem $i \t $ t - files /t $ t - usage \t $ message /n"
else
echo "\t 7 sem $ i \t $ t-files \t $ t-usage\n);
fi
i = 'expr – $i + 1
done
```

Experiment No.10

Program to transfer a file between two stations:–

```
# include <stdio.h>
main ( )
{
int flag = 0, i,
char buffer [80], filename [80];
FILE *FS;
printf ("ENTER NAME OF FILE TO BE TRANSFERED \n");
scanf ("%s", filename);
FS = fopen (filename, "r");
if (FS = = NULL)
{
printf ("FILE NOT PRESENT \n");
exist (0);
}
else
{
while (!feof(FS))
{
k = fgets (buffer, 16, FS);
if (k! = 16)
{
for (i = k + 1; i < = 16; i++)
buffer [i] = ' ';
}
checksum 1 = get parity (buffer, 1, 8);
checksum 2 = get parity (buffer, 9, 16);
flag = 0;
do
{
senddata (buffer, checksum1, checksum2);
k = biosram (2,0,0);
if (k = = 'y')
flag = 1;
}
while (flag);
unsignedchar get parity (buffer, x, y);
unsigned char buffer [10];
int x, y;
{
int i, j;
```

```
unsigned char x = 0 x 00, y;
for(i = x; i < = y; i + +)
}
a = get checksum (buffer [i]);
if (a)
{
y = y | x;
x <<1;
}
else
x <<1;
}
return (y);
}
int getchecksum (unsigned char c)
unsigned char c;
{
int i, count = 0;
for (i = 0; i < 8; i + +)
{
if ( c %2 = = 1)
count++;
c = c >> 2;
}
return (count %2);
}
```

Receiving:–

```
# include<stdio.h>
main ( )
{
int end = 0;
FILE *FD;
FD = fopen ("Destfile", "w");
while (! end)
{
do
{
for (i = 1; i < = 22; i++)
buffer[i] = biosrom (2,0,0); if ((buffer[20] == getparity (buffer, 4, 11) && (buffer [21] ==get
    parity (buffer, 12, 19))
{
biosrom (1, 'r', 0);
```

```
for (i = 4; i < = 16; i++)
fprintf (FD, "%d", buffer [i]);
flag = 0;
}
else
{
biosrom (2, 'N', φ);
flag = 1;
}
}
white (flag);
if (buffer[2] = 0 x 24)
end = 1;
}
```

Experiment No. 11

To implement Djikstra's algorithm of shortest path?

Program :

```
#include <stdio.h>
struct node {
                        int number, cost;
struct node *ptr;
}*head [10], *temp;
#define null (struct node *) 0
int cost (i, j)
int i, j;
{
int value = 9999;
temp = head [i];
while (temp! = null)
{
if (temp -> number = = j)
value = temp -> cost;
temp = temp -> ptr;
}
return(value); /* value is cost of edge between any 2 nodes*/
}
int choose (dist, n,s)
int dist [10], s[10], n;
{
int min = 9999, pos = 1, i;
for (i = 1; i < = n; i++)
if (dist [i] < min)
if (s[i] = = 0)
{
min = dist [i]
post = i;
}
return (pos);
}
void shortest-path (source, dist,n)
   int source, dist [10], n;
{
int num = 2, s[10], w, u, i;
for (i = 1; i < = n; i++)
{
```

```
s[i] = 0;
dist [i] = cost (source, i);
}
s[source] = 1;
dist [source] = 0;
while (num < n)
{
u = choose (dist, s);
/*choose returns an int value 'u' such that s [u] = 1 */
s[u] = 1;
num ++;
for (w =1; w < = n; w++)
if (s[w] == 0
if (dist [u] + cost (u, w) < dist [w])
dist [w] = dist [u] + cost (u, w);
} /* while closes */
}
main ( )
{
int i, j, n, source, dist [10];
char. dec;
printf ("\t Enter value of n :");
scanf ("%d", & n);
for (i = 1; i < = n; i++)
head [i] = null;
for (i = 1; i < n; i++)
for (j = 1; j < = n; j ++)
{
if (i ! = j)  / *As, when i = j then cost = 0 * /
{
dec = ' ' ;
printf ("Does edge exist between %d &%d (y/n): ", i, j);
while (toupper (dec)! 'y' && toupper (dec)! = 'N')
scanf ("%c", & dec);
if (toupper (dec) = = 'y')
{
printf ("\t Enter info (x):");
temp = (struct node *) malloc (size of (struct node));
temp → ptr = head [i];
temp → number = j;
head [i] = temp;
```

```
scanf ("%d", & (temp → cost));
}
}
}
printf ("\t Enter source : ");
scanf ("%d", & source);
shortest-path(source, dist, n);
printf ("\t Adjacency list is : ");
/* print adj. list */
for (i = 1; i < n; i++)
{
printf ("\n %d", i);
temp = head [i];
while (temp! = null)
{
printf ("Number = % d cost = %d", temp → number, temp → cost);
temp = temp → ptr;
}
}
printf ("\n");
printf ("\t shortest path is : ");
for (i = 1; i < = n; i++)
{
if (i! = source & & dist [i] ! = 9999)
{
printf ("shortest dist between node %d and %d in %d \n", source, i, dist [i]);
}
}
}
```

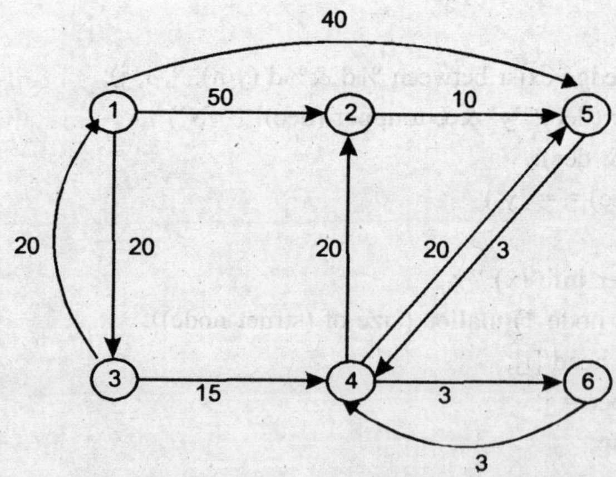

	1	2	3	4	5	6
1	–	50	20	–	40	–
2	–	–	15	–	10	–
3	20	–	–	15	–	–
4	–	20	–	–	20	3
5	–	–	–	3	–	–
6	–	–	–	3	–	–

Source = 6 & destination = 1

∴ shortest – dist between node 6 & 1 is **58**

Example 2:

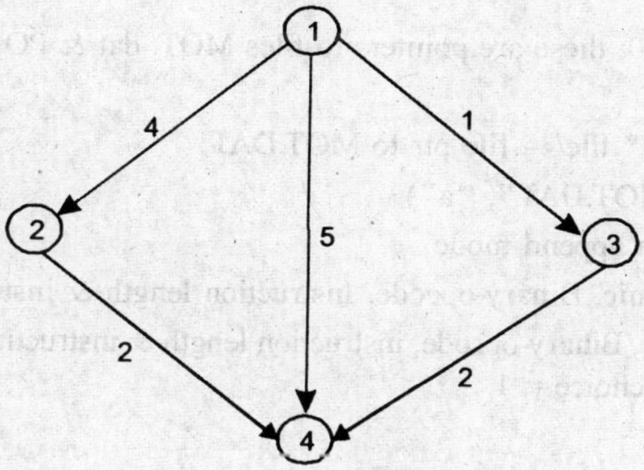

$$\begin{array}{c c} & \begin{array}{cccc} 1 & 2 & 3 & 4 \end{array} \\ \begin{array}{c} 1 \\ 2 \\ 3 \\ 4 \end{array} & \left[\begin{array}{cccc} - & 4 & 1 & 5 \\ - & - & - & 2 \\ - & - & - & 2 \\ - & - & - & - \end{array}\right] \end{array}$$

if source = 1, destination = 4

then $1 \rightarrow 3 \rightarrow 4 \equiv 1 + 2 = 3$

& $1 \rightarrow 4 \equiv 5$

& $1\text{–}2\text{–}4 \equiv 4 + 2 = 6$

∴ **Short path between 1 & 4 is 1–3–4 & its cost is 3**

Experiment No.12

Write a C program to create MOT & POT?

It's Algorithm is:–

Step 1: Display menu as:

1. Add to MOT
2. Add to POT
3. DISPLAY MOT
4. DISPLAY POT
5. Quit

& accept choice

Step 2: file 1 ← file 2 ← 0; these are pointers to files MOT. dat & POT.dat

& flag ← 'y'

Step 3: If choice = 1 /* file/← file ptr to MOT.DAT

file1← fopen ("MOT.DAT", "a")

i.e., open MOT.dat in append mode

Step 4: (a) **Read** mneumonic, Binary-opcode, Instruction length & instruction format

(b) **Write** mneumonic, Binary-opcode, instruction length & instruction format into MOT.DAT

& continue step (4) while choice = 1

Step 5: close MOT.DAT

Step 6: if choice = 2

file 2 ← fopen ("POTDAT", "a")

i.e., open POT.DAT in append mode.

Step 7: (a) **Read** pot-code & pot address

(b) **Write** pot-code & pot address into POT.DAT

& continue step (7) while choice = 2

Step 8: close POT.DAT

Step 9: If choice = 3

fl = fopen ("MOT.DAT", "r")

Read mneumonic, Binary opcode, instruction length, instruction format from MOT.dat

Print menumonic, Binary opcode, instruction length, instruction format, close MOT.DAT

Step 10: If choice = 4 f2 = fopen ("POT.DAT", "r")

/* read mode */

Write "POTCODE ADDRESS"

Read pot-code, pot-addr from POT.DAT

Print pot-code, pot-address,

close POT.DAT

Step 11: Exit

end

So, follow this algorithm. The input given is—

MENU

(i) Add to MOT file

A	5A	10	001
AH	4A	10	001
AL	5E	10	001
MYE	DL	11	100

(ii) Add to POT file

DROP	333
END	444
EQU	ABC
START	DEF

output is–

MOT file;

Mneumonic	**Binary**	**Instruction length**	**format**
A	5A	10	001
AH	4A	10	001
AL	5E	10	001
MVE	DL	11	100

& **POT file**

Pseudo-op	**addr**
DROP	333
END	444
EQU	ABC
START	DEF

PROGRAM–

```
# include <stdio.h>
int mcnu ( )
{
int choice;
system ("CLS");
printf ("\n\n\n\n\n");
printf ("\t\t\t\t MAIN MENU \n");
printf ("\t\t\t 1. ADD TO MOT FILE \n");
printf ("\t\t\t 2. ADD TO POT FILE \n");
printf ("\t\t\t 3. DISPLAY MOT FILE \n")
printf ("\t\t\t 4. DISPLAY POT FILE \n")
printf ("\t\t\t 5.EXIT PROGRAM \n");
printf ("\n\n\n\n\n ");
printf ("\t Enter your choice:)";
scanf ("%d", & choice);
getchar( );
return (choice);
}
```

```
main ( )
{
FILE *filel, *file2;
int choice, createl = 0, create 2 = 0;
char flag = 'y', mne [4], bin [3], ins-len [3], ins-for [4], p-code [5], p-adds [3];
while (1)
{
choice = menu ( ) ;
if (choice > 0 && choice <6)
switch (choice)
{
case 1:
system ("cls");
printf ("\n\n\n\n\n Enter record to MoT File:);
file 1 = fopen ("MOT.DAT", "a");
create 1 = 1;  /* create MOT-file */
flag = 'y';
while (flag) = = 'y')
{
strcpy (mne, " "); strcpy (inslen, " ");
printf ("enter mneumonic. op-code \n");
scanf ("%s", mne);
fprintf (file 1, "%s ",mne);
printf ("enter binary-op code: \n");
scanf ("%s", bin);
fprint f( file 1, "%s ",bin);
printf ("Enter instruction length);
scanf ("%s", ins-len);
fprintf (file 1, "%s", ins-len);
printf ("Enter instruction format);
scanf ("%s", ins-for);
fprintf (file 1, "%s \n", ins-for);
printf ("\n");
printf ("Do you want to append more records? y/n");
getchar( );
scanf ("%c", & flag);
}
fclose (filel);
break;
Case 2:
system ("CLS");
printf "\n\n\n\n\n\n\n ADD RECORD TO POT FILE: \n\n");
```

```
      file 2 = fopen ("POT.DAT","a");
      create 2 = 1;
      flag = 'y';
      while (flag = = 'y')
      {
      printf (Enter pseudo code \n");
      scanf ("%s", p-code);
      printf ("Enter addr of rountine:\n")
      scanf (%s", p-addr);
      fprintf (file2, "%s", p-code);
      fprint (file2, "%s \n", p-addr);
      printf ("\n");
      printf  ("Want to append more records? Enter y/n");
      getchar();
      scanf ("%c", & flag);
      }
      fclose (file 2);
      break;
Case 3:
      system ("tput clear);
      prinft ("\n\n\n\n DISPLAY MOT FILE = \n\n");
      if (create 1 = = 1) /* if MOT was created then */
      {
      printf ("\t\t\t MOT TABLE \n");
      printf ("MENUMONIC \t BINARY-CODE \t INSTRUCTION LENGTH \t INSTRUCTION");
      file 1 = fopen ("MOT.DAT", "r");
      While (! feof (file 1))
      {
      strcpy (mne, " ");    strcpy (bin, "   ");
      strcpy (inst, "");    strcpy (ins-for, " ");
      fscanf (file 1, "%s \n", mne);
      fscanf (file 1, "%s \n", bin);
      fscanf (file 1, "%s \n", ins-len);
      fscanf (file 1, "%s \n", ins-for);
      printf ("\n%s \t\t%s \t \t\t%s \t \t \t %n", mne, bin, ins-len, ins-for);
      }
      fclose (file 1);
      }
      else
      printf ("\n\n MOT TABLE EMPTY:");
      printf ("\n\n Press any key to continue .....: ");
      getchar ( ) ;
      break;
```

```
Case 4:
system ("tput clear");
printf("\n\n\n\n\n DISPLAY POT FILE  \n\n");
if (create 2 = =1)
{
printf ("\t\t\t\t POT TABLE \n");
printf ("PSEUDO opco \t\t\\t\t ADDRESS OF ROUTINE);
file 2 = fopen ("POT.DAT", "r");
while (!feof (file2))
{
strcpy (p-code, ""); strcpy (p-addr, " "),
fscanf (file 2, "%s \t %s \n", p-code, p-addr);
printf("%s \n \t \t \t \t \t%s \n", p-code, p-addr);
}
fclose (file 2);
}
else
printf ("\n\n POT TABLE EMPTY:")
printf ("\n\n PRESS ANY key to continue .....:") ;
getchar ( );
break;
Case 5:
system ("cls");
printf ("\n\n\n\n EXIT PROGRAM \n\n\);
exit ( ) ;
}
else
{
system ("cls");
printf ("\n\n\n\n Enter ascending to month options: \n\n");
printf ("press any key to continue: .....");
getchar ( );
}
}
}
```

Experiment No.13

WAP a C program to find the length of given ALP.

Also find the number of machine opcodes & pseudo-opcodes?

[KUD 1995]

It's algorithm is:–

(1) Start

(2) Instruction length ← 0, length ← 0 motcount ← 0 potcount ← 0;

(3) Read the first line of source-program.

(4) Check opcode

(5) If the opcode is mneumonic, instruction length ← length of instruction, motcount ← motcount + 1, length ← length + motcount

else

potcount ← potcount +1

(6) Check if EOF has been reached

if yes stop

else goto next line

(7) go to step (4)

```
# include <stdio.h>
# include <ctype.h>
FILE *in;
int counter = 0, meant = 0, p = 0,
int potc(str)
char *str;
{
char emp[50], a[20], ppp[5];
int i, com = 0;
if (! strcmp (str, "ds"))
{
fscanf (in, "%s,", emp);
i = 0;
while (isdigit (emp [i])
{
a[i] = emp [i];
i++;
}
a[i] = '\0';
if (emp[i] =='f')
return (4 *atoi(a));
else
return (2*atoi(a));
}
i = 0;
```

```
if (!strcmp (str, "dc"))          /*compares str & dc*/
{
fscanf (in, "%s", emp);
while (emp[i]! = '\0')
{
if (emp[i] == ',')
com++;
i++;
}
if (emp[0] =='f')
return (4 * (com+1));
else
return (2 * (com+1));
}
return (0);
}
int motc (str)
char *str;
{
FILE *mot;
char instr[20], t, c;
mot = fopen ("MOT.DAT", "r");
while (! feof (mot))
{
fscanf (mot, "%3s %c", instr, &c);
if (!strcmp (instr, str))
{
fscanf (mot, "%2s", instr,&c);
fscanf (mot, "%2s", instr);
if (!strcmp (instr, "O1"))
{
mount++;
return (2);
}
if (! strcmp (instr, "10"))
{
mount ++;
return (4);
}
if (! strcmp (instr, "//"))
{
mount ++;
return (6);
```

```
}
}
fscanf (mot, "% [^\n]%c", instr, & t);
}
return (0);
}
main ( )
{
char c, str [20], t;
int flag, x, con = 0;
in = fopen ("so.dat","r");
while (! feof (in))
{
cou++;
flag = 0;
if (feof (in)! = 0)
break;
c = fgetc (in);
if (c ! = 't')
fscanf. (in, "%s", str);
fscanf (in, "%s", str);
if (!strcmp (str, "ltrog"))
{
if (counter %8! = 0)
counter + = 2;
}
else
{
if (x = pofc (str))
flag = 1;
counter + = x;
}
if (! flag)
{
counter + = motc (str);
}
}
fscanf (in, "%[^/n]%c", str, & c);
}
printf ("length of program = % d \n", counter);
printf ("No. of mot instructions = % d\n", mount);
printf ("No. of pot instructions =%d\n", cou-mount);
fclose (in);
}
```

Experiment No. 14

a) /* shell program for counting no. of files */

```
cls
cd/
cd user
today = 'date | cut, -c9-10'
echo "\t Today's date is : $today"
for list in 'ls –d 7 sem 7 *'
do
echo "\n user : $ list"
num = find/user/$list - mtime-/ - print | /wc-l'
echo "No. of files created today is: $num \n\n"
read X
```

OUTPUT → sh filename

Today's date is : 12

user : 7 sem 759

number of files created today is 0

user : 7 sam 713

no. of files created today is : 3

14 b) (Trace) or path - command of UNIX or Tree-Command of DOS

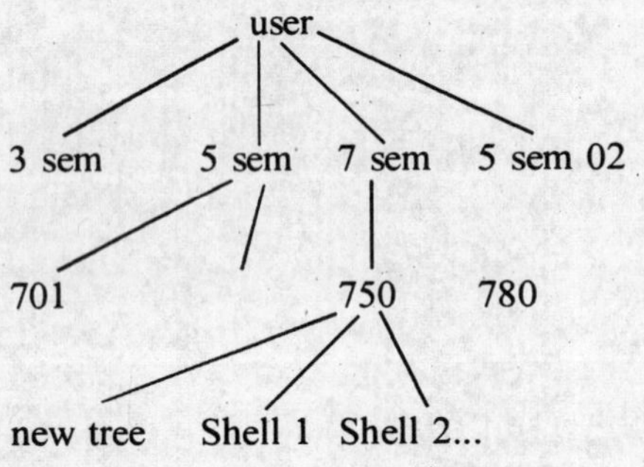


```
cd
cd..
cls
echo        "user-id"
for (sem) in 7sem 759          / * Take a for loop*/
do
for (user-id) in 'ls-d $sem*' /Substitute for all erecules of sem.
do
echo "\t → $ user-id"
cd $ user id
cd $ use - id          /* '$' means access value stored in user id*/
for dir in 'ls - d*'
```

```
do
if [ -d $ dir]            /* 'd' means the file is a dir #
then
echo "\t\t\t\t --- ** $ dir"
cd $dir
read dummy              /*
for file in 'ls *'
do
echo "/t/t/t/t ---- $ file".
read X       print names of all files
done         /* [Note that in 1st FOR-LOOP we took "user-id", in 2nd one-dir& in 3rd -one
file, according to hierarchy] /*
cd..
fi
done
cd..
done
done
```

output → Sh filename

```
user id ------- 7 sem 759 ----- ** root 1
*:No such file or dir ------ ** root 2
*: No such file or dir ----- ** root 3
*: No such file or dir ----- ** Rajiv
--- extra
---- files
----newtree
-----today
----root1;
------- fl.1
--- root2;
/*** No files in root 2 ***/
```

Experiment No.15

WAP in C to sequence n-jobs through 2 machines.

ALGORITHM

1. Write the function read-job configuration ().
2. Write the function find-smallest-point ()
3. Write the function find-sequence ().
4. Write the function print-sequene ().
5. & hence the main program.

PROGRAM -

```
# include <stdio.h>
int no-of-jobs;
int process-times [200] [2];
int Q [200] [2];
void        read-job-configuration ()
{
int i;
printf ("Enter the no. of jobs");
scanf ("%d", &no-of-jobs);
printf ("Enter processing times:");
print f ("Job \t mkl \t mk2 \n");
printf (" ------------ \n");
for (i = 0; i<no-of-jobs; i ++)
{
printf (" %d \n", i +1);
scanf( "%d % d", & process - times [i] [0], &process-times [i] [1]);
}
return;
]
int find-smallest-point (marked)
int marked [200];
{ int i, j;
int small 1 = small 2 = 999;
int Jobl, Job2;
for (i = 0; i <no-of-jobs; i++)
if (! marked [i])
{
if (process-times [i] [0] < small 1)
{
small 1 = process-times [i] [0];
Jobl = i;
{
if (process-times [i] [1] < small 2)
```

```
{
small 2 = process-times [i] [1];
Job 2 = i;
}
}
if (small 1 < small 2)
return (Job 1);
else
if (small 2 < small 1)
return (Job 2);
if (small 1 = = small 2)
if (process-times [job1] [1] < process-times [Job2 ] [0]
                    return (Job 1);
else
                    return (Job 2);
}
}
void find-sequence (sequence)
int sequence [200];
{
int i, j, k:
int marked [200], front, rear, job;
front = 0;
rear = no-of-jobs - 1;
for (i= 0; i < no-of-jobs; i++)
                    marked [i] = 0;
for (i = 0; i< no-of-jobs; i++)
{
Job = find-smallest-point (marked);
                    marked [Job] =1;
if (process-times [Job] [0] < = process-times [job] [1].
Sequence [front ++] = job;
else
sequence [rear --] = job;
}
return;
}
void print-sequence (sequence)
int sequence [200];
{
int i;
printf ("optional sequence");
```

```
for (i = 0; i <no-of-jobs; i++)
printf ("%d ", sequence [i] +1);
printf ("\n");
}
void main ()
{
int sequence {200];
printf (" Sequence n jobs through 2 m/c \n");
read - job-configuration ();
find-sequence (sequence);
print-sequence (sequence);
}
```

Experiment No. 16

To create ST, BT & LT of given ALP.

It's algorithm is:-

1] start, var ← 0 rel ← 0

2] Read first line of source program.

3] Check opcode field.

4] if opcode is mneumonic, var ← length of opcode.

5] if label field is present, rel ← rel + var

6] store the symbol in SYMBOL TABLE

7] If opcode is "LTORG"

check if literal is

f : var ← 4

L: var ← 2

d : var ← 6

8] rel ← rel + var

9] store literal in LITERAL table

10] if opcode is USING check 2nd operand for base reg. content. 1st operand ← base reg.

11] Store a BASE TABLE

12] check if EOF

13] if no go to step 2

14] stop.

```
# include <stdio.h>
# include <ctype.h>
FILE *in, *st, *tt, *bt;
int len =  0, k =  0, n = 0, var = 0, pq = 0;
char str [85] [85], base [30] [30], templl [30] [30];
void lit ()
{
int i =   0, p = 4;
char r = 'r';
len -- ;
while (len > = 0)
{
fprintf (lt, " %s, \t %d, \t% d \t % c, \n ", str [i], lc, p, r);
n + = size (str [i] [0] );
p = size (str [i] [0] );
lc+ = size (str [i] [0] );
len --;
i++;
}
return:
}
```

```
int size (c)
char c;
{
switch (c)
{
case 'f' : return (4);
case 'h': return (2);
default : return (4);
}
}
int mot (z)
char z [20];
{
FILE *mot;
char instr [20], t, c;
mot = fopen ("mot.dat", "r");
while (!f eof (mot)
{
fscanf (mot, "%4s %c", instr, &c);
if (! strcmp (instr, z))
{
fscanf (mot, "% 2s", instr, &c);
fscanf (mot, "% 2s", instr);
If (! strcmp (instr, "01"))
return (2);
if (!strcmp (instr, "10"))
return (4);
if (! strcmp (instr, "11"))
return (6);
}
fscanf (mot, "% [^\n] % c", instr, & c);
}
return (0);
}
void bas ()
{
int i = 0, g, j, f;
char z [100], c, zz [20];
st = fopen ("symbol", "r");
bt = fopen ("bs", "w");
while (var > = 0)
{
```

```
if (! strcmp (temp 1[i], "*");
{
fprintf (bt, "%s \t \n", base[i]);
i ++;
}
st = fopen ("symbol", "r");
while (! feof (st))
{
fscanf (st, "%s", z);
if (! strcmp (temp1 [i], z))
{
fscanf (st, "%s", z);
f = atoi (z);
if (f > 4096)
{
fclose (bt);
bf = fopen ("bs", "r");
while (fgets (z, 80, bt));
fclose (bt);
bt = fopen ("bs", "a");
g= 0;
while (z[g]! = '\t')
g ++;
g ++;
j= 0;
While (z [g]! = '\ 0')
{
zz [j] = z [g];
j ++;
g ++;
}
g = i-1;
f printf (bt, "%s \t %s, \n," base [g], zz);
}
else
fprintf (bt, "%s \t %s \n", base [i], z);
}
fscanf (st, "% [^\n] %c", z, &c);
}
i ++;
var --;
```

```
pg --- ;
}
}
main ()
{
int i, ol, K, flag,, com, m, p =1, q = 4, f = 0;
char z [20], temp [20], c, r;
st = fopen ("symbol", "w");
lt = fopen ("lit", "w");
in = fopen ("source", "r");
ol = 0;
while (!feof (in))
{
flag = 0;
r = 'r';
c = fgetc (in);
if (c! = '\t')
{
fscanf (in, "%s", z);
if (strcmp (z, "end"))
fprintf (st, "%c, %s \t", c, z);
flag = 1;
}
fscanf (in, "%s", z);
if (! strcmp (z, "equ")
{
fscanf(in, "%s", z);
if (! strcmp (z, "*"))
fprintf (st, "%d\t %d \t %c", c, p, r);
else
{
r = 'a';
printf (st, "%s \t %d \t % c\n", c, p, r);
}
r = 'r';
}
else
if (! strcmp (z, "using"))
{
fscanf (in, "%s", z);
i = 0;
while ((z [i]! = ',') && (z [i]! = '\o'))
```

```
{
temp1 [pq] [i] = z [i];
i ++;
}
temp 1 [pq] [i] = '\0';
pq ++;
if (z [i] = = ',')
{
K = 0;
i ++;
while (z [i]! = '\0')
{
temp [k] = z [i];
k ++;
i ++;
}
temp [k] = '\0';
fclose (st);
st = fopen (" symbol", "r");
white (! feof (st))
{
fscanf (st, "%s", z);
if (! strcmp (temp, z))
{
fscanf (st, "%s", z);
strcpy (base [var], z);
f = 1;
var ++;
}
fscanf (st, "%[ ^\n] %c", z, &c);
}
if (f! = 1)
{
strcpy (base [var], temp);
var ++;
}
fclose (st);
st = fopen (" symbol", "a");
}
}
else
```

```
if (! strcmp (z, "ds"))
{
fprintf (st, "%d, \t %d \t % c \n", lc, q, r);
fscanf (in, "%s", z);
i = 0;
while (is digit (z[i]))
{
temp [i] = z [i];
i++
}
temp [i] = '\0';
lc + = atoi (temp) * size (z[i]);
else
if (!strcmp) (z, "dc"))
{
fprintf (st, "%d \t %d \t %c \n", lc, q, r);
fscanf (in, "%s", z);
i = 0;
com = 0;
while (z [i]! = '\0')
{
if (z [i] = = ',')
com + +;
i++;
lc + = (com +1) * size (z[0]);
}
else
if (! strcmp (z, "ltrog"))
{
m = lc % 8;
lc + = 8 - m;
ol = 1;
lit();
{
else
if (x = mof (z))
if (flag)
fprintf (st, "%d \t %d\t%c\n",lc,x,r);
lc + = x;
fscanf (in, "%s", z);
i =  0;
while ((z [i] ! = '=')) && (z [i]! = '\0')
```

```
i++:
if (z [i] = = '=')
{
K = 0;
i++;
while (z [i]! = '\0')
{
temp [k] = Z [i];
k++;
i++;
}
temp [k] = '\0';
strcpy (str [len ++], temp);
}
}
else
if (! strcmp) (z,"start"))
fprintf (st, "%d \t %d \t%c \n", lc, p, r);

fscanf (in, "% ["\n]", z);
fscanf (in, "%c", &c);
}
if (! ol)
lit ();
fclose (st);
fclose (lt);
f close (in);
base ();
}
```

Experiment No. 17

WAP a C program to search for a symbol in ST in expt.16 & print line no. if not FOUND?

(1) Start (i.e., store the symbols in ST in Hash table)

(2) Check 1st line of source program.

(3) Check 1st "operand field".

(4) See if it's present in ST.
If no then print Error message & appropriate line no.

(5) Check IInd "operand field"

(6) If present in ST then read next line
else once again print the error message & appropriate line no.

(7) See if EOF has been reached, if no go to step 2.

(8) Stop

∴ Input is :-

```
RAJ     START   0
        USING   *, 15
        LR      1, INDEXA
        A       2, TIND
        AL      2, INDEX
        SR      1, TOTAL1
        LR      2, ADDA
ADDA    EQU     3
        END
```

& output is:-

Symbol not found on line No. **3**

Symbol not found on line No. **5**

```
# include <stdio.h>
#define new (struct node*) malloc (size of (struct node))
#define null (struct node *)0
#define isnum (C) ((C>='0') && (C<='9') ? 1: 0
        int     found;
        int     line = 0;
struct node {
        char value [25];
        *next;
        };
        struct node * b[5];
        FILE *in, * sym;
        int hash (list)
        char list [25];
        {
        nif sum = 0;
```

```
        int i;
for (i = 0; list [i]! =' \0'; i++)
        sum + = toupper (list [i]) – 'A' + 1;
        sum = sum % 5;
        return (sum) ;
}
void    insert (list)
        char list [25];
         {
                int i;
        struct node *temp, *n;
        i = hash (list);
        temp = b [i];
        if (temp = = null)
        {
        temp = new;
        strcpy (temp → value, list);
        temp → next = null;
        }
        x = new;
        x → next = temp → next;
        temp → next = x;
        strcpy (x → value, list);
        return;
        }
        int search (list)
        char list [25];
        {
        int i, found = 0;
        struct node *temp;
        i = hash (list);
        temp = b [i];
        if (!strcmp (temp → value, list))
        found = 1;
        else
        {
        while (temp! = null)
        {
        temp = temp → next;
        if (! strcmp (temp → value list))
        found = 1;
        }
```

```
            found = 0;
            }
            return (found);
            }
void found-s ()
            {
            char d[25];
            if (found = = 1)
            printf ("The symbol %s is found \n", d);
else
            printf ("The symbol %s is not found on line %d \n", d, line);
}           return;
main ( )
{
int i = 0, j;
char a[25], str1 [25], temp1 [25], str2 [25], array [80], d[25];
      char choice, c;
      choice = 'y';
in = fopen ("in. dat ", "r");
sym = fopen ("sym. dat", "w");
if ((in = = (FILE *0) || (sym = = (FILE *) 0
      {
print f ("Error in opening the file \n\n");
      exit (1);
}
do {
      printf ("Enter the symbol:");
      scanf ("%s", a);
      puts (a);
fprintf (sym, "%s\n", a);
      insert (a);
      getchar( );
      printf ("want to continue (y/n)? : \t"),
      choice = getchar ( );
}
      while (choice = = 'y');
            fclose (sym); /* stop writing into sym now*/
      printf ("the searching starts !!!! \n");
      while (!feof (in))
            {
            line = line +1;
```

```
        fgets (array, 60, in);
        puts (array);
        i = 0;
        found = search (temp 1);
        found-s( ) ;
        fscanf (in, "%s% [^\t]%s", strl, str2);
i = j = 0;
if (! isnum (str 2[j]))
        {
while (str 2[j++]! = ',')
        d[i++] = str 2 [i++];
        found = search (d);
                found-s ( );
        }
        j++;
        i = 0;
if (! isnum (str2 [j]))
        while (str2 [j++]! = '')
d [i++] = str2 [j++];
found = search (d);
}       found-s( );
fscanf (in, "%c[^\n]%s", str2);
}
printf("hello, boss\n");
        fclose (in);
        fclose (sym);
}
```

Experiment No. 18

To process RR-type of instruction?

It's algorithm is:-

(1) Start.

(2) Read 1st line of source program.

(3) Check opcode field of the source program.

(4) If it is 'RR' - type then check Ist operand. If it is a symbol then get its value. Check IInd operand. If it is a symbol then get its value (value2)

(5) Put the instruction in the format.

(6) Check for EOF

If no go to next line & go to step 3

else

(7) stop

∴ Input is a source program:

```
RAJ      START  0
USING           *, 15
BALR            15, 0
SR              1,2
A               1, DATA1
LR              2, DATA 2
L               1, DATA1
AR              3, TOTAL
TOTAL    DC     F'5'
DATAI    EQU    4
DATA2    EQU    2
         END
```

& output is

```
BALR    15, 0
SR      1,2
LR      2,2
AR      3,5
```

```
#include <stdio.h>
#include <string.h>
#include <ctype.h>
char str3 [10];
FILE *f1, *f2, *f3;
int correct (c)
char c;
{
int i;
i = to ascii (c) – 48;
```

```
return (i);
{
int isd (c)
char c;
{
if (c > = '0' && C< = '9')
return (1);
return (0);
}
int mot-search (data)
char data [30];
{
int K = 0;
char opc [30], dummy [10];
rewind (f2);
while       (!feof (f2))
fscanf (f2, "%s", opc);
if (strcmp (data, opc) = = 0)
{
fscanf (f2, "%s %d %s", dummy, & k, str3);
return (1);
}
else
fscanf (f2, "%s, %d %s", dummy, &k, str3);
}
return (0);
}
int search (str)
char str [ ];
{
char str 6 [10];
int value;
rewind (f3);
while (! feof (f3))
{
fscanf (f3, "%s %d", str6, & value);
if (strcmp (str6, str) = = 0)
{
return (value);
}
}
}
```

```
main( )
{
int n, l , i;
int flag = 0, flagl = 0, h = 0;
char c, f;
char data [30], str [20], opr [30], str1 [20], str8[10], opc [10];
fl = fopen ("s.c", "r");
f2= fopen (" mot.dat", "r");
f3 = fopen ("st2.c", "r");
while (!feof (fl))
fscanf (fl, "%s \t", data);
i = mot-search (data);
if (i = =1)
{
if (strcmp (str 3), "rr") = = 0)
{
printf ("%s", data);
flag = flagl = 0;
fscanf (fl, "%s\n", opr);
i = 0;
c = opr [0];
if (isd (c))
{
flag = 1;
n = correct (c);
while (c! = ',')
{
i ++ ;
c = opr [i];
}
}
if (flag = = 0)
{
h = 0;
while (opr [i]! = ',')
{
str [h] = opr [i];
h++;
i++;
}
str [h++] = '\0';
n = search (str);
}
```

```
i++;
f = opr [i];
if (isd (f))
{
flag 1 =1;
l = correct (f);
}
if ( flag1 = = 0)
{
h = 0;
while (i < strlen (opr))
{
strl [h] = opr [i];
h ++;
i++;
]
strl [h ++] = '\0';
l = search (strl);
}
if (flag = = 1 && flag 1 = = 1)
printf ("%s \n", opr);
else
{
printf ("%d %d", n, l);
printf ("\n\n");
}
}
else
fscanf (fl, "%[ ^\n]", str 8);
}
}
}
```

Experiment No. 19

To create MDT, MNT & ALA (for MACROS (Pass1)) for given source proram?

* It's algorithm is:-

(1) Start
(2) MDTC ← MNTC ←1, ALAC ← 0
(3) Read the line of source program
(4) If the opcode is "MACRO" go to next line.
Print the MDTC, the whole line into Macro definition table
Print the macro name in Macro name table.
MDTC ← MDTC + 1
MNTC ← MNTC + 1
(5) go to next line.
(6) Replace the label by #0 in MDT.
(7) MDTC + = 1;
(8) Read the operand field.
(9) Replace the argument by "#" no.
Where no ← the argument no.
(10) Continue until opcode "MEND".
(11) Read next line.
(12) if opcode = name of macro then
(13) store the lable field in ALA
ALAC ← ALAC + 1
(14) Fill the value of ALAC in ALA
(15) Store the 3 argument in ALA along with ALAC value
(16) Are all arguments over
If no then to go 15
(17) Continue until opcode = "END"
(18) END.

∴ Input is source - program:

```
MACRO
&CAB        INCR            &ARG1, &ARG2
&CAB        LR              1, &ARG1
            AR              2, &ARG2
            MEND
LOOP        INCR DATA1, DATA 2
```

MDT:

```
1           &CAB            INCR &ARG1, &ARG2
2           #0              LR              1, #1
3                           AR              2, #2
MEND
```

ALA is

MDT index	Argument
1	" LOOP"
2	"DATA 1"
3	"DATA 2"

So, its program is:-

```
#include <stdio.h.>
#include <string.h>
#include <ctype.h>
main ()
{
int mntc = 1, mdtc = 1, mdtflg = 0, i, j, alac = 0, comma, fstmro = 0, mrohd, labc = 0;
int cmaflg = 0, valac = 0;
char *mro = {"macro"], *mnd = {"mend"};
char lbl [10], opd [10], ond [20], c, ropd [10], temp [10];
FILE *srcf, *mnt, *mdt, *ala;
void mntfn ( );
srcf = fopen ("source-p", "r" );
mnt = fopen ("name", "w+");
mdt = fopen ("defn", "w +");
ala = fopen ("argu", "w + ");
while (! feof (srcf))
{
c = fgetc(srcf);
if (c > 0)
{
i = 0;
while (c! =  ")
{
lbl [i] = c;
i++;
c = fgetc (srcf);
}
if (i == 0)
strcpy (lbl, " ");
else
lbl [i] = '\0';
while ((c = fgetc (srcf)) = = ' ' );
i = 0;
while (c! = ' ')
{
opd [i] = c;
i++;
c =fgctc (srcf);
}
opd [i] = '\0' ;
if (strcmp (opd, mro) = = 0)
mrohd = 1;
if (mrohd = = 2)
```

```
{
fprintf (mnt, "%d \t%s \t \t %d \n",
                    mntc, opd, mdtc);
mntc ++;
mdtflg = 1;
mrohd = 0;
}
while (c = fgetc (srcf)) = = ' ' );
i = 0;
while (c! = '\n')
{
ond [i] = c;
i++;
c = fgetc (srcf);
}
ond [i] = '\0';
if (mdflg = = 1)
{
if (strcmp (opd, mnd) = = 0)
{
fstmro = 1;
mdtflg = 0;
}
if (strcmp (opd, mro)! = 0)
{
comma = 1;
while (ond [i]! ='\0')
{
if (ond[i] = = ',')
comma ++;
i++;
}
fstmro ++;
fprintf (mdt, "%d \t%s \t% s \t %s \n" mdtc, lbl, opd, ond);
mdtc ++;
if (fstmro = = 1)
strcpy (ropd, opd);
}
}
i = 0;
if (fstmno = = 2)
if (strcmp (ropd, opd) = = 0)
{
comma = 1;
while (ond [i]! = '\0')
{
if (ond [i] = = ',')
comma ++;
i++;
}
i = 0;
```

```
do
{
if (labc = = 0)
{
{
if (strcmp (labc, "  ")! = 0)
{
fprintf (ala, "%d \t%s \n", alac, lbl);
alac ++;
}
labc = 1;
}
while (ond [i]! = '\0')
{
if (cmaflg = = 0)
if (ond [i]! = ',')
{
temp [j] = ond [i];
j++;
}
else
cmaflg = 1;
i++;
}
cmaflg = 0;
i = 0;
while (ond [i] ! = ',')
i++;
i ++;
if (j! = 0)
{
temp [j] = '\0';
fprintf (ala, "%d /t%s \n", alac, temp),
alac ++;
j = 0;
}
-- comma;
} while (comma! = 0);
}
i = 0;
j = 0;
if (mrohd = = 1)
mrohd ++;
if (strcmp (ropd, opd) = = 0)
if (fstmro = = 1)
fstmro++;
}
else
break;
}
fclose (srcf);
fclose (mnt);
fclose (mdt);
}
```

(Additional Expts.)

APPENDIX-D

Experiment No. 20

//********PRODUCER-CONSUMER PROBLEM IN BOUNDED BUFFER USING COUNTING SEMAPHORES AND MUTE-X****** ****//

```
# include<stdio.h>
# include<pthread.h>
# include<semaphore.h>

# define TRUE 1

/* the semaphores */
sem_t full, empty, mutex;

/* buffer array */
int buffer[1000];

/* buffer counter */
int counter, in, out;

int BUFFER_SIZE;
int i,m,n;

pthread_t pr_tid[100];
pthread_t cr_tid[100];

pthread_attr_t attr; //Set of thread attributes

void *producer(void *param); /* the producer function */
void *consumer(void *param); /* the consumer function */

/* the function initializeData() is initializing all the semaphores and mutex used in the code*
/
void initializeData()
{
	sem_init(&mutex,0,1); /* Create the binary semaphore used as a lock */
	/* Create the counting semaphore for indicating the full buffer and initialize to 0 */ sem_
init(&full,0,0);
	/* Create the counting semaphore for indicating the empty buffer and initialize to BUFFER_
SIZE */
```

```
        sem_init(&empty,0,BUFFER_SIZE);

        /* Getting the default attributes */
        pthread_attr_init(&attr);

        /* initializing buffer */
        counter = 0; .
        in = 0;//in indicates the position of last inserted item in the buffer
        out = 0;//out indicates the position in the buffer from where the next item will be consumed
}
/* Producer function */
void *producer(void *param)
{
        int item;//the item to be produced

        while (TRUE)
        {
        /* sleep for a period of time */
        sleep(2) ;

/* generate a random number which acts as the item produced */
item = rand()%1000;
if (counter==BUFFER_SIZE)
{
        for(i=0; i<n; i++)
            if(pthread_self() == pr_tid[i] )
                printf("\npresently PRODUCER %d waiting", (i+1));
}
/* calling sem wait on empty semaphore */
sem_wait(&empty);
        /* acquire the semaphore lock */
        sem_wait(&mutex);

        /* item produced is inserted in the buffer, it is the critical section*,

        for(i=0; i<n; i++)
            if (pthread_self() == pr_tid[i] )
                printf("\npresently PRODUCER %d running", (i+l));

        insert_item(item};
```

```
        printf("\nproducer produced %d\n", item);

        printf("BUFFER : ");
        for(i=O; i<BUFFER_SIZE; i++)
        {
                printf("%d",buffer[i]);
        }
        printf ("\n") ;

            /* release the semaphore lock */
            sem_post(&mutex);

            /* calling sem signal on full semaphore */
            sem_post(&full);
        }
}

/* Consumer function */
void *consumer(void *param)
{
        int item;//item to be consumed

        while (TRUE)
        {
            /* sleep for a period of time * /
            sleep(2);

        if (counter==0)
            {
                for(i=0; i<m; i++)
                    if (pthread_self() == cr_tid[i] )
                        printf("\npresently CONSUMER %d waiting", (i+l));
            }
            /* calling the sem wait on the full semaphore */
            sem_wait(&full);

            /* aquire the semaphore lock */
            sem_wait(&mutex);

            for(i=O; i<m; i++)
```

```
            if(pthread_self() == cr_tid[i] }
                printf("\npresently CONSUMER %d running", (i+1));

        /*the item is removed from the buffer, is it the critical section*/
        item = remove_item();
        printf("\nconsumer consumed %d\n", item);

        printf("BUFFER : ");
        for(i=0; i<BUFFER_SIZE; i++)
        {
            printf("%d",buffer[i]);
        }
      printf("\n"};

        /* release the semaphore lock */
        sem_post(&mutex};

        /* calling sem signal on empty semaphore */
        sem_post(&empty);
      }
}
/* function to add an item in the buffer */
int insert_item(int item)
{
      /* When the buffer is not full add the item*/
      buffer[in] = item;
      counter++;
      in = (in+l)%BUFFER_SIZE;
}
/* function to remove an item from the buffer */
int remove_item()
{
      /* When the buffer is not empty remove the item
          and return the item*/
      int item;
      item = buffer[out];
      buffer [out] = -1;
      counter--;
      out = (out+l)%BUFFER_SIZE;
      return item;
```

```
}
/* function main includes all the thread creation and their initialization to their respective functions*/
int main(int argc, char *argv(])
{
    /* Creating the producer threads */
    printf("enter the number of producers: ");
    scanf (" %d", &n) ;

    printf("enter the number of consumers: ");
    scanf("%d",&m) ;

    printf("enter the size of buffer: ");
    scanf("%d",&BUFFER_SIZE);

    if(BUFFER_SIZE <= 0)
    {
        printf ("BUFFER SIZE IS NOT VALID \n");
    exit (0) ;
    }
    else if(BUFFER_SIZE >1000)
    {
        printf("BUFFER SIZE MORE THAN 1000 IS NOT PERMISSIABLE \n");
        exit(0);
    }
    else if(n <= 0)
    {
        printf("NO PRODUCER is here\n");
        exit (0) ;
    }
    else if(m <=0)
    {
        printf("NO CONSUMER is here\n");
        exit(0) ;
    }
    for(i=0; i<BUFFER_SIZE; i++)
    { buffer[i] = -1; }

    /* Initialize the semaphores */
    initializeData() ;
```

```
    for(i = 0; i < n; i++)
    {
        pthread_create(&pr_tid[i],&attr,producer,NULL);
    }
    /* Creating the consumer thread */
    for(i = 0; i < m; i++)
    {
        pthread_create(&cr_tid[i],&attr,consumer,NULL);
    }
    /* Sleep for the specified amount of time in milliseconds */
    sleep (30);
    /* Exit the program */
    printf ("Exit the program\n"};
    exit (0);
    }
```

Expt. No. 21

```
/* Solution.01 (OS)
/* To implement our own linux shell using C— by Dr. Rajiv Chopra */
# include<stdio.h>
# include<string.h>
# include<fcntl.h>
# include<unistd.h>
# include<sys/types.h>
# include<dirent.h>
# include<wait.h>

/* CONSTANTS USED */
# define MAX_VALUE 128;
# define DELIM "\t\n"

/*
    FUNCTION PROTOTYPES USED
*/
void User_Input();
void Start_Shell();
void piping(char*);
void string_token(char*);
void c_direc_excute(char**);
void run_cd(char**);
void exit_FROM_SHELL();
```

```
void excute_command(char**);
void method_CLEAR();
void method_Help();
void method_Design();
void method_Echo(char**);
void method_PWD() ;

/* VARIABLE USED

char *c_direc[201];
char* storage;
int fix_size = 200;
/* PROGRAM EXECUTION STARTS FROM HERE--main(‘) */
*/
int main() {
        int true =1;
        while (true) {
        Start_Shell();
        }
        return 0;
}
/* SHELL STARTS FROM HERE */
void Start_Shell() {
        char buffer[128];
        printf("[MYGROUP_SHELL");
        printf(basename(getcwd(buffer,128)));
        printf("l $ ");
        User_Input();
}
/*      READ USER'S INPUT    */

void User_Input() {
        char storage[128];
        gets(storage);
        if(strlen(storage) >0) {
            if((storage[strlen(storage)] == '&') || strstr(storage,"$")
                || strstr(storage,"|")
                || strstr(storage, ">")
                || strstr(storage,">>")
                || strstr(storage,"<")
```

```
            || strstr(storage,"<<")) {
            piping(storage);
        }
        else{
            string_token(storage);
        }
    }
}
/* TO SIMULATE PIPING */
void  piping(char *storage) {
    char *BUFFER = (char*)malloc(sizeof(char)*1024);
    FILE *file_open = popen(storage, "r");
    fgets(BUFFER,1024,file_open);
    write(STDOUT_FILENO,BUFFER,strlen(BUFFER));
    pclose(file_open);
}
/* TO TOKENIZE STRING */

void string token(char *stock){
    int i, temp;
    char *direc = (char*)malloc(sizeof(char)*128);
    strcpy(direc,stock);
    for(i=0 ; i<fix_size+l;i++) {
        c_direc[i] = (char*)malloc(sizeof(char)*20);
    }
        for(i=0; i<fix_size+l;i++){
            if(i == 0) {
                c_direc[i] = strtok(direc,DELIM);
            }
            else{
                c_direc[i] = strtok(NULL,DELIM);
            }
        }
    excute_command(c_direc);
}
/* TO IMPLEMENT EXCUTE_COMMAND */
void excute_cornmand(char **c_direc){
    int i;
    char new_corre_work_dir[50];
    if(strcmp(c_direc[0],"quit") = = 0) {
```

```
        method_Design();
        exit_FROM_SHELL();
    }
    else if(strcmp(c_direc[0],"cd") = =0){
            if(c_direc[1]) {
                    char corre_work_dir[50];
                    getcwd(corre_work_dir,50);
            chdir(c_direc[1] );
            // char new_corre_work_dir[50];
            getcwd(new_corre_work_dir,50);
                    if(strcmp(corre_work_dir,new_corre_work_dir)){
                            method_Design();
                            printf("\t\t\t                    DIRECTORY IS CHANGE
\t\t\t\t\n\n");
                            if(strcmp(new_corre_work_dir,"1s") = = 0){
                                    excute_command(new_corre_work_dir);
                            }
                    }
                    else if(strcmp(new_corre_work_dir,"pwd"))
                    method_PWD();
            }
        }
        else if(strcmp(c_direc[O],"pwd") ==0 ) {
            method_Design();

            printf("PATH\n");
printf("~~~~~~~~~~~~~~~~~~~~~~~~~~~~~~~~~~~~~~~~~~~~~~~~~~~~~~~~~~~~~~~~~~~")
;
            printf("~~~~~~~~~~~~~~~~~~~~~~~~~~~~\n");
            method_PWD();
printf("~~~~~~~~~~~~~~~~~~~~~~~~~~~~~~~~~~~~~~~~~~~~~~~~~~~~~~~~~~~~~~~~~~~")
;
            printf("~~~~~~~~~~~~~~~~~~~~~~~~~~~~\n");
    }
    else if(strcmp(c_direc[0],"clear") = = 0) {
            method_CLEAR();
            printf(" SCREEN IS CLEAR");
            printf("\n*****************\n\n");
    }
    else if(strcmp(c_direc[0],"help") = = 0){
```

```
            method_Design();
            method_Help();
      }
      else if(strcmp(c_direc[0],"echo") = = 0) {
            method_Design();
            printf("ECHO'S \n");

printf("~~~~~~~~~~~~~~~~~~~~~~~~~~~~~~~~~~~~~~~~~~~~~~~~~~~~~~~~~~~~~~")
;
            printf("~~~~~~~~~~~~~~~~~~~~~~~~~~~~~~\n");
            method_Echo(c_direc);
printf("~~~~~~~~~~~~~~~~~~~~~~~~~~~~~~~~~~~~~~~~~~~~~~~~~~~~~~~~~~~~~~")
;
            printf("~~~~~~~~~~~~~~~~~~~~~~~~~~~~~~\n");
      }
      else{
         c_direc_excute(c_direc);
      }
}

/* DEFINITION OF C_DIREC_EXCUTE */

void c_direc_excute(char **c_direc) {
      pid_t pid;
      int rat;
      pid = fork () ;
      if(pid == 0) {
         if(execvp(c_direc[O],c_direc)<O) {
            system("clear") ;
            printf("\n\t+ + + + + + + + + + + + + + + .: WARNNING");
            printf(" + + + + + + + + + + + + + + +\n\n");
            printf("--------------------------------------------------------------------------------");
            printf("-------------------");
            printf("                                                INVALID COMMAND
ENTERED. . . . . . . . . . . . . .        \n\n");
            printf ("                                                  PLEASE TRY
AGAIN . . . . . . . . . . . . . . . .     \n\n\n");
         }
      }
      else
```

```
        wait(NULL);
    }

/* METHOD DECLARATION */

void exit_FROM_SHELL() {
      exit(0);
}
void method_PWD() {
      system ("pwd") ;
}
void method_CLEAR() {
      system ("clear") ;
}
void method_Help() (
      system ("help") ;
}
void method_Echo (char** statement) {
         int i;
         char *value;
         for( i=1; statement [i] !=NULL;i++) {
             if ((statement[i] [0]) = = '$') {
             statement[i]=statement[i]+1;
             value=(char*)getenv(statement[i]);
             if (value !=NULL)
                 printf("VALUE IS    %s ",*value);
         }
         else
             printf("%s",statement[i]);
    }
    printf("\n") ;
}
void method_Design(){
        system ("clear") ;
        printf("\n\t+ + + + + + + + + + + + + + + RESULT");
        printf(" + + + + + + + + + + + + ~ ++\n\n");
        printf("--------------------------------------------------------------------------------");
        printf("--------------------------");
        printf("                                                        YOU ENTERED A VALID
COMMAND                  \n\n");
```

```
}
```

Expt. No. 21 (Alternative Solution – I)

```
# include<stdio.h>
# include<string.h>
# include<sys/wait.h>
# include<unistd.h>
# include<stdlib.h>
# include<sys/types.h>
# include<signal.h>
# include<fcntl.h>
// ******************** declaring global variables ***********************************
char *inp[20];      // to store the tokenized strings
int no_of_arg;      // storing the no. of arguments after tokenizing the input.
// ********************** PROMPT() **********************************
/* DISPLAYS THE PROMPT
     eg: c:/home/adminstrator/desktop/myshell> */
void prompt ( )
{
     // inbuilt method for getting the current working directory
     printf("%s/myshell> ", (char *)get_current_dir_name()); // for displaying the prompt
}
// ********************** ECHO ( ) ********************************************
/*
     TAKES THE INPUT FROM STANDARD INPUT AND DISPLAYS IT ON STANDARD
OUTPUT
*/
void echol ( )
{
     int i = 1;
     while(inp[i] !=NULL)
     {
          printf ("%s ", inp [i] ) ;
          i++;
     }
     printf("\n") ;
}
// ********************** ENVIRON() *******************************************
/*
     DISPLAYS THE VALUE OF ENVIRONMENT VARIABLES
```

```
        PARAM: char **envp : the reference to environment variables is contained in envp
*/
void environ(char **envp)
{
        int i=0;
        while(envp[i] != NULL)
        {
        printf("%s\n",envp[i]) ;
        i++;
        }
}
// ********************** Pause() **********************************************
/*
        PAUSE THE FUNCTIONING OF SHELL TILL IT GETS NEXT '\n' CHARACTER
*/
void paus ( )
{
        char ch;
        do
        {
        ch = getchar();         // taking the input from standard input device(character by charac
        }while(ch != '\n');     // checks for the newline charater
}
// ********************** DIRECTORY() ******************************************
/*
        OPENS THE DIRECTORY WHOSE NAME IS GIVEN IN THE ARGUMENT
*/
void directory ()
{
        DIR *dr;                // creating a variable of type DIP
        struct dirent *d; char *ch;
        if (no_of_arg = = 1)
        {
inp [1] = ".";
        }
        dr = opendir(inp[1]);
        while(d = readdir(dr)}
        {
            ch = d->d name;
        if((ch[0] = = '.'}   | | strcmp(d->d_name, "."} = = 0   | | strcmp (d->d_name, ". ."} = = 0)
```

```
    {
        continue;
    }
    printf("%s",d->d name}; } printf("\n") ;
    closedir (dr) ;
}
// ********************* CHANGEDIR() ***************************************
/*
    CHANGES THE DIRECTORY FROM EXISTING DIRECTORY TO THE ONE WHOSE
NAME IS GIVEN IN THE ARGUMENTS
*/
void changedir()
{
    // it's checking if only 'cd' is given as the command then it does nothing as it changes to the
currently working directory only
    if (no_of_erg == 1) {}
    else
    {
        // chdir () is an inbuilt function in c which makes the cwd as given in the arguments
    if(chdir(inp[l]))
    {
        printf("NO such file or directory\n"};
    }
    }
}
// ********************** PIPE() ***********************************
/* THE FUNCTION HANDLES THE PIPING
PARAM : char *input :the input string containing the pipe
*/
void pipes1 (char *input}
{
    char *argument 1;        // refers to the argument before the pipe.
    char *argument 2;        // refers to the argument after the pipe.
    char *comm1;             // refers to the temporary file that will be created to handle piping.
    int pid;             // the process id
    int i = 0;               // the number of arguments returned after tokenizing input
    int fd;
// file descriptor of the temporary file.
    int flag;
    // tokenizing with delimitor |
```

```
argument1 = strtok (input, "|");
argument 2 = strtok (NULL, "|");
// Temporary file name
comm1 = "pipe";
// using inbuilt function 'strtok', for breaking the argument1 into substrings inp[i] =
strtok(argument1, " "};
while(inp[i] != NULL)
{
inp[++i] = strtok(NULL, " ");
}
/*
opening the file in read write mode and if the file doesn't, exists then it is created owner, other
members of the same group or any other group can access the file in all the 3 modes
i.e. read, write, execute
*/
fd=open(comm1, O_CREAT | O_RDWR, 0777) ;
flag=0;
if ( (pid=fork() )==0)
{
close (1) ;            // closing the standard output stream
dup2(fd,1) ;           // redirecting the standard output to the file pointed by fd
execvp (inp [0] , inp) ;
printf("\nBad file command");
exit (0) ;
}
// waiting for child to terminate.
wait (&pid) ;
// using inbuilt function 'strtok', breaking the argument1
i = 0;
inp[i] = strtok(argument2, " ");
while(inp[i] != NULL)
{
inp[++i] = strtok(NULL, " ");
}
fd = open (comm1, O_RDONLY) ;
// forking to execute the second command.
if((pid=fork() )==0)
{
close(0) ;             // closing the standard input stream
dup2(fd,0) ;           // coping the standard input to the file pointed by fd
```

```
    execvp(inp[0] , inp);
    printf("\nBad file command");
    exit (0) ;
    }
    wait (&pid) ;
    if (remove ("pipe") )
    {
        printf("error occurred");
    }
}
// ********************* HELP ******************************************
//DISPLAYS THE HELP MANUAL TO THE USER
void help ( )
{
    char cmd [] = "cat helpme | more" ;   // helpme is a manual .file created by us
    pipes 1 (cmd) ;
}
// ********************* EXECUTE() ***************************************
/*THE FUNCTION EXECUTES THE COMMAND USING FORKING AND EXECING ALSO
HANDLES THE BACKGROUND PROCESSES
*/
void execute ()
{
    char *c;          // stores the last argument of the original input string
    int p ;           // process id
c = inp [– – no_of_arg];
// Processes will run in background and checking if an & is enetered.
if (! strcmp (inp [no_of_arg] , "&") )
{
inp[no_of_arg]=NULL;
                      // creates child process
if((p=fork()) = = 0)
{
    execvp(inp[0] ,inp);  // executes the instruction
    printf ("Bad File Command\n");    // give the error if the command is bad or not found
}
    // Processes will run in background and checking if an & is concatenated with the last
argument.
    else if(c[strlen(c)-l] = = '&')
    {
inp[no_of_arg] = strtok(c, "&");
```

```
            // creates child process
    if((p=fork() )==0)
    {
        execvp(inp[0] , inp);              // executes the instruction
        printf("Bad File Command\n");      // give the error if the command is bad or not found
    }
    }
    /* handles the other cases when an & is not entered. That is it will run in background and will
wait for child to terminate. */
    else
    {
            // creates child process
    if((p=fork()) = = 0)
    {
        execvp(inp[0] ,inp);               // executes the instruction
        printf ("Bad File Command\n");     // give the error if the command is bad or not found
        exit(0);
    }
    else
    {
        waitpid(p,0,0) ;                   // waits for the child process to exit
    }
    }
}
// ******************** REDIRECTION (OCCURENCE OF <) ************************
/*
    HANDLES THE REDIRECTION IF THERE IS '<' IN THE COMMAND
    PARAM: char *input : contains the command
*/
void Single_Redirect2(char *input)
{
    char *p;              // reference to first occurence of
    int pid;              // process id
    char *comm;           // contains the command to be executed.
    char *comm1;          // contains the file
    int fd;               // file descriptor
    int i=0;
    if(p = strstr(input,"<"))
    {
    p[0]= ' ';            // removes < from the command
```

```
                        // using inbuilt function 'strtok', breaking the input string into substrings
    inp[i] = strtok(input, " ");
    while (inp[i] != NULL)
    {
        inp [++i] = strtok (NULL, " ");
    }
    no of_arg = i;
    comm1 = inp[no of arg-1];
    inp[no_of_arg-1] = NULL;
    no of_arg - -;
    fd = open(comm1,O_CREAT | O_RDONLY);            // opening file.
    if(fd < 0)
    {
        printf("Insufficient arguments");
        return;
    }
    if((pid=fork()) = = 0)
    {
        close(0) ;
        dup2 (fd, 0) ;
        execvf, inp [0] ,inp) ;
        printf ("Bad file command\n") ;
        exit (0) ;
    }
    }
}
// ********************** REDIRECTION(OCCURENCE OF >>) *********************
***************** *****
/*
    HANLES THE REDIRECTION IF THERE IS >> IN THE COMMAND
    PARAM: char*input : the command to be handled
*/
void double Redirect (char *input)
{
    char *p;            // reference to first occurence of >>
    int pid;            // process id
    char *comm;         // contains the command to be executed.
    char *comm1;        // contains the file
    int fd;             // file descriptor.
    int i = 0;
```

```
    if (p=strstr(input, ">>"))
    {
    p[0] = ' '     // REMOVES THE >> FROM COMMAND
    P [1] = ' ';
    inp[i] = strtok(input, " ");
    while(inp[i] != NULL)
    {
        inp[++i] = strtok (NULL, " ");
    }
    no_of_arg = i;
    comm1 = inp[no of arg-1];
    inp[no of arg-1] = NULL;
    no_of_arg--;
    fd = open(comm1,O_APPEND | O_WRONLY | O_CREAT,0777);
    if((pid=fork()) = = 0)
    {
        close (1);
        dup2 (fd, 1);
        execvp(inp[0], inp);
        printf ("Bad file command\n");
        exit (0);
    }
    }
}
// ****************** REDIRECTION (OCCURENCE OF >) ************************
**********
/*    HANDLES THE REDIRECTION IF THERE IS > IN THE COMMAND
      PARAM: char *input : command to be handled
*/
void Single_Redirect1(char *input)
{
      char *p;                  // reference to first occurence of >
      int pid;                  // process id
      char *comm;               // contains the command to be executed.
      char *comm1;              // contains the file
      int fd;                   // file descriptor.
      int i = 0;
      if(p=strstr(input,">"))
      {
      p[0] = ' '; // REMOVES > FROM THE COMMAND
```

```
inp[i] = strtok(input, " ");
while(inp[i] != NULL)
{
    inp[++i] = strtok(NULL " ");
}
no_of_arg = i;
com1 = inp [no_of_arg-1];
inp[no of arg-1] = NULL;
no of_arg–1;
fd=open (com1, O_CREAT | O_WRONLY | O_TRUNC, 0777);
if ((pid=fork()) = = 0)
{
    close(1);                       // Working to execute 2nd command
    dup2(fd, 1);                    // Closing std input stream
    execvp (inp[0], inp);           // Copying standard input to the file printed by fd.
    printf ("Bad file command\n");  // Execute a file
    exit (0);
}
}
}
// ******************* CALL () ******************************************
// void myshell fn(char *filename, char **envp);
void check(char input[], char **envp)
{
    int i =0;
    char *p;
    if(p=strstr(input,">>"))
    {
    double Redirect (input) ;
    return;
    }
    if (p=strstr(input, ">"))
    {
    Single Redirectl(input);
    return;
    }
    if (p=strstr(input, "<"))
    {
    Single Redirect2(input);
    return;
```

```
}
if(p=strstr(input,“ | ”))
{
pipesl(input);
return;
}
inp[i] = strtok(input, “ ”);
while(inp[i] != NULL)
{
inp[++i] = strtok(NULL, “ ”);
}
no_of_arg = i;
if (no of arg == 0)
{
return;
}
if ((!(strcmp(inp[0],“myshell”))) && (no_of_arg > 1))
{
myshell_fn(inp[1] ,envp);
return;
}
if ((!(strcmp(inp[0],“clr”))) && (no_of_arg = = 1))
{
system (“clear”) ;
return;
}
if ((!(strcmp(inp[0],“environ”))) && (no of arg = = 1))
{
environ(envp);
return;
}
if ((!(strcmp(inp[0],“quit”))) && (no of arg = = 1))
{
exit(1);
if ((!(strcmp(inp[0),“help”))) && (no_of_arg == 1))
{
help () ;
return;
}
if ((!(strcmp(inp[0),“pause”))) && (no_of_arg == 1))
```

```
{
paus() ;
return;
}
if (! (strcmp (inp [0] , "echo" )))
{
echol () ;
return;
}
if ((! (strcmp(inp[0], "dir"))) && (no_of_arg < = 2))
{
directory() ;
return;
}
if ((!(strcmp(inp[0], "cd"))) && (no_of_arg <= 2))
{
changedir() ;
return;
}
execute() ;
}
// ******************** MYSHELL_FN() ***************************************
void myshell_fn(char *filename, char **envp)
{
    char inputl[100];
    FILE *fd; int count=0;
    fd = fopen(filename,"r");        //opening file.
    if (fd == NULL)
    {
    printf("File doesn't exists\n");
    return;
    }
    fgets(input1, 100, fd);
    inputl[strlen(input1)-1] = '\0';
    count = 0; while(strcmp(input1,"eof"))
    {
    if (!strcmp (inputl, "quit"))
    {
    fclose (fd) ;                // closes the file pointed by fd return;
    }
```

```
        else
        {
                printf("\nOutput for line no %d : \n", ++count);
            check (input1, envp) ;
            fgets(input1, 100, fd);
            input1[strlen(input1)-1] = '\0';
            }
        }
        fclose(fd) ;            // closes the file pointed by fd return;
}
// ********************* MAIN *******************************************
/*
        THE MAIN FUNCTION FIRST TOKENIZE THE COMMAND AND CHECKS THE
CONTENTS OF THE COMMAND AND THEN ASSIGN
        THE CORRESPONDING FUNCTION TO IT
        PARAM:    int argc:       stores count
            char **argv: argument vector
            char **envp: reference to environment variables
*/
int main(int argc, char **argv, char **envp)
{
        // the infinite loop will continue taking the input from the user trll it gets quit command for (;;)
        {
        int i =0;
        char input [100] ;
        char *p;
        prompt() ;
        fgets(input, 100, stdin) ;
        input[strlen(input)-1] = '\0';
            if(strstr(input,"myshell"))
        {
                i = 0;
            if ( ! strcmp (input, "myshell"))
                {
            printf ("BAD COMMAND\n") ;
            continue;
                }
                inp[i] = strtok(input, "");
                while(inp[i] != NULL)
                {
```

```
        inp[++i] = strtok(NULL,"");
            }
            no_of_arg = i;
        if ((! (strcmp(inp[0], "myshell"))) && (no_of_arg != 2))
        {
        printf ("BAD COMMAND\n") ;
                continue;
        }
            if ( (! (strcmp (inp [0], "myshell") )) && (no_of_arg == 2))
            {
            myshell_fn(inp[l] , envp);
        for (i=0; i<no_of_arg; i++)
        {
            inp[i] = NULL;
        }
            continue;            // returns back to the loop
        }
    }
    else
    {
        check(input, envp);
        continue;
        }
    }
    return 0;
}
```

Expt. No. 21 (Alternative Solution – II)

```
# define Dos Ox21
# include<dos.h>
# include<stdio.h>
# include<string.h>
# include<process.h>
# include<conio.h>
    int ch;
    void main ()
        {
        clrscr();
    do
        {
        printf("\n\t--------------------------------");
```

```
printf("\n\t1.Display message on screen");
printf ("\n\t2.Create a Subdirectory.");
printf ("\n\t3.Delete a Subdirectory.");
printf ("\n\t4.Change a Directory.");
printf ("\n\t5.List contents of current or Specified Directory.");
printf ("\n\t6.CAT command of LINUX.");
printf ("\n Enter your choice.");
scanf("%d", & ch);
if (ch = = 1)
     void display ();
if (ch = = 2)
     void create ();
if (ch = = 3)
     void del ();
if (ch = = 4)
     void changedir ();
/*  if (ch = = 5)
     void dircontents (int argc, char * argv[]);
if (ch = = 6)
     void cat (int argc, char * argv[]); */
if (ch > 6) break;
}
     while (ch > = 1 | | ch < = 6);
}
void display ()
     {
     union REGS regs;
     char *msg = "shell using C $";
          /* Display string */
          regs.h.ah=9;
          regs.h.dx=FP_OFF (msg);
          int86 (ox21, & regs, & regs);
     }
     void create ()
          {
          Union REGS regs;
          char dirname[18];
          printf ("/n/t Enter name of dir to create :");
          scanf ("%"s, dirname);
          /* Create subdir now */
```

```
                regs.h.ah = ox 39;
                regs.x.dx = FP_OFF (dirname);
                int86(DOS, & regs, & regs);
            if (regs.x.coflag! = 0)
            printf ("Dir already exists—unable to create it");
        }
void del ()
        {
        Union REGS regs;
        char dirname [80];
        printf ("Enter dir name to delete :");
        scan f ("%S", dirname);
        /* Delete subdir now */
        regs.h.ah = Ox3a;
        regs.x.dx = FP_OFF (dirname);
        int86 (DOS, & regs, & regs);
        if (regs.x.cflag ! = 0)
            printf ("Not a dir or dir not empty");
        }
void changedir ()
        {
        Union REGS regs;
        char dirname [18];
        printf ("Enter name of changed dir :");
        scanf ("%S", dirname);
        /* change directory */
            regs.h.ah = ox3b;
            regs.x.dx = FP_OFF (dirname);
            int86(DOS, & regs, & regs);
            if (regs.x.cflag ! = 0)
                printf ("Invalid directory");
            }
            void dircontents (int argc, char * argc[])
                {
                char buffer [25];
                struct find_t find;        // file found block
            put ("List files of current or specified Directory .............");
            if (argc > 1)
                {
                if (! strcmp (argv [1], "?"))
```

```
                {
                printf ("Usage : LF [?] [Listing specification]");
                exit (1);
                }
        }
    if (argc < 2)
        strcpy (buffer, "x.x");
    else
        strcpy (buffer, argv[1]);
    if (! _dos_findfirst (buffer, _A_NORMAL, & find))
        {
        do
            {
            printf ("/n%S", find.name);
            }
            while (! _dos_findnext (&find));
            }
        }
        void cat (int argc, char * argv[])
            {
            char ch;
            struct find_t find;
            FILE *fp;
            int i;
            puts ("CAT command_Displaying file contents...");
            if (argc < 2)
                {
                printf ("Usage : CAT file name | [filename 2 ...]");
            exit (1);
        }
    for (i = 1; i < argc; i++)
        {
        if (! _dos_findfirst (argv[i], _A_NORMAL, & find))
            {
            do
                {
                /* check for current find is not a directory */
            if (! (find.attrib & FA_DIREC))
                {
                printf ("\n ---------------------------/n");
```

```
                printf ("FILE : %S", find.name);
                printf ("\n ---------------------------/n");
            /* Open file for reading */
                fp = fopen (find.name, "r");
            /* Display contents of a file */
            while (!feof (fp))
                {
                ch = getc (fp);
                printf ("%c", ch);
                }
            fclose (fp);
            }
        }
    while (! _dos_findnext (& find));
    }
  }
}
```

SET – II

Linux based Experiments (O.S.)

LAB – 1

Linux or less frequently used in is a unix like and mostly POSIX complaint computer OS assembled under the model of free and open source of software development and distribution.

Linux was originally developed as a free OS for Intel X86 – based personal computers. It has been since ported to more computer between platform than any other OS. It is a leading OS on servers and other big iron systems such as mainframe and super computers. Linux also runs on embedded systems which are ware firm.

Commands for Linux are as follows:

To make a new user:

[root@root~] user add Adiba

[root@root~] password (passwd)

Passwd: It displays the absolute path name, As you navigate the file name with the CD command, you will be using passwd to know your current directory.

[Adiba@root~] $

- **cd:** Through passwd displays the absolute path name, cd doesn't need to use once the command cd progs have means this "change your subdirectory to programs under this directory.

  To make a directory:

  [Adiba@root~] $ mkdir A6

  [Adiba@root~] $ ls

  A_1 A_2 A_3 A_4

- **mkdir:** directories have been created with the mkdir command. This command is followed by the names of the directories to be created & of the directory path is created under the current directory this:

  mkdir Test: mkdir failed to denied, failed to make directory "Test";

  Permission denied

  This can happen due to these reasons. The directory test already, exists.

  Permission set for the current directory dont permit the creation of files $ directories by user you'll most certainly get this msg if you try to create a directory in | bin | etc or in any other directory that has UNIX system files.

- **r m dir:** It processes directories

- **rm dir P** is

  However, the directory must be empty like mkdir, rmdir can also delete more than one directory in one shot. Note, when you delete a directory $ its subdirectory a reverse logic has to be applied.

- **man:** The man command is used to get information about commands, e.g., man mkdir, this command give you the information about mkdir command its syntax & why it is used.

- **ls:** List directory contents list information about the FILES (current directory by default) sort entries alphabetically.

- **ls – *l*:** It lists the file attributes (–*l*) is the long option that reveals most. This option displays the most attributes of file, like its permissions size and ownership details.

- **date:** Shows date and time

[Adiba@root~] $ date

Tue Aug 12 18 : 28 : 14 IST 2014

- **vi editor:** vi uses a no. of internal commands to navigate to any point in a text files and edit the text there. Also allows you to copy and move text within a file and also from one file together.

Simplest type of I/P is ';' for insertion [with : w command you can optionally specify a file name as well as in that case, contents are separately written to another file.

- **:X and : Wq: saving & quitting:** Previous command returns you to command mode so you can continue editting.
- **Abort editing (: q):** It will you just quit, saving wont be done.
- **cp : Copying a file:** It creates an exact image of file on disk with a different name.
- **rm : deleting files:** rm command deletes one or more files : Normally operates silently and should be used with caution. Following command deletes 3 files.
- **rm : Ch01 Ch02 Ch03:** A file once deleted cant be recovered rm wont usually removes a directed directory but can remove files from one.

rm pregs/Ch01 progs/Ch02 rm

* All files are gone.

- **mv : renaming files:** mv command renames files. It has two distinct functions.
  - It renames a file.
  - It moves a group of file to a different directory.

  mv doesn't creates a copy of file, it mainly renames it.

  mv Ch 01 man 01

  mv Chap 01 Ch 02 Ch 03 progs.

  The following command moves three files to progs directly.

  ♦ Make sure you are doing the right thing before you use rm *. Be doubly sure before you are rm – rf *. The first command removes ordinary files in current directly directory second one removes everything files and directories a like it, if root used (super user) invoke rm – rf * in the / directory entire unix systems will be wiped out of the hard disk.

- **who : who are the users**

$ who

Kumar	**console Aug 9**	**09 : 31 (: 0 : 0)**
Vipul	**Pts/4**	**Aug 1208 : 43 (0 : 0)**
Rajiv	**Pts/5 Aug 12**	**08 : 51**
	(Satu)	

♦ These are currently logged in users

- **t put:** To clear the screen

$ t put

$ ps : viewing process

ls : Listening files.

- **Linux commands:**

The format of a command is:

Command [options] arguments

- **Command options:**

– –h

– – – help

– –v

– – – version

- **Command arguments:**

"– – help" is wrong

"– – help" is right

- **MISC command:** man, banner, calender, clear, noh up, tty, echo, printf

(*a*) Manual command:

Shows online manual pages.

eg $man ls

(*b*) Banner command:

banner prints characteres in a sort of ASCII art poster; or we can print letter in big.

eg $ banner Rajiv.

(*c*) Cal command:

Cal command will print the calender on current month by default.

eg $ Cal 8 1996.

(*d*) Clear command:

Clear command clears the screen and puts cursor at beginning of first line:

- **nohup command:**

Nohup command if added in front of any command will continue running the command.

eg $ nohup is

$ cat nohup.out

$ nohup PS

- **tty command:**

tty command will display your terminal.

eg $ tty

– S — – – Silent

– – quiet

– – help

– – version

eg $ tty – S

- **echo command:**

It prints the message on the terminals.

$ echo "Linux made easy by Dr. Rajiv."

- **printf command:**

It prints the formatted message on the terminal.

$ printf

Printf : usage : Printf [–v var]

format [arguments]

$ printf "the amount is % d\n"

10000

O/P

The amount is 10000.

- File management commands:

(*a*) pwd command

It will print your home directory on screen, pwd means print working directory.

$ pwd

O/P:- /home/ajay

- **ls command**

ls command is most widely used command and it displays the contents of directory.

eg $ ls

- **tail command:**

Tail filename by default will display the last 10 lines of a file.

$ tail – 3 nohup.out

- **wc command:**

wc command counts the characters, words or lines a file depending upon the option:

wc [OPTION]...[FILE]...

- **cp command:**

Copying files and directories :

$ cp oldfile newfile

- **mv command:**

mv command is used to more a file from one directory to another directory or to rename a file.

- mv oldfile newfile
- mv – i oldfile newfile
- mv –f oldfile newfile

eg mv –i

- **rm command**

To delete files use rm command

eg rm – i

- **Comparison and searching:**

diff, discrmp, cmp, grep, find, sort

- **diff command:**

diff command will compare the two files and print out the differences between them

eg $ diff test. txt test1. txt

- **dircmp command:**

This dircmp command compares the two directories specified by the Directory1 and Directory2.

eg diff – r

- **sort command:**

sort command sort the lines of a files or files, in alphabetical order

eg $ sort sortdemo.txt

$ sort – r sortdemo.txt

- **Communications**

♦ **cu command**

cu command is used for communication over a modem or direct line with another linux system.

cu options destination.

as – bn, –c, –d, –n

- **login command:**

login command invokes a login session to a Linux system, which then authenticates the login to a system.

- **rlogin command:**

rlogin command is used to log on to remote Linux system, user must have permission on both systems as well as same user rid.

eg rlogin options host

- **Write command:**

Will initiate an interactive conversation with user

Syntax is,

write user try.

- **Storage commands:**

compress, uncompress, cpio, dump, pack, tar, mt.

♦ **Compress command:**

It compresses a file and return the original file with .z extension.

- **pack command:**

Pack command compact each file and combine them together into a filename .z file.

eg Pack options files. [syntax].

- **Uncompress command:**

Uncompress file uncompresses a file and return it to its original form.

uncompress filename .z

♦ **System Status:**

at, chmod, chgrp, chown, crontab, date, df, du, env, finger, ps, ruptime, shutdown, stty, who

- **at command:**

About at

eg at – m 01 : 35 < at job

at – l

at – r

- **chmod command:**

chmod is used to change the permission on a file.

_rw_rw_rw

- **chgrp command**

chgrp command is used to change the group of a file or directory.

eg chgrp hope file.txt

- **chown command**

chown command to change ownership of a file or directory to one or more users.

eg chown chope file.txt

chown – R chope work

- **df command:**

The df (disk free) command reports the amount of space used and available on currently mounted file systems.

df [option [s]] [device (s)]

- **du command:**

The du (disk usage) command reports the sizes of directory trees inclusive of all of their contents and the sizes of individual files

du – h

du – a/etc.

- **Shutdown command:**

Shutdown command can only be executed by root.

eg –gn, –ik & –y.

LAB – 2

root login :Adiba

password :

Last login : Tue Aug 1918 : 11 :

26 on tty2

[Adiba @ root ~] $ ls – l

LS (1)

NAME :

ls – list directory contents

Synopsis:

ls [OPTION]…[FILE]…

- **Description:**

List information about the files (the current directory by default). Sort entries alphabetically if none of –Cftuvsux nor – – sort.

Mandatory args to long options are mandatory for short options too

–a, –all

do not ignore entries starting with

–A, – – almost – all.

do not list implied. and .

– – author

with – *l*, prints author of each file

O/P:

Total 40

drWXr _ xr _ x. 2 Adiba Adiba 4096

Aug 19 18 : 09 Desktop

– rW – rW – r – – . 1 Adiba Adiba

31 Aug 12 18 : 35 l1

[Adiba @ root ~] $ cd

[Adiba @ root ~] $ cd l 2

[Adiba @ root l 2] $ touch try 5

[Adiba @ root l 2] $ vi try 5

File opened

For inserting press i

Now write the data for file

hello, Bye

Press Exc then, : , wq

O/P

"try S" 10L 27 C Written

[Adiba @ root ~]

[Adiba @ root ~] $ grep l

[Adiba @ root l 2] $ grep l try 5

hello, Bye

- **Grep:**

  NAME: grep, egrep, fgrep, –print lines matching a pattern.

- **Synopsis:**

  grep [OPTIONS] PATTERN [FILE…]

  grep [OPTIONS] [–e PATTERN : – f FILE]

  [FILE…]

  Description:

  Grep searches the named I/P files (or std input of no files are named or if a single hyphen – minus (–) is given as file name), for lines containing a match to given PATTERN.

- By default, grep prints the matching lines.

  In addition, 2 variant programs e grep and –f grep are available-e grep is same as grep –E, f grep is same as grep –f. Direct invocation as either e grep or f grep is deprecated, but it is provided to allow historial apps that rely on them to run umodified.

- **OPTIONS:**

  Generic Programs Inform

  – – help print a usage msg briefly summarizing these command line options and bug–reporting address, than exist.

  wc try 5

  6 6 29

lines words characters

- **wc(1)**

  NAME:

  wc – print newlines, word, and byte counts for each file.

- **Synopsis:**

  wc [OPTIONS]… [FILE]…

  wc [OPTIONS]… [FILE O – From f]

Print newline, word, and byte counts for each FILE, and a total line if more than one FILE is specified with no FILE, or when FILE is –, read std I/P.

– C, – – bytes

Print byte counts.

– m, – – chars.

Print characters counts.

– l, – – lines

Print newline counts.

– – files O – from = f

read I/P from files specified by NUL – terminated names in File F; If F is = then read name from std I/Ps

– w, – – words

print word counts

– L, – – max – line – length

Print length of longest line.

– – help display this help and exit.

– – version

O/P version into and exit.

- **Chmod (changing file permission):**

[Adiba @ root ~] $ mKdir j s

[Adiba @ root ~] $ ls

js

[Adiba @ root ~] $ cel js

[Adiba @ root ~] $ touch try 3

[Adiba @ root js] chmod 777

[Adiba @ root js] $ c/s

try 3

[Adiba @ root js] $ ls – 1

total 0

– rw × rw × rw × .1 Adiba Adiba 0

Aug 26 18 : 04 try 3.

- **Chmod 000 filename**

000 will give no permission.

Binary	Octal	Permission	Significance
000	0	– – –	No permission
001	1	_ _x	Executable only
010	2	_ w_	Writable only
011	3	_ w x	Writable and Executable
100	4	r _ _	Readable only
101	5	r_ x	Readable and Executable
110	6	r w_	Readable and Writable
111	7	rwx	Readable, writable and executable

It would be quite easy for you to understand expression 777 which signifies all programming permissions for all categories, while 000 indicates absence of all permissions for all categories. But can we delete a file and can we present file from being deleted we can do that too.

To assign all permissions to owner, read and write permissions to group, and only access permissions to others use this:

Chmod 761 X Start

Cat: Concatenate files of and print on standard O/P.

Synopsis: cat [OPTION]…[FILE]…

```
$    cat    abc
            Name
            Rajiv
            Nidhi
            Ajay.
```

- **more:** more command will display a page of a time and then wait for I/P which is spacebar.

  For eg : If you have a file which is 500 lines and you want to read it all. So you can use more file name.

```
$    more   abc
            Name
            Rajiv
            Nidhi
            Ajay.
```

100% will be displayed at the bottom of page indicating file that file has been displayed completely.

- **commands:** [user Management]

  id, useradd, usermod, user del, group add, group del, group mod, passwd.

Command	Use
Id	prints info. for a certain user
user add	To create a new user
user mod	To modify a users account
user del	To delete a user account
Group add	To create a new group

Group del	delete a group
group mod	to change a group name
password	change the user's pass-word

- **'id' command:**

  The id command prints informtion for a certain user.

  id [–a] [–G] [–g] [–u] [user]

  [Options]

- **useradd command:**

  It enable a super user or root to create a new user or updates default new user information.

eg useradd [–c comment]

  useradd – m

  useradd – s shell

- **Use of 'passwd' command:**

  It is used to change the login passward and password attributes

  Syntax: passwd [login-name]

  passwd – s [–a]

  passwd – s [login-name]

  passwd – P

- **'user mod' command:**

  It enables a super user or root user to modify a user's account

  user mod [–d home-dir] login

  user mod – L

  user mod – U

- **'Userdel' command:**

  It enables a super user to remove a user's account

  userdel [–r] login

- **'groupadd' command:**

  It creates a new group account

  groupadd [–9 gid [–0]] group

- **'groupdel' command:**

  It enables a super user or root to remove a group.

  groupdel group.

♦ **Command to find the current shell:**

  $ echo $ SHELL

- **Mounting and unmounting of Devices into existing file system:**

  Mounting a device means attaching the device to the file system heirarchy (the tree (/)).

  To mount a file system, the mount command is used.

  mount – t file system / device-path-mount point-path.

mount – t vfat/dcv/hda6/mnt/data.

- **Mount options:** The mount command has several options that override the default behaviour.

For example, we can mount a file system read-only by specifying –Oro.

#mount – 0 remount, ro¦back up.

unmount¦mnt¦data

- **The numeric (octal) representation for the file permission:**

if a numeric representation is used, then it is in the octal format and digits involved are 0 to 7:

Examples:

	owner : read & write
644	group : only read
	others : only read
755	owner : read, write and execute
	group : read and execute
	others : read & execute permission

Features:

- **Aliases:**

The alias command is useful if we want to create a shortcut to a command.

The format is alias name = 'command'

$ alias list = 'ls – la'

$ alias

- **Command History:**

$ alias command History:

Sometimes you may end up repeating the previous commands for various reasons.

One key completion:

Automatic file name completion is one of the most useful features of the Linux command line.

$ cat un "and hit the Tab Key".

- **The 'Grep' utility:**

Finding matching pattern using grep utility.

Create text file as follows:

demo-file

hello world!

cartoons are good

especially toon like tom (cat)

what

the no. one song

12221

they love us

I too

After saving file, issue following commands.

$ grep "too" demofile.

O/P

Cartoons are good

especially toon like tom (cat)

Syntax:

grep [Options] "word to find" [file-name]

- **Data manipulation using 'awk' utility**

awk utility is powerful data manipulation/scripting programming language. Aw is a programming language developed in 1977.

Create data file using any text editor or simply is :

inventory

egg order 4

cake good 10

cheese okay 4

pen good 12

floppy good 5.

After creating file issue command.

$ awk '/good/{print $ 3}'

inventory

10

12

$ awk '/good/{print$1"''$3}' inventory

Syntax:

awk 'pattern {action}' file-name

LAB – 3

```
# Shell script to add Numbers supplied by command line arguments.
# !/bin/bash
#
# script to sum two nos
#
if [$ # – nez]
then
echo "usage – $OXY"
echo "where x and y are two nos for which I will print sum"
exit 1
fi
echo" sum of $1 and $2 is "expr $1 + $2".
```

LAB – 4

Script to find out biggest number from the given three numbers supplied by command line argument.

```
# !/bin/bash
```

```
#
# Script to find out biggest number
#
# Algo:
# (1) START: Take three nos as n1, n2, n3
# (2) | Is n | is greater than n2 & n3, if yes
# print n1 is biggest no goto step 5 otherwise goto next step.
# (3) Is n2 is greater than n1 and n3, if yes
print n2 is biggest no goto steps 5, otherwise goto next step.
# (4) Is n3 is greater than n1 & n2, if yes
print n3 is biggest no goto step 5, goto next step.
# (5) END
#
#
if [$# – ne3]
then
echo "$ 0 : number 1 number 2 number 3 are not given" > & 2
exit 1
fi
n1 = $1
n2 = $2
n3 = $3
if [$n1 – gt $n2] && [$n1 – gt $ n3]
then
echo "$n1 is Biggest number"
elif [$n2 – gt $n1] && [$n2 – gt$ n3]
then
echo "n2 is Biggest number"
elif [$n3 – gt $n1] && [$n3 – gt $n2]
then
echo "$n3 is Biggest number"
elif [$1 – eq $2] && [$1 – eq $3] && [$2 – eq $3]
then
echo "All the three no's are equal"
else
echo "I cannot figure out which number is bigger"
fi
```

LAB – 5

Script to print the Numbers as 5, 4, 3, 2, 1 using while loop

```
# !/bin/bash
```

```
# Algo :
# (1) START : Set value of i to 5
(since we want to start from 5, if you want to start from other value put that value)
# (2) Start while loop
# (3) Check, Is value of i is zero, if yes goto step 5 else
# continue with step next step
# (4) print i, decrement i by 1
(i.e., i = i – 1 to goto zero) and
# goto step 3
# (5) END
#
i = 5
while test $i! = 0
do echo "$i"
i = 'expr $ i – 1'
done
```

LAB – 6

Script to print the Given number in Reverse order

```
#!/bin/bash
#script to reverse given no
#
# Algo:
# (1) Input number n
# (2) Set rev = 0, Sd = 0
# (3) Find single digit in sd as n% 10 it will give (left most digit)
# (4) Construct reverse no as rev * 10 + Sd.
# (5) Decrement n by 1
# (6) Is n is greater than zero, if yes goto step 3, otherwise next step
# (7) print rev
#
if [$ # – ne1]
then
echo "Usage : $ 0 number"
echo "I will find reverse of given number"
echo "for eg. $0 123, I will print 321"
exit 1
fi
n = $1
rev = 0
Sd = 0
```

```
while [$n – gt 0]
do
Sd = 'expr $n%10'
rev = 'expr $ rev 1% * 10 + $Sd'
n = 'expr $n/10'
done
echo "Reverse number is $ rev".
```

LAB – 7

Shell script to print the sum of all digits of a given number

```
# !/bin/slash
# Algo :
# (1) Input number n
# (2) Set sum = 0, Sd = 0
# (3) Find single digit in Sd as n% 10 it will give (left most digit)
# (4) Construct sum no as sum = sum + Sd
# (5) Decrement n by 1
# (6) Is n is greater than zero, if yes go to step 3, otherwise next step
#(7) print sum
#
if [$ # – ne 1]
then
echo "Usage : $ 0 number"
echo "I will find sum of all digit for given number"
echo "For e.g. $ 0 123, I will print 6 as sum of all digit (1 + 2 + 3)"
exit 1
fi
n = $ 1
sum = 0
Sd = 0
while [$n – gt 0]
do
Sd = 'expr $n% 10'
sum = 'expr $ sum + $ sd'
n = 'expr $ n/10'
done
echo "sum of digits for number is $ sum".
```

LAB – 8

Script to determine whether given file exist or Not

```
# !/bin/bash
if [$ # – ne 1]
```

```
then
echo "Usage : $ 0 file-name"
exit 1
fi
if [–f $ 1]
then
echo "$1 file exist"
else
echo "Sorry, $ 1 file does not exist"
fi
```

LAB – 9

 # Script using startup file

```
#!/bin/bash
#
temp h = 'date¦cut – C/2 – 13'
dat = 'date +' "% A % d in % B of % Y (% r)"
if [$ temph – lt 12]
then
mess = "Good morning $ LOG NAME, Have a nice day!"
fi
if [$ temph –gt 12 – a $ temph – lc 16]
then
mess = "Good Afternoon $ LOG NAME"
fi
if [$ temph – gt 16 – a $ temph – le 18]
then
mess = "Good evening $ GOG NAME"
fi
if while dialog > /dev/null
then
dialog – – backtitle "Linux shell Script Tutorial"\
– – title "(–: Welcome to Linux :–)"\
– – infobox "\n $ mess\n This is $ dat" 6 60
echo – n "Press a Key to continue…"
read
        clear
        else
echo – e "$ mess\n This is $ dat"
fi
```

LAB – 10

LAB – 10

 # Script using Echo command

```
# !/bin/bash
#
# echo command with escape
Sequence to give different
effects
#
# Syntax : echo – e "escape – code your
# message, var 1, var 2 etc"
# For eg. echo – e "\033 [1m
# Hello World"
# |   |
# |   |
# Escape code message
#
clear
echo – e"\033 [1 m Hello world"
# bold – effect
echo – e " \ 033 [5m Blink"
# blink effect
echo –e"\033 [om Hello world"
# back to normal
echo – e "\033 [31m Hello world"
# Red color
echo – e "\033 [32 m Hello World"
# Green color
echo – e "\033 [33 m Hello world"
# See remaining on Screen
echo – e "\033 [34 m Hello world"
echo – e "\033 [35 m Hello world"
echo – e "\033 [36 m Hello world"
echo – e – n "\033 [om"
# back to normal
echo – e "\033 [41 m Hello world"
echo – e "\033 [42 m Hello world"
echo – e "\033 [43 m Hello world"
echo – e "\033 [44 m Hello world"
echo – e "\033 [45 m Hello world"
echo – e "\033 [46 m Hello world"
echo – e "\033 [0 m Hello world"
```

LAB – 11

 # Script using loops

```
# ! ¦ bin ¦ bash
#
# echo "Stars"
for ((i = 1; i < = 5; i++))
do
for ((j = 1; j < = 9; i ++))
do
echo – n "*"
done
echo " "
done
```

O/P

```
*
* *
* * *
* * * *
* * * * *.
```

LAB – 12

 # Shell script to implement a background process.

```
# ! ¦ bin ¦ bash
# To run type at $ prompt as
#
echo
echo "Digital clock for Linux"
echo "To stop this clock use command kill pid"
echo "press a key to continue..."
while :
do
ti = ' date + "% r"
echo – e – n "\033 [7S" # save current screen position and attributes
#
# show the clock
#
tput cup 0 69 # row 0 and column 69 is used to show clock
echo – n $ ti # put clock on screen
echo – e – n "\033 [8 u" # restore current position and attributes
#
# Delay for 1 second
```

#

Sleep 1

done.

LAB – 13

(1) Redirectional operator:

Input output redirection operators are used to read output to file or the read input from file. There are three main redirection symbols

>, >>, <

Syntax:

Linux ~ command > filename

The output linux commands result to file

eg ls > myfiles

Linux command < filename

< filename

To take input to linux command from the file instead of keyboard.

(2) Pipes:

A pipe to way to connect the output of one program to the input of another program without any temporary file.

Syntax:

Command 1 ¦ Command 2

eg who, wc – l

who said to be piped to wc.

(3) Filter:

It is command that takes is input from standard output and produces its output on standard output, it is known as **filter**.

eg tail + 20 < hotel.txt ¦ head – x30> whist here

head command is a filter which takes its input from tail command.

APPENDIX-E

Projects in OS Lab

Project 1: Shell. Write a Shell (Command Language Interpreter) to parse textual commands entered from the user's keyboard, malloc argument variables, and execute programs directly or as child processes.

Project 2: Scheduler. Write a five-state task scheduler capable of simultaneously executing up to 128 tasks in a preemptive, prioritized, round-robin manner. Implement binary and counting semaphores and schedule you CLI as its first tasks with pseudo-interrupt driven character input. Add timer semaphores and tasks to validate you implementation.

oject 3: Jurassic Park. Jurassic Park is an interprocess communication and synchronization problem between multiple tasks. Visitors to the park purchase a ticket, wait to take a ride on a part tour car to see the dinosaurs, and then visit the museum and gift shops before leaving the park. Since the part is on a limited budget, drivers must perform double duty when not sleeping by selling tickets and driving the tour cars. Visitors, drivers, and cars are represents by concurrent tasks while an additional task is used to display the park status every second.

Project 4: Distributed Mutual Exclusion. Integrate a distributed banking system consisting of nine remote ASTM's (clients) and one centralized Bank (server) into your OS and implement a distributed mutual exclusion mechanism (Lamport's algorithm) to protect asynchronous accesses to the Bank (critical section).

Project 5: Virtual Memory. Add a Memory Management Unit (MMU) to your OS that translates virtual LC-3 addresses to physical addresses in a restricted memory space. Validate your implementation by successfully executing up to 32 LC-3 crawler and/or memory test programs concurrently in 2 frames of physical memory (128 words).

Project 6: Fat File Manager. Add a MSDOS® FAT-12 file manager to your OS that is able to traverse file directories, view file data, and load/execute LC-3 programs from files. Implement creation, access, and modification of FAT-12 files by adding file manager functions and commands that use file system buffering, basic file I/O, file descriptors, and file pointers to modify file allocation tables (FAT), directory structures and cluster chains.

APPENDIX–F
Question Papers
MCA/III Sem. G

Paper—CS.302—OPERATING SYSTEMS

(New Course) Delhi University

(Admission of 2001 and onwards)

Time: 3 hours *Maximum Marks : 60*

(Write your Roll No. on the top immediately on receipt of this question paper.)

Attempt *All* questions

All parts of a question must be attempted together.

1. (*a*) What resources are used when a thread is created? How do they differ from those used when a process is created?

(*b*) Provide two programming examples of multithreading that improve performance over a single-threaded solution. 2 + 2

(*c*) Suppose that a scheduling algorithm favours those processes that have used the least processor time in the recent past. Why will this algorithm favour I/O-bound programs and yet not permanently starve CPU-bound programms? 4

(*d*) Consider the following processes, with the length of CPU burst and arrival time :

Process	Arrival Time	Burst Time
P1	0.0	8
P2	0.4	4
P3	1.0	1

(*i*) What is the average turn around time for these processes with FCFs scheduling algorithm? 2

(*ii*) What is average turn around time with SJF scheduling algorithm ? 2

2. (*a*) Explain the readers-writers problem. Discuss the case when writers have priority over readers. 8

(*b*) What is the meaning' of term busy-waiting? What other kind of waiting are there in an operating systems ? 4

(*c*) Consider the following snapshot of a system :

	Allocation	Max	Available
	A B C D	A B C D	A B C D
P_0	0 0 1 2	0 0 1 2	1 5 2 0
P_1	1 0 0 0	1 7 5 0	
P_2	1 3 5 4	2 3 5 6	
P_3	0 6 3 2	0 6 5 2	
P_4	0 0 1 4	0 6 5 6	

(*i*) What are necessary conditions for a deadlock to occur? Are they also sufficient? Justify. 3

(*ii*) Use bankers algorithm to determine the state of the system. 6

(*iii*) If a request from process P_1 arrives for (0, 4, 2, 0), can the request be granted immediately ? 2

3. (*a*) Why are segmentation and paging some times combined into one scheme? 3

(*b*) Consider the following segment table: 2 + 2

Segment	Base	Length
0	219	600
1	2300	14
2	90	100
3	1327	580
4	1952	96

What are the physical addresses for the following logical addresses ?

(i) 0430;

(ii) 3400.

(*c*) Consider the following page reference string :

1, 2, 3, 4, 2, 1, 5, 6, 2, 1, 2, 3, 7, 6, 3, 2, 1.

How many page faults will occur for LRU and FIFO assuming 4 and 5 frames ? 4+4

4. (*a*) Give an example of an application in which data in a file should be accessed in the following order : 3

(*i*) Sequentially;

(*ii*) Randomly.

(*b*) How are system calls implemented ? 4

MCA/III Sem. F

Paper—CS.302—OPERATING SYSTEMS

(New Course)

(Admission of 2001 and onwards)

Time: 3 hours *Maximum Marks : 60*

(Write your Roll No. on the top immediately on receipt of this question paper.)

Attempt *All* questions

All parts of a question must be attempted together.

1. Illustrate with a suitable example the distinction between:

(*i*) real and virtual address 2

(*ii*) interrupt and trap 2

(*iii*) mode switch and context switch 2

(*iv*) program, process and thread 3

(*v*) user-level threads and kernel-level threads 2

(*vi*) page and frame 1

(*vii*) internal and external fragmentation 1

(*viii*) indexed and linked allocation of free blocks on secondary storage. 2

2. (*a*) A short-term scheduling algorithm increases the priority of a process inversely to its CPU usage. How are the I/O bound and CPU bound processes treated in this environment? Justify your answer. 4

(*b*) What are system calls? How do they relate to the concept of dual-mode operation of CPU? 3

(*c*) What are the conditions that must be satisfied by the solution to critical region problem? 3

(*d*) Implement a counting semaphore using binary semaphore(s). 5

3. (*a*) Three processes share four resource units that can be reserved and released one at a time. Each process needs maximum of two units. Show that a deadlock can not occur. 4

(*b*) What is the difference between deadlock avoidance, detection and prevention? 5

(*c*) Consider a fixed partitioning scheme with equal sized partitions of 2^{16} and main memory of 2^{24} bytes. How many bits are required to maintain a pointer to the partition in the PCB? 1

(*d*) A virtual address '*a*' in a paging system is equivalent to a pair (*p*, *w*) where '*p*' is the page number and '*w*' is the offset in page. Let there be '*z*' bytes in the page. Derive algebraic equations to show relationship between *p*, *w*, *z* and *a*. 5

4. (*a*) What is a byte stream file? How can a structure be imposed on a byte stream file? 3

(*b*) Describe the information maintained by the file manager for each file as a "c structure". Write the algorithm for "open (filename, permissions)". 5

(*c*) Given a page reference stream

W = 2, 3,1,2,3, 2,5, 1,3,4,2,4,5.

Find the number of page faults using LRU, LFU and FIFO page replacement algorithms. Use *m*=3 and *m*=5. Compare the page faults for each algorithm for different values of *m*, and give your observations. 7

MCA/III Sem. A

Paper—MCA 305—OPERATING SYSTEMS

(New Course)

(Admission of 2009 and onwards)

Time: 2 hours *Maximum Marks : 50*

(Write your Roll No. on the top immediately on receipt of this question paper.)

All *questions are compulsory.*

Parts of a question must be answered together.

All *questions carry equal marks.*

1. Consider an application with two concurrent processes, P_1 and P_2 defined as follows: A,B,C,D and E are atomic statements. Show all possible interleavings of the execution, if P_1 and P_2 are invoked at the same time.

```
P2()        P1()
{           {
   A;          D;
   B;          E;
   C;       }
}
```

2. Distinguish between

(*i*) processes and threads

(*ii*) mode switch and context switch

3. Given the following information, calculate the turn around time, waiting time for each process using SJF and RR (quantum = 10 units) algorithms.

Process : p1 p2 p3 p4

Burst time : 35 12 75 25

4. Consider a reference string 1,2,3,4,2,5,6,2,3,2, 1, 6, 7; and a system with four frames, demand paging, and all frames initially empty. How many page faults would occur with a FIFO replacement scheme? How many page faults would occur with a LRU replacement scheme?

5. Given the request for cylinders 10, 15, 40, 2, 18, 54, 27, 83, 50 and the initial position of arm at cylinder 30. If seek takes 5 msec per cylinder, what is the total seek time using (i) FCFS and (ii) SCAN algorithm ?

6. How is a process implemented by an operating system? What is the difference between preemptive and non-preemptive scheduling algorithms for process scheduling?

7. Explain distinctions between multiprocessing and multi programming systems, giving suitable examples.

8. Which of the following instructions should be executed in user/kernel mode? Justify your answer:

(*i*) Disable all interrupts

(*ii*) Read the time of clock

(*iii*) Set the time of clock

(*iv*) Kill a process

(*v*) transfer contents of R1 to R5, where R1 and R2 denote registers.

9. Name two schemes for keeping track of free blocks on disk by the file management system. Give one advantage and one disadvantage of each.

10. What is a deadlock? What are the necessary conditions for a deadlock to occur?

MINOR I OPERATING SYSTEMS (31 Aug 2010)

MCA – III

Time: 1 Hr. *Maximum marks : 30*

1. Do as indicated

i. Suppose a system has several users logged on. Give a command to find if user U2 is logged on to the system?

ii. Create a directory called dir2 under dir1 which is in the current directory

iii. While you are in directory dir2, list the contents of directory dir1.

iv. List all files that have character 'f in them, and display page by page.

v. List the contents of the root directory and the bin directory (see command)

vi. Use 'pipe' to count the number of files in your current directory.

vii. Which command would you use to create a file from the terminal

viii. Display last 4 lines of the file try.txt.

ix. Split the file "test.txt" into multiple files with names starting with "try", each having 5 line

x. Concatenate f1, …, f5 to create 'file "final" (10)

2. Draw and explain a state transition diagram with 5 states? (5)

3. What is the difference between mode switch and contexts switch? (5)

4. Show interrupt processing with the help of a flowchart, segregating the tasks performed by the hardware and the software. (10)

MCA-305 (O.S.)

Time : 1 hours *Maximum Marks: 30*

Q1. Given the code for two processes P_1 & P_2 with "bal" as shared variable

```
P1()                          P2()
{                             {
  :                             :
  bal = bal + amount            bal = bal – amount
  :                             :
}                             }
```

Show how the race condition arises. How can the problem be solved using compare swap Instruction. (10)

Q2. Explain two advantages of threads over processes? (5)

Q3. Draw a neat diagram to show the general organization of SMP. (5)

Q4. Define a counting semiphone and the operations done on it. (3)

Q5. (*i*) Given a file with names, hours worked and rate of wages in three columns. Create a file for the wage bill. (2)

(*ii*) Given a file with sollow, marks in 5 subjects (out of 100) create a file that contains only those roll no. who have secured marks between 50% and 60%. (3)

(*iii*) Point in reverse order the fields of every line. (2)

First Term Examination/Minor (Feb 2013)

Programme: B.Tech Subject: Operating System Code: ETCS-212

Semester: 4th

Time: 1 hr *Max. Marks: 30*

Note: Attempt any three questions including question no. 1 which is compulsory.

Ql (*a*) Why page sizes always powers of 2? (2.5 Marks)

(*b*) What is starvation? What are the possible solutions to solve this problem? (2.5 Marks)

(*c*) What is Belady's Anomaly? (2.5 Marks)

(*d*) What is Convoy effect? Explain with suitable example. (2.5 Marks)

Q2 (*a*) Differentiate between Multiprocessing, Multiprogramming and Multitasking. (5 Marks)

(*b*) Consider there are 4 frames allocated to a process and the reference string is 2,3,4,6,2,4,5,7, 4,8,2,9,8. Calculate the number of page faults for the following page replacement algorithms.

(*i*) FIFO

(*ii*) LRU (5 Marks)

Q3 (*a*) Consider a logical address space of 8 pages of 1024 words, each mapped onto a physical memory of 32 frames.

(*i*) How many bits are there in the logical address?

(*ii*) How many bits are there in the physical address? (3 Marks)

(*b*) What is the difference between logical and physical address? (3 Marks)

(*c*) On a system using segmentation, Compute the physical address for each of the logical addresses given in the following segment table. If the address generates a segment fault, indicate so. (4 Marks)

Segment	Base	Length
0	330	112
1	876	124
2	111	99
3	448	302

(*a*) 0, 99 (b) 2, 78 (*c*) 1,265 (*d*) 3, 222

Q4 (*a*) What are various Scheduling criteria's? (4 Marks)

(*b*) Consider the following set of processes with the CPU burst &;arrival time in milliseconds. (6 Marks)

Process	Arrival Time	Burst Time
A	0	10
B	1	5
C	2	8
D	3	4
E	4	11

Draw the Gantt chart & Find:

(*i*) Average waiting time for these processes with the Shortest Remaining Time First & Round Robin (Time quantum = 3 ms) scheduling algorithm.

(*ii*) Average turnaround time for these processes with the Round Robin scheduling algorithm.

MCA / III Sem.

Paper - MCA. 305 : OPERATING SYSTEMS

(Admission of 2007 and onwards)

Time: 3 hours *Maximum Marks: 60*

(Write your Roll No. on the top of immediately on receipt of this question paper). All questions are compulsory. Parts of a question must be answered together.

Q1. *a.* What is the context of the process? Describe in detail all activities in a context switch. (6)

b. List and define the different metrics by which a scheduler can be evaluated. (4)

c. Compute the completion and waiting times for the following set of jobs for shortest process next and shortest remaining time algorithm. Assume a zero context switch overhead. (5)

Process	Arrival time	Burst
P1	0	10
P2	1	5
P3	2	2
P4	4	3

Q2. *a.* What is the meaning of race condition? Illustrate your answer with the help of an example. (6)

b. Apply Banker's algorithm to check if the following system of four processes with two resources is deadlocked for the given availability vectors? (6)

Current allocation matrix

	R_1	R_2
P1	1	3
P2	4	1
P3	1	2
P4	2	0

Current request matrix

P1	1	2
P2	4	3
P3	1	7
P4	5	1

Availability Vectors <1, 4>, <2, 3>, <4, 4>

(*c*) What is the essential cause for the difference in cost between a context switch for Processes and threads ? (4)

Q3. *a.* Describe the difference between *external* and *internal* fragmentation. Indicate which of the two is likely to be an issue in paging, segmentation and paging with segmentation schemes, and why. (4)

b. Consider a virtual memory architecture with the following parameters:

48 bit virtual addresses, 8K byte page size, 64K segments in a virtual address, 16 gigabytes of real memory. Each virtual page has read, write, and valid bits associated with it. Answer the following:

1. how the various fields of logical address are interpreted,
2. the size of each field (in bits),
3. the maximum number of entries each table could hold, and
4. the maximum size possible for each table (in bytes). 6

Consider a reference string 1, 2, 3, 4, 2, 5, 6, 2, 3, 2, 1, 6, 7 and a demand paging system with four frames; all frames initially empty.

(*i*) How many page faults would occur with a FIFO replacement scheme? What are the pages in the frames when the reference string has completed?

(*ii*) How many page faults would occur with a LRU replacement scheme? What are the pages in the frames when the reference string has completed?

(*iii*) Would increasing the number of frames always decrease the number of page faults for a particular reference string for FIFO? for LRU! Why or why not? (4)

4. (*a*) Give an example where contiguous allocation of tile blocks on disks can be used in practice. (2)

(*b*) What is the difference between supervisor mode and user mode? Why are they needed? (5)

(*c*) What are the tradeoffs between bit map and linked list representations of free space in a file system. (5)

(*d*) List the pros-and-cons of using semaphores and monitors for designing applications with concurrent processes. (3)

Second Term Examination

Fourth semester [B.Tech], April-2014(Regular)

Paper Code: - ETCS-212 **Subject: - Operating System**

Time: 1½ hr *Max. Marks: 30*

Attempt any three questions including **question No. 1** which is compulsory.

Ques No.1 (3, 3, 2, 2)

(*a*) What is the meaning of term busy waiting? Can busy waiting be avoided altogether? Explain your answer.

(*b*) What is the difference between Semaphore & Monitors? Explain with suitable example?

(*c*) Explain Seek time and Rotational Latency in disk scheduling?

(*d*) Consider a system consisting of six tape drives with 'n' processes competing for them. Each process may need two drives. For which values of 'n', the system deadlock free.

Ques No.2

(*a*) Show that the two-phase locking protocol ensures conflict serializability? (4)

(*b*) What is deadlock? List four necessary conditions for the occurrence of deadlock. Is it possible to have a deadlock having one process only? Explain your answer. (6)

Ques No.3

(*a*) What is the difference between Virtual, Dedicated & Shared Devices? (4)

(*b*) Consider the following snapshot of a system: (6)

	Allocation	**Max**	**Available**
	ABCD	ABCD	ABCD
P0	0012	0012	1520
P1	1000	1750	
P2	1354	2356	
P3	0632	0652	
P4	0014	0656	

Answer the following questions using banker's algorithm:

a. What is the content of the matrix Need?

b. Is the system in a safe state? Explain?

c. If a request from process PI arrives for (0, 4, 2, 0) can the request be granted immediately?

Ques No. 4

(*a*) Explain The Dining-Philosophers Problem? (4)

(*b*) Suppose the moving head disk with 200 tracks is currently serving a request for track 143 and just finished a request for track 125. If the queue of requests is kept in a FIFO order: 86,147, 177,94, and 150. Starting from current head position, what is the total head movement for the following scheduling schemes?

1. FCFS 2. SSTF 3. Elevator 4. LOOK 5. C-SCAN 6. C-LOOK (6)

First Term Examination/Minor (Feb 2014)

Programme: B. Tech **Max. Marks: 30**

Subject: Operating System **Semester: 4th**

Code: ETCS-212

Note: Attempt any three questions including question no. 1 which is compulsory.

Q1. (*a*) When do page faults occur? Describe the actions taken by the operating system when a Page fault occurs. (2.5 Marks)

(*b*) What are the differences between user-level threads and kernel –supported threads? (2.5 Marks)

(*c*) What is the purpose of system calls? Write any four system calls for process control. (2.5 Marks)

(*d*) Why page sizes always powers of 2? (2.5 Marks)

Q2. (*a*) Describe the differences among short-term, medium-term and long-term scheduling. (4 Marks)

(*b*) Consider there are 3 frames allocated to a process and the reference string is: 1, 2, 3, 4, 2, 1, 5, 6, 2, 1, 2, 3, 7, 6, 3, 2 ,1, 2, 3, 6. Calculate the number of page faults for the following page replacement algorithms.

(*i*) FIFO (*ii*) LRU (*iii*) Optimal (6 Marks)

Q3. (*a*) A computer system has a 36-bit virtual address space with a page size of 8K, and 4 byte entries per page table. (4 Marks)

(*i*) How many pages are in the virtual address space?

(*ii*) What is the maximum size of addressable physical memory in this system?

(*b*) What is the difference between Multitasking and Multithreading? (3 Marks)

(*c*) What is the cause of thrashing? How does the system detect thrashing? Once it detects thrashing, what can the system do to eliminate this problem? (3 Marks)

Q4. (*a*) In loading programs into memory, what is the difference between load-time dynamic linking and run-time dynamic linking? (4 Marks)

(*b*) Consider the following set of processes with the CPU burst & arrival time in milliseconds. Assume each context switch takes 1 unit of time. (6 Marks)

Process	Arrival Time	Burst Time
P1	3	10
P2	1	1
P3	4	2
P4	3	1
P5	0	5

Draw the Gantt chart & calculate average waiting time and average turnaround time for each of the following scheduling algorithms:

(*i*) Shortest Job First

(*ii*) Shortest Remaining Time First

(*iii*) Round Robin (Time qunatum = 3 ms) scheduling algorithm.

End Term Examination

Fourth Semester [B.TECH] MAY-JUNE 2014

Paper Code: ETCS-212 Subject: operating System

Time: 3 Hours ***Maximum Marks: 75***

Note: Attempt all questions. Internal Choice is indicated.

Q'. (*a*) What do you understand by the following terms:- (6 × 2 = 12)

(*i*) Time Sharing

(*ii*) Race Condition

(*iii*) Concurrency

(*iv*) PCB

(*v*) Light Weight Process

(*vi*) Bootstrapping

(*b*) Compare and contrast the following : - (5 × 2 = 10)

(*i*) Internal and external fragmentation.

(*ii*) Pages vs Frames.

(*iii*) Memory Compaction and garbage collection.

(*iv*) Logical addresses vs Physical addresses.

(*v*) Single stream batch processing and batch multiprogramming.

(*c*) What are semaphores ? What are its drawback ? (3)

Q2. (*a*) What memory management scheme is used in modern operating system? Explain. (4.5)

(*b*) Consider the following page reference stream and then find out the number of page faults for each of the following algorithms (No. of fames: 4)

"7 0 1 2 3 0 1 2 7 3 1 2 0 4 3 2 1 7 0 2 1 3 4 7"

(*i*) FIFO

(*ii*) LRU

(*iii*) Optimal algorithm (8)

OR

(*a*) What do you understand by virtual memory? How is it implemented? What do you understand by page fault and swapping ? (6)

(*b*) What do you understand by thrashing? Explain the concept of working set model. what do you understand by principle of locality and operating incontext. (6.5)

Q3.(*a*) Discuss the Round Robin CPU scheduling algorithm. What are various consideration that affect the size of time quantum ? (6)

(*b*) What is Master/Slave scheduling ? Explain its advantages and disadvantages. (6.5)

OR

(*a*) Distinguish between preemptive, non-preemptive and cooperative scheduling methods. (6)

(*b*) Discuss the critical section problem. Discuss some of the solutions to solve this problem. (6.5)

Q4. (*a*) What are the necessary conditions for the occurrence of deadlocks ? Prove that they are not the sufficient conditions with the help of examples. (6)

(*b*) Given memory partitions of 100K, 500K, 200K, 300K and 600K (in order). How would the Best-fit and Worst-Fit algorithms place processes of 212K, 417K, 112K and 426K (in order) ? Which algorithm makes more efficient use of memory. (6.5)

OR

(*a*) Explain different Disk Scheduling algorithms. (6)

(*b*) Explain the ways to detect and recover from a deadlock. (6.5)

Q5. (*a*) Discuss the method of indexed allocation used in file management. How is information organized in FAT? (6)

(*b*) How are OPEN and CLOSE implemented in a multi-user environment. *i.e.*, when more than one user can use the same file. (6.5)

OR

(*a*) Discuss the relative advantage of different types of directory structures. (6)

(*b*) Why is it difficult to protect a system in which user are allowed to do their own I/O. (6.5)

Appendix G

BIBLIOGRAPHY

1. Galvin S, “Operating System Concepts”, Addision Wesely, 5th Ed., 2001.
2. J. Donovan & E Madnick, “Operating System Concept and Design”, Tata McGraw Hill Intl. Edition 2001.
3. Ekta Walia, “Operating System Concepts”, Khanna Publishers, Edition 2002.
4. John Donovon, “Systems Programming”, Tata McGraw Hill, 23rd Reprint, 2000.
5. P.S. Gill, “Operating Systems Concepts”, Laxmi (Firewall) Publications, 1st Edition 2006.
6. William stallings, “Operating System Internals and Design Principles”, PHI, 6th Edition-2002.
7. Andrew S.Tenenbaum, “Operating System Design”, PHI, Edition 2000.
8. P. Prasad, “Operating Systems”, Sai Tech Publications, Edition Second 2007.
9. Rajesh Mishra, “Operating System Concepts”, Pragati Prakashan, Meerut, Edition First, 2000.
10. R.C. Joshi, “Operating System Concepts”, Wiley Dreamtech, 2005.
11. D.M. Dhamdhere, “Operating Systems: A Concept Based Approach, 2nd edition, Tata McGraw Hill, 2007.
12. Gary Nutt, “Operating Systems: A Modern Approach”, Tata McGrawHill 2nd Edition, 2007.
13. W. Stallings, “Operating System”, Pearson, 4th Edition, 2010.